P9-BYL-291

INVITATIONS TO INSIGHT

SKILL BUILDERS

ARTWORK IN *LOOKING OUT/LOOKING IN*

Like music and poetry, art can capture the essence of interpersonal communication in compelling ways. The commentary below explains some connections between images in *Looking Out/Looking In* and the text that they accompany. Captions are not provided for works that clearly speak for themselves.

www.wadsworth.com

wadsworth.com is the World Wide Web site for
Wadsworth and is your direct source to dozens
of online resources.

At *wadsworth.com* you can find out about supplements,
demonstration software, and student resources. You can
also send email to many of our authors and preview new
publications and exciting new technologies.

wadsworth.com
Changing the way the world learns®

FROM THE WADSWORTH SERIES IN SPEECH COMMUNICATION

LOOKING OUT/LOOKING IN

MEDIA EDITION

TENTH EDITION

RONALD B. ADLER
Santa Barbara City College

NEIL TOWNE
Emeritus, Grossmont College

THOMSON
——✳——™
WADSWORTH

Australia • Canada • Mexico • Singapore • Spain
United Kingdom • United States

THOMSON
™
WADSWORTH

Executive Editor: Deirdre Anderson
Publisher: Holly J. Allen
Assistant Editor: Nicole George
Editorial Assistant: Mele Alusa
Technology Project Manager: Jeanette Wiseman
Marketing Manager: Kimberly Russell
Marketing Assistant: Neena Chandra
Advertising Project Manager: Shemika Britt
Project Manager, Editorial Production: Cathy Linberg

Print/Media Buyer: Barbara Britton
Permissions Editor: Robert Kauser
Production Service: Robin Lockwood Productions
Text Designer: Janet Bollow
Art Researcher: Sherri Adler
Copyeditor: Jennifer Gordon
Cover Printer: R. R. Donnelley & Sons, Willard
Compositor: Thompson Type
Printer: R. R. Donnelley & Sons, Willard

COPYRIGHT © 2003 Wadsworth, a division of Thomson Learning, Inc. Thomson Learning™ is a trademark used herein under license.

ALL RIGHTS RESERVED. No part of this work covered by the copyright hereon may be reproduced or used in any form or by any means—graphic, electronic, or mechanical, including but not limited to photocopying, recording, taping, Web distribution, information networks, or information storage and retrieval systems—without the written permission of the publisher.

Printed in the United States of America
1 2 3 4 5 6 7 06 05 04 03 02

For more information about our products, contact us at:
Thomson Learning Academic Resource Center
1-800-423-0563
For permission to use material from this text,
contact us by:
Phone: 1-800-730-2214
Fax: 1-800-730-2215
Web: http://www.thomsonrights.com

ExamView® and *ExamView Pro*® are registered trademarks of FSCreations, Inc. Windows is a registered trademark of the Microsoft Corporation used herein under license. Macintosh and Power Macintosh are registered trademarks of Apple Computer, Inc. Used herein under license.

COPYRIGHT 2003 Thomson Learning, Inc. All Rights Reserved. Thomson Learning *WebTutor*™ is a trademark of Thomson Learning, Inc.

ISBN 0-534-54986-1

Wadsworth/Thomson Learning
10 Davis Drive
Belmont, CA 94002-3098
USA

Asia
Thomson Learning
5 Shenton Way #01-01
UIC Building
Singapore 068808

Australia
Nelson Thomson Learning
102 Dodds Street
South Melbourne, Victoria 3205
Australia

Canada
Nelson Thomson Learning
1120 Birchmount Road
Toronto, Ontario M1K 5G4
Canada

Europe/Middle East/Africa
Thomson Learning
High Holborn House
50/51 Bedford Row
London WC1R 4LR
United Kingdom

Latin America
Thomson Learning
Seneca, 53
Colonia Polanco
11560 Mexico D.F.
Mexico

Spain
Paraninfo Thomson Learning
Calle/Magallanes, 25
28015 Madrid, Spain

BRIEF CONTENTS

**PART ONE
LOOKING IN**

**PART TWO
LOOKING OUT**

**PART THREE
LOOKING AT
RELATIONAL
DYNAMICS**

v

CONTENTS

**PART ONE
LOOKING IN**

CHAPTER 3
PERCEPTION: WHAT YOU SEE IS WHAT YOU GET   92

CHAPTER 4
EMOTIONS: THINKING, FEELING, AND ACTING   134

CHAPTER 5
LANGUAGE: BARRIER AND BRIDGE   174

**PART TWO
LOOKING OUT**

CHAPTER 8
COMMUNICATION AND RELATIONAL DYNAMICS   313

PART THREE
LOOKING AT
RELATIONAL
DYNAMICS

PREFACE

PREFACE

Professors and students of interpersonal communication are lucky people. We get to explore a topic that has obvious relevance to our lives and the potential for immense personal benefit. As authors, our challenge has been to make sure this edition of *Looking Out/Looking In* does justice to this important subject. If we have succeeded, you are holding a book that provides a solid academic introduction to the field of interpersonal communication and contains information about how to communicate more effectively in everyday life.

WHAT'S FAMILIAR

This tenth edition of *Looking Out/Looking In* retains the approach that has made it the leading interpersonal text for almost 30 years, used by over a million readers. A user-friendly voice links scholarship to everyday life without compromising academic integrity. The attention-grabbing assortment of quotations, music lyrics, cartoons, art, poetry, fiction, and nonfiction highlights and reinforces the text in a compelling way. The prominent treatment of ethical issues helps users explore how to communicate in a principled manner. The Media Edition and the extensive ancillary package (described below in detail) includes resources for both students and professors. *Looking Out/Looking In* emphasizes the transactional nature of relationships. It presents communication not as a

collection of techniques we use on others, but as a process we engage in *with* them. Readers also learn that even the most competent communication doesn't always seek to create warm, fuzzy relationships. The book explains that even impersonal or adversarial interactions often have the best chance of success when they are handled in a constructive, respectful manner.

This edition continues to integrate the discussion of similarities and differences involving gender and culture from beginning to end, rather than isolating them in separate Chapters. It also retains a nonideological approach to these topics, citing research that shows how other variables are often at least as important in shaping interaction. As in recent editions, a series of "Looking at Diversity" profiles give first-person accounts of how culture, physical factors, and technology influence interaction.

Long-time users will also find the same class-tested organizational structure that has proved its value. The number and basic focus of the Chapters has remained constant, and Chapters 2 through 10 can be covered in whatever order works best for individual situations.

NEW TO THE MEDIA EDITION

The Media Edition introduces and integrates CD-ROM and Web technology to enhance features that have served users well in the past. Accompanying each student text is the ***Looking***

Out/Looking In CD-ROM. This CD-ROM consists of four integrated components: access to InfoTrac® College Edition, access to Chapter-by-Chapter resources at the *Looking Out/Looking In* Web site at Wadsworth's Communication Café, *Looking Out/Looking In* Communication Scenarios, and a preview of Thomson Learning WebTutor. Each component of the CD-ROM is represented in the text with an icon. Integrated throughout the Chapter and expanded upon at the end of Chapters in the new *Looking Out/Looking In* Online section, these integrated icons direct students to numerous digital activities and reinforce and enrich the concepts presented.

Looking Out/Looking In **Communication Scenarios icons** prompt students to view and interact with multimedia communication encounters based on the Communication Transcripts feature described under Pedagogical aids on page xv. This multimedia tool makes concepts previously presented in the abstract come alive. Students maximize their experience by reading, watching, listening to, critiquing, and analyzing the model communication encounters.

Marginal **Weblinks** are featured in each Chapter and prompt students to explore Chapter concepts online. **InfoTrac College Edition Exercises** are new to the Media Edition and guide students in using InfoTrac College Edition. InfoTrac College Edition is an online library of full text articles (not abstracts) from top scholarly journals and popular publications—available 24 hours a day, seven days a week. Four months of FREE access to the new and improved InfoTrac College Edition is automatically packaged with each new copy of *Looking Out/Looking In Media Edition.* InfoTrac College Edition offers full text articles from journals such as *Communication Quarterly, Sex Roles, U.S News and World Report* and *Harper's.* Engaging and practical end-of-Chapter InfoTrac College Edition exercises expand Chapter content, guarantee currency of presentation and help students use InfoTrac College Edition in a directed way.

The *Looking Out/Looking In* **Web site** at the Wadsworth Communication Café provides numerous student and instructor resources. For students, Chapter-by-Chapter resources include learning objectives, activities, InfoTrac activities, a digital glossary, and a practice quiz. In addition, all of the URLs included in the book are maintained for each Chapter under WebLinks. Accessible via this Web site is the **Film in Communication Database,** which allows students and faculty to search for feature films that illustrate communication concepts by key term. In addition to these new features, the new edition has been improved in several ways.

Streamlined material Thorough editing has kept the book's length manageable, making way for new material. Readers will find more concise explanations of many concepts that promote clarity without sacrificing content. In fact, if we have done our job well, long-time users will appreciate the improved flow of the text without being able to spot what's been trimmed.

Expanded coverage of gender *Looking Out/Looking In* continues to explore both differences and similarities between male and female communication, avoiding an uncritical acceptance of the *Men Are from Mars, Women Are from Venus* approach.

New material includes a clearer explanation of the difference between "sex" and "gender," the influence of gender on shaping identity (Chapter 2), dangers of gender-related stereotyping (Chapter 3), the influence of gender on emotional expression (Chapter 4), similarities and differences between male and female language use (Chapter 5), and nonverbal communication (Chapter 6). A new section on Gender and Listening (in Chapter 7) discusses both social influences and possible biological differences that affect the way men and women listen. New material explores gender differences in preferred ways of expressing intimacy (Chapter 8) and managing conflict (Chapter 10).

New material on mediated communication Material throughout the book explores how technologies like email, instant messaging, and personal Web pages affect interpersonal communication. For example, Chapters 1 and 8 explore the question of whether computer-mediated communication enhances or reduces the quality of interpersonal relationships. Chapter 2 describes how communicators manage their identities in email and on web pages. Chapter 6 discusses how email users attempt to add a nonverbal dimension to this text-based tool.

Enhanced treatment of culture and diversity This edition of *Looking Out/Looking In* continues to integrate discussions of culture and diversity throughout the book. For example, Chapter 2 outlines the influence of culture on shaping identity, Chapter 5 offers perspectives on immigrants' views of language in the United States, and Chapter 8 discusses how American notions about friendliness and self-disclosure with strangers aren't universally held.

Enhanced design and art program An inviting, provocative design has always distinguished *Looking Out/Looking In*. In this edition, we have paid special attention to choosing artworks that illustrate communication concepts in attractive, provocative ways. In order to stimulate viewers' thinking, we have deliberately presented the images without captions. However, readers who are curious about the placement of a particular work can view the authors' notes, which are located after the Quick Reference Guide, at the front of this book.

Other changes Changes throughout the book keep *Looking Out/Looking In* current with the latest scholarship, without forcing users to overhaul the structure of their courses. For example, Chapter 1 contains new material that previews importance of identity management. Material in Chapter 2 clarifies the relationship between self-concept and self-esteem, as well as showing how factors such as gender, ethnicity, age, and socioeconomic status shape our identity. A new Ethical Challenge explores the degree to which we are responsible for communicating in ways that support others' self-esteem. Stereotyping and punctuation now are discussed in their own sections of Chapter 3, which also has an expanded discussion of how common perceptual errors affect communication. Chapter 4 cites research showing that both underexpression and overexpression of emotions can affect physical health and personal relationships. A new section on verbal expression of emotions explains the value—and the limitations—of revealing emotions clearly and directly. A new section of Chapter 5 titled "Understandings and Misunderstandings" draws a closer connection between linguistic rules and everyday communication challenges. Material in Chapter 8 on managing dialectical tensions has been clarified.

PEDAGOGICAL AIDS

A variety of in-text pedagogical devices help students learn concepts and develop skills most effectively.

Activities throughout the book help readers take a closer look at important concepts. They are labeled by type: *Invitations to Insight* help readers understand how theory and research applies to their own lives. *Skill Builders* help them improve their communication skills. *Ethical Challenge*s highlight some challenges communicators face as they pursue their own goals.

Communication Transcripts describe how the skills and concepts from the text sound when used in everyday life.

Looking at Diversity profiles (half of which are new to this edition) provide first-person accounts of communicators from a variety of backgrounds. New profile subjects include a student with attention-deficit disorder talking about how the disability affects the way people perceive him, a Palestinian woman living in California who describes how people respond to her traditional style of dress, a deaf man describing how his disability shaped his growing up, and a couple who met and fell in love in an Internet chat room.

End-of-Chapter resources *Looking Out/ Looking In* Online appears at the end of each chapter and offers print and media resources that add rich descriptions of the principles introduced in the text. Included in this section is information about how students can access the digital resources that accompany the Media Edition as well as InfoTrac College Edition Exercises, prompts to the Communication in Film Database and a visual prompt to the *Looking Out/Looking In* CD-ROM or Web site.

TEACHING AND LEARNING RESOURCES

A long with the text itself and in addition to the CD-ROM and Web site resources described on page xiv, *Looking Out/Looking In* is accompanied by an extensive array of materials that will make teaching and learning more efficient and effective. A comprehensive **Instructor's Manual** provides tips and tools for both new and experienced professors. The manual also contains hard copy of over 1,200 class-tested exam questions, indexed by page number and level of understanding.

- The **Activity Manual and Study Guide** has been revised by Mary Wiemann to feature the kinds of activities and learning aids requested by users. New "Mediated Messages" activities in each chapter help students explore ways in which communicating via electronic media affect their relationships.

- **ExamView®,** a computerized testing program makes the creation of exams faster and easier. This program comes with more than 1,200 questions covering the entire contents of *Looking Out/Looking In.*

- A revised **Communication in Film** guide (by Russell F. Proctor II) expands on the film tips in each Chapter of *Looking Out/Looking In.* This guide provides detailed suggestions for using both new and classic films to illustrate communication principles introduced in the text.

- **Communication Scenarios for Critique and Analysis Videos Volumes I–III** include the video scenarios included on the *Looking Out/Looking In* CD-ROM as well as additional scenarios covering interviewing and group work. Contact your Wadsworth/ Thomson Learning representative for details.

- **CNN Videos,** allow you to integrate the newsgathering and programming power of CNN into the classroom to show students the relevance of course topics to their everyday lives. Organized by topics covered in a typical course, these videos are divided into short segments, perfect for introducing key concepts. High-interest clips are followed by questions designed to spark class discussion. Contact your Wadsworth/Thomson Learning representative for details.

- **Multimedia Presentation and Lecture Tool** on CD-ROM has been developed by Mary Weimann and includes pre-designed PowerPoint® presentations, containing hundreds of images, text, and cued videos of the Communication Scenarios featured on the *Looking Out/Looking In* CD-ROM. You can customize and manipulate these slides as you see fit.

- **InfoTrac® College Edition Student Activities Workbooks** feature extensive individual and group activities which utilize InfoTrac College Edition. Different workbooks focus on Interpersonal Communication, Intercultural Communication and Public Speaking. These saleable items can be bundled with the text and include guidelines for faculty and students on maximizing this resource.

- **The Teaching Assistant's Guide to the Basic Course** by Katherine Hendrix is a guidebook designed for the new Communication teacher. Based on leading communication teacher training programs, the guide covers general teaching and course management topics as well as specific strategies for communication instruction. For example; providing effective feedback on performance, managing sensitive class discussions, and conducting mock interviews.

- **A Guide to the Basic Course for ESL Students** by Esther Yook is a saleable item which can be bundled with the text and is designed to assist the non-native speaker. Features FAQs, helpful URLs, strategies for accent management and overcoming speech apprehension.

- **Service Learning in Communication Studies: A Handbook** by Rick Isaacson, Bruce Dorries, and Kevin Brown is a handbook for students in a course that integrates or is planning to integrate a service learning component. The handbook provides guidelines for connecting service learning work with classroom concepts and advice for working effectively with agencies and organizations. It also provides model forms and reports and a directory of online resources.

- **MyCourse 2.0,** is a free online course builder. Whether you want only the easy-to-use tools to build a course Web site or *Looking Out/Looking In* content to furnish it, My Course 2.0 is a simple solution for a custom course Web site that allows you to assign, track, and report on student progress; load your syllabus; and more. Contact your representative for details.

■ **WebTutor Advantage on Web CT and Blackboard** offers text-specific, pre-formatted content and total flexibility, you can easily create and manage your own personal Web site or online course. WebTutor Advantage's course management tool gives you the ability to provide virtual office hours, post syllabi, set up threaded discussions, track student progress with the quizzing material, and much more. For students, WebTutor Advantage offers real-time access to a full array of study tools specific to *Looking Out/ Looking In*, including chapter outlines, summaries, learning objectives, glossary flashcards (with audio), practice quizzes, Web links, InfoTrac® College Edition exercises, and Web links. And, WebTutor Advantage features further enhancements, including animations, the videos included on the *Looking Out/Looking In* CD-ROM, and Microsoft® PowerPoint® images, which increase interactivity and bring topics to life. WebTutor Advantage also provides robust communication tools, such as a course calendar, asynchronous discussion, real time chat, a whiteboard, and an integrated email system.

ACKNOWLEDGMENTS

Any project with the magnitude of *Looking Out/Looking In* owes its success to the contributions of many people. The best place to begin is with our students, who over the years have helped us understand how to present material in ways that make sense and make a difference.

We are grateful for the thoughtful suggestions of colleagues who advised us about what to keep and what to change in this revision. Thanks go to Patrick O'Sullivan, Illinois State University; Jim Vickerey, Troy State University; Mark Singer, Baker College of Flint; Jim Chesher and Joe White, Santa Barbara City College; Patricia Amason, University of Arkansas; Robyn Bergstrom, Ricks College; Jon Braddy, Jackson State Community College; Kenneth C. Cisna, University of South Florida; Rebecca O. Fielding, University of Montana; Dan Grossnickle, North Hennepin Community College; Aloysia Hard, Olympia College; Cynthia B. Johnson, College of the Sequoias; Cindy Khoury, Long Beach City College; Meg Kreiner, Spokane Community College; Mary-Jo Popovici, Monroe Community College; Carol Shaw, College of the Desert; Cherié C. White, Muskingum Area Technical College; and Nancy Willets, Cape Cod Community College.

We are grateful on many levels for the good ideas and the friendship of Jeanne Elmhorst, Albuquerque Technical-Vocational Institute; Darin Garard and Mary Wiemann, Santa Barbara City College; Russ Proctor, Northern Kentucky University; and Lawrence B. Rosenfeld, University of North Carolina. Their helpfulness and goodwill have made this book a better one, and us better people.

Our thanks also go to the team of publishing professionals who have played a role in this edition from start to finish: Mele Alusa, Deirdre Anderson, Barbara Britton, Stephen Dalphin, Nicole George, Laura Hanna, Garry Harman, Cathy Linberg, Robin Lockwood, Sandra Lord, Amy McGaughey, Linda McMillan, Cathy Richard, and Caroline Robbins. We also declare our admiration and gratitude to Janet Bollow for her talents in designing the book you are holding, and to Sherri Adler for selecting the art it contains.

Peanuts reprinted by permission of United Features Syndicate, Inc.

INTRODUCING THE AUTHORS

Since this is a book about interpersonal communication, it seems appropriate for us to introduce ourselves to you, the reader. The "we" you'll be reading throughout this book isn't just an editorial device: It refers to us—Ron Adler and Neil Towne.

Ron lives in Santa Barbara, California, with his wife, Sherri, and their sixteen-year-old son, Daniel. Their oldest daughter, Robin (who had just been born when the first edition of this book was published), now works in the publishing industry. Rebecca, their other daughter, is an accomplished designer and a fund-raiser for worthy nonprofit organizations.

Ron spends most of his professional time teaching and writing about communication. In addition to helping create *Looking Out/Looking In*, he has contributed to six other books about topics including business communication, public speaking, small group communication, assertiveness, and social skills. Besides writing and teaching, Ron helps professional and business people improve their communication on the job.

Cycling and hiking help keep Ron physically and emotional healthy. Ron cherishes his family and friends. His biggest challenge remains balancing the demands of his career with the other important parts of his life. His only regret is that there aren't more hours in the day.

Ron Adler

Finally, after four decades of teaching, Neil has retired. He and his wife, Bobbi, now live on the shore of beautiful Clear Lake in Northern California. For them, retirement is not a lean-back and do-nothing time. Instead, they explain that they have been "overworked and underpaid" as they go about making their new house a home and settling into a new community. Neil and Bobbi don't complain and agree that their efforts are truly a labor of love.

Neil stays active in the communication field through his continuing involvement in *Looking Out/Looking In*, and by directing workshops, teaching short classes in Couple Communication with Bobbi, and working with their church community in the area of conflict resolution.

Now, add their growing family—their greatest love—and you have an inkling of why the Townes often experience retirement as exhaustion. Currently the family includes their five adult children, along with their spouses, and eight grandkids. Sharing in the lives of their family members now involves traveling, which is another joy in Neil and Bobbi's lives.

Along with work and family, Neil enjoys reading, water skiing, wind surfing, singing in the choir, learning about the flora and fauna around their new home, volunteering as a docent at the nearby state park, making new friends, walking, and looking for any new adventure that may be just around the corner.

Neil Towne

A FIRST LOOK AT INTERPERSONAL RELATIONSHIPS

THE SILENCING

As his name was called, James J. Pelosi, the 452nd West Point cadet of the class of '73, drew in his breath and went to the podium—steeling himself for one last moment of humiliation. The slender, bespectacled young man accepted his diploma, then turned to face the rows of starched white hats and—so he expected—a chorus of boos. Instead, there was only silence. But when he returned to his classmates, the newly fledged lieutenant was treated to something new—a round of handshakes. "It was just as if I were a person again," he said. Thus ended one of the strangest and most brutal episodes in the long history of the corps.

Nineteen months ago, the Long Island cadet was hauled up before the West Point Honor Committee and charged with cheating on an engineering exam. In spite of conflicting testimony given at his trial and his own determined plea of innocence, the third-year cadet, one of the most respected in his company and himself a candidate for the Honor Committee, was convicted. Pelosi's case was thrown out by the Academy superintendent after his military lawyer proved there had been undue influence over the proceeding by the Honor Committee adviser, but that wasn't the end of it. The Academy honor code reserves a special fate for those thought by the majority to be guilty even when there is insufficient evidence to convict. It is called Silencing.

Pelosi's fellow cadets voted to support the Honor Committee sentence. And so for most of his third and all of his fourth year at West Point, Pelosi was ostracized. He was transferred by the Academy to what one friend called a "straight-strict" company—"one of the toughest in the corps." He ate alone each day at a table for ten; he lived by himself in a room meant for two or three; he endured insult and occasional brickbats tossed in his direction; he saw his mail mutilated and his locker vandalized. And hardly anyone, even a close friend who wept when he heard the Silencing decision, would talk to him in public. Under those conditions, most cadets resign. But even though he lost 26 pounds, Pelosi hung tough. "When you're right," he said later, "you have to prove yourself . . . I told myself I didn't care."

And in the end, James Pelosi survived—one of only a handful of Academy cadets in history to graduate after Silencing. Now that he is out, Lieutenant Pelosi is almost dispassionate in his criticism of the Academy and his fellow cadets. About as far as he will go is to say that "Silencing should be abolished. It says cadets are above the law. This attitude of superiority bothers me." As for his own state of mind during the ordeal he told *Newsweek*'s Deborah Beers: "I've taken a psychology course and I know what isolation does to animals. No one at the Academy asks how it affects a person. Doesn't that seem strange?"

Perhaps you played this game as a child. The group of children chooses a victim—either as punishment for committing a real or imagined offense or just for "fun." Then for a period of time, that victim is given the silent treatment. No one speaks to him or her, and no one responds to anything the victim says or does.

If you were the subject of this silent treatment, you probably experienced a range of emotions. At first you might have felt—or at least acted—indifferent. But after a while the strain of being treated as a nonperson probably began to grow. If the game went on long enough, it's likely you found yourself either retreating into a state of depression or lashing out with hostility—partly to show your anger and partly to get a response from the others.

Children who instigate this sort of silencing intuitively know that communication—the company of others—is one of the most basic human needs and that lack of contact is among the cruelest punishments a person can suffer. Besides being emotionally painful, the lack of contact and companionship is so serious that it can affect life itself.

Evidence demonstrating the importance of communication has existed for centuries. Fredrick II, emperor of Germany from 1196 to 1250, may have been the first person to prove the point systematically. A medieval historian described one of his significant, if inhumane, experiments:

> He bade foster mothers and nurses to suckle the children, to bathe and wash them, but in no way to prattle with them, for he wanted to learn whether they would speak the Hebrew language, which was the oldest, or Greek, or Latin, or Arabic, or perhaps the language of their parents, of whom they had been born. But he labored in vain because all the children died. For they could not live without the petting and joyful faces and loving words of their foster mothers.[1]

Fortunately, contemporary researchers have found less dramatic ways to illustrate the importance of communication. In one study of isolation, subjects were paid to remain alone in a locked room. Of the five subjects, one lasted for eight days. Three held out for two days, one commenting, "Never again." The fifth subject lasted only two hours.[2]

The need for contact and companionship is just as strong outside the laboratory, as individuals who have led solitary lives by choice or necessity have discovered. W. Carl Jackson, an adventurer who sailed across the Atlantic Ocean alone in fifty-one days, summarized the feelings common to most loners:

> I found the loneliness of the second month almost excruciating. I always thought of myself as self-sufficient, but I found life without people had no meaning. I had a definite need for somebody to talk to, someone real, alive, and breathing.[3]

WHY WE COMMUNICATE

You might object to stories like this, claiming that solitude would be a welcome relief from the irritations of everyday life. It's true that all of us need solitude, often more than we get. On the other hand, each of us has a point beyond which we do not want to be alone. Beyond this point solitude changes from a pleasurable to a painful condition. In other words, we all need relationships. We all need to communicate.

Physical Needs

Communication is so important that its presence or absence affects physical health. In extreme cases communication can become even a matter of life or death. When he was a Navy pilot, U.S. Senator John McCain was shot down over North Vietnam and held as a prisoner of war for six years, often in solitary confinement. He describes how POWs set up clandestine codes in which they sent messages by tapping on walls to laboriously spell out words. McCain describes the importance of keeping contact and the risks that inmates would take to maintain contact with one another:

> The punishment for communicating could be severe, and a few POWs, having been caught and beaten for their efforts, had their spirits broken as their bodies were battered. Terrified of a return trip to the punishment room, they would lie still in their cells when their comrades tried to tap them up on the wall. Very few would remain uncommunicative for long. To suffer all this alone was less tolerable than torture. Withdrawing in silence from the fellowship of other Americans . . . was to us the approach of death.[4]

The link between communication and physical well-being isn't restricted to prisoners. Medical researchers have identified a wide range of health threats that can result from a lack of close relationships. For instance:

We must love one another or die.

W. H. Auden

■ A lack of social relationships jeopardizes coronary health to a degree that rivals cigarette smoking, high blood pressure, blood lipids, obesity, and lack of physical activity.[5]

■ Socially isolated people are four times more susceptible to the common cold than those who have active social networks.[6]

■ Social isolates are two to three times more likely to die prematurely than are those with strong social ties. The type of relationship doesn't seem to matter: Marriage, friendship, religious ties, and community ties all seem to increase longevity.[7]

■ Divorced men (before age seventy) die from heart disease, cancer, and strokes at double the rate of married men. Three times as many die from hypertension; five times as many commit suicide; seven times as many die from cirrhosis of the liver; and ten times as many die from tuberculosis.[8]

■ The rate of all types of cancer is as much as five times higher for divorced men and women, compared to their married counterparts.[9]

■ The likelihood of death increases when a close relative dies. In one Welsh village, citizens who had lost a close relative died within one year at a rate more than five times greater than the rate of those who had not lost a relative.[10]

Research like this demonstrates the importance of having satisfying personal relationships. Not everyone needs the same amount of contact, and the quality of communication is almost certainly as important as the quantity. The important point is that personal communication is essential for our well-being.

Identity Needs

Communication does more than enable us to survive. It is the way—indeed, the *only* way—we learn who we are. As chapter 2 explains, our sense of identity comes from the way we interact with other people. Are we smart or stupid, attractive or ugly, skillful or inept? The answers to these questions don't come from looking in the mirror. We decide who we are based on how others react to us.

Deprived of communication with others, we would have no sense of ourselves. In his book *Bridges, Not Walls*, John Stewart dramatically illustrates this fact by citing the case of the famous "Wild Boy of Aveyron," who spent his early childhood without any apparent human contact. The boy was discovered in January 1800 digging for vegetables in a French village garden. He showed no behaviors that one would expect in a social human. The boy could not speak but rather uttered only weird cries. More significant than this lack of social skills was his lack of any identity as a human being. As author Roger Shattuck put it, "The boy had no human sense of being in the world. He had no sense of himself as a person related to other persons."[11] Only with the influence of a loving "mother" did the boy begin to behave—and, we can imagine, think of himself—as a human.

Like the boy of Aveyron, each of us enters the world with little or no sense of identity. We gain an idea of who we are from the way others define us. As chapter 2 explains, the messages we receive in early childhood are the strongest, but the influence of others continues throughout life.

Some scholars have argued that we are most attracted to people who confirm our identity.[12] This confirmation can come in different forms, depending on the self-image of the communicator. People with relatively high self-esteem seek out others who confirm their value and as much as possible avoid others who treat them poorly. Conversely, people who regard themselves as unworthy may look for relationships in which others treat them badly. This principle offers one explanation for why some people maintain damaging or unsuccessful relationships. If you view yourself as a loser, you may associate with others who will confirm that self-perception. Of course, relationships can change a communicator's identity as well as confirm it. Supportive relationships can transform feelings of inadequacy into self-respect, and damaging ones can lower self-esteem.

The role of communication in shaping identity works in a second way. Besides others' messages shaping who we think we are, the messages we create often are attempts (some more conscious than others) to get others to see us the way we want to be seen. For example, the choices we make about how to dress and otherwise shape our appearance are almost always attempts to manage our identity. Table 1-1 offers some examples of identity-based goals.

TABLE 1-1	Functions of Interpersonal Communication: Some Examples

SHAPING/MAINTAINING IDENTITY

Defending yourself when criticized by an influential person
Choosing a distinctive wardrobe to create a desired impression
Acting nonchalant when feeling nervous

MEETING SOCIAL NEEDS

Striking up a conversation with a stranger
Chatting with coworkers
Trying to resolve a conflict or disagreement to keep a relationship positive

ACCOMPLISHING PRACTICAL GOALS

Scheduling a meeting
Seeking advice about a problem
Asking a smoker not to light up around you

Social Needs

Besides helping to define who we are, communication provides a vital link with others. Researchers and theorists have identified a whole range of social needs that we satisfy by communicating. These include pleasure; affection, companionship, escape, relaxation; and control.[13]

Needs like these arise in virtually every relationship—with friends, fellow workers, family members, lovers, spouses, and even strangers. And communication is the primary way we satisfy our social needs. In fact, some social scientists have argued that communication is the principal way by which relationships are created.[14] For example, a study of eighteen hundred southern Californians showed that "good old-fashioned" chats with neighbors are the surest way to build a sense of community.[15]

A variety of evidence suggests that many people aren't very successful at managing their interpersonal relationships. For example, one study revealed that one-quarter of the more than four thousand adults surveyed knew more about their dogs than they did about their neighbors' backgrounds, and 48 percent slept with their dogs in their beds instead of another human.[16] More Americans believe that communication problems "very frequently" cause a marriage or a relationship to end than attribute relationship

problems to money, relatives or in-laws, sex, previous relationships (9 percent), or children (7 percent).[17]

Because relationships with others are so vital, some theorists have gone as far as to argue that communication is the primary goal of human existence. Anthropologist Walter Goldschmidt terms the drive for meeting social needs the "human career."[18] If you pause now and make a mental list of your own relationships, you'll probably see that, no matter how successful your relationships at home, with friends, at school, and at work, there is plenty of room for improvement in your everyday life. The information that follows will help you improve the way you communicate with some of the people who matter most to you.

Who can enjoy alone?

John Milton, *Paradise Lost*

Practical Goals

Besides satisfying social needs and shaping our identity, communication is the most widely used approach to satisfying what communication scholars call **instrumental goals:** getting others to behave in ways we want. Some instrumental goals are quite basic: Communication is the tool that lets you tell the hair stylist to take just a little off the sides, lets you negotiate household duties, and lets you convince the plumber that the broken pipe needs attention *now*!

Other instrumental goals are more important. Career success is the prime example. Communication skills—the ability to speak and listen effectively—are the top factors in helping college graduates find jobs in an increasingly competitive workplace, ranking higher than technical competence, work experience, and specific degree earned.[19] Good communication on the job is just as important. Economist James Flanigan explains: "Communication skills will fetch premium pay. The person who talks on the phone to mutual fund investors will have to be even more knowledgeable, efficient, and personable than the bank teller of old. Competition for such jobs won't be based on pay alone but on skills."[20] The same communication skills are increasingly important for getting along well with fellow workers. Harvard Business School Professor Rosabeth Moss Kanter shows that informal interpersonal relationships are the most dynamic sources of power in organizations today.[21] This means that good personal skills aren't just a social nicety: They can mean the difference between success and failure on the job.

Note the overlap between the kinds of identity, social, and practical goals outlined in Table 1-1. For example, you probably try to handle job-related communication (an instrumental goal) in a way that makes your relationships smooth and enjoyable (a social goal). Likewise, you may tell a joke to look clever or humorous (an identity goal) in a way that builds relationships.

Psychologist Abraham Maslow suggested that the physical, identity, social, and practical needs we have been discussing fall into five hierarchical categories, each of which must be satisfied before we concern ourselves with the less fundamental needs.[22] The most basic of these needs are *physical:* sufficient air, water, food, and rest, and the ability to reproduce as a species. The second of Maslow's needs is *safety:* protection from threats to our well-being. Beyond physical and safety needs are the *social needs* we have mentioned already. Beyond these, Maslow suggests, each of us has *self-esteem* needs: the desire to believe that we are worthwhile, valuable people. The final category of needs described by Maslow is *self-actualization:* the desire to develop our potential to the maximum, to become the best person we can be. As you read on, think about the ways in which communication is often necessary to satisfy each level of need.

THE PROCESS OF COMMUNICATION

We have been talking about *communication* as though the actions described by this word were perfectly clear. Before going further we need to explain systematically what happens when people exchange messages with one another. Doing so will introduce you to a common working vocabulary and, at the same time, preview some of the topics that are covered in later chapters.

A Linear View

As recently as fifty years ago, researchers viewed communication as something that one person "does" to another.[23] In this **linear communication model,** communication is like giving an injection: A **sender encodes** ideas and feelings into some sort of **message** and then conveys them by means of a **channel** (speech, writing, and so on) into a **receiver,** who **decodes** the message (see Figure 1-1).

This perspective does provide some useful information. For instance, it highlights how different channels can affect the way a receiver responds to a message. Should you say "I love you" in person? Over the phone? By renting space on a billboard? By sending flowers and a card? With a singing telegram? Each channel has its differences.

The linear model also introduces the concept of **noise**—a term used by social scientists to describe any forces that interfere with effective communication. Noise can occur at every stage of the communication process. Three types of noise can disrupt communication—external, physiological, and psychological. *External noise* (also called "physical noise") involves those factors outside the receiver that make it difficult to hear, as well as many other kinds of distractions. For instance, too much cigarette smoke in a crowded room might make it hard for you to pay attention to another person, and sitting in the rear of an auditorium might make a speaker's remarks unclear. External noise can disrupt communication

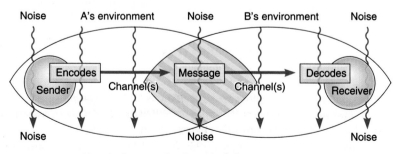

FIGURE 1-1 **Linear Communication Model**

almost anywhere in our model—in the sender, channel, message, or receiver. *Physiological noise* involves biological factors in the receiver or sender that interfere with accurate reception: illness, fatigue, and so on. *Psychological noise* involves forces within a communicator that interfere with the ability to express or understand a message accurately. For instance, a fisherman might exaggerate the size and number of the fish he caught in order to convince himself and others of his talents. In the same way, a student might become so upset upon learning that she failed a test that she would be unable (perhaps *unwilling* is a better word) to understand clearly where she

went wrong. Psychological noise is such an important communication problem that we have devoted much of chapter 9 to investigating its most common form, defensiveness.

A linear model also shows that communicators often occupy different **environments**—fields of experience that help them understand others' behavior. In communication terminology, *environment* refers not only to a physical location but also to the personal experiences and cultural background that participants bring to a conversation.

Consider just some of the factors that might contribute to different environments:

■ Person A might belong to one ethnic group and person B to another.

■ A might be rich and B poor.

■ A might be rushed and B have nowhere to go.

■ A might have lived a long, eventful life and B might be young and inexperienced.

■ A might be passionately concerned with the subject and B indifferent to it.

Environments aren't always obvious. For example, one study revealed that college students who have been enrolled in debate classes become more argumentative and verbally aggressive than those who have not been exposed to this environment.[24]

Notice how the model in Figure 1-1 shows that the environments of persons A and B overlap. This area represents the background that the communicators must have in common. As the shared environment becomes smaller, communication becomes more difficult. Consider a few examples in which different perspectives can make understanding difficult:

- Bosses who have trouble understanding the perspective of their employees will be less effective managers, and workers who do not appreciate the challenges of being a boss are more likely to be uncooperative (and probably less suitable for advancement).

- Parents who have trouble recalling their youth are likely to clash with their children, who have never known and may not appreciate the responsibility that comes with parenting.

- Members of a dominant culture who have never experienced how it feels to be "different" may not appreciate the concerns of people from nondominant cocultures, whose own perspectives make it hard to understand the cultural blindness of the majority.

Differing environments make understanding others challenging, but certainly not impossible. Hard work and many of the skills described in this book provide ways to bridge the gap that separates all of us to a greater or lesser degree. For now, recognizing the challenge that comes from dissimilar environments is a good start. You can't solve a problem until you recognize that it exists.

A Transactional View

Despite its simplicity, the linear view of communication isn't completely accurate. One of its greatest weaknesses is the suggestion that communication flows in one direction, from sender to receiver. Although some types of messages (printed and broadcast messages, for example) do flow in a one-way, linear manner, most types of communication—especially the interpersonal variety—are two-way exchanges.

Consider, for instance, the significance of a friend's yawn as you describe your romantic problems. Or imagine the blush you may see as you tell one of your raunchier jokes to a new acquaintance. Nonverbal behaviors like these show that most face-to-face communication is a two-way affair. The discernible response of a receiver to a sender's message is called **feedback.** Not all feedback is nonverbal, of course. Sometimes it is oral, as when you ask an instructor questions about an upcoming test or volunteer your opinion of a friend's new haircut. In other cases it is written, as when you answer the questions on a midterm exam or respond to a letter from a friend. Figure 1-2 makes the importance of feedback clear. It shows that most communication is, indeed, a two-way affair.

Another weakness of the linear view is the questionable assumption that all communication involves encoding. We certainly do choose symbols to convey most verbal messages. But what about the many nonverbal cues that occur whether or not people speak: facial expressions, gestures, postures, vocal tones, and so on? Cues like these clearly do offer information about others, although they are often unconscious and thus don't involve encoding. For this reason, the transactional model replaces the

Like paths and alleys overgrown with hardy, rank-growing weeds, the words we use are overgrown with our individual, private, provincial associations, which tend to choke the meaning.

Stefan Themerson

term encoding with the broader label **behavior** because it describes both intentional and unintentional actions that can be observed and interpreted.[25]

A **transactional communication model** represents communication accurately in other respects. It reveals that we usually encode, send, receive, and decode messages simultaneously and not in a back-and-forth manner suggested by the linear model. Consider, for example, what might occur when you and

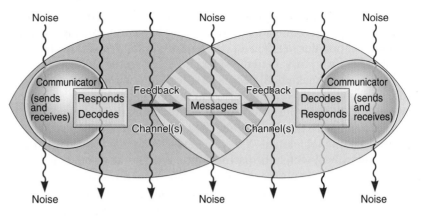

FIGURE 1-2 **Transactional Communication Model**

a housemate negotiate how to handle household chores. As soon as you begin to hear (receive) the words sent by your housemate, "I want to talk about cleaning the kitchen . . . ," you grimace and clench your jaw (sending a nonverbal message of your own while receiving the verbal one). This reaction leads your housemate to interrupt himself, defensively sending a new message: "Now wait a minute. . . ." Because communicators send and receive messages simultaneously, the transactional model pictured in Figure 1-2 combines these functions into the single role of "communicator."[26]

A transactional model of communication shows that it's difficult to isolate a single discrete "act" of communication from the events that precede and follow it.[27] Consider the cartoon on this page. At first glance it appears that Jeremy is the victim of his mother's nagging. On the other hand, if Jeremy would be more responsive to his mother, she might not need to be so persistent. In other words, the communication pattern that Jeremy and his mother have created together contributes to the quality of their relationship.

The transactional model shows that communication isn't something that we do *to* others; rather, it is an activity that we do *with* them. In this sense, person-to-person communication is rather like dancing—at least

Reprinted with special permission of King Features Syndicate.

the kind of dancing we do with partners. Like dancing, communication depends on the involvement of a partner. And like good dancing, successful communication doesn't depend only on the person who takes the lead. A great dancer who forgets to consider and adapt to the skill level of his or her partner can make both people look bad. In communication and dancing, having even two talented partners doesn't guarantee success. When two skilled dancers perform without coordinating their movements, the results feel bad to the dancers and look foolish to an audience. Finally, relational communication—like dancing—is a unique creation that arises out of the way in which the partners interact. The way you dance probably varies from one partner to another. Likewise, the way you communicate almost certainly varies from one partner to another.

http://www.sfc.keio.ac.jp/~masanao/Mosaic_data/com_model.html

This Web site and list of links provides you with visual access to the many various communication models developed over the years in the communication discipline. Compare and contrast communication models by completing Activity 1.2 on the *Looking Out/Looking In* Web site.

INVITATION TO INSIGHT

A MODEL MUDDLE

You can gain appreciation for the transactional communication model by using Figure 1-2 to analyze a communication problem you recently experienced. Which elements described in the model help explain the problem? What steps might you and the other person or persons involved have taken to overcome the difficulties? Share the results with your classmates, and determine which elements of the communication process create the greatest challenges for your group.

The way in which communicators influence one another shows up dramatically in relationships between parents and their children. We normally think of "good parenting" as a skill that some people possess and others lack. We judge the ability of a mother and father in terms of how well their children turn out. In fact, research suggests that the quality of interaction between parents and children is a two-way affair—that children influence parents just as much as the reverse.[28] For example, children who engage in what social scientists call "problematic behavior" evoke more high-control responses from their parents than do cooperative children. By contrast, youngsters with mild temperaments are less likely to provoke coercive reactions by their parents than are more aggressive children. Parents with low self-esteem tend to send more messages that weaken the self-esteem of their children, who in turn are likely to act in ways that make the parents feel even worse about themselves. Thus, a mutually reinforcing cycle arises in which parents and children shape one another's feelings and behavior. In cases like this it's at least difficult and probably impossible to identify who is the "sender" and who is the "receiver" of messages. It's more accurate to acknowledge that parents and children—just like husbands and wives, bosses and employees, teachers and students, or any other people in relationships—act in ways that mutually influence one another.

Now we can summarize the definition of *communication* that we have been developing. **Communication** is a continuous, transactional

Sometimes she thought the trouble was, she and Leon were too well acquainted. The most innocent remark could call up such a string of associations, so many past slights and insults never quite settled or forgotten, merely smoothed over. They could no longer have a single uncomplicated feeling about one another.

Anne Tyler, *Morgan's Passing*

process involving participants who occupy different but overlapping environments and create relationships through the exchange of messages, many of which are affected by external, physiological, and psychological noise. Whether or not you memorize this definition is a matter for you and your instructor to decide. In any case, notice how it reflects a more sophisticated view of the process than you might have had before reading this far.

COMMUNICATION PRINCIPLES AND MISCONCEPTIONS

Before we look at the qualities that distinguish interpersonal communication, it's important to define what communication is and what it isn't and to discuss what it can and can't accomplish.

Communication Principles

It's possible to draw several important conclusions about communication from what you have already learned in this chapter.

Communication Can Be Intentional or Unintentional   Some communication is clearly intentional: You probably plan your words carefully before asking the boss for a raise or offering constructive criticism. Some scholars argue that only intentional messages like these qualify as communication. Others argue that even unintentional behavior is communicative. Suppose, for instance, that a friend overhears you muttering complaints to yourself. Even though you didn't intend for her to hear your remarks, they certainly did carry a message. In addition to these slips of the tongue, we unintentionally send many nonverbal messages. You might not be aware of your sour expression, impatient shifting, or

sigh of boredom, but others view them nonetheless. Scholars have debated without reaching consensus about whether unintentional behavior should be considered communication, and it's unlikely that they will ever settle this issue.[29]

In *Looking Out/Looking In* we will look at the communicative value of both intentional and unintentional behavior.

It's Impossible Not to Communicate

Because both intentional and unintentional behaviors send a message, many theorists agree that it is impossible not to communicate. Whatever you do—whether you speak or remain silent, confront or avoid, act emotional or keep a poker face—you provide information to others about your thoughts and feelings. In this sense we are like transmitters that can't be shut off.

Of course, the people who decode your message may not interpret it accurately. They might take your kidding seriously or underestimate your feelings, for example. The message that you intend to convey may not even resemble the one that others infer from your actions. Thus, when we talk about "a communication breakdown" or "miscommunication," we rarely mean that communication has ended. Instead, we mean that it is inaccurate or unsatisfying.[30]

This explains why the best way to boost understanding is to discuss your intentions and your interpretations of the other person's behavior until you have negotiated a shared meaning. The perception-checking skills described in chapter 3, the tips on clear language offered in chapter 5, and the listening skills introduced in chapter 7 will give you tools to boost the odds that the meanings of messages you send and receive are understandable to both you and others.

Communication Is Irreversible

We sometimes wish that we could back up in time, erasing words or acts and replacing them with better alternatives. Unfortunately, such reversal is impossible. Sometimes, further explanation can clear up another's confusion, or an apology can mollify another's hurt feelings, but other times no amount of explanation can erase the impression you have created. It is no more possible to "unreceive" a message than to "unsqueeze" a tube of toothpaste. Words said and deeds done are irretrievable.

Communication Is Unrepeatable

Because communication is an ongoing process, it is impossible to repeat the same event. The friendly smile that worked so well when meeting a stranger last week might not succeed with the person you meet tomorrow: It might feel stale and artificial to you the second time around, or it might be wrong for the new person or occasion. Even with the same person, it's impossible to re-create an event. Why? Because neither you nor the other person *are* the same persons. You've both lived longer. The behavior isn't original. Your feelings about one another may have changed. You need not constantly invent new ways to act around familiar people, but you should realize that the "same" words and behavior are different each time they are

"C'mon, let's get outta here," I said. "You give me a royal pain in the ass, if you want to know the truth."

Boy, did she hit the ceiling when I said that. I know I shouldn't have said it, and I probably wouldn't've ordinarily, but she was depressing the hell out of me. Usually I never say crude things like that to girls. *Boy,* did she hit the ceiling. I apologized like a madman, but she wouldn't accept my apology.

J. D. Salinger, *Catcher in the Rye*

spoken or performed. Chapter 8 will alert you to the stages through which a relationship progresses.

Communication Misconceptions

It's just as important to know what communication is *not* as to know what it is.[31] Avoiding the following misconceptions can save you a great deal of personal trouble.

Meanings Are Not in Words   The biggest mistake we can make is to assume that *saying* something is the same thing as *communicating* it. To use the terminology of our communication model, there's no guarantee that a receiver will decode a message in a way that matches the sender's intention. (If you doubt this proposition, list all the times you've been misunderstood in the past month.) Chapter 3 outlines the many reasons why people can interpret a statement differently from the way you intended it, and chapter 5 describes the most common types of verbal misunderstandings and suggests ways to minimize them. Chapter 7 introduces listening skills that help ensure that the way you receive messages matches the ideas that a speaker is trying to convey.

"Let's stop this before we both say a lot of things we mean."

©The New Yorker Collection 1996 Bruce Eric Kaplan from cartoonbank.com. All Rights Reserved.

More Communication Is Not Always Better   Whereas not communicating enough can cause problems, there are also situations when *too much* communication is a mistake. Sometimes excessive communication is simply unproductive, as when two people "talk a problem to death," going over the same ground again and again without making progress. There are other times when talking too much actually aggravates a problem. We've all had the experience of "talking ourselves into a hole"—making a bad situation worse by pursuing it too far. As one communication book puts it, "More and more negative communication merely leads to more and more negative results."[32]

There are even times when *no* communication is the best course. Any good salesperson will testify that it's often best to stop talking and let the customer think about the product, and when two people are angry and hurt, they may say things that they don't mean and that they will later regret. In such cases it's probably best to spend time cooling off, thinking about what to say and how to say it. Chapter 4 will help you decide when and how to share feelings.

No Single Person or Event Causes Another's Reaction   Although communicative skill can often make the difference between satisfying and unsatisfying outcomes, it's a mistake to suggest that any single thing we say or do causes an outcome. Many factors play a role in how others will react to your communication in a single situation. Suppose, for example, that you lose your temper and say something to a friend that

I don't care who's wrong or right.
I don't really wanna fight no more.
Too much talking, babe.
Let's sleep on it tonight.
I don't really wanna fight no more.
This is time for letting go.

Tina Turner

you regret as soon as the words escape your lips. Your friend's reaction will depend on a whole host of events besides your unjustified remark: her frame of mind at the moment (uptight or mellow), elements of her personality (judgmental or forgiving), your relational history (supportive or hostile), and her knowledge of any factors in your life that might have contributed to your unjustified remark. Because communication is a transactional, ongoing, collaborative process, it's usually a mistake to think that any event occurs in a vacuum.

Communication Will Not Solve All Problems   Sometimes even the best-planned, best-timed communication won't solve a problem. Imagine, for example, that you ask an instructor to explain why you received a poor grade on a project that you believe deserved top marks. The instructor clearly outlines the reasons why you received the poor grade and sticks to that position after listening thoughtfully to your protests. Has communication solved the problem? Hardly.

Sometimes clear communication is even the *cause* of problems. Suppose, for example, that a friend asks you for an honest opinion of the $200 outfit he has just bought. Your clear and sincere answer, "I think it makes you look fat," might do more harm than good. Deciding when and how to self-disclose isn't always easy. See chapter 8 for suggestions.

THE NATURE OF INTERPERSONAL COMMUNICATION

Now that you have a better understanding of the overall process of human communication, it's time to look at what makes some types uniquely interpersonal.

Two Views of Interpersonal Communication

Scholars have characterized interpersonal communication in a number of ways.[33] The most obvious definition focuses on the number of people involved. A **quantitative** definition of interpersonal communication includes any interaction between two people, usually face to face. Social scientists call two persons interacting a **dyad,** and they often use the adjective *dyadic* to describe this type of communication. So, in a quantitative sense, the terms *dyadic communication* and *interpersonal communication* can be used interchangeably. Using a quantitative definition, a sales clerk and customer or a police officer ticketing a speeding driver would be an example of interpersonal acts, whereas a teacher and class or a performer and audience would not.

Dyadic communication is different from the kind of interaction that occurs in larger groups. For example, two-person exchanges are the earliest form of interaction we experience, and throughout life they are the most common type of communication. Unlike threesomes and other

Having just heard that his dear friend of 25 years had died of a heart attack, stockbroker Bernard Pechter was crying as he drove down Market St. at 6:15 A.M. on his way to work. A policewoman in a patrol car flashed her red lights and motioned him to pull over. She then ordered him out of the car, saying, "You look so sad I figured you need a hug." She held him for a few moments and drove off, leaving Bernard dumbfounded and also open-mouthed. But definitely feeling better.

Herb Caen, San Francisco *Chronicle*

groups, dyads are complete and cannot be subdivided. If one person withdraws from the other, the relationship is finished. This indivisibility means that, unlike groups, the partners in a dyad can't form coalitions to get their needs met: They must work matters out with one another.

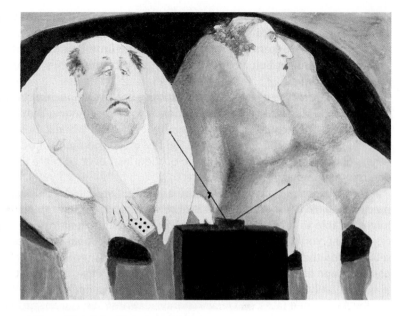

Despite the unique qualities of dyads, you might object to the quantitative definition of interpersonal communication. For example, consider a routine transaction between a sales clerk and customer or the rushed exchange when you ask a stranger on the street for directions. Communication of this sort hardly seems interpersonal—or personal in any sense of the word. In fact, after transactions like this we commonly remark, "I might as well have been talking to a machine." On the other hand, you may have been lucky to have had a personally rewarding relationship with an instructor that went far beyond the normal limits of the teacher-student relationship.[34]

The impersonal nature of some two-person exchanges and the personal nature of others have led some scholars to argue that *quality*, not quantity, is what distinguishes interpersonal communication.[35] Using a **qualitative** definition, interpersonal communication occurs when people treat one another as unique individuals, regardless of the context in which the interaction occurs or the number of people involved. When quality of interaction is the criterion, the opposite of interpersonal communication is **impersonal interaction,** not group, public, or mass communication.

Several features distinguish qualitatively interpersonal communication from less personal communication[36] The first feature is *uniqueness*. Communication in impersonal exchanges is determined by social *rules* (laugh politely at others' jokes, don't dominate a conversation, and so on) and by social *roles* (the customer is always right, be especially polite to senior citizens). Qualitatively interpersonal relationships are characterized by the development of unique rules and roles. For example, in one relationship you might exchange good-natured insults, whereas in another you are careful never to offend your partner. Likewise, you might handle conflicts with one friend or family member by expressing disagreements as soon as they arise, whereas the unwritten rule in another relationship is to withhold resentments until they build up and then clear the air periodically. One communication scholar coined the term *relational culture* to describe people in close relationships who create their own unique ways of interacting.[37]

To know all your neighbors on the global level does not mean that you will automatically love them all; it does not, in and of itself, introduce a reign of peace and brotherhood. But to be potentially in touch with everybody at least makes fighting more uncomfortable. It becomes easier to argue instead.

Isaac Asimov, "The Fourth Revolution"

Even within a single relationship communication can vary from ritualistic to unique. Sometimes your relationship with friends, family, neighbors, or coworkers might fit the standard cultural pattern; but on occasions you might behave in quite different ways that reflect your feelings at the moment.

A second feature of qualitatively interpersonal relationships is *irreplaceability*. Because interpersonal relationships are unique, they can't be replaced. This explains why we usually feel so sad when a close friendship or love affair cools down. We know that no matter how many other relationships fill our lives, none of them will ever be quite like the one that just ended.

Interdependence is a third feature of qualitatively interpersonal relationships. At the most basic level the fate of the partners is connected. You might be able to brush off the anger, affection, excitement, or depression of someone you're not involved with personally, but in an interpersonal relationship the other's life affects you. Sometimes interdependence is a pleasure, and at other times it is a burden. In either case, it is a fact of life in qualitatively interpersonal relationships. Interdependence goes beyond the level of joined fates. In interpersonal relationships, our very identity depends on the nature of our interaction with others. As psychologist Kenneth Gergen puts it: "One cannot be 'attractive' without others who are attracted, a 'leader' without others willing to follow, or a 'loving person' without others to affirm with appreciation."[38] As chapter 2 explains, our identity is shaped by interaction with many people, not just those with whom we have interpersonal relationships. But the "significant others" with whom we communicate in a qualitatively interpersonal manner have a profound influence on how we view ourselves.

A fourth feature of interpersonal relationships is often (though not always) the amount of *disclosure* of personal information. In impersonal relationships we don't reveal much about ourselves, but in interpersonal relationships we feel more comfortable sharing our thoughts and feelings. This doesn't mean that all interpersonal relationships are warm and caring, or that all self-disclosure is positive. It's possible to reveal negative, personal information: "I'm really mad at you . . ."

A fifth feature of interpersonal communication is *intrinsic rewards*. In impersonal communication we seek payoffs that have little to do with the people involved. You listen to professors in class or talk to potential buyers of your used car in order to reach goals that have little to do with developing personal relationships. By contrast, you spend time in qualitatively interpersonal relationships with friends, lovers, and others because you find the time personally rewarding. It often doesn't matter *what* you talk about: The relationship itself is what's important.

Because relationships that are unique, disclosing, and intrinsically rewarding are rare, qualitatively interpersonal communication is relatively scarce. We chat pleasantly with shopkeepers or fellow passengers on the bus or plane; we discuss the weather or current events with most classmates and neighbors; we deal with coworkers and teachers in a polite way, but considering the number of people with whom we communicate, personal relationships are by far in the minority.

The rarity of personal relationships isn't necessarily unfortunate. Most of us don't have the time or energy to create personal relationships with everyone we encounter. In fact, the scarcity of qualitatively interpersonal communication contributes to its value. Like precious jewels and one-of-a-kind artwork, interpersonal relationships are special because of their scarcity.

Technology and Interpersonal Communication

Face-to-face conversation isn't the only way people can create and maintain personal relationships. Along with the telephone and old-fashioned correspondence, **computer-mediated communication** (CMC) provides another way to interact. E-mail is the most popular form of CMC. Instant messaging and online chat are other tools that acquaintances—and even strangers—can use to communicate.

At first, some theorists predicted that CMC would reduce the quality of interpersonal communication. With no nonverbal cues, it seemed that CMC couldn't match the rich interaction that happens in person or even over the phone, where the communicators' voices provide cues about their feelings. Furthermore, some research seems to suggest that CMC reduces communication in important relationships. One survey conducted by Stanford University professor Norman Nie showed that roughly 25 percent of the people who use the Internet regularly spent less time talking in person and on the phone with friends and family members.[39] Even when people replace some of their face-to-face communication with online communication, some observers claim that the quality of the relationship suffers. "E-mail is a way to stay in touch," said Nie, "but you can't share a coffee or a beer with somebody on e-mail or give them a hug."

Despite observations like this, a growing body of research is showing that CMC isn't the threat to relationships that some critics have feared. A UCLA survey that measured the behavior of both Internet users and nonusers revealed that over two-thirds of U.S. adults and children use the Internet and that over three-quarters of these people say they never feel ignored by another household member's spending time online.[40] In fact, the majority of Internet users said that e-mail Web sites and chat rooms had a "modestly positive impact" on their ability to communicate more with family members and make new friends. Another survey reinforces the notion that electronic communication can *enhance*, not diminish, the quantity and quality of interpersonal communication. A survey of over three thousand adults in the United States (again, both Internet users and nonusers) showed how relationships can prosper online.[41] In that survey, 72 percent of the Internet users had communicated with a relative or a friend within the past day, compared with 61 percent for nonusers. Surprisingly, the Internet users were also more likely to have phoned friends and relatives. Even more significant than the amount of communication that occurs online is its quality. Fifty-five percent of Internet users said that e-mail had improved communications with family, and 66 percent said that their contact

Richard, we need to talk.
I'll e-mail you.

© The New Yorker Collection 1997 Aaron Bacall from cartoonbank.com. All Rights Reserved.

with friends had increased because of e-mail. Among women, the rate of satisfaction was even higher: 60 percent reported better contact with family and 71 percent with friends.

Many scholars are discovering what CMC users know from personal experience: Communication via computer can be at least as deep and complex as personal contact.[42] There are several reasons why CMC can increase both the quantity and quality of interpersonal communication. For one thing, CMC makes communication easier. Busy schedules and long distances can make quality time in face-to-face contact difficult or impossible. The challenge of finding time is especially tough for people who are separated by long distances and multiple time zones. In relationships like this, the *asynchronous* nature of e-mail provides a way to share information that otherwise would be impossible. Communicators can create their own message and respond to one another without having to connect in real time. Instant messaging is another way to keep in touch: Discovering that a friend or relative is online and starting an electronic conversation is "like walking down the street and sometimes running into a friend," says Laura Balsam, a New York computer consultant.[43]

Even when face-to-face communication is convenient, some people find it easier to share personal information via CMC. Sociolinguist Deborah Tannen describes how e-mail transformed the quality of two relationships:

> E-mail deepened my friendship with Ralph. Though his office was next to mine, we rarely had extended conversations because he is shy. Face to face he mumbled so, I could barely tell he was speaking. But when we both got on e-mail, I started receiving long, self-revealing messages; we poured our hearts out to each other. A friend discovered that e-mail opened up that kind of communication with her father. He would never talk much on the phone (as her mother would), but they have become close since they both got on line.[44]

Experiences like these help explain why Steve Jobs, the cofounder of Apple Computer, suggested that personal computers be renamed "*inter*-personal computers."[45]

Personal and Impersonal Communication: A Matter of Balance

Now that you understand the differences between qualitatively interpersonal and impersonal communication, we need to ask some important questions. Is interpersonal communication better than impersonal communication? Is more interpersonal communication the goal?

Most relationships aren't *either* interpersonal *or* impersonal. Rather, they fall somewhere on a continuum between these two extremes. Consider, for example, the kinds of communication described in the "Electronic Block Party" on page 21. On one hand, the messages described in the reading sound basically instrumental and impersonal: about repairing water pipes, choosing a car mechanic, and so on. On the other hand, it's easy to imagine how, as neighbors become better acquainted, they might

THE ELECTRONIC BLOCK PARTY

It was bound to happen. Everything else is on line. So why not the neighborhood?

It started when a new arrival to the neighborhood decided to introduce herself not just to her immediate neighbors, but to everyone. When she finished her visits, we had a count of the houses in our enclave and a spreadsheet with everyone's name, street address and E-mail address. She distributed the list at a neighborhood meeting about repaving our streets. Shortly thereafter, the first neighborhood-wide E-mail appeared in our in-boxes. We were networked.

It has been a huge bonus in our busy lives to be able to tackle issues with the tap of a "send" or "reply" button. We've gotten messages about everything from bats—a frantic neighbor killed a bat in her house with a broomstick, then sought advice about what she should have done—to advice on choosing a car mechanic.

Some neighbors have successfully advertised apartments for rent. We used E-mail to raise money for a couple of decorative trees for our newly repaved streets. There were some lively exchanges about whether we should all replace the water pipes leading to our homes as the street was torn up. Would it increase property values? Who had found a good person to do it? What if we all got together and negotiated with one contractor to get a better price for everyone? There are a few households that aren't wired. But we know which ones they are, and we remember to use the telephone when necessary.

Some people claim that it's isolating to communicate using a computer. Most of our neighbors would disagree. We've shared much more on line than we do in our once-a-year block party. We're a community in a whole new sense—one that solves problems and shares news, both good and not so good.

Judy F. Kugel

start to develop unique ways of interacting and discover irreplaceable friendships. Your own experience probably reveals that there is often a personal element in even the most impersonal situations. You might appreciate the unique sense of humor of a grocery checker or connect on a personal level with the person cutting your hair. And even the most tyrannical, demanding, by-the-book boss might show an occasional flash of humanity.

Just as there's a personal element in many impersonal settings, there is also an impersonal element to our relationships with the people we care most about. There are occasions when we don't want to be personal: when we're distracted, tired, busy, or just not interested. In fact, interpersonal communication is rather like rich food—it's fine in moderation, but too much can make you uncomfortable.

The personal-impersonal mixture of communicating in a relationship can change over time. The communication between young lovers who talk only about their feelings may change as their relationship develops,

INVITATION TO INSIGHT

HOW PERSONAL ARE YOUR RELATIONSHIPS?

Use the characteristics of qualitatively interpersonal communication described on pages 17–19 to think about your own relationships.

1. Make a list of several people who are close to you—family members, people you live with, friends, coworkers, and so on.

2. Use the scales that follow to rate each relationship. To distinguish the relationships from one another, use a different color of ink for each one.

3. Consider comparing your results with those of classmates or friends.

After completing the exercise, ask yourself the important question: How satisfied are you with the answers you have found?

Uniqueness

| 1 | 2 | 3 | 4 | 5 |

Standardized, habitual ———————————————— Unique

Replaceability

| 1 | 2 | 3 | 4 | 5 |

Replaceable ———————————————— Irreplaceable

Dependence

| 1 | 2 | 3 | 4 | 5 |

Independent ———————————————— Interdependent

Disclosure

| 1 | 2 | 3 | 4 | 5 |

Low disclosure ———————————————— High disclosure

ETHICAL CHALLENGE

Martin Buber's *I and Thou*

Martin Buber is arguably the most influential advocate of qualitatively interpersonal communication as defined on pages 17–19. His book *Ich und Du* has been a worldwide classic, selling millions of copies since its publication in 1922.

In English, the book's title has sometimes been translated as *I and Thou*, wording that both obscures and explains its central theme. The religious connotations of the word *thou* have led some readers to think that Buber was writing from a theological point of view. In fact, *thou* reflects a distinction in German between two forms of address: the formal *sie* and the personal *du*. Other languages make the same differentiation. In Spanish, for example, the terms are *usted* and *tu*, and in French *vous* and *tu*. Because *thou* connotes formality, the definitive English translation of Buber's work refers to its key concept as "I-You," the best English representation of the kind of intimate relationship that Buber is describing.

Buber states that "I-It" and "I-You" represent two ways in which humans can relate to one another. "I-It" relationships are stable, predictable, detached. In an "I-It" mode we deal with people because they can do things for us: pump gas, laugh at our jokes, buy products we are selling, provide information or amusement. "I-It" is also the approach of science, which attempts to understand what makes people tick in order to explain, predict, and control their behavior. Buber would have regarded advertisers as operating in an "I-It" mode, crafting messages that lead people to buy their products or services. "I-It" relationships exist in personal relationships as well as impersonal ones: On everyday basis parents and children, bosses and employees, service providers and customers—even lovers—deal with one another as objects ("I wish she would leave me alone"; "Can you pick me up after work?" "How can I get him/her to love me?").

In profound contrast to "I-It" relationships, Buber described an "I-You" way of interacting. "I-You" relationships are utterly unique. Because no two teachers or students, parents or children, husbands or wives, bosses or employees are alike, we encounter each person as an individual and not as a member of some category. An "I-You" posture goes further: Not only are people different from one another, but also they themselves change from moment to moment. An "I-You" relationship arises out of how we are now, not how we might have been yesterday or even a moment ago. In an "I-You" relationship, persuasion and control are out of the question: We certainly may explain our point of view, but ultimately we respect the fact that others are free to act.

Buber acknowledges that it is impossible to create and sustain pure "I-You" relationships. But without this qualitatively interpersonal level of contact, our lives are impoverished. To paraphrase Buber, without "I-It" we cannot exist; but if we live only with "I-It," we are not fully human.

Think of your most important relationships. To what degree can they be described as "I-You" or "I-It"? How satisfied are you with this level of relating? What obligation do you have to treat others in an "I-Thou" manner? Based on your answers to these questions, how might you change your style of communication?

An English translation of Martin Buber's *I and Thou* was published in 1970 by Scribner's. For useful descriptions of its central themes, see John Stewart, "A Philosopher's Approach" in J. Stewart, ed., *Bridges, Not Walls* (New York: McGraw-Hill, 1999); and H. J. Paton's chapter "Martin Buber" in *The Modern Predicament* (London: Allen & Unwin, 1955).

so that several years later their communication has become more routine and ritualized, and the percentage of time they spend on personal, relational issues drops and the conversation about less intimate topics increases. Chapter 8 discusses how communication changes as relationships pass through various stages and also describes the role of self-disclosure in keeping those relationships strong. As you read this information, you will see even more clearly that, although interpersonal communication can make life worth living, it isn't possible or desirable all the time.

It's clear that there is a place in our lives for both impersonal and interpersonal communications. Each type has its uses. The real challenge, then, is to find the right balance between the two types.

COMMUNICATING ABOUT RELATIONSHIPS

By now you understand the characteristics that distinguish interpersonal relationships. But what kinds of messages do we exchange as we communicate interpersonally?

Content and Relational Messages

Virtually every verbal statement has a **content** dimension, containing the subject being discussed. The content of such statements as "It's your turn to do the dishes" or "I'm busy Saturday night" is obvious.

Content messages aren't the only thing being exchanged when two people communicate. In addition, almost every message—both verbal and nonverbal—also has a second, **relational** dimension, which makes statements about how the parties feel toward one another.[46] These relational messages deal with one or more social needs, most commonly control, affection, or respect. Consider the two examples we just mentioned:

- Imagine two ways of saying "It's your turn to do the dishes": one that is demanding and another that is matter-of-fact. Notice how the different nonverbal messages make statements about how the sender views control in this part of the relationship. The demanding tone says, in effect, "I have a right to tell you what to do around the house," whereas the matter-of-fact tone suggests, "I'm just reminding you of something you might have overlooked."

- You can easily visualize two ways to deliver the statement "I'm busy Saturday night": one with little affection and the other with much affection.

Notice that in each of these examples the relational dimension of the message was never discussed. In fact, most of the time we aren't conscious of the many relational messages that bombard us every day. Sometimes we are unaware of relational messages because they match our belief about the amount of respect, control, and affection that is appropriate. For example, you probably won't be offended if your boss tells you to do a certain job because you agree that supervisors have the right to direct employees. In other cases, however, conflicts arise over relational messages even though content is not disputed. If your boss delivers the order in a condescending, sarcastic, or abusive tone of voice, you probably will be offended. Your complaint wouldn't be with the order itself but rather with the way it was delivered. "I may work for this company," you might think, "but I'm not a slave or an idiot. I deserve to be treated like a human being."

"You say, 'off with her head,' but what I'm hearing is, 'I feel neglected.'"

How are relational messages communicated? As the boss-employee example suggests, they are usually communicated nonverbally. To test this fact for yourself, imagine how you could act while saying, "Can you help me for a minute?" in a way that communicates each of the following relationships:

superiority	friendliness	sexual desire
helplessness	aloofness	irritation

Although nonverbal behaviors are a good source of relational messages, they are ambiguous. The sharp tone that you receive as a personal insult might be due to fatigue, and the interruption that you assume is an attempt to ignore your ideas might be a sign of pressure that has nothing to do with you. Before you jump to conclusions about relational clues, it's a good idea to check them out verbally. Chapter 3 will introduce you to the skill of perception checking—a useful tool for verifying your hunches about nonverbal behavior.

Types of Relational Messages

The number and variety of content messages are almost infinite, ranging from black holes to doughnut holes, from rock and roll to *Rock of Ages*. But unlike the range of content messages, there is a surprisingly narrow range of relational messages. Virtually all of them fit into one of three categories.

Affinity   An important kind of relational communication involves **affinity**—the degree to which people like or appreciate one another.[47] Not surprisingly, affection is the most important ingredient in romantic relationships.[4*] Not all affinity messages are positive, though: A glare or an angry word shows the level of liking just as clearly as a smile or profession of love. The range of affinity messages shows that interpersonal relationships aren't always friendly. Friends who disagree or lovers who argue are still partners. As long as these relationships possess all the characteristics that distinguish them as interpersonal—uniqueness, irreplaceability, interdependence, and so on—we can say they are interpersonal. In this sense, liking and disliking (both signs that we *care* about the other person) are much more closely related to one another than either is to indifference.

Respect   At first glance respect might seem identical to affinity, but the two attitudes are different.[49] Whereas affinity involves liking, **respect** involves esteem. It's possible to like others without respecting them. For instance, you might like—or even probably love—your two-year-old cousin without respecting her. In the same way, you might have a great deal of affection for some friends, yet not respect the way they behave. The reverse is also true: It's possible to respect people we don't like. You might hold an acquaintance in high esteem for being a hard worker, honest, talented, or clever, yet not particularly enjoy that person's company.

Sometimes being respected is more important than being liked. Think about occasions in school when you were offended because an instructor or fellow students didn't seem to take your comments or questions seriously. The same principle holds on the job, where having your opinions count often means more than being popular. Even in more personal relationships, conflicts often focus on the issue of respect. Being taken seriously is a vital ingredient of self-esteem. For reasons like this, respect is a good predictor of successful relationships.

Control   A final way to look at relationships involves the question of **control**—the degree to which the parties in a relationship have the power to influence one another.

Communication researchers have commonly identified the balance of relational control in two ways. *Conversational control* involves who talks the most, who interrupts whom, and who changes the topic most often.[50] The person who exercises the greatest amount of conversational control doesn't always make decisions. For example, a friend who chatters constantly might not persuade you to accept his beliefs. *Decision control* involves who has the power to determine what will happen in the relationship. What will we do Saturday night? Shall we use our savings to fix up the house or to take a vacation? How much time should we spend together and how much should we spend apart? As these examples suggest, some decisions are minor, whereas others are major. It's important to realize that even the smallest decisions reveal something about the balance of power in the relationship.

There are at least two ways to look at the distribution of control in a relationship.[51] A **complementary relationship** exists when one party exercises control, and the other is willing to go along. As the examples in Table 1-2 show, the person in control is often labeled "one up," and the one who is not in control is labeled "one down." Whereas power is unequal in a complementary relationship, in a **symmetrical relationship** the partners seek the same degree of control. Table 1-2 illustrates that symmetrical communication comes in several forms. In *neutralized symmetry*, each person is comfortable possessing the same amount of power. On the other hand, in *competitive symmetry*, each person strives to be one-up, controlling the other; and in submissive symmetry, everyone wants to avoid being in control and be in a one-down position.

Most healthy relationships handle the distribution of control in a flexible way (sometimes called **parallel**). Rather than clinging to the lopsidedness of complementary relationships and the total equality of neutralized symmetry, partners shift between one-up, one-down, and straight-across roles. John may handle the decisions about car repairs and menu planning, as well as taking the spotlight at parties with their friends. Mary manages the finances and makes most of the decisions about child care, as well as controlling the conversation when she and John are alone. When a decision is very important to one partner, the other willingly gives in, knowing that the favor will be returned later. When issues are important to both partners, they try to share power equally. But when an impasse occurs, each will make concessions in a way that keeps the overall balance of power equal. The same sort of parallel arrangement characterizes many working relationships, even among superiors and subordinates. The boss may assert authority in many cases but defer to employees in other cases when their judgment or experience justifies that approach. And much of the time, both boss and employees will work together to develop a solution that makes sense to everyone.

TABLE 1-2   **Distribution of Control in Relationships**

Complementary **Unequal control (one-up, one-down)**	"Let's go dancing tonight." "Sure. That sounds great." "What do you think I should do?" "I think you should quit the job."
Neutralized Symmetry **Shared control (straight across)**	"We could save money by taking the red-eye flight." "Good idea. And also by checking the Web for hotel deals."
Competitive Symmetry **Both seek control (both up)**	"Women still don't get a fair deal these days." "Oh, sure, they do. Don't be so negative."
Submissive Symmetry **Both avoid control (both down)**	"Do you think we should go out tonight or stay home?" "I don't care. Whatever you want is fine."

MEASURING YOUR RELATIONSHIPS

What kinds of relational messages do you communicate? What do they say about your relationship with others? You can find out by following these steps.

1. Choose an important interpersonal relationship.

2. Place your initials on each of the scales below to represent the kinds of relational messages you communicate to the other person. Be prepared to offer specific examples of situations that illustrate this type of relational communication.

3. Place your partner's initials on each scale representing your perception of his or her relational messages, and be prepared to offer examples to back up your choices.

4. Invite your partner to complete steps 2 and 3, using a different color of ink to distinguish his or her responses from yours.

5. Now compare your answers with your partner's, and answer the following questions:

   a. Are your responses similar or different? If they are different, whose perception is more accurate?

   b. Are you satisfied with the relationship as it is described here? If not, what can you do to improve it?

Low	High
	Affinity

Low	High
	Respect

Complementary	Symmetrical
	Control

Metacommunication

Not all relational messages are nonverbal. Social scientists use the term **metacommunication** to describe messages that people exchange about their relationship. In other words, metacommunication is communication about communication. Whenever we discuss a relationship with others, we are metacommunicating: "I wish we could stop arguing so much" or "I appreciate how honest you've been with me." Verbal metacommunication is an essential ingredient in successful relationships. Sooner or later it becomes necessary to talk about what is going on between you and the other person. The ability to focus on the kinds of issues described in this chapter can keep the relationship on track.

Metacommunication is an important method for solving conflicts in a constructive manner. It provides a way to shift discussion from the content level to relational questions, where the problem often lies. For example, consider the conversation between Macon and Muriel in the

COMMUNICATION TRANSCRIPT

Content and Relational Messages

Both content and relational communication are important. But when each person in a conversation focuses on a different level, problems are likely to arise. In this excerpt from Anne Tyler's novel The Accidental Tourist, Muriel tries to turn Macon's content-related remark about her son into a discussion about the future of their relationship. Until Macon and Muriel agree about whether they will focus on content or relational issues, they are likely to remain at an uncomfortable impasse.

"I don't think Alexander's getting a proper education," he said to her one evening.

"Oh, he's okay."

"I asked him to figure what change they'd give back when we bought the milk today, and he didn't have the faintest idea. He didn't even know he'd have to subtract."

"Well, he's only in second grade," Muriel said.

"I think he ought to switch to a private school."

"Private schools cost money."

"So? I'll pay."

She stopped flipping the bacon and looked over at him. "What are you saying?" she asked.

"Pardon?"

"What are you saying, Macon? Are you saying you're committed?"

Macon cleared his throat. He said, "Committed."

"Alexander's got ten more years of school ahead of him. Are you saying you'll be around for all ten years?"

"Um . . ."

"I can't just put him in a school and take him out again with every passing whim of yours."

He was silent.

"Just tell me this much," she said. "Do you picture us getting married sometime? I mean when your divorce comes through?"

He said, "Oh, well, marriage, Muriel . . ."

"You don't, do you. You don't know what you want. One minute you like me and the next you don't. One minute you're ashamed to be seen with me and the next you think I'm the best thing that ever happened to you."

He stared at her. He had never guessed that she read him so clearly.

"You think you can just drift along like this, day by day, no plans," she said. "Maybe tomorrow you'll be here, maybe you won't. Maybe you'll just go on back to Sarah. Oh yes! I saw you at Rose's wedding. Don't think I didn't see how you and Sarah looked at each other."

Macon said, "All I'm saying is—"

"All I'm saying," Muriel told him, "is take care what you promise my son. Don't go making him promises you don't intend to keep."

"But I just want him to learn to subtract!" he said.

"Communication Transcript" above. Imagine how the discussion might have been more productive if they had focused on the relational issue of Macon's commitment to Muriel and her son. By sticking to the content level—the boy's math skill—Muriel avoided the kind of meta-communication that is often necessary to keep relationships healthy.

Metacommunication isn't just a tool for handling problems. It is also a way to reinforce the satisfying aspects of a relationship: "I really appreciate it when you compliment me about my work in front of the boss." Comments like this serve two functions: First, they let others know that you value their behavior; second, they boost the odds that others will continue the behavior in the future.

Despite the benefits of metacommunication, bringing relational issues out in the open does have its risks. Discussing problems can be interpreted in two ways. On one hand, the other person might see it in a positive light—"Our relationship is working because we can still talk things out." On the other hand, your desire to focus on the relationship might look like a bad omen—"Our relationship isn't working if we have to keep talking it over."[52] Furthermore, metacommunication does involve a certain degree of analysis ("It seems like you're angry with me"), and some people resent being analyzed. These cautions don't mean that verbal metacommunication is a bad idea. They do suggest, though, that it's a tool that needs to be used carefully.

WHAT MAKES AN EFFECTIVE COMMUNICATOR?

It's easy to recognize good communicators and even easier to spot poor ones. But what are the characteristics that distinguish effective communicators from their less successful counterparts? Answering this question has been one of the leading challenges for communication scholars.[53] Although all the answers aren't yet in, research has identified a great deal of important information about communication competence.

Communication Competence Defined

Defining **communication competence** isn't as easy as it might seem. Although scholars are still struggling to agree on a precise definition, most would agree that effective communication involves achieving one's goals in a manner that, ideally, maintains or enhances the relationship in which it occurs.[54] This definition may seem vague on one hand and wordy on the other, but a closer look shows that it suggests several important characteristics of communication competence.

There Is No "Ideal" Way to Communicate   Your own experience shows that a variety of communication styles can be effective. Some very successful communicators are serious, whereas others use humor; some are gregarious, whereas others are quieter; and some are more straightforward, whereas others hint diplomatically. Just as there are many kinds of beautiful music or art, there are many kinds of competent communication. It certainly is possible to learn new, effective ways of communicating from observing models, but it would be a mistake to try to copy others in a way that doesn't reflect your own style or values.

Cultural differences also illustrate the principle that there is no single model of competence. What qualifies as competent behavior in one culture might be completely inept, or even offensive, in another.[55] On an obvious level, customs like belching after a meal or appearing nude in public that might be appropriate in some parts of the world would be considered outrageous in others. But there are more subtle differences in competent communication. For example, qualities like self-disclosing and speaking clearly that are valued in the United States are likely to be considered overly aggressive and insensitive in many Asian cultures, where subtlety and indirectness are considered important.[56] Even within a single society, members of various cocultures may have different notions of appropriate behavior. One study revealed that ideas of how good friends should communicate varied from one ethnic group to another.[57] As a group, Latinos valued relational support most highly, whereas African Americans valued respect and acceptance. Asian Americans prized a caring, positive exchange of ideas, and Anglo Americans prized friends who recognized their needs as individuals. Findings like these mean that there can be no sure-fire list of rules or tips that will guarantee your success as a communicator. They also mean that competent communicators are able to adapt their style to suit the individual and cultural preferences of others.[58]

Competence Is Situational   Even within a culture or relationship, the specific communication that is competent in one setting might be a colossal blunder in another. The joking insults you routinely trade with one friend might offend a sensitive family member, and last Saturday night's romantic approach would probably be out of place at work on Monday morning.

Because competent behavior varies so much from one situation and person to another, it's a mistake to think that communication competence is a trait that a person either has or does not have. It's more accurate to talk about *degrees* or *areas* of competence.[59] You and the people you know are probably quite competent in some areas and less so in others. You might deal quite skillfully with peers, for example, but feel clumsy interacting with people much older or younger, wealthier or poorer, more or less attractive than yourself. In fact, your competence with one person may vary from situation to situation. This means that it's an overgeneralization to say in a moment of distress, "I'm a terrible communicator!" when it's more accurate to say, "I didn't handle this situation very well, even though I'm better in others."

Competence Is Relational   Because communication is transactional—something we do *with* others rather than *to* others—behavior that is competent in one relationship isn't necessarily competent in others. For example, researchers have uncovered a variety of ways by which people deal with jealousy in their relationships.[60] The ways include keeping closer tabs on the partner, acting indifferent, decreasing affection, talking the matter over, and acting angry. The researchers found that no type of behavior was effective or ineffective in every relationship. They concluded that approaches that work with some people would be harmful to others. Findings like these demonstrate that competence arises out of developing ways of interacting that work for you and for the other people involved.[61]

Competence Can Be Learned   To some degree, biology is destiny when it comes to communication style.[62] Studies of identical and fraternal twins suggest that traits including sociability, anger, and relaxation seem to be partially a function of our genetic makeup.

Fortunately, biology isn't the only factor that shapes how we communicate. Communication competence is, to a great degree, a set of skills that anyone can learn. Sometimes competence is studied systematically—for instance, in communication classes. People with high communication apprehension often benefit from communication skills training.[63] Even a modest amount of training can produce dramatic results. For example, after only thirty minutes of instruction, one group of observers became significantly more effective in detecting deception in interviews.[64] One study revealed that college students' communication competence increases over their undergraduate studies.[65]

Characteristics of Competent Communicators

Despite the fact that competent communication varies from one situation to another, scholars have identified several common denominators that characterize effective communication in most contexts.

A Wide Range of Behaviors Effective communicators are able to choose their actions from a wide range of behaviors. To understand the importance of having a large communication repertoire, imagine that someone you know repeatedly tells jokes—perhaps racist or sexist ones—that you find offensive. You could respond to these jokes in a number of ways:

- You could decide to say nothing, figuring that the risks of bringing the subject up would be greater than the benefits.
- You could ask a third party to say something to the joke teller about the offensiveness of the jokes.
- You could hint at your discomfort, hoping that your friend would get the point.
- You could joke about your friend's insensitivity, counting on humor to soften the blow of your criticism.
- You could express your discomfort in a straightforward way, asking your friend to stop telling the offensive jokes, at least around you.
- You could even demand that the friend stop.

With this choice of responses at your disposal (and you can probably think of others as well), you could pick the one that had the best chance of success. But if you were able to use only one or two of these responses when raising a delicate issue—always keeping quiet or always hinting, for example—your chances of success would be much smaller. Indeed, many poor communicators are easy to spot by their limited range of responses. Some are chronic jokers. Others are always belligerent. Still others are quiet in almost every situation. Like a piano player who knows only one tune or a chef who can prepare only a few dishes, these people are forced to rely on a small range of responses again and again, whether or not they are successful.

Ability to Choose the Most Appropriate Behavior   Simply possessing a large range of communication skills is no guarantee of success. It's also necessary to know which of these skills will work best in a particular situation. Choosing the best way to send a message is rather like choosing a gift: What is appropriate for one person won't be appropriate for another person at all. This ability to choose the best approach is essential because a response that works well in one setting would flop miserably in another one.

Although it's impossible to say precisely how to act in every situation, there are at least three factors to consider when you are deciding which response to choose. The first factor is the communication *context*. The time and place will almost always influence how you act. Asking your boss for a raise or your lover for a kiss might produce good results if the time is right, but the identical request might backfire if your timing is poor. Likewise, the joke that would be ideal at a bachelor party would probably flop at a funeral.

Your *goal* will also shape the approach you take. Inviting a new neighbor over for a cup of coffee or dinner could be just the right approach if you want to encourage a friendship; but if you want to maintain your privacy it might be wiser to be polite but cool. Likewise, your goal will determine your approach in situations in which you want to help another person. As you will learn in chapter 7, there are times when offering advice is just what is needed. But when you want to help others develop the ability to solve problems on their own, it's better to withhold your own ideas and function as a sounding board to let them consider alternatives and choose their solutions.

Finally, your *knowledge of the other person* should also shape the approach you take. If you're dealing with someone who is very sensitive or insecure, your response might be supportive and cautious. With an old and trusted friend you might be blunt. The social niche of the other party can also influence how you communicate. For instance, you would probably act differently toward an eighty-year-old person than you would toward a teenager. You would probably act differently toward the president of your institution than you would toward a classmate, even in identical circumstances. Likewise, there are times when it's appropriate to treat a man differently than a woman, even in this age of gender equity.

Skill at Performing Behaviors   After you have chosen the most appropriate way to communicate, it's still necessary to perform the required skills effectively. There is a big difference between knowing *about* a skill and being able to put it into practice. Simply being aware of alternatives isn't much help unless you can skillfully put these alternatives to work.

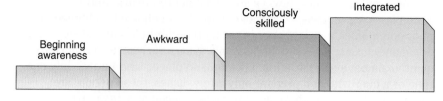

FIGURE 1-3 **Stages in Learning Communication Skills**

Just reading about communication skills in the following chapters won't guarantee that you can start using them flawlessly. As with any other skills—playing a musical instrument or learning a sport, for example—the road to competence in communication is not a short one. As you learn and practice the communication skills in the following pages, you can expect to pass through several stages,[66] shown in Figure 1-3.

Beginning Awareness The first step in learning any new skill is a beginning awareness. This is the point at which you first learn that there is a new and better way of behaving. If you play tennis, for example, awareness might grow when you learn about a new way of serving that can improve your power and accuracy. In the area of communication, *Looking Out/Looking In* should bring this sort of awareness to you.

Awkwardness Just as you were awkward when you first tried to ride a bicycle or drive a car, your initial attempts at communicating in new ways may also be awkward. This doesn't mean that there's anything wrong with these ways, but rather that you need more experience with them. After all, if it's reasonable to expect difficulty learning other skills, you ought to expect the same fumbling with the concepts in this book. As Ringo Starr put it when talking about music, "If you want to play the blues, you gotta pay your dues. . . . It don't come easy."

You have to be willing to look bad in order to get good.

Jack Canfield

Skillfulness If you are willing to keep working at overcoming the awkwardness of your initial attempts, you will arrive at the third learning stage, which is one of skillfulness. At this stage you'll be able to handle yourself well, although you will still need to think about what you're doing. As in learning a new language, this is the time when you're able to speak grammatically and use the correct words, even though you still need to think hard to express yourself well. As an interpersonal communicator, you can expect the stage of skillfulness to be marked by a great deal of thinking and planning and also by good results.

Integration Finally, after a period of time in the skillful stage, you'll find yourself at the final stage—integration. This occurs when you're able to perform well without thinking about it. The behavior becomes automatic, a part of you. Integrated speakers of a foreign language converse without translating mentally from their native tongue. Integrated cyclists ride skillfully and comfortably, almost as if the bike were an extension of each cyclist's own body. And integrated communicators express themselves in skillful ways, not because they are acting self-consciously but rather because that is who they have become.

It's important to keep these stages in mind as you try out the ideas in this book. Prepare yourself for the inevitable awkwardness, knowing that if you're willing to keep practicing the new skills you will become more and more comfortable and successful with them. Realize that the effort is worth it because after you have learned new methods of communicating[67] you'll be rewarded with far more satisfying relationships.

Cognitive Complexity

Cognitive Complexity People have the best chance of developing an effective message when they understand the other person's point of view. And because others aren't always good at expressing their thoughts and feelings clearly, the ability to imagine how an issue might look from the others' point of view is an important skill. In fact, understanding the other person is so important that researchers have labeled *empathy* the most important aspect of communication competence.[68] Because empathy is such an important element of communication competence, much of chapter 3 is devoted to this topic.

Social scientists use the term **cognitive complexity** to describe the ability to construct a variety of frameworks for viewing an issue. Researchers have found that cognitive complexity increases the chances of having satisfying communication among married couples,[69] helping others who are feeling distressed,[70] being persuasive, and achieving career advancement,[71] to name a few contexts.

To understand how cognitive complexity can increase competence, consider an example. Imagine that a long-time friend seems to be angry with you. One possible explanation is that your friend is offended by something you've done. Another possibility is that something has happened in another part of your friend's life that is upsetting. Or perhaps nothing at all is wrong, and you're just being overly sensitive. Considering the issue from several angles might prevent you from overreacting or misunderstanding the situation, increasing the odds of finding a way to resolve the problem constructively. The sections on empathy and perception checking in chapter 3, listening in chapter 7, and preventing defensiveness in chapter 9 provide specific tools for developing your cognitive complexity.

Self-Monitoring

Self-Monitoring Whereas increased cognitive complexity helps you understand others better, self-monitoring is one way to understand yourself better. Psychologists use the term **self-monitoring** to describe the process of paying close attention to one's behavior and using these observations to shape the way one behaves. Self-monitors are able to separate a part of their consciousness and observe their behavior from a detached viewpoint, making observations such as:

"I'm making a fool out of myself."

"I'd better speak up now."

"This approach is working well. I'll keep it up."

Although too much self-monitoring can be problematic (see chapter 2), people who are aware of their behavior and the impression it makes are more skillful communicators than people who are low

Calvin and Hobbes

by Bill Watterson

CALVIN AND HOBBES © Watterson. Reprinted with permission of Universal Press Syndicate. All rights reserved.

self-monitors.[72] For example, they are more accurate in judging others' emotional states, better at remembering information about others, less shy, and more assertive. By contrast, low self-monitors aren't able even to recognize their incompetence. One study revealed that poor communicators were blissfully ignorant of their shortcomings and more likely to overestimate their skill than were better communicators.[73] For example, experimental subjects who scored in the lowest quartile on joke-telling skills were more likely than their funnier counterparts to grossly over-estimate their sense of humor.

Whereas low self-monitors may blunder through life, succeeding or failing without understanding why, high self-monitors have the detach-ment to ask themselves the question "How am I doing?" and to change their behavior if the answer isn't positive.

Commitment   One feature that distinguishes effective communication—at least in qualitatively interpersonal relationships—is commitment. In other words, people who seem to care about relationships communicate better than those who don't.[74] This care shows up in several ways. The first is *commitment to the other person*. Concern for the other person is revealed in a variety of ways: a desire to spend time with him or her instead of rushing, a willingness to listen carefully instead of doing all the talking, the use of language that makes sense to the other person, and openness to change after hearing the other person's ideas.

Effective communicators also care about *the message*. They appear sincere, seem to know what they are talking about, and demonstrate through words and deeds that their ideas matter. Phony communication is a turnoff. So are wishy-washy positions and uninformed, ignorant statements.

How do you measure up as a competent communicator? Competence isn't a trait that people either have or do not have. Rather, it's a state that we achieve more or less frequently. A realistic goal, then, is not to become perfect but rather to boost the percentage of time when you communicate in ways outlined in this section.

LOOKING AT DIVERSITY

Competent Communication in Suburbia and the Inner City

In this profile **Daria Muse** *describes how effective communication varies in two strikingly different environments: her home neighborhood of South-Central Los Angeles and her school in the suburban San Fernando Valley. This account demonstrates some of the elements of communication competence introduced in chapter 1: a wide repertoire of behaviors, the ability to choose the best behavior for a given situation, and skill at performing that behavior.*

During my elementary and middle-school years, I was a well-behaved, friendly student at school and a tough, hard-nosed "bad girl" in my neighborhood. This contrast in behavior was a survival tool, for I lived in a part of South-Central Los Angeles where "goody-goodies" aren't tolerated, and I attended school in Northridge, where trouble-makers aren't tolerated.

Beckford Ave. Elementary School was in the heart of a middle-class suburbia, and I, coming from what has been described as the "urban jungle," was bused there every day for six years.

In a roundabout way, I was told from the first day of school that if I wanted to continue my privileged attendance in the hallowed classrooms of Beckford, I would have to conform and adapt to their standards. I guess I began to believe all that they said because slowly I began to conform.

Instead of wearing the tight jeans and T-shirt which were the style in South-Central at the time, I wore schoolgirl dresses like those of my female classmates. I even changed my language. When asking a question, instead of saying, "Boy! Gimme those scissors before I knock you up you head!" in school, I asked, "Excuse me, would you please hand me the scissors?" When giving a compliment in school I'd say, "You look very nice today," instead of "Girl, who do you think you are, dressin' so fine, Miss Thang."

This conformation of my appearance and speech won me the acceptance of my proper classmates at Beckford Elementary School, but after getting out of the school bus and stepping onto the sidewalks of South-Central, my appearance quit being an asset and became a dangerous liability.

One day, when I got off the school bus, a group of tough girls who looked as though they were part of a gang approached me, looked at my pink and white lace dress, and accused me of trying to "look white." They surrounded me and demanded a response that would prove to them that I was still loyal to my black heritage. I screamed, "Lay off me, girl, or I'll bust you in the eyes so bad that you'll need a telescope just to see!" The girls walked away without causing any more trouble.

From then on, two personalities emerged. I began living a double life. At school I was prim and proper in appearance and in speech, but during the drive on the school bus from Northridge to South-Central, my other personality emerged. Once I got off the bus I put a black jacket over my dress, I hardened my face, and roughened my speech to show everyone who looked my way that I was not a girl to be messed with. I led this double life throughout my six years of elementary school.

Now that I am older and can look back at that time objectively, I don't regret displaying contrasting behavior in the two different environments. It was for my survival. Daria, the hard-nosed bad girl, survived in the urban jungle and Daria, the well-behaved student, survived in the suburbs.

As a teen-ager in high school I still display different personalities: I act one way in school, which is different from the way I act with my parents, which is different from the way I act with my friends, which is different from the way I act in religious services. But don't we all? We all put on character masks for our different roles in life. All people are guilty of acting differently at work than at play and differently with co-workers than with the boss. There's nothing wrong with having different personalities to fit different situations; the trick is knowing the real you from the characters.

CHECK YOUR COMPETENCE

Other people are often the best judges of your competence as a communicator. They can also offer useful information about how to improve your communication skill. Find out for yourself by following these steps:

1. Choose a person with whom you have an important relationship.

2. In cooperation with this person, identify several contexts in which you communicate. For example, you might choose different situations such as "handling conflicts," "lending support to friends," or "expressing feelings."

3. For each situation, have your friend rate your competence by answering the following questions:
   a. Do you have a wide repertoire of response styles in this situation, or do you always respond in the same way?
   b. Are you able to choose the most effective way of behaving for the situation at hand?
   c. Are you skillful at performing behaviors? (Note that knowing how you want to behave isn't the same as being *able* to behave.)
   d. Do you communicate in a way that leaves others satisfied?

4. After reviewing your partner's answers, identify the situations in which your communication is most competent.

5. Choose a situation in which you would like to communicate more competently, and with the help of your partner:
   a. Determine whether your repertoire of behaviors needs to be expanded.
   b. Identify the ways in which you need to communicate more skillfully.
   c. Develop ways to monitor your behavior in the key situation to get feedback on your effectiveness.

SUMMARY

Communication is essential on many levels. Besides satisfying practical needs, effective communication can enhance physical health and emotional well-being. As children, we learn about our identity via the messages sent by others, and as adults our self-concept is shaped and refined through social interaction. Communication also satisfies social needs: involvement with others, control over the environment, and giving and receiving affection.

The process of communication is not a linear one that people "do" to one another. Rather, communication is a transactional process in which participants create a relationship by simultaneously sending and receiving messages, many of which are distorted by various types of noise.

Interpersonal communication can be defined contextually by the number of people involved or qualitatively by the nature of interaction between them. In a qualitative sense, interpersonal relationships are unique, irreplaceable, interdependent, and intrinsically rewarding. Qualitatively interpersonal communication can occur in computer-mediated contexts as well as in traditional ones. Qualitatively interpersonal communication is relatively infrequent, even in the strongest relationships. Both personal and impersonal communications are useful, and most relationships have both personal and impersonal elements.

Communication occurs on two levels: content and relational. Relational communication can be both verbal and nonverbal. Relational messages usually refer to one of three dimensions of a relationship: affinity, respect, or control. Metacommunication consists of messages that refer to the relationship between the communicators.

All communication, whether personal or impersonal, content or relational, follows the same basic principles. Messages can be intentional or unintentional. It is impossible not to communicate. Communication is irreversible and unrepeatable. Some common misconceptions should be avoided when thinking about communication: Meanings are not in words, but rather in people. More communication does not always make matters better. Communication will not solve all problems. Finally, communication—at least effective communication—is not a natural ability.

Communication competence is the ability to get what you are seeking from others in a manner that maintains the relationship on terms that are acceptable to all parties. Competence doesn't mean behaving the same way in all settings and with all people; rather, competence varies from one situation to another. The most competent communicators have a wide repertoire of behaviors, and they are able to choose the best behavior for a given situation and perform it skillfully. They are able to take others' points of view and analyze a situation in a variety of ways. They also monitor their own behavior and are committed to communicating successfully.

KEY TERMS

affinity
behavior
channel
cognitive complexity
communication
communication competence
complementary relationship
computer-mediated communication (CMC)
content message
control (conversational and decision)

decoding
dyad
encoding
environment
feedback
impersonal interaction
instrumental goals
interpersonal communication (quantitative and qualitative)
linear communication model
message
metacommunication

noise (external, physiological, psychological)
parallel relationship
receiver
relational message
respect
self-monitoring
sender
symmetrical relationship
transactional communication model

LOOKING OUT/LOOKING IN ONLINE

Use your *Looking Out/Looking In* CD-ROM for quick access to the electronic resources that accompany this chapter. Included on this CD-ROM are additional study aids and links to the *Looking Out/Looking In* Web site at the Wadsworth Communication Café. The CD-ROM is your gateway to a wealth of resources that will help you understand and further explore the material in this chapter. **Video clips** under *Communication Scenarios* on the CD illustrate the skills introduced in this chapter. Click on the Web site link to complete self-study

review quizzes to help you master new concepts; access a **feature film database** to locate clips and entire movies that illustrate communication principles; find Internet material via the maintained **Web site links;** and complete **online activities** to help you master new concepts.

INFOTRAC COLLEGE EDITION® EXERCISES

Use the InfoTrac College Edition password that was included free with a copy of this new text to answer the following questions. These questions can be completed online and, if requested, submitted to your instructor under InfoTrac College Edition Activities at the *Looking Out/Looking In* Web site.

1. Why We Communicate

Use PowerTrac to locate the article "Men's and Women's Organizational Peer Relationships: A Comparison" by Janie Harden Fritz. What does the research in this article say about the different ways in which men and women form interpersonal relationships on the job? How well do the findings in this article match your personal experience?

2. Practical Goals

Use PowerTrac to locate the article "Walking the Talk: The Relationship Between Leadership and Communication Competence" by Frank J. Flauto. What does this article tell you about the kinds of communication skills that are necessary for effective leaders? How can you use this information to become a better leader?

3. Technology and Interpersonal Communication

Use PowerTrac to locate the article "Rich Media Will Transform Comms By 2005" by Kevin Featherly. (Hint: Use PowerTrac's title and author searching tools to locate the article.) Make a list of the ways in which technology will transform interpersonal communication. Then describe how these changes would be likely to change the nature of your relationships. What advantages do you anticipate if such changes come about? Do you foresee any disadvantages with new communication technologies?

READINGS

Cialdini, Robert B. *Influence: Science and Practice*, 4th ed. Boston: Allyn and Bacon, 2000.

Mutual understanding isn't the only goal of communication. This highly readable digest of social science research captures the range of instrumental goals that communicators try to attain and the ways they do so. Cialdini shows how interpersonal influence operates in a wide range of settings, including business transactions, medicine, religion, politics, and romance.

Littlejohn, Stephen W. *Theories of Human Communication*, 7th ed. Belmont, Calif.: Wadsworth, 2002.

This thorough book surveys the status of theories and research in human communication. Chapter 12 focuses on interpersonal communication and on several topics introduced in Looking Out/Looking In, *including perception, self-disclosure, interpersonal attraction, and conflict.*

Lynch, James J. *The Broken Heart: The Medical Consequences of Loneliness.* New York: Basic Books, 1977; and *The Language of the Heart: The Body's Response to Human Dialogue.* New York: Basic Books, 1985.

Lynch is the former director of the Psychosomatic Clinics at the University of Maryland's School of Medicine. He documents the strong link between poor physical health and inadequate interpersonal relationships.

Mortensen, C. David. *Miscommunication.* Thousand Oaks, Calif.: Sage, 1997.

This book explores the broad range of ways in which communication can go badly when people are unsuccessful at creating shared meanings. It addresses a wide range of problems that will be addressed throughout Looking Out/ Looking In *and steers readers toward the thinking of communication scholars who have explored these challenges.*

Petronio, Sandra, Jess K. Alberts, Michael L. Hecht, and Jerry Buley, eds. *Contemporary Perspectives on Interpersonal Communication.* Madison, Wis.: Brown and Benchmark, 1993.

In this collection of scholarly writings, serious students will find some of the most influential work of social scientists who studied interpersonal communication in the last decades of the twentieth century. Topics include theoretical approaches to the subject, influence, bonding, relational development and maintenance, conversation management, and interpersonal competence.

Redmond, Mark. "Interpersonal Communication: Definitions and Conceptual Approaches" in M. V. Redmond, ed., *Interpersonal Communication: Readings in Theory and Research.* Fort Worth: Harcourt Brace, 1995.

A comprehensive overview of the many ways in which interpersonal communication has been defined and studied by scholars. A good resource for preparing to study interpersonal communication in greater detail.

FILMS

In addition to the films suggested here, go to the **Film in Communication Database** at the *Looking Out/Looking In* Web site to locate movie clips that illustrate various aspects of interpersonal communication.

The Importance of Interpersonal Communication

As Good As It Gets (1997) Rated PG-13

Melvin Udall (Jack Nicholson) is a crotchety, obsessive-compulsive hermit who locks himself in his apartment, where, ironically, he writes romance novels. When people try to talk with him, Melvin drives them away with mean and offensive comments. He seems intent on disproving the notion that "no man is an island."

But one person—and one dog—breaks through Melvin's tough exterior. The person is Carol Connelly (Helen Hunt), a waitress who gives him attention and doesn't put up with his guff. As a result, Melvin ritualistically visits her restaurant every morning. The dog is named Verdell. Melvin is forced to baby-sit Verdell when his owner, Simon (Greg Kinnear), is hospitalized. The dog works his way into Melvin's heart and brings out his softest side.

When both Carol and Verdell temporarily exit Melvin's life, he must come to grips with the fact that he misses interacting with them. His social needs pull him into meaningful relationships with Carol and Simon, and he slowly becomes a more competent communicator through their love and support. The romance novelist finally finds romance in his own life, and he learns that it's not so bad to need—and be needed by—other people.

Communication as a Transactional Process

Ordinary People (1980) Rated R

Conrad (Timothy Hutton) is recovering from a suicide attempt triggered by guilt over surviving the accident in which his brother died. His low self-esteem is also shaped by the (correct) perception that his mother, Beth (Mary Tyler Moore), doesn't seem to love him as much as she did his brother, who died in a boating accident. The well-intentioned father, Calvin (Donald Sutherland), is ready to get on with his life, but he is caught in the middle between his wife and son. Conrad seeks help from a psychiatrist named Berger (Judd Hirsch), and after a difficult beginning he manages to get in touch with the source of his guilt. Despite the breakthrough, the film does not have a neat, happy ending: Calvin confronts his mother about her emotional sterility, and she leaves home. In the final scene, Conrad and Calvin affirm their love for one another.

Ordinary People vividly illustrates the transactional nature of relationships. Virtually every interaction between the three members of the family is affected by the history of their relationship: the brother's death, Conrad's suicide attempt and hospitalization, and the resentment and hurt between Conrad and Beth.

Interpersonal and Impersonal Communication

Big Kahuna (2000) Rated R

In a Wichita hotel hospitality suite, three salesmen nervously plan a cocktail reception. Their company makes industrial lubricants, and their goal is to get the account of a man named Dick Fuller, whom they refer to as "The Big Kahuna." The men are Larry (Kevin Spacey), Phil (Danny DeVito), and Bob (Peter Facinelli). Larry and Phil are long-time friends and colleagues who have grown weary and wise over their years selling lubricants. Bob is a young idealist, and this is his first convention.

After the reception ends, it first seems that the Big Kahuna did not show up. But then Larry and Phil discover that their number one prospective customer was indeed in the room, wearing someone else's name tag—and that Bob talked to him for hours. What did they talk about? About the death of the Big Kahuna's dog and then about Bob's personal savior, Jesus Christ. The topic of industrial lubricants never entered the conversation. "About Christ?" screams Larry. "Did you mention what line of industrial lubricant Jesus uses?"

At one level, the film seems to invite us to explore the priorities in our lives. After all, which is more important: making a sale or achieving personal salvation? But in a late-night speech Phil explains to Bob that even saving souls can be an impersonal task when we treat others as objects to be persuaded—when we treat people as things.

Communication Competence

The Great Santini (1980) Rated PG

Bull Meechum (Robert Duvall) is an ace Marine fighter pilot who views himself as an all-around man: warrior, husband, father, and friend. He expects his family to go along with this image as they move to yet another duty station, this time at a South Carolina Marine air station. Meechum is a stereotype of the aggressive, insensitive male, and his wife, Lillian, is the classic devoted, uncritically supportive southern wife. On one level, the Meechums can be viewed as a dysfunctional family controlled by an insensitive self-centered male who makes life miserable for his wife and children. But despite Bull's many shortcomings, the Meechum family genuinely loves—and even likes—one another. Because this nontextbook set of relationships does work reasonably well, the film illustrates that communication competence varies from one relationship to another.

LOOKING OUT/LOOKING IN WEB SITE

Use your *Looking Out/Looking In* CD-ROM to access the *Looking Out/Looking In* Web site. In addition to the **Film in Communication Database,** you can access online activities such as the **Communication Model** activity suggested under the **Web Link** feature on page 12.

WADSWORTH
THOMSON LEARNING

Looking Out, Looking In,
Media Edition (with
InfoTrac and CD-ROM)
Ronald B. Adler, et al.
10th Edition
ISBN: 0534549861

Close Window

Chapter Resources ▾

1. A First Look at Interpersonal Relationships

Chapter 1 ▾
- Flashcards
- Glossary
- Internet Activities
- Tutorial Quiz
- Web Links

Book Level Resources
- About the Text

Companion Products
- Supplements

Discipline Level ▾
- Communication Links
- Careers
- Events

return to overview page

Complete these activities by visiting the sites given below and entering your answers in the spaces provided. If your instructor would like you to email your responses, be sure to fill in the information in the box at the top of this page. Click on "Submit" at the bottom of this page to send your answers.

Web Exercise 1.1: What Are Your Communication Strengths and Weaknesses?
Take the online survey at Communication Skills Test . Submit your answers to the survey and obtain the results and interpretation. According to these results, which areas of communication do you feel you need to work on? According to the characteristics of competent communicators listed in the textbook, where do your strengths lie and in which areas do you feel you need to improve?

Web Exercise 1.2: Comparing and Contrasting Communication Models
Visit the Models of Communication Web site. This list of links provides you with visual access to the many various communication models developed over the years in the communication discipline. Choose two communication models to compare and contrast. In your own words, describe the similarities and differences between the two models. Referencing the models described in your textbook, what elements are included and left out of the models you chose? Finally, describe how the models you chose are similar or different to the linear and transactional models described in your textbook.

Web Exercise 1.3: Why Communicate Cooperatively?
Visit the Cooperative Communication Skills Internet Resource Center . The author lists 7 benefits/reasons for learning and adopting a more cooperative communication style. What are these 7 reasons? Which of these 7 reasons apply to your own life? Give specific, concrete examples of how these reasons apply in your own life (i.e. if one reason you agree with is "more respect," state that you would like to have more respectful relationships with your children, or with your co-workers). What are the barriers to success? What steps can you take to overcome these barriers?

CHAPTER 2

COMMUNICATION AND IDENTITY: THE SELF AND MESSAGES

Who are you? Take a moment now to answer this question. You'll need the following list as you read the rest of this chapter, so be sure to complete it now. Try to include all the characteristics that describe you:

Your moods or feelings (e.g., happy, sad)

Your appearance (e.g., attractive, unattractive)

Your social traits (e.g., friendly, shy)

Talents you have or do not have (e.g., musical, tone-deaf)

Your intellectual capacity (e.g., smart, stupid)

Your strong beliefs (e.g., religious, environmentalist)

Your social roles (e.g., parent, spouse)

Your physical condition (e.g., healthy, overweight)

Now take a look at what you've written. How did you define yourself? As a student? A man or woman? By your age? Your religion? Your occupation? Of course, there are many ways of identifying yourself. List as many ways as you can. You'll probably see that the words you've chosen represent a profile of what you view as your most important characteristics. In other words, if you were required to describe the "real you," this list ought to be a good summary.

COMMUNICATION AND THE SELF-CONCEPT

What you've done in developing this list is to give a partial description of your **self-concept:** the relatively stable set of perceptions you hold of yourself. If a special mirror existed that reflected not only your physical features but also other aspects of yourself—emotional states, talents, likes, dislikes, values, roles, and so on—the reflection you'd see would be your self-concept.

You probably recognize that the self-concept list you recorded earlier is only a partial one. To make the description complete, you'd have to keep adding items until your list ran into hundreds of words.

Take a moment now to demonstrate the many parts of your self-concept by simply responding to the question "Who am I?" over and over again. Add these responses to the list you started earlier.

Of course, not every item on your self-concept list is equally important. For example, the most significant part of one person's self-concept might consist of social roles, and for another person it might be physical appearance, health, friendships, accomplishments, or skills.

You can discover how much you value each part of your self-concept by rank-ordering the items on your list. Try it now: Place a *1* next to the most fundamental item about you, a *2* next to the second most fundamental item, and continue in this manner until you've completed your list.

This self-concept you've just described is extremely important. To see just how important it is, try the following exercise.

TAKE AWAY

1. Look over the list of words you've just used to describe yourself. If you haven't already done so, pick the ten words that describe the most fundamental aspects of who you are. Be sure that you've organized these words so that the most fundamental one is in first place and the one that is least central to your identity is number 10, arranging the words or phrases in between in their proper order.

2. Now find a comfortable spot where you can think without being interrupted. You can complete this exercise in a group with the leader giving instructions, or you can do it alone by reading the directions yourself when necessary.

3. Close your eyes and get a mental picture of yourself. Besides visualizing your appearance, you should also include in your image your less observable features: your disposition, your hopes, your concerns, of course, including all the items you described in step 1.

4. Keep this picture in mind, but now imagine what would happen if the tenth item on your list disappeared from your makeup. How would you be different? Does the idea of giving up that item leave you feeling better or worse? How hard was it to let go of that item?

5. Now, without taking back the item you just abandoned, give up the ninth item on your list, and see what difference this makes to you. After pausing to experience your thoughts and feelings, give up each succeeding item on your list one by one.

6. After you've abandoned the number one feature of who you are, take a few minutes to regather the parts of yourself that you abandoned, and then read on.

For most people this exercise dramatically illustrates just how fundamental the concept of self is. Even when the item being abandoned is an unpleasant one, it's often hard to give it up. And when asked to let go of their most central feelings or thoughts, most people balk. "I wouldn't be *me* without that," they insist. Of course, this proves our point: The concept of self is perhaps our most fundamental possession. Knowing who we are is essential because without a self-concept it would be impossible to relate to the world.

The self-concept isn't just an individual matter. Entire communities collectively develop an image of themselves. Communication scholar Donal Carbaugh describes how Americans interact in ways that collectively craft their identities in settings as varied as basketball games, the workplace, weddings, and public policy disputes.[1] You can probably understand this phenomenon by reviewing the self-concept list you just created. Several items probably refer to your identity as a member of various groups: ethnic, religious, family, social, and so on.

Self-esteem is the part of the self-concept that involves evaluations of self-worth. A hypothetical communicator's self-concept might include

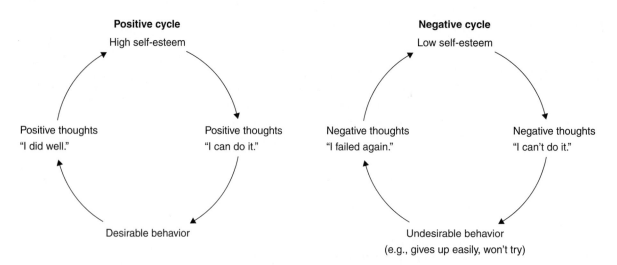

Positive cycle	Negative cycle

Positive cycle
High self-esteem

Positive thoughts
"I did well."

Positive thoughts
"I can do it."

Desirable behavior

Negative cycle
Low self-esteem

Negative thoughts
"I failed again."

Negative thoughts
"I can't do it."

Undesirable behavior
(e.g., gives up easily, won't try)

FIGURE 2-1 **The relationship between self-esteem and communication behavior**

being quiet, argumentative, or serious. His or her self-esteem would be determined by how he or she felt about these qualities: "I'm glad that I am quiet," or "I am embarrassed about being so quiet," for example.

Self-esteem has a powerful effect on communication behavior.[2] People with high self-esteem are more willing to communicate than people with low self-esteem. They are more likely to think highly of others and expect to be accepted by others. They evaluate their behaviors more highly than people who are less secure. They are not afraid of others' reactions and perform well when being watched. They work harder for people who demand high standards of performance, and they are comfortable with others they view as superior in some way. When confronted with critical comments, they are able to defend themselves. By contrast, people with low self-esteem are likely to disapprove of others and expect rejection. They are critical of their own performances. They are sensitive to possible disapproval of others and perform poorly when being watched. They work harder for undemanding, less critical people. They feel threatened by people they view as superior in some way and have difficulty defending themselves against others' negative comments.

Figure 2-1 pictures the relationship between self-esteem and communication behavior. People who feel good about themselves have positive expectations about how they will communicate. These expectations increase the chance that communication will be successful, and successes contribute to positive self-evaluations, which reinforce self-esteem. Of course, the same principle can work in a negative way with communicators who have low self-esteem.

How the Self-Concept Develops

Most researchers agree that we are not born with a self-concept.[3] An infant lying in a crib has no notion of self, no notion—even if the ability to speak were miraculously made available—of how to answer the question

In order to get at any truth about myself, I must have contact with another person. The other is indispensable to my own existence, as well as to my knowledge about myself.

Jean-Paul Sartre

"Who am I?" Consider what it would be like to have no idea of your characteristic moods, physical appearance, social traits, talents, intellectual capacity, beliefs, or important roles. If you can imagine this experience—*blankness*—you can start to understand how the world might appear to someone with no sense of self. Of course, you have to take it one step further and *not know* you do not have any notion of self.

During the first year of life the child begins to recognize "self" as distinct from surroundings. If you've ever watched children at this age

INVITATION TO INSIGHT

"EGO BOOSTERS" AND "EGO BUSTERS"

1. Either by yourself or with a partner, recall someone you know or once knew who was an "ego booster"—who helped enhance your self-esteem by acting in a way that made you feel accepted, competent, worthwhile, important, appreciated, or loved. This person needn't have played a crucial role in your life as long as the role was positive. Often your self-concept is shaped by many tiny nudges as well as by a few giant events. A family member with whom you've spent most of your life can be an "ego booster," but so can the stranger on the street who spontaneously smiles and strikes up a friendly conversation.

2. Now recall an "ego buster" from your life—someone who acted in a large or small way to reduce your self-esteem. As with ego booster messages, ego buster messages aren't always intentional. The acquaintance who forgets your name after you've been introduced or the friend who yawns while you're describing an important problem can diminish your feelings of self-worth.

3. Now that you've thought about how others shape your self-concept, recall a time when you were an ego booster to someone else—when you intentionally or unintentionally boosted another's self-esteem. Don't merely settle for an instance in which you were nice: Look for a time when your actions left another person feeling valued, loved, needed, and so on. You may have to ask the help of others to answer this question.

4. Finally, recall a recent instance in which you were an ego buster for someone else. What did you do to diminish another's self-esteem? Were you aware of the effect of your behavior at the time? Your answer might show that some events we intend as boosters have the effect of busters. For example, you might joke with a friend in what you mean as a friendly gesture, only to discover that your remarks are received as criticism.

After completing the exercise (you *did* complete it, didn't you?), you should begin to see that your self-concept is shaped by those around you. This process of shaping occurs in two ways: reflected appraisal and social comparison.

It is thus with most of us; we are what other people say we are. We know ourselves chiefly by hearsay.

Eric Hoffer

you've probably marveled at how they can stare with great fascination at a foot, hand, and other body parts that float into view, almost as if these were strange objects belonging to someone else. Then the connection is made, almost as if the children were realizing, "The hand is *me*," "The foot is *me*." These first revelations form a child's earliest concept of self. At this early stage, the self-concept is almost exclusively physical, involving the child's basic realization of existing and of possessing certain body parts over which some control is exerted. As the child develops, this rudimentary sense of identity expands into a much more complete and sophisticated picture that resembles the self-concept of adults. This evolution is almost totally a product of social interaction.

Reflected Appraisal: The Looking-Glass Self

As early as 1912, sociologist Charles Cooley used the image of a mirror to identify the process of **reflected appraisal:** the fact that each of us develops a self-concept that matches the way we believe others see us.[4] In other words, we are likely to feel less valuable, lovable, and capable to the degree that others have communicated ego busting signals; and we will probably feel good about ourselves to the degree that others seem to feel good about us. The validity of the principle of reflected appraisal will become clear when you realize that the self-concept you described in the list at the beginning of this chapter is a product of the positive and negative messages you have received throughout your life.

To illustrate this point further, let's start at the beginning. Newborn children aren't born with any sense of identity: They learn to judge themselves only through the way others treat them. At first the evaluations aren't linguistic. Nonetheless, even the earliest days of life are full of messages that constitute the first ego boosters and ego busters that start to shape the child's self-concept. The amount of time that parents allow their baby to cry before attending to its needs nonverbally communicates over a period of time how important it is to them. Their method of handling the child also speaks volumes: Do they affectionately toy with it, or do they treat it like so much baggage, changing diapers, feeding, and bathing it in a brusque, businesslike manner? Does the tone of voice with which they speak express love and enjoyment or disappointment and irritation?

Of course, many of these messages are not intentional ones. It is rare when a parent will intentionally try to tell a child it's not lovable; but whether they're intentional or not doesn't matter—nonverbal statements play a big role in shaping a youngster's feelings of being "OK" or "not OK."

> *We are not only our brother's keeper; in countless large and small ways, we are our brother's maker.*
>
> Bonaro Overstreet

Children Learn What They Live

If a child lives with criticism he learns to condemn.

If a child lives with hostility he learns to fight.

If a child lives with ridicule he learns to be shy.

If a child lives with shame he learns to feel guilty.

If a child lives with tolerance he learns to be patient.

If a child lives with encouragement he learns confidence.

If a child lives with praise he learns to appreciate.

If a child lives with fairness he learns justice.

If a child lives with security he learns to have faith.

If a child lives with approval he learns to like himself.

If a child lives with acceptance and friendship he learns to find love in the world.

Dorothy Law Nolte, *Children Learn What They Live*

As the child learns to speak and understand language, verbal messages also contribute to a developing self-concept. Every day a child is bombarded with scores of messages about him- or herself. Some of these are positive: "You're so cute!" "I love you." "What a big girl." Other messages are negative: "What's the matter with you? Can't you do anything right?" "You're a bad boy." "Leave me alone. You're driving me crazy!"

Evaluations like these are the mirror by which we know ourselves; and because children are trusting souls who have no other way of viewing themselves, they accept at face value both the positive and negative evaluations of the apparently all-knowing and all-powerful adults around them.

These same principles in the formation of the self-concept continue in later life, especially when messages come from what sociologists term a **significant others**—people whose opinions we especially value. (See the story "Cipher in the Snow" on pages 54–55) A look at the ego boosters and ego busters you described in the previous exercise as well as others you can remember will show that the evaluations of a few especially important people can be powerful. Family members are the most obvious type of significant other.[5] Others, though, can also be significant others: a special friend, a teacher, or perhaps a barely known acquaintance whose opinion you value can leave an imprint on how you view yourself. To see the importance of significant others, ask yourself how you arrived at your opinion of yourself as a student, as a person attractive to others, as a competent worker, and you'll see that these self-evaluations were probably influenced by the way others regarded you. During childhood and adolescence, the power of messages from significant others remains.[6] For example, teenage girls whose close friends are overly concerned with weight loss are more likely to view their appearance negatively and become prone to extreme weight-loss behaviors such as radical diets and bulimia.[7]

Although messages from others have a powerful impact on shaping our identity, it is an exaggeration to suggest that feedback is *always* responsible for modifying the self-concept.[8] There are cases where a person's actual abilities play a larger role in shaping both self-evaluations and the perceptions of others. For example, if you are an outstanding athlete or a computer whiz, your accomplishments will probably boost your self-esteem, even if others don't give you much praise.

The influence of significant others becomes less powerful as people grow older. After most people approach the age of thirty, their self-concepts don't change radically, at least without a conscious effort such as psychotherapy.[9] By contrast, the self-concept of younger people is still flexible. For example, between the ages of fourteen and twenty-three, the self-esteem of about two-thirds of the males in one study increased, whereas the self-esteem of about one-third of the males decreased.[10] The same study revealed that about 57 percent of women in the same age group grew to feel *less*

Once riding in old Baltimore,
  Heart-filled, head-filled with glee,

I saw a Baltimorean
  Keep looking straight at me.

Now I was eight and very small,
  And he was no whit bigger,

And so I smiled, but he poked out
  His tongue and called me, "Nigger."

I saw the whole of Baltimore
  From May until December:

Of all the things that happened there
  That's all that I remember.

Countee Cullen

good about themselves, whereas the remaining 43 percent grew to feel better about themselves.

Social Comparison

So far we have looked at the way by which others' messages shape our self-concept. In addition to these messages, each of us forms our self-image by the process of **social comparison:** evaluating ourselves in terms of how we compare with others.

Two types of social comparison need highlighting. In the first, we decide whether we are *superior or inferior* by comparing ourselves to others. Are we attractive or ugly? A success or failure? Intelligent or stupid? It depends on those against whom we measure ourselves.[11]

You might feel just ordinary or inferior in terms of talent, friendships, or attractiveness if you compare yourself with an inappropriate reference group. In one study, young women's perceptions of their bodies changed for the worse after watching just thirty minutes of televised images of the "ideal" female form.[12] You'll probably never be as beautiful as a Hollywood star, as agile as a professional athlete, or as wealthy as a millionaire. When you consider the matter logically, these facts don't mean you're worthless. Nonetheless, many people judge themselves against unreasonable standards and suffer accordingly.[13] You'll read more about how to avoid placing perfectionistic demands on yourself in chapter 4. This principle is especially powerful when we compare ourselves to images in the media. Furthermore, these distorted self-images can lead to serious behavioral disorders such as depression, anorexia nervosa, bulimia, and other eating disorders.

In addition to feelings of superiority and inferiority, social comparison provides a way to decide if we are the *same as* or *different from* others. A child who is interested in ballet and who lives in a setting where such preferences are regarded as weird will start to accept this label if there is no support from others. Likewise, adults who want to improve the quality of their relationships but are surrounded by friends and family who don't recognize or acknowledge the importance of these matters may think of themselves as oddballs. Thus, it's easy to recognize that the **reference groups** against which we compare ourselves play an important role in shaping our view of ourselves.

You might argue that not every part of one's self-concept is shaped by others, insisting that there are certain objective facts that are recognizable by self-observation. After all, nobody needs to tell a person that he is taller than others, speaks with an accent, has acne, and so on. These

Watch me perform!

I walk a tightrope of unique design.

I teeter, falter, recover and bow.

You applaud.

I run forward, backward, hesitate and bow.

You applaud.

If you don't applaud I'll Fall.

Cheer me! Hurray me!

Or you push me

Down.

Lenni Shender Goldstein

facts are obvious. Though it's true that some features of the self are immediately apparent, the *significance* we attach to them—the rank we assign them in the hierarchy of our list and the interpretation we give them—depends greatly on the opinions of others. After all, many of your features are readily observable, yet you don't find them important at all because nobody has regarded them as important.

We once heard a woman in her eighties describing her youth. "When I was a girl," she declared, "we didn't worry about weight. Some people were skinny and others were plump, and we pretty much accepted the bodies God gave us." In those days it was unlikely that weight would have found its way onto the self-concept list you constructed because it wasn't considered significant. Compare this attitude with what you find today: It's seldom that you pick up a popular magazine or visit a book-store without reading about the latest diet fads, and television ads are filled with scenes of slender, happy people. As a result you'll rarely find a person who doesn't complain about the need to "lose a few pounds." Obviously, the reason for such concern comes from the attention paid to fitness. We generally see slimness as desirable because others tell us it is. In a society where obesity is the ideal (and there are such societies), a person who regards herself as extremely heavy would be a beauty. In the same way, the fact that one is single or married, solitary or sociable, aggressive or passive takes on meaning depending on the interpretation that society attaches to those traits. Thus, the importance of a given characteristic in your self-concept has as much to do with the impor-tance that you and others attach to it as with the existence of the characteristic.

By now you might be thinking, "It's not my fault that I've always been shy or insecure. Because I developed a picture of myself as a result of the way others have treated me, I can't help being what I am." Though it's true that to a great extent you are a product of your environment, to believe that you are forever doomed to a poor self-concept would be a big mistake. Having held a poor self-image in the past is no reason for continuing to do so in the future. You *can* change your attitudes and behaviors, as you'll soon read. So don't despair, and most of all don't use the fact that others have shaped your self-concept as an excuse for feeling self-pity or for acting helpless. Now that you know the effect that overly negative evaluations have had on you in the past, you'll be in a better position to raise your perception of yourself in the future.

Characteristics of the Self-Concept

Now that you have a better idea of how your self-concept has developed, we can take a closer look at some of its characteristics.

The Self-Concept Is Subjective Although we may believe that our self-concept is accurate, in truth it may well be distorted. Some people view themselves more favorably than objective facts would suggest. For example, researchers have found that there is no relationship between

©Ziggy and Friends, Inc. Reprinted with permission of Universal Press Syndicate. All rights reserved.

I am not what I think I am. I am not what you think I am. I am what I think you think I am.

Aaron Bleiberg and Harry Leubling

CIPHER IN THE SNOW

It started with tragedy on a biting cold February morning. I was driving behind the Milford Corners bus as I did most snowy mornings on my way to school. It veered and stopped short at the hotel, which it had no business doing, and I was annoyed as I had to come to an unexpected stop. A boy lurched out of the bus, reeled, stumbled, and collapsed on the snowbank at the curb. The bus driver and I reached him at the same moment. His thin, hollow face was white even against the snow.

"He's dead," the driver whispered.

It didn't register for a minute. I glanced quickly at the scared young faces staring down at us from the school bus. "A doctor! Quick! I'll phone from the hotel. . . ."

"No use, I tell you he's dead." The driver looked down at the boy's still form. "He never even said he felt bad," he muttered. "Just tapped me on the shoulder and said, real quiet, 'I'm sorry. I have to get off at the hotel.' That's all. Polite and apologizing like."

At school, the giggling, shuffling morning noise quieted as the news went down the halls. I passed a huddle of girls. "Who was it? Who dropped dead on the way to school?" I heard one of them half-whisper.

"Don't know his name; some kid from Milford Corners" was the reply.

It was like that in the faculty room and the principal's office. "I'd

appreciate your going out to tell the parents," the principal told me. "They haven't a phone and, anyway, somebody from school should go there in person. I'll cover your classes."

"Why me?" I asked. "Wouldn't it be better if you did it?"

"I didn't know the boy," the principal admitted levelly. "And, in last year's sophomore personalities column I note that you were listed as his favorite teacher."

I drove through the snow and cold down the bad canyon road to the Evans place and thought about the boy, Cliff Evans. His favorite teacher! I thought. He hasn't spoken two words to me in two years! I could see him in my mind's eye all right, sitting back there in the last seat in my afternoon literature class.

He came in the room by himself and left by himself. "Cliff Evans," I muttered to myself, "a boy who never talked." I thought a minute. "A boy who never smiled. I never saw him smile once."

The big ranch kitchen was clean and warm. I blurted out my news somehow. Mrs. Evans reached blindly toward a chair. "He never said anything about bein' ailing."

His stepfather snorted. "He ain't said nothin' about anything since I moved in here."

Mrs. Evans pushed a pan to the back of the stove and began to untie her apron. "Now hold on," her husband snapped. "I got to have breakfast before I go to town. Nothin' we can do now anyway. If Cliff hadn't been so dumb, he'd have told us he didn't feel good."

After school I sat in the office and stared blankly at the records spread out before me. I was to close the file and write the obituary for the school paper. The almost bare sheets mocked the effort. Cliff Evans, white, never legally adopted by stepfather, five young half-brothers and sisters. These meager strands of information and the list of D grades were all the records had to offer.

Cliff Evans had silently come in the school door in the mornings and gone out the school door in the evenings, and that was all. He had never belonged to a club. He had never played on a team. He had never held an office. As far as I could tell he had never done one happy, noisy kid thing. He had never been anybody at all.

How do you go about making a boy into a zero? The grade-school records showed me. The first and second grade teachers' annotations read "sweet, shy child," "timid but eager." Then the third grade note had opened the attack. Some teacher had written in a good, firm hand, "Cliff won't talk. Uncooperative. Slow learner." The other academic sheep had followed with "dull"; "slow-witted"; "low I.Q." They became correct. The boy's I.Q. score in the ninth grade was listed as 83. But his I.Q. in the third grade had been 106. The score didn't go under 100 until the seventh grade. Even shy, timid, sweet children have resilience. It takes time to break them.

I stomped to the typewriter and wrote a savage report pointing out what education had done to Cliff Evans. I slapped a copy on the principal's desk and another in the sad, dog-eared file. I banged the typewriter and slammed the file and crashed the door shut, but I didn't feel much better. A little boy kept walking after me, a little boy with a peaked, pale face; a skinny body in faded jeans; and big eyes that had looked and searched for a long time and then had become veiled.

I could guess how many times he'd been chosen last to play sides in a game, how many whispered child conversations had excluded him, how many times he hadn't been asked. I could see and hear the faces and voices that said over and over, "You're a nothing, Cliff Evans."

A child is a believing creature. Cliff undoubtedly believed them. Suddenly it seemed clear to me: When finally there was nothing left at all for Cliff Evans, he collapsed on a snowbank and went away. The doctor might list "heart failure" as the cause of death, but that wouldn't change my mind.

We couldn't find ten students in the school who had known Cliff well enough to attend the funeral as his friends. So the student body officers and a committee from the junior class went as a group to the church, being politely sad. I attended the services with them, and sat through it with a lump of cold lead in my chest and a big resolve growing through me.

I've never forgotten Cliff Evans nor that resolve. He has been my challenge year after year, class after class. I look for veiled eyes or bodies scrouged into a seat in an alien world. "Look, kids," I say silently, "I may not do anything else for you this year, but not one of you is going to come out of here a nobody. I'll work or fight to the bitter end doing battle with society and the school board, but I won't have one of you coming out of here thinking himself a zero."

Most of the time—not always, but most of the time—I've succeeded.

Jean Mizer

the way college students rate their ability as interpersonal communicators, public speakers, or listeners and their true effectiveness. In all cases, the
self-reported communication skill is higher than
actual performance.

Not all distortion of the self-concept is so positive. Many people view themselves much more
harshly than the objective facts warrant. We have
all experienced a temporary case of the "uglies,"
convinced that we look much worse than others
assure us we really look. Research confirms what
common sense suggests: that people are more critical of themselves when they are experiencing these
negative moods than when they are feeling more
positive.[14] Although we all suffer occasional bouts
of self-doubt that affect our communication, some
people suffer from long-term or even permanent
states of excessive self-doubt and criticism.[15] It's
easy to understand how this chronic condition
can influence the way they approach and respond
to others.

Distorted self-evaluations like these can occur for several reasons.
One reason is *obsolete information.* The effects of past failures in school
or social relations can linger long after they have occurred, even though
such events don't predict failure in the future. Likewise, your past
successes don't guarantee future success. Perhaps your jokes used to
be well received or your work was superior, but now the facts have
changed.

Distorted feedback also can create a self-image that is worse or
better than the facts warrant. Overly critical parents are one of the most
common causes of a negative self-image. In other cases the remarks of
cruel friends, uncaring teachers, excessively demanding employers, or
even memorable strangers can have a lasting effect. Other distorted
messages are unrealistically positive. A boss may think of herself as an
excellent manager because her assistants shower her with false praise in
order to keep their jobs or gain promotions. Likewise, a child's inflated
ego may be based on the praise of doting parents.

After communicators fasten onto a self-concept—whether it is
positive or negative—the tendency is to seek out people who confirm it.
Recent studies show that both college students and married couples with
high self-esteem seek out partners who view them favorably, whereas
those with negative self-esteem are more inclined to interact with people
who view them unfavorably.[16] The tendency to look for people who
confirm our self-concept has been called *self-verification.* It suggests
that we are less concerned with learning the "truth" about ourselves
than with reinforcing a familiar self-concept.

Along with obsolete information and distorted feedback, another
cause for a strongly negative self-concept is the emphasis on *perfection,*
which is common in our society. From the time most of us learn to

understand language we are exposed to models who appear to be perfect. Children's stories and advertisements imply that the way to be a hero, the way to be liked and admired, is to show no flaws. Unfortunately, many parents perpetuate the myth of perfection by refusing to admit that they are ever mistaken or unfair. Children, of course, accept this perfectionist façade for a long time, not being in any position to dispute the wisdom of such powerful beings. And from the behavior of the adults around them comes a clear message: "A well-adjusted, successful person has no faults." Thus, children learn that, in order to gain acceptance, it's necessary to pretend to "have it all together," even though they know this isn't the case. Given this naive belief that everyone else is perfect and the knowledge that one isn't, it's easy to see how one's self-concept would suffer.

Don't misunderstand: It's not wrong to aim at perfection as an *ideal*. We're suggesting only that achieving this state of perfection is usually not possible, and to expect that you should do so is a sure ticket to an inaccurate and unnecessarily low self-esteem.

A final reason why people often sell themselves short is connected to *social expectations*. Curiously, the perfectionist society to which we belong rewards those people who downplay the strengths we demand that they possess (or pretend to possess). We term these people "modest" and find their behavior agreeable. On the other hand, we consider those who honestly appreciate their strengths to be "braggarts" or "egotists," confusing them with the people who boast about accomplishments they do not possess.[17] This convention leads most of us to

"Am I the smart one and you're the pretty one or is it the other way around?"

© The New Yorker Collection 2000 Barbara Smaller from cartoonbank.com. All Rights Reserved.

TABLE 2-1	Differences Between Communicators With High and Low Self-Esteem

PERSONS WITH HIGH SELF-ESTEEM

1. Likely to think well of others.
2. Expect to be accepted by others.
3. Evaluate their own performance more favorably than people with low self-esteem.
4. Perform well when being watched: not afraid of others' reactions.
5. Work harder for people who demand high standards of performance.
6. Inclined to feel comfortable with others they view as superior in some way.
7. Able to defend themselves against negative comments of others.

PERSONS WITH LOW SELF-ESTEEM

1. Likely to disapprove of others.
2. Expect to be rejected by others.
3. Evaluate their own performance less favorably than people with high self-esteem.
4. Perform poorly when being watched: sensitive to possible negative reaction.
5. Work harder for undemanding, less critical people.
6. Feel threatened by people they view as superior in some way.
7. Have difficulty defending themselves against others' negative comments; more easily influenced.

Summarized by Don E. Hamachek. *Encounters with the Self* (2d ed.). New York: Holt, Rinehart, and Winston, 1982, pp. 3–5.

talk freely about our shortcomings while downplaying our accomplishments. It's all right to proclaim that you're miserable if you have failed to do well on a project; but it's considered boastful to express your pride at a job well done. It's fine to say that you feel unattractive but egocentric to say that you feel attractive.

After a while we begin to believe the types of statements we repeatedly make. The disparaging remarks are viewed as modesty and become part of our self-concept, and the strengths and accomplishments go unmentioned and are thus forgotten. And in the end we see ourselves as much worse than we are.

Self-esteem may be based on inaccurate thinking, but it still has a powerful effect on the way we relate to others. Table 2-1 summarizes some important differences between communicators with high and low self-esteem. Differences like these make sense when you realize that people who dislike themselves are likely to believe that others won't like them either. Realistically or not, they imagine that others are constantly viewing them critically, and they accept these imagined or real criticisms as more proof that they are indeed unlikable people. To use the well-known terminology of psychiatrist Eric Berne, they adopt an "I'm not OK—you're OK" orientation to life. Sometimes this low self-esteem is manifested in hostility toward others because the communicator takes the approach that the only way to look good is to put others down.

One way to avoid falling into the trap of becoming overly critical is to recognize your strengths. The following exercise will give you a chance to suspend the ordinary rules of modesty and appreciate yourself publicly for a change.

RECOGNIZING YOUR STRENGTHS

1. This exercise can be done either alone or with a group. If you are with others, sit in a circle so that everyone can see one another.

2. Each person should share three personal strengths or accomplishments. These needn't feature areas in which you are an expert, and they don't have to be concerned with momentous feats. On the contrary, it's perfectly acceptable to talk about some part of yourself that leaves you feeling pleased or proud. For instance, you might say that, instead of procrastinating, you completed a school assignment before the last minute, that you spoke up to a friend even though you were afraid of disapproval, that you bake a fantastic chocolate cake, or that you frequently drive hitchhikers to their destinations although it's out of your way.

3. If you're at a loss for items, ask yourself:
   a. What are some ways in which you've grown in the past year? How are you more skillful, wiser, or a better person than you previously were?
   b. Why do certain friends or family members care about you? What features do you possess that make them appreciate you?

4. After you've finished, consider the experience. Did you have a hard time thinking of things to share? Would it have been easier to list the things that are *wrong* with you? If so, is this because you are truly a wretched person or because you are in the habit of stressing your defects and ignoring your strengths? Consider the impact of such a habit on your self-concept, and ask yourself whether it wouldn't be wiser to strike a better balance distinguishing between your strengths and weaknesses.

The Self-Concept Resists Change

Despite the fact that we all change, there is a tendency to cling to an existing self-concept, even when evidence shows that it is obsolete. This tendency to seek and attend to information that conforms to an existing self-concept has been labeled **cognitive conservatism.**

It's understandable why we're reluctant to revise a previously favorable self-concept. A student who did well in earlier years but now has failed to study might be unwilling to admit that the label "good scholar" no longer applies; and a previously industrious worker, pointing to past commendations in a personnel file and insisting that she is a top-notch employee, might resent a supervisor's mentioning increased absences and low productivity. These people aren't *lying* when they insist that they're doing well in spite of the facts to the contrary; they honestly believe that the old truths still hold precisely because their self-concepts have been so resistant to change.

Self-love, My liege, is not so vile a sin as self-neglecting.

Shakespeare, *King Henry V*

Curiously, the tendency to cling to an outmoded self-perception also holds when the new self-perception would be more favorable than the old one. We recall a former student whom almost anyone would have regarded as beautiful, with physical features attractive enough to appear in any glamour magazine. In spite of her appearance, in a class exercise this woman characterized herself as "ordinary" and "unattractive." When questioned by her classmates, she described how as a child her teeth were extremely crooked and how she had worn braces for several years in her teens to correct this problem. During this time she was often kidded by her friends, who never let her forget her "metal mouth," as she put it. Even though the braces had been off for two years, our student reported that she still saw herself as ugly and brushed aside our compliments by insisting that we were just saying these things to be nice—she knew how she *really* looked.

Examples like this show one problem that occurs when we resist changing an inaccurate self-concept. Our student denied herself a much happier life by clinging to an obsolete picture of herself. In the same way, some communicators insist that they are less talented or less worthy of friendship than others would suggest, thus creating their own miserable world when it needn't exist. These unfortunate souls probably resist changing because they aren't willing to go through the disorientation that comes from redefining themselves, correctly anticipating that it *is* an effort to think of oneself in a new way. Whatever their reasons, it's sad to see people in such an unnecessary state.

A second problem arising from the persistence of an inaccurate self-concept is self-delusion and lack of growth. If you hold an unrealistically favorable picture of yourself, you won't see the real need for change that may exist. Instead of learning new talents, working to change a relationship, or improving your physical condition, you'll stay with the familiar and comfortable delusion that everything is all right. As time goes by, this delusion becomes more and more difficult to maintain, leading to a third type of problem: defensiveness.

To understand this problem, you need to remember that communicators who are presented with information that contradicts their self-perception have two choices: They can either accept the new data and change their perception accordingly, or they can keep their original perception and in some way refute the new information. Because most communicators are reluctant to downgrade a favorable image of themselves, their tendency is to opt for refutation, either by discounting the information and rationalizing it away or by counterattacking the person who transmitted it. The problem of defensiveness is so great that we will examine it in chapter 9.

Influences on Identity

We have already seen how experiences in the family, especially during childhood, shape our sense of who we are. Along with the messages we receive at home, many other forces shape our identity, and thus our communication, including age, physical ability/disability, sexual orientation, and socioeconomic status. Along with these forces, culture and gender are powerful forces in shaping how we view ourselves and others and how we communicate. We will examine each of these forces now.

It has become something of a cliché to observe that if we do not love ourselves, we cannot love anyone else. This is true enough, but it is only part of the picture. If we do not love ourselves, it is almost impossible to believe fully that we are *loved* by someone else. It is almost impossible to accept love. It is almost impossible to receive love. No matter what our partner does to show that he or she cares, we do not experience the devotion as convincing because we do not feel lovable to ourselves.

Nathaniel Branden,
The Psychology of Romantic Love

In Japan, in fact, everything had been made level and uniform—even humanity. By one official count, 90 percent of the population regarded themselves as middle-class; in schools, it was not the outcasts who beat up the conformists, but vice versa. Every Japanese individual seemed to have the same goal as every other—to become like every other Japanese individual. The word for "different," I was told, was the same as the word for "wrong." And again and again in Japan, in contexts varying from the baseball stadium to the watercolor canvas, I heard the same unswerving, even maxim: "The nail that sticks out must be hammered down."

Pico Iyer, *Video Night in Katmandu*

Culture   Although we seldom recognize the fact, our sense of self is shaped, often in subtle ways, by the culture in which we have been reared.[18] Most Western cultures are highly individualistic, whereas traditional other cultures—most Asian ones, for example—are much more collective. When asked to identify themselves, individualistic people in the United States, Canada, Australia, and Europe would probably respond by giving their first name, surname, street, town, and country. Many Asians do it the other way around.[19] If you ask Hindus for their identity, they will give you their caste and village as well as their name. The Sanskrit formula for identifying one's self begins with lineage and goes on to state family, house, and ends with one's personal name.[20]

These conventions for naming aren't just cultural curiosities: They reflect a very different way of viewing one's self and of what kinds of relationships are important. In collective cultures a person gains identity by belonging to a group. This means that the degree of interdependence among members of the society and its subgroups is high. Feelings of pride and self-worth are likely to be shaped not only by what the individual does, but also by behavior of other members of the community. This linkage to others explains the traditional Asian denial of self-importance—a strong contrast to the self-promotion that is common in individualistic Western cultures.[21] In Chinese written language, for example, the pronoun *I* looks very similar to the word for selfish.[22] Table 2-2 summarizes some differences between individualistic cultures and more collective ones.

This sort of cultural difference isn't just a matter of interest to anthropologists. It shows up in the level of comfort or anxiety that people feel when communicating. In collective societies, there is a higher degree of communication apprehension. For example, as a group, residents of China, South Korea, and Japan exhibit a significantly higher degree of anxiety about speaking out than do members of individualistic cultures such as the United States and Australia.[23] It's important to realize that different levels of communication apprehension don't mean that shyness is a "problem" in some cultures. In fact, just the opposite is true: In these societies reticence is valued. When the goal is to *avoid* being the nail that sticks out, it's logical to feel nervous when you make yourself appear different by calling attention to yourself. A self-concept that includes "assertive" might make a westerner feel proud, but in much of Asia it would more likely be cause for shame.

The difference between individualism and collectivism shows up in everyday interaction. Communication researcher Stella Ting-Toomey has developed a theory that explains cultural differences in important norms, such as honesty and directness.[24] She suggests that in individualistic Western cultures where there is a strong "I" orientation, the norm of speaking directly is honored; whereas in collectivistic cultures, where the main desire is to build connections between the self and others, indirect approaches that maintain harmony are considered more desirable. "I gotta be me" could be the motto of a westerner, but "If I hurt you, I hurt myself" is closer to the Asian way of thinking.

Ethnicity   Ethnicity can have a powerful effect on how people think of themselves and how they communicate. To appreciate this fact, recall

TABLE 2-2 The Self in Individualistic and Collectivistic Cultures

INDIVIDUALISTIC CULTURES

- Self is separate, unique individual; should be independent, self-sufficient
- Individual should take care of him/herself and immediate family
- Many flexible group memberships; friends based on shared interests and activities
- Reward for individual achievement and initiative; individual decisions encouraged; individual credit and blame assigned
- High value on autonomy, change, youth, individual security, equality

COLLECTIVISTIC CULTURES

- People belong to extended families or in-groups; "we" or group orientation
- Person should take care of extended family before self
- Emphasis on belonging to a very few permanent in-groups that have a strong influence over the person
- Reward for contribution to group goals and well-being; cooperation with in-group members; group decisions valued; credit and blame shared
- High value on duty, order, tradition, age, group security, status, and hierarchy

Adapted by Sandra Sudweeks from material in H. C. Triandis, "Cross-Cultural Studies of Individualism and Collectivism" in J. Berman, ed., *Nebraska Symposium on Motivation* 37 (Lincoln, Neb.: University of Nebraska Press, 1990), pp. 41–133.

how you described yourself in the "Who Am I?" list you created when you began this chapter. If you are a member of a nondominant ethnic group, it's likely that you included your ethnicity in the most important parts of who you are. There's no surprise here: If society keeps reminding you that your ethnicity is important, then you begin to think of yourself in those terms. If you are part of the dominant majority, your probably aren't as conscious of your ethnicity. Nonetheless, it plays an important part in your self-concept. Being part of the majority increases the chances that you have a sense of belonging to the society in which you

cathy®

by Cathy Guisewite

Cathy ©Cathy Guisewite. Reprinted with permission of Universal Press Syndicate. All rights reserved.

live and of entitlement to being treated fairly. These are feelings that members of less privileged ethnic groups often don't have.

Sex and Gender   One way to appreciate the tremendous importance of gender on your sense of self is to imagine how your identity would be different if you had been born as a member of the opposite sex. Would you express your emotions in the same way? Deal with conflict? Relate to friends and strangers? The answer is almost certainly a resounding "no."

From the earliest months of life, being male or female shapes the way others communicate with us and thus how they shape our sense of self. Think about the first questions most people ask when a child is born. One of them is almost always "Is it a boy or a girl?" As the "Cathy" cartoon on this page shows, after most people know what the baby "is," they often behave accordingly.[25] They use different pronouns and often choose gender-related nicknames. With boys, comments often focus on size, strength, and activity; comments about girls more often address beauty, sweetness, and facial responsiveness. It's not surprising that messages like these shape a child's sense of identity and how he or she will communicate. The implicit message is that some ways of behaving are masculine and others feminine. Little girls, for example, are more likely to be reinforced for acting "sweet" than are little boys. The same principle operates in adulthood: A man who stands up for his beliefs might get approval for being "tough" or "persistent," whereas a woman who behaves in the same way could be described by critics as a "nag" or "bitch."[26] It's not hard to see how the gender roles and labels like these can have a profound effect on how men and women view themselves and on how they communicate.

Self-esteem is also influenced by gender. In a society that values competitiveness more in men than in women, it isn't surprising that the self-esteem of adolescent young men is closely related to having abilities that are superior in some way to those of their peers, whereas teenage women's self-worth is tied more closely to the success of their social relationships and verbal skills. [27]

Don't resign yourself to being a prisoner of expectations about your gender. Research demonstrates that our sense of self is shaped strongly by the people with whom we communicate and by the contexts in which we communicate.[28] For example, a nonaggressive young man who might feel unwelcome and inept in a macho environment might gain new self-esteem by finding others who appreciate his style of communicating. A woman whose self-esteem is stifled by the limited expectations of bosses and coworkers can look for more hospitable places to work. Children usually can't choose the reference groups that shape their identities, but adults can.

The Self-Fulfilling Prophecy and Communication

The self-concept is such a powerful force on the personality that it not only determines how you see yourself in the present but also can actually influence your future behavior and that of others. Such occurrences come about through a phenomenon called the self-fulfilling prophecy.

A **self-fulfilling prophecy** occurs when a person's expectations of an event make the event more likely to occur than would otherwise have been true. Self-fulfilling prophecies occur all the time, although you might never have given them that label. For example, think of some instances you may have known.

You expected to become nervous and botch a job interview and later did so.

You anticipated having a good (or terrible) time at a social affair and found your expectations being met.

A teacher or boss explained a new task to you, saying that you probably wouldn't do well at first. You did not do well.

A friend described someone you were about to meet, saying that you wouldn't like the person. The prediction turned out to be correct—you didn't like the new acquaintance.

In each of these cases there is a good chance that the event occurred because it was predicted to occur. You needn't have botched the interview, the party might have been boring only because you helped make it so, you might have done better on the job if your boss hadn't spoken up, and you

There is a joke which goes right to the heart of this matter. It is about a man whose tire goes flat on a dark and lonely country road. When he discovers that he doesn't have a jack, he recalls seeing a farm house about a mile back. And so he starts to walk there in the hopes of borrowing one. While he is walking, he talks to himself about his situation: "Wow, I'm really stranded here. The guy will probably want a few dollars to lend me his jack. Why should he do it for nothing? Everyone wants to make a few bucks. A few bucks! If I don't get the jack, I'll never get out of here. He'll realize that, and probably want fifteen dollars, maybe twenty-five dollars. Twenty-five dollars? This guy's really got me by the old cashews. He'll ask fifty dollars, for sure—maybe a hundred."

Well, he goes on in this way until he reaches the farm house. He knocks at the door. An elderly farmer answers and with a cheerful smile asks, "Is there something I can do for you, young man?" "Do for me? Do for me?" says the man, "I'll tell you what you can do, you can take your goddamn jack and shove it!"

. . . If, as in this case, you predict that you will not be lent a jack in a spirit of gracious cooperation, you prepare yourself for the confrontation in such a way that you guarantee the jack will not be lent in a spirit of gracious cooperation. Your prediction is transformed into a fact, which then becomes the reality.

Neil Postman,
Crazy Talk, Stupid Talk

might have liked the new acquaintance if your friend hadn't given you preconceptions. In other words, what helped make each event occur was the expectation of it.

Types of Self-Fulfilling Prophecies

There are two types of self-fulfilling prophecies. *Self-imposed prophecies* occur when your own expectations influence your behavior. In sports you've probably "psyched" yourself into playing either better or worse than usual, so that the only explanation for your unusual performance was your attitude. Similarly, you've probably faced an audience at one time or another with a fearful attitude and forgotten your remarks, not because you were unprepared, but because you said to yourself, "I know I'll blow it."

Research has demonstrated the power of self-imposed prophecies. In one study, communicators who believed they were incompetent proved less likely than others to pursue rewarding relationships and more likely to sabotage their existing relationships than did people who were less critical of themselves.[29] On the other hand, students who perceived themselves as capable achieved more academically.[30] In another study, subjects who were sensitive to social rejection tended to expect rejection, perceive it where it might not have existed, and overreact to their exaggerated perceptions in ways that jeopardized the quality of their relationships.[31] Research also suggests that communicators who feel anxious about giving speeches seem to create self-fulfilling prophecies about doing poorly that cause them to perform less effectively.[32] The self-fulfilling prophecy also operates on the job. For example, salespeople who view themselves as being effective communicators are more successful than those who view themselves as less effective, despite the fact that there was no difference in the approach that members of each group used with customers. In other words, the apparent reason why some salespeople are successful is that they expect to succeed.

Self-imposed prophecies operate in many ways that affect everyday communication. You've had the experience of waking up in a cross mood and saying to yourself, "This will be a 'bad day.'" After you made such a decision, you may have acted in ways that made it come true. If you approached a class expecting to be bored, you most probably did lose interest, owing partly to a lack of attention on your part. If you avoided the company of others because you expected they had nothing to offer, your expectations would have been confirmed—nothing exciting or new did happen to you. On the other hand, if you approached the same day with the idea that it could be a good one, this expectation probably would have been met also. Researchers have found that putting a smile on your face, even if you're not in a good mood, can lead to a more positive disposition.[33] Likewise, if you approach a class determined to learn something, you probably will—even if it's how not to instruct students! Approach many strangers with the idea that some of them will be good to know, and you'll most likely make

The difference between a lady and a flower girl is not how she behaves, but how she's treated. I shall always be a flower girl to Professor Higgins, because he always treats me as a flower girl, and always will; but I know I can be a lady to you, because you always treat me as a lady, and always will.

G. B. Shaw, *Pygmalion*

"I don't sing because I am happy. I am happy because I sing."

©The New Yorker Collection 1991 Ed Frascino from cartoonbank.com. All Rights Reserved.

some new friends. In these cases and ones like them, your attitude has a great deal to do with how you see yourself and how others will see you.

A second category of self-fulfilling prophecies is imposed by one person on another, so that the expectations of one person govern another's actions. The classic example was demonstrated by Robert Rosenthal and Lenore Jacobson in a study they described in their book *Pygmalion in the Classroom*.[34] The experimenters told teachers that 20 percent of the children in a certain elementary school showed unusual potential for intellectual growth. The names of these 20 percent were drawn by means of a table of random numbers, which is to say that the names were drawn out of a hat. Eight months later these unusual or "magic" children showed significantly greater gains in IQ than did the remaining children, who had not been singled out for the teachers' attention. The change in the teachers' expectations regarding the intellectual performance of these allegedly "special" children had led to an actual change in the intellectual performance of these randomly selected children. In other words, the children did better, not because they were any more intelligent than their classmates, but because they learned that their teachers— significant others—believed they could.

To put this phenomenon in context with the self-concept, we can say that when a teacher communicates to a child the message "I think you're bright," the child accepts that evaluation and changes her self-concept to include it. Unfortunately, we can assume that the same principle holds for students whose teachers send the message "I think you're stupid."

This type of self-fulfilling prophecy has been shown to be a powerful force for shaping the self-concept and thus the behavior of people in a wide range of settings outside the schools.[35] In medicine, patients who unknowingly use placebos—substances such as injections of sterile water or doses of sugar pills that have no curative value—often respond just as favorably to treatment as those who actually received a drug. The patients believe they have taken a substance that will help them feel better, and this belief actually brings about a "cure." In psychotherapy Rosenthal and Jacobson describe several studies suggesting that patients who believe they will benefit from treatment do so regardless of the type of treatment they receive. In the same vein, when a doctor believes that a patient will improve, the patient may do so precisely because of this expectation, whereas another person for whom the doctor has little hope often fails to recover. Apparently the patient's self-concept as sick or well—as shaped by the doctor—plays an important role in determining the actual state of health.

Notice that it isn't just that the observer must *believe* to create a self-fulfilling prophecy for the person who is the target of the expectations. The observer also must communicate that belief in order for the prediction to have any effect. If parents have faith in their children, but the kids aren't aware of that confidence, they won't be affected by their parents' expectations. If a boss has concerns about an employee's ability to do a job but keeps those concerns to herself, the employee won't be influenced. In this sense, the self-fulfilling prophecies imposed by one

There is an old joke about a man who was asked if he could play a violin and answered, "I don't know. I've never tried." This is psychologically a very wise reply. Those who have never tried to play a violin really do not know whether they can or not. Those who say too early in life and too firmly, "No, I'm not at all musical," shut themselves off prematurely from whole areas of life that might have proved rewarding. In each of us there are unknown possibilities, undiscovered potentialities—and one big advantage of having an open self-concept rather than a rigid one is that we shall continue to expose ourselves to new experiences and therefore we shall continue to discover more and more about ourselves as we grow older.

S. I. Hayakawa

person on another are as much a communication phenomenon as a psychological one.

Influence of Self-Fulfilling Prophecies

The influence of self-fulfilling prophecies on communication can be strong, acting either to improve or harm relationships. If, for instance, you assume that another person is unlikable, then you'll probably act in ways that communicate your feelings. In such a case, the other person's behavior will probably match your expectations: We usually don't go out of our way to be nice to people who aren't nice to us. If, on the other hand, you treat the other person as likable, the results are likely to be more positive.

In business, the power of the self-fulfilling prophecy was proved as early as 1890. A new tabulating machine had just been installed at the U.S. Census Bureau in Washington, D.C. In order to use the machine, the bureau's staff had to learn a new set of skills that the machine's inventor believed to be quite difficult. He told the clerks that after some practice they could expect to punch about 550 cards per day; to process any more would jeopardize their psychological well-being. Sure enough, after two weeks the clerks were processing the anticipated number of cards and reported feelings of stress if they attempted to move any faster.

Later an additional group of clerks was hired to operate the same machines. These clerks knew nothing of the machines, and no one had told them about the upper limit of production. After only three days, the new clerks were each punching over two thousand cards per day with no ill effects. Again, the self-fulfilling prophecy seemed to be in operation. The original clerks believed themselves capable of punching only 550 cards and so behaved accordingly, whereas the new clerks had no limiting expectations as part of their self-concepts and so behaved more productively.[36]

The self-fulfilling prophecy operates in families as well. If parents tell a child long enough that he can't do anything right, his self-concept will soon incorporate this idea, and he will fail at many or most of the tasks he attempts. On the other hand, if a child is told that she is a capable or lovable or kind person, there is a much greater chance of her behaving accordingly.

The self-fulfilling prophecy is an important force in interpersonal communication, but it doesn't explain or affect all behavior. There are certainly times when the expectation of an event's outcome won't bring it about. Your hope of drawing an ace in a card game won't in any way affect the chance of that card turning up in an already shuffled deck, and your belief that good weather is coming won't stop the rain from falling. In the same way, believing that you'll do well in a job interview when you're clearly not qualified for the job is unrealistic. Similarly, there will probably be people you don't like and occasions you won't enjoy, no matter what your attitude. To connect the self-fulfilling prophecy with the "power of positive thinking" is an oversimplification.

In other cases your expectations will be borne out because you're a good predictor and not because of the self-fulfilling prophecy. For

http://www.
outsights.com/
systems/theWay/
sss/ssx01.htm

Through description and diagram, the authors of this page feature a specific example of how initial beliefs can influence behavioral outcomes. Based on the example at the Web site, create your own labeled diagram and description of a self-fulfilling prophecy that has played out in your own life by completing Activity 2.1 "My Own Self-Fulfilling Prophecy" on the *Looking Out/Looking In* Web site.

example, some children are not well equipped to do well in school; in such cases it would be wrong to say that the children's performance was shaped by a parent or teacher, even though the behavior did match that which was expected. In the same way, some workers excel and others fail, some patients recover and others don't, in agreement with or contrary to our predictions, but not because of them.

Keeping these qualifications in mind, you will find it important to recognize the tremendous influence that self-fulfilling prophecies play in our lives. To a great extent we are what we believe we are. In this sense we and those around us constantly create our self-concepts and thus ourselves.

Changing Your Self-Concept

After reading this far, you know more clearly just what the self-concept is, how it is formed, and how it affects communication. But we still haven't focused directly on perhaps the most important question of all: How can you change the parts of your self-concept with which you aren't happy? There's certainly no quick method for becoming the person you'd like to be: Personal growth and self-improvement are a lifetime process. But we can offer several suggestions that will help you move closer to your goals.

Have a Realistic Perception of Yourself   One source of a poor self-concept is an inaccurate self-perception. As you've already read, such unrealistic perceptions sometimes come from being overly harsh on yourself, believing that you're worse than the facts indicate. By showing the self-concept list you developed on page 46 to others who know you, you can see whether you have been selling yourself short. Of course, it would be foolish to deny that you could be a better person than you are, but it's also important to recognize your strengths. A periodic session of recognizing your strengths such as you tried earlier in this chapter is often a good way to put your strengths and weaknesses into perspective.

An unrealistically poor self-concept can also arise from the inaccurate feedback of others. Perhaps you are in an environment where you receive an excessive number of prickly messages, many of which are undeserved, and a minimum of fuzzy messages. We've known many homemakers, for example, who have returned to college after many years spent in homemaking, where they received virtually no recognition for their intellectual strengths. It's amazing that these women have the courage to come to college at all, so low are their self-concepts; but come they do, and most are thrilled to find that they are much brighter and more competent intellectually than they suspected. In the

"YOU'RE A VERY FINE FELLOW!"

ECHO POINT

© Gahan Wilson

same way, workers with overly critical supervisors, children with cruel "friends," and students with unsupportive teachers all are prone to low self-concepts owing to excessively negative feedback.

If you fall into this category, it's important to put the unrealistic evaluations you receive into perspective and then to seek out more supportive people who will acknowledge your assets as well as point out your liabilities. Doing so is often a quick and sure boost.

Have Realistic Expectations   It's extremely important to realize that some of your dissatisfaction might come from expecting too much of yourself. If you demand that you handle every act of communication perfectly, you're bound to be disappointed. Nobody is able to handle every conflict productively, to be totally relaxed and skillful in conversations, always to ask perceptive questions, or to be 100 percent helpful when others have problems. Expecting yourself to reach such unrealistic goals is to doom yourself to unhappiness at the start.

Sometimes it's easy to be hard on yourself because everyone around you seems to be handling themselves so much better than you. It's important to realize that much of what seems like confidence and skill in others is a front to hide uncertainty. Others may be suffering from the same self-imposed demands of perfection that you impose on yourself.

Even in cases where others definitely seem more competent than you, it's important to judge yourself against your own growth and not against the behavior of others. Rather than feel miserable because you're not as talented as an expert, realize that you probably are a better, wiser, or more skillful person than you used to be and that this is a legitimate source of satisfaction. Perfection is fine as an ideal, but you're being unfair to yourself if you expect actually to reach it.

Have the Will to Change   Often we say we want to change, but we aren't willing to do the necessary work. In such cases it's clear that the responsibility for growing rests squarely on our shoulders, as the example following the exercise shows.

SKILL BUILDER

REEVALUATING YOUR "CAN'TS"

1. Choose a partner and for five minutes or so take turns making and listing statements that begin with "I can't . . ." Try to focus your statements on your relationships with family, friends, coworkers, students, and even strangers: anyone with whom you have a hard time communicating. Sample statements:

   "I can't be myself with strangers I'd like to get to know at parties."

   "I can't tell a friend how much I care about her."

   "I can't bring myself to ask my supervisor for the raise I think I deserve."

   "I can't ask questions in class."

2. Notice your feelings as you make each statement: self-pity, regret, concern, frustration, and so on, and reveal these to your partner.

3. Now repeat aloud each statement you've just made, except this time change each "can't" to a "won't." After each sentence, tell your partner whatever thoughts you have about what you've just said.

4. After you've finished, decide whether "can't" or "won't" is more appropriate for each item, and explain your choice to your partner.

5. Are there any instances of the self-fulfilling prophecy in your list—times when your decision that you "can't" do something was the only force keeping you from doing it?

As this exercise demonstrates, we often maintain an unrealistic self-concept by claiming that we "can't" be the person we'd like to be when in fact we're simply not willing to do what's required. You *can* change in many ways, if only you are willing to make the effort.

You might, for instance, decide that you'd like to become a better conversationalist. Seeking the advice of your instructor or some other communication adviser, you receive two pieces of advice. First, your adviser suggests that you spend the next three weeks observing people who handle themselves well in conversations and to record exactly what they do that makes them so skillful. Second, your adviser suggests that you read several books on the subject of conversational skills. You begin these tasks with the best intentions, but after a few days the task of recording conversations becomes a burden—it would be so much easier just to listen to others talk. And your diligent reading program becomes bogged down as the press of other work fills up your time. In other words, you find that you just "can't" fit the self-improvement plan into your busy schedule.

Let's be realistic. Becoming a better communicator is probably one of many goals in your life. It's possible that other needs are more pressing, which is completely reasonable. However, you should realize that changing your self-concept often requires a good deal of commitment and that without that commitment your good intentions alone probably won't get you much closer to this goal. In communication, as in most other aspects of life, "there's no such thing as a free lunch."

Have the Skill to Change   Often trying isn't enough. In some instances you would change if you knew how to do so. To see if this is the case for you, go back to your list of "can'ts" and "won'ts," and see if any items there are more appropriately "don't know hows." If so, then the way to change is to learn how. You can do so in two ways.

First, you can seek advice—from books such as this one, the references listed at the end of each chapter, and other printed sources. You can also get advice from instructors, counselors, and other experts, as well as friends. Of course, not all the advice you receive will be useful, but if you read widely and talk to enough people, you have a good chance of learning the things you want to know.

Are We Our Brother's Keeper? Moral Rules Theory

If it is true that our messages help shape others' self-concepts for better or worse, what responsibility do we have to act in their best interests? American philosopher W. D. Ross offered a partial answer to this question by arguing that human beings have certain prima facie moral duties: obligations that are self-evident at first glance. Among these are the duties of

1. Fidelity: to keep promises
2. Reparation: to make up for any wrongs committed
3. Gratitude: to feel and express appreciation for the kindness of others
4. Beneficence: to promote goodness and help others
5. Self-improvement: to become the best person we possibly can
6. Justice: to distribute goods fairly, according to what others have earned and deserve
7. Nonmaleficence: to refrain from injuring others and to prevent injury

Of these moral duties, beneficence and nonmaleficence seem most closely related to the question of our responsibility for shaping others' self-concepts. These rules seem to oblige us to communicate in ways that will, at the very least, avoid hurting others and that ideally will help them.

Ross recognized that the obligation to act with beneficence and nonmaleficence would, on occasion, conflict with other duties. Consider a few examples:

- You promise to be honest (following rule 1) but later realize that your candor would hurt the other person's feelings.

- As a boss, you want to hire the most qualified job-seeker (following rule 6), but passing over a less deserving but more needy candidate might demolish his or her self-confidence.

- In order to grow as a person (rule 5) you need to end a romantic relationship, but doing so would demolish the self-confidence of your partner.

In cases like these, Ross reasoned that we should follow two rules: First, to obey that duty that, under the actual circumstances, is most compelling, and second, to always do that which has the greatest prima facie rightness over prima facie wrongness. It seems to follow that the duty of nonmaleficence would generally take precedence over the other duties: At the very least, duty theory suggests, we are obliged to act in ways that do no harm to others.

Duty theory rests on intuition. Ross can offer no reasons to support the claim that these are, indeed, universal duties belonging to all persons, nor can he offer a reasoned way of determining which duty is more compelling. Ross responded to criticisms of this weakness: "To me it seems as self-evident as anything could be, that to make a promise, for instance, is to create a moral claim on us in someone else. Many readers will perhaps say that they do not know this to be true. If so, I certainly cannot prove it to them. I can only ask them to reflect again, in the hope that they will ultimately agree that they also know it to be true."

Duty theory doesn't seem to provide an answer for every situation in which our behavior might affect the way others feel about themselves, but it does present us with a list of questions to ponder as we consider the effects of our messages.

Apply duty theory to your relationship with someone who is important to you and on whose self-concept your behavior is likely to have some impact. What responsibilities do you have to follow the rules of beneficence and nonmaleficence? How can you communicate in ways that honor these rules?

This abstract is based on William D. Ross, *The Right and the Good* (New York: Oxford University Press, 1930).

Second, you can observe models—people who handle themselves in the ways you would like to master. It's often been said that people learn more from models than in any other way, and by taking advantage of this principle you will find that the world is full of teachers who can show you how to communicate more successfully. Become a careful observer.

Watch what people you admire do and say, not so that you can copy them, but so that you can adapt their behavior to fit your own personal style.

At this point, you might be overwhelmed at the difficulty of changing the way you think about yourself and the way you act. Remember that we never said that this process would be an easy one (although it sometimes is). But even when change is difficult, you know that it's possible if you are serious. You don't need to be perfect, but you can improve your self-concept if you choose.

PRESENTING THE SELF: COMMUNICATION AS IDENTITY MANAGEMENT

So far we have described how communication shapes the way communicators view themselves. In the remainder of this chapter we will turn the tables and focus on the topic of **identity management**—the communication strategies that people use to influence how others view them. In the following pages you will see that many of our messages aim at creating desired identity.

Public and Private Selves

To understand how identity management operates, we have to discuss the notion of self in more detail. So far we have referred to the "self" as if each of us had only one identity. In truth, each of us has several selves, some private and others public. Often these selves are quite different.

The **perceived self** is a reflection of the self-concept. Your perceived self is the person you believe yourself to be in moments of honest self-examination. We can call the perceived self "private" because you are unlikely to reveal all of it to another person. You can verify the private nature of the perceived self by reviewing the self-concept list you developed while reading page 46. You'll probably find some elements of yourself there that you would not disclose to many people and some that you would not share with anyone. You might, for example, be reluctant to share some feelings about your appearance ("I think I'm rather unattractive"), your intelligence ("I'm not as smart as I wish I were"), your goals ("The most important thing to me is becoming rich"), or your motives ("I care more about myself than about others").

TABLE 2-3 Self-Selected Adjectives Describing Perceived and Presenting Selves of College Students

PERCEIVED SELF		PRESENTING SELF	
Men	**Women**	**Men**	**Women**
1. Friendly	1. Friendly	1. Wild	1. Active
2. Active	2. Responsible	2. Able	2. Responsible
3. Responsible	3. Independent	3. Active	3. Able
4. Independent	4. Capable	4. Strong	4. Bright
5. Capable	5. Sensible	5. Proud	5. Warm
6. Polite	6. Active	6. Smart	6. Funny
7. Attractive	7. Happy	7. Brave	7. Independent
8. Smart	8. Curious	8. Capable	8. Proud
9. Happy	9. Faithful	9. Responsible	9. Sensible
10. Funny	10. Attractive	10. Rough	10. Smart

Adapted from C. M. Shaw and R. Edwards, "Self-Concepts and Self-Presentations of Males and Females: Similarities and Differences," *Communication Reports* 10 (1997): 55–62.

In contrast to the perceived self, the **presenting self** is a public image—the way we want others to view us. The presenting self is sometimes called one's **face.** In most cases the presenting self that we seek to create is a socially approved image: diligent student, loving partner, conscientious worker, loyal friend, and so on. Social norms often create a gap between the perceived and presenting selves. For instance, Table 2-3 shows that the self-concepts of one group of male and female college students were quite similar but that their public selves were different in several respects from both their private selves and from the public selves of the opposite sex.[37]

You can recognize the difference between public and private behaviors by recalling a time when you observed a driver, alone in his or her car, behaving in ways that would never be acceptable in public. All of us engage in backstage ways of acting that we would never do in public. Just recall how you behave in front of the bathroom mirror when the door is locked, and you will appreciate the difference between public and private behaviors. If you knew that someone were watching, would you behave differently?

Characteristics of Identity Management

Now that you have a sense of what identity management is, we can look at some characteristics of this process.

We Strive to Construct Multiple Identities   It is an oversimplification to suggest that each of us uses identity management strategies to create just one identity. In the course of even a single day, most people perform a variety of roles: "respectful student," "joking friend," "friendly neighbor," and "helpful worker," to suggest just a few.

The ability to construct multiple identities is one element of communication competence. For example, the style of speaking or even the language itself can reflect a choice about how to construct one's identity. We recall a black colleague who was also minister of a Southern Baptist congregation consisting mostly of black members. On campus his manner of speaking was typically professorial; but a visit to hear him preach one Sunday revealed a speaker whose style was much more animated and theatrical, reflecting his identity in that context. Likewise, one scholar pointed out that bilingual Latinos in the United States often choose whether to use English or Spanish depending on the kind of identity they are seeking in a given conversation.[38]

We strive even to construct different identities with the same person. As you grew up you almost certainly changed characters as you interacted with your parents. In one context you acted as responsible adult ("You can trust me with the car!"), and in another context you were the helpless child ("I can't find my socks!"). At some times—perhaps on birthdays or holidays—you were a dedicated family member, and at other times you may have played the role of rebel. Likewise, in romantic relationships we switch among many ways of behaving, depending on the context: friend, lover, business partner, scolding critic, apologetic child, and so on.

INVITATION TO INSIGHT

YOUR MANY IDENTITIES

You can get a sense of the many roles you try to create by keeping a record of the situations in which you communicate over a one- or two-day period. For each situation, identify a dramatic title to represent the image you try to create. A few examples might be "party animal," "helpful housekeeper," "wise older sibling," and "sophisticated film critic."

Identity Management Is Collaborative   Sociologist Erving Goffman used a dramatistic metaphor to describe identity management.[39] He suggested that each of us is a kind of playwright who creates roles that reflect how we want others to see us as well as the performer who acts out those roles. But unlike the audience for most forms of acting, our "audience" is made up of other actors who are trying to create their own characters. Identity-related communication can be viewed as a kind of process theater in which we collaborate with other actors to improvise scenes in which our characters mesh.

You can appreciate the collaborative nature of identity management by thinking about how you might handle a gripe with a friend or family member who has failed to pass along a phone message that arrived while you were away from home. Suppose that you decide to raise the issue tactfully in an effort to avoid seeming like a nag (desired role for yourself: "nice person") and also to save the other person from the embarrassment of being confronted (hoping to avoid suggesting that the other person's role is "screw-up"). If your tactful bid is accepted, the dialog might sound like this:

You: ". . . By the way, Jenny told me she called yesterday. If you wrote a note, I guess I missed seeing it."

Other: "Oh . . . sorry. I meant to write a note, but as soon as I hung up the doorbell rang, and then I had to run off to class."

You (in friendly tone of voice)**:** "That's okay. I sure would appreciate from now on if you'd leave me a note."

Other: "No problem."

"Hah! This is the Old King Cole nobody ever sees."

©The New Yorker Collection 1983 Dana Fradon from cartoonbank.com. All Rights Reserved.

In this upbeat conversation, both you and the other person accepted one another's bids for identity. As a result, the conversation ran smoothly. Imagine, though, how differently the outcome would be if the other person didn't accept your role as "nice person":

You: ". . . By the way, Jenny told me she called yesterday. If you wrote a note, I guess I missed seeing it."

Other (defensively)**:** "OK, so I forgot. It's not that big a deal. You're not perfect yourself, you know!"

Your first bid as "nice, face-saving person" was rejected. At this point you have the choice of persisting in trying to play the original role: "Hey, I'm not mad at you, and I know I'm not perfect!" Or, you might switch to the new role of "unjustly accused person," responding with aggravation, "I never said I was perfect. But we're not talking about me here . . ."

As this example illustrates, *collaboration* doesn't mean the same thing as *agreement*.[40] The small issue of the phone message might mushroom into a fight in which you and the other person both adopt the role of combatants. The point here is that virtually all conversations provide an arena in which communicators construct their identities in response to the behavior of others. As you read in chapter 1, communication isn't made up of discrete events that can be separated from one another. Instead, what happens at one moment is influenced by what each party brings to the interaction and what happened in their relationship up to that point.

Identity Management Can Be Deliberate or Unconscious At this point you might object to the notion of strategic identity management, claiming that most of your communication is spontaneous and not a deliberate attempt to present yourself in a certain way. You might acknowledge that some of your communication involves a conscious attempt to manage your identity.

There's no doubt that sometimes we are highly aware of managing impressions. Most job interviews and first dates are clear examples of deliberate identity management. But in other cases we unconsciously act in ways that are really small public performances.[41] For example, experimental subjects expressed facial disgust in reaction to eating sandwiches laced with a supersaturated saltwater solution only when there was another person present: When they were alone, they made no faces while eating the same sandwiches.[42] Another study showed that communicators engage in facial mimicry (such as smiling or looking sympathetic in response to another's message) in face-to-face settings only when their expressions can be seen by the other person. When they are speaking over the phone, and their reactions cannot be seen, they do not make the same expressions.[43] Studies like these suggest that most of our behavior is aimed at sending messages to others—in other words, identity management.

The experimental subjects described in the preceding paragraph didn't consciously think, "Somebody is watching me eat this salty sandwich, so I'll make a face" or "Because I'm in a face-to-face conversation, I'll show I'm sympathetic by mimicking the facial expressions of my conversational partner." Decisions like these are often instantaneous and outside of our conscious awareness. In the same way, many of our choices about how to act in the array of daily interactions aren't highly considered strategic decisions. Rather, they rely on "scripts" that we have developed over time. You probably have a variety of roles for managing your identity from which to choose in familiar situations such as dealing with strangers, treating customers at work, interacting with family members, and so on. When you find yourself in familiar situations like these, you probably slip into these roles quite often. Only when those roles don't seem quite right do you deliberately construct an approach that reflects how you want the scene to play out.

Despite the pervasiveness of identity management, it seems like an exaggeration to suggest that *all* behavior is aimed at making impressions. Young children certainly aren't strategic communicators. A baby spontaneously laughs when pleased and cries when sad or uncomfortable without any notion of creating an impression in others. Likewise, there are times when we, as adults, act spontaneously. Despite these exceptions, most people consciously or unconsciously communicate in ways that help construct desired identities for themselves and others.

Identity Management Varies by Situation

The degree to which we consciously manage our identities varies from one situation to another. Not surprisingly, most of us work harder at creating a desired impression in the early stages of a relationship—especially one where we are seeking the approval of people whose opinion we value. If you have ever been in an employment interview where you tried to impress a potential boss, you know how carefully you presented yourself.[44] The same principle operates in courtship situations. For example, college men changed their self-presentation more when they were talking to women they found attractive than they did when talking to less attractive women.[45] After we get to know others, we don't work as hard at managing impressions. The gender of the other person seems to make a difference, though: Research suggests that we are less concerned with identity management among familiar people of the same sex than with less familiar people of the same sex or people of the opposite sex, regardless of how well we know them.[46]

People Differ in Their Degree of Identity Management   Some people are much more aware of their identity management behavior than others. These high self-monitors have the ability to pay attention to their own behavior and others' reactions, adjusting their communication to create the desired impression. By contrast, low self-monitors express what they are thinking and feeling without much attention to the impression their behavior creates.[47] You can get an idea of whether you are a high or a low self-monitor by answering the following questions.

INVITATION TO INSIGHT

SELF-MONITORING INVENTORY

These statements concern personal reactions to a number of situations. No two statements are exactly alike, so consider each statement carefully before answering. If a statement is true, or mostly true, as applied to you, circle the *T*. If a statement is false, or not usually true, as applied to you, circle the *F*.

1. I find it hard to imitate the behavior of other people.   T   F
2. I guess I put on a show to impress or entertain people.   T   F
3. I would probably make a good actor.   T   F
4. I sometimes appear to others to be experiencing deeper emotions than I actually am.   T   F
5. In a group of people I am rarely the center of attention.   T   F
6. In different situations and with different people, I often act like very different persons.   T   F
7. I can argue only for ideas I already believe.   T   F
8. In order to get along and be liked, I tend to be what people expect me to be rather than anything else.   T   F
9. I may deceive people by being friendly when I really dislike them.   T   F
10. I'm not always the person I appear to be.   T   F

Scoring: Give yourself one point for each of questions 1, 5, and 7 that you answered *F*. Give yourself one point for each of the remaining questions that you answered *T*. Add up your points. If you are a good judge of yourself and scored 7 or above, you are probably a high self-monitoring individual; 3 or below, you are probably a low self-monitoring individual.

Source: Mark Snyder, "The Many Me's of the Self-Monitor," *Psychology Today* (March 1983): 34. Reprinted with permission.

What is the ideal score for this self-quiz? There are certainly advantages to being a high self-monitor.[48] People who pay attention to themselves are generally good actors who can create the identity they want, acting interested when bored or friendly when they really feel quite the opposite. This allows them to handle social situations smoothly, often putting others at ease. They are also good "people-readers" who can adjust their behavior to get the desired reaction from others. Along with these advantages, there are some potential disadvantages to being an extremely high self-monitor. The analytical nature of such people may prevent them from experiencing events completely because a portion of their attention will always be viewing the situation from a detached position. High self-monitors' ability to act means that it is difficult to tell how they are really feeling. In fact, because high self-monitors change roles often, they may have a hard time knowing *themselves* how they really feel.

People who score low on the self-monitoring scale live life quite differently from their more self-conscious counterparts. They have a more simple, focused idea of who they are and who they want to be. Low self-monitors are likely to have a narrower repertoire of behaviors, and thus they can be expected to act in more or less the same way regardless of the situation. This means that low self-monitors are easy to read. "What you see is what you get" might be their motto. Although this lack of flexibility may make their social interaction less smooth in many situations, low self-monitors can be counted on to be straightforward communicators.

By now it should be clear that neither extremely high nor low self-monitoring is the ideal. There are some situations when paying attention to yourself and adapting your behavior can be useful, and there are other situations when reacting without considering the effect on others is a better approach. This need for a range of behaviors demonstrates again the notion of communicative competence outlined in chapter 1: Flexibility is the key to successful relationships. In the following reading titled "Will the Real Me Please Stand Up?" writer Barry Stevens describes the challenges of managing identities while being true to oneself.

Why Manage Identities?

Why bother trying to shape others' opinions? Sometimes we create and maintain a front to follow social rules. As children we learn to act polite, even when bored. Likewise, part of growing up consists of developing a set of manners for various occasions: meeting strangers, attending school, going to church, and so on. Young children who haven't learned all the do's and don'ts of polite society often embarrass their parents by behaving inappropriately ("Mommy, why is

"Not the "real you?"
Well, of course it's not the real you.
The real you is bald.

©2001 Wm. Hamilton from cartoonbank.com. All Rights Reserved.

Kholoud Elayyan: Identity and a Sense of Mission

I was born and raised near the Palestinian town of Ramallah. I lived there until I came to the U.S. at the age of 18 to study communication.

I don't dress like the typical female college student in Southern California. I wear modest clothing and a head-scarf, which is called a "hijab" in Arabic. This style of appearance follows a rule of Islam, which says that women should appear in public in a modest, non-provocative manner. That is quite different from a lot of

women on campus and around the town where I live!

Despite what some people think, I don't mind dressing in a way that's not the norm. In fact, I like it. For one thing, it frees me from being examined in a sexual way, which would make me uncomfortable. But even more, my style of dressing leads some people to ask me about my religion. And I believe that sharing Islam with others is an important mission.

I find that many people make stereotypical assumptions about Palestinians and about the Islamic religion. Some think

all of us are militants, or even terrorists. I try to behave calmly and kindly to everyone, and to explain my faith if they are interested in listening. I find that most people respond well when we talk on a person-to-person level.

I choose to study communication so I could explain my beliefs better. Although my choice about appearance isn't a deliberate strategy to reach out to non-Muslims, I find it works as a door-opener. For that, I'm grateful.

---

that man so fat?"); but by the time they enter school, behavior that might have been excusable or even amusing just isn't acceptable. Good manners are often aimed at making others more comfortable. For example, able-bodied people often mask their discomfort upon encountering someone who is disabled by acting nonchalant or stressing similarities between themselves and the disabled person.[49]

Social rules govern our behavior in a variety of settings. It would be impossible to keep a job, for example, without meeting certain expectations. Salespeople are obliged to treat customers with courtesy. Employees need to appear reasonably respectful when talking to the boss. Some forms of clothing would be considered outrageous at work. By agreeing to take on a job, you are signing an unwritten contract that you will present a certain face at work, whether or not that face reflects the way you might be feeling at a particular moment.

Even when social roles don't dictate the proper way to behave, we often manage our own and one another's identities for a second reason: to accomplish personal goals. You might, for example, dress up for a visit to traffic court in hope that your front (responsible citizen) will convince the judge to treat you sympathetically. You might chat sociably with neighbors who you don't find especially interesting so that you can exchange favors or solve problems as they come up.

Sometimes identity management aims at achieving one or more of the relational goals we discussed in chapter 1: affiliation, control, or

WILL THE REAL ME PLEASE STAND UP?

So then there were two of I. One I always doing something that the other I disapproved of. Or other I said what I disapproved of. All this argument in me so much.

In the beginning was I, and I was good.

Then came in other I. Outside authority. This was confusing. And then other I became very confused because there were so many different outside authorities.

Sit nicely. Leave the room to blow your nose. Don't do that, that's silly. Why, the poor child doesn't even know how to pick a bone! Flush the toilet at night because if you don't it makes it harder to clean. DON'T FLUSH THE TOILET AT NIGHT—you wake people up! Always be nice to people. Even if you don't like them, you mustn't hurt their feelings. Be frank and honest. If you don't tell people what you think of them, that's cowardly. Butter knives. It is important to use butter knives. Butter knives? What foolishness! Speak nicely. Sissy! Kipling is wonderful! Ugh! Kipling (turning away).

The most important thing is to have a career. The most important thing is to get married. The hell with everyone. Be nice to everyone. The most important thing is sex. The most important thing is to have everyone like you. The most important thing is to be sophisticated and say what you don't mean and don't let anyone know what you feel. The most important thing is a black seal

In the beginning, I was one person, knowing nothing but my own experience.

Then I was told things, and I became two people: the little girl who said how terrible it was that the boys had a fire going in the lot next door where they were roasting apples (which was what the woman said)—and the little girl who, when the boys were called by their mothers to go to the store, ran out and tended the fire and the apples because she loved doing it.

coat and china and silver. The most important thing is to be clean. The most important thing is to always pay your debts. The most important thing is not to be taken in by anyone else. The most important thing is to love your parents. The most important thing is to work. The most important thing is to be independent. The most important thing is to speak correct English. The most important thing is to go to the right plays and read the right books. The most important thing is to do what others say. And others say all these things.

All the time, I is saying, live with life. That is what is important.

But when I lives with life, other I says no, that's bad. All the different other I's say this. It's dangerous. It isn't practical. You'll come to a bad end. Of course . . . everyone felt that way once, the way you do, but *you'll learn.*

Out of all the other I's some are chosen as a pattern that is me. But there are all the other possibilities of patterns within what all the others say which come into me and become other I which is not myself, and sometimes these take over. Then who am I?

I does not bother about who am I. I is, and is happy being. But when I is happy being, other I says get to work, do something worthwhile! I is happy doing dishes. "You're weird!" I is happy being with people saying nothing. Other I says talk. Talk, talk, talk. I gets lost.

I knows that things are to be played with, not possessed. I likes putting things together, lightly. Taking things apart, lightly. "You'll never have anything!" Making things of things in a way that the things themselves take part in, putting themselves together with surprise and delight to I. "There's no money in that!"

I is human. If someone needs, I gives. "You can't do that! You'll never have anything for yourself! We'll have to support you!"

I loves. I loves in a way that other I does not know. I loves. "That's too warm for friends!" "That's too cool for lovers!" "Don't feel so bad, he's just a friend. It's not as though you loved him." "How can you let him go? I thought you loved him." So cool the warm for friends and hot up the love for lovers, and I gets lost.

So both I's have a house and a husband and children and all that, but both I's are confused because other I says, "You see? You're lucky," while I goes on crying. "What are you crying about? Why are you so ungrateful?" I doesn't know gratitude or ingratitude, and cannot argue. I goes on crying. Other I pushes it out, says, "I am happy! I am very lucky to have such a fine family and a nice house and good neighbors and lots of friends who want me to do this, do that." I is not reasonable either. I goes on crying.

Other I gets tired, and goes on smiling because that is the thing to do. Smile, and you will be rewarded. Like the seal who gets tossed a piece of fish. Be nice to everyone and you will be rewarded. People will be nice to you, and you can be happy with that. You know they like you. Like a dog who gets patted on the head for good behavior. Tell funny stories. Be gay. Smile, smile, smile. . . . I is crying. . . . "Don't be sorry for yourself! Go out and do things for people!" "Go out and be with people!" I is still crying, but now, that is not heard and felt so much.

Suddenly: "What am I doing?" "Am I to go through life playing the clown?" "What am I doing, going to parties that I do not enjoy?" "What am I doing, being with people who bore me?" "Why am I so hollow and the hollowness filled with emptiness?" A shell. How has this shell grown around me? Why am I proud of my children and unhappy about their lives which are not good enough? Why am I disappointed? Why do I feel so much waste?

I comes through, a little. In moments. And gets pushed back by other I.

I refuses to play the clown any more. Which I is that? "She used to be fun, but now she thinks too much about herself." I lets friends drop away. Which I is that? "She's being too much by herself. That's bad. She's losing her mind." Which mind?

Barry Stevens

respect. For instance, you might act more friendly and lively than you feel upon meeting a new person so that you will appear likable. You could sigh and roll your eyes when arguing politics with a classmate to gain an advantage in an argument. You might smile and preen to show the attractive stranger at a party that you would like to get better acquainted. In situations like these you aren't being deceptive as much as putting "your best foot forward."

All these examples show that it is difficult—even impossible—*not* to manage identities. After all, you have to send some sort of message. If you don't act friendly when meeting a stranger, you have to act aloof, indifferent, hostile, or in some other manner. If you don't act businesslike, you have to behave in an alternative way: casual, goofy, or whatever. Likewise, you have to play some role in constructing others' identities. In conversations, you have to act either interested or disinterested. If you don't act friendly with acquaintances, you have to act in some other manner. These examples show that the question usually isn't whether or not to manage identities but rather how you will do so.

How Do We Manage Identities?

How do we create a public face? In an age in which technology provides many options for communicating, the answer depends in part on the communication channel chosen.

Face-to-Face Impression Management   In face-to-face interaction, communicators can manage their front in three ways: manner, setting, and appearance.[50] *Manner* consists of a communicator's words and nonverbal actions. Physicians, for example, display a wide variety of manners as they conduct physical examinations. Some are friendly and conversational, whereas others adopt a brusque and impersonal approach. Still others are polite but businesslike. Much of a communicator's manner comes from what he or she says. A doctor who remembers details about your interests and hobbies is quite different from one who sticks to clinical questions. One who explains a medical procedure creates a different impression than another who reveals little to the patient. Along with the content of speech, nonverbal behaviors play a big role in creating impressions. A doctor who greets you with a friendly smile and a handshake comes across quite differently from one who gives nothing more than a curt nod. Manner varies widely in other professional and personal settings—professors, salespeople, hair stylists, and so on—and the impressions they create vary accordingly. The same principle holds in personal relationships. Your manner plays a major role in shaping how others view you. Chapters 5 and 6 will describe in detail how your words and nonverbal behaviors create impressions. Because you have to speak and act, the question isn't whether your manner sends a message but rather whether these messages will be intentional.

Along with manner, a second dimension of identity management is *appearance*—the personal items that people use to shape an image.

Among the People, every person possessed a Shield of one kind or another. One of the most important things to understand about these Shields is that they were never intended to give physical protection in battle. They were not bade to turn away arrows or bullets, or for people to hide behind . . .

Sometimes they were made from the tough hides of bears or buffalo bulls, but more often they were covered only with the soft skins of deer, antelope, coyote, otter, weasel, or even mice. They were then hung with eagle plumes, cedar pouches, tassels of animal fur, and many other things. They were also painted with various symbolic figures. These signs told who the man was, what he sought to be, and what his loves, fears, and dreams were. Almost everything about him was written there, reflected in the Mirror of his Shield . . .

These Shields were carried by the men among the People in order that anyone they met might know them.

Hyemeyohsts Storm, *Seven Arrows*

Sometimes appearance is part of creating a professional image. A physician's white lab coat and a police officer's uniform both set the wearers apart as someone special. A tailored suit or a rumpled outfit create very different impressions in the business world. Off the job, clothing is just as important. We choose clothing that sends a message about ourselves, sometimes trendy and sometimes traditional. Some people dress in ways that accent their sexuality, whereas others hide it. Clothing can say, "I'm an athlete," "I'm wealthy," or "I'm an environmentalist." Along with dress, other aspects of appearance play a strong role in identity management. Are you suntanned or pale? What is your hairstyle? Do you make an effort to look friendly and confident?

Tattoos offer an interesting example of how appearance can help create an identity. The very act of decorating one's skin makes a statement, and the design or words chosen say even more. One fascinating study explored the communicative function of tattoos worn by some people to announce their HIV-positive condition.[51] At the most obvious level, such tattoos convey important information about the health status of the wearer to medical workers. Beyond being a practical announcement, though, such tattoos can be a vehicle for identity management, intended for both the wearer and others. One tattoo wearer listed the messages that his visible label conveys: the refusal to internalize shame, a commitment to safer sex practices, a challenge to stereotypes about weak "AIDS victims," and an educational tool that generates discussion by making the condition visible.

A final way to manage identities is through the choice of *setting*—physical items that we use to influence how others view us. In modern Western society the automobile is a major part of identity management.

We may be born naked, but we waste little time correcting the oversight. Almost from the moment we wriggle into the world, we start getting dressed. Conventional wisdom claims that clothing is simply a means of survival, but clearly there's more to it. Whether it's a couple of strategically placed shells or a suit of armor, a G-string or a caribou parka, clothing is a set of signals to all we meet. And though clothes may indeed protect us from the elements, their real job is to protect us from social opprobrium, or to make a statement—to a potential boss, a potential bride, or a very real enemy.

Banana Republic Catalog

This explains why many people lust after cars that are far more expensive and powerful than they really need. A sporty convertible or fancy imported sedan doesn't just get drivers from one place to another: It also makes statements about the kind of people they are. The physical setting we choose and the way we arrange it are another important way to manage identities. What colors do you choose for the place you live? What artwork? What music do you play? Of course, we choose a setting that we enjoy; but in many cases we create an environment that will present the desired front to others. If you doubt this fact, just recall the last time you straightened up the house before important guests arrived. Backstage you might be comfortable with a messy place, but your public front—at least to some people—is quite different.

Impression Management in Mediated Communication

Most of the preceding examples involve face-to-face interaction, but impression management is just as common and important in other types of communication. Consider the care you probably take when drafting a resume for a potential employer, a thank you letter in response to a gift, or a love note to a sweetheart. Besides giving careful thought to the wording of your message, you probably make strategic decisions about its appearance. Will you use plain white paper or something more distinctive? Will you type out your words or write them in longhand? People think carefully about considerations like these because they instinctively know that the *way* a message is presented can say as much as the words it contains.

Along with personal correspondence, communicators sometimes manage their identity in the mass print media. Personal newspaper ads in which people seek romantic partners are an obvious case of deliberate identity management. Younger people who describe themselves to potential dating partners emphasize physical appearance and are more likely to play up sexuality. By contrast, ads by people over age fifty are more likely to focus on personality features.[52]

Nationality and gender also play a role in how we manage our identity. A comparison of personal ads placed by men in the *London Review of Books* and ones placed by women in the *New York Review of Books* contrasts the American tendency for unapologetic self-promotion and a feminine focus on romance with the kind of droll understatement and self-deprecation more typical of British men:

New York Review of Books: Petite, pretty, blond professional seeks relationship built around laughter, love and a view that life should continue to be an adventure.

San Francisco screenwriter, mid-30's female, lucid, wry, kind, emotionally generous and forthright, extremely fit and comely blue-eyed bicyclist; desires self-aware, serene, sensual, supple, tall, expressive, loving man for stormy coastlines, books, be-bop, swing dancing, caressing, confessing, voluptuary highs and intimate friendship. Someone who loves to play and who savors the details as we sit across the gothic wooden table laden with sumptuous organic feasts, our well-loved friends coming for Sunday dinners, stories and discourse infused with sovereign thought, self-possessed rebellion, deep compassion and shameless discovery.

London Review of Books: Insensitive 47-year-old lounge lizard (male), seeks woman with energy to suffer periods of self-indulgence. Offers in return good sangria and complete lack of interest in sport.

Shy, ugly man, fond of extended periods of self-pity, middle-aged, flatulent and overweight, seeks the impossible.[53]

At first glance, the new technology of computer-mediated communication (CMC) seems to limit the potential for impression management. E-mail messages, for example, appear to lack the "richness" of other channels. They don't convey the tone of your voice, postures, gestures, or facial expressions. Recently, though, communication scholars have begun to recognize that what is missing in computer-mediated communication can actually be an *advantage* for communicators who want to manage the impressions they make.[54] E-mail authors can edit their messages until they create just the desired impression. They can choose the desired level of clarity or ambiguity, seriousness or humor, logic or emotion. Unlike face-to-face communication, electronic communication allows a sender to say difficult things without forcing the receiver to respond immediately, and it permits the receiver to ignore a message rather than give an unpleasant response. Options like these show that CMC can serve as a tool for impression management at least as well as face-to-face communication.

Like e-mail, personal pages on the World Wide Web provide opportunities for their creators to manage their identities. Every Web surfer has encountered pages "under construction." Some observers have pointed out that the construction involves much more than what appears on the computer screen: Personal home page designers are also constructing their public identities.[55] The words, images, and sounds that Web designers choose make a statement about who they are—or at least how they want to be regarded by others.

Designers create identity both by what they *include* and what they *exclude* from their home page. Consider how including or excluding the following kinds of information affects how Web surfers might regard the creator of a home page: age, personal photo, educational or career accomplishments, sexual orientation, job title, personal interests, personal philosophy and religious beliefs, and organizations to which the page creator belongs. You can easily think of a host of other kinds of material that could be included or excluded and the effect that each would have on how others regard the page creator.

Communicators who want to manage impressions don't always prefer computer-mediated channels. People are generally comfortable with face-to-face interaction when they feel confident that others support the image they want to present. On the other hand, people are more likely to prefer mediated channels when their own self-presentation is threatened.

"On the Internet, nobody knows you're a dog."

©The New Yorker Collection 1993 Peter Steiner from cartoonbank.com. All Rights Reserved.

Identity Management and Honesty

After reading this far, you might think that identity management sounds like an academic label for manipulation or phoniness. If the perceived self is the "real" you, it might seem that any behavior that contradicts it would be dishonest.

There certainly are situations where identity management is dishonest. A manipulative date who pretends to be affectionate in order to gain sexual favors is clearly unethical and deceitful. So are job applicants who lie about academic records to get hired or salespeople who pretend to be dedicated to customer service when their real goal is to make a quick buck. But managing impressions doesn't necessarily make you a liar. In fact, it is almost impossible to imagine how we could communicate effectively without making decisions about which front to present in one situation or another. It would be ludicrous for you to act the same way with strangers as you do with close friends, and nobody would show the same face to a two-year-old as he or she would to an adult.

Each of us has a repertoire of faces—a cast of characters—and part of being a competent communicator is choosing the best face for the situation. Consider a few examples:

- You offer to teach a friend a new skill: playing the guitar, operating a computer program, or sharpening up a tennis backhand. Your friend is making slow progress with the skill, and you find yourself growing impatient.

- At a party you meet someone who you find to be very attractive, and you are pretty sure that the feeling is mutual. On one hand you feel an obligation to spend most of your time with the person whom you came with, but on the other hand the opportunity here is very appealing.

- At work you face a belligerent customer. You don't believe that anyone has the right to treat you this way.

■ A friend or family member makes a joke about your appearance that hurts your feelings. You aren't sure whether to make an issue of the joke or to pretend that it doesn't bother you.

In each of these situations—and in countless others every day—you have a choice about how to act. It is an oversimplification to say that there is only one honest way to behave in each circumstance and that every other response would be insincere and dishonest. Instead, identity management involves deciding which face—which part of yourself—to reveal. For example, when teaching a new skill, you choose to display the "patient" instead of the "impatient" side of yourself. In the same way, at work you have the option of acting defensive or nondefensive in difficult situations. With strangers, friends, or family you can choose whether to disclose your feelings. Which face to show to others is an important decision, but in any case you are sharing a real part of yourself. You may not be revealing everything—but as you will learn in chapter 8, complete self-disclosure is rarely appropriate.

SUMMARY

The self-concept is a relatively stable set of perceptions that individuals hold about themselves. It begins to develop soon after birth, being shaped by both verbal and nonverbal messages from significant others and from reflected appraisal based on comparison with reference groups. The self-concept is subjective and can vary in important ways from the way a person is perceived by others. Although the self may evolve over time, the self-concept resists change.

A self-fulfilling prophecy occurs when a person's expectations of an event influence the outcome. One type of prophecy consists of predictions by others, whereas another type is self-imposed. Self-fulfilling prophecies can be both positive and negative.

It is possible to change one's self-concept in ways that lead to more effective communication. It is necessary to have realistic expectations about how much change is possible and to begin with a realistic assessment of oneself. Willingness to exert the effort to change is important, and in some cases change requires new information or skill.

Identity management consists of strategic communication designed to influence others' perceptions of an individual. Identity management aims at presenting to others one or more faces, which may be different from private, spontaneous behavior that occurs outside of others' presence. Some communicators are high self-monitors who are highly conscious of their own behavior, whereas others are less aware of how their words and actions affect others.

Identity management occurs for two reasons. Many times it aims at following social rules and conventions. At other times it aims at achieving a variety of content and relational goals. In either case, communicators engage in creating an identity by managing their manner, appearance, and the settings in which they interact with others. Identity management occurs both in face-to-face and mediated communications. Although identity management might seem manipulative, it can be an authentic form of communication. Because each person has a variety of faces that he or she can reveal, choosing which one to present need not be dishonest.

KEY TERMS

cognitive conservatism
face
identity
identity management
perceived self

presenting self
reference groups
reflected appraisal
self-concept

self-esteem
self-fulfilling prophecy
significant other
social comparison

LOOKING OUT/LOOKING IN ONLINE

Use your *Looking Out/Looking In* CD-ROM for quick access to the electronic resources that accompany this chapter. Included on this CD-ROM are additional study aids and links to the *Looking Out/Looking In* Web site at the Wadsworth Communication Café. The CD-ROM is your gateway to a wealth of resources that will help you understand and further explore the material in this chapter. **Video clips** under *Communication Scenarios* on the CD illustrate the skills introduced in this chapter. Click on the Web site link to complete self-study **review quizzes** to help you master new concepts; access a **feature film database** to locate clips and entire movies that illustrate communication principles; find Internet material via the maintained **Web site links;** and complete **online activities** to help you master new concepts.

INFOTRAC COLLEGE EDITION EXERCISES

Use the InfoTrac College Edition password that was included free with a copy of this new text to answer the following questions. These questions can be completed online and, if requested, submitted to your instructor under InfoTrac College Edition Activities at the *Looking Out/Looking In* Web site.

1. How the Self-Concept Develops

Read the research study "Family Communication Patterns and Personality Characteristics" by Li-Ning Huang. (Hint: Use PowerTrac's author and title search functions to locate this article.) What connections did the researchers discover between personality characteristics and communication patterns in one's family of origin? In what ways did the environment in which you grew up shape your communication? To what degree do you think it is possible to change your current communication style?

2. Sex and Gender

Read the study "The Effect of Social Context on Gender Self-Concept" by Cynthia J. Smith, Jane A. Noll, and Judith Becker Bryant. (Hint: Use PowerTrac's author and title search functions to locate this article.) What does this article tell you about the stability of one's self-concept? How closely do the findings of the article match your personal experience?

3. Identity Management

Use PowerTrac to locate the article "Symbolic Interactionism Revisited: Potential Liabilities for the Self Constructed in the Crucible of Interpersonal Relationships" by Susan Harter. (Hint: Use the author and title fields to find the article quickly.)

What four problems does the author suggest come from our sense of identity arising from social interaction? Describe how you have observed these problems in your own life. What can you do to avoid these problems?

READINGS

Cupach, William R., and Sandra Metts. *Facework.* Thousand Oaks, Calif.: Sage, 1994.

The authors summarize research on how communicators manage their own identity and maintain the face of others, especially in problematic situations.

Duck, Steve, ed. *Learning about Relationships.* Newbury Park, Calif.: Sage, 1993.

This book describes the lasting effects of early life experiences on later relationships. Most chapters describe the many ways parents influence their children's self-concept and social skills.

Gergen, Kenneth. *The Saturated Self: Dilemmas of Identity in Contemporary Life.* New York: Basic Books, 1992.

Gergen's thesis is that in today's fast-paced society, traditional notions of the self are being crowded out by a variety of alternatives. Chapter 6, "From Self to Relationship," describes how creating (and communicating) any self-image one desires is becoming increasingly possible in emerging postmodern society.

Goffman, Erving. *The Presentation of Self in Everyday Life.* New York: Doubleday Anchor, 1959; *Interaction Ritual: Essays on Face-to-Face Behavior.* New York: Doubleday Anchor, 1967.

These books provide a thorough introduction to the topic of identity management, written by the most influential theorist on the subject. Goffman introduces the notion of face and discusses how individuals communicate in a manner to create and preserve various social fronts.

FILMS

In addition to the films suggested here, go to the **Film in Communication Database** at the *Looking Out/Looking In* Web site to locate movie clips that explore issues of communication and identity.

Influences on the Self-Concept

Boyz in the Hood (1991) Rated R

How important is a parent in shaping a child's self-concept? The movie *Boyz in the Hood* offers dramatic answers to this question. Tre Styles (Cuba Gooding, Jr.) is an angry young man being raised on the mean streets of south-central Los Angeles by his father, Fury (Lawrence Fishburne). Tre becomes comes pals with his neighbors Ricky (Morris Chestnut) and Doughboy (Ice Cube), who are half-brothers. The three young men take different paths in life, due in large part to the parenting they receive.

Tre is the only one of the three with a father to guide him. Tre sometimes resents his father's discipline, but Fury explains, "I'm trying to teach you how to be responsible, unlike your little friends across the street." Fury also fills Tre's mind and heart with messages about how to be a leader and how much he is loved. Tre becomes a strong young man who is able to resist the pressures of the streets that surround him.

Ricky receives words of approval and affection from his mother, which help boost his self-esteem. He also looks to Fury and Tre for guidance and direction that he never received from his absentee father. Doughboy, on the other hand, is told by his mother from an early age that he will never amount to anything. His mother's words become self-fulfilling prophecies for each son. Ricky becomes a star football player, whereas Doughboy struggles, angry and aimlessly, through life. At the movie's conclusion, the moral to the story is clear: A parent's appraisal can make all the difference in the world.

Self-Fulfilling Prophecies

Pay It Forward (2000) Rated PG-13

Trevor (Haley Joel Osment) is a junior high schooler whose father has disappeared. His mother, Arlene (Helen Hunt), is a recovering alcoholic who makes ends meet by working as a Las Vegas cocktail waitress. On the first day of school, Trevor's new teacher, Mr. Simonet (Kevin Spacey), gives a provocative assignment: Think of an idea that could change the world. Trevor's idea is simple but profound. You have to do something that really helps people. It has to be something they can't do by themselves. The recipients of the favor "pay it forward" by doing the same thing for three other people.

Trevor's "pay it forward" acts become powerful self-fulfilling prophecies, helping to transform formerly hopeless and cynical people into powerful agents who really do help make the world a better place. One of his schemes is to get his mom and Mr. Simonet together. Simonet, whose face is covered with scars from burns, is reluctant. It's clear that the emotional scars are more painful than his physical ones, and he resists the idea that he could be loveable. Still, Trevor's persistence guides his teacher and mother into a relationship in which each of them helps boost the self-esteem of the other.

The film ends on a sad note, but its message comes through strongly: Each of us has the power to communicate in ways that shape ourselves, others, and the world. The only question is whether we will use that power consciously and whether we will use it to make life better or worse.

Stand and Deliver (1988) Rated PG-13

Jaime Escalante (Edward James Olmos) is a mild-mannered math teacher who is commissioned to the tough classrooms of Garfield High. He is soft-spoken, cerebral, and demanding—in other words, the kind of teacher who street-hardened students would normally despise and ignore. Although the students do, in fact, regard him suspiciously at first, by the story's end they adore him. Perhaps more important, they achieve top-flight scores on their advance placement calculus exam, which is their ticket to a college education.

How can we account for the students' success? The film suggests that the key is not Escalante's knowledge of math, his lecture techniques, or his classroom charisma. The key is that he believes in his students, who hadn't been believed in before. Because he believes in them, they stop thinking of themselves as losers. Escalante helps them master a subject they thought was impossible and in so doing radically changes their self-concepts. This is a powerful story that offers contemporary support for the "Pygmalion" theory of the self-fulfilling prophecy.

LOOKING OUT/LOOKING IN WEB SITE

Use your *Looking Out/Looking In* CD-ROM to access the *Looking Out/Looking In* Web site. In addition to the **Film in Communication Database,** you can access the InfoTrac College Edition Activities suggested above.

WADSWORTH
THOMSON LEARNING

Close Window

Looking Out, Looking In, Media Edition (with InfoTrac and CD-ROM)
Ronald B. Adler, et al.
10th Edition
ISBN: 0534549861

Chapter Resources ▾

2. Communication and Identity: The Self and ...

Chapter 2 ▾
- Flashcards
- Glossary
- Internet Activities
- Tutorial Quiz
- Web Links

Book Level Resources ▾
- About the Text

Companion Products
- Supplements

Discipline Level ▾
- Communication Links
- Careers
- Events

return to overview page

Research Links Chapter 2: Communication and Identity: The Self and Messages

Communication and Self
This lecture outline is written by a communication instructor and highlights principles and concepts found in Chapter 2 of Looking Out / Looking In by Adler & Towne.

Developing Self Esteem Through Interactions with Others
This page provides a list of annotated citations for academic and popular articles about the relationship between communicating with others and building self-esteem.

Identity Theory Research Links
This page provides a list of direct web links to articles about theories of identity and personality development.

Communication Builds Self Esteem
This article gives practical suggestions and tips for communicating to children in order to build self esteem.

Pygmalion Effect: The Oak Elementary School Experiment
This page describes a classic study illustrating one type of self fulfilling prophecy that can take place in the classroom.

The Penny and Nancy Story
This page features a unique story dialogue that illustrates a self-fulfilling prophecy between teacher and students in the classroom.

Self Fulfilling Prophecy
Through description and diagram, the authors of this page feature a specific example of how initial beliefs can influence behavioral outcomes.

Methods for Changing Our Thoughts, Attitudes, Self-Concept, Motivation, Values, and Expectations
As part of an excellent self-help online book, this skill-based chapter takes a comprehensive look at communication and self. Sub-topics include: changing your self-concept and building self-esteem; increasing self-awareness; challenging irrational ideas; determinism; trying a new lifestyle; paradoxical intention; increasing motivation; straight thinking, common sense and good arguments; developing attitudes that help you cope; and self-hypnosis and mental imagery.

Increasing Self-Awareness
This page provides an excellent description of several chapter concepts including: self-monitoring, perceived self, and resisting self-concept change.

Changing Our Self-Concept and Building Self-Esteem

PERCEPTION: WHAT YOU SEE IS WHAT YOU GET

M. C. Escher's "Relativity" ©2001 Cordon Art B. V. -Baarn -Holland. All rights reserved.

Study M. C. Escher's drawing *Relativity* above. It pictures a strange universe in which the inhabitants of each world exist at right angles, using the same staircase but oblivious to each other's existence. Each has his or her own conception of up and down, right and left. If these characters were introduced to the residents of other worlds, they would find them odd, defying the rule of gravity.

This surreal vision provides a useful metaphor for challenges that we encounter every day. Each of us experiences a different reality, and failing to understand other people's point of view can lead to problems on both practical and relational levels. But perceptual differences can enhance as well as interfere with relationships. By seeing the world through others' eyes you can gain insights that are different—and often more valuable—than those arising out of your own experiences.

This chapter will help you deal with the challenge of communicating in the face of perceptual differences. We will begin by looking at some of the reasons why the world appears different to each of us. In our survey we'll explore several areas: how our psychological makeup, personal needs, interests, and biases shape our perceptions; the physiological factors that influence our view of the world; the social roles that affect our image of events; and finally the role that culture plays in creating our ideas of what behavior is proper. In doing so, we'll cover many of the types of physiological and psychological noise you read about in chapter 1. After examining the perceptual factors that can drive us apart, we will look at two useful skills for bridging the perceptual gap.

THE PERCEPTION PROCESS

We need to begin our discussion of perception by examining the gap between "what is" and what we know. At one time or another you've probably seen photos of sights invisible to the unaided eye: perhaps an infrared photo of a familiar area or the vastly enlarged image of a minute object taken by an electron microscope. You've also noticed how certain animals are able to hear sounds and smell odors that are not apparent to humans. Experiences like these remind us that there is much more going on in the world than we are able to experience with our limited senses, that our idea of reality is in fact only a partial one.

Even within the realm of our senses we're aware of only a small part of what is going on around us. A simple walk in the park would probably be a different experience for companions with different interests. A botanist might notice the vegetation; a fashion designer might pay attention to the way people are dressed; and an artist might be aware of the colors and forms of the people and surroundings. On a personal level, we've all had the experience of failing to notice something unusual about a friend—perhaps a new hairstyle or a sad expression—until it's called to our attention. Sometimes our failure to recognize some events while recognizing others comes from not paying attention to important information. But in other cases it's simply impossible to be aware of everything, no matter how attentive we might be: There is just too much going on.

William James said, "to the infant the world is just a big blooming, buzzing confusion." One reason for this is the fact that infants are not yet able to sort out the myriad impressions with which we're all bombarded. As we grow, we learn to manage all this data, and as we do so, we begin to make sense out of the world.

I've always admired those reporters who can descend on an area, talk to key people, ask key questions, take samplings of opinions, and then set down an orderly report very much like a road map. I envy this technique and at the same time do not trust it as a mirror of reality. I feel that there are too many realities. What I set down here is true until someone else passes that way and rearranges the world in his own style. In literary criticism the critic has no choice but to make over the victim of his attention into something the size and shape of himself. . . .

So much there is to see, but our morning eyes describe a different world than do our afternoon eyes, and surely our wearied evening eyes can only report a weary evening world.

John Steinbeck, *Travels with Charley*

Because this ability to organize our perceptions in a useful way is such a critical factor in our ability to function, we need to begin our study of perception by taking a closer look at this process. We can do so by examining the three steps by which we attach meaning to our experiences: selection, organization, and interpretation.

Selection

Because we're exposed to more input than we can possibly manage, the first step in perception is the **selection** of which impressions we will attend to. There are several factors that cause us to notice some things and ignore others.

Stimuli that are *intense* often attract our attention. Something that is louder, larger, or brighter stands out. This explains why—other things being equal—we're more likely to remember extremely tall or short people and why someone who laughs or talks loudly at a party attracts more attention (not always favorable) than do quiet guests.

Repetitious stimuli, repetitious stimuli, repetitious stimuli, repetitious stimuli, repetitious stimuli, repetitious stimuli also attract attention.[1] Just as a quiet but steadily dripping faucet can come to dominate our awareness, people to whom we're frequently exposed become noticeable.

ATTENTION IS ALSO FREQUENTLY RELATED TO contrast OR change IN STIMULATION. Put differently, unchanging people or things become less noticeable. This principle gives an explanation (excuse?) for why we take wonderful people for granted when we interact with them frequently. It's only when they stop being so wonderful or go away that we appreciate them.

Motives also determine what information we select from our environment. If you're anxious about being late for a date, you'll notice whatever clocks may be around you; and if you're hungry, you'll become aware of any restaurants, markets, and billboards advertising food in your path. Motives also determine how we perceive people. For example, someone on the lookout for a romantic adventure will be especially aware of attractive potential partners, whereas the same person at a different time might be oblivious to anyone but police or medical personnel in an emergency.

Intensity isn't just a matter of physical properties or cues: We also pay more attention to people or behaviors after we have become attuned to them. If you are annoyed with a friend who talks too much or a boss who seems critical, you are likely to tune into behaviors that feed your aggravation. If you find redheads, tall people, Asians, or people with nice smiles attractive, you're likely to spot them more than others who don't fit these attributes.

Selection isn't just a matter of attending to some stimuli: It also involves ignoring other cues. If, for example, you decide that someone is a terrific person, you may overlook his or her flaws. If you are focused on examples of unfair male bosses, you might not recognize unfair female bosses.

We usually see only the things we are looking for—so much that we sometimes see them where they are not.

Eric Hoffer

Organization

Along with selecting information from the environment, we must arrange it in some meaningful way. You can see how the principle of **organization** works by looking at Figure 3-1. You can view the picture either as one of a vase or as one of two twins, depending on whether you focus on the light or the dark areas. In instances such as this we make sense of stimuli by noticing some data that stand out as a *figure* against a less striking *ground*. The "vase-face" drawing is interesting because it allows us to choose between two sets of figure-ground relationships.

FIGURE 3-1

This principle of figure-ground organization operates in communication, too. Recall, for instance, how certain speech can suddenly stand out from a babble of voices. Sometimes the words are noticeable because they include your name, whereas at other times they might be spoken by a familiar voice.

The vase-face drawing suggests that there are only two ways to organize impressions. In fact, there are usually many more. Consider, for example, Figure 3-2. How many ways can you view the boxes? One? Two? Three? Keep looking. If you're stumped, Figure 3-3 will help.

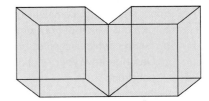

FIGURE 3-2

Just as you were inclined to view these boxes in one way, each of us can organize our impressions of other communicators using a number of schemes (called *perceptual schema* by social scientists). Sometimes we classify people according to their *appearance:* male or female, beautiful or ugly, heavy or thin, young or old, and so on. At other times we classify people according to their *social roles:* student, attorney, wife, and so on. Another way we classify people is by their *interaction style:* friendly, helpful, aloof, and sarcastic are examples. In other cases we classify people by their *psychological traits:* curious, nervous, insecure, and so on. Finally, we can use others' *membership*, classifying them according to the group to which they belong: Republican, immigrant, Christian, and so on.

The perceptual schemas we use shape the way we think about and communicate with others. If you've classified a professor, for example, as "friendly," you'll handle questions or problems one way; if you've classified a professor as "mean," your behavior will probably be quite different. Note that there's an element of selection in the constructs we use: Choosing some constructs means that you ignore others. If you classify people by their age or appearance, for example, you are likely to ignore other characteristics such as their friendliness or intelligence. What constructs do you use to classify the people you

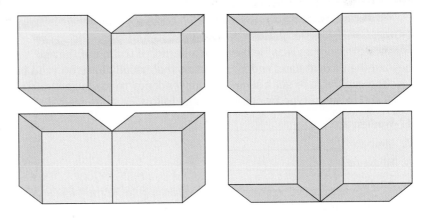

FIGURE 3-3

encounter in your life? Consider how your relationship might change if you used different schema.

INVITATION TO INSIGHT

YOUR PERCEPTUAL FILTERS

1. Identify the constructs described in the preceding section that you would use to classify people in each of the following contexts. Describe both the *general type of organizing scheme* (e.g., "physical," "membership") and the *specific category* within each type (e.g., "attractive," "roughly the same age as me").
   a. Spending time with new acquaintances at a party
   b. Socializing with fellow workers on the job
   c. Choosing teammates for an important class project
   d. Offering help to a stranded motorist

2. Consider how valid the constructs you use are in making decisions about the type of communication in which you engage.
   a. Explain which of your organizing schemes are valid.
   b. Explain which schemes are not valid, and suggest better alternatives.
   c. Describe how your relationships might change if you used different constructs.

Stereotyping   After we have chosen an organizing scheme to classify people, we use that scheme to make generalizations and predictions about members of the groups who fit the categories we use. For example, if you were especially aware of gender you might be alert to the differences between the way men and women behave or the way they are treated. If religion played an important part in your life, you might think of members of your faith differently from others. If ethnicity was an important issue for you, you would probably tune in to the differences between members of various ethnic groups. There's nothing wrong with generalizations as long as they are accurate. In fact, it would be impossible to get through life without them.

But when generalizations lose touch with reality, they lead to **stereotyping**—exaggerated generalizations associated with a categorizing system.[2] Stereotypes may be based on a kernel of truth, but they go beyond the facts at hand and make claims that usually have no valid basis.

You can begin to get a sense of your tendency to make generalizations and to stereotype by completing the following sentences:

1. Women are _____.
2. Men are _____.
3. Hispanics _____.
4. Anglos _____.
5. Blacks _____.
6. Older people _____.

It's likely that you were able to complete each sentence without much hesitation. Does this mean you were stereotyping? You can answer this question by deciding whether your generalizations fit the three characteristics of stereotypes:

- You often categorize people on the basis of this easily recognized characteristic. For example, the first thing you notice about a person is his or her skin color.
- You ascribe a set of characteristics to most or all members of a category. For example, you assume that all older people are doddering or all men are insensitive to women's concerns.
- You apply the set of characteristics to any member of the group. For example, when you meet an older person, you expect him or her to be senile.[3]

Stereotypes can plague interracial communication.[4] Surveys of college student attitudes show that many blacks characterize whites as "demanding" and "manipulative," whereas many whites characterize blacks as "loud" and "ostentatious." Many black women report having been raised with stereotypical characterizations of whites (e.g., "most whites cannot be trusted"). One black college professor reported a personal story revealing a surprising set of stereotypical assumptions from a white colleague. "As the only African American at a university-sponsored party for faculty a few years ago, I was appalled when a white professor (whom I had just met) asked me to sing a Negro spiritual."[5] Although it's possible that behavior like this can be motivated by a desire to be friendly, it is easy to see how it can be offensive.

After we hold stereotypes like these, we seek out isolated behaviors that support our inaccurate beliefs. For example, men and women in conflict often remember only behaviors of the opposite sex that fit their gender stereotypes.[6] They then point to these behaviors—which might not be representative of how the other person typically behaves—as "evidence" to suit their stereotypical and inaccurate claims: "Look! There you go criticizing me again. Typical for a woman!"

Stereotypes don't always lead to communication problems. If the person with whom you are interacting happens to fit the pattern in your mind, there may be no difficulties. But if your mental image does not happen to match the characteristics of the other person, problems can arise. A fascinating series of experiments on perceptions of prejudice and gender bias illustrates this point.[7] In one phase of the experiments, white and black students were presented with stories in which a prejudicial act might or might not have taken place. For example, a man who has been promised a hotel room over the phone is later denied the room when he shows up in person. Four race combinations were used for each story: white perpetrator/black victim, white perpetrator/white victim, black perpetrator/white victim, and black perpetrator/black victim. In almost all instances, participants were more likely to label white-on-black behavior (white perpetrator and black victim) as prejudice than any other combination. In addition, females were more likely than

Farcus by David Waisglass
Gordon Coulthart

"Kid, there are two types of people in this world . . . those who generalize, and those who don't."

Farcus® is reprinted with permission from LaughingStock Licensing Inc., Ottawa. All rights reserved.

males, and blacks were more likely than whites, to label an action as prejudiced. From these results, the researchers conclude that a proto-typic or "model" stereotype exists regarding racism (whites oppress blacks, men oppress women, and not the reverse) and that "participants who belong to traditionally oppressed groups (blacks, women) may be more sensitive to potential prejudice." In other words, we select, organize, and interpret behavior in ways that fit our existing notions about others' motives. One way to avoid the kinds of communication problems that come from excessive stereotyping is to "decategorize" others, giving yourself a chance to treat them as individuals instead of assuming that they possess the same characteristics as every other member of the group to which you assign them.

Punctuation   The process of organizing goes beyond our generalized perceptions of people. We also can organize our interactions with others in different ways, and these differing organizational schemes can have a powerful effect on our relationships with others. Communication theo-rists have used the term **punctuation** to describe the determination of causes and effects in a series of interactions.[8] You can begin to under-stand how punctuation operates by visualizing a running quarrel between a husband and wife. The husband accuses the wife of being too critical, whereas she complains that he is withdrawing from her. Notice that the order in which each partner punctuates this cycle affects how the quarrel looks. The husband begins by blaming the wife: "I withdraw because you're so critical." The wife organizes the situation differ-ently, starting with the husband: "I criticize because you withdraw." After the cycle gets rolling, it is impossible to say which accusation is accurate. The answer depends on how the sentence is punc-tuated. Figure 3-4 illustrates how this process operates.

Punctuation #1

Nagging ⟶ Withdrawing ⟶ Nagging ⟶ Withdrawing

Punctuation #2

Withdrawing ⟶ Nagging ⟶ Withdrawing ⟶ Nagging

FIGURE 3-4   **The Same Event Can Be Punctuated in More Than One Way**

Differing punctuations can lead to a variety of communication prob-lems. Notice how the following situations seem different depending on how they're punctuated:

■ "I don't like your friend because he never has anything to say."

■ "He doesn't talk to you because you act like you don't like him."

■ "I keep talking because you interrupt so much."

■ "I interrupt because you don't give me a chance to say what's on my mind."

The kind of finger pointing that goes along with arguing over which punctuation scheme is correct will probably make matters worse. It's far more productive to recognize that a dispute can look different to each party and then move on to the more important question of "What can we do to make things better?"

PUNCTUATION PRACTICE

You can appreciate how different punctuation patterns can influence attitudes and behavior by following these directions.

1. Use the format pictured in Figure 3-4 to diagram the following situations:

    a. A father and daughter are growing more and more distant. The daughter withdraws because she interprets her father's coolness as rejection. The father views his daughter's aloofness as a rebuff and withdraws further.

    b. The relationship between two friends is becoming strained. One jokes to lighten up the tension, and the other becomes more tense.

    c. A dating couple is on the verge of breaking up. One partner frequently asks the other to show more affection. The other withdraws physical contact.

2. Identify two punctuating schemes for each of the situations described in step 1. Consider how the differing schemes would affect the way the two people in each situation respond to one another.

    Now identify a difficult communication issue in your own life. Punctuate it in two ways: how you would punctuate it and how the other person might punctuate it. Discuss how seeing the issue from the other person's point of view might change the way you communicate as you discuss the issue.

Interpretation

After we have selected and organized our perceptions, we interpret them in a way that makes some sort of sense. **Interpretation** plays a role in virtually every interpersonal act. Is the person who smiles at you across a crowded room interested in romance or simply being polite? Is a friend's kidding a sign of affection or irritation? Should you take an invitation to "drop by any time" literally or not?

Several factors cause us to interpret an event in one way or another:

Degree of involvement with the other person We sometimes view people with whom we have or seek a relationship more favorably than those whom we observe from a detached perspective.[9] One recent study revealed how this principle operates in everyday life. A group of male subjects was asked to critique presentations by women who allegedly owned restaurants. Half of these presentations were designed to be competent and half to be incompetent. The men who were told they would be having a casual date with the female speakers judged their presentations—whether competent or not—more highly than those who didn't expect any involvement with the speakers.[10]

Past experience What meaning have similar events held? If, for example, you've been gouged by landlords in the past, you might be skeptical about an apartment manager's assurances that careful house-keeping will assure you the refund of your cleaning deposit.

Assumptions about human behavior "People generally do as little work as possible to get by." "In spite of their mistakes, people are doing the best they can." Beliefs like these will shape the way we interpret another's actions.

Expectations Anticipation shapes interpretations. If you imagine that your boss is unhappy with your work, you'll probably feel threatened by a request to "see me in my office first thing Monday morning." On the other hand, if you imagine that your work will be rewarded, your weekend will probably be pleasant.

Knowledge If you know that a friend has just been jilted by a lover or been fired from a job, you'll interpret his aloof behavior differently than you would if you were unaware of what had happened. If you know that an instructor speaks sarcastically to all students, you won't be as likely to take her remarks personally.

Self-concept When you're feeling insecure, the world is a very different place from the world you experience when you're feeling secure. For example, the recipient's self-concept has proved to be the single greatest factor in determining whether people who are on the receiving end of being teased interpret the teaser's motives as being friendly or hostile and whether they respond with comfort or defensiveness.[11] The same goes for happiness and sadness or any other opposing emotions. The way we feel about ourselves strongly influences how we interpret others' behavior.

Relational satisfaction The behavior that seems positive when you are happy with a partner might seem completely different when you are unhappy with a partner. For example, unsatisfied partners in a couple are more likely than satisfied partners to blame one another when things go wrong.[12] They are also more likely to believe that their partners are self-ish and have negative intentions. Unhappy spouses are more likely than happy ones to make negative interpretations of their mate's behavior. To see how this principle operates, recall the husband-wife quarrel we dis-

SALLY FORTH   by Greg Howard

Reprinted with special permission of King Features Syndicate.

cussed earlier. Suppose the wife suggests that they get away for a week-end vacation. If the marriage has been troubled, the husband might interpret his wife's suggestion as more criticism ("You never pay attention to me"), and the fight will continue. If the marriage is solid, he is more likely to view the suggestion as a bid for a romantic getaway. It wasn't the event that shaped the reaction, but rather the way the husband interpreted the event.

Although we have talked about selection, organization, and interpretation separately, the three phases of perception can occur in differing sequences. For example, a parent or baby-sitter's past interpretations (such as "Jason is a troublemaker") can influence future selections (his behavior becomes especially noticeable) and the organization of events (when there's a fight, the assumption is that Jason started it). As with all communication, perception is an ongoing process in which it is hard to pin down beginnings and endings.

INFLUENCES ON PERCEPTION

Now that we've explored the psychological processes by which we perceive, it's time to look at some of the influences that cause us to select, organize, and interpret information.

Physiological Influences

The first set of influences we need to examine involves our physical makeup. Within the wide range of human similarities, each of us perceives the world in a unique way because of physiological factors. In other words, although the same events exist "out there," each of us receives a different image because of our perceptual hardware. Consider the long list of factors that shapes our views of the world:

The Senses The differences in how each of us sees, hears, tastes, touches, and smells stimuli can affect interpersonal relationships. Consider the following everyday situations:

"Turn down that radio! It's going to make me go deaf."

"It's not too loud. If I turn it down, it will be impossible to hear it."

"It's freezing in here."

"Are you kidding? We'll suffocate if you turn up the heat!"

"Why don't you pass that truck? The highway is clear for a mile."

"I can't see that far, and I'm not going to get us killed."

These disputes aren't just over matters of opinion. The sensory data we receive are different. Differences in vision and hearing are the easiest to recognize, but other differences exist as well. There is evidence that identical foods taste differently to different individuals.[13] Odors that please some people repel others. Likewise, temperature variations that

To a Laplander, a temperature of fifty-eight degrees may be "hot," to a South African it may be "cold." The statement "It is hot (or cold)" is a statement about what is going on inside one's body. The statement "The temperature is now ninety degrees (or fifty-eight degrees)" is a statement about what is going on outside one's body. . . .

This distinction is by no means trivial. . . . I can never prove to a Laplander that fifty-eight degrees is "cool," but I can prove to him that it is fifty-eight degrees. In other words, there is no paradox in two different people's concluding that the weather is both "hot" and "cold" at the same time. As long as they both know that each of them is talking about a different reality, their conversation can proceed in a fairly orderly way.

Neil Postman, *Crazy Talk, Stupid Talk*

leave some of us uncomfortable are inconsequential to others. Remembering these differences won't eliminate them, but it will make it easier to remember that the other person's preferences aren't crazy, just different.

Age   Older people often view the world differently from younger ones because they have a greater scope and number of experiences. There are also developmental differences that shape perceptions. Swiss psychologist Jean Piaget described a series of stages that children pass through on their way to adulthood.[14] According to Piaget, younger children are incapable of performing mental feats that are natural to the rest of us. Until they approach the age of seven, for example, they aren't able to take another person's point of view. This fact helps explain why children often seem egocentric, selfish, and uncooperative. A parent's exasperated plea, "Can't you see I'm too tired to play?" just won't make sense to a four-year-old full of energy who imagines that everyone else must feel the same.

Health   Recall the last time you came down with a cold, flu, or some other ailment. Do you remember how different you felt? You probably had much less energy. It's likely that you felt less sociable and that your thinking was slower than usual. These kinds of changes have a strong impact on how you relate to others. It's good to realize that someone else may be behaving differently because of illness. In the same way, it's important to let others know when you feel ill so that they can give you the understanding you need.

Fatigue   Just as being ill can affect your relationships, so can being overly tired. Again it's important to recognize the fact that you or someone else may behave differently when fatigued. Trying to deal with important issues at such a time can get you into trouble.

Hunger   People often get grumpy when they haven't eaten and get sleepy after stuffing themselves. A number of physiological changes occur as we eat and become hungry again. Trying to conduct important business at the wrong time in this cycle can lead to problems.

Biological Cycles   Are you a "morning person" or a "night person"? Most of us can answer this question pretty easily, and there's a good physiological reason behind our answer. Each of us is in a daily cycle in which all sorts of changes constantly occur, including body temperature, sexual drive, alertness, tolerance to stress, and mood.[15] Most of these changes are due to hormonal cycles. For instance, adrenal hormones, which affect feelings of stress, are secreted at higher rates during some hours. In the same manner, the male and female sex hormones enter our systems at variable rates. We often aren't conscious of these changes, but they surely influence the way we relate to each other. After we're aware that our own daily cycles and those of others govern our feelings and behavior, it becomes possible to manage our lives so that we deal with important issues at the most effective times.

For some women, the menstrual cycle plays an important role in shaping feelings and thus affects communication. Women aren't the only ones whose communication is affected by periodic changes in mood. Men, too, go through recognizable mood cycles, even though they aren't marked by obvious physical changes. Although they may not be aware of it, many men seem to go through biologically regulated periods of good spirits followed by equally predictable times of depression.[16] The average length of this cycle is about five weeks, although in some cases it's as short as sixteen days or as long as two months. However long it may be, this cycle of ups and downs is quite regular.

Although neither men nor women can change these emotional cycles, simply learning to expect them can be a big help in improving communication. When you understand that a bad mood is predictable from physiological causes, you can plan for it. You'll know that every few weeks your patience will be shorter, and you'll be less likely to blame your bad moods on innocent bystanders. The people around you can also learn to expect your periodic lows. If they can attribute them to biology, maybe they will show you some understanding.

INVITATION TO INSIGHT

NEW BODY, NEW PERSPECTIVE

You can get a clearer idea of how physiology influences perception by trying the following exercise.

1. Choose one of the following situations:
   An evening in a singles' bar
   A volleyball game
   A doctor's physical examination

2. How would the event you chose seem different if
   Your eyesight were much worse (or better).
   You had a hearing loss.
   You were eight inches taller (or shorter).
   You were coming down with a serious cold.
   You were a member of the opposite sex.
   You were ten years older (or younger).

Cultural Differences

So far you have seen how physical factors can make the world a different place for each of us. But there's another kind of perceptual gap that often blocks communication—the gap between people from different backgrounds. Every culture has its own worldview, its own way of looking at the world. Keeping in mind these differing cultural perspectives can be a good way of learning more about both ourselves and others. But at times it's easy to forget that people everywhere don't see things the way we do.

The power of culture to shape perceptions was demonstrated in studies over thirty years ago exploring the domination of vision in one eye

Jason Rothman: Attention Deficit Disorder and Communication

I've had attention deficit disorder (ADD) my whole life. One Web site describes ADD's symptoms as "inattention, distractibility, impulsivity, and in some cases, hyperactivity." This is the way I behaved, especially before my ADD was diagnosed and treated.

When I was a young child, my parents quickly realized that I was having a hard time sitting still. They also realized that I was easily distracted, hyperactive, and impulsive to the point where I said and did anything that came into my mind. At first they didn't know what to do. Eventually we found a therapist who diagnosed my condition and helped me find medication that worked.

Beginning in my earliest years of school, my teachers would single me out for not paying attention. They thought I was misbehaving, but actually I was so overstimulated by what was going on around me

that I couldn't sort out school tasks from everything else. Almost anything would capture my attention— a noise outside the room, music, other kids' movements, or even when somebody dropped a pencil on the ground by mistake. And because ADD limits impulse control, sometimes I would speak out during class at the wrong times. The problem continued into high school. I acquired the reputation as a discipline problem because I couldn't keep focused on school business. It's not that I was deliberately causing trouble: It's just that I was so stimulated and distracted that sitting still and focusing on classwork was almost impossible.

ADD complicated my social life, too. In conversations with friends, my mind would wander, and I would tune out. At other times, I would interrupt. This made people think that I was rude or that I didn't care about what they were saying. Just like in school, it wasn't that I didn't care about other people, but

that I didn't have the control that other people take for granted.

Getting my ADD diagnosed was the beginning of gaining more control over my communication. Medication was a real help, although I've found ways to cope without needing it so much. I've found ways of focusing my attention and tuning out background distractions. I'm doing much better in school, and my social life is running much more smoothly.

If you ever know someone who seems inattentive and impulsive, you might ask whether they have ADD or some other neurological processing problem. If so, you can help a lot by asking them to explain their situation to you and trying to find ways of communicating that work for you and them. Talking one-to-one in a place without distractions can be a big help. Above all, don't take their behavior personally and don't embarrass them about something they can't control.

over the other.[17] Researchers used a binoculars-like device that projects different images to each eye. The subjects were twelve natives of the United States and twelve Mexicans. Each was presented with ten pairs of photographs, each pair containing one picture from U.S. culture (e.g., a baseball game) and one from Mexican culture (e.g., a bullfight). After viewing each pair of images, the subjects reported what they saw. The results clearly indicated the power of culture to influence perceptions: Subjects had a strong tendency to see the image from their own background.

Not all perceptual differences are so subtle. The most obvious cross-cultural problems arise out of poor translation from one language to another:

- General Motors was baffled when its Chevrolet Nova model did not sell well in Latin American countries. Officials from General Motors finally realized the problem: In Spanish, *no va* means "does not go."

- One airline lost customers when it promoted the "rendezvous lounges" on its planes flying Brazilian routes. In Portuguese, *rendezvous* is a place to have sex.

- McDonald's Corporation was chagrined to learn that in French-Canadian slang "big macs" are large breasts.[18]

Nonverbal behaviors, too, differ from one part of the world to another. In many cultures, the American "OK" sign, made by touching the tips of thumb and forefinger, is an obscene gesture representing the female genitalia. To a woman, it is a proposition for sex, and to a man it is an accusation of homosexuality.[19] It's easy to imagine the problems that could result in an unsuspecting American's innocent gesture.

The range of cultural differences is wide. In Middle Eastern countries, personal odors play an important role in interpersonal relationships. Arabs consistently breathe on people when they talk. As anthropologist Edward Hall explains:

> To smell one's friend is not only nice, but desirable, for to deny him your breath is to act ashamed. Americans, on the other hand, trained as they are not to breathe in people's faces, automatically communicate shame in trying to be polite. Who would expect that when our highest diplomats are putting on their best manners they are also communicating shame? Yet this is what occurs constantly, because diplomacy is not only "eyeball to eyeball" but breath to breath.[20]

Even beliefs about the very value of talk differ from one culture to another.[21] Western cultures view talk as desirable and use it for social purposes as well as for task performance. Silence has a negative value in these cultures. It is likely to be interpreted as lack of interest, unwillingness to communicate, hostility, anxiety, shyness, or a sign of interpersonal incompatibility. Westerners are uncomfortable with silence, which they find embarrassing and awkward.

On the other hand, Asian cultures perceive talk quite differently. For thousands of years, Asian cultures have discouraged the expression of thoughts and feelings. Silence is valued, as Taoist sayings indicate: "In much talk there is great weariness," or "One who speaks does not know; one who knows does not speak." Unlike westerners who are uncomfortable with silence, Japanese and Chinese believe that remaining quiet is the proper state when there is nothing to be said. To easterners a talkative person is often considered a show-off or insincere.

It's easy to see how these different views of speech and silence can lead to communication problems when people from different cultures meet. Both the talkative westerner and the silent Asian are behaving in ways they believe are proper; yet each views the other with disapproval and mistrust. Only when they recognize the different standards of behavior can they adapt to one another, or at least understand and respect their differences.

A woman from Texas went to Washington, D.C., for a job in dormitory administration. When the dorm staff got together for meetings, she kept searching for the right time to break in—and never found it. Although back home she was considered outgoing and confident, in Washington she was perceived as shy and retiring. When she was evaluated at the end of a year, she was told to take an assertiveness-training course because of her inability to speak up.

That's why slight differences in conversational style—tiny little things like microseconds of a pause—can have enormous impact on your life. These little signals make up the mechanics of conversation, and when they're even slightly off, conversation is thrown off—or even cut off. The result in this case was a judgment of psychological problems—even in the mind of the woman herself, who really wondered what was wrong with her and signed up for assertiveness training.

Author Anne Fadiman explains why Hmong immigrants from the mountains of Laos preferred their traditional shamanistic healers, called *txiv neeb,* to American doctors.

> A *txiv neeb* might spend as much as eight hours in a sick person's home; doctors forced their patients, no matter how weak they were, to come to the hospital, and then might spend only twenty minutes at their bedsides. *Txiv neebs* were polite and never needed to ask questions; doctors asked about their sexual and excretory habits. *Txiv neebs* could render an immediate diagnosis; doctors often demanded samples of blood (or even urine or feces, which they liked to keep in little bottles), took X rays, and waited for days for the results to come back from the laboratory—and then, after all that, sometimes they were unable to identify the cause of the problem. *Txiv neebs* never undressed their patients; doctors asked patients to take off all their clothes, and sometimes dared to put their fingers inside women's vaginas. *Txiv neebs* knew that to treat the body without treating the soul was an act of patent folly; doctors never even mentioned the soul.[22]

It isn't necessary to travel overseas to encounter differing cultural perspectives. Within this country there are many subcultures, and the members of each one have backgrounds that cause them to see things in different ways. Failure to recognize these differences can lead to unfortunate and unnecessary misunderstandings. For example, an uninformed Anglo teacher or police officer might interpret the downcast expression of a Latino female as a sign of avoidance, or even dishonesty, when in fact this is the proper behavior in her culture for a female being addressed by an older man. To make direct eye contact in such a case would be considered undue brashness or even a sexual come-on.

Eye contact also differs in traditional black and white cultures. Whereas whites tend to look away from a conversational partner while speaking and at the other person when listening, blacks do just the opposite, looking at their conversational partner more when talking and less when listening.[23] This difference can cause communication problems without either person's realizing the cause. For instance, whites are likely to use eye contact as a measure of how closely the other person is listening: The more others look, the more they seem to be paying attention. A white speaker, therefore, might interpret a black partner's lack of eye contact as a sign of inattention or rudeness when quite the opposite could be true. Because this sort of interpretation is usually unconscious, the speaker wouldn't even consider the possibility of testing her assumptions with the kind of perception check you will learn later in this chapter.

Along with ethnicity, geography also can influence perception. A fascinating series of studies revealed that climate and geographic latitude were remarkably accurate predictors of communication predispositions.[24] People living in southern latitudes of the United States are more socially isolated, less tolerant of ambiguity, higher in self-esteem, more likely to touch others, and more likely to verbalize their thoughts and feelings. This sort of finding helps explain why communicators who travel from one part of a country to another find that their old patterns of communicating don't work as well in their new location. A southerner whose

Father, Mother, and Me,
      Sister and Auntie say
All the people like us are We,
      And everyone else is They.
And They live over the sea
      While we live over the way,
But—would you believe it?—
      They look upon We
      As only a sort of They!
We eat pork and beef
      With cow-horn-handled knives.
They who gobble Their rice off a leaf
      Are horrified out of Their lives;
While They who live up a tree,
      Feast on grubs and clay,
(Isn't it scandalous?) look upon We
      As a simply disgusting They!

We eat kitcheny food.
      We have doors that latch.
They drink milk and blood
      Under an open thatch.
We have doctors to fee.
      They have wizards to pay.
And (impudent heathen!) They
      look upon We
      As a quite impossible They!
All good people agree,
      And all good people say,
All nice people, like us, are We
      And everyone else is They:
But if you cross over the sea,
      Instead of over the way,
You may end by (think of it!)
      looking on We
      As only a sort of They!

Rudyard Kipling, *"We and They"*

relatively talkative, high-touch style seemed completely normal at home might be viewed as pushy and aggressive in a new northern home.

Social Roles

So far you have seen how cultural and physiological differences can block communication. Along with these differences, another set of perceptual factors can lead to communication breakdowns. From almost the time we're born, each of us is indirectly taught a whole set of roles that we'll be expected to play. In one sense this set of prescribed parts is necessary because it enables a society to function smoothly and provides the security that comes from knowing what's expected of you. But in another sense, having roles defined in advance can lead to wide gaps in understanding. When roles become unquestioned and rigid, people tend to see the world from their own viewpoint, having no experiences that show them how other people see it. Naturally, in such a situation communication suffers.

Gender Roles   Although people use the terms *sex* and *gender* as if they were identical, there is an important difference. *Sex* refers to biological characteristics of a man or woman, whereas *gender* refers to the social and psychological dimensions of male and female behavior.

In every society gender is one of the most important factors in determining how people perceive one another. Children learn the importance of sex-typed behavior by watching other people and by being exposed to media as well as by receiving reinforcement.[25] After members of a society learn customary gender roles, they tend to regard violations of those roles as unusual—or even undesirable.

Some theorists have suggested that stereotypical masculine and feminine behaviors are not opposite poles of a single continuum, but rather two separate sets of behavior.[26] With this view, an individual can act in a masculine manner or a feminine manner or exhibit both types of characteristics. The male-female dichotomy, then, is replaced with four psychological sex types: masculine, feminine, **androgynous** (combining masculine and feminine traits), and undifferentiated (neither masculine nor feminine). Combining the four psychological sex types with the traditional physiological sex types produces the eight categories listed in Table 3-1.

Each of these eight psychological sex types perceives interpersonal relationships differently. For example, masculine males may be likely to see their interpersonal relationships as opportunities for competitive interaction, as opportunities to win something. Feminine females probably see their interpersonal relationships as opportunities to be nurturing,

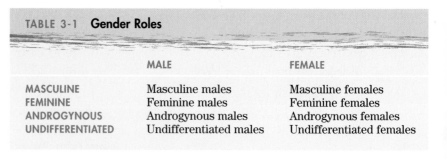

TABLE 3-1 **Gender Roles**		
	MALE	FEMALE
MASCULINE	Masculine males	Masculine females
FEMININE	Feminine males	Feminine females
ANDROGYNOUS	Androgynous males	Androgynous females
UNDIFFERENTIATED	Undifferentiated males	Undifferentiated females

to express their feelings and emotions. Androgynous males and females, on the other hand, probably differ little in their perceptions of their interpersonal relationships.

Androgynous individuals probably see their relationships as opportunities to behave in a variety of ways, depending on the nature of the relationships themselves, the context in which a particular relationship takes place, and the myriad other variables affecting what might constitute appropriate behavior. These variables are usually ignored by the sex-typed masculine males and feminine females, who have a smaller repertoire of behavior.

Occupational Roles The kind of work we do often influences our view of the world. Imagine five people taking a walk through the park. One, a botanist, is fascinated by the variety of trees and other plants. Another, a zoologist, is looking for interesting animals. The third, a meteorologist, keeps an eye on the sky, noticing changes in the weather. The fourth companion, a psychologist, is totally unaware of nature, instead concentrating on the interaction among the people in the park. The fifth person, being a pickpocket, quickly takes advantage of the others' absorption to make some money. There are two lessons in this little scenario. The first, of course, is to watch your wallet carefully. The second is that our occupational roles shape our perceptions.

Even within the same occupational setting, the different roles that participants have can affect their perceptions. Consider a typical college classroom, for example: The experiences of the instructor and students often are quite dissimilar. Having dedicated a large part of their lives to their work, most instructors see their subject matter—whether French literature, physics, or speech communication—as vitally important. Students who are taking the course to satisfy a general education requirement may view the subject quite differently: maybe as one of many obstacles that stand between them and a degree, maybe as a chance to meet new people. Another difference centers on the amount of knowledge possessed by the parties. To an instructor who has taught the course many times, the material probably seems extremely simple; but to students encountering it for the first time, it may seem strange and confusing. Toward the end of a semester or quarter the instructor might be pressing onward hurriedly to cover all the material in the course, whereas the students are fatigued from their studies and ready to move more slowly. We don't need to spell out the interpersonal strains and stresses that come from such differing perceptions.

Perhaps the most dramatic illustration of how occupational roles shape perception occurred in 1971.[27] Stanford psychologist Philip Zimbardo recruited a group of middle-class, well-educated young men. He randomly chose eleven to serve as "guards" in a mock prison set up in the basement of Stanford's psychology building. He issued the guards uniforms, handcuffs, whistles, and billy clubs. The remaining ten subjects became "prisoners" and were placed in rooms with metal bars, bucket toilets, and cots.

"The Accuracy and Power of Sex, Social Class and Ethnic Stereotypes: A Naturalistic Study in Person Perception"

http://psych-server.iastate. edu/faculty/madon/resubshl. fin.htm

This research article examines the accuracy and power of sex, social class, and ethnic stereotypes in person perception. A comprehensive and useful list of related references follows the article.

OPERATION EMPATHY: PREPARATION FOR THE CHANGING POLICE ROLE

We are all aware that it is extremely difficult to immerse the average police officer into situations that will reveal the feelings of the down-and-outer, the social outcast, the have-nots, and show us their perspective of normal law-enforcement procedures. Obviously the officer, in his or her police role, would not fit into a ghetto of any kind. But suppose he or she was a person with a great deal of courage, willing for the sake of experimentation to become a bum, a skid row habitant.

Our Covina officers who were willing to become skid row habitants were carefully selected and conditioned for the role they were about to play. Each was given three dollars with which to purchase a complete outfit of pawn shop clothing. Among other props were such items as a shopping bag filled with collected junk, and a wine bottle camouflaged with a brown paper sack.

Conditioned and ready, our officers, assigned in pairs, moved into the Los Angeles skid row district. They soon discovered that when they tried to leave the area, walking a few blocks into the legitimate retail sections, they were told, "Go back where you belong!" Our officers knew in reality they were not "bums," but they found that other citizens quickly categorized them and treated them accordingly.

During the skid row experiment, our officers ate in the rescue missions and sat through the prayer services with other outcasts and derelicts. They roamed the streets and the alleys and discovered many leveling experiences. Some were anticipated, others were not. Perhaps the most meaningful experience of the skid row exercise occurred to Tom Courtney, a young juvenile officer with five years' police service.

It was dusk, and Tom and his partner were sauntering back to a prearranged gathering place. Feeling a little sporty, the pair decided to "polish off" the bottle of wine. They paused in a convenient parking lot, and Tom tipped the bottle up. As if from nowhere, two uniformed policemen materialized before the surprised pair. Tom and his partner were spread-eagled against a building and searched. Forgetting the admonishment not to reveal identities and purpose unless absolutely necessary, Tom panicked and identified himself.

Later, Tom found it difficult to explain why he was so quick in his revelation. "You wouldn't understand," he told me; then blurted he "thought he might get shot."

I found it difficult to receive this as a rational explanation, especially since Tom stated that the officers, while firm, were courteous at all times. With some additional prodding, Tom admitted that as he was being searched, he suddenly thought of every negative thing he had ever heard about a policeman. He even perceived a mental flash of a newspaper headline: "Police Officer Erroneously Shot While on Field Experiment."

"I know better now," Tom continued, "but when you feel that way about yourself, you believe—you believe."

I attempted to rationalize with Tom his reason for fear. I asked if he was certain that the officers were courteous. He replied in the affirmative, but added, "They didn't smile, or tell me what they were going to do next." Tom had discovered a new emotional reaction within his own personal makeup, and it left a telling impression.

Today, Tom Courtney is still telling our department personnel, "For God's sake, smile when you can. And above all, tell the man you're shaking down what you are going to do. Take the personal threat out of the encounter, if you can."

Equally important as Tom's experience, I believe, is the lesson we learned about personal judgments. Our men in the "Operation Empathy" experiment found they were adjudged by the so-called normal population as "being like" all the other inmates of skid row, simply because their appearance was representative.

Perhaps we would all do well to heed the lesson, for now, more than at any other time in our history, police officers must guard against the natural tendency to lump people into categories simply because they look alike.

Fred Ferguson

Zimbardo let the guards establish their own rules for the experiment. The rules were tough: No talking during meals, rest periods, and after lights-out. Head counts at 2:30 A.M. Troublemakers received short rations.

Faced with these conditions, the prisoners began to resist. Some barricaded their doors with beds. Others went on hunger strikes. Several ripped off their identifying number tags. The guards reacted to the rebellion by clamping down hard on protesters. Some turned sadistic, physically and verbally abusing the prisoners. They threw prisoners into solitary confinement. Others forced prisoners to call each other names and clean out toilets with their bare hands.

Within a short time the experiment had become reality for both prisoners and guards. Several inmates had stomach cramps and lapsed into uncontrollable weeping. Others suffered from headaches, and one broke out in a head-to-toe rash after his request for early "parole" was denied by the guards.

The experiment was scheduled to go on for two weeks, but after six days Zimbardo realized that what had started as a simulation had become too intense. "I knew by then that they were thinking like prisoners and not like people," he said. "If we were able to demonstrate that pathological behavior could be produced in so short a time, think of what damage is being done in 'real' prisons. . . ."

This dramatic exercise in which twenty-one well-educated, middle-class citizens turned almost overnight into sadistic bullies and demoralized victims tells us that *how* we think is a function of our roles in society. It seems that *what* we are is determined largely by society's designation of *who* we are. Fortunately, many officials in the field of law enforcement are aware of the perceptual blindness that can come with one's job. These professionals have developed programs that help to overcome the problem, as the following reading illustrates.

ROLE REVERSAL

Walk a mile in another person's shoes. Find a group that is foreign to you, and try to become a member of it for a while.

If you're down on the police, see if your local department has a ride-along program where you can spend several hours on patrol with one or two officers.

If you think the present state of education is a mess, become a teacher yourself. Maybe an instructor will give you the chance to plan one or more classes.

If you're adventuresome, follow the example of the police officers in the article on pages 112–113 and become a homeless person for a day. See how you're treated.

If you're a political conservative, try getting involved in a radical organization; if you're a radical, check out the conservatives.

Whatever group you join, try to become part of it as best you can. Don't just observe. Get into the philosophy of your new role and see how it feels. You may find that all those weird people aren't so weird after all.

THE INVESTIGATION

John Jonik

Self-Concept

Another factor that influences how we think of ourselves and interact with others is the self-concept. Extensive research shows that a person with high self-esteem is more likely to have a high opinion of others, whereas a person with low self-esteem is likely to have a low opinion of others.[28] Your own experience may bear this out: Persons with low self-esteem are often cynical and quick to ascribe the worst possible motives to others, whereas persons with high self-esteem often think favorably about others. As one writer put it, "What we find 'out there' is what we put there with our unconscious projections. When we think we are looking out a window, it may be, more often than we realize, that we are really gazing into a looking glass."[29]

Besides distorting the facts about others, our self-concepts lead us to have distorted views of ourselves. We already hinted at this fact when we explained in chapter 2 that the self-concept is not objective. "It wasn't my fault," you might be tempted to say, knowing deep inside that you were responsible. "I look horrible," you might think as you look into the mirror, despite the fact that everyone around you sincerely insists that you look terrific.

Shared Narratives

Our interaction with other individuals and groups creates a shared perception of the world. Communication scholars have come to call this kind of shared perception a **narrative**.[30] This term reflects the notion that humans make sense of the world by spinning a kind of story to explain events and behavior. Shared narratives help groups of communicators make sense of themselves and others.[31]

Narratives evolve without any conscious strategy by the participants. One study of sense-making on the job illustrates how the process operates.[32] Researchers located employees who had participated in office discussions about "differential treatment"—cases where a fellow worker had received "differential treatment" from management about matters such as time off, pay, or work assignments. The researchers then analyzed the conversations that employees had about the differential treatment. The analysis revealed that these conversations were where employees created and reinforced the meaning of the employee's behavior and management's response. For example, consider the way employees made sense of Jane Doe's habit of taking late lunches. As Jane's coworkers discuss her behaviors, they might decide that her late lunches aren't fair—or they might agree that late lunches aren't a big deal. Either way, discussion of office events *defines* those events. After they are defined, coworkers tend to seek reinforcement for their perceptions by keeping a mental scorecard rating their fellow employees and management ("Did you notice that Bob came in late again today?" "Did you notice that the boss chose Jane to go on that trip to New York?"). Although most of us like to think we make judgments about others on our own, this research suggests that sense-making is an *interactive* process. In other words, reality in the workplace and elsewhere isn't "out there:" We create it with others through communication.

Research on long-term happy marriages summarized by Judy Pearson demonstrates that shared narratives don't have to be accurate to be powerful.[33] Couples who report being happily married after fifty or more years seem to collude in a relational narrative that doesn't jibe with the facts. They agree that they rarely have conflict, although objective analysis reveals that they have had their share of conflict. Without overtly agreeing to do so, they choose to blame outside forces or unusual circumstances for problems instead of blaming one another. They offer the most charitable interpretations of one another's behavior, believing that their spouse acts with good intentions when things don't go well. They seem willing to forgive, or even forget, transgressions. Pearson concludes

> Should we conclude that happy couples have a poor grip on reality? Perhaps they do, but is the reality of one's marriage better known by outside onlookers than by the players themselves? The conclusion is evident. One key to a long happy marriage is to tell yourself and others that you have one and then to behave as though you do![34]

THE ACCURACY—AND INACCURACY— OF PERCEPTION

By now it's obvious that many factors distort the way we interpret the world. Social scientists use the term **attribution** to describe the process of attaching meaning to behavior. We attribute meaning both to our own actions and to the actions of others, but we often use different yardsticks. Research has uncovered several perceptual errors that lead to inaccurate attributions.[35]

We Often Judge Ourselves More Charitably Than Others

In an attempt to convince ourselves and others that the positive face we show to the world is true, we tend to judge ourselves in the most generous terms possible. Social scientists have labeled this tendency the **self-**

serving bias.[36] On one hand, when others suffer, we often blame the problem on their personal qualities. On the other hand, when we suffer, we blame the problem on forces outside ourselves. Consider a few examples:

> When *they* botch a job, we might think they weren't listening well or trying hard enough; when *we* botch a job, the problem was unclear directions or not enough time.
>
> When *he* lashes out angrily, we say he's being moody or too sensitive; when *we* lash out angrily, it's because of the pressure we've been under.
>
> When *she* gets caught speeding, we say she should have been more careful; when *we* get caught speeding, we deny that we were driving too fast or we say, "Everybody does it."

The egocentric tendency to rate ourselves more favorably than others rate us has been demonstrated experimentally.[37] In one study, members of a random sample of men were asked to rank themselves on their ability to get along with others.[38] Defying mathematical laws, all subjects—every last one—put themselves in the top half of the population. Sixty percent rated themselves in the top 10 percent of the population, and an amazing 25 percent rated themselves in the top 1 percent. In the same study, 70 percent of the men ranked their leadership in the top quarter of the population, whereas only 2 percent ranked their leadership as below average. Sixty percent said they were in the top quarter in athletic abilities, whereas only 6 percent said they were below average.

Distortions like these usually revolve around the desire to maintain a presenting self-concept that has been threatened. The desire to maintain face is often strong. If you want to present yourself as a good student or musician, for example, an instructor who gives you a poor grade or a critic who doesn't appreciate your music *must* be wrong, and you'll find evidence to show it. If you want to think of yourself as a good worker or parent, you'll find explanations for the problems in your job or family that shift the responsibility away from you. Of course, the same principle works for people with excessively negative self-images: They'll go out of the way to explain any information that's favorable to them in terms that show they really are incompetent or undesirable. The list of defense mechanisms in chapter 9 shows how inventive people can be when a presenting self-concept is threatened.

We Tend to Favor Negative Impressions of Others over Positive Ones

What do you think of Harvey? He's handsome, hardworking, intelligent, and honest. He's also very conceited.

Did the last characteristic listed make a difference in your judgment? If it did, you're not alone. Research shows that when people are aware of

"The truth is, Cauldwell, we never see ourselves as others see us."

I have heard students say things like, "It was John's fault, his speech was so confusing nobody could have understood it." Then, two minutes later, the same student remarked, "It wasn't my fault, what I said could not have been clearer. John must be stupid." Poor John! He was blamed when he was the sender and when he was the receiver. John's problem was that he was the other person, and that's who is always at fault.

Stephen W. King

both positive and negative personal characteristics, they tend to be more influenced by the less desirable characteristics. For example, one study revealed that job interviewers were likely to reject a candidate who revealed negative information, even when the rest of the information about the candidate was positive.

We Are Often Influenced by What is Most Obvious

The error of being influenced by what is most obvious is understandable. As you read at the beginning of this chapter, we select stimuli from our environment that are noticeable: intense, repetitious, unusual, or otherwise attention-grabbing. The problem is that the most obvious factor is not necessarily the only one—or the most significant one for an event. For example,

- When two children (or adults, for that matter) fight, it may be a mistake to blame the one who lashes out first. Perhaps the other one was at least equally responsible, teasing or refusing to cooperate.

- You might complain about an acquaintance whose malicious gossiping or arguing has become a bother, forgetting that by putting up with such behavior in the past you have been at least partially responsible.

- You might blame an unhappy working situation on the boss, overlooking other factors beyond her control such as a change in the economy, the policy of higher management, or demands of customers or other workers.

We Cling to First Impressions

Labeling people according to our first impressions is an inevitable part of the perception process. These labels are a way of making interpretations. "She seems cheerful." "He seems sincere." "They sound awfully conceited."

If such first impressions are accurate, they can be useful ways of deciding how to respond best to people in the future. Problems arise, however, when the labels we attach are inaccurate; after we form an opinion of someone, we tend to hang on to it and make any conflicting information fit our opinion.

Suppose, for instance, that you mention the name of your new neighbor to a friend. "Oh, I know him," your friend replies. "He seems nice at first, but it's all an act." Perhaps this appraisal is off-base. The neighbor may have changed since your friend knew him, or perhaps your friend's judgment is simply unfair. Whether the judgment is accurate or not, after you accept your friend's evaluation, it will probably influence the way you respond to the neighbor. You'll look for examples of the insincerity you've heard about—and you'll probably find them. Even if the neighbor were a saint, you would be likely to interpret his behavior in ways that fit your expectations. "Sure he *seems* nice," you might think, "but it's probably just a front." Of course, this sort of suspicion can create a self-fulfilling prophecy, transforming a genuinely nice person into someone who truly becomes an undesirable neighbor.

Given the almost unavoidable tendency to form first impressions, the best advice we can give is to keep an open mind and to be willing to change your opinion as events prove it mistaken.

We Tend to Assume That Others Are Similar to Us

In chapter 2 you read one example of this principle: that people with low self-esteem imagine that others view them unfavorably, whereas people with high self-esteem imagine that others view them favorably, too. The frequently mistaken assumption that others' views are similar to our own applies in a wide range of situations:

- You've heard a slightly raunchy joke that you think is pretty funny. You might assume that it won't offend a somewhat strait-laced friend. It does.

- You've been bothered by an instructor's tendency to get off the subject during lectures. If you were an instructor, you'd want to know if anything you were doing was creating problems for your students, so you decide that your instructor will probably be grateful for some constructive criticism. Unfortunately, you're wrong.

- You lost your temper with a friend a week ago and said some things you regret. In fact, if someone said those things to you, you'd consider that the relationship was finished. Imagining that your friend feels the same way, you avoid making contact. In fact, your friend feels that she was partly responsible and has avoided you because she thinks you're the one who wants to end things.

Examples like these show that others don't always think or feel the way we do and that assuming that similarities exist can lead to problems. How can you find out the other person's real position? Sometimes by asking directly, sometimes by checking with others, and sometimes by making an educated guess after you've thought the matter out. All these alternatives are better than simply assuming that everyone would react as you do.

PERCEPTION CHECKING TO PREVENT MISUNDERSTANDINGS

Serious problems can arise when people treat interpretations as if they were matters of fact. Like most people, you probably resent others jumping to conclusions about the reasons for your behavior.

"Why are you mad at me?" (Who said you were?)

"What's the matter with you?" (Who said anything was the matter?)

"Come on now. Tell the truth." (Who said you were lying?)

As you'll learn in chapter 9, even if your interpretation is correct, a dogmatic, mind-reading statement is likely to generate defensiveness. The skill of **perception checking** provides a better way to handle your interpretations.[39]

Elements of Perception Checking

A complete perception check has three parts:

- A description of the behavior you noticed
- At least two possible interpretations of the behavior
- A request for clarification about how to interpret the behavior

Perception checks for the preceding three examples would look like this:

"When you stomped out of the room and slammed the door," (*Behavior*) "I wasn't sure whether you were mad at me" (*First interpretation*) "or just in a hurry." (*Second interpretation*) "How *did* you feel?" (*Request for clarification*)

"You haven't laughed much in the last couple of days." (*Behavior*) "It makes me wonder whether something's bothering you" (*First interpretation*) "or whether you're just feeling quiet." (*Second interpretation*) "What's up?" (*Request for clarification*)

"You said you really liked the job I did." (*Behavior*) "On the other hand, there was something about your voice that made me think you may not like it." (*First interpretation*) "Maybe it's just my imagination, though." (*Second interpretation*) "How do you really feel?" (*Request for clarification*)

Perception checking is a tool for helping you understand others accurately instead of assuming that your first interpretation is correct. Because its goal is mutual understanding, perception checking is a cooperative approach to communication. Besides leading to more accurate perceptions, it minimizes defensiveness by preserving the other person's face. Instead of saying, in effect, "I know what you're thinking . . ." a perception check takes the more respectful approach that states or implies, "I know I'm not qualified to judge you without some help."

Perception Checking Considerations

Like every communication skill outlined in *Looking Out/Looking In*, perception checking isn't a mechanical formula that will work in every situation. As you develop the ability to check your perceptions fully, consider the following factors in deciding when and how to use this approach.

Completeness   Sometimes a perception check won't need all the parts listed earlier to be effective:

"You haven't dropped by lately. Is anything the matter?" (*Single interpretation combined with request for clarification*)

"I can't tell whether you're kidding me about being cheap or if you're serious." (*Behavior combined with interpretations*) "Are you mad at me?"

"Are you sure you don't mind driving? I can use a ride if it's no trouble, but I don't want to take you out of your way." (*No need to describe behavior*)

Sometimes even the most skimpy perception check—a simple question like "What's going on?"—will do the job. You might also rely on other people to help you make sense of confusing behavior: "Rachelle has been awfully quiet lately. Do you know what's up?" A complete perception check is most necessary when the risk of sounding judgmental is highest.

Nonverbal Congruency A perception check can succeed only if your nonverbal behavior reflects the open-mindedness of your words. An accusing tone of voice or a hostile glare will contradict the sincerely worded request for clarification, suggesting that you have already made up your mind about the other person's intentions.

Cultural Rules The straightforward approach of perception checking has the best chance of working in what chapter 5 identifies as *low-context cultures:* ones in which members use language as clearly and logically as possible. The dominant cultures of North America and western Europe fit into this category, and members of these groups are most likely to appreciate the kind of straight talking that perception checking embodies. On the other hand, members of *high-context cultures* (more common in Latin America and Asia) value social harmony over clarity. High-context communicators are more likely to regard candid approaches like perception checking as potentially embarrassing, preferring instead less direct ways of understanding one another. Thus, a "let's get this straight" perception check that might work well with a Euro American manager who was raised to value clarity could be a serious mistake with a Mexican American or Asian American boss who has spent most of his or her life in a high-context culture.

"Pictures and Perception Checking"

http://www. acd.roch.edu/ lhalverson/Assign/ perceptioncheck.htm

Find a partner and practice your perception checking skills by following the directions on this Web page developed by communication professor Lori Halverson-Wente. Use Activity 3.1 "Perception Checking Practice" on the *Looking Out/Looking In* Web site to guide your work.

SKILL BUILDER

PERCEPTION CHECKING PRACTICE

Practice your perception checking ability by developing three-part verifications for the following situations:

1. You made what you thought was an excellent suggestion to an instructor. The instructor looked uninterested but said she would check on the matter right away. Three weeks have passed, and nothing has changed.

2. A neighbor and good friend has not responded to your "Good morning" for three days in a row. This person is usually friendly.

3. You haven't received the usual weekly phone call from the folks back home in over a month. The last time you spoke, you had an argument about where to spend the holidays.

4. An old friend with whom you have shared the problems of your love life for years has recently changed when around you: The formerly casual hugs and kisses have become longer and stronger, and the occasions where you "accidentally" brush up against one another have become more frequent.

EMPATHY AND COMMUNICATION

Perception checking is a valuable tool for clarifying ambiguous messages. But ambiguity isn't the only cause of perceptual problems. Sometimes we understand *what* people mean without understanding *why* they believe as they do. At times like this we are short on the vital ability to empathize.

Empathy Defined

Empathy is the ability to re-create another person's perspective, to experience the world from the other's point of view. It may be impossible to ever experience another person's perspective completely, but with enough effort we can certainly gain a better idea of how the world appears to him or her. As we'll use the term here, **empathy** involves three dimensions.[40] In one dimension, empathy involves *perspective taking*—an attempt to take on the viewpoint of another person. This requires a suspension of judgment so that for the moment you set aside your own opinions and try to understand the other person. Empathy also has an *emotional* dimension that helps us get closer to experiencing others' feelings: to gain a sense of their fear, joy, sadness, and so on. A third dimension of empathy is a genuine *concern* for the welfare of the other person. When we empathize we go beyond just thinking and feeling as others do and genuinely care about their well-being.

The ability to empathize seems to exist in a rudimentary form in even the youngest children.[41] Research sponsored by the National Institute of Mental Health revealed what many parents know from experience: Virtually from birth, infants become visibly upset when they hear another baby crying, and children who are a few months old cry when they observe another child in tears. Young children have trouble distinguishing others' distress from their own. If, for example, one child hurts its finger, another baby might put its own finger into her mouth as if she was feeling pain. Researchers report cases in which children who see their parents in tears wipe their own eyes, even though they are not crying.

Although children may have a basic capacity to empathize, studies with twins suggest that the degree to which we are born with the ability to sense how others are feeling seems to vary according to genetic factors.[42] Although some people may have an inborn edge, environmental experiences are the key to developing the ability to understand others. Specifically, the way in which parents communicate with their children seems to affect their ability to understand others' emotional states.[43] When parents point out to children the distress that others feel from their misbehavior ("Look how sad Jessica is because you took her toy. Wouldn't you be sad if someone took away your toys?"), those children gain a greater appreciation that their acts have emotional consequences than when parents simply label such behavior as inappropriate ("That was a mean thing to do!").

It is easy to confuse empathy with **sympathy,** but the concepts are different in two important ways. First, sympathy means you feel compas-

ETHICAL CHALLENGE

Empathy and the Golden Rule

Virtually everyone is familiar with the Golden Rule, which most of us learned in the form "Do unto others as you would have them do unto you." By obliging us to treat others as well as we would treat ourselves, this maxim seems to offer the foundation for a civil society in which everyone would behave with consideration.

Some ethicists have pointed out that the Golden Rule doesn't work well in situations where others don't want to be treated the same way you would. You may like to play heavy metal rock and roll at 3 a.m., but appeals to the Golden Rule probably won't placate your neighbors who don't share your musical tastes or late night hours. Likewise, just because you enjoy teasing banter, you aren't entitled to banter with others who might find this type of humor offensive or hurtful. You may be infatuated with a potential lover who doesn't want to reciprocate your affections, but following the Golden Rule might lead to a restraining order against you.

The Golden Rule presents special problems in cases of intercultural

contacts, where norms for what is desirable vary dramatically. For example, most speakers from low-context cultures where English is the first language value honesty and explicit communication, but this level of candor would be offensive in high-context cultures of Asia or the Middle East. A naive communicator following the Golden Rule might justify social blunders by claiming, "I was just communicating the way I'd like to be treated." This sort of ethnocentrism is a recipe for unsuccessful communication and perhaps for very unpleasant consequences.

In response to the challenge of differing wants, Milton Bennett proposed a "Platinum Rule": "Do unto others as they themselves would have done unto them." Unlike the Golden Rule, this rule requires us to understand how others think and what they want before we can determine how to act ethically. Put differently, the Platinum Rule implies that empathy is a prerequisite for moral sensitivity.

Despite its initial appeal, the Platinum Rule poses its own problems. There are certainly cases

where doing unto others what they want might compromise our own needs or even our ethical principles. It is easy to imagine cases in which the Platinum Rule would oblige us to cheat, steal, or lie on others' behalf.

Even if acting on the Platinum Rule is problematic, the benefit of thinking about it seems clear. An essential requirement for benign behavior is the ability to empathize, helping us recognize that what others want may be different than what we would want under the same circumstances.

Describe how applying the Golden Rule and the Platinum Rule would affect one of your important interpersonal relationships. What communication is necessary before you could put each rule into practice? Which rule seems to be preferable?

For a discussion of the Golden and Platinum rules, See M. Bennett, "Overcoming the Golden Rule: Sympathy and Empathy" in D. Nimmo, ed., *Communication Yearbook 3* (New Brunswick, N.J.: Transaction Books, 1979), pp. 407–422; and J. A. Jaksa and M. S. Pritchard, *Communication Ethics: Methods of Analysis*, 2nd ed. (Belmont, Calif.: Wadsworth, 1994), pp. 101–105.

---

sion *for* another person's predicament, whereas empathy means you have a personal sense of what that predicament is like. Consider the difference between sympathizing with an unwed mother or a homeless person and empathizing with them—imagining what it would be like to be in their position. When you sympathize, it is the other's confusion, joy, or pain. When you empathize, the experience becomes your own, at least for the moment.

Empathy is different from sympathy in a second way. We sympathize only when we accept the reasons for another's pain as valid, whereas it's possible to empathize without feeling sympathy. You can empathize with a difficult relative, a rude stranger, and even a

Apart from abstract propositions of comparison (such as two and two make four), propositions which tell us nothing by themselves about concrete reality, we find no proposition ever regarded by any one as evidently certain that has not either been called a falsehood, or at least had its truth sincerely questioned by someone else.

William James, *The Will to Believe*

It was six men of Indostan
        To learning much inclined,
Who went to see the elephant
        Though all of them were blind
That each by observation
        Might satisfy his mind.

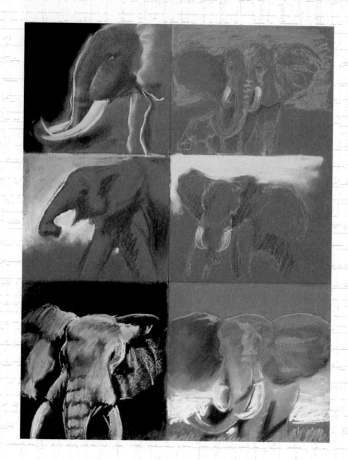

The first approached the elephant
        And, happening to fall
Against the broad and sturdy side,
        At once began to bawl:
"Why, bless me! But the elephant
        Is very much like a wall!"

The second, feeling of the tusk,
        Cried: "Ho! What have we here
So very round and smooth and sharp?
        To me, 'tis very clear,
This wonder of an elephant
        Is very like a spear!"

The third approached the animal,
        And, happening to take
The squirming trunk within his hands
        Thus boldly up he spake:
"I see," quoth he, "the elephant
        Is very like a snake!"

The fourth reached out his eager hand
        And felt about the knee:
"What most this wondrous beast is like
        Is very plain," quoth he:
" 'Tis clear enough the elephant
        Is very like a tree!"

The fifth who chanced to touch the ear
        Said: "E'en the blindest man
Can tell what this resembles most—
        Deny the fact who can:
This marvel of an elephant
        Is very like a fan!"

The sixth no sooner had begun
        About the beast to grope
Than, seizing on the swinging tail
        That fell within his scope,
"I see," quoth he, "the elephant
        Is very like a rope!"

And so these men of Indostan
        Disputed loud and long,
Each in his own opinion
        Exceeding stiff and strong;
Though each was partly in the right,
        And all were in the wrong.

John G. Saxe

criminal without feeling much sympathy for them. Empathizing allows you to understand another person's motives without requiring you to agree with them. After empathizing you will almost certainly understand them better, but sympathy won't always follow.

Neither sympathy nor empathy is identical to the "I know how you feel" type of response that some people offer when faced with another's expression of emotion. Hearing someone else's account—of falling in love or losing a job, for example—might remind you of a similar

"How would you feel if the mouse did that to you?"

©The New Yorker Collection 1997 William Steig from cartoonbank.com. All Rights Reserved.

experience, but it is highly unlikely that your experience matched his or hers. Furthermore, an "I know how you feel" response can be interpreted as a conversational "take-away" in which you disregard the other person's story and begin telling yours. Chapter 7 offers more warnings about the perils of this type of apparent support.

There is no consistent evidence that suggests that the ability to empathize is better for one sex or the other.[44] Some people, however, seem to have a hereditary capacity for greater empathizing than do others.[45] Studies of identical and fraternal twins indicate that identical female twins are more similar to one another in their ability to empathize than are fraternal twins. Interestingly, there seems to be no difference between male twins. Although empathy may have a biological basis, the role of environment can still play an important role. For example, parents who are sensitive to their children's feelings tend to have children who also are sensitive to the feelings of others.[46]

Total empathy is impossible to achieve. Completely understanding another person's point of view is simply too difficult a task for humans with different backgrounds and limited communication skills. Nonetheless, it is possible to get a strong sense of what the world looks like through another person's eyes.[47] The following method will help you become more empathic.

The "Pillow Method": A Tool for Building Empathy

Perception checking is a relatively quick, easy tool for clarifying potential misunderstandings. But some issues are too complex and serious to be handled with this approach. Writer Paul Reps describes a tool for boosting empathy when finding merit in another's position seems impossible.[48]

Developed by a group of Japanese schoolchildren, the **pillow method** gets its name from the fact that a problem has four sides and a middle, just like a pillow (see Figure 3-5). As the examples on pages

127–128 show, viewing the issue from each of these perspectives almost always leads to valuable insights.

Position 1: I'm Right, You're Wrong

This is the perspective that we usually take when viewing an issue. We immediately see the virtues in our position and find fault with anyone who happens to disagree with us. Detailing this position takes little effort and provides little new information.

Position 2: You're Right, I'm Wrong

At this point you switch perspectives and build the strongest possible arguments to explain how another person can view the issue differently from you. Besides identifying the strengths in the other's position, this is the time to play the devil's advocate and find flaws in yours.

Finding flaws in your position and trying to support the other's position requires discipline and a certain amount of courage, even though this is only an exercise and you will soon be able to retreat to position 1 if you choose. But most people learn that switching perspectives shows that there is some merit to the other person's perspective.

There are some issues where it seems impossible to call the other position "right." Criminal behavior, deceit, and disloyalty often seem beyond justification. At times like these it is possible to arrive at position 2 by realizing that the other person's behavior is understandable. For example, without approving you may be able to understand how someone would resort to violence, tell lies, or cheat. Whatever the particulars, the goal of position 2 is to find some way of comprehending how anyone could behave in a way that you originally found impossible to defend.

Position 3: Both Right, Both Wrong

From this position you acknowledge the strengths and weaknesses of each person's arguments. If you have done a good job with position 2, it should be clear that there is some merit in both points of view and that each side has its demerits. Taking a more evenhanded look at the issue can lead you to be less critical and more understanding of another's point of view.

Position 3 can also help you find the commonalities between your position and the other's.

> The test of a first-rate intelligence is the ability to hold two opposed ideas in mind at the same time and still retain the ability to function.
>
> F. Scott Fitzgerald

POSITION 1:
I'm right,
you're wrong

POSITION 3:
Both right,
both wrong

POSITION 5:
There's truth in
all perspectives

POSITION 4:
The issue isn't
important

POSITION 2:
You're right,
I'm wrong

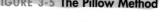

FIGURE 3-5 **The Pillow Method**

The Pillow Method in Action

Example 1: Planning a Wedding
Background

Who would have thought that planning a wedding would be such a nightmare? My fiancé and I are struggling to decide whether we should have a large, festive wedding or a small, intimate one. I'm in favor of having a big, expensive ceremony and party. He wants a smaller, more affordable one.

Position 1: I'm Right, and He Is Wrong

I have a big family, and I would feel guilty not inviting everyone. Also, we have lots of friends who would really miss not being present to celebrate our special day. If we invite one friend or relative, I say we have to invite them all to avoid hurting anybody's feelings. Otherwise, where do you draw the line? As far as money goes, I say that you get married only once, and this is no time to scrimp. My parents are willing to help pay the expenses because they want our entire family to be there at the wedding.

Position 2: He's Right, and I'm Wrong

My fiancé is right to say that we really don't have the funds to spend on a fancy wedding. Every dollar we spend on a lavish event will be one less dollar we have to buy a house, which we hope to do soon. My fiancé is right to say that a big wedding could postpone our house purchase for a year or two—maybe even longer, if real estate prices go up before we can buy. He's also right to say that no matter how many people we invite, someone is always

going to be left out. It's just a case of where we draw the line. Finally, he's right to say that planning a big wedding will be a very stressful process.

Position 3: Both of Us Are Right, and Both Are Wrong

Both of us are right, and both are wrong. I'm right to want to include our extended families and friends on this joyous day, and I'm right to say that a special wedding would be a lifetime memory. He's right that doing so could would still leave some hurt feelings and that it will postpone our house purchase. He also has a good point when he says that planning a big event could drive us crazy and distract us from the real importance of joining our lives.

Position 4: The Issue Isn't Important

After thinking about it, I've realized that *getting* married is different from *being* married. The decision about what kind of ceremony to have is important, but ultimately it won't affect the kind of marriage we have. How we behave *after* we're married will be much more important. And we are going to face a lot of decisions together—about children and jobs, for example—that will have much bigger consequences than this ceremony.

Conclusion

Before using the pillow method to think through all sides of this issue, I was focused on getting my way. This attitude was creating some feelings between my fiancé and I that were not what we should be having as we faced this most important event. I've realized that if one or the other of us "wins" but the result is injured feelings, it won't be much of a victory. I

don't know what kind of ceremony we will finally decide to have, but I'm determined to keep my focus on the really important goal of keeping our relationship positive and respectful.

Example 2: Exotic Dancing
Background

My best friend is an exotic dancer. I have tried to persuade her to find a less degrading way to earn a living, but she doesn't see the need to stop yet. She knows I don't agree with her decision to dance for money, but she tells me it's the only way she can make a decent income at this point in her life.

Position 1: I'm Right, and She Is Wrong

My friend is exaggerating when she says this job is the *only* way she can get the money to put herself through school. She could get a job that doesn't pay as well and make it through until she graduates. It wouldn't be perfect, but other people manage this way, and so can she. My friend is wrong to say this job doesn't intrude into her life away from work. When we lived together, she had some arguments with her boyfriend about a strange man who would send her gifts at the club where she dances. This was really affecting their relationship. Also, sometimes she comes home at 4 o'clock a.m. after eight hours of dancing. I don't see how she can go on like this.

Position 2: She's Right, and I'm Wrong

She is right to say that there is no other job where she can make this much money in so little time, at her age, and with her credentials. No one else supports my friend. She

Continued

earns enough money to pay for rent, food, and pay off some of her loans. She is still physically OK. She is a straight-A student, so it's true that the job isn't affecting her school work. The club where she works is clean and safe.

Position 3: Both of Us Are Right, and Both Are Wrong

I'm right to worry about her and encourage her to think about other options besides exotic dancing. She's right when she says there's no other job that pays so well. She's also right to say that her family

doesn't support her in any way, which puts additional pressure on her that I can't imagine.

Position 4: The Issue Isn't Important

My friend and I both love one another and won't let this disagreement affect that. My friend hasn't let the dancing affect her self-worth. The dancing is just a chapter in her life, and it will be over soon.

Conclusion

Now I can see that this dispute has many sides. I still wish my friend would quit her dancing job,

and I'm still going to keep trying to persuade her to stop. But this method makes it easier for us to talk about the issue without either of us shutting down or rejecting the other.

Using your Looking Out/ Looking In CD-ROM, click on Communication Scenarios and then click on either "The Pillow Method—Planning A Wedding" or "The Pillow Method—Exotic Dancing" icons to watch and analyze dramatized versions of the scenarios described in this box.

Perhaps you've both been right to care so much about the issue, but both wrong to fail to recognize the other person's concerns. Perhaps there are underlying values that you both share and similar mistakes that you've both made. In any case, the perspective of position 3 should help you see that the issue isn't as much a matter of complete right and wrong as it first appeared to be.

Position 4: The Issue Isn't As Important As It Seems   This perspective will help you realize that the issue isn't as important as you thought. Although it is hard to think of some issues as unimportant, a little thought will show that most aren't as important as we make them out to be. The impact of even the most traumatic events—the death of a loved one or the breakup of a relationship, for example—usually fades over time. The effects may not disappear, but we learn to accept them and get on with life. The importance of a dispute can also fade when you realize that you've let it overshadow other equally important parts of your relationship. It's easy to become so wrapped up in a dispute about one subject that you forget about the other ways in which you are close to the other person.

Conclusion: There Is Truth in All Four Perspectives   After completing the first four positions, a final step is to recognize that each of them has some merit. Although logic might suggest that it's impossible for a position to be both right and wrong, both important and unimportant, your own experience will show that there is some truth in each of the positions you have explored. This fifth is very different from the "I'm right and you're wrong" attitude that most people bring to an issue. After you have looked at an issue from these five perspectives, it is almost certain that you will gain new insights. These insights may not cause you to change your mind or even solve the problem at hand. Nonetheless, these new insights can increase your tolerance for the other person's position and thus improve the communication climate.

The belief that one's own view of reality is the only reality is the most dangerous of all delusions.

Paul Watzlawick

SKILL BUILDER

PILLOW TALK

Try using the pillow method in your life. It isn't easy, but after you begin to understand it, the payoff in increased understanding is great.

1. Choose a person or viewpoint with whom or which you strongly disagree. If you've chosen a person, it's best to have him or her there with you; but if that's not possible, you can do it alone.

2. What disagreement should you choose? No doubt there are many in your life:
   Parent-child
   Teacher-student
   Employer-employee
   Brother-sister
   Friend-friend
   Nation-nation
   Republican-Democrat

3. For each disagreement that you choose, really place yourself in each position on the pillow as you encounter it:
   a. Your position is correct, and your opponent's is wrong.
   b. Your opponent's position is correct, and yours is wrong.
   c. Both your positions are correct, and both are wrong.
   d. It isn't important which position is right or wrong.
   e. Finally, affirm the fact that there is truth in all four positions.

4. The more important the disagreement is to you, the harder it will be to accept positions 2 through 5 as valid. But the exercise will work only if you can suspend your present position and imagine how it would feel to hold the other ones.

5. How can you tell if you've been successful with the pillow method? The answer is simple: If, after going over all the steps, you can understand—not necessarily accept but just understand—the other person's position, you've done it. After you've reached this understanding, do you notice any change in how you feel about the other person?

SUMMARY

There is more to the world "out there" than any person is capable of understanding. We make sense of our environment by the three-step process of selecting certain stimuli from the environment, organizing them into meaningful patterns, and interpreting them in a manner that is shaped by past experience, assumptions about human behavior, expectations, knowledge, and personal moods.

A number of factors affect the way we select, organize, and interpret information. Physiological factors such as the five senses, age, and health play an important role. Cultural background also affects the way we view the world, as do social roles and self-concept. Finally, communicators often construct shared narratives that create a common set of perceptions about themselves and others. In addition to these factors, we commonly make a number of perceptual errors when attributing meaning to others' behavior.

Perception checking can be a useful tool for verifying interpretations of others' behavior instead of assuming that the first hunch is correct. A complete perception check includes a description of the other's behavior, at least two plausible interpretations of its meaning, and a request for clarification about what the behavior does mean.

Empathy is the ability to experience another person's point of view. Empathy differs from sympathy because it more closely matches the other's experience and because it does not necessarily require agreement or pity. One means for boosting empathy is the pillow method, which involves viewing an issue from five different perspectives.

KEY TERMS

androgynous	interpretation	pillow method	stereotyping
attribution	narrative	punctuation	sympathy
empathy	organization	selection	
gender role	perception checking	self-serving bias	

LOOKING OUT/LOOKING IN ONLINE

Use your *Looking Out/Looking In* CD-ROM for quick access to the electronic resources that accompany this chapter. Included on this CD-ROM are additional study aids and links to the *Looking Out/Looking In* Web site at the Wadsworth Communication Café. The CD-ROM is your gateway to a wealth of resources that will help you understand and further explore the material in this chapter. **Video clips** under *Communication Scenarios* on the CD illustrate the skills introduced in this chapter. Click on the Web site link to complete self-study **review quizzes** to help you master new concepts; access a **feature film database** to locate clips and entire movies that illustrate communication principles; find Internet material via the maintained **Web site links;** and complete **online activities** to help you master new concepts.

INFOTRAC COLLEGE EDITION EXERCISES

Use the InfoTrac College Edition password that was included free with a copy of this new text to answer the following questions. These questions can be completed online and if requested, submitted to your instructor under InfoTrac College Edition Activities at the *Looking Out/Looking In* Web site.

Use PowerTrac's keyword search feature to locate articles indexed under "person perception" or "communication and perception." Find an article that interests you, and report on how its findings relate to the information in Chapter 3.

1. The Perception Process

Use PowerTrac's keyword search feature to locate articles on stereotyping. Find an article that discusses how stereotyping operates in an area that is important to you, and report on its significance to your classmates and instructor.

2. Influences on Perception

Use PowerTrac to search for articles containing both the keywords "perception" and "gender." Locate one article that contains information on how men and women perceive events differently. Describe how the differences you identify affect interpersonal communication.

3. Empathy and Communication

Locate and read the article "Teaching Empathy" by William J. O'Malley. (Hint: Use "empathy" as your search term.) Does your personal experience match the author's concern about the inability and unwillingness for young people to concern themselves with others' feelings? How empathic are you with the plight of strangers? Are you satisfied with your answer to this question? If not, how can you modify your attitudes and behavior?

READINGS

Eisenberg, Nancy, and Janet Strayer, eds. *Empathy and Its Development.* Cambridge, England: Cambridge University Press, 1987.

This collection of scholarly writings provides a thorough review of the research and theory regarding empathy. Topics include the development of empathy in children and adults, gender and age differences in empathy and sympathy, the affective and cognitive dimensions of empathy, and the relationship between parental empathy and child adjustment.

Ickes, William E., ed. *Empathic Accuracy.* New York: Guilford, 1997.

This book offers an array of scholarly articles describing the nature and importance of empathic accuracy. Topics include the evolutionary and social factors that contribute to empathy, the psychological characteristics and influences that affect empathic ability, and the relationship of empathy and gender.

Macrae, C. Neil, Charles Stangor, and Miles Hewstone, eds., *Stereotypes and Stereotyping.* New York: Guilford, 1996.

This collection of scholarly works provides a comprehensive look at stereotyping. Chapters deal with the formation and development of stereotypes, how stereotyping operates in everyday interaction, and how to minimize the harmful effects of stereotyping.

FILMS

In addition to the films suggested here, go to the **Film in Communication Database** at the *Looking Out/Looking In* Web site to locate movie clips that illustrate principles of perception.

Multiple Perspectives

White Man's Burden (1995) Rated R

A group of well-to-do people are dining together, debating social problems. Thaddeus Thomas (Harry Belafonte) concludes their discussion with a question: "Are these a people who are beyond being helped?" Viewers of *White Man's Burden* realize at this point that the movie is reversing stereotypical roles of blacks and whites in our society. The dinner guests are rich black people who see poor white people as the problem to be solved.

The movie explores what the United States might be like if blacks were the advantaged majority and whites were the disadvantaged minority. Louis Pinnock (John Travolta) is a white man who works at a factory owned by Thomas. Pinnock gets fired over a misunderstanding and begs Thomas—unsuccessfully— for his job back. Pinnock and other whites are in one-down positions throughout the movie. Black people mistrust and mistreat them; they are the butts of racist comments and jokes.

White Man's Burden challenges viewers to look at U.S. society through a different set of perceptual lenses and with a new set of assumptions. For some, it provides a glimpse into advantages and disadvantages they might not have seen because of the limitations of their perceptual standpoints.

Shared Narratives

The First Wives Club (1996) Rated PG, *Waiting to Exhale* (1995) Rated R

Though different in tone, both these films center on women who are unhappy with the men in their lives. *Waiting to Exhale* chronicles the adventures of four friends (played by Whitney Houston, Angela Bassett, Loretta Devine, and Lela Rochon) who seek relational happiness, which is mostly frustrated by disappointing male partners. *The First Wives Club* is a revenge comedy in which five friends (played by Bette Midler, Goldie Hawn, Diane Keaton, Maggie Smith, and Sarah Jessica Parker) join forces to get even with the husbands who have cheated on and swindled them. Some viewers (mostly men) regard these stories as male-bashing, but from a communication perspective, that's precisely the point: Through shared narratives, the female characters form and reinforce their opinions about what they deserve in romantic relationships and how poorly the men in their lives measure up.

Building Empathy

The Doctor (1991) Rated PG-13

Jack McKee (William Hurt) is an ace surgeon and a first-class egotist. He treats his patients with a breezy self-assurance, brushing aside their concerns with jokes and indifference. It's not that McKee is mean-spirited: He just views his patients as objects upon which he can practice his skill and not as human beings with feelings.

McKee receives a major attitude adjustment when his nagging cough is diagnosed as throat cancer, and his surgeon treats him with the same mechanical indifference that he had bestowed on his patients. As McKee suffers the indignities of a hospital patient and confronts his mortality, his attitude toward the human side of medical care predictably changes.

The film should become a part of the medical school curriculum, but it also shows other viewers how walking a mile in another person's shoes can lead to greater tolerance and understanding.

LOOKING OUT/LOOKING IN CD-ROM

Using your *Looking Out/Looking In* CD-ROM, click on Scenarios and then click on either "Planning a Wedding" or "Exotic Dancing" to watch and analyze one of the two scenarios featured in the Communication Transcript "The Pillow Method in Action" on pages 127–128.

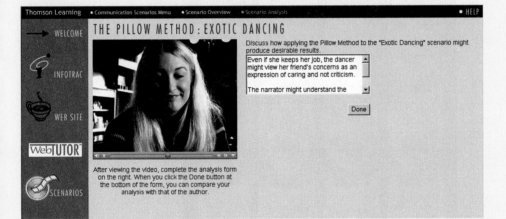

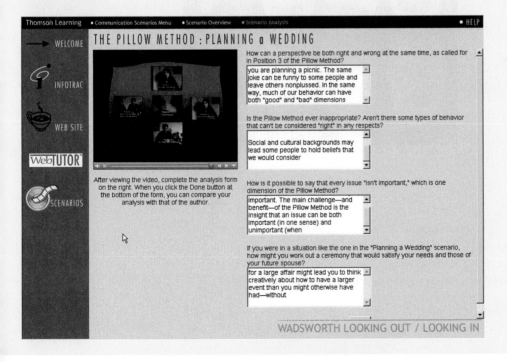

CHAPTER 4

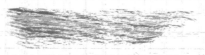

EMOTIONS: THINKING, FEELING, AND ACTING

It's impossible to talk about communication without acknowledging the importance of emotions. Think about it: Feeling confident can make the difference between success and failure in everything from giving a speech to asking for a date, whereas feeling insecure can ruin your chances. Feeling angry or defensive can spoil your time with others, whereas feeling and acting calm will help prevent or solve problems. The way you share or withhold your feelings of affection can affect the future of your relationships. On and on the list of feelings goes: appreciation, loneliness, joy, insecurity, curiosity, irritation. The point is clear: Communication shapes our feelings, and feelings shape our communication.

The role of emotions in human affairs is apparent to social scientists and lay people alike. When Yale University psychologist Robert Sternberg asked people to describe an "intelligent person," one of the skills listed was the ability to understand and get along with others.[1] This ability to get along was characterized by psychologist Daniel Goleman as one aspect of "emotional intelligence."[2] Goleman makes the claim that intellectual ability is not the only way to measure one's talents and that success in the world depends in great part on the ability to understand and manage one's own emotions and be sensitive to others' feelings.

Because this subject of emotions is so important, we'll spend this chapter taking a closer look. Just what are feelings, and how can we recognize them? How are feelings caused, and how can we control them, increasing the productive ones and decreasing ones that are less productive? When and how can we best share our feelings with others?

WHAT ARE EMOTIONS?

Suppose that an extraterrestrial visitor asked you to explain emotions. How would you answer? You might start by saying that emotions are things that we feel. But this doesn't say much because in turn you would probably describe feelings as synonymous with emotions. Social scientists generally agree that there are several components to the phenomena we label as feelings.

Physiological Changes

When a person has strong emotions, many bodily changes occur. For example, the physical components of fear include an increased heartbeat, a rise in blood pressure, an increase in adrenaline secretions, an elevated blood sugar level, a slowing of digestion, and a dilation of pupils. Some of these changes are recognizable to the person having them. These sensations are termed *proprioceptive stimuli*, meaning that they are activated by the movement of internal tissues. Proprioceptive messages can offer a significant clue to your emotions after you become aware of them. A churning stomach or tense jaw can be a signal that something is wrong. You can get a sense of your own proprioceptive messages by trying the following exercise.

Every thought, gesture, muscle tension, feeling, stomach gurgle, nose scratch, fart, hummed tune, slip of the tongue, illness—everything is significant and meaningful and related to the now. It is possible to know and understand oneself on all these levels, and the more one knows the more he is free to determine his own life.

If I know what my body tells me, I know my deepest feelings and I can choose what to do. . . . Given a complete knowledge of myself, I can determine my life; lacking that mastery, I am controlled in ways that are often undesirable, unproductive, worrisome, and confusing.

William Schutz, *Here Comes Everybody*

HOW DOES IT FEEL?

Here's a way to learn more about yourself from your body. You can do this exercise with a group or alone outside the classroom. If you do it alone, read all the steps ahead of time so that you can work through the whole experience without interrupting yourself. However, the exercise will have more impact if you do it for the first time in a group because in this way your facilitator can read the instructions for you. Also, in a group your feelings can be shared and compared. The ellipses (. . .) in the instructions indicate points where you should pause for a moment and examine what you're feeling.

1. Wherever you are, find yourself a comfortable position, either lying or sitting. You'll need to find a quiet place with no distractions. You'll find that the exercise works better if you dim the lights.

2. Close your eyes. The visual sense is so dominant that it's easy to neglect your other senses.

3. Now that your eyes are closed and you're comfortable, take a trip through your body and visit its various parts. As you focus on each part, don't try to change what you find . . . just notice how you are, how you feel.

4. Now let's begin. Start with your feet. How do they feel? Are they comfortable, or do they hurt? Are your toes cold? Do your shoes fit well, or are they too tight?

   Now move your attention to your legs. . . . Is there any tension in them, or are they relaxed? . . . Can you feel each muscle? . . . Are your legs crossed? Is there pressure where one presses against the other? . . . Are they comfortable?

   Now pay attention to your hips and pelvis . . . the area where your legs and backbone join. Do you feel comfortable here, or are you not as relaxed as you'd like to be? If you're seated, direct your attention to your buttocks. . . . Can you feel your body's weight pressing against the surface you're sitting on?

   Now move on to the trunk of your body. How does your abdomen feel? . . . What are the sensations you can detect there? . . . Is anything moving? . . . Focus on your breathing. . . . Do you breathe off the top of your lungs, or are you taking deep, relaxed breaths? . . . Does the air move in and out through your nose or your mouth? Is your chest tight, or is it comfortable?

   Checking your breathing has probably led you to your throat and neck. Is your throat comfortable, or do you feel a lump there you need to keep swallowing? . . . How about your neck? . . . Can you feel it holding your head in its present position? . . . Perhaps moving your head slowly from side to side will help you feel these muscles doing their work. . . . Is there tension in your neck or shoulders?

   Now let's move to your face. . . . What expression are you wearing? . . . Are the muscles of your face tense or relaxed? Which ones?

"The EQ Factor"

http://www.time.com/time/magazine/archive/1995/951002/951002.cover.html

Access the *Time* magazine archive to read a cover article about the concept of emotional intelligence. You can then answer questions about this article by completing Activity 4.3 "What Is Emotional Intelligence" on the *Looking Out/Looking In* Web site.

Your mouth . . . brow . . . jaw . . . temples? Take a few moments and see. . . .

Finally, go inside your head and see what's happening there. . . . Is it quiet and dark, or are things happening there? . . . What are they? Does it feel good inside your head, or is there some pressure or aching? . . .

You've made a trip from bottom to top. Try feeling your whole body now. . . . See what new awareness of it you've gained. . . . Are there any special parts of your body that attract your attention now? . . . What are they telling you?

Now there's another very important part of your body to focus on. It's the part of you where you *feel* when you're happy or sad or afraid. Take a moment and find that spot. . . . See how you are now in there. . . . See what happens when you ask yourself, "How am I now? How do I feel?" . . . See what happens in that place when you think of a personal problem that's been bothering you lately. . . . Be sure it's something that's important to your life now. . . . Now see if you can get the feel of this problem there in the place where you feel things. . . . Let yourself feel all of it. . . . If the feeling changes as you focus on it, that's OK. Just stay with the feeling wherever it goes and see how it is. . . . If what you feel now makes a difference to you, see what that difference is. . . . Now, take a few minutes to use it in whatever way you like, and then slowly open your eyes.

5. Now think about the following questions. If you're with a group, you may want to discuss them there.

   a. Did you find out things about your body that you hadn't noticed before? Did you discover some tensions that you'd been carrying around? How long do you think you've been this way? Did discovering them make any difference to you?

   b. Could you find the part of yourself where you usually feel things? Where was it? Or are there different spots for different feelings? Did focusing on your problem make some kind of difference to you?

Nonverbal Reactions

Not all physical changes that accompany emotions are internal. Feelings are often apparent by observable changes. Some of these changes involve a person's appearance: blushing, sweating, and so on. Other changes involve behavior: a distinctive facial expression, posture, gestures, different vocal tone and rate, and so on.

Although it's reasonably easy to tell when someone is feeling a strong emotion, it's more difficult to be certain exactly what that emotion might be. A slumped posture and sigh may be a sign of sadness, or they may be a sign of fatigue. Likewise, trembling hands might indicate excitement, or they may indicate fear. As you'll learn in chapter 6, nonverbal behavior is usually ambiguous, and it's dangerous to assume that it can be "read" with much accuracy.

Although we usually think of nonverbal behavior as the reaction to an emotional state, there may be times when the reverse is true—when nonverbal behavior actually *causes* an emotional state. In one study, experimental subjects were able to create various emotional states by altering their facial expressions.[3] When subjects were coached to move their facial muscles in ways that appeared afraid, angry, disgusted, amused, sad, surprised, and contemptuous, the subjects' bodies responded as if they were having these feelings. In another experiment, subjects who were coached to smile actually reported feeling better, and when they altered their expressions to look unhappy, they felt worse than before.[4]

Cognitive Interpretations

Although there may be situations in which there is a direct connection between physical behavior and emotional states, in most situations the mind plays an important role in determining emotional states. On page 136 you read that some physiological components of fear are a racing heart, perspiration, tense muscles, and elevated blood pressure. Interestingly enough, these symptoms are similar to the physical changes that accompany excitement, joy, and other emotions. In other words, if we were to measure the physical condition of someone having a strong emotion, we would have a hard time knowing whether that person was trembling with fear or quivering with excitement. The recognition that the bodily components of most emotions are similar led some psychologists to conclude that the experience of fright, joy, or anger comes primarily from the *label* we give to the same physical symptoms at a given time.[5] Psychologist Philip Zimbardo offers a good example of this principle:

> I notice I'm perspiring while lecturing. From that I infer I am nervous. If it occurs often, I might even label myself a "nervous person." Once I have the label, the next question I must answer is "Why am I nervous?" Then I start to search for an appropriate explanation. I might notice some students leaving the room, or being inattentive. I am nervous because I'm not giving a good lecture. That makes me nervous. How do I know it's not good? Because I'm boring my audience. I am nervous because I am a boring lecturer and I want to be a good lecturer. I feel inadequate. Maybe I should open a delicatessen instead. Just then a student says, "It's hot in here, I'm perspiring and it makes it tough to concentrate on your lecture." Instantly, I'm no longer "nervous" or "boring."[6]

©The New Yorker Collection 1981
Robert Weber from cartoonbank.com.
All Rights Reserved.

"What the hell was that? Something just swept over me—like contentment or something."

In his book *Shyness,* Zimbardo discusses the consequences of making inaccurate or exaggerated attributions. In a survey of more than five thousand subjects, over 80 percent described themselves as having been shy at some time in their lives, whereas more than 40 percent described themselves as being presently shy. Most significantly, those who described themselves as "not shy" behaved in virtually the *same way* as their shy counterparts. They would blush, perspire, and feel their hearts pounding in certain social situations. The biggest difference between the two groups seemed to be the label with which they described themselves.[7] This is a significant difference. Someone who notices the symptoms we've described and thinks, "I'm such a shy person!" will most likely feel more uncomfortable and communicate less effectively than another person with the same symptoms who thinks, "Well, I'm a bit shaky (or excited) here, but that's to be expected."

We'll take a closer look at ways to reduce unpleasant emotions through cognitive processes later in this chapter.

Verbal Expression

As you will read in chapter 6, nonverbal behavior is a powerful way of communicating emotion. In fact, nonverbal actions are better at conveying emotions than they are at conveying ideas. But sometimes words are necessary to express feelings. Is your friend's uncharacteristically short temper a sign of anger at you, or does it mean something less personal? Is a lover's unenthusiastic response a sign of boredom with you or the result of a long workday? Is a new acquaintance mistaking your friendliness as a come-on? There are times—especially in our low-context culture—when you can't rely on perceptiveness to be sure that a message is communicated and understood accurately.

The ability to communicate clearly about feelings has been characterized by Daniel Goleman and others as part of "emotional intelligence."[8] Goleman identifies a wide range of problems that arise for people who aren't able to talk about emotions constructively, including social isolation, unsatisfying relationships, feelings of anxiety and depression, and misdirected aggression. Other researchers have shown that the way that parents talk to their children about emotions has a powerful effect on the children's development.[9] The researchers identified two distinct parenting styles: "emotion coaching" and "emotion dismissing." They show how the coaching approach gives children skills for communicating about feelings in later life that lead to much more satisfying relationships. Later in this chapter you will find some guidelines for effectively communicating about emotions.

TYPES OF EMOTIONS

So far our discussion has implied that although emotions may differ in tone, they are similar in most other ways. In truth, emotions vary in many respects.

Emotional Weather Report

Late night and early morning low clouds
  with a chance of fog;
  Chance of showers into the afternoon
  with variable high cloudiness
  and gusty winds, gusty winds . . .

Things are tough all over
  when the thunderstorms start;
  Increasing over the southeast
  and south central portions
  of my apartment.

I get upset and a line of thunderstorms was
  developing in the early morning,
  ahead of a slow moving cold front.
  Cold blooded, with tornado watches issued
  shortly before noon Sunday
  for the areas including the western region
  of my mental health
  and the northern portions of my
  ability to deal rationally with my
  disconcerted precarious emotional situation.

Tom Waits

Primary and Mixed Emotions

Emotions are rather like colors: Some are simple, whereas others are blends. Robert Plutchik's "emotion wheel" (see Figure 4-1) illustrates the difference.[10] For example, jealousy can be viewed as a combination of several different emotions: distress, anger, disgust, contempt, fear, and even shame.[11] Likewise, loneliness can include feelings of anger toward self and others, estrangement, and depression.[12] Plutchik has identified eight **primary emotions,** which are listed inside the wheel. He suggests that these primary emotions can combine to form **mixed emotions,** some of which are listed outside the wheel.

Whether or not you agree with the specific emotions that Plutchik identifies as primary and mixed, the wheel suggests that many feelings need to be described in more than a single term. To understand why, consider the following examples. For each one, ask yourself two questions: How would I feel? What feelings might I express?

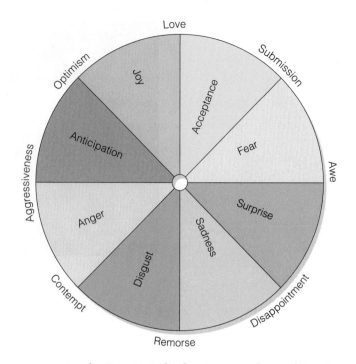

FIGURE 4-1   **The Emotion Wheel: Primary and Mixed Emotions**

An out-of-town friend has promised to arrive at your house at six o'clock. When he hasn't arrived by nine, you are convinced that a terrible accident has occurred. Just as you pick up the phone to call the police and local hospitals, your friend breezes in the door with an offhand remark about getting a late start.

You and your companion have a fight just before leaving for a party. Deep inside, you know that you were mostly to blame, even though you aren't willing to admit it. When you arrive at the party, your companion leaves you to flirt with several other attractive guests.

In situations like these you would probably feel mixed emotions. Consider the case of the overdue friend. Your first reaction to his arrival would probably be relief—"Thank goodness, he's safe!" But you would also be likely to feel anger—"Why didn't he phone to tell me he'd be late?" The second example would probably leave you with an even greater number of mixed emotions: guilt at contributing to the fight, hurt and perhaps embarrassment at your friend's flirtations, and anger at this sort of vengefulness.

Despite the commonness of mixed emotions, we often communicate only one feeling—usually the most negative one. In both of the preceding examples you might show only your anger, leaving the other person with little idea of the full range of your feelings. Consider the different reaction you would get by showing *all* your emotions in these cases and in others.

Intense and Mild Emotions

Another way in which emotions are like colors is in their intensity. Figure 4-2 illustrates this point clearly.[13] Each vertical slice represents the range of a primary emotion from its mildest to its most intense state. This model shows the importance not only of choosing the right emotional family when expressing yourself but also of describing the strength of the emotion. Some people fail to communicate clearly because they understate their emotions, failing to let others know how strongly they feel. To say you're "annoyed" when a friend breaks an important promise, for example, would probably be an understatement. In other cases, people chronically overstate the strength of their feelings. To them, everything is "wonderful" or "terrible." The problem with this sort of exaggeration is that when a truly intense emotion comes along, they have no words left to describe it adequately. If chocolate chip cookies from the local bakery are "fantastic," how does it feel to fall in love?

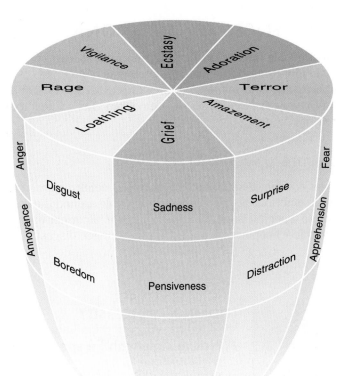

FIGURE 4-2 **Intensity of Emotions**

INVITATION TO INSIGHT

RECOGNIZING YOUR EMOTIONS

Keep a three-day record of your feelings. You can do this by spending a few minutes each evening recalling what emotions you felt during the day, what other people were involved, and the circumstances in which the emotions occurred.

At the end of the three-day period you can understand the role that emotions play in your communication by answering the following questions:

1. How did you recognize the emotions you felt: through proprioceptive stimuli, nonverbal behaviors, or cognitive processes?

2. Did you have any difficulty deciding which emotions you were feeling?

3. What emotions do you have most often? Are they primary or mixed? Mild or intense?

4. In what circumstances do you or don't you show your feelings? What factors influence your decision to show or not show your feelings? The type of feeling? The person or persons involved? The situation (time, place)? The subject that the feeling involves (money, sex, and so on)?

5. What are the consequences of the type of communicating you just described in step 4? Are you satisfied with these consequences? If not, what can you do to become more satisfied?

INFLUENCES ON EMOTIONAL EXPRESSION

Most people rarely express their emotions, at least verbally. People are generally comfortable making statements of fact and often delight in expressing their opinion, but they rarely disclose how they feel. Why is it that people fail to express their emotions? Let's take a look at several reasons.

Culture

Over one hundred years of research has confirmed the fact that certain basic emotions are experienced by people around the world.[14] No matter where a person is born and regardless of his or her background, the ability to feel happiness, sadness, surprise, anger, disgust, and fear seems to

---

LOOKING AT DIVERSITY

A Native American Perspective on Emotional Expression

Todd Epaloose was raised on the Zuñi pueblo, New Mexico. He spent part of his childhood on the reservation and part attending school in the city. He now lives in Albuquerque, where he studies environmental protection technology and works in a medical lab. As an urbanite who still spends time with his family on the reservation, Todd alternates between two worlds. On the reservation he is surrounded by his Native American culture, whereas in the city he has developed the skills necessary to succeed in a technological society. In this profile, Todd reflects on the differences between the ways Zuñi and Anglo cultures deal with emotional expression.

Zuñi and Anglo cultures are as different as night and day in the ways they treat communication about emotions. In mainstream U.S.

culture speaking up is accepted, or even approved. This is true from the time you are a child. Parents are proud when their child speaks up—whether that means showing affection, being curious, or even expressing unhappiness in a way that the parents approve. Being quiet gets a child labeled as "shy," and is considered a problem. Assertiveness is just as important in school, at work, and in adult relationships.

In Zuñi culture, emotions are much less public. We are a private people, who consider a public display of feelings embarrassing. Self-control is considered a virtue. I think a lot of our emotional reticence comes from a respect for privacy. Your feelings are your own, and showing them to others is just as wrong as taking off your clothes in public. It's not that traditional Zuñis have fewer or less intense feelings than people in the city: It's just that

there is less value placed on showing them in obvious ways.

The way we express affection is a good example of Zuñi attitudes and rules for sharing emotions. Our families are full of love—at least as much as families in mainstream American culture. But someone from the city might not recognize this love, since it isn't displayed very much. There isn't a lot of hugging and kissing, even between children and parents. Also, there isn't a lot of verbal expression: People don't say "I love you" to one another very much. The feeling is there, but it's understood without being mentioned. We show our emotions by our actions: by helping one another, by caring for the people we love when they need us. That's enough to keep us happy.

I think that one source of the difference between Anglo and Zuñi communication styles comes from the way each culture treats time. In

---

be universal. People from all cultures also express these emotions in the same way, at least in their facial expressions. A smile or scowl, for example, is understood everywhere.

Of course, this doesn't mean that the same events generate an emotion in all cultures. The notion of eating snails might bring a smile of delight to some residents of France, whereas it would cause many North Americans to grimace in disgust. More to the point of this book, research has shown that fear of strangers and risky situations is more likely to frighten people living in the United States and Europe than those living in Japan, whereas Japanese are more apprehensive about relational communication than Americans and Europeans.[15]

There are also differences in the degree to which people in various cultures display their feelings. For example, social scientists have found support for the notion that people from warmer climates are more

the city, time is precious. There's never enough of it, so people try to do things as quickly as possible. This means that it's important to get your feelings across now. Waiting is uncomfortable, and "wastes" time. In traditional Zuñi culture, time is not such a scarce commodity. There's less of a hurry. This means that getting a message (like how you feel) expressed quickly isn't so important. There's plenty of time to figure out how someone feels, and if the matter is important enough, it will become clear sooner or later.

One way to summarize the difference between the two cultures has to do with talking and listening. Anglo culture places an emphasis on talking—on expressing yourself clearly and completely. Zuñis aren't such great talkers, but that helps make us better listeners. Because we don't speak so much, we have both the need and the

time to be better at paying attention to what other people say and what they do to show their emotions. This listening can be helpful in school, where we care less about competing for a teacher's recognition than in understanding what we are supposed to learn. It also makes us good, steady workers who learn our jobs, concentrate on our duties, and work extremely hard to perfect our efficiency. We may not get the recognition that comes from being good talkers, but in the long run I am confident that our restraint will be rewarded. As the saying goes, "what goes around comes around."

Which approach is best? I think both cultures have strengths. Many Zuñis and other Native Americans who want to join mainstream culture are at a disadvantage. They aren't very good at standing up for their rights, and so they get taken advantage of. Even at home,

there are probably times when it's important to express feelings to prevent misunderstandings. On the other hand, I think some Native American emotional restraint might be helpful for people who are used to Anglo communication styles. Respecting others' privacy can be important: Some feelings are nobody else's business, and prying or demanding that they open up seems pushy and rude. Native American self-control can also add some civility to personal relationships. I'm not sure that "letting it all hang out" is always the best way.

One final word: I believe that in order to really understand the differences between emotional expression in Native American and Anglo cultures you have to live in both. If that isn't possible, at least realize that the familiar one isn't the only good approach. Try to respect what you don't understand.

emotionally expressive than those who live in cooler climates.[16] Over twenty-nine hundred respondents representing twenty-six nationalities reported that people from the southern part of their countries were more emotionally expressive than were northerners.

One of the most significant factors that influences emotional expression is the position of a culture on the individualism-collectivism spectrum. Members of collectivistic cultures (such as Japan and India) prize harmony among members of their "in-group" and discourage expression of any negative emotions that might upset relationships among people who belong to it. By contrast, members of highly individualistic cultures like the United States and Canada feel comfortable revealing their emotions to people with whom they are close.[17] Individualists and collectivists also handle emotional expression with members of out-groups differently: Whereas collectivists are quite frank about expressing negative emotions toward outsiders, individualists are more likely to hide such emotions as dislike.[18] It's easy to see how differences in display rules can lead to communication problems. For example, individualistic North Americans might view collectivistic Asians as less than candid, whereas Asians could easily regard North Americans as overly demonstrative.

Cultural background influences the way we interpret others' emotions as well as the way we express our own. In one experiment, an ethnically varied group of students—Caucasian, black, Asian, and Hispanic—identified the type, intensity, and appropriateness of emotional expression in fifty-six photos representing eight social situations (e.g., alone, with a friend, in public, with someone of higher status).[19] Results indicated that ethnicity led to considerable differences in the way the subjects gauged others' emotional states. For example, blacks perceived the emotions in the photos as more intense than the Caucasian, Asian, and Hispanic subjects; Asians perceived them the least intense. Also, blacks reported a greater frequency of anger expressions than did the other groups. Ethnicity also shaped ideas about appropriate rules for expressing one's own emotions. For example, Caucasians perceived the display of the several emotions as more appropriate than did the other groups; Asians perceived the display as least appropriate. These findings remind us that, in a multicultural society, one element of communicative competence is the ability to understand our own cultural filters when judging others' behaviors.

Gender

Even within our culture, the ways in which men and women have expressed their emotions vary in some significant areas.[20] Research on emotional expression suggests that there is at least some truth in the cultural stereotype of the unexpressive male and the more expressive female. As a group, women are more likely than men to express both positive emotions (love, liking, joy, and contentment) and feelings of vulnerability (including fear, sadness, loneliness, and embarrassment). Men rarely express these emotions, especially to their male friends, although they may open up to the woman they love. On the other hand, men are less bashful about revealing their strengths.[21] On the Internet, the same differences between male and female emotional expressiveness apply. For example, women were more likely than men to use emoticons (such as the symbol :)) to express their feelings than were men.[22]

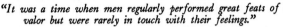

"It was a time when men regularly performed great feats of valor but were rarely in touch with their feelings."

©The New Yorker Collection 1991 Jack Ziegler from cartoonbank.com. All Rights Reserved.

The sexes also differ in their sensitivity to others' emotions. Psychologist Robert Rosenthal and his colleagues developed the Profile of Nonverbal Sensitivity (PONS) test to measure the ability to recognize emotions that are expressed in the facial expressions, movements, and vocal cues of others. Women consistently score slightly higher on this test than men.[23] In fact, gender is the best predictor of the ability to detect and interpret emotional expressions—better than academic background, amount of foreign travel, cultural similarity, or ethnicity.[24]

One's own gender isn't the only factor that affects emotional sensitivity. A second factor is whether the other person is of the same or different sex. For example, men are more likely to express feelings (especially positive ones) with women than with other men.[25] Of course, these gender differences are statistical averages, and many men and women don't fit these profiles. Familiarity with the other person also leads to greater sensitivity. For example, dating and married couples are significantly better at recognizing each other's emotional cues than are strangers.

A final factor is the difference in power between the two parties. People who are less powerful learn—probably from necessity—to read the more powerful person's signals. One experiment revealed that "women's intuition" should be relabeled "subordinate's intuition." In opposite-sex twosomes, the person with less control—regardless of sex—was better at interpreting the leader's nonverbal signals than vice versa.[26]

Social Conventions

In mainstream U.S. society the unwritten rules of communication discourage the direct expression of most emotions.[27] Count the number of genuine emotional expressions that you hear over a two- or three-day period and you'll discover that emotional expressions are rare. People are generally comfortable making statements of fact and often delight in expressing their opinions, but they rarely disclose how they feel.

Not surprisingly, the emotions that people *do* share directly are usually positive. Communicators are reluctant to send messages that embarrass or threaten the "face" of others.[28] Historians offer a detailed description of the ways by which contemporary society discourages expressions of anger.[29] When compared to past centuries, Americans today strive to suppress this "unpleasant" emotion in almost every context, including child-raising, the workplace, and personal relationships. Research supports this analysis. One study of married couples revealed that the partners shared complimentary feelings ("I love you") or face-saving ones ("I'm sorry I yelled at you"). They also willingly disclosed both positive and negative feelings about absent third parties ("I like Fred," "I'm uncomfortable around Gloria"). On the other hand, the husbands and wives rarely verbalized face-threatening feelings ("I'm disappointed in you") or hostility ("I'm mad at you").[30]

Social rules even discourage too much expression of positive feelings.[31] A hug and a kiss for Mother are all right, though a young man should shake hands with Dad. Affection toward friends becomes less and less frequent as we grow older, so that even a simple statement such as "I like you" is seldom heard between adults. Just because we don't express our feelings toward others verbally doesn't mean that we don't communicate them at all. As chapter 6 explains in detail, a tremendous amount of the information carried via nonverbal communication involves relational messages, including our feelings of affinity (or lack of it) toward others.

Fear of Self-Disclosure

In a society that discourages the expression of emotions, revealing them can seem risky.[34] For a parent, boss, or teacher whose life has been built on the image of confidence and certainty, it may be frightening to say, "I'm sorry. I was wrong." A person who has made a life's work out of not relying on others has a hard time saying, "I'm lonesome. I want your friendship."

Moreover, someone who musters up the courage to share feelings such as these still risks unpleasant consequences. Others might misunderstand: An expression of affection might be construed as a romantic invitation, and a confession of uncertainty might be construed as a sign of weakness. Another risk is that emotional honesty might make others feel uncomfortable. Finally, there's always a risk that emotional honesty could be used against you, either out of cruelty or thoughtlessness. Chapter 8 discusses alternatives to complete disclosure and suggests circumstances when it can be both wise and ethical to keep your feelings to yourself.

Social Roles

Expression of emotions is also shaped by the requirements of many social roles. Salespeople are taught always to smile at customers, no

An emotion without social rules of containment and expression is like an egg without a shell: a gooey mess.

Carol Tavris

matter how obnoxious. Teachers and managers are expected to behave rationally and keep their emotions under control. Students are rewarded for asking "acceptable" questions and otherwise being submissive creatures.

Emotional Contagion

Cultural rules and social roles aren't the only factors that affect our feelings. Our emotions are also affected by the feelings of those around us through **emotional contagion:** the process by which emotions are transferred from one person to another.

Most of us recognize the degree to which emotions are "infectious." You can almost certainly recall instances when being around a calm person leaves you feeling more at peace, or when your previously sunny mood was spoiled by contact with a grouch. Researchers have demonstrated that this process occurs quickly and with very little apparent communication.[32] In one study, two volunteers completed a survey that identified their moods. Then they sat quietly, facing each other for a two-minute period, ostensibly waiting for the researcher to return to the room. At the end of that time, they completed another emotional survey. Time after time, the brief exposure resulted in the less expressive partner's moods coming to resemble the moods of the more expressive one. If an expressive communicator can shape another person's emotions with so little input in such a short time, it's easy to understand how emotions can be even more "infectious" with more prolonged contact. As one commentator observed, "We catch feelings from one another as though they were some kind of social virus."[33]

"Im not in one of my moods. I'm in one of your moods."

© The New Yorker Collection 1995 Victoria Roberts from cartoonbank.com. All Rights Reserved.

GUIDELINES FOR EXPRESSING EMOTIONS

A wide range of research supports the value of expressing emotions appropriately. At the most basic physiological level, people who know how to express their emotions are healthier than those who don't. On one hand, underexpression of feelings can lead to serious ailments. Inexpressive people—those who value rationality and self-control, try to control their feelings and impulses, and deny distress—are more likely to get a host of ailments, including cancer, asthma, and heart disease.[35] On the other hand, *overly* expressive people also suffer physiologically. When people lash out verbally, their blood pressure jumps an average of twenty points, and in some people it increases by as much as one hundred points.[36] The key to health, then, is to learn how to express emotions *constructively*.

Beyond the physiological benefits, another benefit of expressing emotions effectively is the chance of improving relationships.[37] As chapter 10 explains, self-disclosure is one path (though not the only one) to intimacy. Even on the job, many managers and organizational researchers are contradicting generations of tradition by suggesting that

The Unexpressed

The unexpressed,
    the unarticulated
    are frightening,
    when as fragments
    they burn
    beneath the skin,
    with no way at all
    to be scratched out,
    plucked out,
    or brought to reason.

Events
    bricked up inside
    cry out in despair:

"We've been forgotten.

We'll be eliminated
    from history:

Let us out!

Let us out!

Suffering rises up
    like a lump in the throat:

We are like stifled sobs.

We long so for our liberation:
    express us!
    express us!"

Yevgeny Yevtushenko

constructively expressing emotions can lead to career success as well as help workers feel better.[38]

Despite its benefits, expressing emotions effectively isn't a simple matter. It's obvious that showing every feeling of boredom, fear, anger, or frustration would get you into trouble. Even the indiscriminate sharing of positive feelings—love, affection, and so on—isn't always wise. On the other hand, withholding emotions can be personally frustrating and can keep relationships from growing and prospering.

The following suggestions can help you decide when and how to express your emotions. Combined with the guidelines for self-disclosure in chapter 9, they can improve the effectiveness of your emotional expression.

Recognize Your Feelings

Answering the question "How do you feel?" isn't as easy for some people as others. Some people (researchers call them "affectively oriented") are much more aware of their own emotional states and use information about those emotional states when making important decisions.[39] By contrast, people with a low affective orientation usually aren't aware of their emotional states and tend to reject feelings as useful, important information. Being in touch with one's feelings has plenty of advantages: positive relationships between parents and children, the ability to comfort others, sensitivity to nonverbal cues, and even skillful use of humor. In other words, being in touch with one's feelings is an important ingredient in communication skill.

As you read earlier in this chapter, feelings become recognizable in a number of ways. Physiological changes can be a clear sign of your feelings. Monitoring nonverbal behaviors is another excellent way to keep in touch with your feelings. You can also recognize your feelings by monitoring your thoughts as well as the verbal messages that you send to others. It's not far from the verbal statement "I hate this!" to the realization that you're angry (or bored, nervous, or embarrassed).

Think about How to Describe Feelings

Most people suffer from impoverished emotional vocabularies. Ask them how they're feeling, and the response will almost always include the same terms: *good* or *bad*, *terrible* or *great*, and so on. Take a moment now to see how many feelings you can write down. After you've done your best, look at Table 4-1 and see which ones you've missed.

Many communicators think they are expressing feelings when, in fact, their statements are emotionally counterfeit. For example, it sounds emotionally

EMOTIONAL ROLLER COASTER

© 2001 Leo Cullum from cartoonbank.com. All Rights Reserved.

revealing to say, "I feel like going to a show" or "I feel we've been seeing too much of each other." But in fact, neither of these statements has any emotional content. In the first sentence the word *feel* really stands for an intention: "I *want* to go to a show." In the second sentence the "feeling" is really a thought: "I *think* we've been seeing too much of each other." You can recognize the absence of emotion in each case by adding a genuine word of feeling to it. For instance, "I'm *bored*, and I want to go to a show" or "I think we've been seeing too much of each other, and I feel *confined.*"

Relying on a small vocabulary to describe feelings is as limiting as relying on a small vocabulary to describe colors. To say that the ocean in all its moods, the sky as it varies from day to day, and the color of your true love's eyes are all "blue" tells only a fraction of the story. Likewise, it's overly broad to use a term like *good* or *great* to describe how you feel in situations as different as earning a high grade, finishing a marathon, and hearing the words "I love you" from a special person.

There are several ways to express a feeling verbally:

■ By using *single words:* "I'm angry" (or "excited," "depressed," "curious," and so on)

■ By describing *what's happening to you:* "My stomach is tied in knots," "I'm on top of the world"

TABLE 4-1 Some Feelings

afraid	concerned	exhausted	hurried	nervous	sexy
aggravated	confident	fearful	hurt	numb	shaky
amazed	confused	fed up	hysterical	optimistic	shocked
ambivalent	content	fidgety	impatient	paranoid	shy
angry	crazy	flattered	impressed	passionate	sorry
annoyed	defeated	foolish	inhibited	peaceful	strong
anxious	defensive	forlorn	insecure	pessimistic	subdued
apathetic	delighted	free	interested	playful	surprised
ashamed	depressed	friendly	intimidated	pleased	suspicious
bashful	detached	frustrated	irritable	possessive	tender
bewildered	devastated	furious	jealous	pressured	tense
bitchy	disappointed	glad	joyful	protective	terrified
bitter	disgusted	glum	lazy	puzzled	tired
bored	disturbed	grateful	lonely	refreshed	trapped
brave	ecstatic	happy	loving	regretful	ugly
calm	edgy	harassed	lukewarm	relieved	uneasy
cantankerous	elated	helpless	mad	resentful	vulnerable
carefree	embarrassed	high	mean	restless	warm
cheerful	empty	hopeful	miserable	ridiculous	weak
cocky	enthusiastic	horrible	mixed up	romantic	wonderful
cold	envious	hostile	mortified	sad	worried
comfortable	excited	humiliated	neglected	sentimental	

- By describing *what you'd like to do:* "I want to run away," "I'd like to give you a hug," "I feel like giving up"

Sometimes communicators inaccurately minimize the strength of their feelings—"I'm a *little* unhappy" or "I'm *pretty* excited" or "I'm *sort of* confused." Of course, not all feelings are strong ones. We do feel degrees of sadness and joy, for example, but some people have a tendency to discount almost every feeling. Do you?

In other cases, communicators express feelings in a coded manner. This happens most often when the sender is uncomfortable about revealing the feeling in question. Some codes are verbal ones, as when the sender hints more or less subtly at the message. For example, an indirect way to say, "I'm lonesome" might be "I guess there isn't much happening this weekend, so if you're not busy, why don't you drop by." Such a message is so indirect that your real feeling may not be recognized. For this reason, people who send coded messages stand less of a chance of having their feelings understood—and their needs met.

If you do decide to express your feeling, you can be most clear by making sure that both you and your partner understand that your feeling is centered on a specific set of circumstances rather than being indicative of the whole relationship. Instead of saying, "I resent you," say, "I resent you when you don't keep your promises." Rather than saying, "I'm bored with you," say, "I'm bored when you talk about your money."

Share Multiple Feelings

Many times the feeling you express isn't the only one you're experiencing. For example, you might often express your anger but overlook the confusion, disappointment, frustration, sadness, or embarrassment that preceded it. In the following examples, notice how sharing multiple feelings increases the accuracy—and the value of the message:

- "I'm mad at you for not showing up. *I'm also disappointed because I was looking forward to seeing you.*"
- "I get mad when you flirt at parties. *I care about you a lot, and I'd hate to think you don't feel the same way about me.*"

■ "I get really angry when you tease me in front of our friends. *It's embarrassing to have you point out my flaws, even though I know you don't mean any harm.*"

Recognize the Difference between Feeling, Talking, and Acting

Just because you feel a certain way doesn't mean you must always talk about it, and talking about a feeling doesn't mean you must act on it. In fact, there is compelling evidence that people who act out angry feelings—even by hitting an inanimate punching bag—actually feel worse than those who experience anger without lashing out.[40]

Understanding the difference between having feelings and acting them out can help you express yourself constructively in tough situations. If, for instance, you recognize that you are upset with a friend, it becomes possible to explore exactly why you feel so upset. Sharing your feeling ("Sometimes I get so mad at you that I could punch you in the nose") might open the door to resolving whatever is bothering you. Pretending that nothing is bothering you, or lashing out at the other person, is unlikely to diminish your resentful feelings, which can then go on to contaminate the relationship.

Accept Responsibility for Your Feelings

It's important to make sure that your language reflects the fact that you're responsible for your feelings. Instead of saying, "You're making me angry," say, "I'm getting angry." Instead of saying, "You hurt my feelings," say, "I feel hurt when you do that." As you'll soon read, people don't make us like or dislike them, and believing that they do denies the responsibility that each of us has for our own emotions. Chapter 5 introduces "I" language, which offers a responsible way to express your own feelings.

Consider When and Where to Express Your Feelings

Often the first flush of a strong feeling is not the best time to speak out. If you're awakened by the racket caused by a noisy neighbor, storming over to complain might result in your saying things you'll regret later. In such a case, it's probably wiser to wait until you have thought out carefully how you might express your feelings in a way that would be most likely to be heard.

Even after you've waited for the first flush of strong feeling to subside, it's still important to choose the time that's best suited to the message. Being rushed or tired or disturbed by some other matter is probably a good reason for postponing the expression of your feeling. Often, dealing with your emotions can take a great amount of time and effort, and fatigue or distraction will make it difficult to follow through on the matter you've started. In the same manner you ought to be sure that the recipient of your message is ready to hear you out before you begin.

I can't choose how I feel, but I can choose what I do about it.

Andy Rooney

Anyone can become angry. That is easy. But to be angry with the right person to the right degree, at the right time for the right purpose, and in the right way: This is not easy.

Aristotle

ETHICAL CHALLENGE

Aristotle's Golden Mean

Almost two and a half millennia ago, the philosopher Aristotle addressed issues that are just as important today as they were in classical Greece. In his *Nicomachean Ethics,* Aristotle examines the question of "moral virtue": What constitutes good behavior, and what ways of acting enable us to function effectively in the world? One important part of his examination addresses the management and expression of emotion: what he defines as "passions and actions."

According to Aristotle, an important dimension of virtuous behavior is moderation, which he defines as "an intermediate between excess and deficit . . . equidistant from the extremes . . . neither too much nor too little." Aristotle introduces the concept of virtue through moderation with a mathematical analogy: If ten is many and two is few, then six is the intermediate. Applying this line of reasoning to emotional expression would reveal that, for example, the preferred form of expressing affection would fall equally between the extremes of being completely unexpressive and passionately animated.

Aristotle points out that a formulaic approach to calculating the "golden mean" doesn't work in human affairs by illustrating the flaws in his mathematical analogy: "If ten pounds are too much for a particular person to eat and two too little, it does not follow that the trainer will order six pounds, for this also is perhaps too much for the person who is to take it." In other words, Aristotle recognizes that people have different personalities; and he acknowledges that it isn't realistic or desirable for a passionate person to strive for the same type of behavior as a dispassionate person. After all, a world in which everyone felt and acted identically would be boring.

Instead of a "one approach fits all" approach to emotional expression, Aristotle urges communicators to moderate their own style, to be "intermediate not in the object, but relative to us." Following Aristotle's injunction, a person with a hot temper would strive to cool down, whereas a person who rarely expresses his or her feelings ought to aim at becoming more expressive. The result would still be two people with different styles, but each of whom behaved better than before seeking the golden mean.

According to Aristotle, moderation also means that emotions should be suited to the occasion: We should feel (and express) them "at the right times, with reference to the right objects, towards the right people, with the right motive, and in the right way." We can imagine times when even a normally restrained person could reasonably act with anger and times when a normally voluble person could reasonably behave with restraint. Even then, too much emotion (rage, for example) or too little emotion falls outside the range of virtue. In Aristotle's words, when it comes to "passions and actions . . . excess is a form of failure and so is deficit."

Aristotle acknowledges that living a life of moderation is a challenge: "It is no easy task to find the middle. . . . Anyone can get angry: That is easy . . . but to do this to the right person, to the right extent, at the right time, with the right motive, and in the right way: That is not for everyone, nor is it easy." He warns us to especially guard against those extreme emotions that come most naturally. "We must drag ourselves away to the contrary extreme; for we shall get into the intermediate state by drawing well away from error."

How would your emotional expression be different if you strived for moderation? Answer this question by identifying which parts of your emotional expression are most extreme, either in their intensity or their absence. How might your relationships change if you acted more moderately? Are there any situations in your life when more extreme forms of emotional expression are both moral and effective?

To read Aristotle's full discussion of the golden mean, see Book Two of his *Nicomachean Ethics,* translated by H. Rachman and published by Harvard University Press in 1934.

FEELINGS AND PHRASES

You can try this exercise alone or with a group.

1. Choose a situation from column A and a receiver from column B.

2. Develop an approach for communicating your feelings for this combination.

3. Now create approaches for the same situation with other receivers from column B. How are the statements different?

4. Repeat the process with various combinations, using other situations from column A.

<u>Column A: Situations</u>

a. You have been stood up for a date or appointment.

b. The other person pokes fun at your schoolwork.

c. The other person compliments you on your appearance, then says, "I hope I haven't embarrassed you."

d. The other person gives you a hug and says, "It's good to see you."

<u>Column B: Receivers</u>

An instructor

A family member
(You decide which one.)

A classmate you don't know well.

Your best friend

MANAGING DIFFICULT EMOTIONS

Although feeling and expressing many emotions add to the quality of interpersonal relationships, not all feelings are beneficial. For instance, rage, depression, terror, and jealousy do little to help you feel better or improve your relationships. The following pages will give you tools to minimize these unproductive emotions.

Facilitative and Debilitative Emotions

We need to make a distinction between **facilitative emotions,** which contribute to effective functioning, and **debilitative emotions,** which detract from effective functioning.

One difference between the two types is their *intensity.* For instance, a certain amount of anger or irritation can be constructive because it often provides the stimulus that leads you to improve the unsatisfying conditions. Rage, on the other hand, will usually make matters worse. The same holds true for fear. A little bit of fear before an important athletic contest or job interview might give you the boost that will improve your performance. (Mellow athletes or employees usually don't do well.) But total terror is something else. Even a little suspicion can make people more effective communicators. One study revealed that mates who doubted that their relational partners were telling the truth were better at detecting deception than were trusting mates.[41] Of course, an extreme case of paranoia would have the opposite and debilitative effect, reducing the ability to interpret the partner's behavior accurately.

Not surprisingly, debilitative emotions like communication apprehension can lead to a variety of problems in personal, business, educational, and even medical settings.[42] When people become anxious, they generally speak less, which means that their needs aren't met; and when they do manage to speak up, they are less effective than their more confident counterparts.[43]

A second characteristic that distinguishes debilitative feelings from facilitative ones is their extended *duration*. Feeling depressed for a while after the breakup of a relationship or the loss of a job is natural. But spending the rest of your life grieving over your loss would accomplish nothing. In the same way, staying angry at someone for a wrong inflicted long ago can be just as punishing to you as to the wrongdoer.

Many debilitative emotions involve communication. Here are a few examples, offered by readers of *Looking Out/Looking In:*

> When I first came to college, I had to leave my boyfriend. I was living with three girls, and for most of the first semester I was so lonesome and unhappy that I was a pretty terrible roommate.

> I got so frustrated with my overly critical boss over several months that I lost my temper and quit one day. I told him what a horrible manager he was and walked off the job right then and there. Now I'm afraid to list my former boss as a reference, and I'm afraid my temper tantrum will make it harder for me to get a new job.

> I've had ongoing problems with my family, and sometimes I get so upset that I can't concentrate on my work or school, or even sleep well at night.

In the following pages you will learn a method for dealing with debilitative feelings like these that can improve your effectiveness as a communicator. This method is based on the idea that one way to minimize debilitative feelings is to minimize unproductive thinking.

Thoughts Cause Feelings

For most people, feelings seem to have a life of their own. You wish you could feel calm when approaching strangers, yet your voice quivers. You try to appear confident when asking for a raise, yet your eye twitches nervously.

Reprinted with special permission of King Feature Syndicate.

At times like these it's common to say that strangers or your boss *make* you feel nervous just as you would say that a bee sting makes you feel pain. The apparent similarities between physical and emotional discomforts become clear if you look at them in the following way:

Event	Feeling
Bee sting	physical pain
Meeting strangers	nervous feelings

When looking at your emotions in this way, you seem to have little control over how you feel. However, this apparent similarity between physical pain and emotional discomfort (or pleasure) isn't as great as it seems to be. Cognitive psychologists argue that it is not *events* such as meeting strangers or being jilted by a lover that cause people to feel bad, but rather the *beliefs they hold* about these events.

Albert Ellis, who developed the cognitive approach called *rational-emotive therapy,* tells a story that makes this point clear. Imagine yourself walking by a friend's house and seeing your friend stick his head out of a window and call you a string of vile names. (You supply the friend and the names.) Under these circumstances it's likely that you would feel hurt and upset. Now imagine that instead of walking by the house you were passing a mental institution when the same friend, who was obviously a patient there, shouted the same vile names at you. In this case, your feelings would probably be quite different—most likely sadness and pity. You can see that in this story the activating event of being called names was the same in both cases, yet the emotional consequences were very different. The reason for your different feelings has to do with your thinking in each case. In the first case, you would most likely think that your friend was very angry with you; further, you might imagine that you must have done something terrible to deserve such a response. In the second case, you would probably assume that your friend had some psychological difficulty, and most likely you would feel sympathetic.

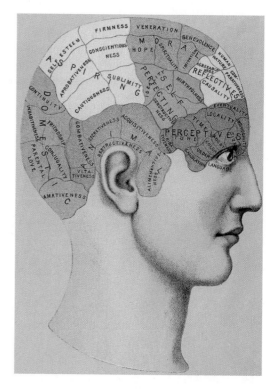

From this example you can start to see that it's the *interpretations* that people make of an event, during the process of self-talk, that determine their feelings.[44]* Thus, the model for emotions looks like this:

Event	Thought	Feeling
Being called names	"I've done something wrong."	hurt, upset
Being called names	"My friend must be sick."	concern, sympathy

The same principle applies in more common situations. In job interviews, for example, people who become nervous are likely to use negative self-talk when they think about their performance: "I won't do well," "I don't know why I'm doing this."[45] In romantic relationships, thoughts shape satisfaction. The words "I love you" can be interpreted in a variety of ways. They could be taken at face value as a genuine expression of deep affection:

Event	Thought	Feeling
Hearing "I love you"	"This is a genuine statement."	delight (perhaps)

The same words might be decoded as a sincere but mistaken declaration uttered in a moment of passion, an attempt to make the recipient feel better, or an attempt at manipulation. For example,

Hearing "I love you"	"S/he's just saying this to manipulate me."	anger

One study revealed that women are more likely than men to regard expressions of love as genuine statements rather than attribute them to some other cause.[46] Other research shows the importance of self-talk in relationships. Members of couples who are unhappy with one another have more negative self-talk about their partner and fewer positive thoughts about their partner and the relationship.[47]

There is nothing good or bad but thinking makes it so.

William Shakespeare, *Hamlet*

INVITATION TO INSIGHT

TALKING TO YOURSELF

You can become better at understanding how your thoughts shape your feelings by completing the following steps.

1. Take a few minutes to listen to the inner voice you use when thinking. Close your eyes now and listen to it. . . . Did you hear the voice? Perhaps it was saying, "What voice? I don't have any voice. . . ." Try again, and pay attention to what the voice is saying.

2. Now think about the following situations, and imagine how you would react in each. How would you interpret them with your inner voice? What feelings would follow from each interpretation?
   a. While sitting on a bus, in class, or on the street, you notice an attractive person sneaking glances at you.
   b. During a lecture your professor asks the class, "What do you think about this?" and looks toward you.
   c. You are telling friends about your vacation, and one yawns.
   d. You run into a friend on the street and ask how things are going. "Fine," she replies and rushes off.

3. Now recall three recent times when you felt a strong emotion. For each one, recall the activating event and then the interpretation that led to your emotional reaction.

The mind is its own place, and in itself can make a Heav'n of Hell, a Hell of Heav'n.

John Milton, *Paradise Lost*

Irrational Thinking and Debilitative Emotions

Focusing on the self-talk that we use to think is the key to understanding debilitative emotions. Many debilitative emotions come from accepting a number of irrational thoughts—we'll call them *fallacies* here—which lead to illogical conclusions and in turn to debilitative emotions. We usually aren't aware of these thoughts, which makes them especially powerful.[48]

1. **The Fallacy of Perfection** People who accept the fallacy of perfection believe that a worthwhile communicator should be able to handle every situation with complete confidence and skill.

   After you accept the belief that it's desirable and possible to be a perfect communicator, the next step is to assume that people won't appreciate you if you are imperfect. Admitting your mistakes, saying, "I don't know," and sharing feelings of uncertainty seem like social defects when viewed in this manner. Given the desire to be valued and appreciated, it's tempting to try to *appear* perfect, but the costs of such deception are high. If others ever find you out, they'll see you as a phony. Even when your act isn't uncovered, such an act uses up a great deal of psychological energy and thus makes the rewards of approval less enjoyable.

   Subscribing to the myth of perfection not only can keep others from liking you, but also can act as a force to diminish your own self-esteem. How can you like yourself when you don't measure up to the way you ought to be? How liberated you become when you can comfortably accept the idea that you are not perfect! That,

   Like everyone else, you sometimes have a hard time expressing yourself.

   Like everyone else, you make mistakes from time to time, and there is no reason to hide this.

   You are honestly doing the best you can to realize your potential, to become the best person you can be.

2. **The Fallacy of Approval** The fallacy of approval is based on the idea that it is not only desirable but also *vital* to get the approval of virtually every person. People who accept this idea go to incredible lengths to seek approval from others even when they have to sacrifice their own principles and happiness to do so. Accepting this fallacy can lead to some ludicrous situations:

   Feeling nervous because people you really don't like seem to disapprove of you

   Feeling apologetic when others are at fault

   Feeling embarrassed after behaving unnaturally to gain another's approval

   In addition to causing the obvious discomfort that arises from denying your own principles and needs, the fallacy of approval is irrational because it implies that others will respect and like you more if you go out of your way to please them. Often this simply isn't true.

I never was what you would call a fancy skater—and while I seldom actually fell, it might have been more impressive if I had. A good resounding fall is no disgrace. It is the fantastic writhing to avoid a fall which destroys any illusion of being a gentleman. How like life that is, after all!

Robert Benchley

How is it possible to respect people who have compromised important values just to gain acceptance? How is it possible to think highly of people who repeatedly deny their own needs as a means of buying approval? Though others may find it tempting to use these individuals to suit their ends or amusing to be around them, these individuals hardly deserve genuine affection and respect.

Striving for universal approval is irrational because it's simply not possible. Sooner or later a conflict of expectations is bound to occur; one person will approve if you behave only in a certain way, but another will accept only the opposite behavior. What are you to do then?

Don't misunderstand: Abandoning the fallacy of approval doesn't mean living a life of selfishness. It's still important to consider the needs of others and to meet them whenever possible. It's also pleasant—we might say even necessary—to strive for the respect of those people you value. The point here is that when you must abandon your own needs and principles in order to seek these goals, the price is too high.

3. **The Fallacy of Shoulds** The fallacy of shoulds is the inability to distinguish between what *is* and what *should be*. You can see the difference by imagining a person who is full of complaints about the world:

"There should be no rain on weekends."

"People ought to live forever."

"Money should grow on trees."

"We should all be able to fly."

Complaints like these are obviously foolish. However pleasant wishing may be, insisting that the unchangeable should be changed won't affect reality one bit. And yet many people torture themselves by engaging in this sort of irrational thinking when they confuse *is* with *should*. They say and think things like this:

"My friend should be more understanding."

"She shouldn't be so inconsiderate."

"They should be more friendly."

"You should work harder."

The message in each of these cases is that you would *prefer* people to behave differently. Wishing that things were better is perfectly legitimate, and trying to change them is, of course, a good idea; but it's unreasonable to *insist* that the world operate just as you want it to or to feel cheated when things aren't ideal.

Imposing the fallacy of shoulds on yourself can also lead to unnecessary happiness. Psychologist Aaron Beck points out some unrealistic self-imposed "shoulds":[49]

"I should be able to find a quick solution to every problem."

"I should never feel hurt; I should always be happy and serene."

"I should always demonstrate the utmost generosity, considerateness, dignity, courage, unselfishness."

A man said to the universe:

"Sir, I exist!"

"However," replied the universe,

"The fact has not created in me

A sense of obligation."

Stephen Crane

Becoming obsessed with "shoulds" like these has three trouble-some consequences. First, it leads to unnecessary unhappiness because people who are constantly dreaming about the ideal are seldom satisfied with what they have or who they are. Second, merely complaining without acting can keep you from doing anything to change unsatisfying conditions. Third, this sort of complaining can build a defensive climate with others, who will resent being nagged. It's much more effective to tell people about what you'd like than to preach: Say, "I wish you'd be more punctual" instead of "You should be on time." We'll discuss ways of avoiding defensive climates in chapter 9.

4. **The Fallacy of Overgeneralization** The fallacy of overgeneralization comprises two types. The first occurs when we base a belief on a *limited amount of evidence.* For instance, how many times have you found yourself saying something like this:

"I'm so stupid! I can't even understand how to do my income tax."

"Some friend I am! I forgot my best friend's birthday."

In cases like these, we focus on a limited type of shortcoming as if it represented everything about us. We forget that along with encountering our difficulties we have solved tough problems and that though we're sometimes forgetful, at other times we're caring and thoughtful.

A second type of overgeneralization occurs when we *exaggerate* shortcomings:

"You *never* listen to me."

"You're *always* late."

"I can't think of *anything.*"

On closer examination, absolute statements like these are almost always false and usually lead to discouragement or anger. You'll feel far better when you replace overgeneralizations with more accurate messages to yourself and others:

"You often don't listen to me."

"You've been late three times this week."

"I haven't had any ideas I like today."

Many overgeneralizations are based on abuse of the verb *to be.* For example, unqualified thoughts such as "He *is* an idiot [all the time?]" and "I *am* a failure [in everything?]" will make you see yourself and others in an unrealistically negative way, thus contributing to debilitative emotions.

5. **The Fallacy of Causation** The fallacy of causation is based on the irrational belief that emotions are caused by others rather than by one's own self-talk.

This fallacy causes trouble in two ways. The first plagues people who become overly cautious about communicating because they don't want to "cause" any pain or inconvenience for others. This attitude occurs in cases such as:

Visiting friends or family out of a sense of obligation rather than a genuine desire to see them

Keeping quiet when another person's behavior is bothering you

Pretending to be attentive to a speaker when you are already late for an appointment or feeling ill

Praising and reassuring others who ask for your opinion even when your honest response would be negative

There's certainly no excuse for going out of your way to say things that will result in pain for others, and there will be times when you choose to inconvenience yourself to make life easier for those you care about. It's essential to realize, however, that it's an overstatement to say that you are the one who causes others' feelings. It's more accurate to say that they *respond* to your behavior with feelings of their own. For example, consider how strange it sounds to suggest that you make others fall in love with you. Such a statement simply doesn't make sense. It would be closer to the truth to say that you act in one way or another, and some people might fall in love with you as a result of these actions, whereas others wouldn't. In the same way, it's incorrect to say that you *make* others angry, upset—or happy, for that matter. It's better to say that others create their own responses to your behavior.

Restricting your communication because of the fallacy of causation can result in three types of damaging consequences. First, as a result of your caution you often will fail to have your own needs met. There's little likelihood that others will change their behavior unless they know that it's affecting you in a negative way. A second consequence is that you're likely to begin resenting the person whose behavior you find bothersome. Obviously, this reaction is illogical because you have never made your feelings known, but logic doesn't change the fact that burying your problem usually leads to a buildup of hostility.

Even when withholding feelings is based on the best intentions, it often damages relationships in a third way—after others find out about your deceptive nature, they will find it difficult ever to know when you are really upset with them. Even your most fervent assurances that everything is fine sound suspicious because there's always the chance that you may be covering up resentments that you're unwilling to express. Thus, in many respects taking responsibility for others' feelings is not only irrational but also counterproductive.

The fallacy of causation also operates when we believe that others cause *our* emotions. Sometimes it certainly seems as if they do, either raising or lowering our spirits by their actions. But think about it for a moment: The same actions that will cause you happiness or unhappiness one day have little effect at other times. The insult or compliment that affected your mood strongly yesterday leaves you unaffected today. Why? Because in the latter case you attached less importance to either.

You certainly wouldn't feel some emotions without others' behavior; but it's your thinking, not their actions, that determines how you feel.

37

EL MUNDO

6. **The Fallacy of Helplessness** The fallacy of helplessness suggests that satisfaction in life is determined by forces beyond your control. People who continuously see themselves as victims make such statements as:

"There's no way a woman can get ahead in this society. It's a man's world, and the best thing I can do is to accept it."

"I was born with a shy personality. I'd like to be more outgoing, but there's nothing I can do about that."

"I can't tell my boss that she is putting too many demands on me. If I did, I might lose my job."

The mistake in statements like these becomes apparent after you realize that there are many things you can do if you really want to. As you read in chapter 2, most "can't" statements can be more correctly rephrased either as "won't" ("I can't tell him what I think" becomes "I won't be honest with him") or as "don't know how" ("I can't carry on an interesting conversation" becomes "I don't know what to say"). After you've rephrased these inaccurate "can'ts," it becomes clear that they're either a matter of choice or an area that calls for your action—both quite different from saying that you're helpless.

When viewed in this light, it's apparent that many "can'ts" are really rationalizations to justify not wanting to change. Lonely people, for example, tend to attribute their poor interpersonal relationships to uncontrollable causes. "It's beyond my control," they think. Also, they expect their relational partners to reject them. Notice the self-fulfilling prophecy in this attitude: Believing that your relational prospects are dim can lead you to act in ways that make you an unattractive prospect. After you persuade yourself that there's no hope, it's easy to give up trying. On the other hand, acknowledging that there is a way to change—even though it may be difficult—puts the responsibility for your predicament on your shoulders. You *can* become a better communicator—this book is one step in your movement toward that goal. Don't give up or sell yourself short!

7. **The Fallacy of Catastrophic Expectations** Fearful communicators who subscribe to the irrational fallacy of catastrophic expectations operate on the assumption that if something bad can possibly happen, it will. Typical catastrophic expectations include:

"If I invite them to the party, they probably won't want to come."

"If I speak up in order to try to resolve a conflict, things will probably get worse."

"If I apply for the job I want, I probably won't be hired."

"If I tell them how I really feel, they'll probably laugh at me."

After you start expecting catastrophic consequences, a self-fulfilling prophecy can begin to build. One study revealed that people who believed that their romantic partners would not change for the better were likely to behave in ways that contributed to the breakup of the relationship.[50]

Although it's naive to assume that all your interactions with others will meet with success, it's just as naive to assume that you'll fail. One way to escape from the fallacy of catastrophic expectations is to think about the consequences that would follow even if you don't communicate successfully. Keeping in mind the folly of trying to be perfect and of living only for the approval of others, realize that failing in a given instance usually isn't as bad as it might seem. What if people do laugh at you? Suppose you don't get the job? What if others do get angry at your remarks? Are these matters really *that* serious?

Before moving on, we need to add a few thoughts about thinking and feeling. First, you should realize that thinking rationally won't completely eliminate debilitative emotions. Some debilitative emotions, after all, are very rational: grief over the death of someone you love, euphoria over getting a new job, and apprehension about the future of an important relationship after a serious fight, for example. Thinking rationally can eliminate many debilitative emotions from your life, but not all of them.

INVITATION TO INSIGHT

HOW IRRATIONAL ARE YOU?

1. Return to the situations described in the exercise "Talking to Yourself" on page 159. Examine each one to see whether your self-talk contains any irrational thoughts.

2. Keep a two- or three-day record of your debilitative emotions. Are any of them based on irrational thinking? Examine your conclusions, and see if you repeatedly use any of the fallacies described in the preceding section.

3. Take a class poll to see which fallacies are most "popular." Also, discuss what subjects seem to stimulate most of this irrational thinking (for example, schoolwork, dating, jobs, family).

Minimizing Debilitative Emotions

How can you overcome such irrational thinking? Social scientists have developed a simple yet effective approach.[51] When practiced conscientiously, it can help you cut down on the self-defeating thinking that leads to many debilitative emotions.

1. *Monitor your emotional reactions.* The first step is to recognize when you're feeling debilitative emotions. (Of course, it's also nice to recognize pleasant emotions when they occur!) As we suggested earlier, one way to recognize emotions is through proprioceptive stimuli: butterflies in the stomach, racing heart, hot flashes, and so on. Although

No one can make you feel inferior unless you agree to it.

Eleanor Roosevelt

such stimuli might be symptoms of food poisoning, more often they are symptoms of a strong emotion. You can also recognize certain ways of behaving that suggest your feelings: stomping instead of walking normally, being unusually quiet, or speaking in a sarcastic tone of voice are some examples.

It may seem strange to suggest that it's necessary to look for emotions—they ought to be immediately apparent. The fact is, however, that we often suffer from debilitative emotions for some time without noticing them. For example, at the end of a trying day you've probably caught yourself frowning and realized that you've been wearing that mask for some time without realizing it.

"So the prince and the princess lowered their expectations and lived reasonably contentedly forever after."

©2001 Steve Delmonte. Used by permission.

2. *Note the activating event.* After you're aware of how you're feeling, the next step is to figure out what activating event triggered your response. Sometimes it is obvious. For instance, a common source of anger is being accused unfairly (or fairly) of foolish behavior; a common source of hurt is being rejected by somebody important to you. In other cases, however, the activating event isn't so apparent.

Sometimes there isn't a single activating event but rather a series of small events that finally builds toward a critical mass and triggers a debilitative emotion. This happens when you're trying to work or sleep and are continually interrupted by a string of interruptions, or when you suffer a series of small disappointments.

The best way to begin tracking down activating events is to notice the circumstances in which you have debilitative emotions. Perhaps they occur when you're around *specific* people. In other cases, you might be bothered by certain *types of individuals* owing to their age, role, background, or some other factor. Or perhaps certain *settings* stimulate unpleasant emotions: parties, work, school. Sometimes the *topic* of conversation is the factor that sets you off, whether it be politics, religion, sex, or some other topic.

3. *Record your self-talk.* This is the point at which you analyze the thoughts that are the link between the activating event and your feeling. If you're serious about getting rid of debilitative emotions, it's important actually to write down your self-talk when first learning to use this method. Putting your thoughts on paper will help you see whether they actually make any sense.

Monitoring your self-talk might be difficult at first. This is a new activity, and any new activity seems awkward. If you persevere, however, you'll find that you will be able to identify the thoughts that lead to your debilitative emotions. After you get in the habit of recognizing this internal monolog, you'll be able to identify your thoughts quickly and easily.

4. *Dispute your irrational beliefs.* Disputing your irrational beliefs is the key to success in the rational-emotive approach. Use the list of

irrational fallacies on pages 160–165 to discover which of your internal statements are based on mistaken thinking.

You can do this most effectively by following three steps. First, decide whether each belief you've recorded is rational or irrational. Next, explain why the belief is rational or irrational. Finally, if the belief is irrational, you should write down an alternative way of thinking that is more rational and that can leave you feeling better when faced with the same activating event in the future.

The approach of replacing self-defeating self-talk with more constructive thinking provides an especially effective tool for improving self-confidence and relational communication.[52] Nonetheless, this approach triggers objections from some readers.

"The rational-emotive approach sounds like nothing more than trying to talk yourself out of feeling bad." This accusation is totally correct. After all, because we talk ourselves *into* feeling bad, what's wrong with talking ourselves *out* of feeling bad, especially when such feelings are based on irrational thoughts? Rationalizing may be an excuse and a self-deception, but there's nothing wrong with being rational.

"The kind of disputing we just read sounds phony and unnatural. I don't talk to myself in sentences and paragraphs." There's no need to dispute your irrational beliefs in any special literary style. You can be just as colloquial as you want. The important thing is to clearly understand what thoughts led you into your debilitative emotions so that you can clearly dispute them. While the approach is new to you, it's a good idea to write or talk out your thoughts in order to make them clear. After you've had some practice, you'll be able to do these steps in a quicker, less formal way.

"This approach is too cold and impersonal. It seems to aim at turning people into cold-blooded, calculating, emotionless machines." This is simply not true. A rational thinker can still dream, hope, and love: There's nothing necessarily irrational about feelings like these. Basically rational people even indulge in a bit of irrational thinking once in a while. But they usually know what they're doing. Like healthy eaters who occasionally indulge in a snack of junk food, rational thinkers occasionally indulge in irrational thoughts, knowing that they'll return to their healthy lifestyle soon with no real damage done.

"This technique promises too much. There's no chance I could rid myself of all unpleasant feelings, however nice that might be." We can answer this objection by assuring you that rational-emotive thinking probably won't totally solve your emotional problems. What it can do is to reduce their number, intensity, and duration. This method is not the answer to all your problems, but it can make a significant difference—which is not a bad accomplishment.

The thought manifests as the word;

The word manifests as the deed;

The deed develops into habit;

And the habit hardens into character.

So watch the thought and its ways with care . . .

As we think, so we become.

From the *Dhammapada* (The sayings of the Buddha)

RATIONAL THINKING

1. Return to the diary of irrational thoughts you recorded on page 165. Dispute the self-talk in each case, and write a more rational interpretation of the event.

2. Now try out your ability to think rationally on the spot. You can do this by acting out the scenes listed in step 4. You'll need three players for each one: a subject, the subject's "little voice"—his or her thoughts—and a second party.

3. Play out each scene by having the subject and second party interact while the "little voice" stands just behind the subject and says what the subject is probably thinking. For example, in a scene where the subject is asking an instructor to reconsider a low grade, the little voice might say, "I hope I haven't made things worse by bringing this up. Maybe he'll lower the grade after rereading the test. I'm such an idiot! Why didn't I keep quiet?"

4. Whenever the little voice expresses an irrational thought, the observers who are watching the skit should call out, "Foul." At this point the action should stop while the group discusses the irrational thought and suggests a more rational line of self-talk. The players should then replay the scene with the little voice speaking in a more rational way.

    Here are some scenes. Of course, you can invent others as well.

    a. Two people are just beginning their first date.
    b. A potential employee has just begun a job interview.
    c. A teacher or boss is criticizing the subject for showing up late.
    d. A student and instructor run across each other in the market.

I believe that courage is all too often mistakenly seen as the absence of fear. If you descend by rope from a cliff and are not fearful to some degree, you are either crazy or unaware. Courage is seeing your fear in a realistic perspective, defining it, considering the alternatives and choosing to function in spite of risk.

Leonard Zunin

COMMUNICATION TRANSCRIPT

Rational Thinking in Action

The following scenarios demonstrate how the rational thinking method described on pages 165–167 applies in everyday challenges. Notice that thinking rationally doesn't eliminate debilitative emotions. Instead, it helps keep them in control, making effective communication more possible.

Situation 1: Dealing with Annoying Customers
Activating Event
I work in a shopping mall that swarms with tourists and locals. Our company's reputation is based on service, but lately I've been losing my patience with the customers. The store is busy from the second we open until we close. Many of the customers are rude, pushy, and demanding. Others expect me to be a tour guide, restaurant reviewer, medical consultant, and even a baby-sitter. I feel like I'm ready to explode.

Beliefs and Self-Talk
1. I'm sick of working with the public. People are really obnoxious!
2. The customers should be more patient and polite instead of treating me like a servant.
3. This work is driving me crazy! If I keep working here, I'm going to become as rude as the customers.
4. I can't quit: I could never find another job that pays this well.

Disputing Irrational Beliefs
1. It's an overgeneralization to say that *all* people are obnoxious. Actually, most of the customers are fine. Some are even very nice. About 10 percent of them cause most of the trouble. Recognizing that most people are OK leaves me feeling less bitter.
2. It's true that obnoxious customers *should* be more polite, but it's unrealistic to expect that everybody will behave the way they ought to. After all, it's not a perfect world.
3. By saying that the customers are driving me crazy I suggest that I have no control over the situation. I'm an adult, and I am able to keep a grip on myself. I may not like the way some people behave, but it's my choice how to respond to them.
4. I'm not helpless. If the job is too unpleasant, I can quit. I probably wouldn't find another job that pays as well as this one, so I have to choose which is more important: money or peace of mind. It's my choice.

Situation 2: Meeting My Girlfriend's Family
Activating Event
Tracy and I are talking about marriage—maybe not soon, but eventually. Her family is very close, and they want to meet me. I'm sure I'll like them, but I am not sure what they think about me. I was married once before, at a young age. It was a big mistake, and it didn't last. Furthermore, I was laid off two months ago, and I'm between jobs. The family is coming to town next week, and I am very nervous about what they will think of me.

Beliefs and Self-Talk
1. They've *got* to like me! This is a close family, and I'm doomed if they think I'm not right for Tracy.
2. No matter how sensibly I act, all they'll think of is my divorce and unemployment.
3. Maybe the family is right. Tracy deserves the best, and I'm certainly not that!

Disputing Irrational Beliefs
1. The family's approval is definitely important. Still, my relationship with Tracy doesn't depend on it. She's already said that she's committed to me, no matter what they think. The sensible approach is to say I *want* their approval, but I don't *need* it.
2. I'm expecting the absolute worst if I think that I'm doomed no matter what happens when we meet. There is a chance that they will dislike me, but there's also a chance that things will work out fine. There's no point in dwelling on catastrophes.
3. Just because I've had an imperfect past doesn't mean I'm wrong for Tracy. I've learned from my past mistakes, and I am committed to living a good life. I know I can be the kind of husband she deserves, even though I'm not perfect.

Using your Looking Out/ Looking In *CD-ROM, click on* Communication Scenarios *and then click on either "Annoying Customers" or "Meeting My Girlfriend's Family" icons to watch and analyze dramatized versions of the everyday challenges described here.*

SUMMARY

Emotions have several dimensions. They are signaled by internal physiological changes, manifested by nonverbal reactions, and defined in most cases by cognitive interpretations. Some emotions are primary, whereas others are combinations of two or more emotions. Some are intense, whereas others are relatively mild.

There are several reasons why people do not verbalize many of the emotions they feel. Social rules discourage the expression of some feelings, particularly negative ones. Many social roles do not allow expression of certain feelings. Finally, fear of the consequences leads people to withhold expression of some emotions.

Because total expression of emotions is not appropriate for adults, several guidelines help define when and how to express emotions effectively. Self-awareness, clear language, and expression of mixed feelings are important. Willingness to accept responsibility for feelings instead of blaming them on others leads to better reactions. Choosing the proper time and place to share feelings is also important.

Whereas some emotions are facilitative, others are debilitative and inhibit effective functioning. Many of these debilitative emotions are caused by various types of irrational thinking. It is often possible to communicate more confidently and effectively by identifying troublesome emotions, identifying the activating event and self-talk that triggered them, and replacing any irrational thoughts with a more logical analysis of the situation.

KEY TERMS

debilitative emotions	fallacy of catastrophic expectations	fallacy of perfection
emotional contagion		fallacy of shoulds
facilitative emotions	fallacy of causation	mixed emotions
fallacy of approval	fallacy of helplessness	primary emotions
	fallacy of overgeneralization	self-talk

LOOKING OUT/LOOKING IN ONLINE

Use your *Looking Out/Looking In* CD-ROM for quick access to the electronic resources that accompany this chapter. Included on this CD-ROM are additional study aids and links to the *Looking Out/Looking In* Web site at the Wadsworth Communication Café. The CD-ROM is your gateway to a wealth of resources that will help you understand and further explore the material in this chapter. **Video clips** under *Communication Scenarios* on the CD illustrate the skills introduced in this chapter. Click on the Web site link to complete self-study **review quizzes** to help you master new concepts; access a **feature film database** to locate clips and entire movies that illustrate communication principles; find Internet material via the maintained **Web site links;** and complete **online activities** to help you master new concepts.

INFOTRAC COLLEGE EDITION EXERCISES

Use the InfoTrac College Edition password that was included free with a copy of this new text to answer the following questions. These questions can be completed online and, if requested, submitted to your instructor under InfoTrac College Edition Activities at the *Looking Out/Looking In* Web site.

1. Gender & Social Conventions

Use PowerTrac to locate and read the article "Gender Differences in Motives for Regulating Emotions" by Monique Timmers, Agneta H. Fische, and Antony S. R. Manstead. What evidence does this study offer for the existence of gender differences in emotional expression? In your experience, how clear are the differences between male and female emotional expression? How much difference can you identify within each gender?

2. Guidelines for Expressing Emotions

Read "EQ vs. IQ," by Cynthia L. Kemper. (Hint: Use PowerTrac's author and title searching tools to find the article.) What is EQ? How does it differ from traditional measures of intelligence? What evidence does the author offer about the importance of EQ?

3. Managing Difficult Emotions

Search for the subject of "self-talk." Find an article that has relevance to your own life and do the following: (a) define the thesis of the article, (b) identify the evidence offered to support that thesis, and (c) apply the valid principles in the article to your own communication.

READINGS

Ben-Ze'ev, Aaron. *The Subtlety of Emotions.* Boston: Bradford/MIT Press, 2000.

This book offers multiple perspectives on human emotions, drawing from the social sciences, literature, and even the Bible. The second half discusses the characteristics of dozens of different emotions.

Burns, D. D. *The Feeling Good Handbook,* rev. ed. New York: Plume/Penguin, 1999.

A useful tool for dealing with debilitative emotions.

Duck, Steve. "Social Emotions: Showing Our Feelings about Other People" in *Human Relationships.* Newbury Park, Calif.: Sage, 1992.

This chapter describes the thoughts and communication behaviors that center on a variety of emotions, including love, jealousy, embarrassment and shyness, and loneliness.

Ellis, Albert. *A New Guide to Rational Living.* North Hollywood, Calif.: Wilshire Books, 1977.

Ellis is probably the best-known advocate of changing feelings by thinking rationally, and this is his most widely read book.

Goleman, Daniel. *Emotional Intelligence: Why It Can Matter More Than I.Q.* New York: Bantam, 1995.

Goleman excels at presenting an impressive array of social science research supporting the importance of effectively managing emotions in human relationships. Topics include emotional expression in families, intimate relationships, and health.

Lewis, Michael, and Jeanette M. Haviland, eds. *Handbook of Emotions*, 2nd ed. New York: Guilford, 2000.

This book is packed with scholarly works on the role of emotions in communication. Chapters deal with topics including how rules for expressing emotions have changed over history, gender and emotion, emotion in personal relationships, and how emotions are expressed in groups.

FILMS

In addition to the films suggested here, go to the **Film in Communication Database** at the *Looking Out/Looking In* Web site to locate movie clips that illustrate emotions.

The Consequences of Unexpressed Feelings

I Never Sang for My Father (1971) Rated PG

When death ends a relationship, those who live on may be left with more regrets about what was not said than about anything they may have said. This is certainly true in *I Never Sang for My Father*, the story of Tom (Melvyn Douglas), an eighty-one-year-old patriarch who is left alone after the death of his wife, and his middle-aged son Gene (Gene Hackman), who has found a new love after the death of his own wife a year earlier. Tom is a man of few personal words: He won't acknowledge that his life is ending, and he certainly won't admit that he loves and needs his son. Gene is no more forthcoming. He won't reveal his marriage plans and his intentions to move thousands of miles away to California, leaving his father behind.

In an intensely emotional scene the father finally does break down and acknowledge his grief, and Gene invites him to come to California with him and his new wife. But the film, like many lives, doesn't have a guaranteed happily-ever-after ending. Tom and his son have lived too many years emotionally isolated to make up for lost time. We see that relationships, like trees, grow and are shaped gradually over the years. After they have established their form, they are not easily or quickly reformed.

Indirect Ways of Expressing Emotions

Smoke (1995) Rated R

The film *Remains of the Day* illustrates the tragedy of unexpressed emotions. Although clear emotional expression can be valuable, the film *Smoke* shows that the communication of affection, especially between men, can sometimes be like the title of this film: barely visible, elusive, yet powerful.

The story is filled with an interesting bunch of characters. Paul Benjamin (William Hurt) is a forlorn writer still recovering from the death of his wife.

Rashid Cole (Harold Perrineau, Jr.) is a bright young man in search of himself and his father (Forest Whitaker). Auggie Wren (Harvey Keitel) is a cigar store owner who befriends Benjamin, hires Cole, and helps his old girlfriend Ruby (Stockard Channing) through a difficult relationship with her (and perhaps his) daughter.

In this story, children are furious with their parents. Friends care deeply for each other. Enemies make amends. Affection is felt on a variety of levels. In some scripts, these emotions would be expressed verbally—"I hate you"; "You mean so much to me"; "I'm sorry"; "I love you"—but not in this movie. Rashid and Auggie "make up" by cursing each other with smiles on their faces. Rashid buries the hatchet with his dad by fighting him, then dining with him in silence. Auggie "tells" Benjamin he cares by showing him photographs, shooting the bull, and sharing stories. Auggie doesn't like it when Ruby cries in appreciation for the money he gives her; he just wants her to know he's concerned. The characters banter, swear, goad each other, and smoke together—and love one another. They don't need to say it; they communicate it quite clearly.

LOOKING OUT/LOOKING IN CD-ROM

Using your *Looking Out/Looking In* CD-ROM, click on *Communication Scenarios* and then click on either one of the two rational thinking scenarios "Annoying Customers" or "Meeting My Girlfriend's Family" featured in the Communication Transcript on page 169.

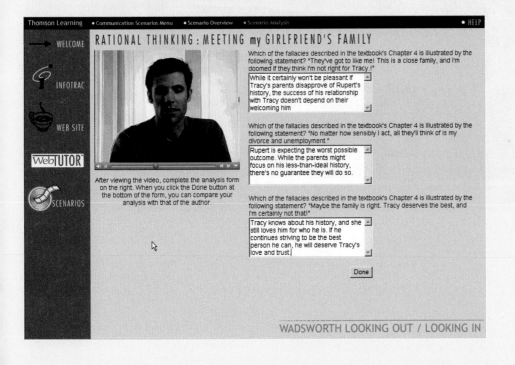

CHAPTER 5

LANGUAGE: BARRIER AND BRIDGE

AND THE WHOLE EARTH WAS OF ONE LANGUAGE AND ONE SPEECH. AND IT CAME TO PASS, AS THEY JOURNEYED FROM THE EAST, THAT THEY FOUND A PLAIN IN THE LAND OF SHINAR; AND THEY DWELT THERE.

AND THEY SAID TO ONE ANOTHER, GO TO, LET US MAKE BRICK, AND BURN THEM THOROUGHLY. AND THEY HAD BRICK FOR STONE, AND SLIME HAD THEY FOR MORTAR.

AND THEY SAID, GO TO, LET US BUILD US A CITY AND A TOWER, WHOSE TOP MAY REACH UNTO HEAVEN; AND LET US MAKE US A NAME, LEST WE BE SCATTERED ABROAD UPON THE FACE OF THE WHOLE EARTH.

AND THE LORD CAME DOWN TO SEE THE CITY AND THE TOWER, WHICH THE CHILDREN OF MEN BUILDED.

AND THE LORD SAID, BEHOLD, THE PEOPLE IS ONE, AND THEY HAVE ALL ONE LANGUAGE; AND THIS THEY BEGAN TO DO: AND NOW NOTHING WILL BE RESTRAINED FROM THEM, WHICH THEY HAVE IMAGINED TO DO.

GO TO, LET US GO DOWN, AND THERE CONFOUND THEIR LANGUAGE, THAT THEY MAY NOT UNDERSTAND ONE ANOTHER'S SPEECH.

SO THE LORD SCATTERED THEM ABROAD FROM THENCE UPON THE FACE OF ALL THE EARTH; AND THEY LEFT OFF TO BUILD THE CITY.

THEREFORE IS THE NAME OF IT CALLED BABEL; BECAUSE THE LORD DID THERE CONFOUND THE LANGUAGE OF ALL THE EARTH; AND FROM THENCE DID THE LORD SCATTER THEM ABROAD UPON THE FACE OF ALL THE EARTH.

GENESIS 11:1–9

The problems that began with Babel live on today. Sometimes it seems as if none of us speaks the same language. Yet, despite its frustrations and challenges, there is no question that language is a marvelous tool. It is the gift that allows us to communicate in a way that no other animals appear to match. Without language we would be more ignorant, ineffectual, and isolated.

In this chapter we will explore the nature of language, taking a look at how to take advantage of its strengths and minimize its weaknesses. After a quick explanation of the symbolic nature of language, we will look at the sources of most misunderstandings. We will then move beyond the challenges of simply understanding one another and explore how the language we use affects the climate of interpersonal relationships. Finally, we will broaden our focus even more to look at how linguistic practices shape the attitudes of entire cultures.

LANGUAGE IS SYMBOLIC

In the natural world, *signs* have a direct connection with the things they represent. For example, smoke is a sign that something's burning, and a high fever is a sign of illness. There's nothing arbitrary about the relationship between natural signs and the things they represent: Nobody made them up, and they exist independent of human opinions.

In human language, the connection between signs and the things they represent isn't so direct. Instead, language is *symbolic*: There's only an arbitrary connection between words and the ideas or things to which they refer. For example, there is nothing particularly fivelike in the number "five." The word represents the number of fingers on your hand only because English speakers agree that it does. To a speaker of French, the symbol "cinq" would convey the same meaning; to a computer programmer, the same value would be represented by the electronically coded symbol "00110101."

Even sign language, as "spoken" by most deaf people, is symbolic in nature and not the pantomime it might seem. Because this form of communication is symbolic and not literal, literally hundreds of sign languages around the world have evolved independently whenever significant numbers of deaf people are in contact.[1] These distinct languages include American Sign Language, British Sign Language, French Sign Language, Danish Sign Language, Chinese Sign Language—even Australian Aboriginal and Mayan Sign Languages.

The symbolic nature of language is a blessing. It enables us to communicate in ways that wouldn't otherwise be possible: about ideas, reasons, the past, the future, and things not present. Without symbolic language, none of this would be possible. On the other hand, the indirect relationship between symbols and the things they represent leads to communication problems only hinted about in the tower of Babel story.

If everyone used symbols the same way, language would be much easier to use and understand. However, your own experience shows that this isn't always the case. Messages that seem perfectly clear to you

"Well, at any rate it's a great comfort," she said as she stepped under the trees, "after being so hot, to get into the—into the—into what?" she went on, rather surprised at not being able to think of the word. "I mean to get under the—under the—under this, you know!" putting her hand on the trunk of the tree. "What does it call itself, I wonder? I do believe it's got no name—why to be sure it hasn't!"

Lewis Carroll, *Through the Looking Glass*

prove confusing or misleading to others You tell the hair stylist to "take a little off the top," and then are stunned to discover that her definition of "a little" was equivalent to your definition of "a lot." You have a heated argument about the merits of "feminism" without realizing that you and the other person have been using the word to represent entirely different ideas.

In Washington, D.C., an uproar developed when the newly appointed Washington, D.C., ombudsman, David Howard, used the word *niggardly* to describe an approach to budgeting.[2] Howard, who is white, was accused by some African-American critics of uttering an unforgivable racial slur. His defenders pointed out that the word, which means "miserly," is derived from Scandinavian languages and that it has no link to the racial slur it resembles. Even though the criticisms eventually died away, they illustrate that, correct or not, the meanings that people associate with words have far more significance than do their dictionary definitions.

UNDERSTANDINGS AND MISUNDERSTANDINGS

Language is rather like plumbing: We pay the most attention to it when something goes wrong. Because misunderstandings are the greatest cause of concern for most people who study language, we'll begin our study by looking at three ways we can misunderstand one another's speech.

Understanding Words: Semantic Rules

Semantic rules reflect the ways in which users of a language make sense of a particular linguistic symbol, usually a word. Semantic rules make it possible for us to agree that "bikes" are for riding and that

Calvin and Hobbes
by Bill Watterson

Calvin and Hobbes © Watterson. Reprinted with permission of Universal Press Syndicate. All rights reserved.

"books" are for reading, and they help us know whom we will and won't encounter when we use rooms marked "men" or "women." Without semantic rules, communication would be impossible because each of us would use symbols in unique ways, unintelligible to one another.

Semantic misunderstandings arise when people use words as if they had different meanings. Semantic misunderstandings come in several forms. In the next few pages, we will look at some of the most common ones.

Equivocation

Equivocal language consists of statements that have more than one commonly accepted definition. Some equivocal misunderstandings are amusing, as the following newspaper headlines illustrate:

Family Catches Fire Just in Time

Man Stuck on Toilet; Stool Suspected

20-Year Friendship Ends at the Altar

Trees Can Break Wind

Some equivocal misunderstandings are trivial. We recall dining at a Mexican restaurant and ordering a "tostada with beans." Instead of being served a beef tostada with beans on the side, we were surprised to see the waiter bring us a plate containing a tostada *filled* with beans. As with most equivocal misunderstandings, hindsight showed that the phrase "tostada with beans" has two equally correct meanings.

Some equivocal misunderstandings can be embarrassing, as one woman recalls:

In the fourth grade the teacher asked the class what a period was. I raised my hand and shared everything I had learned about girls' getting their period. But he was talking about the dot at the end of a sentence. Oops![3]

Other equivocal misunderstandings are less amusing and more problematic. Not long ago we heard about a professor who returned a student paper with the comment "If that's your own work, it's quite good." Instead of feeling complimented, the student took this comment as an indirect accusation of plagiarism. Other equivocal statements can be even more troubling. A nurse gave one of her patients a scare when she told him that he "wouldn't be needing" his robe, books, and shaving materials anymore. The patient became quiet and moody. When the nurse inquired about the odd behavior, she discovered that the poor man had interpreted her statement to mean he was going to die soon. In fact, the nurse meant he would be going home soon.

The reading "The Many Meanings of 'I Love You'" on page 180 illustrates how a seemingly

"Let me get this straight now. Is what you want to build a jean factory or a gene factory?"

THE MANY MEANINGS OF "I LOVE YOU"

"I love you" [is] a statement that can be expressed in so many varied ways. It may be a stage song, repeated daily without any meaning, or a barely audible murmur, full of surrender. Sometimes it means: I desire you or I want you sexually. It may mean: I hope you love me or I hope that I will be able to love you. Often it means: It may be that a love relationship can develop between us or even I hate you. Often it is a wish for emotional exchange: I want your admiration in exchange for mine or I give my love in exchange for some passion or I want to feel cozy and at home with you or I admire some of your qualities. A declaration of love is mostly a request: I desire you or I want you to gratify me, or I want your protection or I want to be intimate with you or I want to exploit your loveliness.

Sometimes it is the need for security and tenderness, for parental treatment. It may mean: My self-love goes out to you. But it may also express submissiveness: Please take me as I am, or I feel guilty about you, I want, through you, to correct the mistakes I have made in human relations. It may be self-sacrifice and a masochistic wish for dependency. However, it may also be a full affirmation of the other, taking the responsibility for mutual exchange of feelings. It may be a weak feeling of friendliness, it may be the scarcely even whispered expression of ecstasy. "I love you"—wish, desire, submission, conquest; it is never the word itself that tells the real meaning here.

J. A. M. Merloo

simple word can be interpreted in many ways. Imagine the troubles that can (and do) arise when people express their love to one another without understanding—at least until it's too late—that they have very different ideas of what their "love" means.

It's difficult to catch every equivocal statement and clarify it while speaking. For this reason, the responsibility for interpreting statements accurately rests in large part with the receiver. Feedback of one sort or another—for example, the kind of perception checking introduced in chapter 3 and the paraphrasing described in chapter 7—can help clear up misunderstandings.

Despite its obvious problems, equivocal language has its uses. As chapter 8 describes in detail, there are times when using language that is open to several interpretations can be useful. It helps people get along by avoiding the kind of honesty and clarity that can embarrass both the speaker and listener. For example, if a friend proudly shows you a newly completed painting and asks your opinion about it, you might respond equivocally by saying, "Gee, it's really unusual. I've never seen anything like it" instead of giving a less ambiguous but more hurtful response such as "This may be the ugliest thing I've ever seen!"

Relative Language   **Relative words** gain their meaning by comparison. For example, do you attend a large or small school? This depends on what you compare it to. Alongside a campus such as the University of Michigan, with over thirty thousand students, your school may look small; but compared with a smaller school, it may seem quite large. Relative words such as *fast* and *slow*, *smart* and *stupid*, *short* and *long* are clearly defined only through comparison.

Some relative terms are so common that we mistakenly assume that they have a clear meaning. In one study, graduate students were asked to assign numerical values to such terms as *doubtful*, *toss-up*, *likely*, *probable*, *good chance*, and *unlikely*.[4] There was a tremendous variation in the meaning of most of these terms. For example, the responses for *probable* ranged from 0 to 99 percent. *Good chance* fell between 35 and 90 percent, whereas *unlikely* fell between 0 and 40 percent.

Using relative terms without explaining them can lead to communication problems. Have you ever responded to someone's question about the weather by saying it was warm, only to find out the person thought it was cold? Have you followed a friend's advice and gone to a "cheap" restaurant, only to find that it was twice as expensive as you expected? Have classes you heard were "easy" turned out to be hard? The problem in each case resulted from failing to link the relative word to a more measurable term.

Static Evaluation   "Mark is a nervous guy." "Karen is short-tempered." "You can always count on Wes." Statements that contain or imply the word *is* lead to the mistaken assumption that people are consistent and unchanging—clearly an incorrect belief. Instead of labeling Mark as permanently and totally nervous, it would probably be more accurate to outline the situations in which he behaves nervously. The same goes for

Karen, Wes, and the rest of us: We are more changeable than the way static, everyday language describes us.

Describing John as "boring" (you can substitute *friendly, immature,* or many other adjectives) is less correct than saying, "The John I encountered yesterday seemed to me to be. . . ." The second type of statement describes the way someone behaved at one point; the first describes him as if he had always been that way.

Subscripting is one linguistic device of dating to reduce **static evaluation.** Adding a subscript whenever appropriate will show the transitory nature of many objects and behaviors. For example, a teacher might write as an evaluation of a student: "Susan $^{May\ 12}$ had difficulty cooperating with her classmates." Although the actual device of superscripting is awkward in writing and impractical in conversation, the idea it represents can still be used. Instead of saying, "I'm shy," a more accurate statement might be "I haven't approached any new people since I moved here." The first statement implies that your shyness is an unchangeable trait, rather like your height, whereas the second one implies that you are capable of changing.

Abstraction   When it comes to describing problems, goals, appreciations, and requests, some language is more specific than others. **Abstract language** is vague in nature, whereas **behavioral language**—as its name implies—refers to specific things that you or the other person says or does. The **"Abstraction Ladder"** in Figure 5-1 illustrates how the same phenomenon can be described at various levels of specificity.

We use higher level abstractions all the time. For instance, rather than saying, "Thanks for washing the dishes," "Thanks for vacuuming the rug," "Thanks for making the bed," it's easier to say, "Thanks for cleaning up." In such everyday situations, abstractions are a useful kind of verbal shorthand.

Although vagueness does have its uses, highly abstract language can cause two types of problems:

Stereotyping   High-level abstractions lead to blanket judgments: "Marriage counselors are worthless," "Skateboarders are delinquents," or "Men are no good." Overly abstract expressions like these can cause people to *think* in generalities, ignoring uniqueness. As you learned in chapter 2, expecting people to act a certain way can become a self-fulfilling prophecy. If you expect the worst of people, you have a good chance of getting it.

Confusing Others   The following conversation illustrates the kind of frustration and confusion that can arise from overly abstract descriptions.

A: We never do anything that's fun anymore.

B: What do you mean?

A: We used to do lots of unusual things, but now it's the same old stuff, over and over.

B: But last week we went on that camping trip, and tomorrow we're going to that party where we'll meet all sorts of new people. Those are new things.

Most abstract

You need to have a better attitude.

You need to be more positive.

You need to complain less.

You need to quit complaining when we have to work late or come in on weekends.

You need to quit complaining every time we have to work late or come in on weekends.

Most specific

FIGURE 5-1 **Abstraction Ladder** A boss gives feedback to an employee about career advancement at various levels of specificity.

A: That's not what I mean. I'm talking about *really* unusual stuff.

B: (*Becoming confused and a little impatient*) Like what? Taking hard drugs or going over Niagara Falls in a barrel?

A: Don't be stupid. All I'm saying is that we're in a rut. We should be living more exciting lives.

B: Well, I don't know what you want.

You can better understand the value of behavioral descriptions by looking at the examples in Table 5-1. Notice how much more clearly they explain the speaker's thought than do the more vague terms.

Overly abstract language can lead to problems of a more serious nature. For instance, accusations of sexual assault can arise because one person claims to have said "no" when the other person insists that no such refusal was ever conveyed. In response to this sort of disagreement, specific rules of sexual conduct have become more common in work and educational settings. Perhaps the best known code of this type is the one developed at Ohio's Antioch College. The code uses low-level abstractions to minimize the chances of anyone claiming confusion about a partner's willingness. For example, the code states:

> To knowingly take advantage of someone who is under the influence of alcohol, drugs, and/or prescribed medication is not acceptable behavior in the Antioch community.

> If sexual contact and/or conduct is not mutually and simultaneously initiated, then the person who initiates sexual contact/conduct is responsible for getting verbal consent of the other individual(s) involved.

> If one person wants to initiate moving to a higher level of sexual intimacy, that person is responsible for getting verbal consent of the other person(s) involved before moving to that level.

> If someone has initially consented but then stops consenting during a sexual interaction, she/he should communicate withdrawal verbally and/or through physical resistance. The other individual(s) must stop immediately.[5]

Some critics have ridiculed rules like these as being unrealistically legalistic and chillingly inappropriate for romantic relationships. Whatever its weaknesses, the Antioch code illustrates how low-level abstractions can reduce the chance of a serious misunderstanding. Specific language may not be desirable or necessary in many situations, but in an era when misinterpretations can lead to accusations of physical assault, it does seem to have a useful place.

Research shows that low-level descriptions can help improve the quality of relationships, even when conflicts arise. One study found that well-adjusted couples had just as many conflicts as poorly adjusted

"Be honest with me, Roger. By 'mid-course correction' you mean divorce, don't you."

©2001 Leo Cullum from cartoonbank.com. All Rights Reserved.

TABLE 5-1 Abstract vs. Behavioral Descriptions

	ABSTRACT DESCRIPTION	BEHAVIORAL DESCRIPTION			REMARKS
		WHO IS INVOLVED	IN WHAT CIRCUMSTANCES	SPECIFIC BEHAVIORS	
PROBLEM	I talk too much.	People I find intimidating	When I want them to like me	I talk (mostly about about myself) instead of giving them a chance to speak or asking about their lives.	Behavioral description more clearly identifies behaviors to change.
GOAL	I want to be more con-structive.	My roommate	When we talk about house-hold duties	Instead of finding fault with her ideas, suggest alternatives that might work.	Behavioral description clearly outlines how to act; abstract description doesn't.
APPRECIATION	"You've really been helpful lately."	(Deliver to fellow worker)	"When I've had to take time off work be-cause of personal problems . . ."	". . . you took my shifts without complaining."	Give both abstract and behavioral descriptions for best results.
REQUEST	"Clean up your act!"	(Deliver to target person)	"When we're around my family . . ."	". . . please don't tell jokes that involve sex."	Behavioral description specifies desired behavior.

couples, but the way well-adjusted couples handled their conflicts was significantly different. Instead of blaming one another by using evaluative language, members of well-adjusted couples expressed their complaints in behavioral terms.[6]

It's hard to overestimate the value of specific, behavioral language because speaking in this way vastly increases the chance not only of thinking clearly about what's on your mind but also of having others understand you. A behavioral description should include three elements: the participants, the circumstances, and the behavior itself.

Who Is Involved?   At first the answer to this question might seem simple. If you're thinking about a personal problem or goal, you might reply, "I am"; if you're expressing appreciation, complaining, or making a request of another person, he or she would be the one who is involved. Although the question of involvement may be easy, it often calls for more detail. Ask yourself whether the problem or goal you're thinking about involves an entire category of people (women, salespeople, strangers), a subclass of the category (attractive women, rude salespeople, strangers you'd like to meet), or a specific person (Jane Doe, the salesclerk at a particular store, a new person in your neighborhood). If you're talking to another person, consider whether your appreciation, complaint, or request is directed solely at him or her or whether it is directed at others also.

In What Circumstances Does the Behavior Occur?   You can identify the circumstances by answering several questions. In what places does the behavior occur? Does it occur at any particular times? When you are discussing particular subjects? Is there anything special about you when it occurs: Are you tired, embarrassed, busy? Is there any trait shared by the other person or persons involved? Are they friendly or hostile, straightforward or manipulative, nervous or confident? In other words, if the behavior you're describing doesn't occur all the time (and few behaviors do), you need to pin down what circumstances set this situation apart from other ones.

What Behaviors Are Involved?   Although such terms as *more cooperative* and *helpful* might sound as if they're concrete descriptions of behavior, they are usually too vague to explain clearly what's on your mind. Behaviors must be *observable*, ideally both to you and to others. For instance, moving down the abstraction ladder from the relatively vague term *helpful*, you might arrive at "does the dishes every other day," "volunteers to help me with my studies," or "fixes dinner once or twice a week without being asked." It's easy to see that phrases like these are easier for both you and others to understand than are more vague abstractions.

There is one exception to the rule that behaviors should be observable, and that involves the internal processes of thoughts and emotions. For instance, in describing what happens to you when a friend has kept you waiting for a long time, you might say, "My stomach felt as if it were in knots—I was really worried. I kept thinking that you had forgotten and that I wasn't important enough to you for you to remember our date." What you're doing when offering such a description is to make unobservable events clear.

"Levels of Abstraction"

http://ol.scc. spokane.cc.wa. us/Jstrever1/ Resources/abstract.htm

Access this Web page for specific examples of levels of abstraction in writing. The author makes suggestions on how to clearly communicate meaning. Practice writing statements at different levels of abstraction by completing Activity 5.1 "Practice Moving Down the Abstraction Ladder" on the *Looking Out/Looking In* Web site.

SKILL BUILDER

DOWN-TO-EARTH LANGUAGE

You can appreciate the value of nonabstract language by translating the following into behavioral terms:

1. An abstract goal for improving your interpersonal communication (for example, "be more assertive" or "stop being so sarcastic")

2. A complaint you have about another person (for example, that he or she is "selfish" or "insensitive")

3. A request for someone to change (for example, "I wish you'd be more punctual" or "Try to be more positive")

4. An appreciation you could share with another person (for example, "Thanks for being so helpful" or "I appreciate your patience")

In each case, describe the person or persons involved, the circumstances in which the behavior occurs, and the precise behaviors involved. What difference will using behavioral descriptions such as the ones you have created here be likely to make?

Understanding Structure: Syntactic Rules

Syntactic rules govern the grammar of a language. You can appreciate how syntax contributes to the meaning of a statement by considering two versions of a letter:

Version 1

Dear John:

I want a man who knows what love is all about. You are generous, kind, thoughtful. People who are not like you admit to being useless and inferior. You have ruined me for other men. I yearn for you. I have no feelings whatsoever when we're apart. I can be forever happy—will you let me be yours?

Mary

Version 2

Dear John:

I want a man who knows what love is. All about you are generous, kind, thoughtful people, who are not like you. Admit to being useless and inferior. You have ruined me. For other men, I yearn. For you, I have no feelings whatsoever. When we're apart, I can be forever happy. Will you let me be?

Yours,

Mary

Semantic rules don't explain why these letters send virtually opposite messages. There's no ambiguity about the meaning of the words they contain: "love," "kind," "thoughtful," and so on. The opposite meanings of the letters came from their different syntax.

Although we usually aren't conscious of the syntactic rules that govern our language, we take notice when they are violated. Sometimes, however, apparently ungrammatical speech is simply following a different set of syntactic rules. For example, consider the way in which some members of the African-American community speak English. This style of speaking (termed "Ebonics" by some) treats forms of the verb *to be* differently than does Standard English.[7] An expression like "I be angry" that would be ungrammatical in Standard English is perfectly correct in Ebonics, where it would be equivalent to the expression "I've been angry for a while." Advocates of using Standard English have argued that people who speak other dialects are at a disadvantage. Even acknowledging this point, it's important to realize that, from an interpersonal perspective, the challenge in cases like this is to look past the different syntax and try to understand what ideas the other communicator is trying to express.

Understanding Context: Pragmatic Rules

Semantic and syntactic problems don't account for all misunderstandings.[8] To appreciate a different type of communication challenge, imagine how a young female employee might struggle to make sense of her older

IT'S A "GIRL" THING FOR WOMEN

When law professor and commentator Susan Estrich sent off her female research assistants after a long day of work, she cheerfully banished them with "Get out of here, girls." When Richard Riordan's press secretary, Noelia Rodriguez, told a TV station official that she was finally taking a week's vacation, the woman executive exclaimed, "You go, girl!"

There was a time when Estrich wouldn't have dreamed of referring to any female adult as anything but a woman. Rodriguez has never used "girl" in her job, and would be stunned if the word ever passed the Los Angeles mayor's lips.

So what's with all the girls? With a significant degree of female equity and parity established in the workplace and other institutions, there has been a gradual social warming among women to the once-ostracized "girl"—a curiously defiant celebration of a word formerly fraught with oppression.

"We've taken back the word and are using it the way we want—girl power, girl talk," said Jane Pratt, the 34-year-old editor of her eponymous new magazine, *Jane*. "It's about girls supporting each other and reveling in what's fun about being a girl. . . . Girl power means something different from feminism."

This is not the old-school, coffee-making, office-slaving, husband's-credit-card-borrowing girl—although the word incorporates a dollop of old-fashioned girlishness. "Girl" has been reborn in the image of a modern woman: It borrows the youthful vigor and spontaneity of female adolescence and discards the meekness of the old-fashioned office girl.

Sometime around the rise of feminism and *Ms.* magazine a quarter of a century ago, "girl" was banned from the vocabulary of smart-thinking men and women when describing any female over 15. It went the way of *stewardesses* and *poetesses*. There were no more office girls fetching coffee, no more college girls getting degrees or career girls working up the job ladder; no more girl Fridays, script girls or hatcheck girls.

So why are "girls" back? "Often after a social movement has been established for a while—like feminism—you can play around with certain terms," said Lynn Chancer, an assistant professor of sociology at Columbia University who studies feminism.

Now "girl" crops up throughout pop culture. "Girls rule" emblazons T-shirts. A college women's crew scrawls, "You row, girl" on the side of the team van.

As murky as the new "girl" may be, it comes with some rules. One is that the conversation should be casual. Neither men—nor women—should be saying, "I'll have my girl call your girl." And no woman wants to use it in a serious office setting—or around impressionable minds. "We have this 'Take Your Daughter to Work Day,'" said Robin Kramer, Riordan's chief of staff, "and the young women range in age from 7 to 17. Listening to both informal conversations and speeches, even those little ones are referred to as young women."

A second rule is that it's generally a woman's prerogative to use the word. Men treading into "girl" territory enter at their own risk. Sometimes a gentle reminder is all it takes to separate the women from the girls. *Ms.* magazine editor Barbara Findlen recalls a recent conversation with a man in which he referred to someone as "the girl who owns that business." "I said, 'God, a girl owns her own company! How old is she?' He laughed. He got it."

Carla Hall

male boss's statement "You look very pretty today." She almost certainly would understand the meaning of the words, and the syntax is perfectly clear. Still, the boss's message could be interpreted in several ways. Was the remark a simple compliment? A come-on? Did it contain the suggestion that she didn't look nice on other days?

If the boss and employee share the same interpretation of the message, their communication would be smooth. But if they bring different perspectives to bear in interpreting it, a problem exists. Table 5-2 shows a number of ways in which different perspectives of the boss and employee would lead to their attaching quite different meanings to the same words.

In cases like this, the meaning comes from the *context* of the message. The example also shows how miscommunication can occur when people—in this case, the boss and employee—use different contexts to make sense of a statement.

In situations like this we rely on **pragmatic rules** to decide how to interpret messages in a given context. Pragmatic rules govern the way speech operates in everyday interaction. You can't look up pragmatic rules in any dictionary: They are almost always unstated,

---

TABLE 5-2 Pragmatic Rules Govern the Use and Meaning of a Statement

Notice how the same message ("You look very nice today") takes on different meaning depending on the perspective of each communicator. Achieving understanding in cases like this requires the participants to negotiate the meaning of their statements.

	BOSS	EMPLOYEE
STATEMENT	"You look very nice today."	
SELF-CONCEPT		
"Who am I?" "Who is s/he?"	Friendly guy	Woman determined to succeed on own merits
EPISODE		
"What's going on in this exchange?"	Casual conversation	Possible come-on by boss?
RELATIONSHIP		
"Who are we to one another?"	Boss who treats employees like like family members	Subordinate employee, dependent on boss's approval for advancement
CULTURE		
"What does my background say about the meaning here?"	Euro-American, raised in United States	Latin American, raised in South America

Adapted from W. B. Pearce and V. Cronen, *Communication, Action, and Meaning.* New York: Praeger, 1980; and E. M. Griffin, *A First Look at Communication Theory,* 4th ed. New York: McGraw-Hill, 2000, p. 74.

---

but they are just as important as semantic and syntactic rules in helping us make sense of one another's messages. When people follow the same set of pragmatic rules, communication is smooth and coordinated. As our boss-employee example shows, problems can arise when communicators don't understand or agree on the pragmatic rules.

The best way to appreciate how pragmatic rules operate is to think of communication as a kind of cooperative game. Like all games, success depends on all the players understanding and following the same set of rules. This is why communication scholars use the term *coordination* to describe the way conversation operates when everyone involved uses the same set of pragmatic rules. [9]

Some pragmatic rules are shared by most people in a culture. In the United States and Canada, for instance, competent communicators understand that the question "How's it going?" usually isn't really a request for information. Anyone familiar with the rules of conversation knows that the proper answer is something like "Pretty good. How's it going with you?" Likewise, most people understand the pragmatic rule that says that "Would you like a drink?" means "Would you like an alcoholic beverage?" whereas "Would you like something to drink?" is a more open-ended question.

Pragmatic rules can be quite complex, as the reading "It's a Girl Thing for Women" on page 187 shows. The ways in which the word *girl* can be used in today's conversations differ from what was more accepted in the past, and who uses the word helps determine how many women might react to hearing it.

Besides following cultural rules, people in individual relationships create their own sets of pragmatic rules. Consider the use of humor: The teasing and jokes you exchange with gusto with one friend might be considered tasteless or offensive in another relationship. [10] One study identified twenty-four different functions that humor can serve in conversations. These include showing the speaker's sense of humor, entertaining others, decreasing another person's aggressive behavior, easing the disclosure of difficult information, expressing feelings, protecting the speaker's ego from attack, avoiding self-disclosure, and expressing aggression. It's easy to imagine how a joke aimed at reducing boredom, for example, might be interpreted by the recipient as an attack.

In situations like this, it's important to make sure that the other person's use of language matches yours before jumping to conclusions about the meaning of his or her statements. The skill of perception checking described in chapter 3 can be a useful tool at times like this.

YOUR LINGUISTIC RULES

To what extent do linguistic rules affect your understanding of and relationships with others? Explore this question by following these steps:

1. Recall a time when you encountered someone whose speech violated the syntactic rules that you are used to. What was your impression of this person? To what degree was this impression influenced by her or his failure to follow familiar linguistic rules? Consider whether this impression was or was not valid.

2. Recall at least one misunderstanding that arose when you and another person followed different semantic rules. Use hindsight to consider whether this misunderstanding (and others like it) could be avoided. If semantic misunderstandings can be minimized, explain what approaches might be useful.

3. Identify at least two pragmatic rules that govern the use of language in one of your relationships. Share these rules with other students. Do they use language in the same way as you and your relational partner?

THE IMPACT OF LANGUAGE

So far we have focused on language only as a medium for helping communicators understand one another. But along with this important function, language can shape our perceptions of the world around us and reflect the attitudes we hold toward one another.

On the broadest level, the language that communicators use can affect the way they view one another and the world around them. This chapter describes how language can shape an entire culture's worldview and how problems can arise when speakers of different languages encounter one another. But even among communicators who speak the same language, the labels we use to describe people, things, events, and ideas can affect our perceptions in a variety of ways.

Naming and Identity

"What's in a name?" Juliet asked rhetorically. If Romeo had been a social scientist, he would have answered "A great deal." Research has demonstrated that names are more than just a simple means of identification: They shape the way others think of us, the way we view ourselves, and the way we act.

Different names have different connotations. In one study, psychologists asked college students to rate over one thousand names according to their likability, how active or passive they seemed, and their masculinity or femininity. In spite of the large number of subjects, the responses were quite similar.[11] Michael, John, and Wendy were likable and active and were rated as possessing the masculine or feminine traits of their sex. Percival, Isadore, and Alfreda were less likable, and their sexual

Naming a child is not easy for parents in America who come from non-European backgrounds, from cultures where Ashutosh, Chae-Hyun and Naeem are common names. We have to ask ourselves a number of important questions. How will the child's foreign name sound to American ears? (That test ruled out Shiva, my family deity; a Jewish friend put her foot down.) Will it provoke bullies to beat him up on the school playground? (That was the end of Karan, the name of a warrior from the Mahabharata, the Hindu epic. A boy called "Karen" wouldn't stand a chance.) Will it be as euphonic in New York as it is in New Delhi? (That was how Sameer failed to get off the ground. "Like a bagel with a schmear!" said one ruthless well-wisher.)

Tunku Varadarajan

identity was less clear. Other research also suggests that names have strong connotative meanings. More common names are generally viewed as being more active, stronger, and better than less common ones.[12] The impact of names does affect first impressions, but the effect doesn't seem so powerful after communicators become more familiar with one another.[13]

The importance of names in defining identity applies to membership in groups. For example, one survey revealed that the majority of individuals who preferred the label *black* chose that term because it is "acceptable" and "based on consensus" of the larger culture.[14] They described themselves as patriotic, accepting of the status quo, and attempting to assimilate into the larger culture. By contrast, people who chose the term *Afro-American* reported deriving a greater part of their identity from their ethnicity and were less interested in assimilating into the larger culture than in merely succeeding in it.

Many women in Western society, aware of the power of names to influence identity, are aware that choosing how to identify themselves after marriage can be a significant decision. They may follow the tradition of taking their husband's last name, hyphenate their own name and their husband's, or keep their birth name. One fascinating survey revealed that a woman's choice is likely to reveal a great deal about herself and her relationship with her husband.[15] Women who took their husband's name placed the most importance on relationships, with social expectations of how they should behave rated second and issues of self coming last. On the other hand, women who kept their birth names put their personal concerns ahead of relationships and social expectations. Women with hyphenated names fell somewhere between the other groups, valuing self and relationships equally.

Female forms of address influence others' perceptions as well as shape the self-concept and behavior of the women who choose them. Research conducted in the late 1980s showed that women who choose the title *Ms.* give the impression of being more achievement oriented, socially assertive, and dynamic—but less interpersonally warm than counterparts who prefer more traditional forms *Miss* or *Mrs.*[16]

The power of naming extends beyond individuals. The terms used to label social groups can shape the way members of those groups regard themselves and the way others regard them. As the reading on the "S word" illustrates, some terms may seem familiar and thus innocuous; but their impact on both the namers and those being named can have subtle but profound effects.

"My mother is black, my father is African-American, and my grandfather is Negro. I can hardly wait to find out about *me*."

©The New Yorker Collection 1996 J. B. Handelsman from cartoonbank.com. All Rights Reserved.

Affiliation, Attraction, and Interest

Besides shaping an individual's identity, speech can build and demonstrate solidarity with others. Research has demonstrated that

CHALLENGING THE "S WORD"

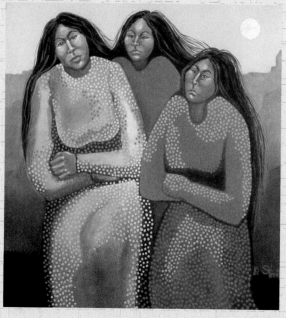

On the Leach Lake Reservation at the Caslic Vena Public School, students gather for Indian Culture class. A group of 11th graders sits in a circle talking about their feelings about the word "squaw."

Ojibwa student Terry Johnson grew up on the Leach Lake Reservation. "I was always taught to respect things, respect the land, respect my people, respect the elders. And one thing I was taught was the word, the S-Q word was very offensive. And I was never to use it."

Terry is one of about twenty students who is active on the Name Change Committee, a group that formed two years ago to get rid of names it deemed derogatory to Native Americans. Students wrote to Crayola Crayon Company asking it to rename the crayon color "Indian Red." Last year the Name Change Committee was successful working with neighboring high school students to change the name of their sports teams from the "Indians" to the "Patriots." The Name Change Committee project started in the classroom of Indian Culture teacher Muriel Charwood Litza, who grew up in Squaw Lake. "I've always been ashamed of that name. It's not a good name. When you're called that, it's a putdown. It is a derogatory, demeaning word."

Two years ago Charwood Litza's daughter and another high school student traced the word *squaw* for a class project. They found an article in a Native American newspaper that said the word is a French corruption of Iroquois slang for *vagina*. Based on that one article, they wrote letters to their state legislators saying the use of the word *squaw* in name places was unacceptable and embarrassing.

The lawmakers responded by passing a mandate to ban the word from lakes, creeks, and geographic features. Squaw Point near the high school is now known as Oak Point. And Squaw Pond is Scout Camp Pond.

Linguists and those who study Native American languages disagree about the word's origins. One linguist at the Smithsonian Institution in Washington, Ives Goddard, says the word originated in an extinct Indian language known as Massachusetts. Goddard says it simply meant "younger woman." Despite this innocent origin, it's generally considered to be demeaning or offensive, most standard dictionaries of English point out.

One of the high school students who started the Name Change Project, Dawn Litza, says that when people have called her *squaw*, it's clearly been meant as an insult. "It's not just about a dictionary. It's not just about a word. It's about people's feelings."

Christina Koening

communicators are attracted to others whose style of speaking is similar to theirs.[17] Likewise, communicators who want to show affiliation with one another adapt their speech in a variety of ways, including their choice of vocabulary, rate of talking, number and placement of pauses, and level of politeness.[18] Adolescents who all adopt the same vocabulary of slang words and speech mannerisms illustrate the principle of linguistic solidarity. The same process works among members of other groups, ranging from street gangs to military personnel. Communication researchers call the process of adapting one's speech style to match that of others with whom the communicator wants to identify **convergence.**

When two or more people feel equally positive about one another, their linguistic convergence will be mutual. But when communicators want or need approval they often adapt their speech to accommodate the other person's style, trying to say the "right thing" or speak in a way that will help them fit in. We see this process when immigrants who want to gain the rewards of material success in a new culture strive to master the host language. Likewise, employees who seek advancement tend to speak more like their superiors, superiors adopt the speech style of managers, and managers converge toward their bosses.

The principle of speech accommodation works in reverse, too. Communicators who want to set themselves apart from others adopt the strategy of **divergence,** speaking in a way that emphasizes their differences from others. For example, members of an ethnic group, even though fluent in the dominant language, might use their own dialect as a way of showing solidarity with one another—a sort of "us against them" strategy. Divergence also operates in other settings. A physician or an attorney, for example, who wants to establish credibility with his or her client might speak formally and use professional jargon to create a sense of distance. The implicit message here is, "I'm different (and more knowledgeable) than you."

Along with convergence and divergence, an individual's choice of words can reflect his or her liking and interest. Social customs discourage us from expressing like or dislike in an overt way. Only a clod would say "I don't like you" in most situations. Likewise, bashful or cautious suitors might not admit their attraction to a potential partner. Even when people are reluctant to speak candidly, the language they use can suggest their degree of interest and attraction toward a person, an object, or an idea. Morton Weiner and Albert Mehrabian outline several linguistic clues that can reveal these attitudes.[19]

- Demonstrative pronoun choice:
  - "These people want our help" indicates greater affinity than "Those people want our help."
- Sequential placement:
  - "Jack and Jill are my friends" may suggest a different level of liking than "Jill and Jack are my friends."

- Negation:
  - For the question "What do you think of it?," the response "It's not bad" is less positive than "It's good."
- Duration:
  - The length of time spent discussing a subject or person also can be a strong indicator of attraction to the subject or person with whom the speaker is talking.

Power

Communication researchers have identified a number of language patterns that add to or detract from a speaker's power to influence others. Notice the difference between these two statements:

> "Excuse me, sir. I hate to say this, but I . . . uh . . . I guess I won't be able to turn in the assignment on time. I had a personal emergency, and . . . well . . . it was just impossible to finish it by today. I'll have it on your desk on Monday, OK?"

> "I won't be able to turn in the assignment on time. I had a personal emergency, and it was impossible to finish it by today. I'll have it on your desk Monday."

Whether or not the professor finds the excuse acceptable, it's clear that the tone of the second one is more confident, whereas the tone of the first is apologetic and uncertain. Table 5-3 identifies several **powerless speech mannerisms** illustrated in the statements you just read. A number of studies have shown that speakers whose talk is free of these

TABLE 5-3	**Examples of Powerless Language**
Hedges	"I'm *kinda* disappointed . . ." "I *think* we should . . ." "I *guess* I'd like to . . ."
Hesitations	"*Uh*, can I have a minute of your time?" "*Well*, we could try this idea . . ." "I wish you would—*er*—try to be on time."
Intensifiers	"*So* that's how I feel . . ." "I'm not *very* hungry."
Polite forms	"Excuse me, *sir* . . ."
Tag questions	"It's about time we got started, *isn't it?*" "*Don't you think* we should give it another try?"
Disclaimers	"*I probably shouldn't say this but* . . ." "*I'm not really sure but* . . ."
Rising inflections	(See reading on page 253 in chapter 6.)

mannerisms are rated as more competent, dynamic, and attractive than speakers who sound powerless.[20] One study revealed that even a single type of **powerless speech mannerism** can make a person appear less authoritative or socially attractive.[21]

Powerful speech that gets the desired results in mainstream North American and European cultures doesn't succeed everywhere with everyone.[22] In Japan, saving face for others is an important goal, so communicators there tend speak in ambiguous terms and use hedge words and qualifiers. In most Japanese sentences the verb comes at the end of the sentence so that the "action" part of the sentence can be postponed. Traditional Mexican culture, with its strong emphasis on cooperation, also uses hedging to smooth over interpersonal relationships. By not taking a firm stand with their speech language, Mexicans believe they will not make others feel ill at ease. The Korean culture represents yet another people who prefer "indirect" (for example, "perhaps," "could be") over "direct" speech.

Even in cultures that value assertiveness, language that is *too* powerful may intimidate or annoy others. Consider these two different approaches to handling a common situation:

> "Excuse me. My baby is having a little trouble getting to sleep. Would you mind turning down the music just a little?"

> "My baby can't sleep because your music is too loud. Please turn it down."

The more polite, if less powerful, approach would probably produce better results than the stronger statement. How can this fact be reconciled with the research on powerful language? The answer lies in the tension between the potentially opposing goals of getting immediate results and developing positive relationships. If you come across as too powerful, you may get what you're seeking in the short term but alienate the other person in ways that will make your relationship more difficult in the long term. Furthermore, a statement that is *too* powerful can convey relational messages of disrespect and superiority—just as likely to antagonize others as to gain their compliance.

In some situations polite, less apparently powerful forms of speech can even enhance a speaker's effectiveness.[23] For example, a boss might say to a secretary, "Would you mind retyping this letter?" In truth, both the boss and secretary know that this is an order and not a request, but the questioning form is more considerate and leaves the secretary feeling better about the boss.[24] The importance of achieving both content and relational goals helps explain why a mixture of powerful speech and polite speech is usually most effective.[25]

Disruptive Language

Not all linguistic problems come from misunderstandings. Sometimes people understand one another perfectly and still wind up in a conflict. Of course, not all disagreements can, or should be, avoided. But eliminating three linguistic habits from your communication repertoire can minimize the kind of disagreements that don't need to happen, allowing you to save your energy for the unavoidable and important disagreements.

Fact-Opinion Confusion

Factual statements are claims that can be verified as true or false. By contrast, opinion statements are based on the speaker's beliefs. Unlike factual statements, they can never be proved or disproved. Consider a few examples of the difference between factual and opinion statements:

FACT	OPINION
You forgot my birthday.	You don't care about me.
You keep interrupting me.	You're a control freak.
You tell a lot of ethnic jokes.	You're a bigot.

When factual and opinion statements are set side by side like this, the difference is clear. In everyday conversation, however, we often present our opinions as if they were facts, and in doing so we invite an unnecessary argument. For example:

"That was a dumb thing to say!"

"Spending that much on a pair of shoes is a waste of money!"

"You can't get a fair shake in this country unless you're a white male."

Notice how much less antagonistic each statement would be if it were prefaced by a qualifier such as "In my opinion . . ." or "It seems to me . . ."

Fact-Inference Confusion

Labeling your opinions can go a long way toward relational harmony, but developing this habit won't solve all linguistic problems. Problems also arise when we confuse factual statements with inferential statements—conclusions arrived at from an interpretation of evidence.

Arguments often result when we label our inferences as facts:

A: Why are you mad at me?

B: I'm not mad at you. Why have you been so insecure lately?

A: I'm not insecure. It's just that you've been so critical.

B: What do you mean, "critical"? I haven't been critical. . . .

Instead of trying to read the other person's mind, a far better course is to use the skill of perception checking that you learned in chapter 3: Identify the observable behaviors (facts) that have caught your attention and describe one or more possible interpretations that you have drawn from them. After describing this train of thought, ask the other person to comment on the accuracy of your interpretation.

"When you didn't return my phone call (*fact*), I got the idea that you're mad at me (*interpretation*). Are you?" (*question*)

© 2001 Marian Henley from cartoonbank.com. All Rights Reserved.

"You've been asking me whether I still love you a lot lately (*fact*), and that makes me think you're feeling insecure (*inference*). Or maybe I'm behaving differently. What's on your mind?" (*question*)

Emotive Language

Emotive language seems to describe something but actually announces the speaker's attitude toward it. If you approve of a friend's roundabout approach to a difficult subject, you might call her "tactful"; if you don't approve of it, you might accuse her of "beating around the bush." Whether the approach is good or bad is more a matter of opinion than of fact, although this difference is obscured by emotive language. Barbra Streisand's tongue-in-cheek description of men and women illustrates how emotive language can describe the same behavior in favorable or unfavorable terms.

You can appreciate how emotive words are really editorial statements when you consider these examples:

If you approve, say	If you disapprove, say
thrifty	cheap
traditional	old-fashioned
extrovert	loudmouth
cautious	coward
progressive	radical
information	propaganda
military victory	massacre
eccentric	crazy

Using emotive words can have ugly consequences. Although experimental subjects who heard a derogatory word used against a member of a minority group expressed annoyance at this sort of slur, the derogatory word did have an impact.[26] Not only did the unwitting subjects rate the minority individual's competence lower when that person performed

A man is commanding—a woman is demanding.
A man is forceful—a woman is pushy.
A man is uncompromising—a woman is a ball-breaker.
A man is a perfectionist—a woman's a pain in the ass.
He's assertive—she's aggressive.
He strategizes—she manipulates.
He shows leadership—she's controlling.
He's committed—she's obsessed.
He's persevering—she's relentless.
He sticks to his guns—she's stubborn.
If a man wants to get it right, he's looked up to and respected.
If a woman wants to get it right, she's difficult and impossible.

Barbra Streisand

poorly, but also they found fault with others who associated socially with that person—even members of the person's own ethnic group.

The best way to avoid arguments involving emotive words is to describe the person, thing, or idea you are discussing in neutral terms and to label your opinions as such. Instead of saying, "I wish you'd quit making those sexist remarks" say, "I really don't like it when you call us 'girls' instead of 'women.'" Not only are nonemotive statements more accurate, but also they have a much better chance of being well received by others.

INVITATION TO INSIGHT

CONJUGATING "IRREGULAR VERBS"

The technique is simple: Just take an action or personality trait, and show how it can be viewed either favorably or unfavorably, according to the label it's given. For example:

I'm casual.
You're a little careless.
He's a slob.
Or try this one:
I'm thrifty.
You're money conscious.
She's a tightwad.

1. Try a few conjugations yourself, using the following statements:

   a. I'm tactful.   d. I'm relaxed.
   b. I'm conservative.   e. My child is high-spirited.
   c. I'm quiet.   f. I have high self-esteem.

2. Now recall at least two situations in which you used emotive language as if it was a description of fact and not an opinion. A good way to recall these situations is to think of a recent disagreement and imagine how the other people involved might have described it differently than you.

The Language of Responsibility

Besides providing a way to make the content of a message clear or obscure, language reflects the speaker's willingness to take responsibility for his or her beliefs and feelings. This acceptance or rejection of responsibility says a great deal about the speaker and can shape the tone of a relationship. To see how, read on.

"It" Statements   Notice the difference between the sentences of each set:

"It bothers me when you're late."

"I'm worried when you're late."

"It's nice to see you."

"I'm glad to see you."

"It's a boring class."

"I'm bored in the class."

As their name implies, **"it" statements** replace the personal pronoun *I* with the less immediate word *it*. By contrast, **"I" language** clearly identifies the speaker as the source of a message. Communicators who use "it" statements avoid responsibility for ownership of a message, instead attributing it to some unidentified source. This habit isn't just imprecise; more important, it is an unconscious way to avoid taking a position. You can begin to appreciate the increased directness of "I" language by trying to use it instead of the less direct and more evasive "it" statements in your own conversations.

"But" Statements   Statements that take the form "*X*-but-*Y*" can be confusing. A closer look at the **"but" statement** explains why. In each sentence, the word *but* cancels the thought that precedes it:

"You're really a great person, but I think we ought to stop seeing each other."

"You've done good work for us, but we're going to have to let you go."

"This paper has some good ideas, but I'm giving it a *D* grade because it's late."

These "buts" often are a strategy for wrapping the speaker's real but unpleasant message between more palatable ideas in a "psychological sandwich." This approach can be a face-saving strategy worth using at times. When the goal is to be absolutely clear, however, the most responsible approach can be to deliver the central idea without the distractions that can come with "but" statements.

Questions   Some questions are sincere requests for information. Other questions, though, are a linguistic way to avoid making a declaration. "What are we having for dinner?" may hide the statement "I want to eat out" or "I want to get a pizza."

"How many textbooks are assigned in that class?" may hide the statement "I'm afraid to get into a class with too much reading."

"Are you doing anything tonight?" can be a less risky way of saying, "I want to go out with you tonight."

"Do you love me?" safely replaces the statement "I love you," which may be too embarrassing, too intimate, or too threatening to say directly.

Sometimes being indirect can be a tactful way to approach a topic that would be difficult to address head on. When used unnecessarily, though, being indirect can be a way to avoid speaking for yourself. See chapter 8 for more details about the value and risks of using questions.

"My hand is doing this movement . . ."
"Is it doing the movement?"
"I am moving my hand like this . . . and now the thought comes to me that . . ."
"The thought 'comes' to you?"
"I have the thought."
"You have it?"
"I think. Yes. I think that I use 'it' very much, and I am glad that by noticing it I can bring it all back to me."
"Bring it back?"
"Bring myself back. I feel thankful for this."
"This?"
"Your idea about the 'it.'"
"My idea?"
"I feel thankful towards you."

"I" and "You" Language   We've seen that "I" language is a way of accepting responsibility for a message. **"You" language** is quite different. It expresses a judgment of the other person. Notice how each of the following statements implies that the subject of the complaint is doing something wrong:

"You left this place a mess!"

"You didn't keep your promise!"

"You're really crude sometimes!"

Despite its name, "you" language doesn't have to contain the pronoun *you*, which is often implied rather than stated outright:

"That was a stupid joke!" ("Your jokes are stupid.")

"Don't be so critical!" ("You're too negative.")

"Mind your own business!" ("You're too nosy.")

Whether the judgment is stated outright or implied, it's easy to see why "you" language can arouse defensiveness. A "you" statement implies that the speaker is qualified to judge the target—not an idea that most listeners are willing to accept, even when the judgment is correct.

Fortunately, "I" language provides a more accurate and less provocative way to express a complaint.[27] "I" language shows that the speaker takes responsibility for the complaint by describing his or her reaction to the other's behavior without making any judgments about its worth.

A complete "I" statement has four elements. It describes

1. the other person's behavior
2. your interpretations
3. your feelings
4. the consequences that the other person's behavior has for you

These elements can appear in any order. A few examples of "I" statements illustrate how they sound in everyday conversation:

"I get embarrassed (*feeling*) when you talk about my bad grades in front of our friends (*behavior*). I'm afraid they'll think I'm stupid (*interpretation*). That's why I got so worked up last night (*consequence*)."

"When you didn't pick me up on time this morning (*behavior*) I was late for class, and I wound up getting chewed out by the professor (*consequences*). It seemed to me that my being on time didn't seem important to you. That's why I got so mad (*feeling*)."

When you point one accusing finger at someone, three of your own fingers point back at you.

Louis Nizer

"I haven't been very affectionate (*consequence*) because you've hardly spent any time with me in the past few weeks (*behavior*). I'm not sure if you're avoiding me, or if you're just busy (*interpretations*). I'm confused (*feeling*) about how you feel about me, and I want to clear it up."

When the risks of being misunderstood or getting a defensive reaction are high, it's a good idea to include all four elements in your "I" message. In some cases, however, only one or two of them will get the job done:

"I went to a lot of trouble fixing this dinner, and now it's cold. Of course, I'm mad!" (The behavior is obvious.)

"I'm worried because you haven't called me up." ("Worried" is both a feeling and a consequence.)

Even the best "I" statement won't work unless it's delivered in the right way. If your words are nonjudgmental, but your tone of voice, facial expression, and posture all send "you" messages, a defensive response is likely to follow. The best way to make sure that your actions match your words is to remind yourself before speaking that your goal is to explain how the other's behavior affects you—not to act like a judge and jury.

Advantages of "I" Language   Using "I" language has three advantages, both for you and for the recipients: defense reduction, honesty, and completeness.

1. *Defense Reduction* Others are more likely to accept your message when it's delivered in "I" language than when you make judgmental "you" statements. Even accurate "you" statements ("you're late," "you broke your promise") are hard to take. By contrast, "I" statements aren't a direct attack on the recipient. Because they describe how the speaker feels, they are easier to accept without justification. This doesn't mean that using "I" language will *eliminate* defensiveness, but it will almost certainly *reduce* it.

2. *Honesty* Even though they are kinder than "you" language, "I" statements are just as honest. They let you speak your mind, sharing what bothers you. They aren't artificially "nice" or watered down to avoid displeasing the other person. In fact, because "I" statements are easier on the recipient, you are more likely to use them when you might be reluctant to blurt out an accusing "you" message.

3. *Completeness* "I" statements deliver more information than "you" statements. Instead of making the other person guess about what's bothering you, they describe the other person's behavior. "I" statements also describe how the other's behavior affects you and how you are feeling—much more information than delivered by most "you" statements.

Problems with "I" Language   Some readers have reservations about using "I" language despite its theoretical appeal. The best way to overcome questions about this communication skill is to answer them.

In interpersonal relationships, I believe first person singular is most appropriate because it places responsibility clearly.

If I say to another person, "I do not like what you did," then no contradiction is possible. No one can correct me because my perception and what I have decided to think about is mine alone. The other person may, however, suggest that I received only a portion of the information, or that I received it unclearly for one reason or another. In such a case, the meaning of the message may be tentative until it can be negotiated. It also is legitimate for me to perceive the message quite differently from the way the other person perceives it.

On the other hand, if I say "You have made me angry," then you may very well contradict me by responding with something such as "No I didn't." In fact, I am eliciting a defensiveness and also inviting "you" to attempt a control of me by your helplessness, suffering, or anger.

Only I am responsible for my behavior. Only I can change what I do. However, when I change my behavior, I may give the other person in the relationship the opportunity to evaluate his behavior and perhaps modify it.

John Narciso and David Burkett,
Declare Yourself

"I" and "You" Language on the Job

For some time, Rebecca has been frustrated by her fellow worker Tom's frequent absences from the job. She hasn't spoken up because she likes Tom and also because she doesn't want to sound like a complainer. Lately, though, Tom's absences have become longer and more frequent. Today he extended his half-hour lunch an extra forty-five minutes. When he returns to the office, Rebecca confronts him with her gripe using "you" language.

Rebecca Where have you been? You were due back at 12:30, and it's almost 1:30 now.

Tom (*Surprised by Rebecca's angry tone, which she has never used before with him*) I had a few errands to run. What's the problem?

Rebecca We all have errands to run, Tom. But it's not fair for you to do yours on company time.

Tom (*Feeling defensive after hearing Rebecca's accusation*) I don't see why you have to worry about how I do my job. Beth (*their boss*) hasn't complained, so why should you worry?

Rebecca Beth hasn't complained because all of us have been covering for you. You should appreciate what a tight spot we're in, making excuses every time you come in late or leave early. (*Again, Rebecca uses "you" language to tell Tom how he should think and act.*)

Tom (*Now too defensive to consider Rebecca's concerns*) Hey, I thought we all covered for one another here. What about the time last year when I worked late for a week so you could go to your cousin's wedding in San Antonio?

Rebecca That's different! Nobody was lying then. When you take off, I have to make up stories about where you are. You're putting me in a very difficult spot, Tom, and it's not fair. You can't count on me to keep covering for you.

Tom (*Feeling guilty, but too angry from Rebecca's judgments and threat to acknowledge his mistakes*) Fine. I'll never ask you for a favor again. Sorry to put you out.

Rebecca may have succeeded in reducing Tom's lateness, but her choice of "you" language left him feeling defensive and angry. The climate in the office is likely to be more strained—hardly the outcome Rebecca was seeking. Notice how she could have handled the same issue using "I" language to describe her problem instead of blaming Tom.

Rebecca Tom, I need to talk to you about a problem. (*Notice how Rebecca identifies the problem as hers instead of attacking Tom.*)

Tom What's up?

Rebecca You know how you come in late to work sometimes or take long lunch hours?

Tom (*Sensing trouble ahead and sounding wary*) Yeah?

Rebecca Well, I need to tell you that it's putting me in a tight spot. (*Rebecca describes the problem in behavioral terms and then goes on to express her feeling.*) When Beth asks where you are, I don't want to say you're not here because that might get you in trouble. So sometimes I make excuses or even lie. But Beth is sounding suspicious of my excuses, and I'm worried about that.

Tom (*Feeling defensive because he knows he's guilty but also sympathetic to Rebecca's position*) I don't want you to get in trouble. It's just that I've got to take care of a lot of personal business.

Rebecca I know, Tom. I just want you to understand that it's getting impossible for me to cover for you.

Tom Yeah, OK. Thanks for helping out.

Notice how "I" language made it possible for Rebecca to confront Tom honestly but without blaming or attacking him personally. Even if Tom doesn't change, Rebecca has gotten the problem off her chest, and she can feel proud that she did so in a way that didn't sound ugly or annoying.

Using your Looking Out/ Looking In CD-ROM, click on Communication Scenarios and then click on the 'I' and 'You' Language on the Job scenario to watch, listen to, and analyze a dramatized version of this conversation.

1. *"I get too angry to use 'I' language."* It's true that when you're angry the most likely reaction is to lash out with a judgmental "you" message. But it's probably smarter to keep quiet until you've thought about the consequences of what you might say than to blurt out something you'll regret later. It's also important to note that there's plenty of room for expressing anger with "I" language. It's just that you own the feeling as yours ("You bet I'm mad at you!") instead of distorting it into an attack ("That was a stupid thing to do!").

2. *"Even with 'I' language, the other person gets defensive."* Like every communication skill described in this book, "I" language won't always work. You may be so upset or irritated that your judgmental feelings contradict your words. Even if you deliver a perfectly worded "I" statement with total sincerity, the other person might be so defensive or uncooperative that nothing you say will make matters better. But using "I" language will almost certainly *improve* your chances for success, with little risk that this approach will make matters worse.

3. *"'I' language sounds artificial."* "That's not the way I talk," you might object. Much of the awkwardness that comes with first using "I" language is due to its novelty. As you become more used to making "I" statements they will sound more and more natural—and become more effective.

One of the best ways to overcome your initial awkwardness is to practice making "I" statements in a safe way: by trying them out in a class, writing them in letters, and delivering them to receptive people on relatively minor issues. After your skill and confidence have grown, you will be ready to tackle really challenging situations in a way that sounds natural and sincere.

SKILL BUILDER

PRACTICING "I" LANGUAGE

You can develop your skill at delivering "I" messages by following these steps:

1. Visualize situations in your life when you might have sent each of the following messages:

   You're not telling me the truth!
   You think only of yourself!
   Don't be so touchy!
   Quit fooling around!
   You don't understand a word I'm saying!

2. Write alternatives to each statement using "I" language.

3. Think of three "you" statements you might make to people in your life. Transform each of these statements into "I" language and rehearse them with a classmate.

"We" Language   Despite its obvious advantages, even the best constructed and delivered "I" message won't always succeed. As author Thomas Gordon points out, "Nobody welcomes hearing that his behavior is causing someone a problem, no matter how the message is phrased."[28] For this reason, Gordon points out that "I" messages can leave the recipient feeling "hurt, sorry, surprised, embarrassed, defensive, argumentative, or even tearful." Furthermore, "I" language in large doses can start to sound egotistical. Research shows that self-absorbed people, also known as "conversational narcissists," can be identified by their constant use of first-person singular pronouns.[29] For this reason, "I" language works best in moderation.

One way to avoid overuse of "I" statements is to consider the pronoun *we*. **"We" statements** imply that the issue is the concern and responsibility of both the speaker and receiver of a message. Consider a few examples:

> "We need to figure out a budget that doesn't bankrupt us."

> "I think we have a problem. We can't seem to talk about money without fighting."

> "We aren't doing a very good job of keeping the place clean, are we?"

It's easy to see how "we" language can help build a constructive climate. Besides being immediate, it suggests a kind of "we're in this together" orientation that reflects the transactional nature of communication. People who use first-person-plural pronouns signal their closeness, commonality, and cohesiveness with others.[30] For example, couples who use "we" language are more satisfied than those who rely more heavily on "I" and "you" language.[31] Chapters 9 and 10 offer detailed advice on the value of achieving a "we" orientation.

On the other hand, "we" statements aren't always appropriate. Sometimes using this pronoun sounds presumptuous because it suggests that you are speaking for the other person as well as yourself. It's easy to imagine someone responding to your statement "We have a problem . . ." by saying, "Maybe *you* have a problem, but don't tell me *I* do!"

Given the pros and cons of both "I" language and "we" language, what advice can we give about the most effective pronouns to use in interpersonal communication? Researchers have found that "I/we" combinations (for example, "I think that we . . ." or "I would like to see us . . .") have a good chance of being received favorably.[32] Because too much of any pronoun comes across as inappropriate, combining pronouns is generally a good idea. If your "I" language reflects your position without being overly self-absorbed, your "you" language shows concern for others without judging them, and your "we" language includes others without speaking for them, you will probably come as close as possible to the ideal use of pronouns. Table 5-4 summarizes the advantages and disadvantages of each type of language and offers suggestions for approaches that have a good chance of success.

TABLE 5-4 Pronoun Use and Its Effects

	ADVANTAGES	DISADVANTAGES	TIPS
"I" language	Takes responsibility for personal thoughts, feelings, and wants. Less defense-provoking than "you" language.	Can be perceived as egotistical, narcissistic, and self-absorbed.	Use "I" messages when other person doesn't perceive a problem. Combine "I" with "we" language.
"We" language	Signals inclusion, immediacy, cohesiveness, and commitment.	Can speak improperly for others.	Combine with "I" language. Use in group settings to enhance unity. Avoid when expressing personal thoughts, feelings, and wants.
"You" language		Can sound evaluative and judgmental.	Use "I" language during confrontations. Use "You" language when praising or including others.

GENDER AND LANGUAGE

So far we have discussed language use as if it were identical for both sexes. Some theorists and researchers take a "Men Are from Mars, Women Are from Venus" approach, arguing that there are significant differences between the way men and women speak.[33] Other scholars have suggested that the differences are few and mostly not significant.[34] What are the similarities and differences between male and female language use?

Content

Although there is a great deal of variation within each gender, on the average men and women discuss a surprisingly different range of topics. The first research on conversational topics was conducted over seventy years ago. Despite the changes in male and female roles since then, the results of several studies are remarkably similar.[35] In these studies, women and men ranging in age from seventeen to eighty described the range of topics each discussed with friends of the same sex. Certain topics were common to both men and women: work, movies, and television proved to be frequent topics for both groups. Both men and women reserved discussions of sex and sexuality for members of the same sex. The differences between men and women were more striking than the similarities. Female friends spent much more time discussing personal and domestic subjects, relationship problems, family, health and reproductive matters, weight, food and clothing, men, and other women. Men, on the other hand, were more likely to discuss music, current events, sports, business, and other men. Both men and women were equally likely to discuss personal appearance, sex, and dating in same-sex conversations. True to one common stereotype, women were more likely to gossip about close friends and family. By contrast, men spent more time gossiping about sports figures and media personalities. Women's gossip was no more derogatory than men's.

These differences can lead to frustration when men and women try to converse with one another. Researchers report that "trivial" is the word often used by both men and women to describe topics discussed by the opposite sex. "I want to talk about important things," a woman might say, "like how we're getting along. All he wants to do is talk about the news or what we'll do this weekend."

"Talk to me, Alice. I speak woman."

© The New Yorker Collection 1992 Mick Stevens from cartoonbank.com. All Rights Reserved.

Reasons for Communicating

Both men and women, at least in the dominant cultures of the United States and Canada, use language to build and maintain social relationships. Regardless of the sex of the communicators, the goals of almost all ordinary conversations include making the conversation enjoyable by being friendly, showing interest in what the other person says, and talking about topics that interest the other person.[36] *How* men and women accomplish these goals is often different, though. Although most communicators try to make their interaction enjoyable, men are more likely than women to emphasize making conversation fun. Their discussions involve a greater amount of joking and good-natured teasing. By contrast, women's discussions involve feelings, relationships, and personal problems. In fact, communication researcher Julia Wood flatly states that "for women, talk *is* the essence of relationships."[37] When members of a group of women were surveyed to find out what kinds of satisfaction they gained from talking with their friends, the most common theme mentioned was a feeling of empathy—"To know you're not alone," as some put it.[38] Whereas men commonly described same-sex conversations as something they *liked*, women described their same-sex conversations as a kind of contact they *needed*. The characteristically female orientation for relational communication is supported by studies of married couples showing that wives spend proportionately more time than husbands communicating in ways that help maintain their relationship.[39]

Because they use conversation to pursue social needs, women typically use statements showing support for the other person, demonstrations of equality, and efforts to keep the conversation going.[40] With these goals, it's not surprising that traditionally female speech often contains statements of sympathy and empathy: "I've felt just like that myself," "The same thing happened to me!" Women are also inclined to ask lots of questions that invite the other person to share information: "How did you feel about that?" "What did you do next?" The importance of nurturing a relationship also explains why female speech is often somewhat powerless and tentative. Saying, "This is just my opinion . . ." is less likely to put off a conversational partner than a more definite "Here's what I think . . ."

The greater frequency of female conversations reflects their importance. Nearly 50 percent of the women surveyed said they called friends at least once a week just to talk, whereas less than half as many men did so. In fact, 40 percent of the men surveyed reported that they never called another man just to chat.

Men's speech is often driven by quite different goals than women's speech. Men are more likely to use language to accomplish the job at hand than to nourish relationships. This explains why men are less likely than women to disclose their vulnerabilities, which would be a sign of weakness. When someone is sharing a problem, instead of empathizing, men are prone to offer advice: "That's nothing to worry about . . ." "Here's what you need to do. . . ." Besides taking care of business, men are more likely than women to use conversations to exert control, preserve their independence, and enhance their status. This explains why men are more prone to dominate conversations and one-up their partners. Men interrupt their conversational partners to assert their own experiences or point of view. (Women interrupt, too, but they usually do so to offer support: quite a different goal.) Just because male talk is competitive doesn't mean it's not enjoyable. Men often regard talk as a kind of game: When researchers asked men what they liked best about their all-male talk, the most frequent answer was its ease.[41] Another common theme was appreciation of the practical value of conversation: new ways to solve problems. Men also mentioned enjoying the humor and rapid pace that characterized their all-male conversations.

Differences like these begin early in childhood. Sociolinguist Deborah Tannen summarizes a variety of studies showing that boys use talk to assert control over one another, whereas girls use talk to maintain harmony.[42] Transcripts of conversations between preschoolers aged two to five showed that girls were far more cooperative than boys.[43] They preceded their proposals for action by saying "let's," as in "Let's go find some" or "Let's turn back." By contrast, boys gave orders like "Lie down" or "Gimme your arm."

Conversational Style

Women behave differently in conversations than do men.[44] For example, although both men and women use expletives, men swear more than women.[45] Women ask more questions in mixed-sex conversations than do men—nearly three times as many, according to one study. Other research has revealed that in mixed-sex conversations, men interrupt women far more than the other way around. Some theorists have argued that differences like these result in women's speech that is less powerful and more

"Gender Games: Doing Business with the Opposite Sex"

http://www. tymson.com.au/ home.html

Click on "Articles & Stories." This site includes several articles written by business educator and speaker Candy Tymson about differences between male and female communication styles. The author suggests concrete skills for dealing effectively with the opposite gender in business. Test your knowledge of gender communication differences by completing Activity 5.4 "Gender Survey" on the *Looking Out/Looking In* Web site.

emotional than men's. Research has supported these theories—at least in some cases. Even when clues about the speakers' sex were edited out, raters found clear differences between transcripts of male and female speech. In one study women's talk was judged more aesthetic, whereas men's talk was judged more dynamic, aggressive, and strong. In another, male job applicants were rated more fluent, active, confident, and effective than female applicants.

Research suggests that women behave somewhat differently in conversations than do men. For example, men are more likely than women to use judgmental adjectives ("Reading can be a drag"), directives ("Think of some more"), and "I" references ("I have a lot to do").[46] Women are more likely to use intensive adverbs ("He's *really* interested"), emotional references ("If he really cared about you . . ."), uncertainty verbs ("It seems to me . . ."), and contradictions ("it's cold, but that's OK"). Differences like these show that men's speech is more typically direct, succinct, personal, and task-oriented. By contrast, women's speech is characterized as more typically indirect, elaborate, and focused on relationships.

Given these differences, a pessimist might wonder how men and women manage to communicate with one another at all. One reason why cross-sex conversations do run smoothly so often is because women accommodate to the topics that men raise. Both men and women often regard topics introduced by women as tentative, whereas topics introduced by men are more likely to be pursued. Thus, women seem to characteristically grease the wheels of conversation by doing more work than men in maintaining conversations. A complementary difference between men and women also promotes cross-sex conversations: Men are more likely to talk about themselves with women than with other men; and because women are willing to adapt to this topic, conversations are likely to run smoothly, if one-sidedly.

An accommodating style isn't always a disadvantage for women. One study revealed that women who spoke tentatively were actually more persuasive with men than those who used more powerful speech.[47] On the other hand, this tentative style was less effective in persuading women. (Language use had no effect on men's persuasiveness.) This study suggests that women who are willing and able to be flexible in their approach can persuade both other women and men—as long as they are not dealing with a mixed-sex audience.

Nongender Variables

Despite the differences in the way men and women speak, the link between gender and language use isn't as clear-cut as it might seem. Despite the differences identified earlier, several research reviews have found that the ways women and men communicate are much more similar than different. For example, one analysis of over twelve hundred research studies found that only 1 percent of variance in communication behavior resulted from gender difference.[48] There is no significant difference between male speech and female speech in areas such as use of profanity, use of qualifiers such as "I guess" or "This is just my opinion," tag questions, and vocal fluency.[49] Some on-the-job research shows that male and female supervisors in similar positions behave the same way and are equally effective. In light of the considerable similarities between the sexes and the relatively minor differences, some communication scholars suggest that the "Men Are from Mars, Women Are from Venus" metaphor should be replaced by the metaphor that "men are from North Dakota, women are from South Dakota."[50]

A growing body of research explains some of the apparent contradictions between the similarities and differences between male speech and female speech. Research has revealed other factors that influence language use as much or more than does gender.[51] For example, social philosophy plays a role. Feminist wives talk longer than their partners, whereas nonfeminist wives speak less than their partners. Orientation toward problem-solving also plays a role in conversational style. The cooperative or competitive orientations of speakers have more influence on how they interact than does their gender.

The speaker's occupation also influences speaking style. For example, male day-care teachers' speech to their students resembles the language of female teachers more closely than it resembles the language of fathers at home. Overall, doctors interrupt their patients more often than the reverse, although male patients do interrupt female doctors more often than their male counterparts. A close study of trial transcripts showed that the speaker's experience on the witness stand and occupation had more to do with language use than did gender. If women generally use "powerless" language, this fact probably reflects their historical role in society at large.

To the degree that women use powerless language, there may be two explanations. The first involves their historical role in society at large: Powerless speech may reflect the relative lack of power held by women. If this explanation is valid, the male-female differences in powerful speech and powerless speech are likely to diminish. A second, equally compelling explanation for the finding that women use more powerless language comes from scholars including Julia Wood[52] and Deborah Tannen,[53] who point out that what powerless speech loses in potency it gains by building rapport between speaker and receiver. Because women have historically been more concerned with building harmonious relationships, it follows that typically feminine speech will sound less powerful.

Another powerful force that influences the way individual men and women speak is their *sex role*. Recall the sex types described in chapter 3 (page 110): masculine, feminine, and androgynous. Remember that these sex types don't necessarily line up neatly with gender. There are "masculine" females, "feminine" males, and androgynous communicators

Consider the marriage of a man who has had most of his conversations with other men, to a woman who has had most of hers with other women. . . . He is used to fast-paced conversations that typically stay on the surface with respect to emotions, that often enable him to get practical tips or offer them to others and that are usually pragmatic or fun. She is used to conversations that, while practical and fun too, are also a major source of emotional support, self-understanding and the understanding of others. Becoming intimate with a man, the woman may finally start expressing her concerns to him as she might to a close friend. But she may find, to her dismay, that his responses are all wrong. Instead of making her feel better, he makes her feel worse. The problem is that he tends to be direct and practical, whereas what she wants more than anything else is an empathetic listener. Used to years of such responses from close friends, a woman is likely to be surprised and angered by her husband's immediate "Here's what ya do. . . ."

Mark Sherman and Adelaide Haas

who combine traditionally masculine and feminine characteristics. These sex types can influence a communicator's style more than his or her biological sex. For example, one study revealed that masculine sex-type subjects used significantly more dominance language than did either feminine or androgynous subjects.[54] Feminine subjects expressed slightly more submissive behaviors and more equivalence behaviors than did the androgynous subjects, and their submissiveness and equivalence were much greater than those of the masculine subjects.

By now it should be clear that there are differences between the way men and women speak but that these differences are determined by a wide variety of factors that have little or nothing to do with biological sex. As men and women grow to have equal opportunities and more similar social experiences, we can expect that there will be fewer differences in the ways they speak.

LANGUAGE AND CULTURE

Anyone who has tried to translate ideas from one language to another knows that conveying the same meaning isn't always easy.[55] Sometimes the results of a bungled translation can be amusing. For example, the American manufacturers of Pet milk unknowingly introduced their product in French-speaking markets without realizing that the word *pet* in French means "to break wind."[56] Likewise, the English-speaking representative of a U.S. soft drink manufacturer naively drew laughs from Mexican customers when she offered free samples of Fresca soda pop. In Mexican slang the word *fresca* means "lesbian."

Even choosing the right words during translation won't guarantee that nonnative speakers will use an unfamiliar language correctly. For example, Japanese insurance companies warn their policy holders who are visiting the United States to avoid their cultural tendency to say "excuse me" or "I'm sorry" if they are involved in a traffic accident.[57] In Japan, apologizing is a traditional way to express goodwill and maintain social harmony, even if the person offering the apology is not at fault. But in the United States an apology can be taken as an admission of fault and result in Japanese tourists being wrongly held responsible for accidents.

Difficult as it may be, translation is only a small part of the differences in communication between members of different cultures. Differences in the way language is used and the very worldview that a language creates make communicating across cultures a challenging task.

Verbal Communication Styles

Using language is more than just choosing a particular group of words to convey an idea. Each language has its own unique style that distinguishes it from others. Matters like the amount of formality or informality, precision or vagueness, and brevity or detail are major ingredients in speaking competently. And when a communicator tries to use the verbal style from one culture in a different one, problems are likely to arise.[58]

One way in which verbal styles vary is in their *directness*. Anthropologist Edward Hall identified two distinct cultural ways of using language.[59] **Low-context cultures** generally value using language to express thoughts, feelings, and ideas as clearly and logically as possible. Low-context communicators look for the meaning of a statement in the words spoken. By contrast, **high-context cultures** value using language to maintain social harmony. Rather than upset others by speaking clearly, high-context communicators learn to discover meaning from the context in which a message is delivered: the nonverbal behaviors of the speaker, the history of the relationship, and the general social rules that govern interaction between people. Table 5-5 summarizes some key differences between the way low- and high-context cultures use language.

North American culture falls toward the low-context end of the scale. Residents of the United States and Canada value straight talk and grow impatient with "beating around the bush." By contrast, most Asian and Middle Eastern cultures fall toward the high-context end of the scale. In many Asian cultures, for example, maintaining harmony is important, and so communicators will avoid speaking clearly if that would threaten another person's face. For this reason, Japanese and Koreans are less likely than Americans to offer a clear "no" to an undesirable request. Instead they will probably use roundabout expressions like "I agree with you in principle, but . . ." or "I sympathize with you. . . ."

The same sort of clash between directness and indirectness can aggravate problems between straight-talking, low-context Israelis who value speaking clearly and Arabs, whose high-context culture stresses smooth interaction. It's easy to imagine how the clash of cultural styles could lead to misunderstandings and conflicts between Israelis and their Palestinian neighbors. Israelis could view the Palestinians as evasive, whereas the Palestinians could view the Israelis as insensitive and blunt.

"Your Japanese Guests"

http://fly.hiwaay. net/~eueda/ japguest.htm

This page is an account of what often happens when Japanese and U.S. Americans meet. Japanese translator Ueda writes about the differences between Japanese and U.S. American culture and communication styles and emphasizes intercultural understanding for sake of the global economy. Access this page and complete Activity 5.7 "High-Context and Low-Context Cultures" on the *Looking Out/Looking In* Web site.

TABLE 5-5 **Low- and High-Context Communication Styles**

LOW CONTEXT	HIGH CONTEXT
Majority of information carried in explicit verbal messages, with less focus on the situational context.	Important information carried in contextual cues (time, place, relationship). Less reliance on explicit verbal messages.
Self-expression valued. Communicators state opinions and desires directly and strive to persuade others to accept their own viewpoint.	Relational harmony valued and maintained by indirect expression of opinions. Communicators abstain from saying "no" directly.
Clear, eloquent speech considered praiseworthy. Verbal fluency admired.	Communicators talk "around" the point, allowing the other to fill in the missing pieces. Ambiguity and use of silence admired.

Mikako Garard: "Speaking" the Culture

Mikako Garard came to the United States at age twenty-one to study at Southern Illinois University. In this profile, she describes how learning to communicate competently in a new language demands skills that aren't usually taught in school.

Before coming to the U.S. from Japan, I studied English for eight years in junior high, high school, and college. I thought I would get along just fine at the university at Carbondale, Illinois. It didn't take long for me to learn that my formal education hadn't prepared me for communicating in the real world of American English.

I knew the rules of English grammar well enough and my vocabulary was pretty large, but that didn't help me understand the way all those Midwestern professors and students spoke. They talked so fast! And their accents didn't sound at all like the way my Japanese and British English instructors spoke back in Japan. Also, they used words that we never were taught in school—like "dude," and "stoked." Understanding colloquial phrases was also hard at first. I finally figured out that the question "What's up?" meant "What's happening in your life?" Since most people answered "Not much." I thought Americans were living pretty boring lives! For my first six months in the U.S., I was exhausted from trying to figure out what people were saying. Also, I was afraid to speak myself because I knew I would make all sorts of mistakes.

After earning a M.A. degree in communication, I took a job as an interpreter in the Kentucky factory of an automotive parts company. My job was to help the Japanese managers and the American staff understand one another. By that time I was really comfortable speaking and understanding English, so I thought this job would be a snap. Was I surprised!

I learned that translating wasn't simply a matter of taking words from one language and saying them in another one. I had to switch the whole style of a message. For example, American business people communicate much more informally than Japanese. Because of this, I couldn't directly translate an American engineer's statement like "What's going on here? This doesn't make any sense!" If I translated that message directly, the Japanese manager would have been very offended. So to make the message fit the Japanese style, I would have to say something like "I'm having a great deal of trouble understanding this problem. I'm sure it's my fault. Could you please explain it to me in more detail?" I had to do the same thing in reverse too, translating and transforming more formal messages from Japanese managers into the style that American engineers, factory workers, and customers were used to.

These experiences have taught me that there's a lot more to learning a language than grammar and vocabulary. If you want to have smooth relationships with people, you have to "speak" the culture, too.

Even within a single country, cocultures can have different notions about the value of direct speech. For example, one series of studies revealed that Asian Americans were more offended by indirectly racist statements than were African Americans, Hispanics, and Anglo Americans.[60] Researchers Laura Leets and Howard Giles suggested that the traditional Asian tendency to favor high-context messages explains the difference: Adept at recognizing hints and nonverbal cues, high-context communicators are more sensitive to messages that were overlooked by people from cultural groups that rely more heavily on unambiguous, explicit low-context messages.

It's worth noting that even generally straight-talking residents of the United States raised in the low-context Euro-American tradition often rely on context to make their point. When you decline an unwanted invitation by saying, "I can't make it," it's likely that both you and the other person know that the choice of attending isn't really beyond your control. If your goal was to be perfectly clear, you might say, "I don't want to get together." As chapter 10 explains in detail, we often equivocate precisely because we want to obscure our true thoughts and feelings.

Besides their degrees of clarity and vagueness, another way in which language styles can vary across cultures is whether they are *elaborate* or *succinct*. Speakers of Arabic, for instance, commonly use language that is much more rich and expressive than that of most communicators who use English. Strong assertions and exaggerations that would sound ridiculous in English are a common feature of Arabic. This contrast in linguistic styles can lead to misunderstandings between people from different backgrounds. As one observer put it,

> First, an Arab feels compelled to overassert in almost all types of communication because others expect him [or her] to. If an Arab says exactly what he [or she] means without the expected assertion, other Arabs may still think that he [or she] means the opposite. For example, a simple "no" by a guest to the host's requests to eat more or drink more will not suffice. To convey the meaning that he [or she] is actually full, the guest must keep repeating "no" several times, coupling it with an oath such as "By God" or "I swear to God." Second, an Arab often fails to realize that others, particularly foreigners, may mean exactly what they say even though their language is simple. To the Arabs, a simple "no" may mean the indirectly expressed consent and encouragement of a coquettish woman. On the other hand, a simple consent may mean the rejection of a hypocritical politician.[61]

Succinctness is most extreme in cultures where silence is valued. In many Native American cultures, for example, the favored way to handle ambiguous social situations is to remain quiet.[62] When you contrast this silent style to the talkativeness that is common in mainstream American cultures when people first meet, it's easy to imagine how the first encounter between an Apache or Navajo and an Anglo might feel uncomfortable to both people.

Along with differences such as directness and indirectness and elaborate and succinct styles, a third way in which languages differ from one culture to another involves *formality* and *informality*. The informal

What mattered to Abu was the *music* of the sentence . . . in general, it was the poetics, the music of things that tossed his confetti . . .

Everywhere, the Arabic alphabet wiggled and popped . . . with outbursts of linguistic jazz, notations from the DNA songbook, energetic markings as primal as grunts and as modern as the abstract electricity of synthesizer feedback.

Tom Robbins, *Skinny Legs and All*

"The Eskimos have eighty-seven words for snow and not one for malpractice."

© 2001 Leo Cullum from cartoonbank.com. All Rights Reserved.

approach that characterizes relationships in countries like the United States, Canada, Australia, and the Scandinavian countries is quite different from the great concern for using proper speech in many parts of Asia and Africa. Formality isn't so much a matter of using correct grammar as of defining social position. In Korea, for example, the language reflects the Confucian system of relational hierarchies.[63] It has special vocabularies for different sexes, for different levels of social status, for different degrees of intimacy, and for different types of social occasions. For example, there are different degrees of formality for speaking with old friends, nonacquaintances whose background one knows, and complete strangers. One sign of being a learned person in Korea is the ability to use language that recognizes these relational distinctions. When you contrast these sorts of distinctions with the casual friendliness that many North Americans use even when talking with complete strangers, it's easy to see how a Korean might view communicators in the United States as boorish and how an American might view communicators in Korea as stiff and unfriendly.

Language and Worldview

Different linguistic styles are important, but there may be even more important differences that separate speakers of various languages. For almost 150 years, some theorists have put forth the notion of **linguistic determinism:** that the worldview of a culture is unavoidably shaped and reflected by the language its members speak. The best-known example of linguistic determinism is the notion that Eskimos have a large number of words (estimated at everything from seventeen to one hundred) for what we simply call "snow." Different terms are used to describe conditions like a driving blizzard, crusty ice, and light powder. This example suggests how linguistic determinism operates. The need to survive in an Arctic environment led Eskimos to make distinctions that would be unimportant to residents of warmer environments, and after the language makes these distinctions, speakers are more likely to see the world in ways that match the broader vocabulary.

Even though there is some doubt that Eskimos really have so many words for snow,[64] other examples do seem to support the principle of linguistic determinism.[65] For instance, bilingual speakers seem to think differently when they change languages. In one study, French-American people were asked to interpret a series of pictures. When they described the pictures in French, their descriptions were far more romantic and emotional than when they described the pictures in English. Likewise, when students in Hong Kong were asked to complete a values test, they expressed more traditional Chinese values when they answered in Cantonese than when they answered in English. In Israel, both Arab and Jewish students saw bigger distinctions between their group and "outsiders" when using their native language than when they used English, a neutral tongue. Examples like these show the power of language to shape cultural identity—sometimes for better and sometimes for worse.

LANGUAGE AND HERITAGE

"Mi'ja, it's me. Call me when you wake up." It was a message left on my phone machine from a friend. But when I heard that word "mi'ja," a pain squeezed my heart. My father was the only one who ever called me this. Because his death is so recent, the word overwhelmed me and filled me with grief.

"Mi'ja" (MEE-ha) from "mi hija" (me ee-HA). The words translate as "my daughter." Daughter, my daughter, daughter of mine: They're all stiff and clumsy, and have nothing of the intimacy and warmth of the word "mi'ja" "Daughter of my heart," maybe. Perhaps a more accurate translation of "mi'ja," is I love you.

Sometimes a word can be translated into more than a meaning. In it is the translation of a worldview, a way of looking at things and, yes, even a way of accepting what others might not perceive as beautiful. "Urraca," for example, instead of "grackle." Two ways of looking at a black bird. One sings, the other cackles. Or, "tocayola," your name-twin, and therefore, your friend. Or the beautiful "estrenar," which means to wear something for the first time. There is no word in English for the thrill and pride of wearing something new.

Spanish gives me a way of looking at myself and the world in a new way. For those of us living between worlds, our job in the universe is to help others see with more than their eyes during this period of chaotic transition.

I think of those two brave women in Amarillo who lost their jobs for speaking Spanish, and I wonder at the fear in their employer. Did he think they were talking about him? What an egocentric! Doesn't he understand that speaking another language is another way of seeing, a way of being at home with one another, of saying to your listener, I know you, I honor you, you are my sister, my brother, my mother, my father, my family. If he learns Spanish, or any other language, he would be admitting I love and respect you, and I love to address you in the language you love.

Sandra Cisneros

Linguistic influences start early in life. English-speaking parents often label the mischievous pranks of their children as "bad," implying that there is something immoral about acting wild. "Be good!" they are inclined to say. On the other hand, French parents are more likely to say *"Sois sage!"*—"Be wise." The linguistic implication is that misbehaving is an act of foolishness. Swedes would correct the same action with the words *"Var snall!"*—"Be friendly," "Be kind." By contrast, Germans use the command *"Sei artig!"*—literally "Be of your own kind"—in other words, get back in step, conform to your role as a child.[66]

The best-known declaration of linguistic determinism is the **Sapir–Whorf hypothesis,** formulated by Edward Sapir and Benjamin Whorf.[67] Following Sapir's theory, Whorf observed that the language spoken by Hopi Native Americans represents a view of reality that is dramatically different from that of more familiar tongues. For example, the Hopi language makes no distinction between nouns and verbs. Therefore, the people who speak it describe the entire world as being constantly in process. Whereas in English we use nouns to characterize people or objects as being fixed or constant, Hopi view them more as verbs, constantly changing. In this sense English represents much of the world rather like a snapshot camera, whereas Hopi language represents the world more like a motion picture.

Although there is little support for the extreme notion that it is *impossible* for speakers of different languages to view the world identically, the more moderate notion of **linguistic relativism**—that language exerts a strong influence on perceptions—does seem valid. As one scholar put it, "The differences between languages are not so much in what *can* be said, but in what it is *relatively easy* to say."[68] Some languages contain terms that have no English equivalents.[69] For example, consider a few words in other languages that have no English equivalents:

Nemawashi (Japanese): The process of informally feeling out all the people involved with an issue before making a decision

Lagniappe (French/Creole): An extra gift given in a transaction that wasn't expected by the terms of a contract

Lao (Mandarin): A respectful term used for older people, showing their importance in the family and in society

Dharma (Sanskrit): Each person's unique, ideal path in life and knowledge of how to find it

Koyaanisquatsi (Hopi): Nature out of balance; a way of life so crazy it calls for a new way of living

After words like these exist and become a part of everyday life, the ideas that they represent are easier to recognize. But even without such words, each of the ideas just listed is still possible to imagine. Thus, speakers of a language that includes the notion of *lao* would probably treat its older members respectfully, and those who are familiar with *lagniappe* might be more generous. Despite these differences, the words aren't essential to follow these principles. Although language may shape thoughts and behavior, it doesn't dominate them absolutely.

The importance of language as a reflection of worldview isn't just a matter of interest for anthropologists and linguists. The labels we use in everyday conversation both reflect and shape the way we view ourselves and others. This explains why businesses often give employees impressive titles and why a woman's choice of the label *Ms.* or *Mrs.* can be a statement about her identity.

Relational titles aren't the only linguistic elements that may shape attitudes about men and women. Language reforms like avoiding *he* as a gender-neutral pronoun can lead to less discriminatory thinking. A recent study examined precisely this question.[70] Students were corrected every time they used *he* as a generic pronoun in their writing. At the end of a semester, results showed that the corrections did reduce the use of gender-biased language. However, students did not change their mental images or their attitudes toward language reforms.

Along with gender, labeling can both affect and reflect the way members of an ethnic group define themselves. Through the years labels of racial identification have gone through cycles of popularity. In North America, the first freed slaves preferred to be called "Africans." In the late nineteenth and early twentieth centuries "colored" was the term of choice, but later "Negro" became the respectable word. Then, in the sixties, the term "black" grew increasingly popular—first as a term for militants and later as a term preferred by more moderate citizens of all colors. More recently "African American" has gained popularity. Surveys have found that between 60 and 72 percent of blacks prefer the term "black," whereas between 15 and 25 percent prefer the term "African American." The rest either had no opinion or chose other terms.[71]

SUMMARY

Language is both a marvelous communication tool and the source of many interpersonal problems. Every language is a collection of symbols, governed by a variety of rules: semantic, syntactic, and pragmatic. Because of its symbolic nature, language is not a precise vehicle: Meanings rest in people, not in words themselves.

Language both reflects and shapes the perceptions of its users. Terms used to name people influence the way the people are regarded. The terms used to name speakers and the language they use reflect the level of affiliation, attraction, and interest of a speaker toward a subject. Language patterns also reflect and shape a speaker's perceived power.

When used carelessly, language can lead to a variety of interpersonal problems. The level of precision or vagueness of messages can affect a receiver's understanding of them. Both precise messages and vague, evasive ones have their uses in interpersonal relationships, and a competent communicator has the ability to choose the optimal level of precision for the situation at hand. Language also acknowledges or avoids the speaker's acceptance of responsibility for his or her positions, and competent communicators know how to use "I" and "we" statements to accept the optimal level of responsibility and relational harmony. Some language habits—such as confusing facts with opinions or inferences and using emotive terms—can lead to unnecessary disharmony in interpersonal relationships.

The relationship between gender and language is a confusing one. There are some differences in the ways men and women speak: The contents of their conversations varies, as do their reasons for communicating and their conversational styles. However, not all differences in language use can be accounted for by the speaker's gender. Occupation, social philosophy, and orientation toward problem-solving also influence the use of language, and psychological sex role can be more of an influence than biological sex.

Different languages often shape and reflect the views of a culture. Low-context cultures like the United States use language primarily to express feelings and ideas as clearly and unambiguously as possible. High-context cultures such as Japan and Saudi Arabia, however, avoid specificity in order to promote social harmony. Some cultures value brevity and the succinct use of language, whereas others value elaborate forms of speech. In some societies formality is important, whereas in others informality is important. Beyond these differences, there is evidence to support linguistic relativism—the notion that language exerts a strong influence on the worldview of the people who speak it.

KEY TERMS

abstract language
abstraction ladder
behavioral language
"but" statement
convergence
divergence
emotive language
equivocal language

high-context cultures
"I" language
"it" statements
linguistic relativism
low-context cultures
powerless speech mannerisms
pragmatic rules
relative words

Sapir–Whorf hypothesis
semantic rules
sex roles
static evaluation
syntactic rules
"we" statements
"you" language

LOOKING OUT/LOOKING IN ONLINE

Use your *Looking Out/Looking In* CD-ROM for quick access to the electronic resources that accompany this chapter. Included on this CD-ROM are additional study aids and links to the *Looking Out/Looking In* Web site at the Wadsworth Communication Café. The CD-ROM is your gateway to a wealth of resources that will help you understand and further explore the material in this chapter. **Video clips** under *Communication Scenarios* on the CD illustrate the skills introduced in this chapter. Click on the Web site link to complete self-study **review quizzes** to help you master new concepts; access a **feature film database** to locate clips and entire movies that illustrate communication principles; find Internet material via the maintained **Web site links;** and complete **online activities** to help you master new concepts.

INFOTRAC COLLEGE EDITION EXERCISES

Use the InfoTrac College Edition password that was included free with a copy of this new text to answer the following questions. These questions can be completed online and, if requested, submitted to your instructor under InfoTrac College Edition Activities at the *Looking Out/Looking In* Web site.

1. The Impact of Language

Read "The Problem of Labeling: The Semantics of Behavior" by Walter V. Clarke. (Hint: Use PowerTrac's author and title search tools to find the article.) Apply the author's arguments to your own life by considering what labels you have used to characterize other people and things as either positive or negative. In what ways has others' labeling affected the way you perceive yourself and how others regard you?

2. Gender and Language

Use InfoTrac College Edition's subject search function to find a list of articles on sexist language. Pick one article and (a) define its thesis, (b) identify the evidence offered to support that thesis, and (c) use material from your own experience and reading to either support or argue against the thesis.

3. Language and Culture

Use the subject search function to find a list of articles combining the topics of language and culture. Pick one article and explain its significance in a brief paper or talk to your classmates.

LOOKING OUT/LOOKING IN CD-ROM

Using your *Looking Out/Looking In* CD-ROM, click on *Communication Scenarios* and then click on the "'I' and 'You' Language on the Job" icon to watch and analyze a dramatized version of the conversation featured in the Communication Transcript on page 202.

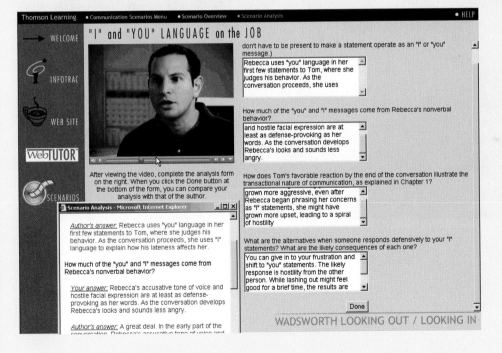

CHAPTER 6

NONVERBAL COMMUNICATION: MESSAGES WITHOUT WORDS

THE ADVENTURES OF SHERLOCK HOLMES

I was seized with a keen desire to see Holmes again, and to know how he was employing his extraordinary powers. His rooms were brilliantly lit, and, even as I looked up, I saw his tall, spare figure pass twice in a dark silhouette against the blind. He was pacing the room swiftly, eagerly, with his head sunk upon his chest and his hands clasped behind him. To me, who knew his every mood and habit, his attitude and manner told their own story. He was at work again. He had risen out of his drug-created dreams and was hot upon the scent of some new problem. I rang the bell and was shown up to the chamber which had formerly been in part my own.

His manner was not effusive. It seldom was; but he was glad, I think, to see me. With hardly a word spoken, but with kindly eye, he waved me to an armchair, threw across his case of cigars, and indicated a spirit case and a gasogene in the corner. Then he stood before the fire and looked me over in his singular introspective fashion.

"Wedlock suits you," he remarked. "I think, Watson, that you have put on seven and a half pounds since I saw you."

"Seven!" I answered.

"Indeed, I should have thought a little more. Just a trifle more, I fancy, Watson. And in practice again, I observe. You did not tell me that you intended to go into harness."

"Then, how do you know?"

"I see it, I deduce it. How do I know that you have been getting yourself very wet lately, and that you have a most clumsy and careless servant girl?"

"My dear Holmes," said I, "this is too much. You would certainly have been burned, had you lived a few centuries ago. It is true that I had a country walk on Thursday and came home in a dreadful mess, but as I have changed my clothes I can't imagine how you deduce it. As to Mary Jane, she is incorrigible, and my wife has given her notice; but there, again, I fail to see how you work it out."

He chuckled to himself and rubbed his long, nervous hands together.

"It is simplicity itself," said he; "my eyes tell me that on the inside of your left shoe, just where the firelight strikes it, the leather is scored by six almost parallel cuts. Obviously they have been caused by someone who has very carefully scraped round the edges of the sole in order to remove crusted mud from it. Hence, you see, my double deduction that you had been out in vile weather, and that you had a particularly malignant boot-slitting specimen of the London slavey. As to your practice, if a gentleman walks into my rooms smelling of iodoform, with a black mark of nitrate of silver upon his right forefinger, and a bulge on the right side of his top hat to show where he has secreted his stethoscope, I must be dull, indeed, if I do not pronounce him to be an active member of the medical profession."

I could not help laughing at the ease with which he explained his process of deduction. "When I hear you give your reasons," I remarked, "the thing always appears to me to be so ridiculously simple that I could easily do it myself, though at each successive instance of your reasoning I am baffled until you explain your process. And yet I believe that my eyes are as good as yours."

"Quite so," he answered, lighting a cigarette, and throwing himself down into an armchair. "You see, but you do not observe."

Arthur Conan Doyle
A Scandal in Bohemia

Sometimes it's difficult to know how other people really feel. Often they don't know for sure themselves, and other times they have some reason for not wanting to tell you. In either case, there are cases when you can't find out what is going on inside another's mind simply by asking.

What should you do in these cases? They happen every day and often in the most important situations. Sherlock Holmes said the way to understand people is to watch them—not only to see, but also to observe.

Observing yourself and others is what this chapter is about. In the following pages you'll become acquainted with the field of nonverbal communication—the way we express ourselves, not by what we say but rather by what we *do*. Some social scientists have argued that 93 percent of the emotional impact of a message comes from nonverbal sources. Others have reasoned more convincingly that the figure is closer to 65 percent.[1] Whatever the precise figure, the point remains: Nonverbal communication plays an important role in how we make sense of one another's behavior. It stands to reason, then, that the ability to understand nonverbal messages is an important part of communicative competence.

We need to begin our study of nonverbal communication by defining that term. At first this might seem like a simple task: If *non* means "not" and *verbal* means "words," then *nonverbal communication* means "communicating without words." In fact, this literal definition isn't completely accurate. For instance, most communication scholars don't define American Sign Language (used by many people with hearing impairments) as nonverbal even though the messages are unspoken. On the other hand, you'll soon read that certain aspects of the voice aren't really verbal, although they are vocal. (Can you think of any? Table 6-1 will help you.)

This isn't the place to explore the rather complex debate about exactly what is and what isn't nonverbal. Interesting as that subject may be, we can move along in this introduction by defining **nonverbal communication** as "those messages expressed by other than linguistic means." This rules out not only sign languages but also written words, but it includes messages transmitted by vocal means that don't involve language—the sighs, laughs, and other assorted noises we alluded to earlier. In addition, our definition allows us to explore the nonlinguistic dimensions of the spoken word—volume, rate, pitch, and so on.

Our brief definition only hints at the richness of nonverbal messages. You can begin to understand their prevalence by trying a simple experiment.

Nonverbal Communication Means

Smiling, frowning

laughing, crying, sighing

standing close to others

being standoffish

The way you look:

your hair, your clothing

your face, your body

your handshake (sweaty palms?)

your postures

your gestures

your mannerisms

Your voice:

soft-loud

fast-slow

smooth-jerky

The environment that you create:

your home, your room

your office, your desk

your kitchen

your car

TABLE 6-1 Types of Communication

	VOCAL COMMUNICATION	NONVOCAL COMMUNICATION
VERBAL COMMUNICATION	Spoken words	Written words
NONVERBAL COMMUNICATION	Tone of voice, sighs, screams, vocal quality, pitch, loudness, etc.	Gestures, movement, appearance, facial expression, touch, etc.

"Types of Communication" adapted from *Together: Communicating Interpersonally* by J. Stewart and G. D'Angelo. ©1980 Addison-Wesley. Used courtesy McGraw-Hill Inc.

INVITATION TO INSIGHT

VERBAL AND NONVERBAL COMMUNICATION

Here's an experiment you can try either at home or in class. It will help you begin learning how nonverbal communication works.

1. Pick a partner, and find a place where you have some space to your-selves.

2. Now sit back-to-back with your partner, making sure that no parts of your bodies are touching. You should be seated so that you can talk easily without seeing each other.

3. After you're seated, take two minutes to carry on a conversation about whatever subject you like. The only requirement is that you not look at or touch each other. Communicate by using words only.

4. Next, turn around so that you're facing your partner, seated at a comfortable distance. Now that you can both see and hear each other, carry on your conversation for another two minutes.

5. Continue to face each other, but for the next two minutes don't speak. Instead, join hands with your partner and communicate whatever messages you want to through sight and touch. Try to be aware of how you feel as you go through this step. There isn't any right or wrong way to behave here—there's nothing wrong with feeling embarrassed, silly, or any other way. The only requirement is to *remain silent.*

After you've finished the experiment, take some time to talk it over with your partner. Start by sharing how you felt in each part of the experience. Were you comfortable, nervous, playful, affectionate? Did your feelings change from one step to another? Could your partner tell these feelings without your expressing them? If so, how? Did your partner communicate his or her feelings, too?

What you are speaks so loudly I cannot hear what you say.

Ralph Waldo Emerson

CHARACTERISTICS OF NONVERBAL COMMUNICATION

If this experiment seemed strange to you, we hope you still went through with it because it points out several things about nonverbal communication.

Nonverbal Communication Exists

Even when you and your partner were in the nontalking part of the experiment, you probably could pick up some of your partner's feelings by touching hands and noting posture and expressions—maybe more than you could during your conversation. We hope that this experiment showed you that there are other languages besides words that carry messages about your relationships.

The point isn't so much *how* you or your partner behaved during the experiment—whether you were tense or relaxed, friendly or distant. We wanted to show you that even without any formal experience you can recognize and to some degree interpret messages that other people send nonverbally. In this chapter we want to sharpen the skills you already have, to give you a better grasp of the vocabulary of nonverbal language, and to show you how this knowledge can help you understand yourself and others better.

All Nonverbal Behavior Has Communicative Value

The fact that communication without words took place between you and your partner brings us to this second important feature of nonverbal communication. To understand what we mean here, think about the experiment that you just finished. Suppose we'd asked you not to communicate any messages at all while with your partner. What would you have done? Closed your eyes? Withdrawn into a ball? Left the room? You can probably see that even these behaviors communicate messages—that you're avoiding contact. One study demonstrated this fact.[2] When communicators were told not to express nonverbal clues, others viewed them as dull, withdrawn, uneasy, aloof, and deceptive.

Take a minute now to try *not* communicating. Join a partner, and spend some time trying not to reveal any messages to one another. What happens?

This impossibility of not communicating is extremely important to understand because it means that each of us is a kind of transmitter that cannot be shut off. No matter what we do, we give off information about ourselves.[3]

Stop for a moment, and examine yourself as you read this. If someone were observing you now, what nonverbal clues would that person get about how you're feeling? Are you sitting forward or reclining back? Is your posture tense or relaxed? Are your eyes wide open, or do they keep closing? What does your facial expression communicate? Can you make your face expressionless? Don't people with expressionless faces communicate something to you?

"I tell you, Mr. Arthur, this survey has no way of registering a non-verbal response."

Reproduced by Special Permission of *Playboy* magazine: ©1977 by Playboy.

Writer [to movie producer Sam Goldwyn]: Mr. Goldwyn, I'm telling you a sensational story. I'm only asking for your opinion, and you fall asleep.

Goldwyn: Isn't sleeping an opinion?

Of course, we don't always intend to send nonverbal messages. Unintentional nonverbal behaviors differ from intentional ones.[4] For example, we often stammer, blush, frown, and sweat without meaning to do so. Whether or not our nonverbal behavior is intentional, others recognize it and make interpretations about us based on their observations.

Some theorists argue that unintentional behavior may provide information but that it shouldn't count as communication. We draw the boundaries of nonverbal communication more broadly, suggesting that even unconscious and unintentional behavior conveys messages and thus is worth studying as communication.

Much Nonverbal Communication Is Culture-Bound

Cultures have different nonverbal languages as well as verbal ones. Fiorello LaGuardia, legendary mayor of New York from 1933 to 1945, was fluent in English, Italian, and Yiddish. Researchers who watched films of his campaign speeches found that they could tell with the sound turned off which language he was speaking by noticing the changes in his nonverbal behavior.[5]

Some nonverbal behaviors have different meanings from culture to culture. The "OK" gesture made by joining the tips of thumb and forefinger to form a circle is a cheery affirmation to most Americans, but it has less positive meanings in other parts of the world.[6] In France and Belgium it means "You're worth zero." In Greece and Turkey it is a vulgar sexual invitation, usually meant as an insult. Given this sort of cross-cultural ambiguity, it's easy to imagine how an innocent tourist might wind up in serious trouble.

Less obvious cross-cultural differences can damage relationships without the parties ever recognizing exactly what has gone wrong. Anthropologist Edward Hall points out that, whereas Americans are comfortable conducting business at a distance of roughly four feet, people from the Middle East stand much closer.[7] It is easy to visualize the awkward advance-and-retreat pattern that might occur when two diplomats or businesspeople from these

Dilbert reprinted by permission of United Feature Syndicate, Inc.

cultures meet. The middle easterner would probably keep moving forward to close the gap that feels so wide, whereas the American would continually back away. Both would feel uncomfortable, probably without knowing why.

Communicators become more tolerant of others after they understand that unusual nonverbal behaviors are the result of cultural differences. In one study, American adults were presented with videotapes of speakers from the United States, France, and Germany.[8] When the sound was eliminated, viewers judged foreigners more negatively than their fellow citizens. But when the speakers' voices were added (allowing viewers to recognize that the speakers were from a different country), the critical ratings dropped.

Like distance, patterns of eye contact vary around the world.[9] A direct gaze is considered appropriate for speakers in Latin America, the Arab world, and southern Europe. On the other hand, Asians, Indians, Pakistanis, and northern Europeans gaze at a listener peripherally or not at all. In either case, deviations from the norm are likely to make a listener uncomfortable.

Differing cultural norms for nonverbal behavior make the potential for cross-cultural misunderstandings great. For example, many Anglo schoolteachers use quasi-questions that hint at the information they are seeking: "Does the name 'Hamilton' ring a bell?" An elementary school instructor might encourage the class to speak up by making an incorrect statement that demands refutation: "So twelve divided by four is six, right?" Most Anglo students would recognize this behavior as a way of testing their understanding. But this style of questioning is unfamiliar to many students raised in traditional black cultures, who aren't likely to respond until they are directly questioned by the instructor.[10] Given this difference, it is easy to imagine how some teachers might view minority children as unresponsive or slow, when in fact the children are simply playing by a different set of rules.

Despite differences like these, many nonverbal behaviors are universal. Certain expressions have the same meanings around the world. Smiles and laughter are universal signals of positive emotions, for example, whereas sour expressions are universal signals of displeasure.[11] Charles Darwin believed that expressions like these are the result of evolution, functioning as survival mechanisms that allowed early humans to convey emotional states before the development of language. The innateness of some facial expressions becomes even more clear when we examine the behavior of children born deaf and blind.[12] Despite a lack of social learning, these children display a broad range of expression. They smile, laugh, and cry in ways virtually identical to those of seeing and hearing children.

Although nonverbal expressions like these may be universal, the way they are used varies widely around the world. Some cultures discourage the overt demonstration of feelings like happiness or anger. In other cultures the same feelings are perfectly appropriate. Thus, a Japanese might appear much more controlled and placid than an Arab, when in fact their feelings might be identical.

The men walked hand-in-hand, laughing sleepily together under blinding vertical glare. Sometimes they put their arms round each other's necks; they seemed to like to touch each other, as if it made them feel good to know the other man was there. It wasn't love; it didn't mean anything we could understand.

Graham Greene, *Journey without Maps*

The same principle operates closer to home among members of different co-cultures. And, as Table 6-2 shows, differences can lead to misunderstandings. For example, observations have shown that black women in all-black groups are nonverbally more expressive and interrupt each other more than white women in all-white groups. This doesn't mean that black women always feel more intensely than their white counterparts. A more likely explanation is that the two groups follow different cultural rules. The researchers found that in racially mixed groups both black and white women moved closer to each others' style.[13] This nonverbal convergence shows that skilled communicators can adapt their behavior when interacting with members of other cultures or subcultures in order to make the exchange more smooth and effective.

TABLE 6-2   Cultural Differences in Nonverbal Communication Can Lead to Misunderstandings

Behaviors that have one meaning for members of the same culture or co-culture can be interpreted differently by members of other groups.

BEHAVIOR	PROBABLE IN-GROUP PERCEPTION	POSSIBLE OUT-GROUP PERCEPTION
Avoidance of direct eye (Latino/a)	Used to communicate attentiveness or respect	A sign of inattentiveness; direct eye contact is preferred
Aggressively challenging a point with which one disagrees (African American)	Acceptable means of dialogue; not regarded as verbal abuse or a precursor to violence	Arguments are viewed as inappropriate and a sign of potential imminent violence.
Use of finger gestures to beckon others (Asian American)	Appropriate if used by adults for children, but highly offensive if directed at adults	Appropriate gesture to use with both children and adults
Silence (Native American)	A sign of respect, thoughtfulness, and/or uncertainty/ambiguity	Interpreted as boredom, disagreement, or refusal to participate/respond
Touch (Latino/a)	Normal and appropriate for interpersonal interactions	Deemed appropriate for some intimate or friendly interactions; otherwise perceived as a violation of personal space
Public display of intense emotions (African American)	Accepted and valued as measure of expressiveness. Appropriate in most settings.	Violates expectations for self-controlled public behaviors; inappropriate in most public settings
Touching or holding hands of same-sex friends (Asian American)	Acceptable behavior that signifies closeness in platonic relationships	Perceived as inappropriate; especially for male friends

Table from *Interracial Communication Theory Into Practice (with Info Trac)*, 1st edition, by M. P. Orbe and T. M. Harris ©2001. Reprinted with permission of Wadsworth, an imprint of Wadsworth Group, a division of Thomson Learning. Fax 800-730-2215.

LEARNING TO GRIN AND BEAR IT

It's Wednesday night, and Hiroshi Ieyoshi and three dozen other gas station attendants are gathered for some tough after-hours training. They're learning how to smile. Or rather, trying to learn.

Relax the muscle under your nose, teacher Akio Emi commands. Loosen up your tongue. Put your hands on your stomach and laugh out loud, feeling the "poisons" escape. Even if you're down in the dumps, Emi tells his sullen audience, deliver an artificial smile and your emotions are likely to follow suit.

Getting employees to smile on the job has become serious business in Japan. Many retail and service businesses are sending workers to "smile schools," which teach techniques such as biting on a chopstick, in hopes that sales and corporate morale will rise along with employees' lips.

It's all a radical change for dour Japan, where smiling at strangers— even if they are customers—has long been, well, frowned upon. Clerks greet customers with a simple "Irasshaimase"— "Welcome"—but usually don't give a friendly grin, make chitchat or even offer a casual "How are you?" or "Have a nice day."

Japanese tradition calls for suppressing emotions—be they happy, sad or angry—to keep the *wa*, or group harmony. In this formal society, families rarely touch, hug or otherwise display physical affection in public, even after long absences. Jokes that foreigners crack at the start of speeches are usually met with dead silence.

"It's so deep in our Japanese consciousness that it's not proper to move the face or body too much," explains Hiroto Murasawa of the Pola Research Institute of Beauty and Culture in Tokyo, who studies faces for a living. Until this century, he notes, some Japanese women shaved their eyebrows and blackened their teeth to veil natural expression. Many Japanese women still hide their mouths behind a hand when they speak or laugh. For men, too, concealing emotion has been considered a virtue.

The Japanese are not humorless. It's just that their expressions are so much more reserved than those of most other countries, including Asian neighbors such as South Korea and China, says Murasawa.

So in the past few years, teachers such as Emi, a retired department store executive, and Yoshihiko Kadokawa, a former retailer who noticed that his friendliest clerks racked up the strongest sales, have made importing joviality their mission. "Japanese are too serious," Emi tells his class. "We have to learn a sense of humor from other countries."

Some foreign firms, such as McDonald's Corp., put such a premium on smiling faces in Japan these days that they discriminate against poker faces in the hiring process. How? In interviews, job applicants are asked to describe their most pleasant experience, and managers evaluate whether their faces reflect the pleasure they're discussing, says Yuichiro Koiso, dean of the company's training institute, known as Hamburger University. If otherwise qualified but unable to crack a smile, they're banished to a job making burgers instead of meeting customers.

After all, employees must provide friendliness at the price promised on menus at each of the chain's nearly 3,000 restaurants in Japan: "Smiles, 0 yen."

Valerie Reifman

Male and Female Nonverbal Communications Differ in Some Ways

It's easy to identify stereotypical differences in male and female styles of nonverbal communication. Just think about exaggerated caricatures of macho men and delicate woman that appear from time to time. Many humorous films and plays have been created around the results that arise when characters try to act like members of the opposite sex. (For some examples, see the "Film Resources" section at the end of this chapter.)

Although few of us behave like over-the-top, stereotypically masculine or feminine movie characters, there are recognizable differences in the way men and women look and act. Some of these differences are biological. Men are generally taller than women. They have deeper, louder voices and more body hair. As a group, women are shorter and less muscular. They have rounder hips, larger breasts, and narrower waists.

Although there's no denying these physical differences, most communication scholars agree that culture has far more influence than biology does in shaping how men and women behave. For example, consider how fashions in the industrialized world accentuate women's physiology: Push-up bras emphasize breast size, high heels force women to wiggle their hips while walking, and the practice of shaving armpits and legs minimizes body hair. Customs like these reflect a cultural emphasis on differences rather than similarities.[14]

Beyond appearance, there are cultural norms in the Western world that distinguish male from female behaviors. For example,

- Women make more eye contact than do men with conversational partners.
- Women are more vocally expressive than men.
- Women interact at closer distances, both with men and with other women, than do men in same-sex conversations.
- Men are more likely to lean forward in conversations than women.
- Men require and are given more personal space than women.
- Women are more likely to face conversational partners head on, whereas men more typically angle their bodies obliquely when speaking.
- Women express more feelings via facial expressions than men. Most noticeably, women smile considerably more than men.
- Women gesture more, whereas men use more expansive gestures.[15]

After looking at differences like these, it might seem as if men and women communicate in radically different ways. In fact, quite the opposite is true: Exhaustive research has shown that sex differences in communication are so minor that men's and women's communication are about 99 percent similar and only 1 percent different.[16] Of course, this 1 percent can be powerful, as we note when we see a masculine-acting woman or a feminine-acting man. Despite this fact, we can say that when it comes to nonverbal communication, it's wrong to claim that men are from Mars and women from Venus. Communication researcher Kathleen Dindia put it well when she said that "Men are from North Dakota, and women are from South Dakota."[17]

Nonverbal Communication Is Primarily Relational

Some nonverbal messages serve utilitarian functions. For example, a police officer directs the flow of traffic, and a team of street surveyors uses hand motions to coordinate its work. But nonverbal communication more commonly expresses the kinds of relational messages (affinity, control, and respect) that you read about in chapter 1 and the kinds of identity messages that you read about in chapter 2.[18]

Consider, for example, the role of nonverbal communication in *identity management.* Chapter 2 discussed how we strive to create an image of ourselves as we want others to view us. Nonverbal communication plays an important role in this process—in many cases more important than verbal communication. Consider, for example, what happens when you attend a party where you are likely to meet strangers you would like to get to know better. Instead of projecting your image verbally ("Hi! I'm attractive, friendly, and easygoing"), you behave in ways that will present this identity. You might smile a lot and perhaps try to strike a relaxed pose. It's also likely that you dress carefully—even if the image involves looking as though you hadn't given a lot of attention to your appearance.

Along with identity management, nonverbal communication allows us to *define the kinds of relationships we want to have with others*. Think about the wide range of ways you could behave when greeting another person. You could wave, shake hands, nod, smile, clap the other person on the back, give a hug, or avoid all contact. Each one of these decisions would send a message about the nature of your relationship with the other person.

Nonverbal behavior can be more powerful than words in defining the kind of relationship you are seeking. Recall all the times and ways you have learned that someone you know is upset with you. Most often the first clues don't come from direct statements but rather from nonverbal clues. Perhaps the message is conveyed through a lack of eye contact, different facial expressions, an increase in distance, or decreased touch. In any case, the change in behavior clearly proves the power of nonverbal communication to define the status of a relationship.

Nonverbal communication performs a third valuable social function: *conveying emotions* that we may be unwilling or unable to express—or ones that we may not even be aware of. In fact, nonverbal communication is much better suited to expressing attitudes and feelings than ideas. You can prove this for yourself by imagining how you could express each item on the following list nonverbally:

You're tired.

You're in favor of capital punishment.

You're attracted to another person in the group.

No matter how eloquently a dog may bark, he cannot tell you that his parents were poor but honest.

Bertrand Russell

You think prayer in the schools should be allowed.

You're angry at someone in the room.

This experiment shows that, short of charades, nonverbal messages are much better at expressing attitudes than other sorts of messages. Among other limitations, nonverbal messages can't convey

Simple matters of fact ("The book was written in 1997.")

The past or future tenses ("I was happy yesterday"; "I'll be out of town next week.")

An imaginary idea ("What would it be like if . . .")

Conditional statements ("If I don't get a job, I'll have to move out.")

As technology develops, an increasing number of Internet messages will include the sender's voice. Until then, e-mail messages offer fewer nonverbal cues about the speaker's feelings than do face-to-face encounters, or even telephone conversations. New e-mail users soon learn that their messages can be and often are misunderstood. Probably the biggest problems arise from joking remarks being taken as serious statements. To solve these problems, e-mail correspondents have developed a series of symbols—called *emoticons* or *smileys*—that can be created using keyboard characters to simulate nonverbal dimensions of a message. The following list contains some of the most common ones. (Because of formatting limitations that come with e-mail, emoticons appear in a side-to-side orientation rather than up and down.) Note that, like most nonverbal messages, emoticons can have multiple meanings.

:-)	Basic smile. Most commonly used to indicate humorous intent ("No offense intended.")
:- D	Big smile
;-)	Wink and grin. Sometimes used to indicate sarcasm or say, "Don't hit me for what I just said."
:- (	Frown
:- I	Indifference
:- @	Screaming, swearing, very angry
:- |	Disgusted, grim
:~- (	Crying
:-/ or :-\	Skeptical
:- O	Surprised, yelling, realization of an error ("Oops!")

Symbols like these may be helpful, but they clearly aren't an adequate substitute for the rich mixture of nonverbal messages that flows in face-to-face exchanges, or even in telephone conversations. That fact explains why the International Academy of Digital Arts & Sciences offered a $10,000 grant to the person or group that devises "a viable way to infuse digital communication with the same individuality and unspoken cues common in face-to-face interactions."[19]

Nonverbal Communication Serves Many Functions

Just because this chapter deals with nonverbal communication, don't get the idea that our words and our actions are unrelated. Quite the opposite is true: Verbal and nonverbal communications are interconnected elements in every act of communication. Nonverbal behaviors can operate in several relationships with verbal behaviors.

1. **Repeating** If someone asked you for directions to the nearest drugstore, you could say, "North of here about two blocks," repeating your instructions nonverbally by pointing north.

2. **Substituting** When a friend asks, "What's up?" you might shrug your shoulders instead of answering in words. Many facial expressions operate as substitutes for speech. It's easy to recognize expressions that function like verbal interjections and say "gosh," "really?," "oh, please!," and so on.[20] Nonverbal substituting can be useful when communicators are reluctant to express their feelings in words. Faced with a message you find disagreeable, you might sigh, roll your eyes, or yawn when speaking out would not be appropriate.

   Courtship is another situation in which nonverbal gestures can signal "I'm interested" when the same message would be awkward to express verbally. Psychologist Monica Moore and a team of graduate students spent hundreds of hours observing women and men courting one another, recording every nonverbal step of the process.[21] Moore discovered that the woman most commonly makes the initial decision about whether to encourage contact by nonverbally signaling her interest to a man.

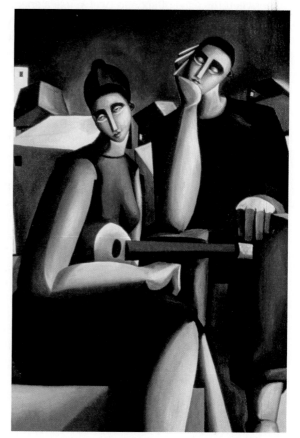

3. **Complementing** If you saw a student talking to a teacher, and the student's head was bowed slightly, his voice was low and hesitating, and he shuffled slowly from foot to foot, you might conclude that he felt inferior to the teacher, possibly embarrassed about something he did. The nonverbal behaviors you observed provided the context for the verbal behaviors—they conveyed the relationship between the teacher and student. Complementing nonverbal behaviors signal the attitudes that people in conversation have about one another.

4. **Accenting** Just as we use italics to emphasize an idea in print, we use nonverbal devices to emphasize oral messages. Pointing an accusing finger adds emphasis to criticism (as well as probably creating defensiveness in the receiver). Accenting certain words with the voice ("It was *your* idea!") is another way to add nonverbal emphasis.

5. **Regulating** Nonverbal behaviors can serve a regulating function by influencing the flow of verbal communication. For example, parties in a conversation often unconsciously send and receive turn-taking cues.[22] When you are ready to yield the floor, the unstated rule is this: Create a rising vocal intonation pattern, then use a falling intonation pattern or draw out the final syllable of the clause at the end of your statement. Finally, stop speaking. If you want to maintain your turn when another speaker seems ready to cut you off, you can suppress the attempt by taking an audible breath, using a sustained intonation pattern (because rising and falling patterns suggest the end of a statement), and avoiding any pauses in your speech. There are other nonverbal cues for gaining the floor and for signaling that you do not want to speak.

6. **Contradicting** People often simultaneously express different and even contradictory messages in their verbal and nonverbal behaviors. A common example of this sort of **mixed message** is the experience we've all had of hearing someone with a red face and bulging veins yelling, "Angry? No, *I'm not angry!*"

   Even though some of the ways in which people contradict themselves are subtle, mixed messages have a strong impact. As we grow older we become better at interpreting these mixed messages. Children between the ages of six and twelve use a speaker's words to make sense of a message. But as adults, we rely more on nonverbal cues to form many impressions. For example, audiences put more emphasis on nonverbal cues than on words to decide whether speakers are honest.[23] They also use nonverbal behaviors to judge the character of speakers as well as their competence and composure; and differences in nonverbal behaviors influence how much listeners are persuaded by a speaker.[24]

7. **Deceiving** Deception is perhaps the most interesting type of double message. Signals of deception—often called **leakage**—can occur in every type of nonverbal behavior. A strong indicator of deception is inconsistency. Changes in a person's normal pattern of behavior alert us that deception may be occurring.[25] Some nonverbal channels are more revealing than others. Facial expressions are less revealing than body clues, probably because deceivers pay more attention to controlling their faces. Even more useful is the voice, which offers a rich variety of leakage clues.[26] In one experiment, subjects who were encouraged to be deceitful made more speech errors, spoke for shorter periods of time, and had a lower rate of speech than did others who were encouraged to express themselves honestly. Another experiment revealed that the vocal frequency of a liar's voice tends to be higher than that of a truth teller. Research also shows that deceivers delivering a prepared lie responded more quickly than truth tellers, mainly because there was less thinking involved. When unprepared, however, deceivers generally took longer than both prepared deceivers and truth tellers.

I suppose it was something you said
That caused me to tighten and pull away.
And when you asked,

"What is it?"

I, of course, said,

"Nothing."

Whenever I say, "Nothing,"

You may be very certain

there is something.

The something is a cold,

hard lump of

Nothing.

Lois Wyse

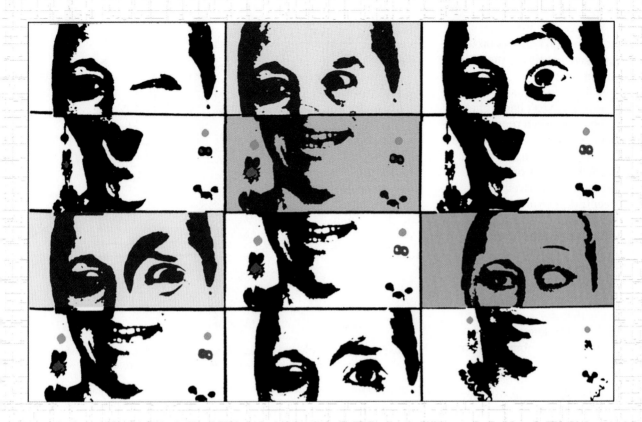

she dresses in flags
comes on
like a mack truck
she paints
her eyelids green
and her mouth
is a loud speaker
rasping out
profanity
at cocktail parties
she is everywhere
like a sheep dog
working a flock
nipping at your sleeve
spilling your drink

bestowing
wet sloppy kisses
but i
have received
secret messages
carefully written
from the shy
quiet woman
who hides
in this
bizarre
gaudy castle

Ric Masten

As this research shows, deceivers don't always broadcast cues that reveal their lies. Nonverbal evidence of lying is most likely to occur when deceivers haven't had a chance to rehearse, when they feel strongly about the information that they are hiding, or when they feel anxious or guilty about their lies. Even when deception cues are abundant, they aren't necessarily direct signals of lying itself; rather, they may signal the anxiety that some liars feel. Table 6-3 outlines some conditions under which liars are likely to betray themselves through nonverbal leakage.

"I knew the suspect was lying because of certain telltale discrepancies between his voice and non verbal gestures. Also his pants were on fire."

©2001 Robert Mankoff from cartoonbank.com. All Rights Reserved.

Despite the abundance of nonverbal deception cues, it isn't always easy to detect deception. The range of effectiveness in uncovering deceptive messages is broad, ranging from 45 percent to 70 percent.[27] Sometimes the very suspicion that someone is lying can improve the deceiver's attempts to hide the truth. Research shows that communicators who probe the messages of deceptive communicators are no better at detecting lies than are those who don't investigate the truth of a message.[28] One explanation for this surprising finding is that deceivers who are questioned become more cautious about revealing the truth and that their greater caution results in a better cover-up of deception cues.

Some people are better than others at uncovering deception. For example, younger people are better than older ones at uncovering lies.[29] Women are consistently more accurate than men at detecting lying and what the underlying truth really is.[30] The same research shows that, as people become more intimate, their accuracy in detecting lies declines. This is a surprising fact: Intuition suggests that we ought to be better at judging honesty as we become more familiar with others. Despite their overall accuracy at detecting lies, women are more inclined to fall for the deception of intimate partners than are men. No matter how skillful or unskillful we may be at interpreting nonverbal behavior, training can make us better.[31]

Before we finish considering how nonverbal behaviors can deceive, it is important to realize that not all deceptive communication is aimed at taking advantage of the recipient. Some deceptive communications are a polite way to express an idea that would be difficult to handle if expressed in words. For example, recall a time when you became bored

TABLE 6-3 Leakage of Nonverbal Cues to Deception

DECEPTION CUES ARE MOST LIKELY WHEN THE DECEIVER	DECEPTION CUES ARE LEAST LIKELY WHEN THE DECEIVER
Wants to hide emotions being felt at the moment	Wants to hide information unrelated to his or her emotions
Feels strongly about the information being hidden	Has no strong feelings about the information being hidden
Feels apprehensive about the deception	
Feels guilty about being deceptive	Feels confident about the deception
Gets little enjoyment from being deceptive	Experiences little guilt about the deception
Needs to construct the message carefully while delivering it	Enjoys the deception
	Knows the deceptive message well and has rehearsed it

Based on "Mistakes When Deceiving" by Paul Ekman in Thomas A. Sebeok and Robert Rosenthal, eds., *The Clever Hans Phenomenon: Communication with Horses, Whales, Apes, and People* (New York: New York Academy of Sciences, 1981), pp. 269–278.

with a conversation while your companion kept rambling on. At such a time the most straightforward statement would be, "I'm tired of talking to you and want to get away." It's obvious that the less direct nonverbal signal—glancing at your watch, for example—is a kinder way to express yourself. In this sense, the ability to deliberately send nonverbal messages that contradict your words can be a kind of communication competence.

Nonverbal Communication Is Ambiguous

You learned in chapter 5 that verbal messages are ambiguous; but nonverbal messages are even more ambiguous. Consider the example of a wink: In one study, college students interpreted this nonverbal signal as meaning a variety of things, including an expression of thanks, a sign of friendliness, a measure of insecurity, a sexual come-on, and an eye problem.[32]

Even the most common nonverbal behavior can be ambiguous. Imagine two possible meanings of silence from a normally talkative friend. Or suppose that a much-admired person with whom you've worked suddenly begins paying more attention to you than ever before. What could some possible meanings of this behavior be? Although nonverbal behavior can be very revealing, it can have so many possible meanings that it's impossible to be certain which interpretation is correct.

The ambiguous nature of nonverbal behavior becomes clear in the area of courtship and sexuality. Does a kiss mean "I like you a lot" or "I want to have sex"? Does pulling away from a romantic partner mean "Stop now" or "Keep trying"? Communication researchers Grace Lim and Michael Roloff explored this question by surveying one hundred college

Safeway Clerks Object to "Service with a Smile" Policy

Twelve Safeway employees have filed grievances over the supermarket chain's smile-and-make-eye-contact rule, complaining that they are being propositioned by shoppers who mistake company-required friendliness for flirting.

Under Safeway's "Superior Service" policy, employees are expected to anticipate customers' needs, take them to items they cannot find, make selling suggestions, thank them by name if they pay by check or credit card and offer to carry out their groceries.

Richelle Roberts, a produce clerk, said she is hit on every day by men who think she is coming on to them. Another produce worker, who spoke on condition of anonymity, said she has hidden in a back room to avoid customers who have harassed her, propositioned her and followed her to her car.

San Francisco Chronicle

students about sexual consent in twelve dating scenarios in order to discover under what conditions verbal approaches (e.g., "Do you want to have sex with me?") were considered preferable to nonverbal indicators (e.g., kissing as an indicator of a desire to have sex).[33] In every scenario, verbal consent was seen as less ambiguous than nonverbal consent. This doesn't mean that romantic partners don't rely on nonverbal signals; many of the respondents indicated that they interpret nonverbal cues (such as kissing) as signs of sexual willingness. However, nonverbal cues were far less likely to be misunderstood when accompanied by verbal cues. The conclusions of this research seem obvious: Verbal messages are clearer than nonverbal messages in matters of sexual consent. Just because they are clearer, however, doesn't mean that they are practiced. Using clearer and less ambiguous verbal messages could reduce a variety of unfortunate outcomes, ranging from a spoiled evening to lawsuits to date rape.

Not all nonverbal behavior is equally ambiguous. In laboratory settings, subjects are better at identifying positive facial expressions of feelings such as happiness, love, surprise, and interest than negative expressions of feelings such as fear, sadness, anger, and disgust.[34] In real life, however, spontaneous nonverbal expressions are so ambiguous that observers are unable to identify the emotions they convey with accuracy any better than blind guessing.[35]

Despite the ambiguity of nonverbal messages, some people are more skillful decoders than others.[36] Those who are better senders of nonverbal messages are also better receivers. Decoding ability also increases with age and training, though there are still differences in ability because of personality and occupation. For instance, extroverts are relatively accurate judges of nonverbal behavior, whereas dogmatists are not. Women seem to be better than men at decoding nonverbal messages. Over 95 percent of the studies examined in one analysis showed that women are more accurate at interpreting nonverbal signals.[37] Despite these differences, even the best nonverbal decoders do not approach 100 percent accuracy. To test this principle for yourself, try the following experiment.

INVITATION TO INSIGHT

READING "BODY LANGUAGE"

While going through the supermarket checkout stand or waiting for a plane, you've probably noticed books that promise to teach you how to read "body language." These books claim that you can become a kind of mind reader, learning the deepest secrets of everyone around you. But it's not quite as simple as it sounds. Here's an exercise that will both increase your skill in observing nonverbal behavior and show you the dangers of being too sure that you're a perfect reader of body language. You can try the exercise either in or out of class, and the period of time over which you do it is flexible, from a single class period to several days. In any case, begin by choosing a partner, and then follow these directions:

Proceed with Caution If Using Hand Signals

A drivers' group has developed a guide to gestures that motorists can give one another on the road, but the one you're most familiar with is not among them.

The National Motorists Association, whose mission includes "the enhancement of motorist-to-motorist communication," has developed signals that drivers can use to deliver such messages as "I'm sorry," "Danger ahead," Pull over to let me pass" and "There is a problem with your car."

Traffic experts, however, urge drivers to use caution in flashing signals to another driver who may mistake one finger for another.

Earlier this month, a motorist on the Ventura Freeway was shot after giving an obscene gesture to a driver who flashed her headlights—the generally accepted signal for prodding slower vehicles to move over. Several years ago an off-duty California Highway Patrol officer, who flashed his headlights in frustration at a pickup drover who cut him off on the freeway, was pursued for several miles and then fatally shot.

And in multicultural Los Angeles, one man's "thumbs up" might mean an insult to another. Or be misinterpreted as a gang sign.

Los Angeles Times

1. For the first period of time (however long you decide to make it), observe the way your partner behaves. Notice movements, mannerisms, postures, style of dress, and so on. To remember your observations, jot them down. If you're doing this exercise out of class over an extended period of time, there's no need to let your observations interfere with whatever you'd normally be doing: Your only job here is to compile a list of your partner's behaviors. In this step you should be careful *not to interpret* your partner's behaviors; just record what you see.

2. At the end of the time period, share what you've seen with your partner, who should do the same with you.

3. For the next period of time your job is not only to observe your partner's behavior but also to *interpret* it. This time in your conference you should tell your partner what you thought his or her behaviors revealed. For example, does careless dressing suggest oversleeping, loss of interest in appearance, or the desire to feel more comfortable? If you noticed frequent yawning, did you think this meant boredom, fatigue after a late night, or sleepiness after a big meal? Don't feel bad if your guesses weren't all correct. Remember that nonverbal clues tend to be ambiguous. You may be surprised how checking out the nonverbal clues you observe can help build a relationship with another person.

I was at a stop light, behind a car with a bumper sticker that said "Honk if you love Jesus." I honked. The driver leaned out his window, flipped me the bird, and yelled "Can't you see the light is still red, you moron?"

Dilbert Newsletter

This exercise should have shown you the difference between merely observing somebody's behavior and actually interpreting it. Noticing someone's shaky hands or smile is one thing, but deciding what such behaviors mean is quite another. If you're like most people, you probably found that a lot of your guesses were incorrect. Now, if that was true here, it may also be true in your daily life. Being a sharp nonverbal observer can give you some good hunches about how people are feeling, but the only way you can find out if these hunches are correct is to *check them out* verbally, using the skill of perception checking you learned in chapter 3.

DIFFERENCES BETWEEN VERBAL AND NONVERBAL COMMUNICATION

Both verbal and nonverbal messages are indispensable: It's hard to imagine how we could function without either one. Much of the value of these two ways of communicating comes from their differences.

Single vs. Multiple Channels

Most verbal messages—words, sentences, and paragraphs—reach us one at a time, rather like pearls on a string. In fact, it's physically impossible

Brent Staples: Nonverbal Stereotyping

My first victim was a woman—white, well dressed, probably in her early twenties. I came upon her late one evening on a deserted street in Hyde Park, a relatively affluent neighborhood in an otherwise mean, impoverished section of Chicago. As I swung onto the avenue behind her, there seemed to be a discreet, uninflammatory distance between us. Not so. She cast back a worried glance. To her, the youngish black man—a broad six feet two inches with a beard and billowing hair, both hands shoved into the pockets of a bulky military jacket—seemed menacingly close. After a few more quick glimpses, she picked up her pace and was soon running in earnest. Within seconds she disappeared into a cross street. As a softy who is scarcely able to take a knife to a raw chicken—let alone hold on to a person's throat—I was surprised, embarrassed, and dismayed all at once.

That first encounter, and those that followed, signified that a vast, unnerving gulf lay between nighttime pedestrians—particularly women—and me.

After dark, on the warrenlike streets of Brooklyn where I live, I often see women who fear the worst from me. They seem to have set their faces on neutral, and with their purse straps strung across their chests bandolier-style, they forge ahead as though bracing themselves against being tackled. I understand, of course, that the danger they perceive is not a hallucination. Women are particularly vulnerable to street violence, and young black males are drastically overrepresented among the perpetrators of that violence. Yet these truths are no solace against the kind of alienation that comes of being ever the suspect, a fearsome entity with whom pedestrians avoid making eye contact.

Over the years, I learned to smother the rage I felt at so often being taken for a criminal. Not to do so would surely have led to madness. I now take precautions to make myself less threatening. I move about with care, particularly late in the evening. I give a wide berth to nervous people on subway platforms during the wee hours, particularly when I have exchanged business clothes for jeans. If I happen to be entering a building behind some people who appear skittish, I may walk by, letting them clear the lobby before I return, so as not to seem to be following them. I have been calm and extremely congenial on those rare occasions when I've been pulled over by the police.

And on late-evening constitutionals I employ what has proved to be an excellent tension-reducing measure: I whistle melodies from Beethoven and Vivaldi and the more popular classical composers. Even steely New Yorkers hunching toward nighttime destinations seem to relax, and occasionally they even join in the tune. Virtually everybody seems to sense that a mugger wouldn't be warbling bright, sunny selections from Vivaldi's *Four Seasons*. It is my equivalent of the cowbell that hikers wear when they know they are in bear country.

Brent Staples,
from "Black Men and Public Spaces"

for a person to speak more than one word at a time. Unlike the spoken word, however, nonverbal messages don't arrive in such an orderly, sequential manner. Instead, they bombard us simultaneously from a multitude of channels. Consider the everyday act of meeting a stranger for the first time. On a verbal level there's relatively little information exchanged in the clichés that occupy the first few minutes of most conversations ("How's it going? . . . " "Great weather we've been having . . ."

"What's your major?"). But at the same moment the number of nonverbal messages available to you is overwhelming: the other person's facial expressions, postures, gestures, clothing, the distance that the person stands from you, and so on. In one way this multichannel onslaught of nonverbal messages is a boon because it provides so many ways of learning about others. In another way, however, the number of simultaneous nonverbal messages is a problem because it's difficult to recognize the overwhelming amount of nonverbal information we receive from others every moment.

Intermittent vs. Continuous

Verbal messages—words, sentences, and paragraphs—form messages with clear beginnings and endings. In this sense we can judge whether others are communicating verbally by observing whether they are speaking or writing. Unlike the written and spoken word, however, nonverbal communication is continuous and never ending. As we've already said, nonverbal communication is a constant, unstoppable process. The postures, gestures, and other types of messages described in the following pages provide a constant flow of messages. Even the absence of a message (an unanswered letter or an unreturned phone call) is a message. As one communication expert said when referring to nonverbal communication, "Nothing never happens."

Clear vs. Ambiguous

Although verbal communication can be vague, we have already seen that most nonverbal cues are even more vague. Nonverbal messages aren't completely ambiguous, of course: It's probably accurate to guess that a frown signifies some sort of negative feeling and that a smile signifies some sort of positive feeling. But we often need language to tell us *why* others feel as they do. Is the boss smiling because she likes your idea or because she finds it amusing, although completely impractical? Does your instructor's frown indicate confusion with your remarks or disagreement? The best way to find out is to ask for a verbal clarification, not to depend on your reading of the nonverbal cues.

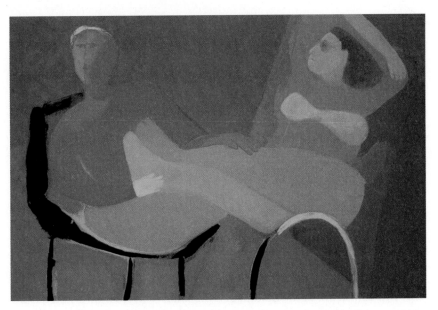

Verbal vs. Nonverbal Impact

When we are exposed to both verbal and nonverbal messages, research shows that we find the nonverbal messages much more powerful.[38] In a variety of settings (including job interviews, therapy sessions, first meetings), adults rely more on nonverbal messages than on words when interpreting the messages of others. Nonverbal cues are especially likely to carry weight when they contradict a speaker's words. In one series of experiments, friendly, neutral, and unfriendly verbal messages were paired with parallel nonverbal messages. Raters who judged the verbal and nonverbal messages separately found them equal in strength. But when the two messages were combined, the nonverbal ones accounted for as much as 12.5 times as much power as did the verbal messages.[39]

Deliberate vs. Unconscious

Although we usually think about what we want to say before speaking or writing, most nonverbal messages aren't deliberate. In one study, less than a quarter of experimental subjects who had been instructed to show increased or decreased liking of a partner could describe the nonverbal behaviors they used.[40] Of course, we do pay attention to some of our nonverbal behavior: smiling when we want to convince others we're happy or making sure our handshake is firm to show that we're straightforward and decisive. But there are so many nonverbal channels that it's impossible to think about and control all of them. Thus, our slumping shoulders might contradict our smiles, and our sweating palms might contradict all the self-confidence of our firm handshakes. The unconscious nature of most nonverbal behavior explains why it offers so many useful cues about how others are feeling.

TYPES OF NONVERBAL COMMUNICATION

Keeping the five characteristics of nonverbal communication in mind, let's take a look at some of the ways we communicate in addition to words.

The first area of nonverbal communication we'll discuss is the broad field of **kinesics,** or body position and motion. In this section we'll explore the role that posture, gestures, body orientation, facial expressions, and eye behaviors play in our relationships with each other.

Body Orientation

We'll start with **body orientation**—the degree to which we face toward or away from someone with our body, feet, and head. To understand how this kind of physical positioning communicates nonverbal messages, you might try an experiment. You'll need two friends to help you. Imagine that two of you are in the middle of a personal conversation when a third person approaches and wants to join you. You're not especially glad to see this person, but you don't want to sound rude by asking him to leave. Your task is to signal to the intruder that you'd rather be alone, using only the position of your bodies. You can talk to the third person if you wish, but you can't verbally tell him that you want privacy.

When you've tried this experiment, or if you've ever been in a real situation similar to it, you know that by turning your body slightly away from an intruder you can make your feelings very clear. An intruder finds himself in the difficult position of trying to talk over your shoulder, and it isn't long before he gets the message and goes away. The nonverbal message here is "We're interested in each other right now and don't want to include you in our conversation." The general rule that this situation describes is that facing someone directly signals your interest, and facing away signals a desire to avoid involvement. This explains how we can pack ourselves into intimate distance with total strangers in places like a crowded elevator without offending others. Because there's a very indirect orientation here (everyone is usually standing shoulder to shoulder, facing in the same direction), we understand that despite the close quarters everyone wants to avoid personal contact.

By observing the way people position themselves you can learn a good deal about how they feel. Next time you're in a crowded place where people can choose whom to face directly, try observing who seems to be included in the action and who is being subtly shut out. And in the same way, pay attention to your own body orientation. You may be surprised to discover that you're avoiding a certain person without being conscious of it or that at times you're "turning your back" on people altogether. If this is the case, it may be helpful to figure out why. Are you avoiding an unpleasant situation that needs clearing up, communicating your annoyance or dislike for the other, or sending some other message?

Posture

Another way we communicate nonverbally is through our **posture.** To see if this is true, stop reading for a moment, and notice how you're sitting. What does your position say nonverbally about how you feel? Are there any other people near you now? What messages do you get from their present posture? By paying attention to the postures of those around you, as well as your own, you'll find another channel of nonverbal communication that can furnish information about how people feel about themselves and each other.

An indication of how much posture communicates is shown by our language. It's full of expressions that link emotional states with body postures:

I won't take this lying down!

Take a load off your back.

He can stand on his own two feet.

She has to carry a heavy burden.

Phrases like these show that an awareness of posture exists for us even if it's often unconscious. The main reason we miss most posture messages is that they aren't very obvious. It's seldom that a person who feels weighted down by a problem hunches over so much that she stands out in a crowd, and when we're bored, we usually don't lean back and slump enough to embarrass the other person. In the reading of posture, then, the key is to look for small changes that might be shadows of the way people feel.

For example, a teacher who has a reputation for interesting classes told us how he uses his understanding of postures to do a better job. "Because of my large classes I have to lecture a lot," he said. "And that's an easy way to turn students off. I work hard to make my talks entertaining, but you know that nobody's perfect, and I do have my off days. I can tell when I'm not doing a good job of communicating by picking out three or four students before I start my talk and watching how they sit throughout the class period. As long as they're leaning forward in their seats, I know I'm doing OK, but if I look up and see them starting to slump back, I know I'd better change my approach."

Psychologist Albert Mehrabian has found that other postural keys to feelings are tension and relaxation. He says that we take relaxed postures in nonthreatening situations and tighten up in threatening situations.[41]

Based on this observation, he says, we can tell a good deal about how others feel simply by watching how tense or loose they seem to be. For example, he suggests that watching tenseness is a way of detecting status differences: The lower-status person is generally the more rigid, tense-appearing one, whereas the higher-status person is more relaxed. This is the kind of situation that often happens when an employee sits ramrod straight while the boss leans back in her chair. The same principle applies to social situations, where it's often possible to tell who's uncomfortable by looking at pictures. Often you'll see someone laughing and talking as if he were perfectly at home, but his posture almost shouts nervousness. Some people never relax, and their posture shows it.

Sometimes posture communicates vulnerability in situations far more serious than mere social or business ones. One study revealed that rapists sometimes use postural clues to select victims they believe are easy to intimidate.[42] Easy targets are more likely to walk slowly and tentatively, stare at the ground, and move their arms and legs in short, jerky motions.

*Fie, fie upon her!
There's language in her
eyes, her cheek, her lip.
Nay, her foot speaks;
her wanton spirits look
out at every joint and
motive in her body.*

William Shakespeare, *Troilus and Cressida*

Gestures

Gestures—movements of the hands and arms—are an important type of nonverbal communication. In fact, they are so fundamental that people who have been blind from birth use them.[43] The most common forms of gestures are what social scientists call **illustrators**—movements that accompany speech and that can't stand alone.[44] Scratching your head when searching for an idea and snapping your fingers when you find an idea are examples of illustrators that complement verbal messages. Research shows that North Americans use illustrators more often when they are emotionally aroused—trying to explain ideas that are difficult to put into words when they are furious, horrified, very agitated, distressed, or excited.[45]

A second type of gestures is **emblems**—deliberate nonverbal behaviors that have a very precise meaning, known to virtually everyone within a cultural group. For example, we all know that a head nod means "yes," a head shake means "no," a wave means "hello" or "goodbye," and a hand to the ear means "I can't hear you." And almost everybody over the age of seven knows the meaning of a raised middle finger.

A third type of gestures is **adaptors**—self-touching behaviors. (To make matters confusing, sometimes these behaviors go by the name of *manipulators*.) Whereas we usually use emblems consciously to express a message, adaptors are usually unconscious. For example, you might fiddle nervously with your hands or click a pen during a high-stress job interview. Research confirms what common sense suggests—that increased use of manipulators is often a sign of discomfort.[46] But not *all* fidgeting signals uneasiness. People also are likely to use adaptors when relaxed. When they let their guard down (either alone or with friends), they will be more likely to fiddle with an earlobe, twirl a strand of hair, or clean their fingernails. Whether or not the fidgeter is hiding something, observers are likely to interpret an adaptor

THE LOOK OF A VICTIM

Little Red Riding Hood set herself up to be mugged. Her first mistake was skipping through the forest to grandma's house. Her second mistake was stopping to pick flowers. At this point, as you might remember in the story, the mean, heavy wolf comes along and begins to check her out. He observes, quite perceptively, that she is happy, outgoing, and basically unaware of any dangers in her surrounding environment. The big bad wolf catches these nonverbal clues and splits to grandma's house. He knows that Red is an easy mark. From this point we all know what happens.

Body movements and gestures reveal a lot of information about a person. Like Little Red Riding Hood, pedestrians may signal to criminals that they are easy targets for mugging by the way they walk.

When was the last time you assessed your "muggability rating"? In a recent study two psychologists set out to identify those body movements that characterized easy victims. They assembled "muggability ratings" of sixty New York pedestrians from the people who may have been the most qualified to judge—prison inmates who had been convicted of assault.

The researchers unobtrusively videotaped pedestrians on weekdays between 10:00 A.M. and 12:00 P.M. Each pedestrian was taped for six to eight seconds, the approximate time it takes for a mugger to size up an approaching person. The judges (prison inmates) rated the "assault potential" of the sixty pedestrians on a ten-point scale. A rating of one indicated someone was "a very easy rip-off," of two, "an easy dude to corner."

Toward the other end of the scale, nine meant a person "would be heavy; would give you a hard time," and ten indicated that the mugger "would avoid it, too big a situation, too heavy." The results revealed several body movements that characterized easy victims: "Their strides were either very long or very short; they moved awkwardly, raising their left legs with their left arms (instead of alternating them); on each step they tended to lift their whole foot up and then place it down (less muggable sorts took steps in which their feet rocked from heel to toe). Overall, the people rated most muggable walked as if they were in conflict with themselves; they seemed to make each move in the most difficult way possible."

Loretta Malandro and Larry Barker

as a signal of dishonesty. Because not all fidgeters are dishonest, it's important not to jump to conclusions about the meaning of adaptors.

Actually, *too few* gestures may be as significant an indicator of mixed messages as *too many*.[47] Lack of gesturing may signal a lack of interest, sadness, boredom, or low enthusiasm. Illustrators also decrease whenever someone is cautious about speaking. For these reasons, a careful observer will look for either an increase or a decrease in the usual level of gestures.

Face and Eyes

The face and eyes are probably the most noticed parts of the body, but this doesn't mean that their nonverbal messages are the easiest to read. The face is a tremendously complicated channel of expression for several reasons.

First, it's hard even to describe the number and kind of expressions we commonly produce with our face and eyes. For example, researchers have found that there are at least eight distinguishable positions of the eyebrows and forehead, eight more of the eyes and lids, and ten for the lower face.[48] When you multiply this complexity by the number of emotions we feel, you can see why it would be almost impossible to compile a dictionary of facial expressions and their corresponding emotions.

Second, facial expressions are difficult to understand because of the speed with which they can change. For example, slow-motion films show expressions fleeting across a subject's face in as short a time as it takes to blink an eye.[49] Also, it seems that different emotions show most clearly in different parts of the face: happiness and surprise in the eyes and lower face; anger in the lower face, brows, and forehead; fear and sadness in the eyes; and disgust in the lower face.

Ekman and Friesen have identified six basic emotions that facial expressions reflect—surprise, fear, anger, disgust, happiness, and sadness. Expressions reflecting these emotions seem to be recognizable in and between members of all cultures. Of course, *affect blends*—the combination of two or more expressions in different parts of the face—are possible. For instance, it's easy to imagine how someone would look who is fearful and surprised or disgusted and angry.

People are quite accurate at judging facial expressions for these emotions. Accuracy increases when people know the target or the context in which the expression occurs, or when they have seen several samples of the target's expressions.

In spite of the complex way in which the face shows emotions, you can still pick up messages by watching it. One of the easiest ways is to look for expressions that seem to be overdone. Often when someone is trying to fool himself or another, he'll emphasize his mask to a point that it seems too exaggerated to be true. Another way to detect a person's feelings is to watch her expression at moments when she isn't likely to be thinking about her appearance. We've all had the experience of glancing into another car while stopped in a traffic jam, or of looking around at a sporting event and seeing expressions that the wearer would probably never show in more guarded moments. At other times, it's possible to watch a **microexpression** as it flashes across a person's face. For just a

"Exploring Nonverbal Communication"

http://zzyx.ucsc. edu/~archer/ intro.html#continue

This interactive site previews a new video series available from the University of California on nonverbal communication. Scroll down and see sample pictures from the videos. Guess about the meaning in the sample pictures and then scroll down further to get the answers. For additional Web links and activities regarding nonverbal communication, access the *Looking Out/Looking In* Web site.

moment we see a flash of emotion quite different from the one a speaker is trying to convey. Finally, you may be able to spot contradictory expressions on different parts of someone's face: The eyes say one thing, but the mouth or eyebrows might say something quite different.

The eyes themselves can send several kinds of messages. Meeting someone's glance with your eyes is usually a sign of involvement, whereas looking away is often a sign of a desire to avoid contact. This principle has a practical application in commerce: Customers leave larger tips when their servers (whether male or female) maintain eye contact with them.[50]

Another kind of message the eyes communicate is a positive or negative attitude. When someone looks toward us with the proper facial expression, we get a clear message that the looker is interested in us—hence the expression "making eyes." At the same time, when our long glances toward someone else are avoided by her, we can be pretty sure that the other person isn't as interested in us as we are in her. (Of course, there are all sorts of courtship games in which the receiver of a glance pretends not to notice any message by glancing away, yet signals interest with some other part of the body.)

The eyes communicate both dominance and submission. We've all played the game of trying to stare down somebody, and in real life there are also times when downcast eyes are a sign of giving in. In some religious orders, for example, subordinate members are expected to keep their eyes downcast when addressing a superior.

Even the pupils of our eyes communicate. Researchers measured the amount of pupil dilation while showing men and women various types of pictures.[51] The results of the experiment were interesting: A person's eyes grow larger in proportion to the degree of interest in an object. For example, men's pupils grew about 18 percent larger when looking at pictures of a naked woman, and women's pupils grew 20 percent when looking at pictures of a naked man. Interestingly enough, the greatest increase in pupil size occurred when women looked at a picture of a mother and an infant. A good salesperson can increase profits by being aware of pupil dilation, as Edward Hall describes. He was once in a middle eastern bazaar, where an Arab merchant insisted that a customer looking at his jewelry buy a certain piece that the customer had been ignoring. But the merchant had been watching the pupils of the customer's eyes and had known what the customer really wanted.[52]

THE EYES HAVE IT

Prove for yourself the role that eye contact plays in social influence by trying a simple experiment.

1. Choose a situation in which you can make simple requests from a series of strangers. You might, for example, ask to cut in line to use a photocopying machine, or you could ask passersby for a small amount of change to make an important phone call.

2. Make similar requests to at least twenty people. Use the same words for each request, but alternate your nonverbal behavior. Half of the time make direct eye contact, and the other half of the time avoid making direct eye contact with the other person when you make your request.

3. Record your results, and see if your eye behavior played any role in generating compliance with your request.

4. If eye contact does make a difference, describe how you could apply your findings to real-life situations.

It was terribly dangerous to let your thoughts wander when you were in any public place or within range of a telescreen. The smallest thing could give you away. A nervous tic, an unconscious look of anxiety, a habit of muttering to yourself—anything that carried with it the suggestion of abnormality, of having something to hide. In any case, to wear an improper expression on your face (to look incredulous when a victory was announced, for example) was itself a punishable offense. There was even a word for it in Newspeak: facecrime, it was called.

George Orwell, 1984

Voice

The voice itself is another channel of nonverbal communication. Social scientists use the term **paralanguage** to describe nonverbal, vocal messages. The way a message is spoken can give the same word or words many meanings. For example, note how many meanings come from a single sentence just by shifting the emphasis from one word to another:

This is a fantastic communication book. (Not just any book, but *this* one in particular.)

This is a *fantastic* communication book. (This book is superior, exciting.)

This is a fantastic *communication* book. (The book is good as far as communication goes; it may not be so great as literature or drama.)

This is a fantastic communication *book*. (It's not a play or record; it's a book.)

There are many other ways through which our voice communicates— through its tone, speed, pitch, volume, number and length of pauses, and **disfluencies** (such as stammering, use of "uh," "um," "er," and so on). All these factors can do a great deal to reinforce or contradict the message that our words convey.

Researchers have identified the power of paralanguage through the use of content-free speech—ordinary speech that has been electronically manipulated so that the words are unintelligible, but the paralanguage remains unaffected. (Hearing a foreign language that you don't understand has the same effect.) Subjects who hear content-free speech can consistently recognize the emotion being expressed as well as identify its strength.[53]

The impact of paralinguistic cues is strong. In fact, when asked to determine a speaker's attitudes, listeners pay more attention to paralanguage than to the content of the words. Furthermore, when vocal factors contradict a verbal message (as when a speaker shouts, "I am *not*

A pause in the wrong place, an intonation misunderstood, and a whole conversation went awry.

E. M. Forster, *A Passage to India*

cathy®

by Cathy Guisewite

Cathy ©Cathy Guisewite. Reprinted with permission of Universal Press Syndicate. All rights reserved.

angry!"), listeners judge the speaker's intention from the paralanguage, not from the words themselves.[54] Young children respond to the paralanguage of adults, warming up to those who speak warmly and shying away from those who speak in a less friendly manner.[55]

Paralanguage can affect behavior in many ways, some of which are rather surprising. Researchers have discovered that communicators are most likely to comply with requests delivered by speakers whose rate was similar to their own: People who spoke rapidly responded most favorably to rapid talkers, whereas slow speakers preferred others whose rate was also slow.[56] Besides complying with same-rate speakers, listeners also feel more positively about people who speak at their own rate.

Vocal changes that contradict spoken words are not easy to conceal. If the speaker is trying to hide fear or anger, the voice will probably sound higher and louder, and the rate of talk may be faster than normal. Sadness produces the opposite vocal pattern: quieter, lower-pitched speech delivered at a slower rate.[57]

Sarcasm is one instance in which we use both emphasis and tone of voice to change a statement's meaning to the opposite of its verbal message. Experience this reversal yourself with the following three statements. First say them literally, and then say them sarcastically.

"Thanks a lot!"

"I really had a wonderful time on my blind date."

"There's nothing I like better than lima beans."

As they do with other nonverbal messages, people often ignore or misinterpret the vocal nuances of sarcasm. Members of certain groups—children, people with weak intellectual skills, and poor listeners—are more likely to misunderstand sarcastic messages than others.[58]

Communication through paralanguage isn't always intentional. Often our voices give us away when we're trying to create an impression different from our actual feelings. For example, you've probably had experiences of trying to sound calm and serene when you were really seething with inner nervousness. Maybe your deception went along perfectly for a while—just the right smile, no telltale fidgeting of the hands, posture appearing relaxed—and then, without being able to do a thing about it, right in the middle of your relaxed comments, your voice squeaked! The charade was over.

Besides reinforcing or contradicting messages, some vocal factors influence the way a speaker is perceived by others. For example, communicators who speak loudly and without hesitations are viewed as more confident than those who pause and speak quietly.[59] People with more attractive voices are rated more highly than those with less attractive voices.[60] Just what makes a voice attractive can vary. As Figure 6-1 shows, culture can make a difference. Surveys show that there are both similarities and differences between what Mexicans and Americans view as the "ideal" voice. Accent plays an important role in shaping perceptions. Generally speaking, accents that identify a speaker's membership in a group lead to more positive evaluations (if the group is high status) or to negative evaluations (if the group is low status).[61] Other factors combine with accent to

Harold Grace can attest that beauty truly is only skin deep. The Edmonton man, who lost his vision 15 years ago, was selected to judge the Miss Alberta and Miss Teen Alberta pageants.

"I couldn't believe it when I was asked to do this—I was quite taken aback at first," said Mr. Grace, an employee with the Canadian National Institute for the Blind in Edmonton.

"I asked how I was supposed to do the beauty part but they told me not to worry about that, I'd be judging personality, intelligence and volunteer experience."

Mr. Grace said he has become so used to picking up subtle clues to personality from how a person speaks that he can make a good guess at facial expression.

"I can feel it when someone smiles," he said.

Toronto Globe and Mail

shape perceptions. For instance, the apparent age reflected by a speaker's voice affects the preferences of listeners.[62] Older-sounding communicators whose language was accent-free were rated as most competent, whereas older-sounding communicators who did not speak in a culturally standard way were rated as least competent.

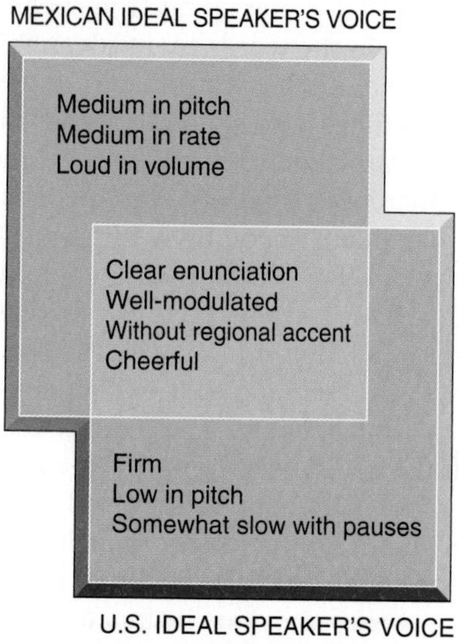

MEXICAN IDEAL SPEAKER'S VOICE

Medium in pitch
Medium in rate
Loud in volume

Clear enunciation
Well-modulated
Without regional accent
Cheerful

Firm
Low in pitch
Somewhat slow with pauses

U.S. IDEAL SPEAKER'S VOICE

FIGURE 6-1 **A Comparison of the Ideal Speakers' Voice Types in Mexico and the United States**

Adapted from "Communicative Power: Gender and Culture as Determinants of the Ideal Voice" in *Women and Communicative Power: Theory, Research and Practice* edited by Carol A. Valentine and Nancy Hoar, ©1988 by SCA. Reprinted by permission.

SKILL BUILDER

BUILDING VOCAL FLUENCY

You can become more adept at both conveying and interpreting vocal messages by following these directions.

1. Join a partner, and designate one person A and the other B.
2. Partner A should choose twenty-five to fifty items from the telephone directory, using his or her voice to convey one of the following attitudes:
   a. egotism
   b. friendliness
   c. insecurity
   d. irritation
   e. confidence
3. Partner B should try to detect the attitude being conveyed.
4. Switch roles, and repeat the process. Continue alternating roles until each of you has both conveyed and tried to interpret at least four attitudes.
5. After completing the preceding steps, discuss the following questions:
   a. What vocal cues did you use to make your guesses?
   b. Were some attitudes easier to guess than others?
   c. Given the accuracy of your guesses, how would you assess your ability to interpret vocal cues?
   d. How can you use your increased sensitivity to vocal cues to improve your everyday communication competence?

Touch

Touch can communicate many messages and signal a variety of relationships.[63]

Functional/professional (dental exam, haircut)

Social/polite (handshake)

Friendship/warmth (clap on back, Spanish *abrazo*)

Sexual arousal (some kisses, strokes)

Aggression (shoves, slaps)

You might object to the examples following each of these categories, saying that some nonverbal behaviors occur in several types of relationships. A kiss, for example, can mean anything from a polite but superficial

THE WAY YOU TALK CAN HURT YOU?

Women also have a distinctive style of speaking: "I was shopping last night? And I saw this wonderful dress? It was so black and slinky?" It's hard to convey intonation in print, but the question marks indicate a rise in pitch at the end of the sentence, as in a question. Many women, especially younger women, use this intonation in declarative sentences: "This is Sally Jones? I have an appointment with Dr. Smith? And I'd like to change it to another day?"

I cringe when I hear this. The rising intonation sounds timid and lacking in self-confidence; the speaker seems to be asking for approval or permission to speak when there's no need to. She should make her point straightforwardly, in an assertion that drops in pitch as it ends.

And I worry that rising intonation harms women. It gets them taken less seriously than they should be in public debates; it encourages salesmen and car mechanics to cheat them when they wouldn't try cheating a man.

A woman friend who studies languages says I've got it wrong. Unlike men, who use conversation to fight for status, she tells me, women see it as co-operative. And they use rising pitch to convey this to their audience. Their tone encourages the supportive interjections, such as "Uh-huh," "Exactly," and "I know what you mean," with which women far more than men interlard each other's speech. And it asks listeners to contribute their ideas on the speaker's topic.

At the very least, women's use of rising intonation involves an ambiguity. It uses a sound that in other contexts conveys timidity, for a very different purpose. Given this ambiguity, we shouldn't be surprised if female speakers who are trying to be co-operative are often heard as hesitant.

It's clearly idiotic to treat conversation as a contest, as so many men do. We'd all benefit from a more co-operative approach. But we need a new symbol to express this, one with no connotations of weakness.

If we find this symbol, we can all, men and women, speak in friendly but firm tones. We can tell anecdotes without lecturing but also without seeming to kowtow. When we call the doctor's, we can say: "This is Sally (or Sam) Jones." (No question about it.) "I have an appointment with Dr. Smith." (I'm reminding you of a fact.) "And I'd like to change it to another day." (Now: Can you help me?)

Thomas Hurka, *Principles: Short Essays on Ethics*

greeting to the most intense arousal. What makes a given touch more or less intense? Researchers have suggested a number of factors:

Which part of the body does the touching

Which part of the body is touched

How long the touch lasts

How much pressure is used

Whether there is movement after contact is made

Whether anyone else is present

The situation in which the touch occurs

The relationship between the persons involved[64]

From this list you can see that there is, indeed, a complex language of touch. Because nonverbal messages are inherently ambiguous, it's no surprise that this language can often be misunderstood. Is a hug playful or suggestive of stronger feelings? Is a touch on the shoulder a friendly gesture or an attempt at domination? The ambiguity of nonverbal behavior often leads to serious problems.

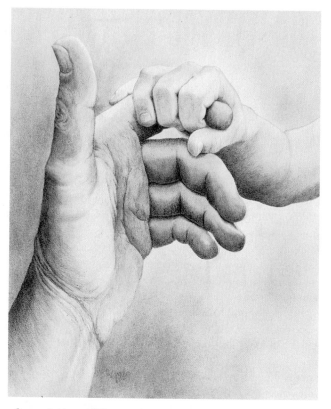

Touch plays a powerful role in shaping how we respond to others. For instance, in a laboratory task, subjects evaluated partners more positively when they were touched (appropriately, of course) by them.[65] Besides increasing liking, touch also increases compliance. In one study, subjects were approached by a female confederate who requested that they return a dime left in the phone booth from which they had just emerged. When the request was accompanied by a light touch on the subject's arm, the probability that the subject would return the dime increased significantly.[66] In a similar experiment, subjects were asked by a male or female confederate to sign a petition or complete a rating scale. Again, subjects were more likely to cooperate when they were touched lightly on the arm. In the rating-scale variation of the study, the results were especially dramatic: 70 percent of those who were touched complied, whereas only 40 percent of those who were untouched did (indicating a predisposition not to comply).[67] An additional power of touch is its on-the-job utility: A restaurant waiter's fleeting touches on the hand and shoulder result in larger tips,[68] and both women and men in taverns increase their alcohol consumption when touched by a waitress.[69]

Besides being the earliest means we have of making contact with others, touching is essential to our healthy development. During the nineteenth and early twentieth centuries a large percentage of children born every year died. In some orphanages the mortality rate was nearly 100 percent, but even children in the most "progressive" homes, hospitals, and other institutions died regularly. When researchers finally tracked down the causes of this mortality, they found that the infants suffered from lack of physical contact with parents or nurses, rather than lack of nutrition, medical care, or other factors. They hadn't been touched enough, and as a result they died. From this knowledge came the practice of "mothering" children in institutions—picking a baby up, carrying it around, and handling it several times each day. At one hospital that began this practice, the death rate for infants fell from between 30 and 35 percent to below 10 percent.[70]

Contemporary research confirms the relationship between touch and health. Studies at the University of Miami's School of Medicine's Touch Research Institute have shown that premature babies grow faster and gain more weight when massaged.[71] The same institute's researchers demonstrated that massage can help premature children gain weight, help colicky children to sleep better, improve the mood of depressed adolescents, and boost the immune function of cancer and HIV patients. Research shows that touch between therapists and clients has the potential to encourage a variety of beneficial changes: more self-disclosure, client self-acceptance, and more positive client-therapist relationships.[72]

INVITATION TO INSIGHT

THE RULES OF TOUCH

Like most types of nonverbal behavior, touching is governed by cultural and social rules. Imagine that you are writing a guidebook for visitors from another culture. Describe the rules that govern touching in the following relationships. In each case, describe how the gender of the participants affects the rules.

1. An adult and a five-year-old child
2. An adult and a twelve-year-old
3. Two good friends
4. Boss and employee

Physical Attractiveness

The importance of physical attractiveness has been emphasized in the arts for centuries. More recently, social scientists have begun to measure the degree to which physical attractiveness affects interaction between people.[73] For example, women who are perceived as attractive have more dates, receive higher grades in college, persuade males with greater ease, and receive lighter court sentences. Both men and women whom others perceive as attractive are rated as being more sensitive, kind, strong, sociable, and interesting than their less fortunate brothers and sisters.

In our now more than slightly cockeyed world, there seems to be little provision for someone to get touched without having to go to bed with whoever does the touching. And that's something to think about. We have mixed up simple healing, warm touching with sexual advances. So much so, that it often seems as if there is no middle way between "Don't you dare touch me!" and "Okay, you touched me, so now we should make love!" A nation which is able to distinguish the fine points between offensive and defensive pass interference, bogies, birdies, and par, a schuss and a slalom, a technical, a personal, and a player-control foul should certainly be able to make some far more obvious distinctions between various sorts of body contact.

Sidney Simon

Cathy © Cathy Guisewite. Reprinted with permission of Universal Press Syndicate. All rights reserved.

Who is most likely to succeed in business? Place your bet on the attractive job applicant. For example, shorter men have more difficulty finding jobs in the first place, and men over six feet two inches receive starting salaries that average 12.4 percent higher than comparable applicants under six feet.

The influence of attractiveness begins early in life. Preschoolers were shown photographs of children their own age and asked to choose potential friends and enemies. The researchers found that children as young as three agreed as to who was attractive ("cute") and unattractive ("homely"). Furthermore, the children valued their attractive counterparts—both of the same and the opposite sex—more highly. Also, preschool children rated by their peers as pretty were most liked, and those rated as least pretty were least liked. Children who were interviewed rated attractive children positively ("He's friendly to other children") and unattractive children negatively ("He hits other children without reason").

Teachers also are affected by students' attractiveness. Attractive students are usually judged more favorably—as being more intelligent, friendly, and popular—than their less attractive counterparts.[74] Fortunately, attractiveness is something we can control without having to call a plastic surgeon. We view others as beautiful or ugly not just on the basis of the "original equipment" they come with but also on the basis of how they use that equipment. Posture, gestures, facial expressions, and other behaviors can increase the attractiveness of an otherwise unremarkable person. Exercise can improve the way each of us looks. Finally, the way we dress can make a significant difference in the way others perceive us, as you'll now see.

Clothing

Besides being a means of protecting us from the elements, clothing is a means of communicating nonverbally. One writer has suggested that clothing conveys at least ten types of messages to others:[75]

- Economic level
- Economic background
- Educational level
- Social background
- Trustworthiness
- Educational background
- Social position
- Level of success
- Level of sophistication
- Moral character

Research shows that we do make assumptions about people based on their clothing. Communicators who wear special clothing often gain

"Tell me about yourself, Kugelman—your hopes, dreams, career path, and what that damn earring means."

From *The Wall Street Journal,* permission. Cartoon Features Syndicate.

persuasiveness. For example, experimenters dressed in uniforms resembling police officers were more successful than those dressed in civilian clothing in requesting pedestrians to pick up litter and in persuading them to lend a dime to an overparked motorist.[76] Likewise, solicitors wearing sheriff's and nurse's uniforms increased the level of contributions to law enforcement and health care campaigns.[77] Uniforms aren't the only kind of clothing that carries influence. In one study, a male and a female were stationed in a hallway so that anyone who wished to go by had to avoid them or pass between them. In one condition the couple wore "formal daytime dress"; in the other, they wore "casual attire." Passersby behaved differently toward the couple, depending on the style of clothing: They responded positively with the well-dressed couple and negatively with the casually dressed couple.[78]

Similar results in other situations show the influence of clothing. College students judged victims of sexual harassment differently depending on their clothing. Victims dressed in black were rated as less honest and more aggressive than those dressed in light colors.[79] We are more likely to obey people dressed in a high-status manner. Pedestrians were more likely to return lost coins to people dressed in high-status clothing than to those dressed in low-status clothing.[80] We are also more likely to follow the lead of high-status dressers, even when it comes to violating social rules. Eighty-three percent of the pedestrians in one study followed a jaywalker dressed in higher-status clothing who violated a "wait" crossing signal, whereas only 48 percent followed a confederate dressed in lower-status clothing.[81] Women who are wearing a jacket are rated as being more powerful than those wearing only a dress or skirt and blouse.[82]

Despite the frequency with which we make them, our clothing-based assumptions aren't always accurate. The stranger wearing wrinkled, ill-fitting old clothes might be a manager on vacation, a normally stylish person on the way to clean a fireplace, or even an eccentric millionaire. As we get to know others better, the importance of clothing shrinks.[83] This fact suggests that clothing is especially important in the early stages of a relationship, when making a positive first impression is necessary to encourage others to know us better. This fact is equally important in personal situations and in employment interviews. In both cases, our style of dress (and personal grooming) can make all the difference between the chance to progress further and outright rejection.

Distance

Proxemics is the study of the way people and animals use space. As you'll see by the end of this chapter, you can sometimes tell how people feel toward each other simply by noting the distance between them. To begin to understand how this is so, try this exercise:

INVITATION TO INSIGHT

DISTANCE MAKES A DIFFERENCE

1. Choose a partner, and go to opposite sides of the room and face each other.

2. Very slowly begin walking toward each other while carrying on a conversation. You might simply talk about how you feel as you follow the exercise. As you move closer, try to be aware of any change in your feelings. Continue moving slowly toward each other until you are only an inch or so apart. Remember how you feel at this point.

3. Now, while still facing each other, back up until you're at a comfortable distance for carrying on your conversation.

4. Share your feelings with each other and/or the whole group.

During this exercise your feelings probably changed at least three times. During the first phase, when you were across the room from your partner, you probably felt unnaturally far away. Then, as you neared a point about three feet from him or her, you probably felt like stopping; this is the distance at which two people in our culture normally stand while conversing socially. If your partner wasn't someone you're emotionally close to, you probably began to feel quite uncomfortable as you moved through this normal range and came closer; it's possible that you had to force yourself not to move back. Some people find this phase so uncomfortable that they can't get closer than twenty inches or so to their partner.

What was happening here? Each of us carries around a sort of invisible bubble of personal space wherever we go. We think of the area inside this bubble as our private territory—almost as much a part of us as our own bodies. As you moved closer to your partner, the distance between your bubbles narrowed and at a certain point disappeared altogether: Your space had been invaded, and this is the point at which you probably felt uncomfortable. As you moved away again, your partner retreated out of your bubble, and you felt more relaxed.

Of course, if you were to try this experiment with someone very close to you—your mate, for example—you might not have felt any discomfort at all, even while touching. The reason is that our willingness to get close to others—physically as well as emotionally—varies according to the person we're with and the situation we're in. And it's precisely the distance that we voluntarily put between ourselves and others that gives a nonverbal clue about our feelings and the nature of the relationship.

Some thirty inches from my nose
The frontier of my Person goes,
And all the untilled air between
Is private *pagus* or demesne.
Stranger, unless with bedroom
   eyes
I beckon you to fraternize,
Beware of rudely crossing it:
I have no gun, but I can spit.

W. H. Auden

Anthropologist Edward T. Hall has defined four distances that we use in our everyday lives.[84] He says that we choose a particular distance depending on how we feel toward the other person at a given time, the context of the conversation, and our interpersonal goals.

Intimate Distance   The first of Hall's four spatial zones begins with skin contact and ranges out to about eighteen inches. We usually use **intimate distance** with people who are emotionally very close to us, and then mostly in private situations—making love, caressing, comforting, protecting. By allowing someone to move into our intimate distance we're letting that person enter our territory. When we do this voluntarily, it's usually a sign of trust: We've willingly lowered our defenses. On the other hand, when someone invades this most personal area without our consent, we usually feel threatened. This explains the discomfort we sometimes feel when forced into crowded places like buses or elevators with strangers. At times like these the standard behavior in our society is to draw away or tense our muscles and avoid eye contact. This is a nonverbal way of signaling, "I'm sorry for invading your territory, but the situation forced it." Invasions of intimate distance can be taken as a form of sexual harassment, even if the invader has no malicious intentions. For this reason, it's important to honor the cultural rules of spatial integrity.

Personal Distance   The second spatial zone, **personal distance**, ranges from eighteen inches at its closest point to four feet at its farthest. Its closer range is the distance at which most couples stand in public. But if someone of the opposite sex stands this near one partner at a party, the other partner is likely to feel uncomfortable. This "moving in" often is taken to mean that something more than casual conversation is taking place. The far range of personal distance runs from about two and a half to four feet. It's the zone just beyond the other person's reach. As Hall puts it, at this distance we can keep someone "at arm's length." This choice of words suggests the type of communication that goes on at this range: The contacts are still reasonably close, but they're much less personal than the ones that occur a foot or so closer.

Social Distance   The third spatial zone, **social distance,** ranges from four to about twelve feet. Within it are the kinds of communication that usually occur in business. Its closer range, from four to seven feet, is the distance at which conversations usually occur between salespeople and customers and between people who work together. Most people feel uncomfortable when a salesclerk comes as close as three feet, whereas four or five feet nonverbally signals "I'm here to help you, but I don't mean to be too personal or pushy."

We use the far range of social distance—seven to twelve feet—for more formal and impersonal situations. This is the distance at which we sit from our boss (or other authority figure) as she stares across her desk at us. Sitting at this distance signals a far different and less relaxed type of conversation than would pulling a chair around to the boss's side of the desk and sitting only three or so feet away.

Choosing the optimal distance can have a powerful effect on how we regard others and how we respond to them. For example, students are more satisfied with teachers who reduce the distance between themselves and their classes. They also are more satisfied with a course itself, and they are more likely to follow a teacher's instructions.[85] Likewise, medical patients are more satisfied with physicians who are not standoffish.[86]

Public Distance   **Public distance** is Hall's term for the farthest zone, running outward from twelve feet. The closer range of public distance is the one that most teachers use in the classroom. In the farther ranges of public space—twenty-five feet and beyond—two-way communication is almost impossible. In some cases, it's necessary for speakers to use public distance because of the size of their audience, but we can assume that anyone who voluntarily chooses to use it when he or she could be closer is not interested in having a dialogue.

Territoriality

Whereas personal space is the invisible bubble we carry around as an extension of our physical being, **territory** remains stationary. Any geographical area such as a work area, room, house, or other physical space to which we assume some kind of "rights" is our territory. What's interesting about territoriality is that there is no real basis for the assumption of proprietary rights of "owning" many areas, but the feeling of ownership exists nonetheless. Your room at home probably feels like *yours* whether you're there or not, unlike personal space, which is carried around with you. In the same way, you may feel proprietary about the seat you always occupy in class, even though you have no illusions about owning that piece of furniture.

The way people use space can communicate a good deal about power and status. Generally we grant people with higher status more personal territory and greater privacy. We knock before entering the boss's office, whereas she can usually walk into our work area without hesitating. In traditional schools professors have offices, dining rooms, and even toilets that are private, whereas students, who are presumably less important, have no such sanctuaries. Among the military greater space and privacy usually come with rank: Privates sleep forty to a barrack, sergeants have their own private rooms, and generals have government-provided houses.

> Stickshifts and safetybelts,
> Bucket seats have all got to go.
> When we're driving in the car,
> It makes my baby seem so far.
> I need you here with me,
> Not way over in a bucket seat.
> I need you to be here with me,
> Not way over in a bucket seat.
>
> By John McCrea
> Performed by CAKE on CD *Fashion Nugget*.

Physical Environment

In this section, we want to emphasize the ways in which physical settings, architecture, and interior design affect our communication. Begin by recalling for a moment the different homes you've visited lately. Were some of these homes more comfortable to be in than others? Certainly a lot of these kinds of feelings are shaped by the people you were with, but there are some houses where it seems impossible to relax, no matter how friendly the hosts are. We've spent what seemed like endless evenings in what Mark Knapp calls "unliving rooms," where the spotless ashtrays, furniture coverings, and plastic lamp covers seem to send nonverbal messages telling us not to touch anything, not to put our feet up, and not to be comfortable. People who live in houses like this probably wonder why nobody ever seems to relax and enjoy themselves at their parties. One thing is quite certain: They don't understand that this environment they have created can communicate discomfort to their guests.

The impressions that home designs communicate can be remarkably accurate. Researchers showed ninety-nine students slides of the insides or outsides of twelve upper-middle-class homes and then asked them to infer the personality of the owners from their impressions.[87] The students were especially accurate after glancing at interior photos. The decorating schemes communicated accurate information about the homeowners' intellectualism, politeness, maturity, optimism, tenseness, willingness to take adventures, and family orientations. The home exteriors also gave viewers accurate perceptions of the owners' artistic interests, graciousness, privacy, and quietness.

Besides communicating information about the designer, an environment can shape the kind of interaction that takes place in it. In one experiment, subjects working in a "beautiful" room were more positive and energetic than those working in "average" or "ugly" spaces.[88] In another experiment, students perceived professors who occupied well-decorated offices as being more credible than those occupying less attractive offices.[89] Doctors have shaped environments to improve the

A good house is planned from the inside out. First, you decide what it has to do for its occupants. Then, you let the functions determine the form. The more numerous and various those functions, the more responsive and interesting the house should be. And it may not look at all like you expect.

Dan MacMasters, *Los Angeles Times*

quality of interaction with their patients. Simply removing a doctor's desk makes patients feel almost five times more at ease during office visits.[90] Redesigning a convalescent ward of a hospital greatly increased the interaction between patients. In the old design, seats were placed shoulder to shoulder around the edges of the ward. By grouping the seats around small tables so that patients faced each other at a comfortable distance, the amount of conversations doubled.

Time

Social scientists use the term **chronemics** to describe the study of how humans use and structure time. The way we handle time can express both intentional and unintentional messages.[91] For instance, in a culture like ours that values time highly, waiting can be an indicator of status. "Important" people (whose time is supposedly more valuable than that of others) may be seen by appointment only, whereas it is acceptable to intrude without notice on lesser beings. To see how this rule operates, consider how natural it is for a boss to drop into a subordinate's office unannounced, whereas the subordinate would never intrude into the boss's office without an appointment. A related rule is that low-status people must never make high-status people wait. It would be a serious mistake to show up late for a job interview, whereas the interviewer might keep you cooling your heels in the lobby. Important people are often whisked to the head of a restaurant or airport line, whereas presumably less exalted masses are forced to wait their turn.

The use of time depends greatly on culture.[92] In some cultures, punctuality is critically important, whereas in others it is barely considered. Punctual mainlanders often report welcoming the laid-back Hawaiian approach toward time. One psychologist discovered the difference between North and South American attitudes when teaching at a university in Brazil.[93] He found that some students arrived halfway through a two-hour class and that most of them stayed put and kept asking questions when the class was scheduled to end. A half-hour after the official end of the class, the psychologist finally closed off discussion because there was no indication that the students intended to leave. This flexibility of time is quite different from what is common in most North American colleges!

Even within a culture, rules of time vary. Sometimes the variations are geographic. In New York City, the party invitation may say 9:00, but nobody would think of showing up before 9:30. In Salt Lake City, guests are expected to show up on time, or perhaps even a bit early. Even within the same geographic area, different groups establish their own rules about the use of time. Consider your own experience. In school, some instructors begin and end class punctually, whereas others are more casual. With some people you feel comfortable talking for hours in person or on the phone, whereas with others time seems to be precious and not "wasted."

SUMMARY

Nonverbal communication consists of messages expressed by nonlinguistic means such as distance, touch, body posture and orientation, expressions of the face and eyes, movement, vocal characteristics, clothing, physical environment, and time.

Nonverbal communication is pervasive; in fact, it is impossible to not send nonverbal messages. Most nonverbal communication reveals attitudes and feelings, in contrast to verbal communication, which is better suited to expressing ideas. Although many nonverbal behaviors are universal, their use and significance vary from one culture to another. Nonverbal communication serves many functions. It can repeat, substitute for, complement, accent, regulate, and contradict verbal communication.

Nonverbal messages differ from verbal ones in several ways. They involve multiple channels, are continuous instead of discrete, are usually more ambiguous, and are more likely to be unconscious. When presented with conflicting verbal and nonverbal messages, communicators are more likely to rely on the nonverbal ones.

KEY TERMS

accenting	gestures	personal distance
adaptors	illustrators	posture
body orientation	intimate distance	proxemics
chronemics	kinesics	public distance
complementing	leakage	regulating
contradicting	microexpression	repeating
deceiving	mixed message	social distance
disfluencies	nonverbal communication	substituting
emblems	paralanguage	territory

LOOKING OUT/LOOKING IN ONLINE

Use your *Looking Out/Looking In* CD-ROM for quick access to the electronic resources that accompany this chapter. Included on this CD-ROM are additional study aids and links to the *Looking Out/Looking In* Web site at the Wadsworth Communication Café. The CD-ROM is your gateway to a wealth of resources that will help you understand and further explore the material in this chapter. **Video clips** under *Communication Scenarios* on the CD illustrate the skills introduced in this chapter. Click on the Web site link to complete self-study **review quizzes** to help you master new concepts; access a **feature film database** to locate clips and entire movies that illustrate communication principles; find Internet material via the maintained **Web site links;** and complete **online activities** to help you master new concepts.

INFOTRAC COLLEGE EDITION EXERCISES

Use the InfoTrac College Edition password that was included free with a copy of this new text to answer the following questions. These questions can be completed online and, if requested, submitted to your instructor under InfoTrac College Edition Activities at the *Looking Out/Looking In* Web site.

1. Nonverbal Communication Scholarship

Use Easy Search to find a list of articles under the term "nonverbal communication." How many articles did you find? Choose and read the three articles that look most interesting to you. Write a brief summary of each article you have chosen. Include a citation (title, author, publication, date), brief description of the article's main idea, and your reaction to the point it makes.

2. Male and Female Nonverbal Communication Differs

Read the article "The New Flirting Game" by Deborah A. Lott. (Hint: Use PowerTrac's author and title search functions to locate the article.) How does your personal experience match the findings reported in this article? How can you use this information to make your relational communication operate more smoothly?

3. Gestures

Locate and read the article "Living Hand to Mouth" by Sharon Begley. You will discover how gesturing can help us remember information that might otherwise be beyond recall. See if increasing your gestures can expand your ability to remember obscure information.

READINGS

Andersen, Peter A. *Nonverbal Communication: Forms and Functions.* Mountain View, Calif.: Mayfield, 1999.

Most surveys of nonverbal communication are organized around various types of behavior such as distance, movement, and language. By contrast, this book is organized around nonverbal communication's major functions, purposes, and uses. Chapters describe the role of nonverbal communication in emotion, immediacy, and power. A useful chapter describes similarities and differences in nonverbal communication between men and women. Other topics include nonverbal communication in intimate relationships, influence, and deception.

Buller, David B. "Deception." In *Strategic Inter-personal Communication.* John A. Daly and John M. Wiemann, eds. Hillsdale, N.J.: Erlbaum, 1994.

This article summarizes the nonverbal and verbal behaviors that characterize both intentional and unintentional deceptions as well as discusses the role of deception in interpersonal relationships.

Levine, Robert. *A Geography of Time, or How Every Culture Keeps Time Just a Little Differently.* New York: Basic Books, 1997.

Levine's central argument is that lacking an understanding of time is one of the biggest barriers between cultures. He describes how the meaning of time differs around the world by comparing the effects of time in thirty-six U.S. cities and thirty-one countries around the world. This brief, readable book demonstrates many ways in which differing senses of time affect the flow of communication.

FILMS

In addition to the films suggested here, go to the **Film in Communication Database** at the *Looking Out/Looking In* Web site to locate movie clips illustrating principles of nonverbal communication.

The Power and Limitations of Nonverbal Communication

At First Sight (1999) Rated PG-13

Virgil Adamson (Val Kilmer) has been blind since he was three years old. He works as a massage therapist in a small resort town where Amy Benic (Mira Sorvino) stops for a visit. Despite his lack of sight, Virgil's other senses are strong and keen. He introduces Amy to touch she has never felt and sounds she has never heard—and soon they fall in love.

Amy learns of a surgical procedure that can restore Virgil's sight; he reluctantly agrees to undergo the procedure. When the bandages are removed, he opens his eyes to a world that is confusing and terrifying. (He cries, "There's something wrong—this can't be seeing!"). A therapist (Nathan Lane) explains that Virgil lacks a "visual vocabulary," which keeps him from making connections between the foreign things he sees, the familiar things he hears and touches, and the words that represent them.

The movie, based on a true story, illustrates how sighted people can take for granted their understanding of nonverbal messages. Virgil often asks Amy, "What does that face mean?" He is unfamiliar with the relational cues being sent in a coy smile, a pained grimace, or an embarrassed blush. Amy even has to teach Virgil when not to look, such as when he stares at a homeless person on the street. Ultimately, they both learn that assigning meaning to sensory information and nonverbal behavior is not a natural skill—it is a skill that must be learned and honed.

Masculine and Feminine Nonverbal Behaviors

The Birdcage (1996) Rated R

Mrs. Doubtfire (1993) Rated PG-13

Tootsie (1982) Rated PG

One way to recognize differences between masculine and feminine styles of nonverbal communication is to observe the same person playing different gender-related roles. Filmmakers have found this notion intriguing enough to produce several movies in which characters disguise themselves with makeup and costumes—and nonverbal cues—related to masculine and feminine roles.

In *Tootsie*, Michael Dorsey (Dustin Hoffman) is an aspiring New York actor who can't get any roles—at least as a man. In a flash of inspiration, he transforms himself into Dorothy Michaels, a middle-aged woman, and wins a part in a daytime soap opera.

Robin Williams takes on a Tootsie-like role in *Mrs. Doubtfire*. He plays Daniel Hillard, a divorced man who cannot bear to live without his children. His ex-wife (Sally Field) needs a housekeeper for the kids, so Daniel asks his gay, makeup-artist brother (Harvey Fierstein) to turn him into Mrs. Doubtfire.

In yet another twist on the masculine/feminine theme, Robin Williams plays a man who teaches his gay partner to be more macho in *The Birdcage*. The goal, once again, is disguise: The partners want their soon-to-be in-laws to believe they are brothers, not lovers.

From *Some Like It Hot* to *Victor/Victoria* (where a woman plays a man playing a woman), films through the years have capitalized on masculine/feminine differences to entertain and intrigue. In each case, the success of the characters is determined not only by what they say, but also by how they say it.

CHAPTER 7

LISTENING: MORE THAN MEETS THE EAR

i have just
wandered back
into our conversation
and find
that you
are still
rattling on
about something
or other
i think i must
have been gone
at least
twenty minutes
and you
never missed me
now this might say

something
about my acting ability
or it might say
something about
your sensitivity
one thing
troubles me tho
when it
is my turn
to rattle on
for twenty minutes
which i
have been known to do
have you
been missing too

Ric Masten

R ic Masten's poem above shows that there's more to listening
than gazing politely at a speaker and nodding your head every so
often. As you will soon learn, listening is a demanding and complex
activity—and just as important as speaking in the communication
process.

If frequency is a measure of importance, then listening easily qualifies as the most important kind of communication. We spend more time
in listening to others than in any other type of communication. One study
(summarized in Figure 7-1) revealed that college students spent an average of 14 percent of their communicating time writing, 16 percent
speaking, 17 percent reading, and a whopping 53 percent listening.
Listening was broken down further into listening to mass communication
media, such as radio and television, and listening to face-to-face messages. The former category accounted for 21 percent of the students'
communication time, and the latter accounted for 32 percent—more than
any other type of communication.[1] On the job, listening is just as important. Studies show that most employees of major corporations in North
America spend about 60 percent of each workday listening to others.[2]
Besides being the most frequent form of communication, listening is
arguably just as important as speaking in terms of making relationships
work. In committed relationships, listening to personal information in
everyday conversations is considered an important ingredient of satisfaction.[3] In one survey, marital counselors identified "failing to take the
other's perspective when listening" as one of the most frequent

If you think
communication is all
talk, you haven't been
listening.

Ashleigh Brilliant

communication problems in the couples with whom they worked.[4] When a group of adults was asked what communication skills were most important in family and social settings, listening was ranked first.[5]

Listening well is just as important in the job as in personal relationships. A study examining the link between listening and career success revealed that better listeners rose to higher levels in their organizations.[6] When one thousand human resource executives were asked to identify skills of the ideal manager, the ability to listen effectively ranked at the top of the list.[7] In problem-solving groups, effective listeners are judged as having the most leadership skills.[8] When a diverse group of senior executives was asked what skills were most important on the job, listening was identified more often than any other skill, including technical competence, computer knowledge, creativity, and administrative talent.[9]

This chapter will explore the nature of listening. After looking at all the elements that make up the process of listening, we will look at a variety of poor listening habits and their causes. After reviewing this gloomy picture, you will learn some ways to improve your listening skills so that your chances of understanding others are better. Finally we'll explore listening and responding skills that can help others solve their problems.

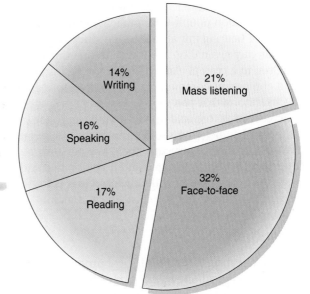

FIGURE 7-1 **Types of Listening Activities**

ELEMENTS IN THE LISTENING PROCESS

Before we go any further, it is important to offer a clear definition of *listening*. There's more to this activity than passively absorbing a speaker's words. In truth, **listening** is a process that consists of five elements: hearing, attending, understanding, responding, and remembering.

Hearing

Hearing is the physiological dimension of listening. It occurs when sound waves strike the ear at a certain frequency and loudness. Hearing is influenced by background noise. If there are other loud noises, especially at the same frequency as the message we are trying to hear, we find it difficult to sort out the important signals from the background. Hearing is also influenced by auditory fatigue, a temporary loss of hearing caused by continuous exposure to the same tone or loudness. If you spend an evening at a loud party, you may have trouble hearing well, even after getting away from the crowd. If you are exposed to loud noise often enough, permanent hearing loss can result.

Hearing can be difficult enough for people with no physical problems. But for many communicators, the challenge of hearing is even

All speech . . . is a dead language until it finds a willing and prepared hearer.

Robert Louis Stevenson

more difficult. In the United States alone, more than thirteen million people communicate with some degree of hearing impairment. One study revealed that, on any given day, one-fourth to one-third of the children in a typical classroom did not hear normally.[10] As a competent communicator, you need to recognize the likelihood that you may be speaking to someone with a hearing loss and to adjust your approach accordingly. Speaking slowly, loudly, and clearly can be helpful. Making sure that the other person can see your face is also important. And if you do not understand what the person with a hearing loss is saying, be sure to ask him or her to repeat the statement.

Attending

Whereas hearing is a physiological process, **attending** is a psychological one and is part of the process of selection that we described in chapter 4. We would go crazy if we attended to every sound we hear, so we filter out some messages and focus on others. Needs, wants, desires, and interests determine what is attended to. Not surprisingly, research shows that we attend most carefully to messages when there's a payoff for doing so.[11] If you're planning to see a movie, you'll listen to a friend's description more carefully than you otherwise would have. And when you want to get better acquainted with others, you'll pay careful attention to almost anything they say, in hopes of improving the relationship.

Surprisingly, attending doesn't help just the listener: It also helps the message sender. Participants in one study viewed brief movie segments and then described them to listeners who varied in their degree of attentiveness to the speakers. Later on the researchers tested the speakers' long-term recall of details from the movie segments. Those who had recounted the movie to attentive listeners remembered more details of the film.[12]

Understanding

Understanding occurs when we make sense of a message. It is possible to hear and attend to a message without understanding it at all. And, of course, it's possible to misunderstand a message. This chapter describes the many reasons why we misunderstand others—and why they *misunderstand* us. It also outlines skills that will help you improve your own understanding of others.

Responding

Responding to a message consists of giving observable feedback to the speaker. Although listeners don't always respond visibly to a speaker, research suggests that they should do so more often. One study of 195 critical incidents in banking and medical settings showed that a major difference between effective and ineffective listening was the kind of feedback offered.[13] Good listeners showed that they were attentive by nonverbal behaviors such as keeping eye contact and reacting with appropriate facial expressions. Their verbal behavior—answering questions and exchanging ideas, for example—also demonstrated their attention. It's easy to imagine how other responses would signal less effective listening. A slumped posture, bored expression, and yawning send a clear message that you are not tuned in to the speaker.

Adding responsiveness to our listening model demonstrates a fact that we discussed in chapter 1: Communication is *transactional* in nature. Listening isn't just a passive activity. As listeners we are active participants in a communication transaction. At the same time that we receive messages we also send them.

Remembering

Remembering is the ability to recall information. If we don't remember a message, listening is hardly worth the effort. Research suggests that most people remember only about 50 percent of what they hear *immediately* after hearing it. Within eight hours the 50 percent remembered drops to about 35 percent. After two months, the average recall is only about 25 percent of the original message. Given the amount of information we process every day—from teachers, friends, the radio, TV, and other sources—the *residual message* (what we remember) is a small fraction of what we hear. Although the tendency to forget information is common, there are ways to improve your retention and recall. You'll learn some of those ways later in this chapter. For now, though, you can begin to get a sense of how tough it is to listen effectively by trying this exercise.

We should all know this: that listening, not talking, is the gifted and great role, and the imaginative role. And the true listener is much more beloved, magnetic, than the talker, and he is more effective, and learns more and does more good. And so try listening. Listen to your wife, your husband, your father, your mother, your children, your friends; to those who love you and those who don't, to those who bore you, to your enemies. It will work a small miracle. And perhaps a great one.

Brenda Ueland

INVITATION TO INSIGHT

LISTENING BREAKDOWNS

You can overcome believing in some common myths about listening by recalling specific instances when

1. you heard another person's message but did not attend to it.

2. you attended to a message but forgot it almost immediately.

3. you attended to and remembered a message but did not understand it accurately.

4. you understood a message but did not respond sufficiently to convey your understanding to the sender.

5. you failed to remember some or all of an important message.

MANKOFF

"I'm sorry, dear. I wasn't listening. Could you repeat what you've said since we've been married?"

© The New Yorker Collection 2000 Robert Mankoff from cartoonbank.com. All Rights Reserved.

Bruce C. Anderson: The Challenges of Hearing Disabilities

Bruce Anderson *is a student at Minneapolis Community and Technical College, where he is preparing for a career teaching middle school students who are hard of hearing and deaf. He is committed to making sure that nobody is deprived of an education or successful career because of his or her physical condition.*

I grew up with a mild hearing disability. The word "mild" doesn't begin to describe how this affected my life. I couldn't hear many of the sounds or tones that are part of most peoples' voices. You can get an idea what this is like by imagining how hard it would be to listen to a muffled, quiet voice that is being drowned out by loud TV and radio playing at the same time, or trying to understand somebody whispering words while your ears are covered and your head is turned away.

When I flunked the school hearing tests in elementary school, I was put in a "special education" program. The other kids saw us as being different, and we were called the very worst names. I'm not perfect, so I fought back when I was picked on. I knew that I needed to escape this situation, so I devised a plan. In the next hearing test, I just followed the other students. When they heard a tone

and raised their hands, I raised mine too. Believe it or not, this satisfied whoever was in charge and I got back into the regular classes. This didn't change the trouble I had hearing and understanding speech.

Back in the regular classes I would sit next to people who I knew, and they would let me copy their work. I changed it just enough so it wouldn't look identical. I watched how to do the assignments and either handed them in late or not at all. I also taught myself to read lips. I took all of the shop classes that I could, and I watched the demonstrations carefully so I could follow along. Many of my teachers let me slide by so I could either continue to play on the school athletic teams, or just to move me out of their classroom. The service sector of society needed workers and I (and people like me) would be filling those jobs.

I was very lucky in some ways: I'm mechanically inclined, and I have been working since I was 14 years old in the maintenance field. Since high school I have been a maintenance engineer, a welder on the railroad, and a service engineer for a commercial laundry equipment company. I have always had to learn things through a hands-on approach because I have never been able to understand completely what a person says to me unless it is in a environment that is quiet.

I chose to become a teacher because I don't want anybody to go through what I did in school. I want to expose hard of hearing and deaf students to options that they may never have considered because of their disabilities. I also want to educate hearing people that the hard of hearing and deaf are able to communicate, but as in all communication it must be a two-way process to be successful.

If you're communicating with someone who has a hearing disability, here are a few tips. Have patience when asked to repeat something over once, twice or even three times. Remember: the deaf and hard of hearing are doing the best they can. Help is very hard to ask for and it is very difficult to draw attention to yourself by asking others what was said. If this still has not solved the problem try another avenue such as using different words or moving to a more quiet location to talk. Even writing something down may be necessary. Hard of hearing and deaf people listen with our eyes, so make sure you're standing or sitting so that the other person can see your face and your gestures.

If you make efforts like these, you will help people with hearing disabilities. And you might also get a new appreciation and respect for their world.

GENDER AND LISTENING

So far we have described the process of listening as if it was the same for both men and women. In fact, there is compelling evidence that gender plays a role the way people listen. To learn how, read on.

Social Influences

For over two thousand years, Western culture has defined different roles for men and women. In classical Greece women were regarded as emotional creatures capable of expressing opinions but not truth.[14] Men, by contrast, were regarded as creatures capable of recognizing and expressing facts. Because of these different perceived traits, women's place was the home, where they could play a nurturing role. Men's place was the public world, where they had the right to speak out to shape civic life.

This characterization of men as rational speakers and women as emotionally oriented listeners has persisted over time. Notice how the traits associated with speaking—forcefulness, power, and confidence—line up with stereotypically male behavior, whereas the traits associated with listening—caring, empathizing, other-centeredness, patience, and understanding—are stereotypically feminine.[15] Research supports the persistence of sex roles. For example, in conversations men interrupt to assert their own point of view, whereas women interrupt to offer encouragement and support.[16] In heterosexual couples, women are more likely than men to seek information about their partner's emotions, whereas men are more likely to speak about and listen for facts.[17] As you read in chapter 6, women are more likely than men to act nonverbally in ways that characterize attentive listening: gazing at the speaker, smiling, leaning forward, nodding the head, and so on.

When men and women deviate from social expectations like these, the results can be problematic. A warmly empathic man risks being viewed by others as somewhat odd, and a highly verbal woman might be viewed with disapproval.[18] (To prove this for yourself, think of the derogatory terms that might be used to describe an attentive, receptive man or a forcefully assertive woman.) Although these gender-specific expectations for listening have their roots in Western civilization, they exist in other cultures. In one study, these stereotypes were found in thirty countries around the world.[19]

From one perspective, sex-role stereotyping doesn't so much favor men and diminish women as define different expectations for each sex,

with men cast as assertive speakers and women as nurturing listeners. A second perspective argues that if women's voices are devalued, then they lose the ability to shape their personal worlds and society at large. A third perspective is that both men and women lose when their range of communication options is narrowed.[20]

Biological Influences

Although few scholars doubt the powerful role of social conditioning on listening behavior, some new research suggests that physiological differences between men and women might play a role, too. Using a brain-scanning technique called functional magnetic resonance imaging, scientists found differences in neural activity between men and women as they listened to a message.[21] A majority of the men showed exclusive activity on the left side of the brain, in the temporal lobe, which is associated with listening and speech. A majority of the women showed activity in the temporal lobe on both sides of the brain, although most activity was in the left lobe. The researchers don't know whether these gender differences in adults may be the physical result of powerful social conditioning about sexual roles that begins in infancy. "As scientists, we're figuring out what normal is, and more and more often it seems that normal for men may be different than normal for women," said Michael Phillips, coauthor of the study.[22] In the future, more research will help discover the degree to which listening, and other dimensions of communication, is shaped by biology.

TYPES OF INEFFECTIVE LISTENING

The preceding exercise demonstrated some of the most common types of poor listening. As you read on, you'll begin to recognize them as behaviors that you and those around you probably use quite often. Although you'll soon learn that a certain amount of ineffective listening is

Calvin and Hobbes
by Bill Watterson

Calvin and Hobbes © Watterson. Reprinted with permission of Universal Press Syndicate. All rights reserved.

inescapable and sometimes even understandable, it's important to be aware of these types so that you can avoid them when understanding others is important to you.

Pseudolistening

Pseudolistening is an imitation of the real thing. Pseudolisteners give the appearance of being attentive: They look you in the eye, nod and smile at the right times, and may even answer you occasionally. Behind that appearance of interest, however, something entirely different is going on because pseudolisteners use a polite façade to mask thoughts that have nothing to do with what the speaker is saying. Often pseudolisteners ignore you because of something on their minds that's more important to them than your remarks. Other times they may simply be bored or think that they've heard what you have to say before and so tune out your remarks. Whatever the reasons, the significant fact is that pseudolistening is really counterfeit communication.

Stage-Hogging

Stage-hogs (sometimes called "conversational narcissists") try to turn the topic of conversations to themselves instead of showing interest in the speaker.[23] One stage-hogging strategy is a "shift-response"—changing the focus of the conversation from the speaker to the narcissist:

A: "I had a great time mountain-biking last weekend!"

B: "Mountain biking's OK, but I'd rather go running."

C: "My math class is really tough."

D: "You think math is tough? You ought to try my physics class!"

Interruptions are another hallmark of stage-hogging. Besides preventing the listener from learning potentially valuable information, they can damage the relationship between the interrupter and the speaker. For example, applicants who interrupt the questions of employment interviewers are likely to be rated less favorably than applicants who wait until the interviewer has finished speaking before they respond.[24]

When confronted with stage-hogs, people react in one of two ways. Sometimes they react passively: talking less, tuning out the speaker, showing disinterest nonverbally, and leaving the conversation. Sometimes they react actively: trying to recapture the floor, hinting about the stage-hog's dominance, or confronting the speaker about his or her narcissism. Reactions like these give stage-hogs a taste of their own medicine, turning the conversation into a verbal tug-of-war.

Not all interruptions are attempts at stage-hogging. One study revealed a difference between male and female interrupters.[25] Men typically interrupted conversations far more often than women. Their goals were usually to control the conversation. Women interrupted for very different reasons: to communicate agreement, to elaborate on the speaker's idea, or to participate in the topic of conversation. These sorts of responses are more likely to be welcomed as a contribution to the discussion and not as attempts to grab the stage.

Everybody's talkin'
at me

I don't hear a word
they're sayin'

Only the echoes of my
mind.

Selective Listening

Selective listeners respond only to the parts of your remarks that interest them, rejecting everything else. All of us are selective listeners from time to time, such as, for instance, when we screen out radio commercials and music and keep an ear cocked for a weather report or an announcement of the time. In other cases, selective listening occurs in conversations with people who expect a thorough hearing but pay attention to their partner only when the conversation turns to their favorite topic—perhaps money, sex, a hobby, or some particular person. Unless and until you bring up one of these pet topics, you might as well talk to a tree.

Insulated Listening

Insulated listeners are almost the opposite of their selective cousins just mentioned. Instead of looking for something, these people avoid it. Whenever a topic arises that they'd rather not deal with, insulated listeners simply fail to hear or acknowledge it. You remind them about a problem, perhaps an unfinished job, poor grades, or the like, and they'll nod or answer you and then promptly forget what you've just said.

Defensive Listening

Defensive listeners take others' remarks as personal attacks. The teenager who perceives her parents' questions about her friends and activities as distrustful snooping is a defensive listener, as is the insecure breadwinner who explodes any time his mate mentions money, or the touchy parent

Not comprehending,
they hear like the deaf.

Heraclitus

who views any questioning by her children as a threat to her authority and parental wisdom. As chapter 9 will suggest, it's fair to assume that many defensive listeners are suffering from shaky presenting images and avoid admitting it by projecting their own insecurities onto others.

Ambushing

Ambushers listen carefully to you, but only because they're collecting information that they'll use to attack what you say. The cross-examining prosecution attorney is a good example of an ambusher. Needless to say, using this kind of strategy will justifiably initiate defensiveness in the other person.

Insensitive Listening

Insensitive listeners offer the final example of people who don't receive another person's messages clearly. As we've said before, people often don't express their thoughts or feelings openly but instead express them through a subtle and unconscious choice of words or nonverbal clues or both. Insensitive listeners aren't able to look beyond the words and behavior to understand their hidden meanings. Instead, they take a speaker's remarks at face value.

WHY WE DON'T LISTEN BETTER

After thinking about the styles of ineffective listening described in the previous pages, most people begin to see that they listen carefully only a small percentage of the time. It's pretty discouraging to realize that much of the time you aren't hearing others and they aren't getting your messages, but this is a fact of life. Sad as it may be, it's impossible to listen *all* the time, for several reasons.

Message Overload

The first reason is that the amount of speech that most of us encounter every day makes careful listening to everything we hear impossible. As you have already read, many of us spend almost half the time we're awake listening to verbal messages—from teachers, coworkers, friends, family, salespeople, and total strangers, not to mention radio and television. This means that we often spend five hours or more a day listening to people talk. It's impossible to keep our attention totally focused for this amount of time. Therefore, at times we have to let our attention wander. Given the onslaught of messages, it's understandable—perhaps even justifiable—to use pseudolistening and other less-than-admirable responses.

Preoccupation

Another reason why we don't always listen carefully is that we're often wrapped up in personal concerns that are of more immediate importance

Bore, n. A person who talks when you wish him to listen.

Conversation, n. A fair for the display of the minor mental commodities, each exhibitor being too intent upon arrangement of his own wares to observe those of his neighbor.

Egotist, n. A person of low taste more interested in himself than me.

Heaven, n. A place where the wicked cease from troubling you with talk of their personal affairs, and the good listen with attention while you expound your own.

Ambrose Bierce, *The Devil's Dictionary*

At the Party

Unrhymed, unrhythmical, the chatter goes:
Yet no one hears his own remarks as prose.
Beneath each topic
tunelessly discussed
The ground-bass is
reciprocal mistrust.
The names in fashion
shuttling to and fro
Yield, when deciphered,
messages of woe.
You cannot read me like
an open book.

I'm more myself than you will ever look.
Will no one listen to my
little song?
Perhaps I shan't be with
you very long.
A howl for recognition,
shrill with fear,
Shakes the jam-packed apartment, but each
    ear
Is listening to its hearing,
so none hear.

W. H. Auden

to us than are the messages that others are sending. It's hard to pay attention to someone else when you're anticipating an upcoming test or thinking about the wonderful time you had last night with good friends. Yet we still feel we have to "listen" politely to others, and so we continue with our charade.

Rapid Thought

Listening carefully is also difficult for a physiological reason. Although we're capable of understanding speech at rates of up to 600 words per minute, the average person speaks between 100 and 150 words per minute.[26] Thus, we have a lot of "spare time" to spend with our minds while someone is talking. And the temptation is to use this time in ways that don't relate to the speaker's ideas, such as thinking about personal interests, daydreaming, planning a rebuttal, and so on. The trick is to use this spare time to understand the speaker's ideas better rather than to let your attention wander.

Effort

Listening effectively is hard work. The physical changes that occur during careful listening show the effort it takes: The heart rate quickens, respiration increases, and body temperature rises.[27] Notice that these changes are similar to the body's reaction to physical effort. This is no coincidence because listening carefully to a speaker can be just as taxing as more obvious efforts.

External Noise

The physical world in which we live often presents distractions that make it hard to pay attention to others. The sound of traffic, music, others' speech, and so on interferes with our ability to hear well. Consider, for example, how the efficiency of your listening decreases when you are seated in a crowded, hot, stuffy room that is surrounded by traffic and other noises. In such circumstances even the best intentions aren't enough to ensure clear understanding.

Hearing Problems

Sometimes a person's listening ability suffers from a physiological hearing problem. After a hearing problem has been diagnosed, it's often possible to treat it. The real tragedy occurs when a hearing problem goes undetected. In such cases both the person with the problem and others can become

As friends, we don't see eye to eye. But then, we don't hear ear to ear either.

Buster Keaton

Bright-eyed college students in lecture halls aren't necessarily listening to the professor, the American Psychological Association was told yesterday.

If you shot off a gun at sporadic intervals and asked the students to encode their thoughts and moods at that moment, you would discover that:

- About 20 percent of the students, men and women, are pursuing erotic thoughts.
- Another 20 percent are reminiscing about something.
- Only 20 percent are actually paying attention to the lecture; 12 percent actively listen.
- The others are worrying, daydreaming, thinking about lunch or—surprise—religion (8 percent).

This confirmation of the lecturer's worst fears was reported by Paul Cameron, an assistant professor at Wayne State University in Detroit. Cameron's results were based on a nine-week course in introductory psychology for 85 college sophomores. A gun was fired 21 times at random intervals, usually when Cameron was in the middle of a sentence.

The San Francisco Sunday Examiner and Chronicle

frustrated and annoyed at the ineffective communication that results. If you suspect that you or someone you know suffers from a hearing loss, it's wise to have a physician or audiologist perform an examination.

Faulty Assumptions

We often make faulty assumptions that lead us to believe that we're listening attentively when quite the opposite is true. When the subject is a familiar one, it's easy to think that you've "heard it all before" although in fact the speaker is offering new information. A related problem arises when you assume that a speaker's thoughts are too simple or too obvious to deserve careful attention, when the truth is that you ought to be listening carefully. At other times just the opposite occurs: You think that another's comments are too complex to be understood (as in some lectures), so you give up trying to make sense of them. A final mistake that people often make is to assume that a subject is unimportant and to stop paying attention when they ought to be listening carefully.

Lack of Apparent Advantages

It often appears that we have more to gain by speaking than by listening. One big advantage of speaking is that it gives you a chance to control others' thoughts and actions. Whatever your goal—to be hired by a prospective boss, to convince others to vote for the candidate of your choice, or to describe the way you want your hair cut—the key to success seems to be the ability to speak well.

Another apparent advantage of speaking is the chance it provides to gain the admiration, respect, or liking of others. Tell jokes, and everyone will think you're a real wit. Offer advice, and they'll be grateful for your help. Tell them all you know, and they'll be impressed by your wisdom. But keep quiet—and you think you'll look like a worthless nobody.

Finally, talking gives you the chance to release energy in a way that listening can't. When you're frustrated, the chance to talk about your problems can often help you feel better. In the same way, you can often lessen your anger by letting it out verbally. It is also helpful to share your excitement with others by talking about it because keeping it inside often makes you feel as if you might burst.

Although it's true that talking does have many advantages, it's important to realize that listening can have advantages, too. As you'll soon read, being a good listener is one good way to help others with their problems; and what better way is there to have others appreciate you? As for controlling others, it may be true that it's hard to be persuasive while you're listening, but your willingness to hear others out will often encourage them to think about your ideas in return. Like defensiveness, listening is often reciprocal: You get what you give.

Deafness Lite

So slight is the bereftness of my belated ear-
fault
that "Deafness Lite" became the name
that I call it.

In a simpler word: things heard are blurred
on the left as well (or as weakly) as right.

Neither half's loss is a matter too drastic
both partly "cured" by batteries in
plastic.

But if eyeing such signs of silence, Hearer,
or (harder to do) spying a less visible
clue
try, by turning your speech slow and
clearer
to reach those few who must
communicate anew.

And so
that is why
as their advocate I
ask you unafflicted this:

Make me your talking's target
and practice, practice, practice.

Address then the wise assistive eyes
of sisters and brothers with hindered ear
and so come to know, then to
de-stranger-ize
those kindred other souls who less than I
can hear.

Repeat. Reword. For patience may reward
yourself;

Not by some sense of the charity kind
but by sharing the very daringest
adventure:
eyes meeting eyes and mind mating with
mind.

Sal Parlato, Jr.

Lack of Training

Even if we want to listen well, we're often hampered by a lack of training. A common but mistaken belief is that listening is like breathing—an
activity that people do well naturally. "After all," the common belief goes,
"I've been listening since I was a child. I don't need to study the subject
in school."

The truth is that listening is a skill much like speaking: Virtually
everybody does it, though few people do it well. Unfortunately, there is
no connection between how competently most communicators *think*
they listen and how competent they really are in their ability to understand others.[28] One survey illustrates this point. In the survey, 144
managers were asked to rate their listening skills. Astonishingly, not one
of the managers described himself or herself as a "poor" or "very poor"
listener, whereas 94 percent rated themselves as "good" or "very good."[29]

TABLE 7-1	**Comparison of Communication Activities**			
	LISTENING	SPEAKING	READING	WRITING
LEARNED	First	Second	Third	Fourth
USED	Most	Next to most	Next to least	Least
TAUGHT	Least	Next to least	Next to most	Most

The favorable self-ratings contrasted sharply with the perceptions of the managers' subordinates, many of whom said their boss's listening skills were weak. As we have discussed, some poor listening is inevitable. The good news is that listening can be improved through instruction and training.[30] Despite this fact, the amount of time spent teaching listening is far less than that spent on other types of communication. Table 7-1 reflects this upside-down arrangement.

Media Influences

A final challenge to serious listening is the influence of contemporary mass media, especially television and radio. A growing amount of programming consists of short segments: news items, commercials, music videos, and so on. (Think of *Sesame Street* and MTV.) In the same vein, news stories (for example, *USA Today* and the television news) consist of brief stories with a declining portion of text and a growing amount of graphical information. These trends discourage the kind of focused attention that is necessary for careful listening, especially to complicated ideas and feelings.

INFORMATIONAL LISTENING

After reading the last few pages, you might decide that listening well is impossible. Fortunately, with the right combination of attitude and skill, you can do a reasonably good job of listening. The first step is to realize that different types of listening are suited for different purposes. With informational listening the goal is to make sure that you are accurately receiving the thoughts that the other person is trying to convey—not always an easy feat when you consider the forces that interfere with understanding.

The situations that call for informational listening are endless and varied: following the directions of an instructor or boss, listening to a friend's account of a vacation, learning about your family history from a relative's tales, swapping ideas in a discussion about religion or politics—the list goes on and on. You can become a more effective informational listener by following several guidelines.

Learn to listen. Opportunity could be knocking at your door very softly.

Frank Tyger

The Chinese characters that make up the verb *to listen* tell us something significant about this skill.

LEND AN EAR

EAR

EYES

UNDIVIDED
ATTENTION

HEART

Calligraphy by Angie Au

The first time the car broke down we were somewhere in North Carolina," my mother-in-law told me over the phone. "We had it fixed, and then it stalled again in Delaware. But the worst was on the Verrazano Bridge during rush hour. It seemed as if we'd never get home."

"That sounds horrible," I said, ready to launch into my own horror story—a car that conked out at 9:30 p.m. in a deserted mall parking lot.

But someone knocked at her door, so she had to say good-bye.

"Thank you for listening," she added, "but most of all for not telling me your worst car story."

My cheeks burning, I hung up. In the days ahead I found myself thinking about the wisdom of her parting words. I can't count the number of times I've begun to complain—about a fight, a professional disappointment, or even car problems—only to have my friend cut me off with "The same thing just happened to me." Suddenly we're talking about *her* ungrateful kid, *her* leaky fuel line. And I'm left nodding my head in all

the right places, wondering if we haven't all come down with a bad case of emotional attention deficit disorder.

What we all hope for when we're feeling low or agitated or wildly happy is to find a friend who sounds as if he or she has all the time in the world to listen. We don't always want answers or advice. Sometimes we just want company.

Roberta Isrealoff

Talk Less

Zeno of Citium put it most succinctly: "We have been given two ears and but a single mouth, in order that we may hear more and talk less." If your true goal is to understand the speaker, avoid the tendency to hog the stage and shift the conversation to your ideas. Talking less doesn't mean you should remain completely silent. As you'll soon read, giving feedback that clarifies your understanding and seeks new information is an important way to understand a speaker. Nonetheless, most of us talk too much when we're claiming to understand others. Other cultures, including many Native American ones, value listening at least as much as talking.[31] You can appreciate the value of this approach by trying the following exercise.

> The greatest compliment that was ever paid me was when one asked me what I thought, and attended to my answer.
>
> Henry David Thoreau

INVITATION TO INSIGHT

SPEAKING AND LISTENING WITH A "TALKING STICK"

Explore the benefits of talking less and listening more by using a "Talking Stick." This exercise is based on the Native American tradition of "council." Gather a group of people in a circle, and designate a particular object as the talking stick. (Almost any manageable object will do.) Participants then pass the object around the circle. Each person may speak

a. when holding the stick,
b. for as long as he or she holds the stick, and
c. without interruption from anyone else in the circle

When a member is through speaking, the stick passes to the left, and the speaker surrendering the stick must wait until it has made its way around the circle before speaking again.

After each member of the group has had the chance to speak, discuss how this experience differed from more common approaches to listening. Decide how the desirable parts of this method could be introduced into everyday conversations.

Get Rid of Distractions

Some distractions are external: ringing telephones, radio or television programs, friends dropping in, and so on. Other distractions are internal: preoccupation with your own problems, an empty stomach, and so on. If the information you're seeking is really important, do everything possible to eliminate the internal and external distractions that interfere with careful listening.

Don't Judge Prematurely

Most people would agree with the principle that it's essential to understand a speaker's ideas before judging them. Despite this commonsense

> So the first simple feeling I want to share with you is my enjoyment when I can really hear someone. I think perhaps this has been a long-standing characteristic of mine. I can remember this in my early grammar school days. A child would ask the teacher a question and the teacher would give a perfectly good answer to a completely different question. A feeling of pain and distress would always strike me. My reaction was, "But you didn't hear him!" I felt a sort of childish despair at the lack of communication which was (and is) so common.
>
> Carl R. Rogers

principle, all of us are guilty of forming snap judgments, evaluating others before hearing them out. This tendency is greatest when the speaker's ideas conflict with our own. Conversations that ought to be exchanges of ideas turn into verbal battles, with the "opponents" trying to ambush one another in order to win a victory. Disagreements aren't the only kind of conversation in which the tendency to judge others is strong: It's also tempting to counterattack when others criticize you, even when those criticisms may contain valuable truths and when understanding them may lead to a change for the better. Even if there is no criticism or disagreement, we tend to evaluate others based on sketchy first impressions, forming snap judgments that aren't at all valid. Not all premature judgments are negative. It's also possible to jump to overly positive conclusions about the quality of a speaker's remarks when we like that person or agree with the ideas being expressed. The lesson contained in these negative examples is clear: Listen first. Make sure you understand. *Then* evaluate.

"You haven't been listening. I keep telling you that I don't want a product fit for a king."

©2001 Ted Goff from cartoonbank.com. All Rights Reserved.

Look for Key Ideas

It's easy to lose patience with long-winded speakers who never seem to get to the point—or *have* a point, for that matter. Nonetheless, most people do have a central idea. By using your ability to think more quickly than the speaker can talk, you may be able to extract the central idea from the surrounding mass of words you're hearing. If you can't figure out what the speaker is driving at, you can always ask in a tactful way by using the skills of questioning and paraphrasing, which we'll examine now.

Ask Questions

So far we have been discussing listening methods that are basically passive in nature; that is, those that can be carried out silently. It's also possible to verify or increase your understanding in a more active way by asking questions to be sure you are receiving the speaker's thoughts and feelings accurately.

Despite their apparent benefits, not all questions are equally helpful. Whereas **sincere questions** are aimed at understanding others, **counterfeit questions** are aimed at sending a message, not receiving one. Counterfeit questions come in several varieties:

■ *Questions that trap the speaker.* When your friend says, "You didn't like that movie, did you?," you're being backed into a corner. It's clear that your friend disapproves, so the question leaves you with two choices: You can disagree and defend your position, or you can devalue your reaction by lying or equivocating—"I guess it wasn't perfect." Consider how much easier it would be to respond to the sincere question, "What did you think of the movie?"

■ *A tag question like "did you?"* or "isn't that right?" at the end of a question can be a tip-off that the asker is looking for agreement, not information. Although some tag questions are genuine requests for confirmation, counterfeit ones are used to coerce agreement: "You said you'd call at 5 o'clock, but you forgot, didn't you?" Similarly, leading questions that begin with "Don't you" (such as, "Don't you think he would make a good boss?") direct others toward a desired response. As a simple solution, changing "Don't you?" to "Do you?" makes the question less leading.

■ *Questions that make statements.* "Are you finally off the phone?" is more of a statement than a question—a fact unlikely to be lost on the targeted person. Emphasizing certain words can also turn a question into a statement: "You lent money to *Tony?*" We also use questions to offer advice. The person who responds with "Are you going to stand up to him and give him what he deserves?" clearly has stated an opinion about what should be done.

■ *Questions that carry hidden agendas.* "Are you busy Friday night?" is a dangerous question to answer. If you say "No," thinking the person has something fun in mind, you won't like hearing, "Good, because I need some help moving my piano." Obviously, such questions are not designed to enhance understanding: They are setups for the proposal that follows. Other examples include, "Will you do me a favor?" and "If I tell you what happened, will you promise not to get mad?" Wise communicators answer questions that mask hidden agendas cautiously, with responses like "It depends" or "Let me hear what you have in mind before I answer."

■ *Questions that seek "correct" answers.* Most of us have been victims of questioners who want to hear only a particular response. "Which shoes do you think I should wear?" can be a sincere question—unless the asker has a predetermined preference. When this happens, the asker isn't interested in listening to contrary opinions, and "incorrect" responses get shot down. Some of these questions may venture into delicate territory. "Honey, do you think I look ugly?" can be a request for a "correct" answer.

■ *Questions based on unchecked assumptions.* "Why aren't you listening to me?" assumes that the other person isn't paying attention. "What's the matter?" assumes that something is wrong. As chapter 3 explains, perception checking is a much better way of checking out assumptions. As you recall, a perception check offers a description and interpretations, followed by a sincere request for clarification: "When you kept looking over at the TV I thought you weren't listening to me, but maybe I was wrong. *Were* you paying attention?"

Unlike the counterfeit questions we've just examined, sincere questions are genuine requests for new information that clarifies a speaker's thoughts or feelings. Although the value of sincere questioning might seem obvious, there are two reasons why people often don't use this information-seeking approach. First, communicators are often reluctant to show their ignorance by asking for explanation of what seems to be an obvious point. At times like this it's a good idea to recall a quote attributed to Confucius: "He who asks a question is a fool for five minutes. He who does not ask is a fool for life."

A second reason why people are often disinclined to ask questions is because they think they already understand a speaker; but do we in fact understand others as often or as well as we think? You can best answer by thinking about how often people misunderstand *you* while they feel certain that they know what you've meant. If you are aware that others should ask questions of you more often, then it's logical to assume that the same principle holds true in reverse.

INVITATION TO INSIGHT

COUNTERFEIT QUESTIONS

Check your understanding of counterfeit questions by looking at Jill and Mark's conversation on page 306. Create examples of poor responses that Mark could have given Jill by showing how and where he could have:

1. asked a question that was really a statement.

2. asked a question with a hidden agenda.

3. asked a question that begged for a "correct" answer.

4. asked a question based on an unchecked assumption.

5. denied Jill the right to her feelings.

6. minimized the significance of the situation.

7. focused on "then and there" rather than "here and now."

8. cast judgment on Jill.

In each case, speculate how Jill might have reacted to Mark's poor response.

Paraphrase

Questioning is often a valuable tool for increasing understanding. Sometimes, however, it won't help you understand a speaker's ideas any more clearly, and it can even lead to greater confusion. Consider the common example of asking directions to a friend's home. Suppose that you've received these directions: "Drive about a mile and then turn left at the traffic signal." Now imagine that a few common problems exist in this simple message. First, suppose that your friend's idea of a mile differs from yours: Your mental picture of the distance is actually closer to two miles, whereas your friend's is closer to three hundred yards. Next, consider that "traffic signal" really means "stop sign"; after all, it's common for us to think one thing and say another. Keeping these problems in mind, suppose that you tried to verify your understanding of the directions by asking, "After I turn at the light, how far should I go?," to which your friend replied that the house is the third from the corner. Clearly, if you parted after this exchange, you would encounter a lot of frustration before finding the elusive residence.

"Listening More Carefully and Responsively"

http://www. coopcomm.org/ w7chal1.htm

This page is a chapter in an excellent, comprehensive online book that explores seven challenging interpersonal communication skills. The chapter addresses the practice of responsive listening and focuses on the practice of separating the acknowledgment of the thoughts and feelings that a person expresses from approving, agreeing, advising, or persuading. Once you have read this page, complete Activity 7.5, "Learning to Acknowledge What You Hear" on the *Looking Out/Looking In* Web site.

What was the problem here? It's easy to see that questioning might not have helped you because your original ideas of how far to drive and where to turn were mistaken. Such mistakes exemplify the biggest problem with questioning: Your inquiries don't tell you whether you have accurately received information that has *already* been sent.

The need to understand others is even more important in a variety of everyday situations: making sure you know just what the boss wants, clarifying a school assignment before leaving class, knowing exactly what's behind critical comments others might direct at you, and understanding what others mean when they offer advice.

Because questioning doesn't always provide the information you need, consider another kind of feedback—one that would tell you whether you understood what had already been said before you asked additional questions. This type of feedback involves restating in your own words the message you thought the speaker had just sent, without adding anything new. Statements that reword the listener's interpretation of a message are commonly termed **paraphrasing** or **active listening.** Sometimes a paraphrase will reflect the *ideas* that you think a speaker has expressed:

> (To a direction-giver) "You're telling me to drive down to the traffic light by the high school and turn toward the mountains, is that it?"

> (To the boss) "So you need me both this Saturday *and* next Saturday—right?"

> (To a professor) "When you said 'Don't worry about the low grade on the quiz,' did you mean it won't count against my grade?"

> In other cases, a paraphrase will reflect your understanding of the speaker's *feelings:*

> "You said you understand, but you look confused. Are you?"

> "You seem to be in a hurry. I get the idea you don't want to talk now. Is that right?"

> "You said 'Forget it,' but it sounds like you're mad. Are you?"

Types of Paraphrasing Statements   Whether your paraphrasing reflects a speaker's thoughts or feelings, and whether it focuses on a specific comment or a general theme, the key to success is to restate the other person's comments in your own words as a way of cross-checking the information. If you simply repeat the other person's comments verbatim, you will sound foolish—and you still might well be misunderstanding what has been said. Notice the difference between simply parroting a statement and true paraphrasing:

> Speaker: "I'd like to go, but I can't afford it."

> Parroting: "You'd like to go, but you can't afford it."

> Paraphrasing: "So if we could find a way to pay for you, you'd be willing to come. Is that right?"

Speaker: "Gawd, do you look awful!"

Parroting: "You think I look terrible."

Paraphrasing: "You think I've put on too much weight?"

As these examples suggest, effective paraphrasing is a skill that takes time to develop. You can make your paraphrasing sound more natural by taking any of three approaches, depending on the situation:

1. **Change the speaker's wording.**

   Speaker: "Bilingual education is just another failed idea of bleeding heart liberals."

   Paraphrase: "Let me see if I've got this right. You're mad because you think bilingual ed sounds good, but it doesn't work?"

2. **Offer an example of what you think the speaker is talking about.**

   When the speaker makes an abstract statement, you may suggest a specific example or two to see if your understanding is accurate.

   Speaker: "Lee is such a jerk. I can't believe the way he acted last night."

   Paraphrase: "You think those jokes were pretty offensive, huh?"

3. **Reflect the underlying theme of the speaker's remarks.**

   When you want to summarize the *theme* that seems to have run through another person's comments, a complete or partial perception check is appropriate:

   Paraphrase: "You keep reminding me to be careful. Sounds like you're worried that something might happen to me. Am I right?"

Paraphrasing won't always be accurate. But expressing your restatement *tentatively* gives the other person a chance to make a correction. (See the examples above for illustrations of open-minded paraphrasing).

Besides increasing the chance of understanding others, paraphrasing is an excellent way to keep the tone of a confrontation positive. When you are sincerely trying to understand the other person, you are less likely to engage in the kind of hostile behavior that can lead to a destructive battle. For this reason, some communication experts suggest that the ratio of active listening to other responses should be at least 5:1, if not more.[32]

Because it's an unfamiliar way of responding, paraphrasing may feel awkward at first; but if you start by paraphrasing occasionally and then gradually increase the frequency of such responses, you can begin to learn the benefits.

"I have a pet at home."

"Oh, what kind of a pet?"

"It is a dog."

"What kind of a dog?"

"It is a cocker spaniel."

"Grown up or a puppy?"

"It is full grown."

"What color is it?"

"It is black and white."

"Why didn't you say you had a full-grown, black-and-white cocker spaniel as a pet in the first place?"

PARAPHRASING PRACTICE

This exercise will help you see that it is possible to understand someone who disagrees with you, without arguing or sacrificing your point of view.

1. Find a partner. Designate one person as *A* and the other as *B*.

2. Find a subject on which you and your partner apparently disagree—a current events topic, a philosophical or moral issue, or perhaps simply a matter of personal taste.

3. Person *A* begins by making a statement on the subject. Person *B*'s job is then to paraphrase the statement. *B*'s job is simply to understand here, and doing so in no way should signify agreement or disagreement with *A*'s remarks.

4. *A* then responds by telling *B* whether her response was accurate. If there was some misunderstanding, *A* should make the correction, and *B* should feed back her new understanding of the statement. Continue this process until you're both sure that *B* understands *A*'s statement.

5. Now it's *B*'s turn to respond to *A*'s statement and for *A* to help the process of understanding by correcting *B*.

6. Continue this process until each partner is satisfied that she has explained herself fully and has been understood by the other person.

7. Now discuss the following questions:

   a. How did your understanding of the speaker's statement change after you used active listening?
   b. Did you find that the gap between your position and that of your partner narrowed as a result of active listening?
   c. How did you feel at the end of your conversation? How does this feeling compare to your usual feeling after discussing controversial issues?
   d. How might your life change if you used active listening at home? At work? With friends?

It is hard to know what to say to a person who has been struck by tragedy, but it is easier to know what not to say. Anything critical of the mourner ("don't take it so hard," "try to hold back your tears, you're upsetting people") is wrong. Anything which tries to minimize the mourner's pain ("it's probably for the best," "it could be a lot worse," "she's better off now") is likely to be misguided and unappreciated. Anything which asks the mourner to disguise or reject his feelings ("we have no right to question God," "God must love you to have selected you for this burden") is wrong as well.

Harold S. Kushner, *When Bad Things Happen to Good People*

FINDING COMMON GROUND THROUGH LISTENING

The reports from the front lines of the abortion wars are as dispiriting as ever. Hostilities have only escalated and opponents have now become enemies.

But in a vine-covered building behind a wooden fence in suburban Boston, a small group of family therapists is trying to establish a demilitarized zone. The Public Conversations Project they have created is on a leading edge of the nascent movement struggling to defuse the civil wars.

Their project grew out of a question that director Laura Chasin asked herself and her colleagues in 1990: "Do we as family therapists have skills that can be helpfully applied 'out there'?"

Over the past year and a half, they invited groups of people to join a different sort of conversation.

Some of their names were provided by Planned Parenthood and Massachusetts Citizens for Life; all identified themselves as pro-choice or pro-life.

Under the ground rules, people were not allowed to try to persuade each other. Instead, over three hours and under the guidance of a project member, they talked and listened. They explored stereotypes of each other, acknowledged ambivalence and watched what emerged from this process. Some questions indeed led down hopeless, dead ends. When does life begin? Is the fetus a person? Who should decide? But of the 50 people who went through the process, only two were totally unable to find new ways of talking.

"The main thing that happened was the way these people perceived each other," says Chasin. "They came in thinking, oh my God, I'm going to be meeting with them. They went out thinking these people are compassionate, principled and share concerns that I have."

Indeed at moments in the videotaped conversations, it is impossible to know the opponents without a label. Which side said, for example, "How do we get people who are in the business of making laws to start thinking about a world in which there would be no need for abortion?"

"These people were in such pitched battles," said another project member, "they didn't have a clue what they had in common." But gradually they uncovered a shared concern about the well-being of children and mothers. Both sides agreed that using abortion as a form of birth control was wrong. They agreed as well about the importance of preventing unintended pregnancy and about the need for sex education.

Chasin and her colleagues harbor no grand illusions that this process will forge A Great Compromise on abortion—take your placards and go home.

But, once a pattern has been "busted," once people are no longer defined as demons, they hope that the public, like the family, may be able to come up with some solutions. Indeed, there are hints of this success in other parts of this movement.

In Missouri, Wisconsin, Texas and California, pro-life and pro-choice people are meeting and talking—carefully.

Ellen Goodman

LISTENING TO HELP

One motive for listening is to advance our own self-interest. Another motive for listening, however, is to help others with their problems. Sometimes the problem is a major one: "I don't know whether we should stay together or split up"; or "I keep getting turned down for jobs I want." At other times the problem is less profound. A friend might be trying to decide what birthday gift to buy or how to spend the weekend.

There's no question about the value of receiving help with personal problems. One survey showed that "comforting ability" was among the most important communication skills a friend could have.[33] The value of receiving help with personal problems is clear when big problems arise, but research shows that the smaller, everyday distresses and upsets can actually take a bigger toll on mental health and physical well-being.[34]

Whether the problem is large or small, knowing how to help is a valuable skill. To understand your present style of helping, try the following exercise before reading on.

INVITATION TO INSIGHT

WHAT WOULD YOU DO?

1. In a moment you'll read a list of situations in which someone tells you of a problem. In each situation, write out the words that you'd use in responding to this person.

2. Here are the statements:
   a. I don't know what to do about my parents. It seems as if they just don't understand me. Everything I like seems to go against their values, and they just won't accept my feelings as being right for me. It's not that they don't love me—they do. But they don't accept me.
   b. I've been pretty discouraged lately. I just can't get a good relationship going with any guys. . . . I mean a romantic relationship . . . you know. I have plenty of men whom I'm good friends with, but that's always as far as it goes. I'm tired of being just a pal. . . . I want to be more than that.
   c. (Child to parents) I hate you guys! You always go out and leave me with some stupid sitter. Why don't you like me?
   d. I'm really bummed out. I don't know what I want to do with my life. I'm pretty tired of school, but there aren't any good jobs around, and I sure don't want to join the service. I could just drop out for a while, but that doesn't really sound very good, either.
   e. Things really seem to be kind of lousy in my marriage lately. It's not that we fight too much or anything, but all the excitement seems to be gone. It's like we're in a rut, and it keeps getting worse. . . .
   f. I keep getting the idea that my boss is angry at me. It seems as if lately he hasn't been joking around very much, and he hasn't said anything at all about my work for about three weeks now. I wonder what I should do.

3. After you've written your response to each of these messages, imagine the probable outcome of the conversation that would have followed. If you've tried this exercise in class, you might have two group members role-play each response. Based on your idea of how the conversation might have gone, decide which responses were productive and which were unproductive.

Most of the responses that you made probably fell into one of several kinds. None of these ways of responding is good or bad in itself, but there's a proper time and place for each kind of response. The problem usually occurs, however, when we use them in the wrong situations or depend on one or two kinds of responses for all situations.

As you read the following descriptions of these ways of responding, see which ones you used most frequently in the previous exercise, and think about the results that probably would have occurred from your response.

Advising

When we are approached with another's problem, our tendency is an **advising response**: to help by offering a solution.[35] Although such a response is sometimes valuable, often it isn't as valuable as you might think.[36]

Often your response may not offer the best course to follow, in which case it can be even harmful. There's often a temptation to tell others how we would behave in their place, but it's important to realize that what's right for one person may not be right for another. A related consequence of advising is that it often allows others to avoid responsibility for their decisions. A partner who follows advice of yours that doesn't work out can always pin the blame on you. Finally, often people simply don't want advice: They may not be ready to accept it, needing instead simply to talk out their thoughts and feelings.

Before offering advice, then, you need to be sure that four conditions are present:[37]

1. Be confident that the advice is accurate. You may be certain about some matters of fact, such as the proper way to solve a school problem or the cost of a piece of merchandise, but resist the temptation to act like an authority on matters you know little about. Furthermore, it is both unfair and risky to make suggestions when you aren't positive that they are the best choice. Realize that just because a course of action worked for you doesn't guarantee that it will work for everybody.

2. Ask yourself whether the person seeking your advice seems willing to accept it. In this way you can avoid the frustration of making good suggestions, only to find that the person with the problem had another solution in mind all the time.

> I've learned that it is best to give advice in only two circumstances: When it is requested and when it is a life-threatening situation.
>
> Andy Rooney

3. Be confident that the receiver won't blame you if the advice doesn't work out. You may be offering advice, but the choice and responsibility for accepting it are up to the recipient.

4. Deliver your advice supportively, in a face-saving manner. Advice that is perceived as being offered constructively, in the context of a solid relationship, is much better received than critical comments offered in a way that signals a lack of respect for the receiver.[38] In fact, advice given in a respectful, caring way has been identified as a key ingredient in keeping platonic male-female friendships strong.[39]

Judging

A **judging response** evaluates the sender's thoughts or behaviors in some way. The judgment may be favorable—"That's a good idea" or "You're on the right track now"—or unfavorable—"An attitude like that won't get you anywhere." But in either case it implies that the person doing the judging is in some way qualified to pass judgment on the speaker's thoughts or actions.

Sometimes negative judgments are purely critical. How many times have you heard such responses as "Well, you asked for it!" or "I *told* you so!" or "You're just feeling sorry for yourself"? Although responses like these can sometimes serve as a verbal slap that brings problem-holders to their senses, they usually make matters worse.

In other cases negative judgments are less critical. These involve what we usually call *constructive criticism*, which is intended to help the problem-holder improve in the future. This is the sort of response given by friends about everything from the choice of clothing to jobs to friends. Another common setting for constructive criticism occurs in school, where instructors evaluate students' work to help them master concepts and skills. But whether it's justified or not, even constructive criticism runs the risk of arousing defensiveness because it may threaten the self-concept of the person at whom it is directed.

Judgments have the best chance of being received when two conditions exist.

THEY LEARN TO AID CUSTOMERS BY BECOMING GOOD LISTENERS

Do you need someone to listen to your troubles? Have your hair done. Beauty salon chairs may be to today's women what conversation-centered backyard fences were to their grandmothers and psychiatrists' couches are to their wealthier contemporaries.

"We are not as family-oriented as our ancestors were," says counselor-trainer Andy Thompson. "They listened to and helped each other. Now that we have become a society of individuals isolated from one another by cars, telephones, jobs and the like, we have had to find other listeners."

Community training program director for Crisis House, Thompson has designed and is conducting human relations training sessions for workers to whom customers tend to unburden their woes most frequently—cosmetologists, bartenders and cabdrivers.

"People can definitely help others just by letting them talk," he said.

"Relatives, friends or spouses who listen do a lot to keep the mental health of this country at a reasonable rate. Workers in situations that encourage communications can make the same meaningful contribution."

Thompson explained that his training is not meant to replace, or be confused with, professional treatment or counseling. His students fill a gap between family and professionals.

"There are not enough psychiatrists or psychologists to go around," he said. "And some professionals become so technical that their help doesn't mean much to persons who just need a someone who will let them get problems and questions out in the open where they can look at them."

Thompson's first course of training, completed recently, was for cosmetologists.

The human relations training program attempts to make the most of these built-in assets by using a method Thompson calls "reflective listening."

"The purpose is to let the customer talk enough to clarify her own thinking," he said. "We are not interested in having cosmetologists tell women what to do, but to give them a chance to choose their own course of action.

"There is a tendency among listeners to try to rescue a person with problems and pull them out of negative situations. People don't really want that. They just want to discuss what is on their minds and reach their own conclusions."

Cosmetologists are taught to use phrases that aid customers in analyzing their thoughts. Some of the phrases are, "You seem to think . . ." "You sound like . . ." "You appear to be . . ." "As I get it, you . . ." and "It must seem to you that . . ."

There also are barriers to conversation that the cosmetologists are taught to avoid.

"A constant bombardment of questions can disrupt communications," Thompson said. "Commands will have the same effect. Many of them are impossible to follow anyway.

"How many can respond to orders to 'Stop feeling depressed,' 'Don't be so upset,' or 'Don't think about it.'

"The same applies to negative criticism, 'That's dumb,' for instance; and evaluations, such as 'Oh, you're just confused.'

"Comments that seem threatening—'You had better stop feeling sad,' as an example—will end a conversation as quickly as changing the subject or not paying attention."

San Diego Union

1. The person with the problem should have requested an evaluation from you. Occasionally an unsolicited evaluation may bring someone to his or her senses, but more often unsolicited evaluation will trigger a defensive response.

2. The intent of your judgment should be genuinely constructive and not designed as a put-down. If you are tempted to use judgments as a weapon, don't fool yourself into thinking that you are being helpful. Often the statement "I'm telling you this for your own good . . ." simply isn't true.

If you can remember to follow these two conditions, your judgments will probably be less frequent and better received.

Analyzing

In an **analyzing statement,** the listener offers an interpretation of a speaker's message. Analyses like these are probably familiar to you:

"I think what's really bothering you is . . ."

"She's doing it because . . ."

"I don't think you really meant that."

"Maybe the problem started when she . . ."

Interpretations are often effective ways to help people with problems consider alternative meanings—meanings they would have never thought of without your help. Sometimes a clear analysis will make a confusing problem suddenly clear, either suggesting a solution or at least providing an understanding of what is occurring.

In other cases, an analysis can create more problems than it solves. There are two problems with analyzing. First, your interpretation may not be correct, in which case the speaker may become even more confused by accepting it. Second, even if your analysis is correct, telling it to the problem-holder might not be useful. There's a chance that it will arouse defensiveness (because analysis implies superiority and evaluativeness), and even if it doesn't, the person may not be able to understand your view of the problem without working it out personally.

How can you know when it's helpful to offer an analysis? There are several guidelines to follow:

1. Offer your interpretation as tentative rather than as absolute fact. There's a big difference between saying "Maybe the reason is . . ." or "The way it looks to me . . ." and insisting, "This is the truth."

2. Your analysis ought to have a reasonable chance of being correct. An incorrect interpretation—especially one that sounds plausible—can leave a person more confused than before.

3. You ought to be sure that the other person will be receptive to your analysis. Even if you're completely accurate, your thoughts won't help if the problem-holder isn't ready to consider them.

4. Be sure that your motive for offering an analysis is truly to help the other person. It can be tempting to offer an analysis to show how brilliant you are or even to make the other person feel bad for not having thought of the right answer in the first place. Needless to say, an analysis offered under such conditions isn't helpful.

Questioning

A few pages ago we talked about questioning as one way for you to understand others better. A **questioning response** can also be a way to help others think about their problems and understand them more clearly. For example, questioning can help a problem-holder define vague ideas more precisely. You might respond to a friend with a line of questioning: "You said Greg has been acting 'differently' toward you lately. What has he been doing?" Another example of a question that helps clarify is: "You told your roommates that you wanted them to be more helpful in keeping the place clean. What would you like them to do?"

Questions can also encourage a problem-holder to examine a situation in more detail by talking either about what happened or about personal feelings—for example, "How did you feel when they turned you down? What did you do then?" This type of questioning is particularly helpful when you are dealing with someone who is quiet or is unwilling under the circumstances to talk about the problem very much.

Although questions have the potential to be helpful, they also have the potential to confuse or distract the person with the problem. The best questioning follows these principles:

1. Don't ask questions just to satisfy your own curiosity. You might become so interested in the other person's story that you will want to hear more. "What did he say then?" you might be tempted to ask. "What happened next?" Responding to questions like these might confuse the person with the problem or even leave him or her more agitated than before.

2. Be sure that your questions won't confuse or distract the person you're trying to help. For instance, asking someone, "When did the problem begin?" might provide some clue about how to solve it—but it could also lead to a long digression that would only confuse matters. As with advice, it's important to be sure that you're on the right track before asking questions.

3. Don't use questions to disguise your suggestions or criticism. We've all been questioned by parents, teachers, or other figures who seemed to be trying to trap us or indirectly to guide us. In this way, questioning becomes a strategy that can imply that the questioner already has some idea of what direction the discussion should take but isn't willing to tell you directly.

The reality of the other person is not in what he reveals to you, but in what he cannot reveal to you.

Therefore, if you would understand him, listen not to what he says but rather to what he does not say.

Kahlil Gibran

Supporting

There are times when other people want to hear more than a reflection of how *they* feel: They would like to know how *you* feel. **Supportive responses** reveal a listener's solidarity with the speaker's situation.

There are several types of support:

Agreement	"You're right—the landlord is being unfair."
	"Yeah, that class was tough for me, too."
Offers to help	"I'm here if you need me."
	"Let me try to straighten him out. Maybe he'll listen to me."
Praise	"I don't care what the boss said: I think you did a great job!"
	"You're a terrific person, and if she doesn't recognize it, that's her problem!"
Reassurance	"The worst part is over. It will get easier from here."
	"I know you'll do a great job."
Diversion	"Let's catch a movie and get your mind off this."
	"That reminds me of the time we . . ."

Women are more likely than men to value supporting messages and to offer supporting messages to others.[40] This fact reinforces the importance of choosing a helping style that is likely to be appreciated by the person you are trying to help. Supporting may be a better response when dealing with women than men.

Despite their apparent value, supporting responses may not be helpful. In fact, they can even make things worse. Telling a person who is obviously upset that everything is fine or joking about what seems like a serious problem can leave others thinking that you don't regard their problems as very significant. They might interpret your comments as putdowns, leaving them feeling worse than before.

It's easy to identify what effective support *doesn't* sound like. There are certain phrases that usually indicate a lack of empathy on the part of a listener. You're probably not being supportive if you:

■ *Deny others the right to their feelings.* Many nonempathic responses imply that certain emotions are wrong or should be stifled. Consider the stock remark "Don't worry about it." Although the remark may be intended as a reassuring comment, the underlying message is that the speaker wants the person to feel differently. The irony is that the suggestion probably won't work—after all, it's unlikely that people can or will stop worrying just because you tell them to do so. Other examples of statements that deny feelings to others include "It's nothing to get so upset about" and "That's a silly way to feel." Research about such responses is clear: "Messages that explicitly acknowledge, elaborate, and legitimize the feelings and perspective of a distressed person are perceived as more helpful messages than those which only implicitly recognize or deny the feelings and perspective of the other."[41]

■ *Minimize the significance of the situation.* Consider the times you've been told, "Hey, it's only ——————." You can probably fill in the blank in a variety of ways: "a job," "her opinion," "a test," "puppy love," "a party." How did you react when you were told this? You probably thought the person who said it "just didn't understand." To someone who has been the victim of verbal abuse, the hurtful message isn't "just words"; to a child who didn't get an invitation, it isn't "just a party"; to a worker who has been chewed out by the boss, it isn't "just a job." When you minimize the significance of someone else's experience, you aren't responding empathically. Instead, you are interpreting the experience from your perspective and rendering judgment—rarely a helpful response.

■ *Focus on "then and there" rather than "here and now."* Although it is sometimes true that "you'll feel better tomorrow," it sometimes isn't. You can probably remember times when you felt *worse* the next day. More important, focusing on the future avoids empathizing in the present. Even if the prediction that "ten years from now you won't remember her name" proves correct, it provides little comfort to someone experiencing heartbreak today. "Everything is going to turn out fine" and "There are lots of other fish in the sea—you'll land one soon" are variations on the same theme. They are platitudes because everything may not "turn out fine" and the person might not "land one soon." There are times when "the bigger picture" offers reassurance (see "Analyzing"), but most "then and there" clichés suggest that the listener is uncomfortable dealing with the present.

■ *Cast judgment.* It usually isn't encouraging to hear "You know, it's your own fault—you really shouldn't have done that" after you've confessed to making a poor decision. This response suggests that the listener is playing judge rather than walking in your shoes. As we'll discuss in chapter 9, evaluative and condescending statements are more likely to engender defensiveness than to help people change for the better.

■ *Defend yourself.* When your response to others' concerns is to defend yourself ("Don't blame me; I've done my part"), it's clear that you are more concerned with yourself than with the other person. Chapter 9 offers detailed advice for responding nondefensively to criticism. Until then, realize that justifying yourself isn't compatible with understanding or helping others.

Reprinted with special permission of King Feature Syndicate.

So Penseroso

Come, megrims, mollygrubs and
    collywobbles!
Come, gloom that limps and misery that
    hobbles!
Come also, most exquisite melancholiage,
As dank and decadent as November
    foliage!
I crave to shudder in your moist embrace,
To feel your oystery fingers on my face.

This is my hour of sadness and of
    soulfulness,
And cursed be he who dissipates my
    dolefulness.
I do not desire to be cheered,
I desire to retire, I am thinking of growing a
    beard,
A sorrowful beard, with a mournful, a
    dolorous hue in it,
With ashes and glue in it.
I want to be drunk with despair,
I want to caress my care,
I do not wish to be blithe,
I wish to recoil and writhe,
I will revel in cosmic woe,
And I want my woe to show.
This is the morbid moment,
This is the ebony hour.
Anoint thee, sweetness and light!
I want to be dark and sour!
Away with the bird that twitters!
All that glitters is jitters!
Roses, roses are gray,
Violets cry Boo! and frighten me.
Sugar is stimulating,
And people conspire to brighten me.
Go hence, people, go hence!
Go sit on a picket fence!
Go gargle with mineral oil,
Go out and develop a boil!
Melancholy is what I brag and boast of,
Melancholy I mean to make the most of,
You beaming optimists shall not destroy it.
But while I am at it, I intend to enjoy it.
Go, people, stuff your mouths with soap,
And remember, please, that when I mope, I
    mope!

Ogden Nash

■ *Rain on the speaker's parade.* Most of the preceding examples deal with difficult situations or messages about pain. Empathizing, however, involves identifying with others' joys as well as their sorrows. Many of us can recall coming home with exciting news, only to be told: "A 5 percent raise? That isn't so great"; "An A-minus? Why didn't you get an A?"; or "Big deal—I got one of those years ago." Taking the wind out of someone's sails is the opposite of empathizing.

Despite the potential drawbacks, supporting responses *can* be helpful. Guidelines for effective support include:

1. Recognize that you can support another person's struggles without approving of his or her decisions. Suppose, for instance, that a friend has decided to quit a job that you think she should keep. You could still be supportive by saying, "I know you've given this a lot of thought and that you're doing what you think is best." Responses like this can provide support without compromising your principles.

2. Monitor the other person's reaction to your support. If it doesn't seem to help, consider other types of responses that let him or her explore the issue.

Even if your advice, judgments, and analysis are correct and your questions are sincere, and even if your support comes from the best motives, these responses often fail to help. One survey demonstrated how poorly such traditional responses work.[42] Mourners who had recently suffered from the death of a loved one reported that 80 percent of the statements made to them were unhelpful. Nearly half of the "helpful" statements were advice: "You've got to get out more." "Don't question God's will." Despite their frequency, these suggestions were helpful only 3 percent of the time. The next most frequent response was reassurance, such as "She's out of pain now." Like advice, this kind of support was helpful only 3 percent of the time. Far more helpful were expressions that acknowledged the mourner's feelings. The remainder of this chapter will explore two kinds of responses that make just this sort of acknowledgment possible: prompting and paraphrasing.

Prompting

Advising, judging, analyzing, questioning, and supporting are all active styles of helping that call for a great deal of input from the respondent. Another approach to helping is more passive. **Prompting** involves using silences and brief statements of encouragement to draw others out and in so doing to help them solve their own problems. Consider this example:

Pablo: Julie's dad is selling a complete computer system for only $1,200, but if I want it I have to buy it now. He's got another interested buyer. It's a great deal. But buying it would wipe out my savings. At the rate I spend money, it would take me a year to save up this much again.

Tim: Uh-huh.

Most conversations seem to be carried out on two levels, the verbal level and the emotional level. The verbal level contains those things which are socially acceptable to say, but it is used as a means of satisfying emotional needs. Yesterday a friend related something that someone had done to her. I told her why I thought the person acted the way he had and she became very upset and started arguing with me. Now, the reason is clear. I had been listening to her words and had paid no attention to her feelings. Her words had described how terribly this other person had treated her, but her emotions had been saying, "Please understand how I felt. Please accept my feeling the way I did." The last thing she wanted to hear from me was an explanation of the other person's behavior.

Hugh Prather

Pablo: I wouldn't be able to take that ski trip over winter break . . . but I sure could save time with my schoolwork . . . and do a better job, too.

Tim: That's for sure.

Pablo: Do you think I should buy it?

Tim: I don't know. What do *you* think?

Pablo: I just can't decide.

Tim: (*silence*)

Pablo: I'm going to do it. I'll never get a deal like this again.

Prompting works especially well when you can't help others make a decision. At times like this your presence can act like a catalyst to help others find their own answers. Prompting will work best when it's done sincerely. Your nonverbal behaviors—eye contact, posture, facial expression, tone of voice—have to show that you are concerned with the other person's problem. Mechanical prompting is likely to irritate instead of help.

Paraphrasing

A few pages ago you read about the value of paraphrasing to understand others. The same skill can be used as a helping tool. When you use paraphrasing, be sure to reflect both the *thoughts* and the *feelings* you hear being expressed. The "Communication Transcript" on page 306 suggests several reasons why paraphrasing can be so helpful.[43] First, listeners who reflect the speaker's thoughts and feelings (instead of judging or analyzing, for example) show their involvement and concern. The nonevaluative nature of reflecting encourages the problem-holder to discuss the matter further. Reflecting feelings as well as thoughts allows the problem-holder to unload more of the concerns he or she has been carrying around, often leading to the relief that comes from catharsis. Finally, paraphrasing helps the problem-holder to sort out the problem. The clarity that comes from this sort of perspective can make it possible to find solutions that weren't apparent before.

Although the immediate payoff of reflective listening is helping the other person, an additional payoff is improving the relationship between speaker and listener. For example, couples who communicate in ways that show they understand one another's feelings and ideas are more satisfied with their marriages than couples who express less understanding.[44] The opposite is also true: In marriages where husbands do not give emotional responses to their wives, the stress level grows.

Because empathy is the ingredient that makes paraphrasing thoughts and feelings helpful, it's a mistake to think of reflective listening as a technique that you can use mechanically.[45] It's essential to realize that empathy is a relational matter and not something that can be created just by paraphrasing or by any other kind of behavior. Carl Rogers, the psychologist generally considered the foremost advocate of active listening, made the case against mechanical paraphrasing strongly: "I am *not* trying

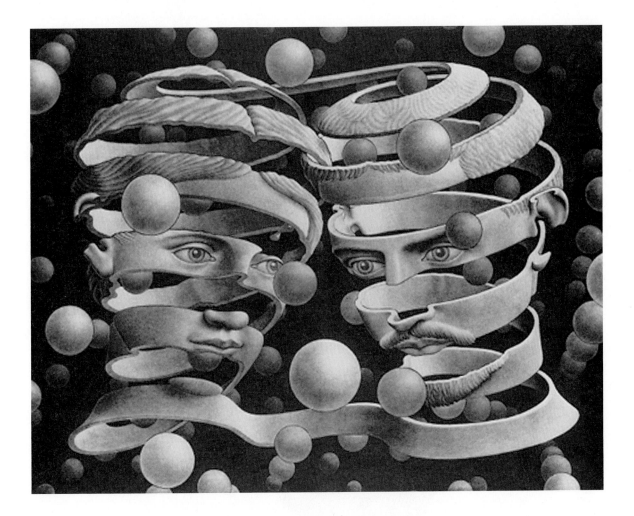

to 'reflect feelings.' I am trying to determine whether my understanding of the client's inner world is correct—whether I am seeing it as he or she is experiencing it at this moment."[46] In other words, reflecting is not an end in itself; rather, it is one way to help others by understanding them better.

There are several factors to consider before you decide to paraphrase:

1. *Is the problem complex enough?* Sometimes people are simply looking for information and not trying to work out their feelings. At times like this, paraphrasing would be out of place. If someone asks you for the time of day, you'd do better simply to give her the information than to respond by saying, "You want to know what time it is." If you're fixing dinner, and someone wants to know when it will be ready, it would be exasperating to hear "You're interested in knowing when we'll be eating."

Trouble me, disturb me with all
    your cares and your worries.
Trouble me on the days when you feel spent.
Why let your shoulders bend underneath
    this burden
when my back is sturdy and strong?
Trouble me.

Speak to me, don't mislead me.
The calm I feel means a storm is swelling;
there's no telling where it starts or how it
    ends.

Speak to me, why are you building this thick
    brick wall to defend me
when your silence is my greatest fear?
Why let your shoulders bend underneath
    this burden
when my back is sturdy and strong?

Speak to me.

Natalie Merchant and Dennis Drew

2. *Do you have the necessary time and concern?* The kind of paraphrasing we've been discussing takes a good deal of time. Therefore, if you're in a hurry to do something besides listen, it's wise to avoid starting a conversation you won't be able to finish. Even more important than time is concern. It's not necessarily wrong to be too preoccupied to help or even to be unwilling to exert the considerable effort that active listening requires: You can't help everyone with every problem. It's far better to state honestly that you're unable or unwilling to help than to pretend to care when you really don't.

3. *Are you genuinely interested in helping the other person?* Sometimes as you listen to others, it's easy to relate their thoughts to your own life or to seek more information just to satisfy your own curiosity. Remember that paraphrasing is a form of helping someone else. The general obligation to reciprocate the other person's self-disclosure with information of your own isn't necessary when the goal is to solve a problem. Research shows that speakers who reveal highly intimate personal information don't expect, or even appreciate, the same kind of disclosure from a conversational partner.[47] Rather, the most competent and socially attractive response is one that sticks to the same topic but is lower in intimacy. In other words, when we are opening up to others, we don't appreciate their pulling a conversational take-away such as "You're worried? So am I! Let me tell you about how I feel . . ."

4. *Can you withhold judgment?* You've already seen that paraphrasing allows other people to find their own answers. You should use paraphrasing only if you can comfortably paraphrase without injecting your own judgments. It's sometimes tempting to rephrase others' comments in a way that leads them toward the solution you think is best without ever clearly stating your intentions. As you will read in chapter 9, this kind of strategy is likely to backfire by causing defensiveness if it's discovered. If you think the situation meets the criteria for advice described earlier in this chapter, you should offer your advice openly.

5. *Is your paraphrasing in proportion to other responses?* Although active listening can be a very helpful way of responding to others' problems, it can become artificial and annoying when it's overused. This is especially true if you suddenly begin to use it as a major response. Even if such responses are potentially helpful, this sudden switch in your behavior will be so out of character that others might find it distracting. A far better way to use paraphrasing is gradually to introduce it into your repertoire of helpfulness so that you can become comfortable with it without appearing too awkward. Another way to become more comfortable with paraphrasing is to start using it on real but relatively minor problems so that you'll be more adept at knowing how and when to use it when a big problem does occur.

> When the day is long and the night, the night is yours alone,
>
> When you're sure you've had enough of this life, well hang on.
>
> Don't let yourself go—Everybody cries and everybody hurts sometimes.
>
> By William Berry, Michael Stipe, Peter Buck & Mike Mills. Recorded by R.E.M.

COMMUNICATION TRANSCRIPT

Paraphrasing on the Job

The following conversation between two coworkers shows how paraphrasing can help listeners find solutions to their problems. Notice how Jill comes to a conclusion about her problem without advice from Mark. Notice also how the paraphrasing sounds natural when combined with occasional sincere questions and other helping styles.

Jill I've had the strangest feeling about John (*their boss*) lately.

Mark What's that? (*A simple question invites Jill to go on.*)

Jill I'm starting to think maybe he has this thing about women—or maybe it's just about me.

Mark You mean he's coming on to you? (*Mark paraphrases what he thinks Jill has said.*)

Jill Oh, no, not at all! But it seems like he doesn't take women—or at least me—seriously. (*Jill corrects Mark's misunderstanding and explains herself.*)

Mark What do you mean? (*Mark asks another simple question to get more information.*)

Jill Well, whenever we're in a meeting or just talking around the office and he asks for ideas, he always seems to pick men. He gives orders to women—men, too—but he never asks the women to say what they think.

Mark So you think maybe he doesn't take women seriously, is that it? (*Mark paraphrases Jill's last statement.*)

Jill Yeah. Well, he sure doesn't seem interested in their ideas. But that doesn't mean he's a total woman-hater. I know he counts on some women in the office. Teresa has been here forever, and he's always saying he couldn't live without her. And when Brenda got the new computer system up and running last month, I know he appreciated that. He gave her a day off and told everybody how she saved our lives.

Mark Now you sound confused. (*Reflects her apparent feeling*)

Jill I am confused. I don't think it's just my imagination. I mean I'm a good producer, but he has never—not once—asked me for my ideas about how to improve sales or anything. And I can't remember a time when he's asked any other women. But maybe I'm overreacting.

Mark You're not positive whether you're right, but I can tell that this has you concerned. (*Mark paraphrases both Jill's central theme and her feeling.*)

Jill Yes. But I don't know what to do about it.

Mark Maybe you should . . . (*Starts to offer advice but catches himself and decides to ask a question instead.*) So what are your choices?

Jill Well, I could just ask him if he's aware that he never asks women's opinions. But that might sound too aggressive and angry.

Mark And you're not angry? (*Tries to clarify how Jill is feeling*)

Jill Not really. I don't know whether I should be angry because he's not taking ideas seriously, or whether he just doesn't take my ideas seriously, or whether it's nothing at all.

Mark So you're mostly confused. (*Reflects Jill's apparent feeling again*)

Jill Yes! I don't know where I stand with John, and not being sure is starting to get to me. I wish I knew what he thinks of me. Maybe I could just tell him I'm confused about what is going on here and ask him to clear it up. But what if it's nothing? Then I'll look insecure.

Mark (*Mark thinks Jill should confront the boss, but he isn't positive that this is the best approach, so he paraphrases what Jill seems to be saying.*) And that would make you look bad.

Jill I'm afraid maybe it would. I wonder if I could talk it over with anybody else in the office and get their ideas . . .

Mark . . . see what they think . . .

Jill Yeah. Maybe I could ask Brenda. She's easy to talk to, and I do respect her judgment. Maybe she could give me some ideas about how to handle this.

Mark Sounds like you're comfortable with talking to Brenda first. (*Paraphrases*)

Jill (*Warming to the idea*) Yes! Then if it's nothing, I can calm down. But if I do need to talk to John, I'll know I'm doing the right thing.

Mark Great. Let me know how it goes.

Using your Looking Out/ Looking In *CD-ROM, click on* Communication Scenarios *and then "Paraphrasing on the Job" to watch and analyze a dramatized version of this conversation.*

By now you can see that there are many ways to help others—probably more than you use. You can also see that each way has its advantages and disadvantages. This leads us to the important question of which way or ways are most helpful. There isn't a simple answer to this question.

When and How to Help?

Before committing yourself to helping another person—even someone in obvious distress—make sure that your help is welcome. There are many cases when others prefer to keep their concerns to themselves. In these cases your efforts to get involved may not be useful and can be even harmful. In one survey, some people reported occasions when social support wasn't necessary because they felt capable of handling the problem themselves.[48] Many regarded uninvited support as an intrusion, and some said it left them feeling more nervous than before. The majority of respondents expressed a preference for being in control of whether their distressing situation should be discussed with even the most helpful friend.

When help is welcome, there is no single best style with which to provide it. Research shows that *all* styles can help others accept their situation, feel better, and have a sense of control over their problems.[49] But there is enormous variability in which style will work with a given person.[50] This fact explains why communicators who use a wide variety of helping styles are usually more effective than those who use just one or two styles.[51]

You can boost the odds of choosing the best helping style in each situation by considering three factors. First, think about the *situation*, and match your response to the nature of the problem. Sometimes people need your advice. At other times people need your encouragement and support, and at still other times people need your analysis or judgment. And, as you have seen, sometimes your probes and paraphrasing can help people find their own answers.

Besides considering the situation, you should also consider the *other person* when deciding which style to use. Some people are able to consider advice thoughtfully, whereas others use advice to avoid making their own decisions. Many communicators are extremely defensive and aren't capable of receiving analysis or judgments without lashing out. Still others aren't equipped to think through problems clearly enough to profit from paraphrasing and probing. Sophisticated helpers choose a style that fits the person.

Finally, consider *yourself* when deciding how to respond. Most of us reflexively use one or two helping styles. You may be best at listening quietly, offering a prompt from time to time. Or perhaps you are especially insightful and can offer a truly useful analysis of the problem. Of course, it's also possible to rely on a response style that is *unhelpful.* You may be overly judgmental or too eager to advise, even when your suggestions aren't invited or productive. As you think about how to respond to another's problems, consider both your strengths and weaknesses.

Unconditional Positive Regard

Carl Rogers is the best-known advocate of paraphrasing as a helping tool. As a psychotherapist, Rogers focused on how professionals can help others, but he and his followers were convinced that the same approach can work in all interpersonal relationships.

Rogers used several terms to describe his approach: Sometimes he labeled it "nondirective," sometimes "client-centered," and at other times "person-centered." All these terms reflect his belief that the best way to help another is to offer a supportive climate in which the person seeking help can find his or her own answers. Rogers believed that advising, judging, analyzing, and questioning are not the best ways to help others solve their problems. Instead, Rogers and his followers were convinced that people are basically good and that they can improve without receiving any guidance from others, after they accept and respect themselves.

An essential ingredient for person-centered helping is what Rogers called "unconditional positive regard." This attitude requires the helper to treat the speaker's ideas respectfully and nonjudgmentally. Unconditional positive regard means accepting others for who they are, even when you don't approve of their posture toward life. Treating a help-seeker with unconditional positive regard doesn't oblige you to agree with everything the help-seeker thinks, feels, or does; but it does oblige you to suspend judgment about the rightness or wrongness of the help-seeker's thoughts and actions.

A person-centered approach to helping places heavy demands on the listener. At the skill level, it demands an ability to reflect the speaker's thoughts and feelings perceptively and accurately. Even more difficult, though, is the challenge of listening and responding without passing judgment on the speaker's ideas or behavior.

Unconditional positive regard is especially hard when we are faced with the challenge of listening and responding to someone whose beliefs, attitudes, and values differ profoundly from our own. This approach requires the helper to follow the scriptural injunction of loving the sinner while hating the sin. One of the best models of this approach is illustrated in the movie *Dead Man Walking*. (See the "Film Resources" section at the end of this chapter.) This movie re-creates the true story of Sister Helen Prejean, a Catholic nun who took on the role of counseling a convicted murderer named Matthew Poncelet. Sister Helen confronts the awful truth of Poncelet's crime while managing to maintain her genuine concern for him as a human being. Few communicators can manage to achieve the level of unconditional positive regard that Sister Helen demonstrates, but her story is a model for those who accept a person-centered approach to helping—and the values it embodies.

For a better understanding of unconditional positive regard, see the following work by Carl Rogers: *On Becoming a Person* (Boston: Houghton Mifflin, 1961); *Carl Rogers on Personal Power* (New York: Delacorte Press, 1977); "A Theory of Therapy, Personality and Interpersonal Relationships, As Developed in the Client-Centered Framework" in S. Koch, ed., *Psychology: A Study of Science* (New York: McGraw-Hill, 1959).

SUMMARY

Listening is the most common—and perhaps the most overlooked—form of communication. Listening consists of five elements: hearing, attending, understanding, responding, and remembering.

A number of responding styles masquerade as listening but actually are only poor imitations of the real thing. We listen poorly for a variety of reasons. Some reasons have to do with the tremendous number of messages that bombard us daily and with the personal preoccupations and rapid thoughts that distract us from focusing on the information we are exposed to. Another set of reasons has to do with the considerable effort involved in listening carefully and the mistaken belief that listening is a natural ability that doesn't require skill or work and that lacks the rewards that come from speaking. A few listeners fail to receive messages due to physical hearing defects. One important type of listening involves seeking information from others. Some keys to success in this type of listening are to talk less, reduce distractions, avoid making premature judgments, and seek the speaker's key ideas. Asking questions and paraphrasing are two important ways of seeking information.

A second type of listening focuses on helping others solve their problems. Some common helping styles are advising, judging, analyzing, questioning and supporting. Prompting and paraphrasing are less common but effective response styles. The most helpful communicators use a variety of these styles, choosing the one most appropriate for themselves, the situation at hand, and the person with the problem.

KEY TERMS

active listening
advising response
ambushing
analyzing statement
attending
counterfeit questions
defensive listening
hearing

insensitive listening
insulated listening
judging response
listening
paraphrasing
prompting
pseudolistening
questioning response

remembering
responding
selective listening
sincere questions
stage-hogging
supporting response
understanding

LOOKING OUT/LOOKING IN ONLINE

Use your *Looking Out/Looking In* CD-ROM for quick access to the electronic resources that accompany this chapter. Included on this CD-ROM are additional study aids and links to the *Looking Out/Looking In* Web site at the Wadsworth Communication Café. The CD-ROM is your gateway to a wealth of resources that will help you understand and further explore the material in this chapter. **Video clips** under *Communication Scenarios* on the CD illustrate the skills introduced in this chapter. Click on the Web site link to complete self-study **review quizzes** to help you master new concepts; access a **feature film database** to locate clips and entire movies that illustrate communication principles; find Internet material via the maintained **Web site links;** and complete **online activities** to help you master new concepts.

INFOTRAC COLLEGE EDITION EXERCISES

Use the InfoTrac College Edition password that was included free with a copy of this new text to answer the following questions. These questions can be completed online and, if requested, submitted to your instructor under InfoTrac College Edition Activities at the *Looking Out/Looking In* Web site.

1. Gender and Listening

Using InfoTrac College Edition's subject search feature, see how many articles you can find on listening. Browse until you find one that has information that is useful to you. Write a brief summary of the article you have chosen. Include a citation (title, author, publication, date), brief description of the article's main idea, and your reaction to the point it makes.

2. Faulty Assumptions

Use PowerTrac to find the article "Giving Good Feedback" by Marc Hequet. (Hint: Use the author and title search fields to locate the article.) Based on the article, what value does feedback offer in a workplace environment? What role does listening play in offering good feedback? How can you use the information in this article to improve your on-the-job effectiveness?

3. Ask Questions

Use PowerTrac's subject and author fields to locate the article "Cultural Differences in Listening Style Preferences: A Comparison of Young Adults in Germany, Israel, and the United States" by Christian Kiewitz, James B. Weaver III, Hans-Bernd Brosius, and Gabriel Weimann. What research do the authors cite regarding similarities and differences among listening styles in different cultures? To what degree is the way people listen shaped by their cultural background?

READINGS

Albrecht, Terence L., Brant R. Burleson, and Deana Goldsmith. "Supportive Communication." In *Handbook of Interpersonal Communication*, 2nd ed., Mark L. Knapp and Gerald R. Miller, eds. Newbury Park, Calif.: Sage, 1994.

This chapter describes the damaging consequences of a lack of social support and explains how communicators can provide support for one another in a variety of ways, including listening.

Brownell, Judi. *Listening: Attitudes, Principles, and Skills*. Boston: Allyn & Bacon, 1996.

Brownell offers a discussion of each step in the listening process and then goes on to describe the role of listening in a variety of contexts, including family, education, the helping professions, and work.

Burleson, Brant R. "Comforting Messages: Features, Functions, and Outcomes." In *Strategic Interpersonal Communication*, John A. Daly and John M. Wiemann, eds. Hillsdale, N.J.: Erlbaum, 1994.

Burleson is a leading researcher on comforting communication. This survey describes the nature and results of supportive responses.

Purdy, Michael, and Deborah Borisoff. *Listening in Everyday Life: A Personal and Professional Approach*. Lanham, Md.: University Press of America, 1997.

As its title suggests, this collection of readings offers practical information about listening in a variety of contexts, including health care, legal, and service industries. In addition, chapters discuss the influences of gender, culture, and group settings on listening.

FILMS

In addition to the films suggested here, go to the **Film in Communication Database** at the *Looking Out/Looking In* Web site to locate movie clips that illustrate listening principles.

Ineffective Listening and Its Alternatives

Jerry Maguire (1996) Rated R

Jerry Maguire (Tom Cruise) is a high-powered pro sports agent with a bulging Rolodex and a stable of multimillionaire athletes. Jerry is so successful that he doesn't have time to truly listen to any of his clients. In an early scene, we see him juggle the callers on his multiline office phone, slinging clichés as he switches between athletes. At this point we think that success is the reason Jerry is such an awful listener; but after he loses his job and scrambles to keep his last client, we learn that he is just as inattentive and insensitive when desperate as when successful. Rich or poor, the egocentric Maguire treats people in his life as props. In true Hollywood fashion, Jerry learns the importance of listening only when he is close to losing the most important people in his life.

Supportive Listening

Good Will Hunting (1997) Rated R

Will Hunting (Matt Damon) is a janitor and natural born math genius who spends most of his free time hanging around with his friends from their lower-middle-class Boston neighborhood. Will turns down offers of jobs that take advantage of his gift, preferring a lifestyle of brawling and boozing that seems to point him toward jail or worse.

The film depicts the efforts of four people who try to head Will away from a life of self-destruction: Will's best friend Chuckie (Ben Affleck), his girlfriend Skylar (Minnie Driver), MIT professor Lambeau (Stellan Skarsgard), who discovered Will's talents, and Lambeau's college roommate, Sean McGuire (Robin Williams), a gifted counselor.

From a communication perspective, it is instructive to see the array of communication styles these four characters use to help Will turn his life around. As in real life, no single style is the best. Will's breakthrough occurs in response to McGuire's skilled counseling, but it is clear that his hope for change and growth depends on the genuine concern of all four characters—each of whom offers help in a highly personal way.

LOOKING OUT/LOOKING IN CD-ROM

Using your *Looking Out/Looking In* CD-ROM, click on *Communication Scenarios* and then click on the "Paraphrasing" icon to watch and analyze a dramatized version of the conversation featured in the Communication Transcript on page 306.

CHAPTER 8

COMMUNICATION AND RELATIONAL DYNAMICS

"We have a terrific relationship."

"I'm looking for a better relationship."

"Our relationship has changed a lot."

Relationship is one of those words that people use all the time but have trouble defining. Take a moment to see if you can define the term in your own words. It isn't as easy as it might seem.

The dictionary defines a *relationship* as "the mode in which two or more things stand to one another." This is true enough: You are tall in relationship to some people and short in relationship to others, and we are more or less wealthy only in relationship to others. But physical and economic relationships don't tell us much that is useful about interpersonal communication.

Interpersonal relationships involve the way people deal with one another *socially*. But what is it about social interaction that defines a relationship? This chapter will offer some insights. It will offer explanations for why we form relationships with some people and not with others. It will look at how communication operates as people form, manage, and sometimes end their relationships. You will see that relationships aren't static, like a painting or photograph. Rather, they change over time, like an ongoing dance or drama. Even the most stable and satisfying relationships wax and wane in a variety of ways as communication patterns change. Finally, this chapter will examine the subject of self-disclosure and its alternatives. By the time you finish reading the following pages you will have a better sense of how communication both defines and reflects our interpersonal world.

> For communication to have meaning it must have a life. It must transcend "you" and "me" and become "us". . . . In a small way we then grow out of our old selves and become something new.
>
> Hugh Prather

WHY WE FORM RELATIONSHIPS

What makes us seek relationships with some people and not with others? This is a question that social scientists have studied extensively. Though it would take an entire book to describe their findings, we can summarize a number of explanations. As you read them, consider which ones fit you.

Attraction

Sometimes we establish personal relationships because we find others attractive in one way or another. Physical attraction is an obvious plus in some types of relationships, but there are other bases of attraction as well.

Similarity and Complementarity A large body of research confirms the fact that we like people who are similar to us, at least in most cases.[1] For example, friends in middle and high school report being similar to each other in many ways, including having mutual friends, enjoying the same sports, liking the same social activities, and using (or not using) alcohol and cigarettes to the same degree.[2] For adults, similarity is more important to relational happiness than even communication ability:

©The New Yorker Collection 1998 John O'Brien from cartoonbank.com. All Rights Reserved.

Friends who have low levels of communication skills are just as satisfied with their relationships as are friends having high levels of communication skills.[3]

Attraction is greatest when we are similar to others in a high percentage of important areas. For example, two people who support each other's career goals, like the same friends, and have similar beliefs about human rights can tolerate trivial disagreements about the merits of sushi or rap music. With enough similarity in key areas, they can even survive disputes about more important subjects, such as how much time to spend with their families or whether separate vacations are acceptable. But if the number and content of disagreements become too great, the relationship may be threatened.

The familiar saying that "opposites attract" seems to contradict the principle of similarity we just described. In truth, though, both are valid. Differences strengthen a relationship when they are *complementary*— when each partner's characteristics satisfy the other's needs. Individuals, for instance, are often likely to be attracted to each other when one partner is dominant and the other passive. Relationships also work well when the partners agree that one will exercise control in certain areas ("You make the final decisions about money") and the other will exercise control in different areas ("I'll decide how we ought to decorate the place"). Strains occur when control issues are disputed.

Studies that have examined successful and unsuccessful couples over a twenty-year period show the interaction between similarities and differences. The studies demonstrate that partners in successful marriages were similar enough to satisfy each other physically and mentally but were different enough to meet each other's needs and keep the relationship interesting. The successful couples found ways to keep a balance between their similarities and differences, adjusting to the changes that occurred over the years.

Reciprocal Attraction

We like people who like us—usually. The power of reciprocal attraction is especially strong in the early stages of a relationship. At that time we are attracted to people who we believe are attracted to us. Conversely, we will probably not care for people who either attack or seem indifferent toward us.

It's no mystery why reciprocal liking builds attractiveness. People who approve of us bolster our feelings of self-esteem. This approval is rewarding in its own right, and it can also confirm a presenting self-concept that says, "I'm a likable person."

You can probably think of cases where you haven't liked people who seemed to like you. These experiences usually fall into two categories. Sometimes you might think the other person's supposed liking is counterfeit—an insincere device to get something from you. This sort of behavior really isn't "liking" at all. At other times the liking may not fit with your own self-concept. When someone says you're good-looking, intelligent, and kind, but you believe you're ugly, stupid, and mean, you may choose to disregard the flattering information and remain in your familiar state of unhappiness. Groucho Marx summarized this attitude when he said he would never join any club that would consider having him as a member.

Competence

We like to be around talented people, probably because we hope their skills and abilities will rub off on us. On the other hand, we are uncomfortable around those who are *too* competent—probably because we look bad by comparison. Given these contrasting attitudes, it's no surprise that people are generally attracted to those who are talented but who have visible flaws that show that they are human, just like us. There are some qualifications to this principle. People with especially high or low self-esteem find "perfect" people more attractive than those who are competent but flawed, and some studies suggest that women tend to be more impressed by uniformly superior people of both sexes, whereas men tend to be more impressed by desirable but "human" subjects. On the whole, though, the principle stands: The best way to gain the liking of others is to be good at what you do but to admit your mistakes.

Disclosure

Revealing important information about yourself can help build liking. Sometimes the basis of this liking comes from learning about how we are similar, either in experiences ("I broke off an engagement myself") or in attitudes ("I feel nervous with strangers, too"). Self-disclosure also builds liking because it is a sign of regard. When people share private information with you, it suggests that they respect and trust you—a kind of liking that we've already seen increases attractiveness.

Not all disclosure leads to liking. People whose sharing is badly timed often meet with bad results. It's probably unwise, for example, to talk about your sexual insecurities with a new acquaintance or to express your pet peeves to a friend at her birthday party. In addition to using bad timing, opening up too much can also be a mistake. Research shows that people are judged as attractive when they match the amount and content of what they share with that of the other person in a relationship. See pages 347–349 for more guidelines about when and how to self-disclose.

Proximity   As common sense suggests, we are likely to develop relationships with people we interact with frequently. We're more likely to develop friendships with close neighbors than with distant ones, for instance; and several studies show that the chances are good that we'll choose a mate with whom we often cross paths.

Familiarity, on the other hand, can also breed contempt. Evidence to support this fact comes from police blotters as well as university laboratories. Thieves frequently prey on nearby victims, even though the risk of being recognized is greater. Spouse abuse and child abuse are distressingly common. Most aggravated assaults occur within the family or among close neighbors. Within the law, the same principle holds: You are likely to develop strong personal feelings of either like or dislike regarding others you encounter frequently.

"Interpersonal Attraction and Relationships"

http://www.bath. ac.uk/~hsstjc/ Relref.html

For a bibliography of scholarly resources related to interpersonal attraction and relationships, access this Web page developed by Tina Cartwright of the University of Bath in Bath, England. To apply the concepts of attraction, complete Activity 8.2 "Factors of Attraction in Your Own Relationships" at the *Looking Out/Looking In* Web site.

INVITATION TO INSIGHT

ANALYZING INTERPERSONAL ATTRACTION

1. List the names of five people with whom you have strong positive personal relationships. Use the list that follows to identify the basis of your attraction.

   a. Are their interests, attitudes, values, beliefs, or backgrounds similar to yours?
   b. Do they fill a complementary need for you?
   c. Are they attracted to you?
   d. Are they competent but human?
   e. Have they shared personal information with you?
   f. Do you encounter them frequently?

2. Now consider five people with whom you would like to build a stronger relationship. Use the same list to decide whether you are the kind of person they would be attracted to.

Intimacy

Research on attraction helps explain why we seek out relationships with some people more than others. But the question of what we *want* in those relationships can be answered in part by looking at the need for intimacy.

The 1970s singing group Three Dog Night said it well: One *can* be the loneliest number. Empirical research confirms the value of intimacy. People who report having satisfying intimate relationships have higher self-esteem, stronger sense of identity, and greater feelings of control over their lives than those without close relationships.[4] In one study, researchers asked people who were dying in hospices and hospitals what mattered most in life. Fully 90 percent of these terminally ill patients put intimate relationships at the top of the list. As a fifty-year-old mother of three children who was dying of cancer put it, "You need not wait until you are in my condition to know nothing in life is as important as loving relationships."[5]

Dimensions of Intimacy

Intimacy has several dimensions. The first dimension is *physical.* Even before birth, the fetus experiences a physical closeness with its mother that will never happen again, "floating in a warm fluid, curling inside a total embrace, swaying to the undulations of the moving body and hearing the beat of the pulsing heart."[6] As they grow up, fortunate children are continually nourished by physical intimacy: being rocked, fed, hugged, and held. As we grow older, the opportunities for physical intimacy are less regular but still possible and important. Some, but by no means all, physical intimacy is sexual. In one survey, only a one-quarter of the respondents (who were college students) stated that intimacy necessarily contains a romantic or sexual dimension.[7] Companions who have endured physical challenges together—in athletics or emergencies, for example—form a bond that can last a lifetime.

A second dimension of intimacy comes from *intellectual* sharing. Not every exchange of ideas counts as intimacy, of course. Talking about next week's midterm with your professor or classmates isn't likely to forge strong relational bonds. But when you engage another person in an exchange of important ideas, a kind of closeness develops that can be powerful and exciting.

A third dimension of intimacy is *emotional:* exchanging important feelings. Sharing personal information can both reflect and create feelings of closeness. Surprisingly, this sort of personal communication needn't happen in face-to-face encounters. One study revealed that almost two-thirds of a randomly selected group of e-mail users said they had formed a personal relationship with someone they had met for the first time through an Internet newsgroup.[8] The electronic friends characterized their relationships in ways that sound remarkably similar to traditional friendships: interdependence (e.g., "We would go out of our way to help each other"), breadth ("Our communication ranges over a wide variety of topics"), depth ("I feel I could confide in this person about almost anything"), and commitment ("I am very committed to maintaining this relationship").

If we define intimacy as being close to another person, then *shared activities* is a fourth dimension that can achieve intimacy. Shared activities can include everything from working side by side at a job to meeting regularly for exercise workouts. When partners spend time together, they can develop unique ways of relating that transform the relationship from an impersonal one to an interpersonal one. For example, both friendships and romantic relationships are often characterized by several forms of play. Partners invent private codes, fool around by acting like other people, tease one another, and play games—everything from having punning contests to arm wrestling.[9] Not all shared activities create and express intimacy, of course, but the bond that comes from experiencing significant events with another person is too frequent and significant to ignore.

Some intimate relationships exhibit all four dimensions: physical, intellectual, emotional, and shared. Other intimate relationships exhibit only one or two. Some relationships, of course, aren't intimate in any way. Acquaintances, roommates, and coworkers may never become intimate. In some cases even family members develop smooth but relatively impersonal relationships.

Not even the closest relationships always operate at the highest level of intimacy. At times you might share all your thoughts or feelings with a friend, family member, or lover; at other times you might withdraw. You might freely share your feelings about one topic and stay more aloof about another one. The same principle holds for physical intimacy, which waxes and wanes in most relationships.

The locker room had become a kind of home to me . . . I relax, my concerns lost among relationships that are warm and real, but never intimate, lost among the constants of an athlete's life. The lines of communication are clear and simple. . . . We are at ease in the setting of satin uniforms and shower nozzles.

Bill Bradley

Masculine and Feminine Intimacy Styles

Until recently most social scientists believed that women are better than men at developing and maintaining intimate relationships.[10] This view grew from the assumption that the disclosure of personal information is the most important ingredient of intimacy. Most research *does* show that women (taken as a group, of course) are somewhat more willing than men to share their thoughts and feelings, although the differences aren't as dramatic as some people might think.[11] In terms of the amount and depth of information exchanged, female-female relationships are at the top of the disclosure list. Male-female relationships come in second, whereas male-male relationships involve less disclosure

You construct intricate rituals which allow you to touch the skin of other men.

than any other type. At every age, women disclose more than men, and the information they disclose is more personal and more likely to involve feelings. Although both sexes are equally likely to reveal negative information, men are less likely to share positive feelings.[12]

Through the mid-1980s many social scientists interpreted the relative lack of male self-disclosure as a sign that men are unwilling or even unable to develop close relationships. Some argued that the female trait of disclosing personal information and feelings makes women more "emotionally mature" and "interpersonally competent" than men. Personal-growth programs and self-help books urged men to achieve closeness by learning to open up and share their feelings.

But scholarship conducted in the past decade has shown that emotional expression isn't the *only* way to develop close relationships. Unlike women, who value personal talk, men grow close to one another by doing things. In one study, more than 75 percent of the men surveyed said that their most meaningful experiences with friends came from activities other than talking.[13] They reported that, through shared activities, they "grew on one another," developed feelings of interdependence, showed appreciation for one another, and demonstrated mutual liking. Likewise, men regarded practical help as a measure of caring. Research like this shows that, for many men, closeness grows from activities that don't depend heavily on disclosure: A friend is a person who does things *for* you and *with* you.

The same pattern holds in communication between fathers and their sons. Whereas mothers typically express their love toward sons directly through words and nonverbal behaviors like hugs and kisses, fathers are less likely to be so direct with their young adult sons.[14] Instead, they showed their sons affection by doing favors and helping the sons with tasks and challenges.

Actually, it isn't biological sex that is most significant in shaping how men express intimacy. Rather, it's the *gender role* that a particular man adopts. Recall that chapter 3 explained how both men and women can adopt a gender role—masculine, feminine, or androgynous—that may or may not match their biological sex. Applying this range of styles to intimacy reveals that masculine men are most likely to express caring via helping behaviors and shared activities.[15] Men whose communication style includes some stereotypically feminine elements are more likely to express affection more directly, especially to other men.

The difference between male and female measures of intimacy helps explain some of the stresses and misunderstandings that can arise between the sexes. For example, a woman who looks for emotional disclosure as a measure of affection may overlook an "inexpressive" man's efforts to show he cares by doing favors or spending time together. Fixing a leaky faucet or taking a hike may look like ways to avoid getting close, but to the man who proposes them, they may be measures of affection and bids for intimacy. Likewise, differing ideas about the timing and meaning of sex can lead to misunderstandings. Whereas many women think of sex as a way to express intimacy that has already developed, men are more likely to see it as a way to *create* that intimacy.[16] In this sense,

Reprinted with special permission of King Feature Syndicate.

the man who encourages sex early in a relationship or after a fight may not be just a testosterone-crazed lecher: He may view the shared activity as a way to build closeness. By contrast, the woman who views personal talk as the pathway to intimacy may resist the idea of physical closeness before the emotional side of the relationship has been discussed.

Cultural Influences on Intimacy   Historically, the notions of public and private behavior have changed dramatically.[17] What would be considered private behavior in modern terms was quite public at times in the past. For example, in sixteenth-century Germany, a new husband and wife were expected to consummate their marriage upon a bed carried among witnesses who would validate the marriage![18] Conversely, at the same time in England as well as in colonial America, the customary level of communication between spouses was rather formal: not much different from the way acquaintances or neighbors spoke to one another.

Even today, the notion of intimacy varies from one culture to another. In one study, researchers asked residents of Britain, Japan, Hong Kong, and Italy to describe their use of thirty-three rules that governed interaction in social relationships.[19] The rules governed a wide range of communication behaviors: everything from using humor to shaking hands to managing money. The results showed that the greatest differences between Asian and European cultures focused on the rules for dealing with intimacy: showing emotions, expressing affection in public, conducting sexual activity, respecting privacy, and so on.

Disclosure is especially high in mainstream North American society. In fact, people from the United States are more disclosing than members of any culture studied.[20] They are likely to disclose more about themselves to acquaintances and even strangers. One British travel book captured this tendency to disclose personal information with this tongue-in-cheek description:

> Sit next to an American on an airplane and he will immediately address you by your first name, ask "So how do you like it in the States?," explain his recent divorce in intimate detail, invite you home for dinner, offer to lend you money, and wrap you in a warm hug on parting. This does not necessarily mean he will remember your name the next day.[21]

By contrast, Germans and Japanese tend to disclose little about themselves except in personal relationships with a select few. Within American culture, intimacy varies from one group to another. For example, working-class black men are much more disclosing than their white counterparts.[22] By contrast, upwardly mobile black men communicate more like white men with the same social agenda, disclosing less with their male friends.

In some collectivist cultures such as Taiwan and Japan there is an especially great difference in the way people communicate with members of their "in-groups" (such as family and close friends) and with their "out-groups."[23] They generally do not reach out to outsiders, often waiting until they are properly introduced before entering into a conversation. After they are introduced, they address outsiders with a degree of formality. They go to extremes to hide unfavorable information about in-group members from outsiders, on the principle that one doesn't wash dirty laundry in public. By contrast, members of more individualistic cultures like the United States and Australia make less distinction between personal relationships and casual ones. They act more familiar with strangers and disclose more personal information, making them excellent "cocktail party conversationalists." Social psychologist Kurt Lewin captured the difference nicely when he noted that Americans are easy to meet but difficult to get to know, whereas Germans are difficult to meet but easy to get to know.[24]

Differences like these mean that the level of self-disclosure appropriate in one culture may seem completely inappropriate in another one. If you were raised in the United States or Canada you might view people from other cultures as undisclosing, or even standoffish. But the amount of information that the nonnatives share might actually be quite personal and revealing according to the standards of their culture. The converse is also true: To members of other cultures, North Americans probably appear like exhibitionists who spew personal information to anyone within earshot.

Even in cultures that value high amounts of personal communication, intimacy is not a priority in every relationship. Many fellow workers, neighbors, and community members often interact in satisfying ways without ever achieving any real degree of intimacy. Even some family members get along well by deliberately keeping their physical and emotional distance from one another. Relationships of this sort might achieve a modest degree of integration but never go further.

The Limits of Intimacy   It's impossible to have a close relationship with everyone: There just isn't enough time and energy. Even if we could seek intimacy with everyone we encountered, few of us would want that much closeness. Consider the various everyday contacts that don't require any sort of intimacy. Some are based on economic exchange (for example, the people at work or the shopkeeper you visit several times a week); some are based on group membership (for example, church or school); some on physical proximity (for example, neighbors, carpooling); and some grow out of third-party connections (for example, mutual friends, child care). Simply engaging in conversational give-and-take can be a kind of enjoyable recreation, not too different from the impromptu "jamming" of musicians who gather to create music without revealing any personal information.[25]

Some scholars have pointed out that an obsession with intimacy can lead to *less* satisfying relationships.[26] People who consider intimate communication as the only kind worth pursuing place little value on relationships that don't meet this standard. This can lead them to regard interaction with strangers and casual acquaintances as superficial, or at best as the groundwork for deeper relationships. When you consider the pleasure that can come from polite but distant communication, the limitations of this view become clear. Intimacy is definitely rewarding, but it isn't the only way of relating to others.

INVITATION TO INSIGHT

YOUR IQ (INTIMACY QUOTIENT)

What is the level of intimacy in your important relationships? Find out by following these directions.

1. Identify the point on each scale below that best describes one of your important relationships.
   a. Your level of physical intimacy

      1   2   3   4   5
      low   high

   b. Your amount of emotional intimacy

      1   2   3   4   5
      low   high

   c. The extent of your intellectual intimacy

      1   2   3   4   5
      low   high

   d. The degree of shared activities in your relationship

      1   2   3   4   5
      low   high

2. Now answer the following questions:
   a. What responses to each dimension of intimacy seem most significant to you?
   b. Are you satisfied with the intimacy profile outlined by your responses?
   c. If you are not satisfied, what steps can you take to change your degree of intimacy?

Rewards

Intimacy can be satisfying, but it isn't the only payoff that drives us to seek out and stay in relationships. Some social scientists have argued that all relationships—both impersonal and personal—are based on a semieconomic model called *social exchange theory*.[27] This model suggests that we often seek out people who can give us rewards that are greater than or equal to the costs we encounter in dealing with them. Rewards may be tangible (a nice place to live, a high-paying job) or intangible (prestige, emotional support, companionship). Costs are undesirable outcomes: unpleasant work, emotional pain, and so on. A simple formula captures the social exchange theory of why we form and maintain relationships:

Rewards – Costs = Outcome

According to social exchange theorists, we use this formula (often unconsciously) to decide whether dealing with another person is a "good deal" or "not worth the effort," based on whether the outcome is positive or negative.

At its most blatant level, an exchange approach seems cold and calculating; but in some types of relationships it seems quite appropriate. A healthy business relationship is based on how well the parties help one another, and some friendships are based on an informal kind of barter: "I don't mind listening to the ups and downs of your love life because you rescue me when the house needs repairs." Even close relationships have an element of exchange. Friends and lovers often tolerate each other's quirks because the comfort and enjoyment they get make the less-than-pleasant times worth accepting.

At first glance, the social exchange approach seems to present a view of relationships very different from one based on the need to seek intimacy. In fact, the two approaches aren't incompatible. Seeking intimacy of any type—whether emotional, physical, or even intellectual—has its costs; and our decision about whether to "pay" those costs is, in great measure, made by considering the likely payoffs. If the costs of seeking and maintaining an intimate relationship are too great or the payoffs not worth the effort, we may decide to back off.

"I'd like to buy everyone a drink. All I ask in return is that you listen patiently to my shallow and simplistic views on a broad range of social and political issues."

©The New Yorker Collection 1996 J. B. Handelsman from cartoonbank.com. All Rights Reserved.

MODELS OF RELATIONAL DEVELOPMENT AND MAINTENANCE

So far we have looked at some factors that influence why we form relationships. But your own experience demonstrates that beginnings are a unique time. How does communication change as we spend time with others and get to know them? Communication scholars have different perspectives on this question. To learn two major perspectives, read on.

Developmental Models

One of the best-known models of relational stages was developed by Mark Knapp, who broke down the rise and fall of relationships into ten stages, contained in the two broad phases of "coming together" and "coming apart."[28] Other researchers have suggested that any model of relational communication ought to contain a third phase of **relational maintenance**—communication aimed at keeping relationships operating smoothly and satisfactorily.[29] Figure 8-1 shows how Knapp's ten stages fit into this three-phase view of relational communication.

The following stages are especially descriptive of intimate, romantic relationships and close friendships. The pattern for other intimate relationships, such as families, would follow different stages. Some valuable associations don't require a high level of intimacy. They are based on other, equally important foundations: career activities, shared political interests, and religion, to mention just a few.[30]

Initiating The goals in the first stage are to show that you are interested in making contact and to show that you are the kind of person worth talking to. Communication during this **initiating** stage is usually brief, and it generally follows conventional formulas: handshakes, remarks about innocuous subjects like the weather, and friendly expressions. These kinds of behavior may seem superficial and meaningless, but they are a way of signaling that we're interested in building some kind of relationship with the other person. They allow us to say without saying, "I'm a friendly person, and I'd like to get to know you."

Experimenting After we have made contact with a new person, the next stage is to decide whether we are interested in pursuing the relationship further. This involves *uncertainty reduction*—the process of getting to know others by gaining more information about them.[31] A usual part of uncertainty reduction is the search for common ground, and it involves the conversational basics such as "Where are you from?" or "What's your major?" From there we look for other similarities: "You're a runner, too? How many miles do you do a week?"

The hallmark of the **experimenting** stage is small talk. As Mark Knapp says, this small talk is like Listerine: "We hate it, but we take large quantities every day."[32] Small talk serves several functions. First, it is a useful way to find out what interests we share with the other person. It also provides a way to "audition" the other person—to help us decide whether a relationship is worth pursuing. In addition, small talk is a safe way to ease into a

Gail and I had come up with something we called the "Weeja bug." Positioning myself directly behind her, I would clasp her around the waist, and then we would walk, sometimes down a busy street, as if we were this mythical four-legged Weeja bug. I don't know how it got started, but we came to associate it with silly high spirits and bursts of great affection.

Cut to a year later, and a woman named Jessica. Overcome with sudden high spirits and a burst of great affection, I clasp her on a busy corner, in the embrace of the Weeja bug and attempt to cross the street.

"What are you doing?" she screams, leaping away.

Robert Masello, "The Private Language of Lovers"

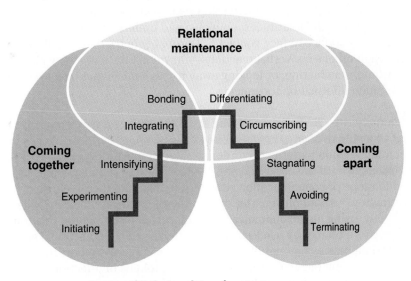

FIGURE 8-1 **Stages of Relational Development**

From *Interpersonal Communication and Human Relationships* (4th edition) by Mark L. Knapp and Anita L. Vangelsti. ©2000 by Allyn & Bacon. Adapted by permission.

relationship. You haven't risked much as you decide whether to proceed further. Finally, small talk can provide a link to others. Some people even enjoy it.

The willingness to pursue relationships with strangers is partly a matter of personal style. Some people are outgoing, and others are more shy, but culture also shapes behavior toward newcomers, especially ones from a different background. Research suggests that members of high-context cultures are more cautious in their first encounters with strangers and make more assumptions about them based on their backgrounds than do members of low-context cultures.[33] This fact might explain why people from certain backgrounds appear unfriendly, when in fact they are simply operating by a set of rules different from those common in low-context North America.

The kind of information we look for during the experimenting stage depends on the nature of the relationship we want.[34] For example, both men and women who are seeking short-term relationships look for someone with an exciting personality and a good sense of humor. Qualities of being trustworthy and romantic become more important when people seek long-term relationships.

For communicators who are interested in one another, the move from initiating to experimenting seems to occur even more rapidly in cyberspace than in person. One study found that people who develop relationships via e-mail begin asking questions about attitudes, opinions, and preferences more quickly than those in face-to-face contact.[35] It probably helps that e-mailers can't see each other's nonverbal reactions—they don't have to worry about blushing, stammering, or looking away if they realize that they asked for too much information too quickly.

The Far Side® by Gary Larson ©1991 FarWorks, Inc. All Rights Reserved. Used with permission.

Intensifying In the **intensifying** stage the kind of truly interpersonal relationship defined in chapter 1 begins to develop. Several changes in communication patterns occur during intensifying. The expression of feelings toward the other becomes more common. Dating couples use a wide range of communication strategies to describe their feelings of attraction.[36] About one-quarter of the time they express their feelings directly, using metacommunication to discuss the state of the relationship. More often they use less-direct methods of communication: spending an increasing amount of time together, asking for support from one another, doing favors for the partner, giving tokens of affection, hinting and flirting, expressing feelings nonverbally, getting to know the partner's friends and family, and trying to look more physically attractive.

Kelly Vodden: Building a Relationship Online

Keith and I are one of those successful online romances you read about from time to time. We met in an Internet chat room where I was having a conversation with a communication major at another college. Keith had been "listening" to us. Since he had studied T.V. broadcasting and had been working in the field, he joined the conversation and suggested some courses we should take.

After a while the other person left the conversation. Keith and I continued talking about various subjects like family, religion, pets—the kind of things you would ask someone you were interested in getting to know. We found we came from similar backgrounds and eventually when the conversation came to a close, we exchanged e-mail addresses so we could keep in touch.

We began e-mailing each other every day and would meet in a chat room a few times a week. Eventually, we swapped pictures through e-mail and decided to talk over the phone. Our first conversation lasted three hours! We were surprised how much we had in common and how well we related to each other. We began talking about once a week. Then we started talking a few times each week, and eventually we phoned every day.

After four and a half months of communicating via e-mail, chat rooms, and through the telephone, we decided it was time to meet in person. Keith flew from Chicago to California where I live. Before meeting Keith, my family was concerned about my safety, so we met at my work. It was a great meeting! It felt as normal as talking with a friend you hadn't seen in a while. Keith passed the test with my parents, and he wound up staying for ten days.

After that first meeting, we continued traveling back and forth between Chicago and California to see one other. Over the months, our relationship grew more serious and committed. We decided to spend Thanksgiving together in California and New Year's together in Chicago. The following Spring, Keith made the important decision to move to California. That summer we found a house together, moved in, and got a dog. It has been almost a year since Keith moved to California. Our dog is now 6 months old and our life continues as a completely normal couple.

Our experience shows that the Internet can be one way for people to meet and develop relationships. We're grateful for the technology. Without it, we never would have met and started a life together.

Other changes mark the intensifying stage. Forms of address become more familiar. The parties begin to see themselves as "we" instead of as separate individuals, and both their talk and actions show it: "What should we do today?" "A party? Sure, we'd love to come." It is during the intensifying stage that we begin to express directly feelings of commitment to one another: "I'm sure glad we met." "You're the best thing that's happened to me in a long time."

The intensifying stage is usually a time of relational excitement and even euphoria. For romantic partners, it's often filled with starstruck gazes, goosebumps, and daydreaming. As a result, it's a stage that's regularly depicted in movies and romance novels—after all, we love to watch lovers in love. The problem, of course, is that the stage doesn't last forever. Sometimes romantic partners who stop feeling goosebumps begin to question whether they're still in love. Although it's possible that they're not, it's also possible that they've simply moved on to a different stage in their relationship—integrating.

Integrating As the relationship strengthens, the parties begin to take on an identity as a social unit. In romantic relationships, invitations begin to come addressed to the couple. Social circles merge. The partners begin to take on each other's commitments: "Sure, we'll spend Thanksgiving with your family." Common property may begin to be designated—our apartment, our car, our song.[37] Partners develop unique, ritualistic ways of behaving.[38] They may even begin to speak alike, using personal idioms and sentence patterns.[39] In this sense, the **integrating** stage is a time when we give up some characteristics of our old selves and develop shared identities.

As we become more integrated with others, our sense of obligation to them grows.[40] We feel obliged to provide a variety of resources such as class notes and money, whether or not the other person asks for them. Surprisingly, although integration is characterized by more relational solidarity, partners make fewer straightforward requests than they did in earlier relational stages. In dating relationships, for example, there is a curvilinear relationship (shown in Figure 8-2) between the relational stage and the number of explicit requests.[41] This pattern isn't as surprising as it might at first seem: As partners become better acquainted, their knowledge of one another makes overt requests less necessary. But later, as the relationship inevitably begins to change, the need for more explicit statements of wants and needs will increase again.

Bonding During the **bonding** stage, the parties make symbolic public gestures to show the world that their relationship exists. The most common form of bonding in romantic relationships is a wedding ceremony and the legal ties that come with it. Bonding generates social support for the relationship. Custom and law both impose certain obligations on partners who have officially bonded.

Bonding marks a turning point in a relationship. Up to now the relationship may have developed at a steady pace: Experimenting gradually moved into intensifying and then into integrating. Now, however, there is

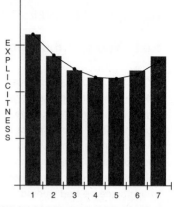

STAGE OF RELATIONAL DEVELOPMENT

FIGURE 8-2 **Stage of Relational Development Explicitness of Requests Varies across Relational Stages**

Adapted from D. H. Solomon, "A Developmental Model of Intimacy and Date Request Explicitness," *Communication Monographs* 64 (1997): 99–118.

Reprinted with special permission of King Feature Syndicate.

a spurt of commitment. The public display and declaration of exclusivity make this a distinct stage in the relationship.

Differentiating   Bonding is the peak of what Knapp calls the "coming together" phase of relational development. But people in even the most committed relationships need to assert their individual identities. This **differentiating** stage is the point where the "hold me tight" orientation that has existed shifts, and "put me down" messages begin to occur. Partners use a variety of strategies to gain privacy from one another.[42] Sometimes they confront the other party directly, explaining that they don't want to continue a discussion. At other times they are less direct, offering nonverbal cues, changing the topic, or leaving the room.

Differentiation is likely to occur when a relationship begins to experience the first, inevitable stress. This need for autonomy needn't be a negative experience, however. People need to be individuals as well as parts of a relationship, and differentiation is a necessary step toward autonomy. The key to successful differentiation is maintaining a commitment to the relationship while creating the space for being an individual as well. (This is a challenge that we will discuss in more detail later in this chapter when we discuss dialectical tensions in relationships.)

Circumscribing   So far we have been looking at the growth of relationships. Although some reach a plateau of development, going on successfully for as long as a lifetime, others pass through several stages of decline and dissolution.

In the **circumscribing** stage communication between members decreases in quantity and quality. Restrictions and restraints characterize this stage. Rather than discuss a disagreement (which requires energy on both sides), members opt for withdrawal—either mental (silence or daydreaming and fantasizing) or physical (where people spend less time together). Circumscribing doesn't involve total avoidance, which may come later. Rather, it involves a certain shrinking of interest and commitment.

Stagnating   If circumscribing continues, the relationship enters the **stagnating** stage. Members behave toward each other in old, familiar ways without much feeling. No growth occurs. The relationship is a hollow shell of its former self. We see stagnation in many workers who have lost enthusiasm for their job yet continue to go through the motions for years. The same sad event occurs for some couples who unenthusiastically have the same conversations, see the same people, and follow the same routines without any sense of joy or novelty.

Avoiding   When stagnation becomes too unpleasant, parties in a relationship begin to create physical distance between each other. This is the **avoiding** stage. Sometimes they do it indirectly under the guise of excuses ("I've been sick lately and can't see you") and sometimes directly ("Please don't call me; I don't want to see you now"). In either case, by this point the handwriting is on the wall about the relationship's future.

The deterioration of a relationship from bonding through circumscribing, stagnating, and avoiding isn't inevitable. One of the key

Some Western cultures have rituals to mark the progress of a friendship and to give it public legitimacy and form. In Germany, for example, there's a small ceremony called *Duzen*, the name itself signifying the transformation in the relationship. The ritual calls for the two friends, each holding a glass of wine or beer, to entwine arms, thus bringing each other physically close, and to drink up after making a promise of eternal brotherhood with the word *Bruderschaft*. When it's over, the friends will have passed from a relationship that requires the formal *Sie* mode of address to the familiar *du*.

Lillian B. Rubin, *Just Friends: The Role of Friendship in Our Lives*

differences between marriages that end in separation and those that are restored to their former intimacy is the communication that occurs when the partners are unsatisfied.[44] Unsuccessful couples deal with their problems by avoidance, indirectness, and less involvement with one another. By contrast, couples who "repair" their relationship communicate much more directly. They confront one another with their concerns and spend time and effort negotiating solutions to their problems.

Terminating   Characteristics of the final stage, **terminating,** include summary dialogues of where the relationship has gone and the desire to dissociate. The relationship may end with a cordial dinner, a note left on the kitchen table, a phone call, or a legal document. Depending on each person's feelings, this stage can be quite short, or it may be drawn out over time, with bitter jabs at each other.

Relationships don't always move toward termination in a straight line. Rather, they take a back-and-forth pattern, where the trend is toward dissolution.[45] Regardless of how long it takes, termination doesn't have to be totally negative. Understanding each other's investments in the relationship and needs for personal growth may dilute the hard feelings. In fact, many relationships aren't so much terminated as redefined. A divorced couple, for example, may find ways to relate to each other in a less-intimate way.

In romantic relationships, the best predictor of whether the parties will become friends is whether they were friends before their emotional involvement.[46] The way the couple split up also makes a difference. It's no surprise to find that friendships are most possible when communication during the breakup was positive: expressions that there were no regrets for time spent together and other attempts to minimize hard feelings. When communication during termination is negative (manipulative, complaining to third parties), friendships are less likely.

According to Knapp, a relationship can exist in only one stage at a time. At any moment it will exhibit the most dominant traits of just one of the ten stages described on pages 324–330. Despite this fact, elements of other stages are usually present. For example, two lovers deep in the throes of integrating may still do their share of experimenting and have differentiating disagreements. Likewise, family members who spend most of their energy avoiding one another may have an occasional good spell in which their former closeness briefly intensifies. Even though there may be overtones of several stages, one will predominate.

When he pictured their introduction . . . it seemed nothing more than the beginning of their parting. When she had looked up at him that first night and rattled the ice cubes in her paper cup, they were already moving toward their last edgy, miserable year together, towards those months when anything either of them said was wrong, toward that sense of narrowly missed connections. They were like people who run to meet, holding out their arms, but their aim is wrong; they pass each other and keep running. It had all amounted to nothing, in the end.

Knapp also argues that movement between stages is generally sequential, so that relationships typically move from one stage to another in a step-by-step manner as they develop and deteriorate. This doesn't mean that every relationship will move through all ten stages. Some reach a certain point and then go no further. When this occurs, movement is usually across the staircase to the corresponding point of deterioration. There are exceptions to the rule of sequential development. Occasionally partners may skip a stage: Sudden elopements and desertions are an example. Nonetheless, most of the time sequential, one-step-at-a-time progression allows the relationship to unfold at a pace that is manageable for the partners.

At first glance, Knapp's ten stages of relational communication seem to suggest that all relationships follow the same trajectory, from initiation through termination. Your own experience almost certainly shows that this isn't necessarily the case. Many never make it past the early stages of initiating and experimenting. Others (with fellow workers, for example) develop as far as integrating or even intensifying without ever reaching the stage of bonding. The ten-stage model illustrates the range of possibilities, but it doesn't describe a guaranteed pathway for every relationship.

INVITATION TO INSIGHT

YOUR RELATIONAL STAGE

You can gain a clearer appreciation of the accuracy and value of relational stages by answering the following questions.

1. If you are in a relationship, describe its present stage and the behaviors that characterize your communication in this stage. Give specific examples to support your assessment.

2. Discuss the trend of the communication in terms of the stages described on pages 324–330. Are you likely to remain in the present stage, or do you anticipate movement to another stage? Which one? Explain your answer.

3. Describe your level of satisfaction with the answer to question 2. If you are satisfied, describe what you can do to increase the likelihood that the relationship will operate at the stage you described. If you are not satisfied, discuss what you can do to move the relationship toward a more satisfying stage.

4. Because both parties define a relationship, define your partner's perspective. Would she or he say that the relationship is at the same stage as you describe it? If not, explain how your partner would describe it. What does your partner do to determine the stage at which your relationship operates? (Give specific examples.) How would you like your partner to behave in order to move the relationship to or maintain it at the stage you desire? What can you do to encourage your partner to behave in the way you desire?

Dialectical Perspectives

Not all theorists agree that stage-related models like the one described in the preceding pages are the best way to explain interaction in relationships. Some theorists suggest that communicators grapple with the same kinds of challenges whether a relationship is brand new or decades old. They argue that communicators seek important but inherently incompatible goals throughout virtually all of their relationships. The struggle to achieve these goals creates **dialectical tensions**: conflicts that arise when two opposing or incompatible forces exist simultaneously. In recent years, communication scholars have identified the dialectical forces that make successful communication challenging.[47] They suggest that the struggle to manage these dialectical tensions creates the most powerful dynamics in relational communication. In the following pages we will discuss three powerful dialectical tensions.

Connection vs. Autonomy   No one is an island. Recognizing this fact, we seek out involvement with others. But, at the same time, we are unwilling to sacrifice our entire identity to even the most satisfying relationship. The conflicting desires for connection and autonomy are embodied in the **connection-autonomy dialectic.**

Research on relational breakups demonstrates the consequences for relational partners who can't find a way to manage these very different personal needs.[48] Some of the most common reasons for relational breakups involve failure of partners to satisfy one another's needs for connection: "We barely spent any time together"; "S/he wasn't committed to the relationship"; "We had different needs." But other relational complaints involve excessive demands for connection: "I was feeling trapped"; "I needed freedom."

The levels of connection and autonomy that we seek can change over time. In his book *Intimate Behavior*, Desmond Morris suggests that each of us repeatedly goes through three stages: "Hold me tight," "Put me down," and "Leave me alone."[49] This cycle becomes apparent in the first years of life when children move from the "hold me tight" stage that characterizes infancy into a new "put me down" stage of exploring the world by crawling, walking, touching, and tasting. The same three-year-old who insists "I can do it myself" in August may cling to parents on the first day of pre-school in September. As children grow into adolescents, the "leave me alone" orientation becomes apparent. Teenagers who used to happily spend time with their parents now may groan at the thought of a family vacation or even the notion of sitting down at the dinner table each evening. As adolescents move into adulthood, they typically grow closer to their families again.[50]

In adult relationships, the same cycle of intimacy and distance repeats itself. In marriages, for example, the "hold me tight" bonds of the first year are often followed by a desire for autonomy. This desire can manifest itself in a number of ways, such as the desire to make friends or engage in activities that don't include the spouse or the need to make a career move that might disrupt the relationship. As the discussion of relational stages earlier in this chapter explained, this movement from connection to autonomy may lead to the breakup of relationships, but it can also be part of a cycle that redefines the relationship in a new form that can recapture or even surpass the intimacy that existed in the past.

Predictability vs. Novelty

Stability is an important need in relationships, but too much of it can lead to feelings of staleness. The **predictability-novelty dialectic** reflects this tension. Humorist Dave Barry exaggerates only slightly when he talks about the boredom that can come when husbands and wives know each other too well:

> After a decade or so of marriage, you know *everything* about your spouse, every habit and opinion and twitch and tic and minor skin growth. You could write a seventeen-pound book solely about the way your spouse *eats*. This kind of intimate knowledge can be very handy in certain situations—such as when you're on a TV quiz show where the object is to identify your spouse from the sound of his or her chewing—but it tends to lower the passion level of a relationship.[51]

Although too much familiarity can lead to the risk of boredom and stagnation, nobody wants a completely unpredictable relational partner. Too many surprises can threaten the foundations upon which the relationship is based ("You're not the person I married!").

The challenge for communicators is to juggle the desire for predictability with the desire for novelty that keeps the relationship fresh and interesting. People differ in their desire for predictability and novelty, so there is no optimal mixture of the two. As you will read shortly, people can use a number of strategies to manage these contradictory drives.

Openness vs. Privacy

As chapter 1 explained, intimacy is one characteristic of interpersonal relationships. Yet, along with intimacy, we have an equally important need to maintain some space between

[Porcupines] huddle together for warmth, but their sharp quills prick each other, so they pull away. But then they get cold. They have to keep adjusting their closeness and distance to keep from freezing and from getting pricked by their fellow porcupines—the source of both comfort and pain.

We need to get close to each other to have a sense of community, to feel we're not alone in the world. But we need to keep our distance from each other to preserve our independence, so others don't impose on or engulf us. This duality reflects the human condition. We are individual and social creatures. We need other people to survive, but we want to survive as individuals.

Deborah Tannen, *That's Not What I Meant!*

"And do you, Rebecca, promise to make love only to Richard, month after month, year after year, and decade after decade, until one of you is dead?"

©The New Yorker Collection 1997 Tom Cheney from cartoonbank.com. All Rights Reserved.

ourselves and others. These sometimes-conflicting needs create the **openness-privacy dialectic.**

Even the strongest interpersonal relationships require some distance. On a short-term basis, the desire for closeness waxes and wanes. Lovers may go through periods of much sharing and periods of relative withdrawal. Likewise, they experience periods of passion and then periods of little physical contact. Friends have times of high disclosure when they share almost every feeling and idea and then disengage for days, months, or even longer. Figure 8-3 illustrates some patterns of variation in openness uncovered in a study of college students' communication patterns.[52] The students reported the degree of openness in one of their important relationships—a friendship, romantic relationship, or marriage—over a range of thirty conversations. The graphs show a definite pattern of fluctuation between disclosure and privacy in every stage of the relationships.

Although all of the dialectical tensions play an important role in managing relationships, some occur more frequently than others. In one study, young married couples reported that connection-autonomy was the most frequent tension (30.8 percent of all reported contradictions).[53] Predictability-novelty was second (21.7 percent). Least common was openness-privacy (12.7 percent).

Managing Dialectical Tensions Managing the dialectical tensions outlined in these pages presents communication challenges. There are a number of ways these challenges can be met.[54]

1. **Denial** In the strategy of denial, communicators respond to one end of the dialectical spectrum and ignore the other. For example, a couple caught between the conflicting desires for predictability and novelty might find their struggle for change too difficult to manage and choose to follow predictable, if unexciting, patterns of relating to one another.

2. **Disorientation** In this strategy, communicators feel so overwhelmed and helpless that they are unable to confront their problems. In the face of dialectical tensions they might fight, freeze, or even leave the relationship. Two people who discover soon after the honeymoon that a "happily ever after" conflict-free life isn't realistic might become so terrified that they would come to view their marriage as a mistake.

3. **Alternation** Communicators who use this strategy choose one end of the dialectical spectrum at some times and the other end on other times. Friends, for example, might manage the connection-autonomy dialectic by alternating between times when they spend a large amount of time together and other times when they live independent lives. In the cartoon on the next page, Jeremy realizes he has forgotten to use his usual approach of segmentation to manage the openness-privacy dialectic with his inquisitive parents.

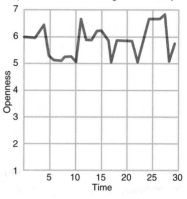

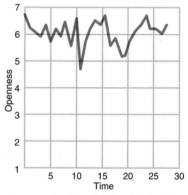

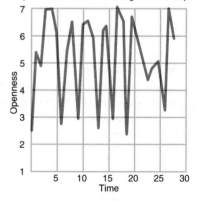

FIGURE 8-3 **Cyclical Phases of Openness and Withdrawal in Relationships**

Figures: From "Testing a Cyclical Model of Communication Openness in Relationship Development: Two Longitudinal Studies" by C. A. VanLear. Published in *Communication Monographs* 59 (1991) © Speech Communication Association.

Reprinted with special permission of King Feature Syndicate.

4. **Balance** Communicators who try to balance dialectical tensions recognize that both forces are legitimate and try to manage them through compromise. As chapter 10 points out, compromise is inherently a situation in which everybody loses at least a little of what he or she wants. A couple caught between the conflicting desires for predictability and novelty might seek balance by compromising with a lifestyle that is neither as predictable as one wants nor as surprise-filled as the other wants—not an ideal outcome.

5. **Integration** With this strategy, communicators simultaneously accept opposing forces without trying to diminish them. Communication researcher Barbara Montgomery describes a couple who accept the needs for both predictability and novelty by devising a "predictably novel" approach: Once a week they would do something together that they had never done before.[55] In a similar way, some step-families manage the tension between the "old family" and the "new family" by adapting and blending their family rituals.[56]

6. **Recalibration** Communicators can respond to dialectical challenges by reframing them so that the apparent contradiction disappears. For example, a change in thinking can transform your attitude from loving someone *in spite* of your differences to loving him or her *because* of those differences.[57] Or consider how two people who each felt hurt by one another's unwillingness to share parts of his or her past might redefine the secrets as creating an attractive aura of mystery instead of being a problem to be solved. The desire for privacy would still remain, but it would no longer compete with a need for openness about every aspect of the past.

7. **Reaffirmation** This strategy acknowledges that dialectical tensions will never disappear. Instead of trying to make them go away, reaffirming communicators accept—or even embrace—the challenges that the tensions present. The metaphorical view of relational life as a kind of roller coaster reflects this strategy, and communicators who use reaffirmation view dialectical tensions as part of the ride.

Love one another, but make not a bond of love:

Let it rather be a moving sea between the shores of your souls.

Fill each other's cup but drink not from one cup.

Give one another of your bread but eat not of the same loaf.

Sing and dance together and be joyous, but let each one of you be alone,

Even as the strings of a lute are alone though they quiver with the same music.

Kahlil Gibran, The Prophet

INVITATION TO INSIGHT

YOUR DIALECTICAL TENSIONS

Describe how each of the dialectical tensions described in these pages operates in one of your important relationships. Which incompatible goals do you and your relational partner(s) seek? Which of the strategies described on pages 334–335 do you use to manage these tensions? Are you satisfied with this strategy, or can you suggest better strategies?

Characteristics of Relational Development and Maintenance

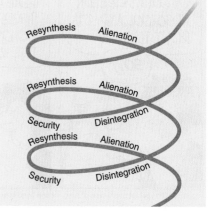

FIGURE 8-4 A Helical Model of Relational Cycles

Whether you analyze a relationship in terms of stages or dialectical tensions, two characteristics are true of every interpersonal relationship. As you read about each, consider how it applies to your own experience.

Relationships Are Constantly Changing   Relationships are certainly not doomed to deteriorate. But even the strongest ones are rarely stable for long periods of time. In fairy tales a couple may live "happily ever after," but in real life this sort of equilibrium is less common. Consider a husband and wife who have been married for some time. Although they have formally bonded, their relationship will probably shift from one dimension of a relational dialectic to another, and forward or backward along the spectrum of stages. Sometimes the partners will feel the need to differentiate from one another, and at other times they will need to seek intimacy. Sometimes they will feel secure in the predictable patterns they have established, and at other times one or both will feel hungry for novelty. The relationship may become more circumscribed or even stagnant. From this point the marriage may fail, but this fate isn't certain. With effort, the partners may move from the stage of stagnating to experimenting, or from circumscribing to intensifying.

Communication theorist Richard Conville describes the constantly changing, evolving nature of relationships as a cycle in which partners move through a series of stages, returning to ones they previously encountered, although at a new level[58] (see Figure 8-4). In this cycle, partners move from security (integration, in Knapp's terminology) to disintegration (differentiating) to alienation (circumscribing) to resynthesis (intensifying, integrating) to a new level of security. This process repeats itself again and again.

Movement Is Always to a New Place   Even though a relationship may move back to a stage it has experienced before, it will never be the same. For example, most healthy long-term relationships will go through several phases of experimenting, when the partners try out new ways of behaving with one another. Though each phase is characterized by the same general features, the specifics will feel different each time. As you learned in chapter 1, communication is irreversible. Partners can never go back to "the way things were." Sometimes this fact may lead to regrets: It's impossible to take back a cruel comment or to forget a crisis. On the other hand, the irreversibility of communication can make relationships exciting because it lessens the chance for boredom.

SELF-DISCLOSURE IN RELATIONSHIPS

One way by which we judge the strength of relationships is the amount of information we share with others. "We don't have any secrets," some people proudly claim. Opening up certainly is important. As chapter 1 explained, one ingredient in qualitatively interpersonal relationships is disclosure. Given the obvious importance of self-disclosure, we need to take a closer look at the subject. Just what is it? When is it desirable? How can it best be done?

The best place to begin is with a definition. *Self-disclosure* is the process of deliberately revealing information about oneself that is significant and that would not normally be known by others. Let's take a closer look at some parts of this definition. Self-disclosure must be *deliberate*. If you accidentally mention to a friend that you're thinking about quitting a job or proposing marriage, that information doesn't qualify as self-disclosure. Besides being deliberate, the information must also be *significant*. Volunteering trivial facts, opinions, or feelings—that you like fudge, for example—hardly counts as disclosure. The third requirement is that the information being disclosed is *not known by others*. There's nothing noteworthy about telling others that you are depressed or elated if they already know that.

Degrees of Self-Disclosure

Although our definition of self-disclosure is helpful, it doesn't reveal the important fact that not all self-disclosure is equally revealing—that some disclosing messages tell more about us than others.

Social psychologists Irwin Altman and Dalmas Taylor describe two ways in which communication can be more or less disclosing.[59] Their model of **social penetration** is pictured in Figure 8-5. The first dimension of self-disclosure in this model involves the **breadth** of information volunteered—the range of subjects being discussed. For example, the breadth of disclosure in your relationship with a fellow

he stripped
the dark circles
of mystery off
revealed his eyes
and thus
he waited
exposed

and I
did sing the song
around
until I found
the chorus
that speaks
of windows

looking out
means looking in
my friend
and I'm all right
now
I'm fine
I have seen
the beauty
that is mine

you can
watch the sky
for signals
but look
to the eyes
for signs

Ric Masten

worker will expand as you begin revealing information about your life away from the job as well as on-the-job information. The second dimension of self-disclosure is the **depth** of information volunteered, the shift from relatively nonpersonal messages to more personal ones.

Depending on the breadth and depth of information shared, a relationship can be defined as casual or intimate. In a casual relationship the breadth may be great, but not the depth. A more intimate relationship is likely to have high depth in at least one area. The most intimate relationships are those in which disclosure is great in both breadth and depth. Altman and Taylor see the development of a relationship as a progression from the periphery of their model to its center, a process that typically occurs over time. Each of your personal relationships probably has a

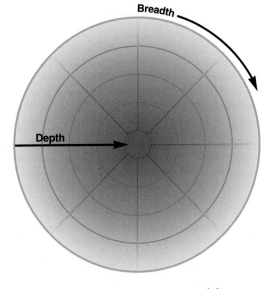

FIGURE 8-5 **Social Penetration Model**

different combination of breadth of subjects and depth of disclosure. Figure 8-6 pictures a student's self-disclosure in one relationship.

What makes the disclosure in some messages deeper than others? One way to measure depth is by how far it goes on two of the dimensions that define self-disclosure. Some revelations are certainly more *significant* than others. Consider the difference between saying, "I love my family" and "I love you." Other revelations qualify as deep disclosure because they are *private.* Sharing a secret that you've told to only a few close friends is certainly a revealing act of self-disclosure, but it's even more revealing to divulge information that you've never told anyone.

Another way to measure the depth of disclosure is to look at the types of information we share.

Clichés **Clichés** are ritualized, stock responses to social situations—virtually the opposite of self-disclosure: "How are you doing? "Fine!" "We'll have to get together soon."

Although they sound superficial, clichés can also serve as codes for messages we don't

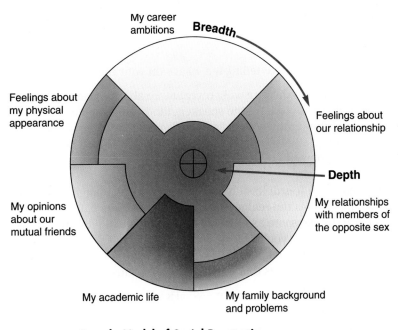

FIGURE 8-6 **Sample Model of Social Penetration**

usually express directly, such as "I want to acknowledge your presence" (for instance, when two acquaintances walk past each other). Additional unstated messages often contained in clichés are "I'm interested in talking if you feel like it" or "Let's keep the conversation light and impersonal; I don't feel like disclosing much about myself right now." Accompanied by a different set of nonverbal cues, a cliché can say, "I don't want to be impolite, but you'd better stay away from me for now." In all these cases clichés serve as a valuable kind of shorthand that makes it easy to keep the social wheels greased and that indicates the potential for further, possibly more profound conversation.

Facts   Not all facts qualify as self-disclosure: They must fit the criteria of being intentional, significant, and not otherwise known:

> "This isn't my first try at college. I dropped out a year ago with terrible grades."

> "I'm practically engaged." (On meeting a stranger while away from home)

> "That idea that everyone thought was so clever wasn't really mine. I read it in a book last year."

Facts like these can be meaningful in themselves, but they also have a greater significance in a relationship. Disclosing important information suggests a level of trust and commitment to the other person that signals a desire to move the relationship to a new level.

Opinions   Still more revealing is the level of opinions:

> "I used to think abortion was no big deal, but lately I've changed my mind."

> "I really like Karen."

> "I don't think you're telling me what's on your mind."

Opinions like these usually reveal more about a person than facts alone. If you know where the speaker stands on a subject, you can get a clearer picture of how your relationship might develop. Likewise, every time you offer a personal opinion, you are giving others valuable information about yourself.

Feelings   The fourth level of self-disclosure—and usually the most revealing one—is the realm of feelings. At first glance, feelings might appear to be the same as opinions, but there is a big difference. As we saw, "I don't think you're telling me what's on your mind" is an opinion. Now notice how much more we learn about the speaker by looking at three different feelings that might accompany this statement:

> "I don't think you're telling me what's on your mind, *and I'm suspicious.*"

> "I don't think you're telling me what's on your mind, *and I'm angry.*"

> "I don't think you're telling me what's on your mind, *and I'm hurt.*"

The difference between these four levels of communication suggests why relationships can be frustrating. Sometimes the communicators might never get to the levels of personal opinions and feelings. At other times communicators can spend *too much* time at these more personal levels. Just as a diet of rich foods can become unappealing if carried to excess, too much personal information can also become unappealing. Another sort of problem occurs when two communicators want to communicate on different levels. If one person is willing to deal only with facts and perhaps an occasional opinion, and the other insists on revealing personal feelings, the results are likely to be uncomfortable for both.

INVITATION TO INSIGHT

EXAMINING YOUR SELF-DISCLOSURE

Here's a chance to explore the levels of self-disclosure that you use with some important people in your life.

1. Choose a "significant other" as the subject of this exercise.

2. Spend a three-day period recording the number of statements you make in each category: clichés, facts, opinions, and feelings.

3. Try to be aware of the topics that you discuss on each level, along with the number of statements in each category.

4. Based on your findings, answer these questions:
   a. Which categories of self-disclosure do you engage in most frequently? Least frequently?
   b. What type of disclosure (fact, opinion, or feeling) do you use in each topic area?
   c. Explain the reason for omitting topical categories (for example, conflicts, the future) or levels of disclosure or both (for example, feelings).
   d. Explain the consequences of any omissions described in part c.

A Model of Self-Disclosure

One way to look at the important part that self-disclosure plays in interpersonal communication is by means of a device called the **Johari Window**.[60] (The window takes its name from the first names of its creators, Joseph Luft and Harry Ingham.) Imagine a frame like Figure 8-7 that contains everything there is to know about you: your likes and dislikes, your goals, your secrets, your needs—everything.

Of course, you aren't aware of everything about yourself. Like most people, you're probably discovering new things about yourself all the time. To represent this, we can divide the frame containing everything about you into two parts: the part you know about and the part you do not know about, as in Figure 8-8.

We can also divide this frame containing everything about you in another way. In this division one part represents the things about you

FIGURE 8-7

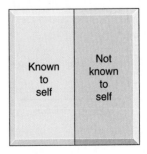

FIGURE 8-8

that others know, and the second part represents the things about you that you keep to yourself. Figure 8-9 represents this view.

When we impose these two divided frames one atop the other, we have a Johari Window. By looking at Figure 8-10 you can see the *everything about you* divided into four parts.

Part 1 represents the information of which both you and the other person are aware. This part is your *open area.* Part 2 represents the *blind area:* information of which you are unaware but of which the other person is aware. You learn about information in the blind area primarily through feedback. Part 3 represents your *hidden area:* information that you know but aren't willing to reveal to others. Items in this hidden area become public primarily through self-disclosure, which is the focus of this chapter. Part 4 represents information that is *unknown* to both you and others. At first the unknown area seems impossible to verify. After all, if neither you nor others know what it contains, how can you be sure it exists? We can deduce its existence because we are constantly discovering new things about ourselves. It is not unusual to discover, for example, that you have an unrecognized talent, strength, or weakness. Items either move directly from the unknown area into the open area when you disclose your insight or move through one of the other areas first.

The relative size of each area in our personal Johari Windows changes from time to time, according to our moods, the subject we are discussing, and our relationship with the other person. Despite these changes, most people's overall style of disclosure could be represented by a single Johari Window. Figure 8-11 pictures windows representing four extreme interaction styles.

Style I depicts a person who is neither receptive to feedback nor willing to self-disclose. This person takes few risks and may appear aloof and uncommunicative. The largest quadrant is the unknown area: Such people have a lot to learn about themselves, as do others. Style II depicts a person who is open to feedback from

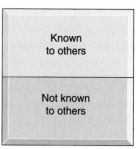

FIGURE 8-9

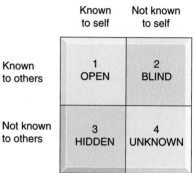

FIGURE 8-10

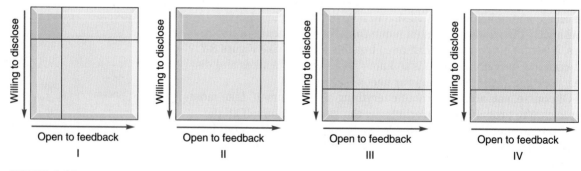

FIGURE 8-11

others but does not voluntarily self-disclose. This person may fear exposure, possibly because of not trusting others. People who fit this pattern may appear highly supportive at first. They want to hear *your* story and appear willing to deny themselves by remaining quiet. Then this first impression fades, and eventually you see them as distrustful and detached. A Johari Window describing such people has a large hidden area.

Style III in Figure 8-11 describes people who discourage feedback from others but disclose freely. Like the people pictured in diagram II, they may distrust others' opinions. They certainly seem self-centered. Their largest quadrant is the blind area: They do not encourage feedback and so fail to learn much about how others view them.

Diagram IV depicts people who are both willing to disclose information about themselves and open to others' ideas. They are trusting enough to seek the opinions of others and disclose their own. In extreme, this communication style can be intimidating and overwhelming because it violates the usual expectations of how nonintimates ought to behave. In moderation, however, this open style provides the best chance for developing highly interpersonal relationships.

Interpersonal communication of any depth is virtually impossible if the individuals involved have little open area. Going a step further, you can see that a relationship is limited by the individual who is less open—that is, who possesses the smaller open area. Figure 8-12 illustrates this situation with Johari Windows. Person A's window is set up in reverse so that A's and B's open areas are adjacent. Notice that the amount of communication (represented by the arrows connecting the two open areas) is dictated by the size of the smaller open area of A. The arrows originating from person B's open area and being turned aside by A's hidden and blind areas represent unsuccessful attempts to communicate.

You have probably found yourself in situations that resemble Figure 8-12. Perhaps you have felt the frustration of not being able to get to know someone who was too reserved. Perhaps you have blocked another person's attempts to build a relationship with you in the same way. Whether you picture yourself more like person A or person B, the fact is that self-disclosure on both sides is necessary for the development of any interpersonal relationship. This chapter will describe just how much self-disclosure is optimal and of what type.

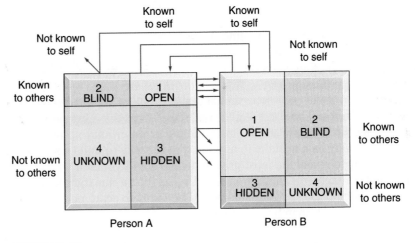

FIGURE 8-12

BUILDING A JOHARI WINDOW

You can use the Johari Window model to examine the level of self-disclosure in your own relationships.

1. Use the format described in the preceding section to draw two Johari Windows representing the relationship between you and one other person. Remember to reverse one of the windows so that your open area and that of the other person face each other.

2. Describe which parts of yourself you keep in the hidden area. Explain your reasons for doing so. Describe the advantages or disadvantages or both of not disclosing these parts of yourself.

3. Look at the blind area of your model. Is this area large or small because of the amount of feedback (much or little) that you get from your partner or because of your willingness to receive the feedback that is offered?

4. Explain whether you are satisfied with the results illustrated by your answers. If you are not satisfied, explain what you can do to remedy the problem.

Characteristics of Self-Disclosure

By now it's clear that self-disclosure isn't a common type of communication, even in close relationships. The following characteristics show the place of self-disclosure in interpersonal affairs.

Self-Disclosure Usually Occurs in Dyads

Although it is possible for people to disclose a great deal about themselves in groups, such communication usually occurs in one-to-one settings. Because revealing significant information about yourself involves a certain amount of risk, limiting the disclosure to one person at a time minimizes the chance that your revelations will lead to unhappy consequences.

Self-Disclosure Occurs Incrementally

Although occasions do occur in which partners start their relationship by telling everything about themselves to each other, such occasions are rare. In most cases the amount of disclosure increases over time. We begin relationships by revealing relatively little about ourselves; then if our first bits of self-disclosure are well received and bring on similar responses from the other person, we're willing to reveal more. This principle is important to remember. It would usually be a mistake to assume that the way to build a strong relationship is to reveal the most private details about yourself when first making contact with another person. Unless the circumstances are unique, such baring of your soul would be likely to scare potential partners away rather than bring them closer.

Relatively Few Transactions Involve High Levels of Self-Disclosure

Just as it's unwise to seek great self-disclosure too soon, it's also unwise to reveal yourself too often. Except for unique settings—such as in therapy—there's usually no need to disclose frequently or steadily. When used properly, self-disclosure may strengthen relationships, but like most medicines, large amounts of disclosure are not necessary to produce good results.

Self-Disclosure Is Relatively Scarce   What is the optimal amount of self-disclosure? You might suspect that the correct answer is "the more, the better," at least in personal relationships. Research has shown that the matter isn't this simple, however.[61] For example, there seems to be a curvilinear relationship between openness and satisfaction in marriage, so that a moderate amount of openness produces better results than either extreme openness or withholding. Most conversations—even among friends—focus on everyday, mundane topics and disclose little or no personal information.[62] Even partners in intimate relationships rarely talk about personal information.[63] One good measure of happiness is how well the level of disclosure matches the expectations of communicators: If we get what we believe is a reasonable amount of candor from others, we are satisfied. If they tell us too little—or too much—we become less satisfied.

Self-Disclosure Usually Occurs in the Context of Positive Relationships   This principle makes sense. We're generally more willing to reveal information about ourselves when we feel accepted by the other person. This doesn't mean that you should avoid making disclosing statements that contain negative messages (for example, "I feel uncomfortable about what happened last night"). Such statements are likely to be successful if they're designed to be constructive, to help your relationship grow. On the other hand, disclosure that has the effect of attacking the other person ("You sure aren't very bright") is almost guaranteed to be destructive. For this reason, it's especially important to phrase negative messages in the supportive, assertive ways described in chapters 9 and 10.

Reasons for Self-Disclosure

Self-disclosure has the potential to improve and expand interpersonal relationships, but it serves other functions as well.[64] As you read each of the following reasons why people reveal themselves, see which apply to you.

Catharsis   Sometimes you might disclose information in an effort to "get it off your chest." In a moment of candor you might, for instance, reveal your regrets about having behaved badly in the past.

Reciprocity A well-documented conclusion from research is that one act of self-disclosure begets another.[65] There is no guarantee that your self-disclosures will trigger self-disclosures by others, but your own honesty can create a climate that makes others feel safer and perhaps even obligated to match your level of honesty. Sometimes revealing personal information will cause the other person to do so. It's easy to imagine how telling a partner how you feel about the relationship ("I've been feeling bored lately . . .") would generate the same degree of candor ("You know, I've felt the same way!"). Reciprocity doesn't always occur on a turn-by-turn basis: Telling a friend today about your job-related problems might help her feel comfortable opening up to you later about her family history, when the time is right for this sort of disclosure.

"Bob, as a token of my appreciation for this wonderful lunch I would like to disclose to you my income-tax returns for the past four years."

©The New Yorker Collection 1984 Jack Ziegler from cartoonbank.com. All Rights Reserved.

Self-Clarification Sometimes you can clarify your beliefs, opinions, thoughts, attitudes, and feelings by talking about them with another person. This sort of "talking the problem out" occurs with psychotherapists, but it also goes on with others, all the way from good friends to bartenders or hairdressers.

Self-Validation If you disclose information ("I think I did the right thing . . .") with the hope of obtaining the listener's agreement, you are seeking validation of your behavior—confirmation of a belief that you hold about yourself. On a deeper level, this sort of self-validating disclosure seeks confirmation of important parts of your self-concept.

Identity Management Sometimes we reveal personal information to make ourselves more attractive. Some observers have made this point bluntly, asserting that self-disclosure has become another way of "marketing" ourselves.[66] Consider two people on their first date. It's not hard to imagine how one or both partners might share personal information to appear more sincere, interesting, sensitive, or interested in the other person. The same principle applies in other situations. A salesperson might say, "I'll be honest with you . . ." primarily to show that she is on your side, and a new acquaintance might talk about the details of his past to seem more friendly and likable.

Relationship Maintenance and Enhancement A large body of research supports the role of self-disclosure in relational success.[67] For example, there is a strong relationship between the quality of self-disclosure and marital satisfaction.[68] The same principle applies in other personal relationships. The bond between grandparents and grandchildren, for example, grows stronger when the honesty and depth of sharing between them are high.[69]

Social Control   Revealing personal information may increase your control over the other person and sometimes over the situation in which you and the other person find yourselves. For example, an employee who tells the boss that another firm has made overtures probably will have increased chance of getting raises and improvements in working conditions.

Manipulation   Although most of the preceding motives might strike you as being manipulative, they often aren't premeditated. There are cases, however, when an act of self-disclosure is calculated to achieve a desired result. Of course, if a disclosure's hidden motive ever becomes clear to the receiver, the results will most likely be quite unlike those intended.

The motives for disclosing vary from one situation to another, depending on several factors. The strongest factor in why we disclose seems to be how well we know the other person.[70] When the target of disclosure is a friend, the most important reason that people give for disclosing is relationship maintenance and enhancement. In other words, we disclose to friends in order to strengthen the relationship. The second important reason is self-clarification—to sort out confusion to understand ourselves better.

With strangers, reciprocity becomes the most common reason for disclosing. We offer information about ourselves to strangers to learn more about them, so that we can decide whether and how to continue the relationship. The second most common reason is impression formation. In other words, we often reveal information about ourselves to strangers to make ourselves look good. This information, of course, is usually positive—at least in the early stages of a friendship.

Guidelines for Self-Disclosure

By now it should be clear that deciding when and how much personal information to disclose is not a simple matter. The following guidelines can help you choose the level of self-disclosure that is appropriate in a given situation.

Is the Other Person Important to You?   There are several ways in which someone might be important to you. Perhaps you have an ongoing relationship deep enough so that sharing significant parts of yourself justifies keeping your present level of togetherness intact. Or perhaps the person to whom you're considering disclosing is someone with whom you've previously related on a less personal level. But now you see a chance to grow closer, and disclosure may be the path toward developing that personal relationship.

Is the Risk of Disclosing Reasonable?   Take a realistic look at the potential risks of self-disclosure. Even if the probable benefits are great, opening yourself up to almost certain rejection may be asking for trouble.

On the other hand, knowing that your partner is trustworthy and supportive makes the prospect of disclosing more reasonable.

Revealing personal thoughts and feelings can be especially risky on the job.[71] The politics of the workplace sometimes requires communicators to keep feelings to themselves in order to accomplish both personal and organizational goals. You might, for example, find the opinions of a boss or customer personally offensive but decide to bite your tongue rather than risk your job or lose goodwill for the company.

In anticipating risks, be sure that you are realistic. It's sometimes easy to indulge in catastrophic expectations and imagine all sorts of disastrous consequences when in fact such horrors are quite unlikely to occur.

Is the Disclosure Relevant to the Situation at Hand?

The kind of disclosure that is often a characteristic of highly personal relationships usually isn't appropriate in less personal settings. For instance, a study of classroom communication revealed that sharing all feelings—both positive and negative—and being completely honest resulted in less cohesiveness than did a "relatively" honest climate in which pleasant but superficial relationships were the norm.[72]

Even in personal relationships—with close friends, family members, and so on—constant disclosure isn't a useful goal. Even during a phase of high disclosure sharing *everything* about yourself isn't necessarily constructive. Usually the subject of appropriate self-disclosure involves the relationship rather than personal information. Furthermore, it is usually most constructive to focus your disclosure about the relationship on the "here and now" as opposed to "there and then." "How am I feeling now?" "How are we doing now?" These are appropriate topics for sharing personal thoughts and feelings. At times it's relevant to bring up the past, but only as it relates to what's going on in the present.

Are the Amount and Type of Disclosure Appropriate?

It is usually a mistake to share too much information too soon. Research shows that in most relationships the process of disclosure is gradual.[73] At first most of the information that is exchanged

"I'm a very sensual person. How about you, Mr. Gellerman?"

©The New Yorker Collection 1982 Stan Hunt from cartoonbank.com. All Rights Reserved.

is relatively nonintimate. As the parties move into the intensifying, integrating, and bonding stages of the relationship, the rate of disclosure begins to grow.

As we've already seen, even in relationships in which disclosure is an important feature, the amount of intimate information is relatively small when compared to nonintimate information. Most long-term relationships aren't characterized by a constant exchange of intimate information. Rather, they are a mixture of much everyday, nonintimate information and less frequent but more personal messages.

Besides being moderate in amount, self-disclosure should consist of positive information as well as negative information. Hearing nothing but a string of dismal confessions or complaints can be discouraging. In fact, people who disclose an excess of negative information are often considered "negatively adjusted."[74]

Finally, when considering the appropriateness of disclosure in any relationship, timing is also important. If the other person is tired, preoccupied, or in a bad mood it may be best to postpone an important conversation.

Will the Effect Be Constructive?
Self-disclosure can be a vicious tool if it's not used carefully. As Chapter 10 explains, every person has a psychological "beltline." Below that beltline are areas about which the person is extremely sensitive. Bach says that jabbing at a "below-the-belt" area is a sure-fire way to disable another person, though usually at great cost to the relationship. It's important to consider the effects of your candor before opening up to others. Comments such as "I've always thought you were pretty unintelligent" or "Last year I made love to your best friend" *may* sometimes resolve old business and thus be constructive, but they also can be devastating—to the listener, to the relationship, and to your self-esteem.

Is the Self-Disclosure Clear and Understandable?
When you are expressing yourself to others, it's important that you reveal yourself in a way that's intelligible. This means using the guidelines for clear language outlined in chapter 5. For instance, it's far better to describe another's behavior by saying, "When you don't answer my phone calls or drop by to visit anymore . . ." than to complain vaguely, "When you avoid me . . ."

Is the Self-Disclosure Reciprocated?
The amount of personal information you reveal will usually depend on how much the other person reveals. As a rule, disclosure is a two-way street. For example, couples are happiest when their levels of openness are roughly equal.[75]

There are few times when one-way disclosure is acceptable. Most of them involve formal, therapeutic relationships in which a client approaches a trained professional with the goal of resolving a problem. For instance, you wouldn't necessarily expect to hear about a doctor's personal ailments during a visit to the doctor's office.

SKILL BUILDER

APPROPRIATE SELF-DISCLOSURE

Use the guidelines on pages 347–349 to develop one scenario where you might reveal a self-disclosing message. Create a message of this type, and use the information in this chapter to discuss the advantages and disadvantages of sharing this message.

ALTERNATIVES TO SELF-DISCLOSURE

Although self-disclosure plays an important role in interpersonal relationships, it isn't the only type of communication available. To understand why complete honesty isn't always an easy or ideal choice, consider some familiar dilemmas:

A new acquaintance is much more interested in becoming friends than you are. She invites you to a party this weekend. You aren't busy, but you don't want to go. What would you say?

Your boss asks you what you think of his new wardrobe. You think it's cheap and flashy. Would you tell him?

You're attracted to your best friend's mate, who has confessed that he feels the same way about you. You both agreed that you won't act on your feelings and that even bringing up the subject would make your friend feel terribly insecure. Now your friend has asked whether you're attracted at all to the mate. Would you tell the truth?

You've just been given a large, extremely ugly painting as a gift by a relative who visits your home often. How would you respond to the question "Where will you hang it?"

Situations like these highlight some of the issues that surround deceptive communication. On one hand, our moral education and common sense lead us to abhor anything less than the truth. Ethicists point out that the very existence of a society seems based on a foundation of truthfulness.[76] Although isolated cultures do exist where deceit is a norm, they are dysfunctional and on the verge of breakdown.

Although honesty is desirable in principle, the preceding examples show that it can have potentially unpleasant consequences. It's tempting to avoid situations where self-disclosure would be difficult, but examples like the preceding ones show that evasion isn't always possible. Research and personal experience show that communicators—even those with the best intentions—aren't always completely honest when they find themselves in situations in which honesty would be uncomfortable.[77] Three common alternatives to self-disclosure are lying, equivocating, and hinting. We will take a closer look at each one.

Lying

To most of us, lying appears as a breach of ethics. At first glance it appears that the very existence of a society depends on the acceptance

To watch and analyze a dramatized version of the conversation featured in the Communication Transcript on the next page, click on "Self-Disclosure" under Communication Scenarios on your Looking Out/Looking In CD-ROM.

COMMUNICATION TRANSCRIPT

Appropriate and Inappropriate Self-Disclosure

Ramon has been working in an entry-level sales job for almost a year after graduating from the university. He likes the company, but he is growing more and more frustrated at his lack of advancement. After much thought, he decides to share his concerns with his boss, Julie. As you read the following transcript, notice that self-disclosure has the potential to enhance or jeopardize personal goals and relationships, depending on whether it follows the guidelines on pages 347–349.

Ramon Do you have a few minutes to talk?

Julie Sure, no problem. Come on in.

Ramon Do you mind if we close the door?

Julie *(looking a bit surprised)* Sure.

Ramon I'd like to talk to you about the future.

Julie The future?

Ramon Well, it's been over a year since I started to work here. One of the things you told me in the interview back then was that people move up fast here . . .

Julie Well, . . .

Ramon . . . and I'm confused because I've been doing pretty much the same work since I was hired.

Julie Well, we do think a lot of your work.

Ramon I'm glad to hear that. But I'm starting to wonder how much of a chance I'll have to grow with this company. *(Ramon is disclosing his concerns about career advancement—a very appropriate topic to raise with his boss. There is some risk in this sort of disclosure, but given Ramon's apparently good*

standing with his boss, it seems reasonable. Note that Ramon is deliberately vague about "his future." At this stage, the high-level abstraction is probably a good idea.)

Julie I can understand that you're anxious about taking on more responsibility. I can tell you that you've got a good shot at advancing, if you can just hang in there for a little while.

Ramon *(Impatiently)* That sounds good, but I've been waiting—a lot longer than I expected to. I'm starting to wonder if some of the things I've heard around here are true.

Julie *(suspiciously)* What kinds of things are you talking about, Ramon?

Ramon Well, Bill and Latisha were telling me about some people who left here because they didn't get the promotions they were promised. *(Ramon discloses information that was told to him in confidence, jeopardizing the standing of two coworkers with Julie.)*

Julie *(firmly)* Ramon, I'm sure you understand that I can't talk about personnel decisions involving former employees. I can tell you that we try to give people all the challenges and rewards they deserve, though it can take a while.

Ramon *(with some sarcasm)* A year seems like more than "a while." I'm starting to think this company is more interested in having somebody with a Hispanic name on the payroll than giving me a real shot at promotion. *(Ramon's concern may be legitimate, but the sarcastic tone of his disclosure isn't constructive.)*

Julie Look: I probably shouldn't be saying this, but I'm as frustrated as you are that it's taking so long to get a promotion arranged for you. I

can tell you that there will be some personnel changes soon that will give you a good chance to make the kinds of changes you want. I think you can expect to see some changes in the next six weeks. *(Julie offers two items of self-disclosure that encourage Ramon to reciprocate.)*

Ramon That's really good to hear! I have to tell you that I've started to think about other career options. Not because I *want* to leave here, but because I just can't afford to stand still. I really need to start bringing home more money. I don't want to be one of those losers who still can't afford to buy his own house by the time he's forty. *(Ramon makes a big mistake disclosing his opinion about home ownership—a topic that has no relevance to the discussion at hand.)*

Julie Gee, I'm still renting . . .

Ramon Oh. I didn't mean that the way it sounded . . . *(But the damage from the inappropriate disclosure is already done.)*

Julie Anyway, I'm glad you let me know about your concerns. I hope you can hang in there for just a little while longer.

Ramon Sure. Six weeks, huh? I'll keep an eye on the calendar!

After the conversation, Julie still thinks Ramon is a candidate for promotion, but some of his inappropriate disclosures have left her with doubts about his maturity and good judgment, which she didn't have before they spoke. Julie makes a mental note to keep an eye on Ramon and to reconsider the amount of responsibility she gives him until he has demonstrated the ability to share his personal feelings and concerns more constructively.

of truthfulness as a social norm. Although lying to gain unfair advantage over an unknowing victim seems clearly wrong, another kind of mistruth—the "white lie"—isn't so easy to dismiss as completely unethical. A **"white lie"** is defined (at least by the teller) as unmalicious, or even helpful, to the person to whom it is told. Whether or not they are innocent, white lies are certainly common. In one study, 130 subjects were asked to keep track of the truthfulness of their everyday conversational statements.[78] Only 38.5 percent of these statements—slightly more than a third—proved to be totally honest.

Reasons for Lying   What reasons do people give for being so deceitful? When subjects in the study were asked to give a lie-by-lie account of their reasons for concealing or distorting the truth, five major reasons emerged.

"Remember when I said I was going to be honest with you, Jeff? That was a big, fat lie."

©The New Yorker Collection 2000 Leo Cullum from cartoonbank.com. All Rights Reserved.

1. *To save face.* Over half the lies were justified as a way to prevent embarrassment. Such lying is often given the approving label "tact" and is used "when it would be unkind to be honest, but dishonest to be kind."[79] Sometimes a face-saving lie saves face for the recipient, as when you pretend to remember someone at a party in order to save that person from the embarrassment of being forgotten. At other times a lie protects the teller from humiliation. You might, for instance, cover up your mistakes by blaming them on outside forces: "You didn't receive the check? It must have been delayed in the mail."

2. *To avoid tension or conflict.* Sometimes it seems worthwhile to tell a small lie to prevent a large conflict. You might, for example, say you're not annoyed at a friend's teasing in order to prevent the hassle that would result if you expressed your annoyance. It's often easier to explain your behavior in dishonest terms than to make matters worse. You might explain your apparent annoyance by saying, "I'm not mad at you; it's just been a tough day."

3. *To guide social interaction.* Sometimes we lie to make everyday relationships run smoothly. You might, for instance, pretend to be glad to see someone you actually dislike or fake interest in a dinner companion's boring stories to make a social event pass quickly. Children who aren't skilled or interested in these social lies are often a source of embarrassment for their parents.

4. *To expand or reduce relationships.* Some lies are designed to make relationships grow: "You're going downtown? I'm headed that way. Can I give you a ride?" In one study, a majority of college students (both men and women) willingly lied to improve their chances of getting a date with an attractive partner. Their exaggerations and untruths covered a wide range of topics, including their attitudes about love, personality traits, income, past relationships, career skills,

and intelligence—all in the direction of making themselves more similar to the attractive prospects.[80]

Sometimes we tell untruths to *reduce* interaction with others: "I really have to go. I should be studying for a test tomorrow." At other times people lie to end a relationship entirely: "You're really great, but I'm just not ready to settle down yet."

5. *To gain power.* Sometimes we tell lies to show that we're in control of a situation. Turning down a last-minute request for a date by claiming you're busy can be one way to put yourself in a one-up position, saying in effect, "Don't expect me to sit around waiting for you to call." Lying to get confidential information—even for a good cause—also falls into the category of lying to gain power.

This five-part scheme isn't the only way to categorize lies. The taxonomy outlined in Table 8-1 is more complicated and covers some types of

TABLE 8-1   Types of White Lies and Their Frequency

	BENEFIT SELF	BENEFIT OTHER	BENEFIT THIRD PARTY
BASIC NEEDS	68	1	1
A. Acquire resources	29	0	0
B. Protect resources	39	1	1
AFFILIATION	128	1	6
A. Positive	65	0	0
1. Initiate interaction	8	0	0
2. Continue interaction	6	0	0
3. Avoid conflict	48	0	0
4. Obligatory acceptance	3	0	0
B. Negative	43	1	3
1. Avoid interaction	34	1	3
2. Leave-taking	9	0	0
C. Conversational control	20	0	3
1. Redirect conversation	3	0	0
2. Avoid self-disclosure	17	0	3
SELF-ESTEEM	35	63	1
A. Competence	8	26	0
B. Taste	0	18	1
C. Social desirability	27	19	0
OTHER	13	5	0
A. Dissonance reduction	3	5	0
B. Practical joke	2	0	0
C. Exaggeration	8	0	0

From "White Lies in Interpersonal Communication: A Taxonomy and Preliminary Investigation of Social Motivations" *Western Journal of Speech Communication* 48 (1984) (1984); P. 315

lies that don't fit into the simpler scheme. Exaggerations, for example, are lies told to boost the effect of a story. In exaggerated tales the fish grow larger, hikes grow longer and more strenuous, and so on. The stories may be less truthful, but they become more interesting—at least to the teller.

Most people think that white lies are told for the benefit of the recipient. In the study cited earlier, the majority of subjects claimed that such lying is "the right thing to do." Other research paints a less-flattering picture of who benefits most from lying. One study found that two out of every three lies are told for "selfish reasons."[81] A look at Table 8-1 seems to make this figure too conservative. Of the 322 lies recorded, 75.8 percent were for the benefit of the liar. Less than 22 percent were for the benefit of the person hearing the lie, whereas a mere 2.5 percent were intended to aid a third party.

Before we become totally cynical, however, the researchers urge a charitable interpretation. After all, most intentional communication behavior—truthful or not—is designed to help the speaker achieve a goal. Therefore, it's unfair to judge white lies more harshly than other types of messages. If we define selfishness as the extent to which some desired resource or interaction is denied to the person hearing the lie or to a third party, then only 111 lies (34.5 percent) can be considered truly selfish. This figure may be no worse than the degree of selfishness in honest messages.

Effects of Lies What are the consequences of discovering that you've been lied to? In an interpersonal relationship, the discovery can be traumatic. As we grow closer to others, our expectations about their honesty grow stronger. After all, discovering that you've been lied to requires you to redefine not only the lie you just discovered, but also many of the messages you previously took for granted. Was last week's compliment really sincere? Was your joke really funny, or was the other person's laughter a put-on? Does the other person care about you as much as he or she claimed?

Research has shown that lying does, in fact, threaten relationships.[82] Not all lies are equally devastating, however. Feelings like dismay and betrayal are greatest when the relationship is most intense, when the importance of the subject is high, and when there was previous suspicion that the other person wasn't being completely honest. Of these three factors, the importance of the information lied about proved to be the key factor in provoking a relational crisis. We may be able to cope with "misdemeanor" lying, but "felonies" are a grave threat.

An occasional white lie in an otherwise honest relationship doesn't pose much threat. Major deception, though—especially when it is part of a pattern of deceit—is likely to provoke a relational crisis. In fact, the discovery of major deception can lead to the end of the relationship. More than two-thirds of the subjects in one study reported that their relationship had ended because they discovered a lie. Furthermore, they attributed the breakup directly to the lie.

IS MISLEADING YOUR SPOUSE FRAUD OR TACT?

When their marriage of more than a decade ended in divorce, Anaheim banker Ronald Askew sued his ex-wife for fraud because she admittedly concealed the fact that she had never felt sexually attracted to him. On Wednesday, an Orange County jury agreed, and ordered Bonnette Askew to pay her ex-husband $242,000 in damages.

"I'm astonished by this verdict and I've looked at divorce in 62 societies," said Helen Fisher, an American Museum of Natural History anthropologist who authored the recent book *Anatomy of Love: The Natural History of Monogamy, Adultery and Divorce*.

Bonnette Askew, 45, acknowledged in court that she had never been sexually attracted to her husband. But she said she always loved him and noted that their marriage was not sexless and that they had two children together.

She first admitted her lack of sexual desire for him during a joint therapy session in 1991. "I guess he confused sex with love," Bonnette Askew said, adding that she concealed her lack of desire because she "didn't want to hurt his male ego."

But Ronald Askew, 50, said his lawsuit had more to do with honesty and integrity than sex. He felt deceived, especially because he said he repeatedly asked her before their marriage to be honest with him and reveal any important secrets.

If Ronald Askew believes total honesty is the foundation of good marriages, Fisher has a message for him: "Grow up."

"Since when is anyone truly honest with anyone?" Fisher said. "Did this man really want her to say: 'You're short, fat and you're terrible in bed'? Much of the world is amazed at what they see as brutal honesty in America. She was operating on an entirely different set of social values, which much of the world operates on—delicacy as opposed to brutal honesty."

Maria Cone, *Los Angeles Times*

The injunction against bearing false witness, branded in stone and brought down by Moses from the mountaintop, has always provoked ambivalent, conflicting emotions. On the one hand, nearly everyone condemns lying. On the other, nearly everyone does it every day. How many of the Ten Commandments can be broken so easily and with so little risk of detection over the telephone?

Paul Gray

The lesson here is clear: Lying about major parts of your relationship can have the most grave consequences. If preserving a relationship is important, honesty—at least about important matters—really does appear to be the best policy.

Equivocating

Lying isn't the only alternative to self-disclosure. When faced with the choice between lying and telling an unpleasant truth, communicators can—and often do—equivocate. As chapter 5 explained, **equivocal language** has two or more equally plausible meanings. Sometimes people send equivocal messages without meaning to, resulting in confusion. "I'll meet you at the apartment" could refer to more than one place. But at other times we are deliberately vague. For instance, when a friend asks what you think of an awful outfit, you could say "It's really unusual—one of a kind!" Likewise, if you are too angry to accept a friend's apology but don't want to appear petty, you might say, "Don't mention it."

The value of equivocation becomes clear when you consider the alternatives. Consider the dilemma of what to say when you've been given an unwanted present—that ugly painting we mentioned before, for example—and the giver asks what you think of it. How can you respond? On one hand, you need to choose between telling the truth and lying. On the other hand, you have a choice of whether to make your response clear or vague. Figure 8-13 displays these choices. After considering the choices, it's clear that the first—an equivocal, true response—is far preferable to the others in several respects.

- **It spares the receiver from embarrassment.** For example, rather than flatly saying, "No" to an unappealing invitation, it may be kinder to say, "I have other plans"—even if those plans are to stay home and watch TV.

- **It can save face for both the sender and receiver.** Because equivocation is often easier to take than the cold, hard truth, it spares the teller from feeling guilty. It's less taxing on the conscience to say, "I've never tasted anything like this" than to say, "This meal tastes terrible," even though the latter comment is more precise. Few people want to lie, and equivocation provides an alternative to deceit.

A study by communication researcher Sandra Metts and her colleagues shows how equivocation can save face in difficult situations.[83] Several hundred college students were asked how they would turn down

	Equivocal	
True	OPTION I: (Equivocal, True Message) "What an unusual painting! I've never seen anything like it!"	OPTION II: (Equivocal, False Message) "Thanks for the painting. I'll hang it as soon as I can find just the right place."
	OPTION III: (Clear, True Message) "It's just not my kind of painting. I don't like the colors, the style, or the subject."	OPTION IV: (Clear, False Message) "What a beautiful painting! I love it."	**False**
	Clear	

FIGURE 8-13 Dimensions of Truthfulness and Equivocation

DILBERT® BY SCOTT ADAMS

DOGBERT, SOMETIMES I THINK YOU'RE THE ONLY ONE WHO RESPECTS ME.

WRONG.

MAYBE I SHOULD DROP IT WHILE THERE'S STILL SOME AMBIGUITY.

Dilbert reprinted by permission of United Feature Syndicate, Inc.

unwanted sexual overtures from a person whose feelings were important to them: either a close friend, a prospective date, or a dating partner. The majority of students chose a diplomatic reaction ("I just don't think I'm ready for this right now") as being more face-saving and comfortable than a direct statement ("I just don't feel sexually attracted to you"). The diplomatic reaction seemed sufficiently clear to get the message across but not so blunt as to embarrass or even humiliate the other person.

■ **It provides an alternative to lying.** If a potential employer asks about your grades during an interview, you would be safe saying, "I had a *B* average last semester," even though your overall grade average is closer to *C*. The statement isn't a complete answer, but it is honest as far as it goes. As one team of researchers put it, "equivocation is neither a false message nor a clear truth, but rather an alternative used precisely when both of these are to be avoided."[84]

Given these advantages, it's not surprising that most people will usually choose to equivocate rather than tell a lie. In a series of experiments, subjects chose between telling a face-saving lie, telling the truth, and equivocating. Only 6 percent chose the lie, and only between 3 and 4 percent chose the hurtful truth. By contrast, over 90 percent chose the equivocal response.[85] People *say* they prefer truthtelling to equivocating, but given the choice, they prefer to finesse the truth.[86]

Hinting

Hints are more direct than equivocal statements. Whereas an equivocal statement isn't necessarily aimed at changing others' behavior, a hint does aim to get a desired response from others.[87]

How does a business person provide a positive reference for an incompetent friend? Lehigh University professor Robert Thorton suggests that equivocation provides a middle way between the brutal truth and a misleading lie. A few examples:

For a lazy worker:
"You will be lucky to get this person to work for you."

For someone with no talent:
"I recommend this candidate with no qualifications."

For a candidate who should not be hired under any circumstances:
"I can assure you that no person will be better for the job" or "Waste no time hiring this person."

Mixed Blessings

DIRECT STATEMENT	FACE-SAVING HINT
I'm too busy to continue with this conversation.	I wish you would let me go. I know you're busy; I'd better let you go.
Please don't smoke here because it is bothering me.	I'm pretty sure that smoking isn't permitted here.
I'd like to invite you out for lunch, but I don't want to risk a "no" answer.	Gee, it's almost lunchtime. Have you ever eaten at that new Italian restaurant around the corner?

The face-saving value of hints explains why communicators are more likely to be indirect than fully disclosing when they deliver a potentially embarrassing message.[88] The success of a hint depends on the other person's ability to pick up the unexpressed message. Your subtle remarks might go right over the head of an insensitive receiver—or one who chooses not to respond. If this happens, you may decide to be more direct. On the other hand, if the costs of a direct message seem too high, you can withdraw without risk.

The Ethics of Evasion

It's easy to see why people choose hints, equivocations, and white lies instead of complete self-disclosure. These strategies provide a way to manage difficult situations that is easier than the alternatives for both the speaker and the receiver of the message. In this sense, successful liars, equivocators, and hinters can be said to possess a certain kind of communicative competence. On the other hand, there are certainly times when honesty is the right approach, even if it's painful. At times like these, evaders could be viewed as lacking the competence or the integrity to handle a situation most effectively.

Are hints, white lies, and equivocations ethical alternatives to self-disclosure? Some of the examples in these pages suggest that the answer is a qualified "yes." Many social scientists and philosophers agree. As the "Ethical Challenge" on page 359 shows, some argue that the morality of a speaker's *motives* for lying, not the lie itself, ought to be judged, and others ask whether the *effects* of a lie will be worth the deception.

Another measure of the acceptability of some lies is the fact that most people are willing to accept them without challenging the person who they know is lying. In fact, there are some circumstances when lies are judged as *more* appropriate than the undiluted truth.[89] For example, there are some circumstances when we are likely to not challenge statements that we know are untruthful:[90]

1. When we expect others tell a fib. (You listen with amusement to a friend's or relative's tall tales, even though you know they are exaggerations.)
2. When the lie is mutually advantageous. (A fellow employee's self-serving account of a job mixup might get you off the hook, too.)

ETHICAL CHALLENGE

Must We Always Tell the Truth?

"Is there really a Santa Claus?"

"Am I talking too much?"

"Isn't this the cutest baby you've ever seen?"

"Was it good for you?"

Questions like these often seem to invite answers that are less than totally honest. The research summarized on pages 350–358 reveals that, at one time or another, virtually everyone avoids telling the complete truth. Sometimes we remain silent, sometimes we tell "white lies," and sometimes we equivocate. We seem to be caught between the time-honored commandment "Thou shall not lie" and the fact that everybody *does* seem to bend the truth, if only for altruistic reasons. What, then, are the ethics of honesty?

Philosopher Immanuel Kant had a clear answer: We may be able to evade unpleasant situations by keeping quiet, but we must always tell the complete truth when there is no way to avoid speaking up. He said that "truthfulness in statements which cannot be avoided is the formal duty of an individual . . . however great may be the disadvantage accruing to himself or another." Kant's unbending position didn't make any exception for lies or equivocations told in the best interests of the receiver. In his moral code, lying is wrong—period.

Kant's unbending position grows from his *categorical imperative*: the

dictum that the morality of an action is determined by whether it could be practiced universally. At one level, the categorical imperative demands that we ask, "What if everybody lied?" Because it would be intolerable—even impossible—to function in a world in which everyone lied, we have an ethical obligation to refrain from lying, even once.

Not all ethicists have shared Kant's rigid standards of truthtelling. Utilitarian philosophers claim that the way to determine the morality of a behavior is to explore whether it leads to the greatest happiness for the greatest number of people. Philosopher Sissela Bok adopts this stance when she argues that the morality (or immorality) of an untruth can be calculated only by comparing its effect to that of telling the unvarnished truth. She offers some circumstances in which deception may be justified: doing good, avoiding harm, and protecting a larger truth.

Despite her tolerance for some lies, Bok doesn't consider benign falsehoods to be just as acceptable as the truth. Her *principle of veracity* asserts that "truthful statements are preferable to lying in the absence of special considerations." In other words, she encourages truthtelling whenever possible. Of course, the phrase "wherever possible" is open to interpretation, and Bok is realistic enough to recognize that liars are

prone to self-deceptive justifications. For this reason, she tempers her utilitarian position with a *test of publicity*. She suggests that we ask how others would respond if they knew that we were being untruthful. If most disinterested observers with all the facts supported untruthful speech as the best course, then it passes the test of publicity.

Submit your case for avoiding the truth to a "court of self-disclosure":

1. Recall recent situations in which you have used each of the following evasive approaches: lying, equivocating, and hinting.

2. Write an anonymous description of each situation, including a justification for your behavior, on a separate sheet of paper. Submit the cases to a panel of "judges" (most likely fellow students), who will evaluate the morality of these decisions.

Read Kant's own words on truthtelling in the following works: "On a Supposed Right to Lie from Altruistic Motives" in *Critique of Practical Reason and Other Writings in Moral Philosophy,* Lewis White Beck, trans. and ed., Chicago: University of Chicago Press, 1964; and *Groundwork of the Metaphysic of Morals,* H. J. Paton, trans., New York: Harper Torchbooks, 1964. Bok's arguments are detailed in her book *Lying: Moral Choice in Public and Private Life,* New York: Vintage, 1979. See also Charles Fried's essay "The Evil of Lying" in *Right and Wrong,* Cambridge, Mass.: Harvard University Press, 1978.

3. When a lie helps us avoid embarrassment. (You assure your host that a meal was delicious, even though it tasted awful.)

4. When the lie helps us avoid confronting an unpleasant truth. (A family acts as if there is nothing wrong when they know that one member is an alcoholic.)

5. When we have asked the other person to lie. (One partner tells the other: "If you're ever unfaithful to me, I don't want to know about it.")

In light of these facts, perhaps the right questions to ask are whether an indirect message is truly in the interests of the receiver and whether this sort of evasion is the only, or the best, way to behave in a given situation.

SUMMARY

People form interpersonal relationships for a variety of reasons. Some reasons involve the degree of interpersonal attraction that communicators feel for one another. Attraction can come from perceived similarity, complementary personality features, reciprocal interest, perceived competence, disclosure of personal information, and proximity. People also form relationships to satisfy their need for intimacy, which they can achieve through physical means, intellectual and emotional exchanges, and shared activities. Intimacy is not essential to all relationships, and even in relationships where it is important, it is not important all the time. Gender and culture exert a strong influence on both the amount of intimacy in a relationship and how that intimacy is communicated. People also form relationships to achieve various types of rewards. Social exchange theory presents a method for explaining when people will choose to form and remain in relationships by showing how they compare their present situation to other alternatives.

Two models offer somewhat different perspectives on how communication operates in the development and maintenance of interpersonal relationships. A stage-related model characterizes communication as exhibiting different characteristics as people come together and draw apart. A dialectical model characterizes communicators in every stage as being driven by the need to manage a variety of mutually incompatible needs. Both models share a variety of characteristics.

An important issue in interpersonal relationships is the appropriate type and degree of self-disclosure: honest, revealing messages about the self that are intentionally directed toward others. Self-disclosing communication contains information that is generally unavailable via other sources. Revealing personal information does not guarantee that this information will be perceived by others as disclosing. A number of factors govern whether a communicator will be judged as being a high- or low-level discloser. The social penetration model describes two dimensions of self-disclosure: breadth and depth. Disclosure of feelings is usually more revealing than disclosure of opinions, and disclosure of opinions is usually more revealing than disclosure of facts. Clichés are the least revealing.

The Johari Window model is a useful way to illustrate self-disclosure. A window representing a single person can illustrate the amount of information that individual reveals to others, hides, is blind to, and is unaware of. Windows representing two communicators reveal how differing levels of disclosure can affect the level of intimacy in a relationship.

Communicators disclose personal information for a variety of reasons: catharsis, self-clarification, self-validation, reciprocal obligations, impression formation, relationship maintenance and enhancement, social control, and manipulation.

The percentage of messages that are self-disclosing is relatively low. Three alternatives to revealing personal facts, feelings, and opinions are lying, equivocating, and hinting. Unmalicious "white lies" serve a variety of functions: saving face for the sender or receiver, avoiding tension or conflict, guiding social interaction, managing relationships, and gaining power. When discovered by the recipient, lies have the potential to provoke a relational crisis, especially if the content of the information lied about is significant. Equivocal messages are an attractive alternative to lies and direct honesty.

They allow a communicator to be honest without being blunt and causing undesirable reaction. Hints, which are more direct than equivocal statements, are used primarily to avoid embarrassment. Hints are risky because they depend on the other person's ability to pick up unexpressed messages. Lies, equivocations, and hints may be ethical alternatives to self-disclosure; however, whether they are depends on the speaker's motives and the effects of the deception.

KEY TERMS

avoiding	differentiating	openness-privacy dialectic
bonding	equivocal language	predictability-novelty dialectic
breadth	experimenting	relational maintenance
circumscribing	initiating	self-disclosure
clichés	integrating	social penetration
connection-autonomy dialectic	intensifying	stagnating
depth	intimacy	terminating
dialectical tension	Johari Window	"white lie"

LOOKING OUT/LOOKING IN ONLINE

Use your *Looking Out/Looking In* CD-ROM for quick access to the electronic resources that accompany this chapter. Included on this CD-ROM are additional study aids and links to the *Looking Out/Looking In* Web site at the Wadsworth Communication Café. The CD-ROM is your gateway to a wealth of resources that will help you understand and further explore the material in this chapter. **Video clips** under *Communication Scenarios* on the CD illustrate the skills introduced in this chapter. Click on the Web site link to complete self-study **review quizzes** to help you master new concepts; access a **feature film database** to locate clips and entire movies that illustrate communication principles; find Internet material via the maintained **Web site links;** and complete **online activities** to help you master new concepts.

INFOTRAC COLLEGE EDITION EXERCISES

Use the InfoTrac College Edition password that was included free with a copy of this new text to answer the following questions. These questions can be completed online and, if requested, submitted to your instructor under InfoTrac College Edition Activities at the *Looking Out/Looking In* Web site.

1. Why We Form Relationships

Using PowerTrac, search for articles on starting and maintaining a relationship. Find at least one piece of information that expands your understanding of how relationships develop. Write a brief summary of the article you have chosen. Include a citation (title, author, publication, date), brief description of the article's main idea, and your reaction to the point it makes.

2. Intimacy

Use PowerTrac to locate the article "Intimacy: The Art of Working out Your Relationships" by Lori H. Gordon (Hint: Use the author and title fields to locate this article.) On what dimensions of intimacy defined in Chapter 8 does the author focus? What level of intimacy does she advocate? What advice does she offer for achieving the desired level of intimacy? How could you apply the suggestions in this article to your important relationships?

3. Guidelines for Self-Disclosure

Use PowerTrac to locate the article "Nothing But the Truth . . ." by Caralee Adams. (Hint: Use the author and title fields to locate this article.) Based on what you read here, decide (a) to what extent are you willing to share sensitive personal information with people in your important relationships? (b) How much information do you really want others to disclose to you? If you prefer less than total disclosure, explain the criteria that determine what information you are and aren't interested in disclosing and receiving.

READINGS

Aronson, Eliot. *The Social Animal*, 8th ed. New York: Worth, 1999.

Chapter 9 of this well-written book is titled "Liking, Loving, and Interpersonal Sensitivity." It offers a clear, readable survey of the factors influencing interpersonal attraction.

Baxter, Leslie, and Barbara Montgomery. *Relating: Dialogues and Dialectics.* New York: Guilford, 1996.

This book explains in detail the dialectical perspective on relational maintenance. For serious readers, it offers a compelling argument that relationships are in constant flux and suggests ways that communicators can manage the inevitable tensions that will never disappear.

Chovil, Nicole. "Equivocation as an Interactional Event" in *The Dark Side of Interpersonal Communication*, William R. Cupach and Brian H. Spitzberg, eds. Hillsdale, N.J.: Erlbaum, 1994.

This chapter describes how equivocal communication can be a form of "strategic ambiguity" that greases the wheels of social interaction. Chovil outlines the types of equivocal messages and identifies situations that elicit them.

Petronio, Sandra. *Balancing the Secrets of Private Disclosures.* New York: Lawrence Erlbaum, 2000.
This collection of readings examines how we juggle disclosure, privacy, and secrecy in our relationships with one another. Chapters by top scholars in the field offer useful resources for readers who want to explore these issues in greater depth.

FILMS

In addition to the films suggested here, go to the **Film in Communication Database** at the *Looking Out/Looking In* Web site to locate movie clips that illustrate various relational dynamics.

Gender and Intimacy

Diner (1982) Rated R

This story takes place in the late 1950s, but update a few of the details, and it could take place today. Members of a group of guys have been out of high school for a year or two. Billy (Timothy Daly) has gone away to college. Boogie (Mickey Rourke) is working his way through school while holding down a job. Shrevie (Daniel Stern) has married his high school sweetheart, Beth (Ellen Barkin). Eddie (Steve Gutenberg) is engaged but isn't quite sure why he is getting married. Fenwick (Kevin Bacon) is probably the smartest of the group, but he is drowning the unhappiness of his life in alcohol.

Viewed from one perspective, the film looks like an indictment of the lack of intimacy in contemporary society. The guys have been friends for years, but they never express their obvious caring for one another. Their relationships with women seem distant at best: Shrevie confesses that marriage has taken the fun out of sex, and the strongest emotion he seems to feel toward his wife is anger when she forgets to put his records back on the shelf in alphabetical order. Boogie tries to pay back his gambling debts by seducing women while his friends watch in hiding. Eddie states that he will marry his fiancée only if she passes a football trivia test. This movie hardly seems like a textbook example of interpersonal communication.

However, a closer viewing of the movie shows some strong examples of close relationships. Fenwick swallows his pride and asks his sanctimonious brother for money to save Boogie from a beating by the small-time hoods who have lent him money. Boogie confesses his seductive strategy to Beth, when he could have gotten away with his plan and paid off his debt. Under director Barry Levinson's guidance, the buddies from the diner behave in ways that make their affection—even their love—for one another clear. This story is a clear illustration of traditionally male approaches to intimacy discussed on pages 319–321 of this chapter. The friends may not talk about their feelings toward one another, but through shared activities and the exchange of favors, they show they care. They know, and we know, too.

Dialectical Tensions in Male-Female Relationships

The Brothers McMullen (1995) Rated R

Gender research suggests that when it comes to dialectical tensions in relationships, men and women often have competing goals. The data generally indicate that men want autonomy whereas women want connection; men are more private whereas women are more open; men like novelty whereas women like predictability.

At first glance, *The Brothers McMullen* seems to illustrate this sort of gender difference. Three brothers—Barry (Edward Burns), Patrick (Mike McGlone), and Jack (Jack Mulcahy)—live up to male stereotypes. Barry is a carefree bachelor who doesn't want commitment. Patrick has mixed emotions about two women and doesn't know how to say what he feels (at least to them). Jack is married but is having an affair. Respectively, they typify autonomy, privacy, and novelty.

But it's not that simple. By movie's end, Barry recognizes and acts on his need for an intimate relationship. Patrick gets in touch with his feelings and declares them to the woman he loves. Jack returns to his marriage after his affair proves unfulfilling. The moral to the story? Dialectical tensions are a part of every human relationship, regardless of gender. Although there may be gender-based tendencies, every person in a relationship must come to grips with both the push and the pull of relational dialectics.

Self-Disclosure

Liar, Liar (1997) Rated PG-13

Fletcher Reed (Jim Carey) is a charming, smooth-talking attorney who says whatever is necessary to get what he wants, regardless of the truth. Reed tells expedient lies away from work, too, and now his five-year-old son Max (Justin Cooper) no longer believes a word his father says. "My dad's a liar," the boy announces in school. "You mean a *lawyer*," his teacher says. Max shrugs his shoulders, as if to say, "What's the difference?"

When Fletcher fails to show up for Max's birthday party, the boy makes a wish as he blows out the candles: that for just one day his dad won't tell a single lie. This wish comes true, and we are treated to a vision of what life would be like if people were totally honest. Much of the film draws laughs by presenting humorous scenarios arising from the fantasy of an attorney telling the entire truth. But the film isn't just an exercise in lawyer-bashing: Viewers also get an amusing look at why total self-disclosure is unrealistic in everyday situations. "How are you today?" a judge asks Fletcher. "I'm a little upset about a bad sexual episode last night," he replies. In a hilarious scene, Fletcher creates an uproar at work by telling his colleagues and bosses his true opinion of them.

At the most simplistic level, *Liar, Liar* argues that healthy relationships demand honesty and attention. But, for more sophisticated communication analysts, it also argues that total honesty can be as risky as lying.

Secrets & Lies (1996) Rated R

Secrets & Lies chronicles the relational fallout when a black, adopted London optometrist named Hortense (Marianne Jean-Baptiste) discovers that her birth mother, Cynthia (Brenda Blethyn), is white. Hortense persuades the reluctant Cynthia that they should meet. The well-educated daughter and working-class mother strike a bond and over time grow steadily closer. Despite her affection and pride for Hortense, Cynthia keeps her daughter's existence a secret from the rest of her family.

The film's other plot line revolves around Cynthia's relationship with her affluent brother Maurice (Timothy Spall), who hasn't called her in over two years. Cynthia blames Maurice's style-conscious wife Monica (Phyllis Logan) for the long silence. As the story develops, we learn that the childless Maurice and Cynthia have their own secrets.

The family's secrets and lies begin to unravel when Cynthia brings Hortense to a family party, introducing her as a "friend from work." In the film's breathtakingly funny and poignant finale we see the characters emerge from their web of secrets and lies and move toward relationships based on a closer understanding of one another.

Despite the emotionally explosive material, *Secrets & Lies* is an enjoyable film. And though few viewers are likely to experience the specific dilemmas faced by its characters, the story offers a compelling look at the advantages and disadvantages of self-disclosure that all of us face.

LOOKING OUT/LOOKING IN CD-ROM

Using your *Looking Out/Looking In* CD-ROM, click on *Communication Scenarios* and then click on the "Self-Disclosure" icon to watch and analyze a dramatized version of the conversation featured in the Communication Transcript on page 351.

CHAPTER 9

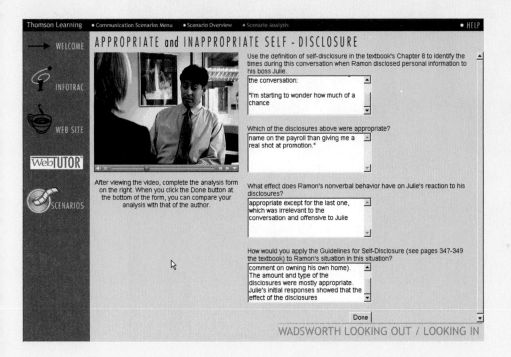

IMPROVING COMMUNICATION CLIMATES

Personal relationships are a lot like the weather. Some are fair and warm, whereas others are stormy and cold; some are polluted, and others healthy. Some relationships have stable climates, whereas others change dramatically—calm one moment and turbulent the next. You can't measure the interpersonal climate by looking at a thermometer or glancing at the sky, but it's there nonetheless. Every relationship has a feeling, a pervasive mood that colors the interactions of the participants.

Although we can't change the external weather, we *can* change an interpersonal climate. This chapter will explain the forces that make some relationships pleasant and others unpleasant. You will learn what kinds of behavior contribute to defensiveness and hostility and what kinds lead to more positive feelings. After reading these pages you will have a better idea of the climate in each of your important relationships—and even more important, how to improve it.

COMMUNICATION CLIMATE: THE KEY TO POSITIVE RELATIONSHIPS

The term **communication climate** refers to the emotional tone of a relationship. A climate doesn't involve specific activities as much as the way people feel about each other as they carry out those activities. Consider two interpersonal communication classes, for example. Both meet for the same length of time and follow the same syllabus. It's easy to imagine how one of these classes might be a friendly, comfortable place to learn, whereas the other could be cold and tense—even hostile. The same principle holds in other contexts. The role of climate in families and friendships is obvious. So is the impact of climate in the workplace. Have you ever held a job where backbiting, criticism, and suspicion were the norm? Or have you been lucky enough to hold a job where the atmosphere was positive, encouraging, and supportive? If you've experienced both, you know what a difference climate makes.

It's hard to overstate the importance of a positive communication climate. It is the best predictor of marital satisfaction.[1] Satisfied couples have a 5:1 ratio of positive to negative statements, whereas the ratio for dissatisfied couples is 1:1.[2] Positive, confirming messages are just as important in families. For example, the satisfaction that siblings feel with one another drops sharply as aggressive, disconfirming messages increase.[3] The same principle holds on the job: Employees have a higher level of commitment at jobs in which they experience a positive communication climate.[4] Studies also show that performance and job satisfaction increase when the communication climate is positive.[5] In school, teacher confirmation plays a significant role in college students' learning.[6] Whether it's the workplace, the classroom, or the home, people thrive in communication climates that affirm and support them.

Like their meteorological counterparts, communication climates are shared by everyone involved. It's rare to find one person describing a relationship as open and positive whereas another describes it as cold and hostile. Also, just like the weather, communication climates can change over time. A relationship can be overcast at one time and sunny at another. Carrying the analogy to its conclusion, we need to acknowledge that communication climate forecasting is not a perfect science. Unlike the weather, however, people can change the communication climates in their relationships. In this chapter we will explore ways to make your communication climates as satisfying as possible. We will begin by describing how communication climates develop. Next, we will explain how and why communicators respond defensively in certain climates. Finally—and most important—we will discuss what can be done to create positive climates and transform negative ones.

I've learned that being kind is more important than being right.

Andy Rooney

Confirming and Disconfirming Communications

What makes a communication climate positive or negative? In large part, the answer is surprisingly simple. The climate of a relationship is shaped by the degree to which the people believe themselves to be *valued* by one another.

Social scientists use the term **confirming communication** to describe messages that convey valuing, and **disconfirming communication** to describe those that show a lack of regard. It's obvious that confirming messages are more desirable than disconfirming ones. But what characteristics distinguish them? Actually, it's an oversimplification to talk about one type of confirming message.

Like beauty, the decision about whether a message is confirming or disconfirming is up to the beholder.[7] Consider, for example, times when you took a comment that might have sounded unsupportive to an outsider ("You turkey!") as a sign of affection within the context of your personal relationship. Likewise, a comment that the sender might have meant to be helpful ("I'm telling you this for your own good . . .") could easily be regarded as a disconfirming attack.

Types of Confirming Messages

Even though there's no guarantee that others will receive even your best attempts at confirming messages the way you intend them, research shows that three increasingly positive types of messages have the best chance of being confirming.[8]

- *Recognition* The most fundamental act of confirmation is to recognize the other person. Recognition seems easy and obvious, and yet there are many times when we do not respond to others on this basic level. Failure to write or visit a friend is a common example. So is failure to return a phone message. Avoiding eye contact and not approaching someone you know on campus at a party or on the street

DISCONFIRMING MESSAGES

Disconfirming messages convey a lack of respect or appreciation. Like their confirming counterparts, these messages can shape the climate of an entire relationship.

Verbal Abuse

The most obvious type of disconfirming response is **verbal abuse:** communication that appears to be meant to cause psychological pain to another person. Where verbal abuse exists in a relationship, it is seldom an isolated event. Some abuse is overt, but at other times it can be disguised in malicious humor or sarcasm:

"Come here, fatty."

"You're such a bitch!"

Complaining

Simple **complaining** may be less intense than verbal abuse, but it can still send a powerful disconfirming message. Complaints may be about specific behavior. More abstract complaints can be especially disconfirming because they suggest that the flaw extends beyond one incident:

"I wish you would be more friendly."

"Why can't you clean up after yourself?"

"You need to have a more positive attitude."

Impervious Responses

Ignoring the other person's attempt to communicate characterizes an **impervious response.** Refusing to answer another person in a face-to-face conversation is the most obvious kind of impervious response, though not the most common. Failing to return a phone call and failing to write back in answer to a letter are more common impervious responses. So is not responding to a smile or a wave.

Interrupting

Beginning to speak before the other person has finished speaking can show a lack of concern about what the other person has to say. The occasional **interrupting response** is not likely to be taken as a disconfirmation, but repeatedly interrupting a speaker can be both discouraging and irritating.

Irrelevant Responses

A: comment unrelated to what the other person has just said is an **irrelevant response.**

A: What a day! I thought it would never end. First the car overheated, and I had to call a tow truck, and then the computer broke down at work.

B: Listen, we have to talk about a present for Ann's birthday. The party is on Saturday, and I have only tomorrow to shop for it.

A: I'm really beat. Could we talk about it in a few minutes? I've never seen a day like this one.

B: I just can't figure out what would suit Ann. She's got everything . . .

Tangential Responses

Conversational "take-aways" are called **tangential responses.** Instead of ignoring the speaker's remarks completely, the other party uses them as a starting point for a shift to a different topic.

A: I'd like to know for sure whether you want to go skiing during vacation. If we don't decide whether to go soon, it'll be impossible to get reservations anywhere.

B: Yeah. And if I don't pass my botany class, I won't be in the mood to go anywhere. Could you give me some help with this homework? . . .

Impersonal Responses

Impersonal responses are loaded with clichés and other statements that never truly respond to the speaker.

A: I've been having some personal problems lately, and I'd like to take off work early a couple of afternoons to clear them up.

B: Ah, yes. We all have personal problems. It seems to be a sign of the times.

Ambiguous Responses

Ambiguous responses contain messages with more than one meaning, leaving the other party unsure of the responder's position.

A: I'd like to get together with you soon. How about Tuesday?

B: Uh, maybe so.

A: Well, how about it? Can we talk Tuesday?

B: Oh, probably. See you later.

Incongruous Responses

An **incongruous response** contain two messages that seem to deny or contradict each other. Often at least one of these messages is nonverbal.

A: Darling, I love you.

B: I love you, too. (*giggles*)

put me in your human eye
come taste
the bitter tears
that I cry
touch me
with your human hand

hear me with your ear
but notice me
damn you
notice me
I'm here.

Ric Masten

send a negative message. Of course, this lack of recognition may simply be an oversight. You might not notice your friend, or the pressures of work and school might prevent you from staying in touch. Nonetheless, if the other person *perceives* you as avoiding contact, the message has the effect of being disconfirming.

■ *Acknowledgment* Acknowledging the ideas and feelings of others is a stronger form of confirmation. Listening is probably the most common form of acknowledgment. Of course, counterfeit listening—ambushing, stage-hogging, pseudolistening, and so on—has the opposite effect of acknowledgment. More active acknowledgment includes asking questions, paraphrasing, and reflecting. Not surprisingly, employees rate highly managers who solicit their opinions—even when the managers don't accept every opinion.[9] As you read in chapter 7, reflecting the speaker's thoughts and feelings can be a powerful way to offer support when others have problems.

■ *Endorsement* Whereas acknowledgment means that you are interested in another's ideas, endorsement means that you agree with them or otherwise find them important. It's easy to see why endorsement is the strongest type of confirming message because it communicates the highest form of valuing. The most obvious form of endorsement is agreeing. Fortunately, it isn't necessary to agree completely with another person in order to endorse her or his message. You can probably find something in the message that you endorse. "I can see why you were so angry," you might reply to a friend, even if you don't approve of his outburst. Of course, outright praise is a strong form of endorsement and one that you can use surprisingly often after you look for opportunities to compliment others. Nonverbal endorsement can also enhance the quality of a relational climate. For example, women rate men who agree with them as more physically attractive than those who fail to do so.[10]

In contrast to confirming communication, disconfirming communication shows a lack of regard for the other person, either by disputing or

Of all the Ten Commandments, "Thou shalt not murder" always seemed to me the one I would have to worry least about, until I got old enough to see that there are many different kinds of death, not all of them physical. There are murders as subtle as a turned eye. Dante was inspired to instill Satan in ice, cold indifference being so common a form of evil.

Anne Truitt, *Daybook*

The worst sin towards our fellow creatures is not to hate them, but to be indifferent to them; that's the essence of inhumanity.

George Bernard Shaw

ignoring some important part of that person's message.[11] Disagreement can be one way to disconfirm others, but not all disagreements are disconfirming—especially when compared to a total lack of acknowledgment. Most experts agree that it is psychologically healthier to have someone disagree with you than ignore you.[12] At its worst, a brutal disagreeing message can so devastate another person that the benefits of recognition and acknowledgment are lost. But in more constructive forms, disagreement includes two confirming components: recognition and acknowledgment. Communication researchers have demonstrated that constructive disagreements can lead to such benefits as enhanced self-concept,[13] communicative competence,[14] and positive climate in the workplace.[15] The key to maintaining a positive climate while arguing is the way you present your ideas. It is crucial to attack issues, not people. In addition, a sound argument is better received when it's delivered in a supportive, affirming manner.[16] The types of supportive messages outlined on pages 380–385 in this chapter show how it is possible to argue in a respectful, constructive way.

"Honey, please don't talk to Daddy when he's in a chat room."

©The New Yorker Collection 1997 Jack Ziegler from cartoonbank.com. All Rights Reserved.

Being ignored can be more disconfirming than being dismissed or attacked. The list of disconfirming responses on page 370 shows how impervious, interrupting, irrelevant, tangential, impersonal, ambiguous, and incongruous responses can show lack of respect for a communicator's importance.

It's important to note that disconfirming messages, like virtually every other kind of communication, are a matter of perception. Communicators are likely to downplay the significance of a potentially hurtful message that they consider to be unintentional.[17] On the other hand, even messages that aren't intended to devalue the other person can be interpreted as disconfirming. Your failure to return a phone call or respond to the letter of an out-of-town friend might simply be the result of a busy schedule; but if the other person views the lack of contact as a sign that you don't value the relationship, the effect can be powerful.

How Communication Climates Develop

As soon as two people start to communicate, a relational climate begins to develop. If their messages are confirming, the climate is likely to be a positive one. If their messages are disconfirming, the relationship is likely to be hostile, cold, or defensive.

Verbal messages certainly contribute to the climate of a relationship, but many climate-shaping messages are nonverbal. The very act of approaching others is confirming, whereas avoiding them can be disconfirming. Smiles or frowns, the presence or absence of eye contact, tone of voice, the use of personal space—all these and other cues send messages about how the parties feel toward one another.

After a climate is formed, it can take on a life of its own and grow in a self-perpetuating **spiral:** a reciprocating communication pattern in which each person's message reinforces the other's.[18] In positive spirals, one partner's confirming message leads to a similar message from the other person. This positive reaction leads the first person to be even more confirming. Negative spirals are just as powerful, though they leave the partners feeling worse about themselves and each other. Research shows how spirals operate in relationships to reinforce the principle that "what goes around comes around." In one study of married couples, each spouse's response in conflict situations was similar to the other's statement.[19] Conciliatory statements (for example, supporting, accepting responsibilities, agreeing) were likely to be followed by conciliatory responses. Confrontive acts (such as criticism, hostile questions, and faultfinding) were likely to trigger confrontive responses. The same pattern held for other kinds of messages: Avoidance begat avoidance, analysis begat analysis, and so on. Table 9-1

TABLE 9-1   Positive and Negative Reciprocal Communication Patterns

NEGATIVE RECIPROCAL PATTERNS

Pattern	Example
Complaint-countercomplaint	A: I wish you weren't so self-centered. B. Well, I wish you weren't so critical.
Disagreement-disagreement	A: Why are you so hard on Marta? She's a great boss. B. Are you kidding? She's the biggest phony I've ever seen. A. You wouldn't know a good boss if you saw one. B. Neither would you.
Mutual indifference	A: I don't care if you want to stay: I'm exhausted, and I'm getting out of here. B. Go ahead if you want, but find your own way home.
Arguments involving metacommunication	A: How can I talk when you won't listen? B. How can I listen when you won't talk?

POSITIVE RECIPROCAL PATTERNS

Pattern	Example
Validation of other's perspective	A: This assignment is really confusing. Nobody can figure out what we're supposed to do. B. I can understand how it might be unclear. Let me explain . . .
Recognizing similarities	A: I can't believe you want to take an expensive vacation! We should be saving money, not spending more! B: I agree we should be saving. But I think we can take this trip and still save some money. Let me show you what I've figured out . . .
Supportiveness	A: I'm going crazy with this job. It was supposed to be temporary. I have to do something different, and soon. B: I can see how much you hate it. Let's figure out how we can get the project finished soon, so you can get back to your regular work.

Adapted from *Competence in Interpersonal Conflict* by W. R. Cupach and D. J. Canary. Reproduced by permission The McGraw-Hill Companies.

illustrates some reciprocal communication patterns that have the potential to create positive and negative spirals.

Escalatory conflict spirals are the most visible way that disconfirming messages reinforce one another.[20] One attack leads to another until a skirmish escalates into a full-fledged battle:

A: (*mildly irritated*) Where were you? I thought we agreed to meet here a half-hour ago.

B: (*defensively*) I'm sorry. I got hung up at the library. I don't have as much free time as you do, you know.

A: I wasn't *blaming* you, so don't get so touchy. I do resent what you just said, though. I'm plenty busy. And I've got lots of better things to do than wait around for you!

B: Who's getting touchy? I just made a simple comment. You've sure been defensive lately. What's the matter with you?

Although they are less obvious, **de-escalatory conflict spirals** can also be destructive.[21] Rather than fighting, the parties slowly lessen their dependence on one another, withdraw, and become less invested in the relationship.

Spirals—whether positive or negative—rarely go on indefinitely. Most relationships pass through cycles of progression and regression. If the spiral is negative, partners may find the exchange growing so unpleasant that they switch from negative to positive messages without discussing the matter. In other cases they may engage in metacommunication. "Hold on," one might say. "This is getting us nowhere." In some cases, however, partners pass the "point of no return," leading to the breakup of a relationship. Even positive spirals have their limit: Even the best relationships go through periods of conflict and withdrawal, although a combination of time and communication skills can eventually bring the partners back into greater harmony.

INVITATION TO INSIGHT

EVALUATING COMMUNICATION CLIMATES

You can probably recognize the communication climate in each of your relationships without much analysis. But taking the following steps will help explain why these climates exist. Taking these steps may also suggest how to improve negative climates.

1. Identify the communication climate of an important interpersonal relationship. Using weather metaphors (sunny, gloomy, calm) may help.

2. List the confirming or disconfirming communications that created and now maintain this climate. Be sure to list both verbal and nonverbal messages.

3. Describe what you can do either to maintain the existing climate (if positive) or to change it (if negative). Again, list both verbal and nonverbal messages.

There is something I don't know
that I am supposed to know.
I don't know what it is I don't know,
and yet am supposed to know,
and I feel I look stupid if I seem both not to
    know it
and not know what it is I don't know.

Therefore I pretend I know it. This is
    nerve-wracking
since I don't know what I must pretend to know.
Therefore I pretend to know everything!

R. D. Laing

DEFENSIVENESS: CAUSES AND REMEDIES

Probably no type of communication pollutes an interpersonal climate more often than defensive spirals. One verbal attack leads to another, and soon the dispute mushrooms out of control, leaving an aftermath of hurt and bitterness that is difficult—sometimes even impossible—to repair.

The word **defensiveness** suggests guarding oneself from attack, but what kind of attack? Surely, few if any of the times you become defensive involve a physical threat. If you're not threatened by bodily injury, what *are* you guarding against? To answer this question we need to talk more about the notions of the presenting self and face introduced in chapter 2.

Recall that a person's face consists of the physical traits, personality characteristics, attitudes, aptitudes, and all the other parts of the image that he or she wants to present to the world. Actually, it is a mistake to talk about a single face: We try to project different faces to different people. You might, for instance, try to impress a potential employer with your seriousness but want your friends to see you as a joker. Of course, not all parts of your presenting self are equally significant. Letting others know that you are right-handed or a Gemini is probably less important to you than convincing them that you are good-looking or loyal.

When others are willing to accept and acknowledge important parts of our presenting image, there is no need to feel defensive. On the other hand, when others confront us with **face-threatening acts**—messages that seem to challenge the image we want to project—we are likely to resist their messages. Defensiveness, then, is the process of protecting our presenting self, our face.

You can understand how defensiveness operates by imagining what might happen if an important part of your presenting self were attacked. Suppose, for instance, that your boss criticized you for making a stupid

It is a curious psychological fact that the man who seems to be "egotistic" is not suffering from too much ego, but from too little.

Sydney J. Harris

mistake. Or consider how you would feel if a friend called you self-centered or your boss called you lazy. You would probably feel threatened if these attacks were unjustified. But notice that you might very well react defensively even if you knew deep inside that the attacks were justified. For instance, you have probably responded defensively at times when you *did* make a mistake, act selfishly, or cut corners on your work. In fact, we often feel most defensive when criticism is right on target.[22] The drive to defend a presenting image—even when it is false—leads some people to act in destructive ways, such as being sarcastic or verbally abusive.[23]

One reason for such defensiveness has to do with our need for approval. In response to the question "Why am I afraid to tell you who I am?" author John Powell quotes one actual response: "Because if I tell you who I am, you may not like who I am, and that is all I have."[24] So one reason why we wear defensive masks is to appear to be the kind of person who will gain the approval of others.

Responding defensively to unpleasant but accurate criticism involves fooling not only others but also ourselves. We want to believe the act we're putting on because it's uncomfortable to admit that we are not the person we would like to be. When faced with a situation where the truth might hurt, we are tempted to convince ourselves that we do fit the idealized picture we have constructed.

Types of Defensive Reactions

When a part of your presenting self is attacked by others and you aren't willing to accept their judgment, you are faced with what psychologists call **cognitive dissonance**—an inconsistency between two conflicting pieces of information, attitudes, or behavior.[25] Dissonance is an uncomfortable condition, and communicators strive to resolve it by seeking consistency. One way to eliminate the dissonance, of course, is to accept the critic's judgment and revise your presenting self accordingly. You could agree that you were stupid or mistaken, for example. Sometimes, however, you aren't willing to accept judgments. The accusations of your critic may be false. And even if they are true, you may be unwilling to admit their truth. It isn't pleasant to admit that you were lazy, unfair, or foolish. There are three broad ways to resolve dissonance without agreeing with a critic. Each of them is characterized by **defense mechanisms:** psychological devices that resolve dissonance by maintaining a positive presenting image.

Attacking the Critic
Counterattacking follows the old maxim that the best defense is a good offense. Attacking defensive maneuvers can take several forms.

- *Verbal aggression* Sometimes the recipient uses **verbal aggression** to assault the critic directly. "Where do you get off calling me sloppy?" you might storm to a roommate. "You're the one who leaves globs of

I seem to get the most defensive when I think something I have done is "bad." The judgment as to what is bad is a judgment of mine as well as others around me. It cuts the most when someone else's judgment of me agrees with my own bad impression of myself.

John T. Wood

toothpaste in the sink and dirty clothes all over the bedroom!" This sort of response shifts the blame onto the critic, without acknowledging that the original judgment might be true. Other attacks on the critic are completely off the subject: "You're in no position to complain about my sloppiness. At least I pay my share of the bills on time." Again, this response resolves the dissonance without ever addressing the validity of the attack.

■ *Sarcasm* Disguising the counterattack in a barbed, humorous message of **sarcasm** is a less-direct form of aggression. "You think I ought to study more? Thanks for taking a break from watching soap operas and eating junk food to run my life." Sarcastic responses might score high on wit and quick thinking, but their hostile, disconfirming nature usually leads to a counterattack and a mutually destructive defensive spiral.

Distorting Critical Information
A second way of defending a perceived self under attack is to somehow distort the critical information in a manner that leaves the presenting self intact—at least in the eyes of the defender. There are a number of ways to distort critical information.

■ *Rationalization* **Rationalization** is the invention of logical but untrue explanations of behavior that is unacceptable to the self. "I would help you out, but I really have to study," you might say as a convenient way to avoid an unpleasant chore. "I'm not overeating," you might protest to another critic who you secretly admit is on target. "I have a busy day ahead, and I need to keep my strength up." (See Table 9-2 for other examples.)

■ *Compensation* Those using **compensation** emphasize a strength in one area to cover up a weakness in another. A guilty parent might keep up the façade of being conscientious by protesting, "I may not be around much, but I give those kids the best things money can buy!"

TABLE 9-2 **Rationalization Reader for Students**

SITUATION	WHAT TO SAY
When the course is offered in lecture format:	We never get a chance to say anything.
When the course is offered in discussion format:	The professor just sits there. We don't know how to teach the course.
When all aspects of the course are covered in class:	All she does is follow the text.
When you're responsible for covering part of the course outside class:	She never covers half the things we're tested on.
When you're given objective tests:	They don't allow for any individuality.
When you're given essay tests:	They're too vague. We never know what's expected.
When the instructor gives no tests:	It isn't fair! She can't tell how much we really know.

Likewise, you might try to convince yourself and others that you are a good friend by compensating: "Sorry I forgot your birthday. Let me give you a hand with that job." There's nothing wrong with most acts of compensation in themselves. The harm comes when they are used not sincerely but rather insincerely to maintain a fictitious presenting image.

- *Regression* Another way to avoid facing attack is to play helpless, claiming you *can't* do something when in truth you *don't want* to do it. "I'd like to have a relationship with you, but I just can't: I'm not ready." "I wish I could do the job better, but I just can't: I just don't understand it." The test for **regression** is to substitute the word *won't* for *can't*. In many cases it becomes clear that "It's not my fault" is a fiction.

Avoiding Dissonant Information

A third way to protect a threatened presenting image is to avoid information altogether. Avoidance can take several forms.

- *Physical avoidance* Steering clear of people who attack a presenting self is an obvious way to avoid dissonance. Sometimes **physical avoidance** may be wise. There's little profit in being battered by hostile or abusive criticism. At other times, however, the relationship may be important enough and the criticism valid enough that avoiding the situation makes matters only worse.

- *Repression* Sometimes we mentally block out dissonant information. You might, for instance, know that you ought to discuss a problem with a friend, boss, or instructor, yet you put the idea out of your mind whenever it arises. It's possible even to repress a problem in the face of a critic. Changing the subject, acting as if you don't understand, and even pretending you don't hear the criticism all fall into the category of **repression.**

- *Apathy* Another avoidance response, **apathy,** involves acknowledging unpleasant information but pretending that you don't care about it. You might, for instance, sit calmly through a friend's criticism and act as if it didn't bother you. Similarly, you might respond to the loss of a job by acting indifferent: "Who cares? It was a dumb job anyhow."

- *Displacement* **Displacement** occurs when we vent aggressive or hostile feelings against people or objects that are seen as less threatening than the people or objects that threatened us originally. You may be mad at your boss, but rather than risk getting fired, you could displace your aggression by yelling at the people you live with. Despite its obvious costs, displacement almost always lets us preserve (at least to ourselves) the image that we're *potent*—that we're in control and can't be pushed around by forces beyond our control. The very act of displacing proves this a lie, of course—but a lie that the displacer fails to recognize.

I Am a Rock

A winter's day
In a deep and dark December
I am alone
Gazing from my window
To the streets below
On a freshly fallen silent shroud of snow
I am a rock
I am an island.

I built walls
A fortress deep and mighty
That none may penetrate
I have no need of friendship
Friendship causes pain
Its laughter and its loving I disdain
I am a rock
I am an island.

Don't talk of love
Well, I've heard the word before
It's sleeping in my memory
I won't disturb the slumber
Of feelings that have died
If I'd never loved I never would have cried
I am a rock
I am an island.

I have my books
And my poetry to protect me.
I am shielded in armor
Hiding in my room
Safe within my womb
I touch no one and no one touches me
I am a rock
I am an island.

And a rock feels no pain
And an island never cries.

Paul Simon

INVITATION TO INSIGHT

DEFENSE MECHANISM INVENTORY

List the three defense mechanisms you use most often, and describe three recent examples of each. You can arrive at your list both by thinking about your own behavior and by asking others to share their impressions of you. Conclude your inventory by describing:

1. The people with whom you become defensive most often

2. The parts of your presenting self you frequently defend

3. The usual consequences of using defense mechanisms

4. Any more-satisfying ways you could act in the future

Preventing Defensiveness in Others

So far, we have talked about defensiveness as if it is the responsibility of only the person who feels threatened. If this was the case, then the prescription would be simple: Grow a thick skin, admit your flaws, and stop trying to manage impressions. This prescription isn't just unrealistic: It ignores the role played by those who send face-threatening messages. In fact, competent communicators protect others' face needs as well as their own.[26]

You probably recognize that the best chances for creating a favorable response come from sending messages that honor the other person's face by supporting his or her presenting self.[27] These facts might leave you caught in an apparent bind, asking yourself how to send a face-honoring message when you have a genuine gripe with someone.

The solution to this dilemma lies in the two-dimensional nature of communication. On a content level you can express dissatisfaction with the other person, but on a relational level you can say—verbally or nonverbally—that you value him or her. The possibility of handling potentially delicate issues in ways that improve your relationships may seem overwhelming, but the influential work of researcher Jack Gibb offers some useful tools for controlling defensiveness.[28] After observing groups for several years, Gibb was able to isolate six types of defense-arousing communication and six contrasting behaviors that seemed to reduce the level of threat and defensiveness by conveying face-honoring relational messages of respect. The **Gibb categories** are listed in Table 9-3 and summarized in the following pages.

Evaluation vs. Description The first type of defense-arousing behavior that Gibb noted is **evaluative communication.** Most people become irritated at judgmental statements, which they are likely to interpret as indicating a lack of regard. One form of evaluation is "you" language, described in chapter 5.

Unlike evaluative "you" language, **descriptive communication** focuses on the

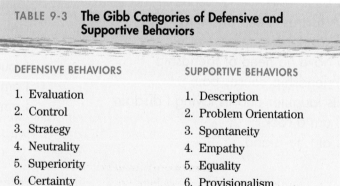

TABLE 9-3 **The Gibb Categories of Defensive and Supportive Behaviors**

DEFENSIVE BEHAVIORS	SUPPORTIVE BEHAVIORS
1. Evaluation	1. Description
2. Control	2. Problem Orientation
3. Strategy	3. Spontaneity
4. Neutrality	4. Empathy
5. Superiority	5. Equality
6. Certainty	6. Provisionalism

speaker's thoughts and feelings instead of judging the speaker. Descriptive messages often are expressed in "I" language, which tends to provoke less defensiveness than "you" language.[29] Contrast the following evaluative "you" claims with their descriptive "I" counterparts:

> Evaluation: "You don't know what you're talking about!"
> Description: "I don't understand how you came up with that idea."

> Evaluation: "This place is a mess!"
> Description: "When you don't clean up, I have to either do it or live with your mess. That's why I'm mad!"

> Evaluation: "Those jokes are disgusting!"
> Description: "When you tell those off-color jokes, I get really embarrassed."

Note how each of the descriptive statements focuses on the speaker's thoughts and feelings without judging the speaker. Despite its value, descriptive language isn't the only element necessary for success. Its effectiveness depends in part on when, where, and how the language is used. You can imagine how each of the preceding descriptive statements would go over if said in front of a room full of bystanders or in a whining tone of voice. Even the best timing and delivery of a descriptive message won't guarantee success. Some people will react defensively to anything you say or do. Nonetheless, it's easy to see that describing how the other person's behavior affects you is likely to produce better results than judgmentally attacking the other person.

Control vs. Problem Orientation

A second defense-provoking message involves some attempt to control another. **Controlling communication** occurs when a sender seems to be imposing a solution on the receiver with little regard for the receiver's needs or interests. The object of controls can involve almost anything: where to eat dinner, what TV program to watch, whether to remain in a relationship, or how to spend a large sum of money. Whatever the situation, people who act in controlling ways create a defensive climate. Researchers have found that the communication of abusive couples was characterized by opposition to one another's viewpoints.[30] None of us likes to feel that our ideas are worthless and that nothing we say will change other people's determination to have their way—yet this is precisely the attitude that a controller communicates. Whether it is done through words, gestures, tone of voice, or some other channel, whether control is accomplished through status, insistence on obscure or irrelevant rules, or physical power, the controller generates hostility wherever he or she goes. The unspoken message that such behavior communicates is "I know what's best for you, and if you do as I say, we'll get along."

In contrast, in **problem orientation** communicators focus on finding a solution that satisfies both their needs and those of the others involved. The goal here isn't to "win" at the expense of your partner but rather to work out some arrangement in which everybody feels like a winner. Chapter 10 has a great deal to say about "win-win" problem-solving as a way to find problem-oriented solutions.

Strategy vs. Spontaneity   Gibb uses the word **strategy** to characterize defense-arousing messages in which speakers hide their ulterior motives. The words *dishonesty* and *manipulation* capture the essence of strategy. Even if the motives of strategic communication are honorable, the victim of such deception who discovers the attempt to deceive is likely to feel offended at being played for a naive sucker.

Spontaneity is the behavior that contrasts with strategy. *Spontaneity* simply means expressing yourself honestly. Despite the misleading label that Gibb chose for this kind of behavior, spontaneous communication needn't be blurted out as soon as an idea comes to you. You might want to plan the wording of your message carefully so that you can express yourself clearly. The important thing is to be honest. Often spontaneity won't get you what you want, but in the long run it's usually better to be candid and perhaps miss out on some small goal than to say all the right things and be a fraud. More than once we've heard people say, "I didn't like what he said, but at least I know he was being honest."

Although it sounds paradoxical at first, spontaneity can be a strategy, too. Sometimes you'll see people using honesty in a calculating way, being just frank enough to win someone's trust or sympathy. This "leveling" is probably the most defense-arousing strategy of all because after we've learned that someone is using frankness as a manipulation, there's almost no chance we'll ever trust that person again.

You may be getting the idea that using supportive behaviors such as description, problem orientation, and so on is a good way to manipulate others. Before going any further, we want to say loudly and clearly that if you ever act supportively without being sincere in what you're saying, you've misunderstood the idea behind this chapter, and you're running a risk of causing even more defensiveness than before. None of the ideas that we present in this book can go into a "bag of tricks" that can be used to control others: If you ever find yourself using them in this way, beware!

Neutrality vs. Empathy   Gibb uses the term **neutrality** to describe a fourth behavior that arouses defensiveness. Probably a better descriptive word would be *indifference*. A neutral attitude is disconfirming because it communicates an indifference for the welfare of the other person and implies that the other person isn't very important to you. This perceived indifference is likely to promote defensiveness because people do not like to think of themselves as worthless, and they'll protect a self-concept that pictures themselves as worthwhile.

The negative effects of neutrality become apparent when you consider the hostility that most people have for the large, impersonal organizations with which they have to deal: "They think of me as a number instead of a person"; "I felt as if I were being handled by computers and not human beings." These two common statements reflect reactions to being handled in an indifferent way. Gibb has found that **empathy** helps rid communication of the quality of indifference. When people show that they care for the feelings of another person, there's little chance that the person's self-concept will be threatened. Empathy means accepting another's feelings, putting yourself in another's place. This doesn't mean that you need to agree with that person. By simply letting that person know of your care and respect, you'll be acting in a supportive way. Gibb noted the importance of nonverbal messages in communicating empathy. He found that facial and bodily expressions of concern are often more important to the receiver than the words used.

Superiority vs. Equality   A fifth behavior that arouses defensiveness is **superiority**. Any message that suggests "I'm better than you" is likely to arouse feelings of defensiveness in the recipients. A body of research confirms that patronizing messages irritate recipients ranging from young students to senior citizens, at least in Western cultures.[31] As humorist Dave Barry suggests in the reading on page 384, some superiority comes from the content of messages. In other cases, the *way* we deliver messages suggests a one-up approach. Consider, for example, how using simplified grammar and vocabulary, talking loudly and slowly, not listening, and varying speaking pitch convey a patronizing attitude.

Superior communication can trigger a variety of defensive responses: "turning off" the speaker, justifying one's self, attacking the speaker, or even walking away.

There are plenty of occasions when we communicate with others who possess talents or knowledge greater than ours, but on these occasions the other persons needn't communicate an attitude of superiority. Gibb has found ample evidence that many people who have superior skills and talents are capable of projecting feelings of **equality** rather than superiority. Such people convey that, although they may have greater talent in certain areas, they see others as having just as much worth as human beings.

Equality is put to the test when a person *doesn't* have superior skills yet is in a position of authority.[32] This condition often exists on the job, where supervisors may have less expertise in certain areas than their subordinates but believe it would be beneath them to admit it. You've probably been in situations where you knew more about the subject than the person in charge—a boss, teacher, parent, or salesperson—yet this person acted as if he or she knew more. Did you feel defensive? No doubt. Did that person feel defensive? No doubt as well. You both were challenging each other's presenting self, so the climate probably became hostile. A truly secure person can treat others with equality even when there are obvious differences in knowledge, talent, and status. Doing so creates a positive climate in which ideas are evaluated not on the merit of who contributed them, but rather on the merit of the ideas themselves.

Certainty vs. Provisionalism   Have you ever run into people who are positive that they're right, who know that theirs is the only or proper way of doing something, who insist that they have all the facts and need no additional information? If you have, you've met individuals who project the defense-arousing behavior that Gibb calls **certainty.** Communicators who regard their own opinions with certainty while disregarding the ideas of others demonstrate a lack of regard for the ideas that others

"Creating Positive Relationships"

http://www. positive-way.com/ communic.htm

Take the quiz featured in this site to assess the level of effective and positive communication in your relationship with a partner. Then read the explanations that follow for suggestions on how to more effectively communicate in your relationship. You can use Activity 9.4 "Analyzing Communication Climate in Your Own Relationship" to guide your work.

HOW TO ARGUE EFFECTIVELY

I argue very well. Ask any of my remaining friends. I can win an argument on any topic, against any opponent. People know this and steer clear of me at parties. Often, as a sign of their great respect, they don't even invite me. You too can win arguments. Simply follow these rules:

Drink Liquor

Suppose you are at a party and some hotshot intellectual is expounding on the economy of Peru, a subject you know nothing about. If you're drinking some health-fanatic drink like grapefruit juice, you'll hang back, afraid to display your ignorance, while the hotshot enthralls your date. But if you drink several large martinis, you'll discover you have *strong views* about the Peruvian economy. You'll be a *wealth* of information. You'll argue forcefully, offering searing insights and possibly upsetting furniture. People will be impressed. Some may leave the room.

Make Things Up

Suppose, in the Peruvian economy argument, you are trying to prove that Peruvians are underpaid, a position you base solely on the fact that *you* are underpaid, and you'll be damned if you're going to let a bunch of Peruvians be better off. *Don't* say: "I think Peruvians are underpaid." Say instead: "The average Peruvian's salary in 1981 dollars adjusted for the revised tax base is $1,452.81 per annum, which is $836.07 below the mean gross poverty level."

NOTE: Always make up exact figures. If an opponent asks you where you got your information, make *that* up too. Say: "This information comes from Dr. Hovel T. Moon's study for the Buford Commission published on May 9, 1982. Didn't you read it?" Say this in the same tone of voice you would use to say, "You left your soiled underwear in my bathroom."

Use Meaningless But Weighty-Sounding Words and Phrases

Memorize this list:

Let me put it this way
In terms of
Vis-a-vis
Per se
As it were
Qua
So to speak

You should also memorize some Latin abbreviations such as "Q.E.D.," "e.g.," and "i.e." These are all short for "I speak Latin, and you don't." Here's how to use these words and phrases. Suppose you want to say, "Peruvians would like to order appetizers more often, but they don't have enough money." You never win arguments talking like that. But you WILL win if you say, "Let me put it this way. In terms of appetizers vis-a-vis Peruvians qua Peruvians, they would like to order them more often, so to speak, but they do not have enough money per se, as it were. Q.E.D." Only a fool would challenge that statement.

Use Snappy and Irrelevant Comebacks

You need an arsenal of all-purpose irrelevant phrases to fire back at your opponents when they make valid points. The best are:

You're begging the question.
You're being defensive.
Don't compare apples to oranges.
What are your parameters?

This last one is especially valuable. Nobody (other than engineers and policy wonks) has the vaguest idea what "parameters" means. Here's how to use your comebacks:

You say: "As Abraham Lincoln said in 1873 . . ." "Your opponent says: "Lincoln died in 1865." "You say: "You're begging the question."

You say: "Liberians, like most Asians . . ." Your opponent says: "Liberia is in Africa." You say: "You're being defensive."

Compare Your Opponent to Adolf Hitler

This is your heavy artillery, for when your opponent is obviously right and you are spectacularly wrong. Bring Hitler up subtly. Say, "That sounds suspiciously like something Adolf Hitler might say," or "You certainly do remind me of Adolf Hitler."

So that's it. You now know how to out-argue anybody. Do not try to pull any of this on people who generally carry weapons.

Dave Barry

hold to be important. It's likely that the receiver will take the certainty as a personal affront and react defensively.

In contrast to certainty is **provisionalism,** in which people may have strong opinions but are willing to acknowledge that they don't have a corner on the truth and will change their stand if another position seems more reasonable.

There is no guarantee that using Gibb's supportive, confirming approach to communication will build a positive climate. The other person may simply not be receptive. But the chances for a constructive relationship will be greatest when communication consists of the constructive approach described here. Besides boosting the odds of getting a positive response from others, supportive communication can leave you feeling better in a variety of ways: more in control of your relationships, more comfortable, and more positive toward others.

The need to be right—the sign of a vulgar mind.

Albert Camus

INVITATION TO INSIGHT

DEFENSIVENESS FEEDBACK

1. Approach an important person in your life, and request some help in learning more about yourself. Inform the other person that your discussion will probably take at least an hour, so make sure that both of you are prepared to invest the necessary amount of time.

2. Begin by explaining all twelve of the Gibb behaviors to your partner. Be sure to give enough examples so that each category is clearly understood.

3. When your explanation is complete and you've answered all your partner's questions, ask him or her to tell you which of the Gibb categories you use. Seek specific examples so that you are certain to understand the feedback fully. (Because you are requesting an evaluation, be prepared for a little defensiveness on your own part at this point.) Inform your partner that you are interested in discovering both the defense-arousing and the supportive behaviors you use and that you are sincerely interested in receiving a candid answer. (Note: If you don't want to hear the truth from your partner, don't try this exercise.)

4. As your partner speaks, record the categories that he or she lists in sufficient detail for both of you to be sure that you have understood the comments.

5. When you have finished your list, show it to your partner. Listen to your partner's reactions, and make any corrections that are necessary to reflect an accurate understanding of the comments. When your list is accurate, have your partner sign it to indicate that you have understood it clearly.

6. In a concluding statement note:
   a. how you felt as your partner was describing you
   b. whether you agree with the evaluation
   c. what effect your use of the Gibb categories has on your relationship with your partner

"What do you mean 'Your guess is as good as mine?' My guess is a hell of a lot better than your guess!"

©The New Yorker Collection 1983 Al Ross from cartoonbank.com. All Rights Reserved.

LOOKING AT DIVERSITY

Police Work and Facework

In addition to his regular duties as a police officer in Santa Barbara, California, **Lorenzo Duarte** *works with local schoolchildren and hosts a weekly call-in radio program for the city's Spanish-speaking residents. Duarte spent most of his childhood in California's agricultural regions, where his Mexican-born parents lived and worked. During his five years in the U.S. Air Force, he earned several awards, both as a weightlifter and for his work in security.*

Saving face is a big part of a police officer's job. It's easy to understand why people feel threatened when they see a flashing red light, a badge, gun, baton, and handcuffs. This is true for law-abiding citizens, but it's especially true when people know they've done something wrong. In situations like this your most important tools as a police officer are your mind and communication skills. If you can make people feel less threatened, you can get them to cooperate without using force.

I've found that the best way to get cooperation is to treat everybody—and I really mean everybody—with respect. This might seem hard to do with some "bad guys," but it is possible. Let me give you an example. A while back we arrested a man we were sure had been stealing from some

of the poorest people in our town. It would have been easy to treat the guy like scum, but that wouldn't have helped us get a confession, which was what we wanted. When he told us what we knew were a bunch of lies, we laid out his options without being critical or judgmental. We told him that the courts would be investigating his story, and that he held his own destiny in his hands. He could do himself a favor and tell the truth or he could lie and take the consequences later. Not only did he confess, but he identified other burglars and took us to the place where the stolen property was kept. Because we were honest and respectful with him, we got four criminal convictions and put the stolen goods back in the hands of their owners. I'm sure that if we had disrespected this guy, he wouldn't have cooperated with us.

This story shows that there are several parts to being respectful. The obvious one is being polite: no name calling or scorn. Another part is giving people a sense of control over their lives. We didn't demand that this suspect confess; we laid out his options and then let him choose what would happen next. Letting people choose how they want an encounter to wind up usually works better than threatening them. Another part of respect is honesty, even with troublemakers. People may not always like police officers, but they'll

cooperate more if they know we're telling the truth. The last way to save face is by listening. Cutting somebody off is disrespectful. If you hear them out, even if they're obviously lying or jabbering, they're more likely to give you what you want.

Most of being respectful is just common sense: treating others the way you would like to be treated. Sometimes, though, knowing the customs or rules of a particular culture can help. For example, if I'm going to investigate a complaint in a home where the people were raised in a Hispanic culture, it's important to approach the man of the house—the husband or father. Questioning the wife or children first would be an insult. I would be making the man lose face by suggesting he wasn't the authority figure. This might not seem fair, especially if the man is the focus of a complaint; but I can still get the guy to cooperate more if I treat him the way he'd like to be treated. This is a small price to pay to solve a problem.

I'm not pretending that you can always be nice as a police officer. Sometimes you're forced to get rough. But it is always best to start by being polite and respectful. You can escalate if you have to. If you start an encounter by being aggressive, the other person is likely to get defensive. Once this happens, it's hard for everybody to back off.

RESPONDING NONDEFENSIVELY TO CRITICISM

The world would be a happier place if everyone communicated supportively. But how can you respond nondefensively when others use evaluation, control, superiority, and all the other attacking behaviors that Gibb identified? Despite your best intentions, it's difficult to be reasonable when you're being attacked. Being attacked is hard enough when the criticism is clearly unfair, but it's often even harder when the criticism is on target. Despite the accuracy of your critic, the tendency is either to counterattack aggressively with a barrage of verbal aggression or to withdraw nonassertively.

Because neither of these counterattacks is likely to resolve a dispute, we need alternative ways of behaving. There are two such ways. Despite their apparent simplicity, they have proved to be among the most valuable skills many communicators have learned.[33]

Seek More Information

The response of seeking more information makes good sense when you realize that it's foolish to respond to a critical attack until you understand what the other person has said. Even attacks that on first consideration appear to be totally unjustified or foolish often prove to contain at least a grain of truth and sometimes much more.

Many readers object to the idea of asking for details when they are criticized. Their resistance stems from confusing the act of *listening open-mindedly* to a speaker's comments with *accepting* the comments. After you realize that you can listen to, understand, and even acknowledge the most hostile comments without necessarily accepting them, it becomes much easier to hear another person out. If you disagree with a person's criticism, you will be in a much better position to explain yourself after you understand the criticism. On the other hand, after carefully listening to the person's criticism, you might just see that it is valid, in which case you have learned some valuable information about yourself. In either case, you have everything to gain and nothing to lose by paying attention to the critic.

Of course, after one has spent years of instinctively resisting criticism, learning to listen to the other person will take some practice. To make matters clearer, here are several ways in which you can seek additional information from your critics.

Ask for Specifics   Often the vague attack of a critic is virtually useless even if you sincerely want to change. Abstract attacks such as "You're being unfair" or "You never help out" can be difficult to understand. In such cases it is a good idea to request more specific information from the sender. "What do I *do* that's unfair?" is an important question to ask before you can judge whether the attack is correct. "When haven't I helped out?" you might ask before agreeing with or disagreeing with the attack.

If you have already asked for specifics and are still accused of reacting defensively, the problem may be in the *way* you ask. Your tone of voice and facial expression, posture, and other nonverbal clues can give the same words radically different connotations. For example, think of how you could use the words "Exactly what are you talking about?" to communicate either a genuine desire to know or your belief that the speaker is crazy. It's important to request specific information only when you genuinely want to learn more from the speaker because asking under any other circumstances will make matters only worse.

Guess about Specifics   On some occasions even your sincere and well-phrased requests for specific information won't meet with success. Sometimes your critics won't be able to define precisely the behavior that they find offensive. At these times, you'll hear such comments as "I can't tell you exactly what's wrong with your sense of humor—all I can say is that I don't like it." At other times, your critics may know the exact behaviors they don't like but for some reason seem to get a perverse satisfaction out of making you struggle to figure it out. At times like this, you hear such comments as, "Well, if you don't know what you did to hurt my feelings, I'm certainly not going to tell you!"

Needless to say, failing to learn the specifics of another's criticism when you genuinely want to know can be frustrating. In instances like these, you can often learn more clearly what is bothering your critic by *guessing* at the specifics of a criticism. In a sense you become both detective and suspect, the goal being to figure out exactly what "crime" you have committed. Like the technique of asking for specifics, guessing must be done with goodwill if it's to produce satisfying results. You need to convey to the critic that for both your sakes you're truly interested in finding out what is the matter. After you have communicated this intention, the emotional climate generally becomes more comfortable because, in effect, both you and the critic are seeking the same goal.

Here are some typical questions you might hear from someone guessing about the specifics of another's criticism:

> "So you object to the language I used in writing the paper. Was my language too formal?"

> "OK, I understand that you think the outfit looks funny. What is it that's so bad? Is it the color? Does it have something to do with the fit? The fabric?"

> "When you say that I'm not doing my share around the house, do you mean that I haven't been helping enough with the cleaning?"

Nothing is weaker than water;
Yet, for attacking what is hard and tough,
Nothing surpasses it, nothing equals it.
The principle, that what is weak overcomes what is strong,
And what is yielding conquers what is resistant, is known to everyone.
Yet few utilize it profitably in practice . . .

Lao Tzu, *Tao Te Ching*

Paraphrase the Speaker's Ideas   Another strategy is to draw out confused or reluctant speakers by paraphrasing their thoughts and feelings and using the active listening skills described in chapter 7. Paraphrasing is especially good in helping others solve their problems; and because people generally criticize you because your behavior creates some problem for them, the strategy is especially appropriate at such times.

One advantage of paraphrasing is that you don't have to guess about the specifics of your behavior that might be offensive. By clarifying or amplifying what you understand critics to be saying, you'll learn more about their objections. A brief dialogue between a disgruntled customer and an especially talented store manager using paraphrasing might sound like this:

Customer: The way you people run this store is disgusting! I just want to tell you that I'll never shop here again.

Manager: (*reflecting the customer's feeling*) It seems that you're quite upset. Can you tell me your problem?

Customer: It isn't *my* problem; it's the problem your salespeople have. They seem to think it's a great inconvenience to help a customer find anything around here.

Manager: So you didn't get enough help locating the items you were looking for, is that it?

Customer: Help? I spent twenty minutes looking around in here before I even talked to a clerk. All I can say is that it's a hell of a way to run a store.

Manager: So what you're saying is that the clerks seemed to be ignoring the customers?

Customer: No. They were all busy with other people. It just seems to me that you ought to have enough help around to handle the crowds that come in at this hour.

Manager: I understand now. What frustrated you the most was the fact that we didn't have enough staff to serve you promptly.

Customer: That's right. I have no complaint with the service I get after I'm waited on, and I've always thought you had a good selection here. It's just that I'm too busy to wait so long for help.

Manager: Well, I'm glad you brought this to my attention. We certainly don't want loyal customers going away mad. I'll try to see that it doesn't happen again.

This conversation illustrates two advantages of paraphrasing. First, the critic often reduces the intensity of the attack after he or she realizes that the complaint is being heard. Often criticism grows from the frustration of unmet needs—which in this case was partly a lack of attention. As soon as the manager genuinely demonstrated interest in the customer's plight, the customer began to feel better and was able to leave the store relatively calm. Of course, this sort of active listening won't always mollify your critic, but even when it doesn't, there's still another benefit that

Placing the blame is a bad habit, but taking the blame is a sure builder of character.

O. A. Battista

makes the strategy worthwhile. In the sample conversation, for instance, the manager learned some valuable information by taking time to understand the customer. The manager discovered that there were certain times when the number of employees was insufficient to help the crowd of shoppers and also that the delays at these times seriously annoyed at least some shoppers, thus threatening a loss in business. This knowledge is certainly important, and by reacting defensively to the customer's complaint, the manager would not have learned from it. As you read earlier, even apparently outlandish criticism often contains at least a grain of truth, and thus a person who is genuinely interested in improving would be wise to hear it out.

Ask What the Critic Wants   Sometimes your critic's demand will be obvious.

"Turn down that music!"

"I wish you'd remember to tell me about phone messages."

"Would you clean up your dirty dishes *now!*"

At other times, however, you'll need to do some investigating to find out what the critic wants from you:

Alex:	I can't believe you invited all those people over without asking me first!
Barb:	Are you saying you want me to cancel the party?
Alex:	No, I just wish you'd ask me before you make plans.
Cynthia:	You're so critical! It sounds like you don't like *anything* about this paper.
Donna:	But you asked for my opinion. What do you expect me to do when you ask?
Cynthia:	I want to know what's wrong, but I don't *just* want to hear criticisms. If you think there's anything good about my work, I wish you'd tell me that, too.

This last example illustrates the importance of accompanying your questions with the right nonverbal behavior. It's easy to imagine two ways in which Donna could have responded to "What do you expect me to do when you ask?" One would show a genuine desire to clarify what Cynthia wanted, whereas the other would have been clearly hostile and defensive. As with all the styles in this section, your responses to criticism have to be sincere to work.

Ask about the Consequences of Your Behavior   As a rule, people criticize your behavior only when some need of theirs is not being met. One way to respond to this kind of criticism is to find out exactly what troublesome consequences your behavior has for them. You'll often find that behaviors that seem perfectly legitimate to you cause some difficulty for your critic; after you have understood this, criticisms that previously sounded foolish take on a new meaning.

ETHICAL CHALLENGE

Nonviolence: A Legacy of Principled Effectiveness

Among the most familiar and challenging biblical injunctions is Christ's mandate, "If someone strikes you on one cheek, turn to him the other . . ."

The notion of meeting aggression with nonviolence is an ancient one. The Taoist doctrine of *wu-wei*, promulgated over twenty-four hundred years ago in China, advocates non-action in the face of an attack. In ancient India, the principle of *ahimsa*—nonharming—was shared by Buddhists, Jains, and many Hindus. In the West, some Greek stoics advocated nonaction in the face of threats.

Pacifism has a moral foundation, but by the nineteenth century it was used as a potent strategy for achieving political goals. In the United States, abolitionist William Lloyd Garrison advocated the use of nonviolence to protest slavery. On both sides of the Atlantic, the suffragette movement used nonviolent resistance as a tool to secure rights for women. In czarist Russia, Count Leo Tolstoy led a pacifist movement rejecting war and advocating civil disobedience as a tool for inhibiting violence.

In the twentieth century, nonviolence proved to be a powerful tool for political change. Mahatma Gandhi was demonstrably the most successful practitioner of this tool, first in South Africa and later in India, where his approach of *satyagraha* (truth-force) played a decisive role in the 1947 withdrawal of imperial Britain from India. In the 1950s and 1960s, Martin Luther King and his followers used nonviolence to demonstrate the evils of racial segregation, contributing to the passage of groundbreaking civil rights laws.

The effectiveness of nonviolence in achieving social change suggests that the strategies of seeking more information from and agreeing with one's critic can be effective in interpersonal situations. These non-confrontational strategies provide communicators with a communication tool that is both principled and pragmatic.

For more information on nonviolent strategies see Peter Ackerman and Christopher Kruegler, *Strategic Nonviolent Conflict: The Dynamics of People Power in the Twentieth Century.* Westport, Conn.: Praeger, 1994; and Robert L. Holmes, ed., *Nonviolence in Theory and Practice.* Belmont, Calif.: Wadsworth, 1990.

Neighbor A: You say that I ought to have my cat neutered. Why is that important to you?

Neighbor B: Because at night he picks fights with my cat, and I'm tired of paying the vet's bills.

Worker A: Why do you care whether I'm late to work?

Worker B: Because when the boss asks, I feel obligated to make up some story so you won't get in trouble, and I don't like to lie.

Husband: Why does it bother you when I lose money at poker? You know I never gamble more than I can afford.

Wife: It's not the cash itself. It's that when you lose, you're in a grumpy mood for two or three days, and that's no fun for me.

Ask What Else Is Wrong It might seem crazy to invite more criticism, but sometimes asking about other complaints can uncover the real problem:

Raul: Are you mad at me?

Tina: No. Why are you asking?

Raul: Because the whole time we were at the picnic you hardly spent any time talking to me. In fact, it seemed like whenever I came over to where you were, you went off somewhere else.

Tina: Is anything else wrong?

Raul: Well, I've been wondering lately if you're tired of me.

This example shows that asking if anything else bothers your critic isn't just an exercise in masochism. If you can keep your defensiveness in check, probing further can lead the conversation to issues that are the source of the critic's real dissatisfaction.

COMMUNICATION TRANSCRIPT

Responding Nondefensively to Criticism

Defending yourself— even when you're right—isn't always the best approach. This dialogue shows the importance of using self-control and thinking before responding when you are being criticized. The employee realizes that arguing won't change his boss's mind, and so he decides to reply as honestly as he can without becoming defensive.

Boss How'd things go while I was out?

Employee Pretty well, except for one thing. Mr. Macintosh—he said you knew him—came in and wanted to buy about $200 worth of stuff. He wanted me to charge him wholesale, and I asked him for his tax resale number, just like you told me. He said he didn't have it, and so I told him he'd have to pay retail. He got pretty mad.

Boss He's a good customer. I hope you gave him the discount.

Employee (*beginning to sound defensive*) Well, I didn't. You told me last week that the law said we had to charge full price and sales tax unless the customer had a resale number.

Boss Oh, my gosh! Didn't Macintosh tell you he had a number?

Employee (*becoming more defensive*) He did, but he didn't have it with him. I didn't want to get you mad at me for breaking the law.

Boss (*barely concealing his exasperation*) Well, customers don't always have their resale numbers memorized. Macintosh has been coming here for years, and we just fill in his number on the records later.

Employee (*deciding to respond nondefensively instead of getting into an argument that he knows he can't win*) I can see why it looks like I gave Mr. Macintosh a hard time. You don't ask him for the number, and I insisted on having it. (*agrees with the boss's perception*)

Boss Yes! There's a lot of competition in this business, and we have to keep our customers happy—especially the good ones— or we'll lose them. Macintosh drives across town to do business with us. There are places right near him. If we jerk him around he'll go there, and we'll lose a good customer.

Employee That's true. (*agrees with the fact that it is important to keep customers happy*) And I want to know how to treat customers right. But I'm confused about how to handle people who want a discount and don't have resale numbers. What should I do? (*asks what the boss wants*)

Boss Well, you need to be a little flexible with good customers.

Employee How should I do that? (*asks for specifics*)

Boss Well, it's OK to trust people who are regulars.

Sometimes soliciting more information from a critic isn't enough. What do you do, for instance, when you fully understand the other person's criticism and still feel a defensive response on the tip of your tongue? You know that if you try to defend yourself, you'll wind up in an argument; on the other hand, you simply can't accept what the other person is saying about you. The solution to such a dilemma is outrageously simple and is discussed in the following section.

Agree with the Critic

But, you protest, how can you honestly agree with criticisms that you don't believe are true? The following pages will answer this question by showing that there's virtually no situation in which you can't honestly

Employee So I don't need to ask regular customers for their resale numbers. I should look them up later? (*paraphrases to clarify boss's ambiguous directions to "trust" regular customers*)

Boss That's right. You've got to use your head in business!

Employee (*ignores the indirect accusation about not "using his head," recognizing that there's no point in defending himself*) OK, so when regular customers come in, I won't even ask them for their resale numbers . . . right? (*paraphrases again to be sure he has the message correct. The employee has no desire to get criticized again about this matter.*)

Boss No, go ahead and ask for the number. If they have it, we won't have to look it up later. But if they don't have the number, just say OK and give them the discount.

Employee Got it. I only have one question: How can I know who

the regular customers are? Should I take their word for it? (*asks for specifics*)

Boss Well, you'll get to know most of them after you've been here a while. But it's OK to trust them until then. If they say they're regulars, just take their word for it. You've got to trust people sometimes, you know!

Employee (*ignores the fact that the boss originally told him not to trust people but rather to insist on getting their number. Decides instead to agree with the boss.*) I can see how important it is to trust good customers.

Boss Right.

Employee Thanks for clearing up how to handle the resale numbers. Is there anything else I ought to know so things will run smoothly when you're not in the store? (*asks if anything else is wrong*)

Boss I don't think so. (*patronizingly*) Don't get discouraged; you'll catch on. It took me twenty

years to build this business. Stick with it, and some day you could be running a place like this.

Employee (*trying to agree with his boss without sounding sarcastic*) I guess I could.

The employee's refusal to act defensively turned what might have been a scolding into a discussion about how to handle a business challenge in the future. The employee might not like the boss's patronizing attitude and contradictory directions, but his communication skill kept the communication climate positive—probably the best possible outcome for this situation.

Using your Looking Out/ Looking In CD-ROM, click on Communication Scenarios and then click on the "Responding to Criticism" scenario to watch and analyze a dramatized version of this conversation.

accept the other person's point of view and still maintain your position. To see how this can be so, you need to realize that there are two different types of agreement, one of which you can use in almost any situation.

Love your enemies, for they tell you your faults.

Benjamin Franklin

Agree with the Facts This is the easiest type of agreement to understand, though not always to practice. Research suggests that it is also highly effective in restoring a damaged reputation with a critic.[34] You agree with your critic when the accusation is factually correct:

"You're right, I am angry."

"I suppose I *was* being defensive."

"Now that you mention it, I did get pretty sarcastic."

Agreeing with the facts seems quite sensible when you realize that certain facts are indisputable. If you agree to be somewhere at 4:00 and don't show up until 5:00, you *are* tardy, no matter how good your explanation for tardiness. If you've broken a borrowed object, run out of gas, or failed to finish a job you started, there's no point in denying it. In the same way, if you're honest, you will have to agree with many interpretations of your behavior even when they're not flattering. You do get angry, act foolishly, fail to listen, and behave inconsiderately. After you rid yourself of the myth of perfection, it's much easier to acknowledge these truths.

If many criticisms aimed at you are accurate, why is it so difficult to accept them without being defensive? The answer to this question lies in a confusion between agreeing with the *facts* and accepting the *judgment* that so often accompanies them. Most critics don't merely describe the action that offends them; they also evaluate it, and it's this evaluation that we resist:

"It's silly to be angry."

"You have no reason for being defensive."

"You were wrong to be so sarcastic."

PEANUTS

Reprinted by permission of United Feature Syndicate, Inc.

It's evaluations like these that we resent. By realizing that you can agree with—and even learn from—the descriptive part of many criticisms and still not accept the accompanying evaluations, you'll often have a response that is both honest and nondefensive.

Of course, in order to reduce defensiveness, your agreements with the facts must be honest ones admitted without malice. It's humiliating to accept descriptions that aren't accurate, and maliciously pretending to accept these leads only to trouble. You can imagine how unproductive the conversation given earlier would have been if the manager had spoken the same words in a sarcastic tone. Agree with the facts only when you can do so sincerely. Though this won't always be possible, you'll be surprised at how often you can use this simple response.

Agree with the Critic's Perception   Agreeing with your critics may be fine when you acknowledge that the criticisms are justified, but how can you agree when they seem to be completely unjustified? You've listened carefully and asked questions to make sure you understand the criticisms, but the more you listen, the more positive you are that the critics are totally out of line. Even in these cases there is a way of agreeing—this time not with the critics' conclusions but with their right to see things their way.

A: I don't believe that you've been all the places you were just describing. You're probably just making all this up to impress us.

B: Well, I can see how you might think that. I've known people who lie to get approval.

C: I want to let you know right from the start that I was against hiring you for the job. I think you got it because you're a woman.

D: I can understand why you'd believe that with all the antidiscrimination laws on the books. I hope that after I've been here for a while, you'll change your mind.

E: I don't think you're being totally honest about your reason for wanting to stay home. You say that it's because you have a headache, but I think you're avoiding Mary and Walt.

F: I can see why that would make sense to you because Mary and I got into an argument the last time we were together. All I can say is that I do have a headache.

One key to feeling comfortable with acknowledging accurate criticism is to understand that *agreeing* with a critic doesn't necessarily oblige you to *apologize*. Sometimes you aren't responsible for the behavior that your critic finds objectionable, in which case an explanation might be more appropriate than an apology:

"I know I'm late. There was an accident downtown, and the streets are jammed." (Spoken in an explanatory, nondefensive tone)

In other cases, your behavior might be understandable, if not perfect. When this happens, you can acknowledge the validity of the criticism without apologizing:

"You're right. I *did* lose my temper. I've had to remind you three or four times, and I guess I finally used up all my patience." (Again, delivered as an explanation, not a defense or counterattack)

In still other cases, you can acknowledge your critic's right to see things differently than you without backing off from your position.

"I can understand why you think I'm overreacting. I know this doesn't seem as important to you as it does to me. I hope you can understand why I think this is such a big deal."

Apologizing is fine if you can do so sincerely; but you will be able to agree with critics more often if you understand that doing so doesn't require you to grovel.

Some critics don't seem to deserve the kinds of respectful responses outlined here. They seem more interested in attacking you than explaining themselves. Before you counterattack these hostile critics, ask yourself whether a defensive response will be worth the consequences.

SKILL BUILDER

COPING WITH CRITICISM

Take turns practicing nondefensive responses with a partner:

1. Choose one of the following criticisms, and brief your partner on how it might be directed at you:
   a. You're so selfish sometimes. You think only of yourself.
   b. Don't be so touchy!
   c. You say you understand me, but you don't really.
   d. I wish you'd do your share around here.
   e. You're so critical!

2. As your partner criticizes you, answer with the appropriate response from the preceding pages. As you do so, try to adopt an attitude of genuinely wanting to understand the criticism and finding parts that you can sincerely agree with.

3. Ask your partner to evaluate your response. Does it follow the forms described in the previous pages? Does it sound sincere?

4. Replay the same scene, trying to improve your response.

SUMMARY

Every relationship has a communication climate. Positive climates are characterized by confirming messages, which make it clear that the parties value one another. Negative climates are usually disconfirming. In one way or another, messages in disconfirming relationships convey indifference or hostility. Communication climates develop early in a relationship, from both verbal and nonverbal messages. After they are created, reciprocal messages create either positive or negative spirals in which the frequency and intensity of either positive or negative messages are likely to grow.

Defensive spirals are among the most destructive types of communication. Most defensiveness occurs when people try to protect key parts of a presenting self-image that they believe is under attack. Defensive communicators respond by attacking their critic, distorting critical information, or avoiding critical messages. Using the supportive behaviors defined by Jack Gibb when expressing potentially threatening messages can reduce the likelihood of triggering defensive reactions in others.

When faced with criticism by others, it is possible to respond nondefensively by attempting to understand the criticism and by agreeing with either the facts or the critic's perception.

KEY TERMS

ambiguous response
apathy
certainty
cognitive dissonance
communication climate
compensation
complaining
confirming communication
controlling communication
de-escalatory conflict spiral
defense mechanism
defensiveness
descriptive communication
disconfirming communication

displacement
empathy
equality
escalatory conflict spiral
evaluative communication
face-threatening act
Gibb categories
impersonal response
impervious response
incongruous response
interrupting response
irrelevant response
neutrality
physical avoidance

problem orientation
provisionalism
rationalization
regression
repression
sarcasm
spiral
spontaneity
strategy
superiority
tangential response
verbal abuse
verbal aggression

LOOKING OUT/LOOKING IN ONLINE

Use your *Looking Out/Looking In* CD-ROM for quick access to the electronic resources that accompany this chapter. Included on this CD-ROM are additional study aids and links to the *Looking Out/Looking In* Web site at the Wadsworth Communication Café. The CD-ROM is your gateway to a wealth of resources that will help you understand and further explore the material in this chapter. **Video clips** under *Communication Scenarios* on the CD illustrate the skills introduced in this chapter. Click on the Web site link to complete self-study **review quizzes** to help you master new concepts; access a **feature film database** to locate clips and entire movies that illustrate communication principles; find Internet material via the maintained **Web site links;** and complete **online activities** to help you master new concepts.

INFOTRAC COLLEGE EDITION EXERCISES

Use the InfoTrac College Edition password that was included free with a copy of this new text to answer the following questions. These questions can be completed online and, if requested, submitted to your instructor under InfoTrac College Edition Activities at the *Looking Out/Looking In* Web site.

1. Defensiveness

Use PowerTrac to locate the article "The Effects of Sense of Humor, Defensiveness, and Gender on the Interpretation of Ambiguous Messages" by Aimee Futch and Renee Edwards. (Hint: Use the author and title fields to locate this article.) Read the review of previous research as well as the findings in this research study. What useful information did you discover about the factors that contribute to defensive reactions? How can you use this information to make your relationships more satisfying?

2. Responding Nondefensively to Criticism

Use the subject search function to find a list of articles on "personal criticism." Find and read one of the articles within this area that provides useful information for you. Summarize the key points the article makes and explain how you can apply them in your work. Do the points you read here support information in this chapter? How?

READINGS

Abel, Richard L. *Speaking Respect, Respecting Speech.* Chicago: University of Chicago Press, 1998.

Abel identifies the unmet desire for respect as a major cause of disputes in modern civic life. He shows how many conflicts could be avoided if the people involved treated one another with the kind of confirming behavior described in this chapter.

Tannen, Deborah. *The Argument Culture.* New York: Random House, 1998.

Sociolinguist Tannen argues (note the combative metaphor) that our culture is suffused with an orientation toward combat that often pushes personal relationships away from cooperation and toward conflict. She offers examples from areas such as the media, politics, and law to support her points. Tannen also profiles other cultures with more collaborative approaches toward managing differences.

Vangelisti, Anita L. "Messages That Hurt" in *The Dark Side of Interpersonal Communication*, William R. Cupach and Brian H. Spitzberg, eds. Hillsdale, N.J.: Erlbaum, 1994.

Vangelisti reports on research about hurtful messages. This chapter describes the types of messages that experimental subjects report as hurtful as well as outlines the personal and relational factors that make some messages more painful than others. The material is a useful supplement to the information in this chapter of Looking Out/Looking In.

FILMS

In addition to the films suggested here, go to the **Film in Communication Database** at the *Looking Out/Looking In* Web site to locate movie clips that illustrate various communication climates.

Confirming and Disconfirming Behaviors

Mr. Holland's Opus (1996) Rated PG

Glenn Holland (Richard Dreyfus) begins his career as a high school music teacher poorly: his students are as bored as he is boring. Holland slowly learns to change the climate in his classroom. He begins teaching lessons from the students' music, rock and roll. He spends countless hours working one on one with those who need extra help. Most importantly, he confirms his students' worth and dignity by investing himself in their lives.

An interesting subplot involves Holland's son, Cole (Joseph Anderson). When Holland learns that his young son is virtually deaf, Holland is devastated because he believes they will never share a passion for music. Although his students feel his constant confirmation, Holland continually disconfirms Cole by ignoring him and the events of his life.

Fortunately, Holland is awakened to the problem and redresses it in a variety of ways (including the sharing of music). By movie's end, their relationship is repaired. The story thus has many morals: A person can send both confirming and disconfirming messages; disconfirmation can be unintentional; patterns of disconfirmation can be reversed. Ultimately, *Mr. Holland's Opus* is a testimony to the transforming power of confirming communication.

LOOKING OUT/LOOKING IN CD-ROM

Using your *Looking Out/Looking In* CD-ROM, click on *Communication Scenarios* and then click on the "Responding to Criticism" icon to watch and analyze a dramatized version of the conversation featured in the Communication Transcript on pages 392–393.

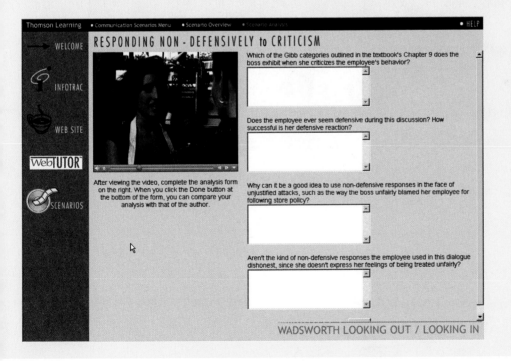

CHAPTER 10

MANAGING INTERPERSONAL CONFLICTS

For most people, conflict has about the same appeal as a trip to the dentist. A quick look at the thesaurus offers a clue about the distasteful nature of conflict. Synonyms for the term include *battle, brawl, clash, competition, discord, disharmony, duel, fight, strife, struggle, trouble,* and *violence.* Even the metaphors we use to describe our conflicts show that we view conflict as something to be avoided.[1] We often talk about conflict as a kind of war: "He shot down my arguments." "OK, fire away." "Don't try to defend yourself!" Another metaphor suggests that conflict is explosive: "Don't blow up!" "I needed to let off steam." "You've got a short fuse." Sometimes conflict seems like a kind of trial, in which one party accuses another: "Come on, admit you're guilty." "Stop accusing me!" "Just listen to my case." Language that suggests that conflict is a mess is also common: "Let's not open this can of worms." "That's a sticky situation." "Don't make such a stink!" Even the metaphor of a game implies that one side has to defeat the other: "That was out of bounds." "You're not playing fair." "I give up; you win!"

Despite images like these, the truth is that conflict *can* be constructive. With the right set of communication skills, conflict can be less like a struggle and more like a kind of dance in which partners work together to create something that would be impossible without their cooperation. You may have to persuade the other person to become your partner, and you may be clumsy at first; but with enough practice and goodwill, you can work together instead of at cross-purposes.

The attitude you bring to your conflicts can make a tremendous difference between success and failure. One study revealed that college students in close romantic relationships who believed that conflicts are destructive were most likely to neglect or quit the relationship and less likely to seek a solution than student couples who had less negative attitudes.[2] Of course, attitudes alone won't always guarantee satisfying solutions to conflicts. The kinds of skills you will learn in this chapter can help well-intentioned partners handle their disagreements constructively. But without the right attitude, all the skills in the world will be little help.

There are no magic tricks to resolve all the conflicts in your life. On the other hand, there are ways to manage these conflicts constructively. If you follow these ways you may find that your relationships are actually stronger and more satisfying than before.

THE NATURE OF CONFLICT

Before focusing on how to solve interpersonal problems constructively, we need to take a brief look at the nature of conflict. What is it? Why is it an inevitable part of life? How can it be beneficial?

Conflict Defined

Before reading farther, make a list of the interpersonal conflicts in your life. They probably involve many different people, revolve around very different subjects, and take many different forms. Some become loud, angry arguments. Others may be expressed in calm, rational discussions. Still others might simmer along most of the time with brief but bitter flare-ups.

Whatever form they may take, all interpersonal conflicts share certain characteristics. Joyce Hocker and William Wilmot provide a thorough definition when they define **conflict** as *an expressed struggle between at least two interdependent parties who perceive incompatible goals, scarce rewards, and interference from the other party in achieving their goals.*[3] A closer look at the key parts of this definition will help you recognize how conflict operates in your life.

Expressed Struggle

A conflict can exist only when both parties are aware of a disagreement. For instance, you may be upset for months because a neighbor's loud stereo keeps you awake at night, but no conflict exists between the two of you until the neighbor learns of your problem. Of course, the expressed struggle doesn't have to be verbal. You can show your displeasure with somebody without saying a word. A dirty look, the silent treatment, and avoiding the other person are all ways of expressing yourself. One way or another, both parties must know that a problem exists before they're in conflict.

Perceived Incompatible Goals

All conflicts look as if one party's gain would be another's loss. For instance, consider the neighbor whose stereo keeps you awake at night. Doesn't somebody have to lose? If the neighbor turns down the noise, she loses the enjoyment of hearing the music at full volume; but if the neighbor keeps the volume up, you're still awake and unhappy.

The goals in this situation really aren't completely incompatible—there are solutions that allow both parties to get what they want. For instance, you could achieve peace and quiet by closing your windows or getting the neighbor to close hers. You might use a pair of earplugs, or perhaps the neighbor could get a set of earphones, allowing the music to be played at full volume without bothering anyone. If any of these solutions prove workable, the conflict disappears.

Unfortunately, people often fail to see mutually satisfying solutions to their problems. As long as they *perceive* their goals to be mutually exclusive, a conflict exists.

Perceived Scarce Rewards

Conflicts also exist when people believe there isn't enough of something to go around. The most obvious example of a scarce resource is money—a cause of many conflicts. If a worker asks for a raise in pay and the boss would rather keep the money or use it to expand the business, the two parties are in conflict.

Time is another scarce commodity. As authors and family men, both of us constantly face struggles about how to use the limited time we have at home. Should we work on this book? Visit with our wives? Play with our children? Enjoy the luxury of being alone? With only twenty-four hours in a day, we're bound to wind up in conflicts with our families, editors, students, and friends—all of whom want more of our time than we have to give.

Interdependence   However antagonistic they might feel, the parties in conflict are usually dependent on each other. The welfare and satisfaction of one depend on the actions of another. If not, then even in the face of scarce resources and incompatible goals there would be no need for conflict. Interdependence exists between conflicting nations, social groups, organizations, friends, and lovers. In each case, if the two parties didn't need each other to solve the problem, they would go their separate ways. In fact, many conflicts go unresolved because the parties fail to understand their interdependence. One of the first steps toward resolving a conflict is to take the attitude that "we're all in this together."

Interference from the Other Party   No matter how much one person's position may differ from another's, a full-fledged conflict won't occur until the participants act in ways that prevent one another from reaching their goals. For example, you might let some friends know that you object to their driving after drinking too much alcohol, but the conflict will escalate if you act in ways that prevent them from getting behind the wheel. Likewise, a parent-child dispute about what clothing and music are appropriate will blossom into a conflict when the parents try to impose their position on the child.

Conflict Is Natural

Every relationship of any depth at all has conflict.[4] No matter how close, how understanding, how compatible you and other people are, there will be times when your ideas or actions or needs or goals won't match. You like rap music, but your companion likes classical; you want to date other people, but your partner wants to keep the relationship exclusive; you think a paper that you've written is fine, but your instructor wants it changed; you like to sleep late on Sunday mornings, but your housemate likes to play the stereo—loudly! There's no end to the number and kinds of disagreements possible. College students who have kept diaries of their relationships report that they take part in about seven arguments per week. Most have argued with the other person before, often about the same topic.[5] In another survey, 81 percent of the respondents acknowledged that they had conflicts with friends.[6] Even the 19 percent who claimed that their friendships were conflict-free used terms like "push and pull" or "little disagreements" to describe the tensions that inevitably occurred. Among families, conflict can be even more frequent. Researchers recorded dinner conversations for fifty-two families and found an average of 3.3 "conflict episodes" per meal.[7]

We struggled together, knowing. We prattled, pretended, fought bitterly, laughed, wept over sad books or old movies, nagged, supported, gave, took, demanded, forgave, resented—hating the ugliness of each other, yet cherishing that which we were. . . . Will I ever find someone to battle with as we battled, love as we loved, share with as we shared, challenge as we challenged, forgive as we forgave? You used to say that I saved up all of my feelings so that I could spew forth when I got home. The anger I experienced in school I could not vent there. How many times have I heard you chuckle as you remembered the day I would come home from school and share with you all of the feelings I had kept in. "If anyone had been listening they would have thought you were punishing me, striking out at me. I always survived and you always knew that I would still be with you when you were through." There was an honesty about our relationship that may never exist again.

Vian Catrell

Just as conflict is a fact of life, so are the feelings that go with it—hurt, anger, frustration, resentment, and disappointment. Because these feelings are usually unpleasant, there is a temptation to avoid them or pretend they don't exist. But as sure as conflicts are bound to arise, so are the feelings that go with them.

At first this might seem depressing. If problems are inevitable in even the best relationships, does this mean that you're doomed to relive the same arguments, the same hurt feelings, over and over? Fortunately, the answer to this question is a definite "no." Even though conflict is a part of a meaningful relationship, you can change the way you deal with it.

Conflict Can Be Beneficial

Because it is impossible to *avoid* conflicts, the challenge is to handle them well when they do arise. Effective communication during conflicts can actually keep good relationships strong. People who use the constructive skills described in this chapter are more satisfied with their relationships[8] and with the outcomes of their conflicts.[9]

Perhaps the best evidence of how constructive conflict skills can benefit a relationship focuses on communication between husbands and wives. Over twenty years of research shows that both happy and unhappy marriages have conflicts but that they manage conflict in very different ways.[10] One nine-year study revealed that unhappy couples argued in ways that we have cataloged in this book as destructive.[11] They were more concerned with defending themselves than with being problem-oriented; they failed to listen carefully to one another, had little or no empathy for their partners, used evaluative "you" language, and ignored one another's nonverbal relational messages.

Many satisfied couples think and communicate differently when they disagree. They view disagreements as healthy and recognize that conflicts need to be faced.[12] Although they may argue vigorously, they use skills like perception checking to find out what the other person is thinking, and they let one another know that they understand the other side of the argument.[13] They are willing to admit their mistakes, both contributing to a harmonious relationship and helping to solve the problem at hand.

In the following pages, we will review communication skills that can make conflicts constructive, and we will introduce still more skills that you can use to resolve the inevitable conflicts you face. Before doing so, however, we need to examine how individuals behave when faced with a dispute.

PERSONAL CONFLICT STYLES

People can act in several ways when their needs aren't met (see Table 10-1). Each way has very different characteristics, as we can show by describing a common problem. At one time or another almost everyone has been bothered by neighbors' barking dog. You know the story: Every

> Not everything that is faced can be changed, but nothing can be changed until it is faced.
>
> James Baldwin

> Are there genuinely nice, sweet people in this world? Yes, absolutely yes, and they get angry as often as you and I. They must—otherwise they would be full of vindictive feelings and slush, which would prevent genuine sweetness.
>
> Theodore Isaac Rubin

TABLE 10-1 Individual Styles of Conflict

	NONASSERTIVE	DIRECTLY AGGRESSIVE	PASSIVE AGGRESSIVE	INDIRECT	ASSERTIVE
APPROACH TO OTHERS	I'm not OK, you're OK.	I'm OK, you're not OK.	I'm OK, you're not OK. (But I'll let you think you are.)	I'm OK, you're not OK or I'm not OK, you're OK.	I'm OK, you're OK.
DECISION MAKING	Lets other choose.	Chooses for others. They know it.	Chooses for others. They don't know it.	Chooses for others. They don't know it.	Chooses for self.
SELF-SUFFICIENCY	Low	High or low	Looks high, but usually low.	High or low	Usually high
BEHAVIOR IN PROBLEM SITUATIONS	Flees; gives in.	Outright attack	Concealed attack	Strategic, oblique	Direct confrontation
RESPONSE OF OTHERS	Disrespect, guilt, anger, frustration	Hurt, defensiveness, humiliation	Confusion, frustration, feelings of manipulation	Unknowing compliance or resistance	Mutual respect
SUCCESS PATTERN	Succeeds by luck or charity of others.	Feels compelled to beat out others.	Wins by manipulation.	Gains unwitting compliance of others.	Attempts "win-win" solutions.

Adapted with permission from *The Assertive Woman* by Stanlee Phelps and Nancy Austin. 3rd edition ©1997 by Impact Publishers, Inc., P. O. Box 1094, San Luis Obispo, CA 93406. Further reproduction prohibited.

passing car, distant siren, pedestrian, and falling leaf seem to set off a fit of barking that makes you unable to sleep, socialize, or study. In a description of the possible ways of handling this kind of situation, the differences between nonassertive, directly aggressive, passive aggressive, indirect, and assertive behavior should become clear.

Nonassertive Behavior

Nonassertion is the inability or unwillingness to express thoughts or feelings in a conflict. Sometimes nonassertion comes from a lack of confidence. At other times people lack the awareness or skill to use a more direct means of expression. Sometimes people know how to communicate in an assertive way but choose to behave nonassertively.

Nonassertion is a surprisingly common way of dealing with conflicts. One study revealed that dating partners do not express roughly 40 percent of their relational grievances to one another.[14] Another study examined the conflict level of spouses in "nondistressed" marriages. Over a five-day period, spouses reported that their partner engaged in an

Reprinted by permission of United Features Syndicate, Inc.

average of thirteen behaviors that were "displeasurable" to them but that they had only one confrontation during the same period.[15]

Nonassertion can take a variety of forms. One is **avoidance**—either physical (steering clear of a friend after having an argument) or conversational (changing the topic, joking, or denying that a problem exists). People who avoid conflicts usually believe that it's easier to put up with the status quo than to face the conflict head-on and try to solve it. **Accommodation** is another type of nonassertive response. Accommodators deal with conflict by giving in, putting the other's needs ahead of their own.

Faced with the annoyance of a barking dog next door, a nonassertive person might try to ignore the noise by closing the windows and turning up the radio. Other nonassertive responses would be to deny that the problem even exists or to hope that it would go away. None of these alternatives sounds very appealing. They probably would lead the nonassertive communicator to grow more and more angry at the neighbors, making a friendly relationship difficult. Nonassertion also can lead to a loss of self-respect: It's hard to respect yourself when you can't cope with even an everyday irritation.[16]

Nonassertion isn't always a bad idea. You might choose to keep quiet or give in if the risk of speaking up is too great: getting fired from a job you can't afford to lose, being humiliated in public, or even risking physical harm. You might also avoid a conflict if the relationship that it involves isn't worth the effort. Even in close relationships, though, nonassertion has its logic. If the issue is temporary or minor, you might let it pass. It might even make sense to keep your thoughts to yourself and give in if the issue is more important to the other person than it is to you. These reasons help explain why the communication of many happily married couples is characterized by "selectively ignoring" the other person's minor flaws.[17] This doesn't mean that a key to successful relationships is avoiding *all* conflicts. Instead, it means that it's smart to save energy for the truly important ones.

Like avoidance, accommodation can also be appropriate, especially in cases in which the other person's needs may be more important than yours. For instance, if a friend wants to have a serious talk and you feel playful, you'd most likely honor her request, particularly if the friend is

Silence needs no
messenger.
Stillness runs in all
directions
Building thoughts and
feelings, each a realm,
To well up and drown
the senses,
And overwhelm.
Your silence needs no
messenger.
Yet, it makes prisoner
my mind.
Wonder becomes worry,
then dread
About that which wasn't
soundly said.

Neil Towne

facing some kind of crisis and wants your help. In most cases, however, nonassertive accommodators fail to assert themselves either because they don't value themselves sufficiently or because they don't know how to ask for what they want.

Direct Aggression

In contrast to nonassertion, **direct aggression** occurs when a communicator expresses a criticism or demand that threatens the face of the person at whom it is directed. Communication researcher Dominic Infante identified several types of direct aggression: character attacks, competence attacks, physical appearance attacks, maledictions (wishing the other ill fortune), teasing, ridicule, threats, swearing, and nonverbal emblems.[18]

Direct aggression can have a severe impact on the target. Recipients can feel embarrassed, inadequate, humiliated, hopeless, desperate, or depressed. These results can lead to decreased effectiveness in personal relationships, on the job, and in families.[19] There is a significant connection between verbal aggression and physical aggression,[20] but even if the attacks never lead to blows, the psychological effects can be devastating. For example, siblings who were teased by a brother or sister reported less satisfaction and trust than those whose relationships were relatively free of this sort of aggression,[21] and high school teams with aggressive coaches lose more games than those whose coaches are less aggressive.[22]

Aggressive behavior can punish the attacker as well as the victim. Men who view conversations as contests and partners as opponents are 60 percent more apt to die earlier than those who are less aggressive.[23] Newly married couples whose disagreements were marked by sarcasm, interruptions, and criticism suffered a drop in the effectiveness of their immune systems.[24]

Verbal aggression can affect the relationship as well as the individuals involved. One aggressive remark can lead to an equally aggressive reaction, starting a destructive spiral that can expand beyond the original dispute and damage the entire relationship.[25] This fact explains why verbally abusive couples report significantly less relational satisfaction than do couples who communicate about their conflicts in other ways.[26] Even among well-adjusted couples, negative communication is more likely to be reciprocated than positive—and after hostility is expressed, it usually escalates.[27]

You could handle the barking dog problem with direct aggression by abusively confronting your neighbors, calling them names and threatening to call the dogcatcher the next time you see their dog running loose. If your town has a leash law, you would be within your legal rights to do so, and thus you would gain your goal of bringing peace and quiet to the neighborhood. Unfortunately, your direct aggression would have other, less productive consequences. Your neighbors and you would probably cease to be on speaking terms, and you could expect a complaint from them the first time you violated even the most inconsequential of city ordinances. If you live in the neighborhood for any time at all, this state of hostilities isn't very appealing. This example shows why research confirms what common sense suggests: Unlike other conflict styles, direct aggression is judged incompetent by virtually everyone who encounters it.[28]

Passive Aggression

Passive aggression occurs when a communicator expresses hostility in an obscure way. As the "Ethical Challenge" on page 411 explains, this behavior has been termed **"crazymaking."** It occurs when people have feelings of resentment, anger, or rage that they are unable or unwilling to express directly. Instead of keeping these feelings to themselves, a crazymaker sends aggressive messages in subtle, indirect ways, thus maintaining the front of kindness. This amiable façade eventually crumbles, however, leaving the crazymaker's victim confused and angry at having been fooled. The targets of the crazymaker can either react with aggressive behavior of their own or retreat to nurse their hurt feelings. In either case passive aggression seldom has anything but harmful effects on a relationship.[29]

You could respond to your neighbors and their barking dog in several crazymaking, passive-aggressive ways. One way would be to complain anonymously to the city pound and then, after the dog has been hauled away, express your sympathy. Or you could complain to everyone else in the neighborhood, hoping that their hostility would force the offending neighbors to quiet the dog or face being social outcasts.

There are a number of shortcomings to this sort of approach, each of which illustrates the risks of passive aggression. First, there is the chance that the crazymaking won't work: The neighbors might simply miss the point of your veiled attacks and continue to ignore the barking. On the other hand, they might get your message clearly, but either because of your lack of sincerity or because of sheer stubbornness, they might simply refuse to do anything about it. In either case, it's likely that in this and other instances passive aggression won't satisfy your unmet need.

Even when passive aggression proves successful in the short run, a second shortcoming lies in its consequences over the longer term. You might manage to intimidate your neighbors into shutting up their dog, for instance, but in winning the battle you could lose what would become a war. As a means of revenge, they could wage their own campaign of crazymaking by such tactics as badmouthing your sloppy gardening to other neighbors or phoning in false complaints about your loud parties. It's obvious that feuds such as this one are counterproductive and outweigh the apparent advantages of passive aggression.

Indirect Communication

The clearest communication is not necessarily the best approach. **Indirect communication** conveys a message in a roundabout manner, in order to save face for the recipient. Although indirect communication lacks the clarity of aggressive or assertive communication, it involves more initiative than nonassertion. It also has none of the hostility of passive-aggressive crazymaking. The goal is to get what you want without arousing the hostility of the other person. Consider the case of the barking dog. One indirect approach would be to strike up a friendly conversation with the owners and ask if anything you are doing is too noisy for them, hoping they would get the hint.

Because it saves face for the other party, indirect communication is often kinder than blunt honesty. If your guests are staying too long, it's probably kinder to yawn and hint about your big day tomorrow than to bluntly ask them to leave. Likewise, if you're not interested in going out with someone who has asked you for a date, it may be more compassionate to claim that you're busy than to say, "I'm not interested in seeing you."

At other times we communicate indirectly in order to protect ourselves. You might, for example, test the waters by hinting instead of directly asking the boss for a raise, or by letting your partner know indirectly that you could use some affection instead of asking outright. At times like these, an indirect approach may get the message across while softening the blow of a negative response.

The advantages of self-protection and face-saving for others help explain why indirect communication is the most common way by which people make requests.[30] The risk of an indirect message, of course, is that the other party will misunderstand you or fail to get the message at all. There are also times when an idea is so important that hinting lacks the necessary punch. When clarity and directness are your goals, an assertive approach is in order.

Assertion

Assertion occurs when a message expresses the speaker's needs, thoughts, and feelings clearly and directly without judging or dictating to others. Most assertive messages follow the format described later in this chapter on pages 415–423.

Dirty Fighting with Crazymakers

Psychologist George Bach uses the term "crazymakers" to describe passive-aggressive behavior. His term reflects the insidious nature of indirect aggression, which can confuse and anger a victim who may not even be aware of being victimized. Although a case can be made for using all of the other approaches to conflict described in this chapter, it is difficult to find a justification for passive-aggressive crazymaking.

The following categories represent a nonexhaustive list of crazymaking. They are presented here as a warning for potential victims, who might choose to use perception checking, "I" language, assertion, or other communication strategies to explore whether the user has a complaint that can be addressed in a more constructive manner.

The Avoider

Avoiders refuse to fight. When a conflict arises, they leave, fall asleep, pretend to be busy at work, or keep from facing the problem in some other way. Because avoiders won't fight back, this strategy can frustrate the person who wants to address an issue.

The Pseudoaccommodator

Pseudoaccommodators pretend to give in and then continue to act in the same way.

The Guiltmaker

Instead of expressing dissatisfaction directly, guiltmakers try to make others feel responsible for causing pain. A guiltmaker's favorite line is "It's OK; don't worry about me . . ." accompanied by a big sigh.

The Mind Reader

Instead of allowing their partners to express feelings honestly, mind readers go into character analysis, explaining what the partner really means or what's wrong with the partner. By behaving this way mind readers refuse to handle their own feelings and leave no room for their partners to express themselves.

The Trapper

Trappers play an especially dirty trick by setting up a desired behavior for their partners and then, when it's met, attacking the very behavior they requested. An example of this technique is for the trapper to say, "Let's be totally honest with each other," and then attack the partner's self-disclosure.

The Crisis Tickler

Crisis ticklers almost bring what's bothering them to the surface but never quite come out and express themselves. Instead of admitting concern about the finances, they innocently ask, "Gee, how much did that cost?" dropping a rather obvious hint but never really dealing with the crisis.

The Gunnysacker

These people don't share complaints as they arise. Instead, they put their resentments into a psychological gunnysack, which after a while begins to bulge with both large and small gripes. Then, when the sack is about to burst, the gunnysacker pours out all the pent-up aggressions on the overwhelmed and unsuspecting victim.

The Trivial Tyrannizer

Instead of honestly sharing their resentments, trivial tyrannizers do things they know will get their part-ners' goat—leaving dirty dishes in the sink, clipping fingernails in bed, belching out loud, turning up the television too loud, and so on.

The Beltliner

Everyone has a psychological "beltline," and below it are subjects too sensitive to be approached without damaging the relationship. Beltlines may have to do with physical characteristics, intelligence, past behavior, or deeply ingrained personality traits that a person is trying to overcome. In an attempt to "get even" or hurt their partners, beltliners will use intimate knowledge to hit below the belt, where they know it will hurt.

The Joker

Because they are afraid to face conflicts squarely, jokers kid around when their partners want to be serious, thus blocking the expression of important feelings.

The Withholder

Instead of expressing their anger honestly and directly, withholders punish their partners by keeping back something—courtesy, affection, good cooking, humor, sex. As you can imagine, this is likely to build up even greater resentments in the relationship.

The Benedict Arnold

These characters get back at their partners by sabotage, by failing to defend them from attackers, and even by encouraging ridicule or disregard from outside the relationship.

For more information about crazymaking, see George Bach and Peter Wyden, *The Intimate Enemy* (New York: Avon, 1968); and George Bach, *Aggression Lab: The Fair Fight Manual* (Dubuque, Iowa: Kendall-Hunt, 1971).

I was angry with my friend.
I told my wrath, my wrath did end.
I was angry with my foe:
I told it not, my wrath did grow.
And I watered it in fears,
Night and morning with my tears;
And I sunned it with smiles,
And with soft deceitful wiles.

And it grew both day and night,
Till it bore an apple bright;
And my foe beheld it shine,
And he knew that it was mine,
And into my garden stole
When the night had veiled the pole:
In the morning glad I see
My foe outstretched beneath the tree.

William Blake

An assertive course of action in the case of the barking dog would be to wait a few days to make sure that the noise is not just a fluke. If the barking continues, you could introduce yourself to your neighbors and explain your problem. You could tell them that although they might not notice it, the dog often plays in the street and keeps barking at passing cars. You could tell them why this behavior bothers you. It keeps you awake at night and makes it hard for you to do your work. You could point out that you don't want to be a grouch and call the pound. Rather than resort to that, you could tell them that you've come to see what kind of solution you can find that will satisfy both of you. This approach may not work, and you might then have to decide whether it is more important to avoid bad feelings or to have peace and quiet. But the chances for a happy ending are best with this assertive approach. And no matter what happens, you can keep your self-respect by behaving directly and honestly.

"Conflict Styles: What Are You Like?"

http://204.98. 1.2/high/wotc/ confli1.htm

This page provides a brief explanation of five different conflict styles. Also included is a self-test to determine your own conflict style. You can follow up on this self-test by completing Activity 10.2 "What Is Your Conflict Style?" at the *Looking Out/Looking In* Web site.

INVITATION TO INSIGHT

YOUR CONFLICT STYLE

1. Think back over your recent history, and recall five conflicts you've had. The more current they are, the better, and they should be ones that occurred with people who are important to you, people with whom your relationship matters.

2. Turn an 8½-by-11 sheet of paper horizontally and copy the following chart. To give yourself plenty of room you might extend your chart onto a second page.

I THE CONFLICT	II HOW I MANAGED IT	III THE RESULTS
(Describe whom it was with, what it was about.)	(What did you say? How did you act?)	(How did you feel? How did the others involved feel? Are you happy with the results?)

3. For each of the conflicts, fill in the appropriate spaces on your chart.

4. Based on what you've written here, answer the following questions:
   a. Are you happy with the way you've handled your conflicts? Do you come away from them feeling better or worse than before?
   b. Have your conflicts made your relationships stronger or weaker?
   c. Do you recognize any patterns in your conflict style? For example, do you hold your angry feelings inside? Are you sarcastic? Do you lose your temper easily?
   d. If you could, would you like to change the way you deal with your conflicts?

[handwritten margin notes: assertion, flexible in process & outcome, good listening skills, open to feedback about self & assertion, healthy self-esteem]

Which Style Is Best?

After reading this far, you might think that assertive communication is clearly superior to other styles. It allows you to express yourself honestly and seems to have the greatest chance of success. Actually, it's an over-simplification to say that any communication style is always best. A competent, successful communicator will choose the most effective style for a given situation.

How can you decide which style will be most effective? There are several factors to consider.

1. *The Relationship* When someone else clearly has more power than you, nonassertion may be the best approach. If the boss tells you to fill that order "*now!*" it may be smart to do so without comment. The more assertive response ("When you use that tone of voice, I feel defensive . . .") might be more clear, but it also could cost you your job.

2. *The Situation* In every relationship, different situations call for different conflict styles. Even the most mild-mannered parents will testify that sooner or later yelling seems to be the only way to get a child to respond: "I've told you three times not to bother the cat. Now *stop it*, or you'll be sorry!" In other cases, it might be smart to replace a normally direct approach with hints or silence.

3. *The Other Person* Although assertiveness has the best chance of success with most people, some receivers respond better to other approaches. One businessman illustrated this point when he described how his normally even-tempered boss used shouting in a phone conversation with a particularly difficult person:

   > I've never heard him so angry. He was enraged. His face was red, and the veins were bulging on his neck. I tried to get his attention to calm him down, but he waved me away impatiently. As soon as the call was over, he turned to me and smiled. "There," he said. "That ought to do it." If I were the guy he'd been shouting at, let me tell you, that would have done it, too. But it was all a put-on.[31]

4. *Your Goals.* When you want to solve a problem, assertiveness may seem like the best approach, but there are other reasons for communicating in a conflict. The other person might not like you as much when you assert your rights as when you keep quiet, so if the goal is to maintain harmony, nonassertion may be the best course.[32] The problem might not be worth the potential conflict. In other cases, your overriding concern may be to calm down an enraged or upset person. Tolerating an outburst from your crotchety and sick neighbor, for example, is probably better than standing up for yourself and triggering a stroke. Likewise, you might choose to sit quietly through the nagging of a family member rather than ruin Thanksgiving dinner. In still other cases, your moral principles might compel an aggressive statement even though it might not get you what you originally sought: "I've had enough of your racist jokes. I've tried to explain why they're so offensive, but you obviously haven't listened. I'm leaving!"

ASSERTION WITHOUT AGGRESSION: THE CLEAR MESSAGE FORMAT

Knowing *when* to behave assertively isn't the same as knowing *how* to assert yourself. The next few pages will describe a method for communicating assertively. It works for a variety of messages: your hopes, problems, complaints, and appreciations.[33] Besides giving you a way to express yourself directly, the clear message format makes it easy for others to understand you. Finally, because assertive messages are phrased in the kind of descriptive "I" language you learned in chapter 5, they are less likely than aggressive attacks to cause a defensive reaction that will start a needless fight or shut down discussion altogether.

A complete assertive message has five parts. We'll examine each part one by one and then discuss how to combine them in your everyday communication.

Behavior

As you read in chapter 5, a **behavioral description** describes the raw material to which you react. A behavioral description should be *objective*, describing an event without interpreting it.

Two examples of behavioral descriptions might look like this.

Example 1

"One week ago John promised me that he would ask my permission before smoking in the same room with me. Just a moment ago he lit up a cigarette without asking for my OK."

Example 2

"Chris has acted differently over the last week. I can't remember her laughing once since the holiday weekend. She hasn't dropped by my place like she usually does, hasn't suggested we play tennis, and hasn't returned my phone calls."

Notice that in both cases the descriptive statements record only data that are available through the senses. The observer has not attached any meaning. The value of describing the problem without using emotive language was demonstrated by a study examining conflicts between couples. The study revealed that satisfied partners tend to offer behavioral complaints ("You always throw your socks on the floor"), whereas unsatisfied partners make more complaints aimed at personal characteristics ("You're a slob").[34] Other research confirmed the fact that personal complaints are more likely to result in an escalated conflict episode.[35] The reason should be obvious—complaints about personal characteristics attack a more fundamental part of the presenting self. Complaining about socks deals with a habit that can be changed; complaining that someone is a slob is a character assault that is unlikely to be forgotten when the conflict is over.

Interpretation

Interpretation is the process of attaching meaning to behavior. The important thing to realize about interpretations is that they are *subjective.* That is, we can attach more than one interpretation to any behavior. For example, look at these two different interpretations of each of the preceding descriptions:

Example 1

Interpretation A "John must have forgotten about our agreement that he wouldn't smoke without asking me first. I'm sure he's too considerate to go back on his word on something he knows I feel strongly about."

Interpretation B "John is a rude, inconsiderate person. After promising not to smoke around me without asking, he's just deliberately done so. This shows that he cares only about himself. In fact, I bet he's deliberately doing this to drive me crazy!"

Example 2

Interpretation A "Something must be bothering Chris. It's probably her family. She'll probably just feel worse if I keep pestering her."

Interpretation B "Chris is probably mad at me. It's probably because I kidded her about losing so often at tennis. I'd better leave her alone until she cools off."

These examples show that interpretations are based on more than simple sense data. They grow out of many factors, including:

- *Your past experience* "John has always (never) kept his promises in the past" or "When I'm preoccupied with personal problems I draw away from my friends."
- *Your assumptions* "An unkept promise is a sign of uncaring (forgetfulness)" or "Lack of communication with friends is a sign that something is wrong."
- *Your expectations* "John probably wants (doesn't want) to fight" or "I thought the family visit (or kidding about tennis) would upset her."
- *Your knowledge* "Longtime, habitual cigarette smokers aren't even aware of lighting up" or "I know Chris's dad has been sick lately."
- *Your current mood* "I feel good about John and about life in general" or "I've been awfully sarcastic lately. I went too far when I kidded Chris about her tennis game."

After you become aware of the difference between observable behavior and interpretation, some of the reasons for communication breakdowns become clear. Many problems occur when a sender fails to describe the behavior on which an interpretation is based. For instance, imagine the difference between hearing a friend say

"You are a tightwad!" (*no behavioral description*)

and explaining

"When you never offer to pay me back for the coffee and snacks I often buy you, I think you're a tightwad." (*behavior plus interpretation*)

The first speaker's failure to specify behavior would probably confuse the receiver, who has no way of knowing what prompted the speaker's remarks. This failure to describe behavior also reduces any chance that the receiver will change the offensive behavior, which, after all, is unknown to that person.

Just as important as specifying behavior is the need to label an interpretation as such instead of presenting it as a matter of fact. Consider the difference between saying

"It's obvious that if you cared for me you'd write more often." (*interpretation presented as fact*)

and

"When I didn't get a letter or even a postcard from you, I thought that you didn't care for me." (*interpretation made clear*)

As you learned in chapter 5, your comments are much less likely to arouse defensiveness in others when you present them using "I" language.

It's important to avoid making statements that appear to describe behavior but that are, in fact, interpretations. For instance, don't mistake these kinds of statements as objective descriptions:

"I see you're tired." (*Tired* is an interpretation. Your behavioral description might have been "I see your eyes closing and your head nodding.")

"I see you're in a hurry." (*Hurry* is an interpretation. The behavioral description could have been "I see you gathering up your books and looking at the clock.")

"I can tell that you're hungry." (*Hungry* is an interpretation. The behavior you heard was the sound of your friend's stomach growling.)

"You look anxious to get started." (*Anxious* is an interpretation. What could the behavior be in this case? The short time that it took your friend to answer the doorbell? The outside clothing in which the person was already dressed?)

There's nothing wrong with making these interpretations. In fact, this is a necessary step because only by interpreting behavior do we arrive at a meaning. However, we often make inaccurate interpretations, and when we don't separate behavior from our interpretations, we fool ourselves into believing that our interpretations are reality—that is, what we *think* is what exists.

BEHAVIORS AND INTERPRETATIONS

1. Tell two other group members several interpretations that you have recently made about other people in your life. For each interpretation, describe the behavior on which you based your interpretations.

2. With your partners' help, consider some alternate interpretations of the behavior that might be as plausible as your original one.

3. After considering the alternate interpretations, decide
   a. which one was most reasonable
   b. how you might share that interpretation (along with the behavior) with the other person involved in a tentative, nondogmatic way

Feeling

Reporting behavior and sharing your interpretations are important, but *feeling statements* add a new dimension to a message. For example, consider the difference between saying

"When you kiss me and nibble on my ear while we're watching television (*behavior*), I think you probably want to make love (*interpretation*), and *I feel excited.*"

and

"When you kiss me and nibble on my ear while we're watching television, I think you probably want to make love, and *I feel disgusted.*"

Notice how the expression of different feelings can change the meaning of another message.

"When you laugh at me (*behavior*), I think you find my comments foolish (*interpretation*), and *I feel embarrassed.*"

and

"When you laugh at me, I think you find my comments foolish, and *I feel angry.*"

No doubt you can supply other examples in which different feelings can radically affect a speaker's meaning. Recognizing this, we find it logical to say that we should identify our feelings in our conversations with others. Yet if we pay attention to the everyday acts of communication, we see that no such disclosure occurs.

It's important to recognize that some statements *seem* as if they're expressing feelings but are actually interpretations or statements of intention. For instance, it's not accurate to say "I feel like leaving" (really an intention) or "I feel you're wrong" (an interpretation). Statements like these obscure the true expression of feelings.

Why do people not share their feelings? Certainly one reason is that making such statements can bring on a great deal of anxiety. It's often frightening to come right out and say, "I'm angry," "I feel embarrassed," or

"I love you," and often we aren't willing to take the risks that come with such clear-cut assertions.

A second reason why people don't share their feelings clearly is simply because they don't recognize them. We aren't always aware that we're angry, confused, impatient, or sad. Asking yourself, "How do I feel?" can often uncover important information that needs to be communicated to your partner.

SKILL BUILDER

NAME THE FEELING

Add a feeling that you would be likely to have to each of the following messages:

1. I felt _____ when I found out you didn't invite me on the camping trip. You said you thought I wouldn't want to go, but I have a hard time accepting that.

2. I felt _____ when you offered to help me move. I know how busy you are.

3. When you tell me you still want to be a friend but you want to "lighten up a little," I get the idea you're tired of me, and I feel _____ .

4. You told me you wanted my honest opinion about your paintings, and then when I tell you what I think, you say I don't understand them. I'm _____ .

    How would the impact of each message be different if it didn't include a feeling statement?

Consequence

A **consequence statement** explains what happens as a result of the behavior you have described, your interpretation, the ensuing feeling, or all three. There are three types of consequences:

■ What happens to you, the speaker

  ■ "When I didn't get the phone message yesterday (*behavior*), I didn't know that my doctor's appointment was delayed and that I would end up sitting in the office for an hour when I could have been studying or working (*consequences*). It seems to me that you don't care enough about how busy I am to even write a simple note (*interpretation*), and that's why I'm so mad (*feeling*)."

  ■ "I appreciate (*feeling*) the help you've given me on my term paper (*behavior*). It tells me you think I'm on the right track (*interpretation*), and this gives me a boost to keep working on the idea (*consequences*)."

■ What happens to the person you're addressing

  ■ "When you have four or five drinks at a party after I've warned you to slow down (*behavior*), you start to act strange: You make crude

"Expressing Yourself More Clearly and Completely"

http://www. coopcomm.org/ w7chal3.htm

This page is a chapter in an excellent, comprehensive online book that explores seven challenging interpersonal communication skills. The chapter offers a step-by-step methodology for assertively expressing yourself in a clear and complete manner (a variation on the assertive message format described on these pages). To practice expressing yourself more effectively complete Activity 10.1 "Delivering Your Own Clear and Complete Messages" on the *Looking Out/Looking In* Web site.

jokes that offend everybody, and on the way home you drive poorly (*consequences*). For instance, last night you almost hit a phone pole while you were backing out of the driveway (*more behavior*). I don't think you realize how differently you act (*interpretation*), and I'm worried (*feeling*) about what will happen if you don't drink less."

■ What happens to others

- ■ "You probably don't know because you couldn't hear her cry (*interpretation*), but when you rehearse your lines for the play without closing the doors (*behavior*), the baby can't sleep (*consequence*). I'm especially concerned (*feeling*) about her because she's had a cold lately."

- ■ "I thought you'd want to know (*interpretation*) that when you kid Bob about his height (*behavior*), he gets embarrassed (*feeling*) and usually quiets down or leaves (*consequences*)."

Consequence statements are valuable for two reasons. First, they help you understand more clearly why you are bothered or pleased by another's behavior. Just as important, telling others about the consequences of their actions can clarify for them the results of their behavior. As with interpretations, we often think that others *should* be aware of consequences without being told; but the fact is that they often aren't. By explicitly stating consequences, you can be sure that you or your message leaves nothing to the listener's imagination.

When you are stating consequences, it's important simply to describe what happens without moralizing. For instance, it's one thing to say, "When you didn't call to say you'd be late, I stayed up worrying," and another to rant on, "How can I ever trust you? You're going to drive me crazy!" Remember that it's perfectly legitimate to express your thoughts and feelings, but it's important to label them as such. And when you want to request change from someone, you can use intention statements, which we'll now describe.

It's easy to confuse some interpretation, feeling, or intention statements with consequences. For example, you might say, "As a consequence of your turning down my invitation (*behavior*), I got the idea (*interpretation*) you're mad at me. I'm worried (*feeling*), and I want to know what you're thinking (*intention*)." To say that these are not consequences as we're using the term is more than semantic hairsplitting. Confusing interpretations, feelings, and intentions with consequences might prevent you from mentioning the true consequence—what has happened as a result of this event. In our example, a real consequence statement might be ". . . and that's why I've been so quiet lately." As you'll read on pages 422–423, sometimes a consequenceis combined with another message element. The important point to remem-ber is that you somehow need to explain the consequences of an incident ifthe other person is to understand your concern completely.

Intention

Intention statements are the final element of the assertive clear message format. They can communicate three kinds of messages:

- Where you stand on an issue
  - "When you call us 'girls' after I've told you we want to be called 'women' (*behavior*), I get the idea you don't appreciate how important the difference is to us (*interpretation*) and how demeaning it feels (*feeling*). Now I'm in an awkward spot: Either I have to keep bringing the subject up, or else drop it and feel bad (*consequence*). I want you to know how much this bothers me (*intention*)."
  - "I'm really grateful (*feeling*) to you for speaking up for me in front of the boss yesterday (*behavior*). That must have taken a lot of courage (*interpretation*). Knowing that you're behind me gives me a lot of confidence (*consequence*), and I want you to know how much I appreciate your support (*intention*)."
- Requests of others
  - "When I didn't hear from you last night (*behavior*), I thought you were mad at me (*interpretation*). I've been thinking about it ever since (*consequence*), and I'm still worried (*feeling*). I'd like to know whether you are angry (*intention*)."
  - "I really enjoyed (*feeling*) your visit (*behavior*), and I'm glad you had a good time, too (*interpretation*). I hope you'll come again (*intention*)."
- Descriptions of how you plan to act in the future
  - "I've asked you to repay the twenty-five dollars I lent you three times now (*behavior*). I'm getting the idea that you've been avoiding me (*interpretation*), and I'm pretty angry about it (*feeling*). I want you to know that unless we clear this up now, you shouldn't expect me ever to lend you anything again (*intention*)."
  - "I'm glad (*feeling*) you liked (*interpretation*) the paper I wrote. I'm thinking about taking your advanced writing class next term (*intention*)."

Why is it so important to make your intentions clear? Because failing to do so often makes it hard for others to know what you want from them or how to act. Consider how confusing the following statements are because they lack a clear statement of intention.

"Wow! A frozen Snickers. I haven't had one of those in years." (Does the speaker want a bite, or is she just making an innocent remark?)

"Thanks for the invitation, but I really should study Saturday night." (Does the speaker want to be asked out again, or is she indirectly suggesting that she doesn't ever want to go out with you?)

"To tell you the truth, I was asleep when you came by, but I should have been up anyway." (Is the speaker saying that it's OK to come by in the future, or is he hinting that he doesn't appreciate unannounced visitors?)

You can see from these examples that it's often hard to make a clear interpretation of another person's ideas without a direct statement of intention. Notice how much more direct statements become when the speakers make their position clear.

"Wow! A frozen Snickers. I haven't had one of those in years. *If I hadn't already eaten, I'd sure ask for a bite.*"

"Thanks for the invitation, but I really should study Saturday night. *I hope you'll ask me again soon.*"

"To tell you the truth, I was asleep when you came by, but I should have been up anyway. *Maybe the next time you should phone before dropping in so I'll be sure to be awake.*"

As in the preceding cases, we are often motivated by one single intention. Sometimes, however, we act from a combination of intentions, which may even be in conflict with each other. When this happens, our conflicting intentions often make it difficult for us to reach decisions.

"I want to be truthful with you, but I don't want to violate my friend's privacy."

"I want to continue to enjoy your friendship and company, but I don't want to get too attached right now."

"I want to have time to study and get good grades, but I also want to have a job with some money coming in."

Although revealing your conflicting intentions is guaranteed to clear up confusion, sometimes an outright statement, such as the preceding, can help you come to a decision. Even when you remain mixed up, expressing your conflicting intentions has the benefit of letting others know where you stand.

Using the Clear Message Format

Before you try to deliver messages by using the clear message format, there are a few points to remember.

1. *The elements may be delivered in mixed order.* As the examples on the preceding pages show, it's sometimes best to begin by stating your feelings. At other times you can start by sharing your intentions or interpretations or by describing consequences.

2. *Word the message to suit your personal style.* Instead of saying, "I interpret your behavior to mean . . ." you might choose to say "I think . . ." or "It seems to me . . ." or perhaps "I get the idea. . . ." In the same way, you can express your intentions by saying, "I hope you'll understand (or do) . . ." or perhaps, "I wish you would. . . ." The words that you choose should sound authentic in order to reinforce the genuineness of your statement.

3. *When appropriate, combine two elements in a single phrase.* The statement ". . . and ever since then I've been wanting to talk to you" expresses both a consequence and an intention. In the same way, saying, ". . . and after you said that, I felt confused" expresses a consequence and a feeling. Whether you combine elements or state them separately, the important point is to be sure that each one is present in your statement.

4. *Take your time delivering the message.* It isn't always possible to deliver messages such as the ones here all at one time, wrapped up in neat paragraphs. It will often be necessary to repeat or restate one part many times before your receiver truly understands what you're saying. As you've already read, there are many types of psychological and physical noise that make it difficult for us to understand each other. In communication, as in many other activities, patience and persistence are essential.

Now try your hand at combining all these elements in this exercise.

SKILL BUILDER

PUTTING YOUR MESSAGE TOGETHER

1. Join with two other class members. Each person in turn should share a message that he or she might want to send to another person, being sure to include behavior, interpretation, feeling, consequence, and intention statements in the message.

2. The others in the group should help the speaker by offering feedback about how the message could be made clearer if there is any question about the meaning.

3. After the speaker has composed a satisfactory message he or she should practice actually delivering it by having another group member play the role of the intended receiver. Continue this practice until the speaker is confident that he or she can deliver the message effectively.

4. Repeat this process until each group member has had a chance to practice delivering a message.

CONFLICT IN RELATIONAL SYSTEMS

So far we have focused on individual conflict styles. Even though the style you choose in a conflict is important, your style isn't the only factor that will determine how a conflict unfolds. In reality, conflict is *relational:* Its character usually is determined by the way the parties interact with one another.[36] You might, for example, be determined to handle a conflict with your neighbor assertively, only to be driven to aggression by his uncooperative nature—or even to nonassertion by his physical threats. Likewise, you might plan to hint to a professor that you are bothered by her apparent indifference, but wind up discussing the matter in an open, assertive way in reaction to her constructive response. Examples like these suggest that conflict doesn't depend on just individual choice. Rather, it depends on how the partners interact. When two or more people are in a long-term relationship they develop their own **relational conflict style**—a pattern of managing disagreements. The mutual influence that parties have on one another is so powerful that it can overcome our disposition to handle conflicts in the manner that comes most easily to one or the other.[37] As we will soon see, some relational conflict styles are constructive, whereas others can make life miserable and threaten relationships.

Complementary, Symmetrical, and Parallel Styles

Partners in interpersonal relationships—and impersonal ones, too—can use one of three styles introduced in chapter 1 to manage their conflicts. In relationships with a **complementary conflict style** the partners use different but mutually reinforcing behaviors. In a **symmetrical conflict style,** both partners use the same behaviors. In a **parallel conflict style,** both partners shift between complementary and symmetrical patterns from one issue to another. Table 10-2 illustrates how the same conflict can unfold in very different ways, depending on whether the partners' communication is symmetrical or complementary. A parallel style would alternate between these two patterns, depending on the situation.

Research shows that a complementary "fight-flight" style is common in many unhappy marriages. One partner—most commonly the wife—addresses the conflict directly, whereas the other—usually the husband—withdraws.[38] It's easy to see how this pattern can lead to a cycle of increasing hostility and isolation because each partner punctuates the conflict differently, blaming the other for making matters worse. "I withdraw because she's so critical," a husband might say. The wife wouldn't organize the sequence in the same way, however. "I criticize because he withdraws" would be her perception.

Complementary styles aren't the only ones that can lead to problems. Some

Cathy © Cathy Guisewite. Reprinted with permission of Universal Press Syndicate. All rights reserved.

TABLE 10-2 **Complementary and Symmetrical Conflict Styles**

SITUATION	COMPLEMENTARY STYLES	SYMMETRICAL STYLES
Example 1:		
Wife upset because husband is spending little time at home.	Wife complains; husband withdraws, spending even less time at home.	Wife complains. Husband responds angrily and defensively.
Example 2:		
Female employee offended when boss calls her "sweetie."	Employee objects to boss, explaining her reasons for being offended. Boss apologizes for his unintentional insult.	Employee turns the tables by calling the boss "cutie." Boss gets the hint and stops using the term.
Example 3:		
Parents uncomfortable about teenager's new friends.	Parents express concerns. Teen dismisses them, saying "There's nothing to worry about."	Teen expresses concern that parents are being too protective.

distressed marriages suffer from destructively symmetrical communication. If both partners treat one another with matching hostility, one threat or insult leads to another in an escalatory spiral. If the partners both withdraw from one another instead of facing their problems, a deescalatory spiral results, in which the satisfaction and vitality ebb from the relationship, leaving it a shell of its former self.

As Table 10-2 shows, both complementary and symmetrical behaviors can produce "good" results as well as "bad" results. If the complementary behaviors are positive, then a positive spiral results and the conflict stands a good chance of being resolved. This is the case in example 2 in Table 10-2, where the boss is open to hearing the employee's concerns, listening willingly as the employee talks. Here, a complementary talk-listen pattern works well.

Symmetrical styles can also be beneficial, as another look at the boss-employee example shows. Many women have found that giving insensitive men a taste of their own sexist medicine is an effective way to end harassment without provoking an argument. The clearest example of constructive symmetry occurs when both parties communicate assertively, listening to one another's concerns and working together to resolve them. The potential for this sort of solution occurs in example 3, in the parent-teenager conflict. With enough mutual respect and careful listening, both the parents and their teenager can understand one another's concerns and very possibly find a way to give both parties what they want.

INVITATION TO INSIGHT

UNDERSTANDING CONFLICT STYLES

You can gain a clearer idea of how conflict styles differ by completing the following exercise.

1. Join a partner, and choose one of the following conflicts to work on. If you prefer, you may substitute a conflict of your own.
    Roommates disagree about the noise level in their apartment.
    Parents want their college sophomore son or daughter to stay home for the winter vacation. The son or daughter wants to travel with friends.
    One person in a couple wants to spend free time socializing with friends. The other wants to stay at home together.

2. Role-play the conflict four times, reflecting each of the following styles:
    Nonintimate-aggressive   Intimate-aggressive
    Nonintimate-nonaggressive   Intimate-nonaggressive

3. After experiencing each of these styles, determine which of them characterizes the way conflict is managed in one of your interpersonal relationships. Are you satisfied with this approach? If not, describe what style would be more appropriate.

Intimate and Aggressive Styles

Another way to look at conflict styles is to examine the interaction between intimacy and aggression. The following scheme was originally used to describe communication between couples, but it also works well for other types of relationships.

■ *Nonintimate-Aggressive* These partners fight but are unsuccessful at satisfying important content and relational goals. In some relationships aggression is expressed directly: "Forget it. I'm not going to another stupid party with your friends. All they do is gossip and eat." In other relationships, indirect aggression is the norm: (*Sarcastically*) "Sure I'd *love* to go to another party with your friends." Neither of these approaches is satisfying because there are few rewards to justify the costs of the unpleasantness.

■ *Nonintimate-Nonaggressive* The parties avoid conflicts—and one another—instead of facing issues head-on: "You won't be coming home for the holidays? Oh, well, I guess that's OK. . . ." Relationships of this sort can be quite stable, but because this pattern of communication doesn't confront and resolve problems, the vitality and satisfaction can decline over time.

■ *Intimate-Aggressive* This pattern combines aggression and intimacy in a manner that might seem upsetting to outsiders but that can work well in some relationships. Lovers may argue like cats and dogs, but then make up just as intensely. Coworkers might argue heatedly about how to get the job done, but cherish their association.

Intimate-Nonaggressive This sort of relationship has a low amount of attacking or blaming. Partners may confront one another directly or indirectly, but one way or another they manage to prevent issues from interfering with their relationship.

The pattern that partners choose may reveal a great deal about the kind of relationship they have chosen. Communication researcher Mary Ann Fitzpatrick identified three types of couples: separates, independents, and traditionals.[39] Further research revealed that partners in each type of relationship approached conflict in a different manner.[40] Separates and independents tended to avoid conflict. Traditionals, by contrast, spent the most time focusing on their interaction. They also felt most secure about their relationships. They expressed negative emotions frequently but also sought and revealed a large amount of personal information. Satisfied traditional couples fit the intimate-nonaggressive pattern, communicating more positive and less negative information than independents.

Findings like this suggest that there's no single "best" relational conflict style. Some families or couples may fight intensely but love one another just as strongly. Others might handle issues more rationally and calmly. Even a nonintimate-nonaggressive style can work well when there's no desire to have an interpersonal relationship. You might, for example, be willing to accommodate the demands of an eccentric professor for a semester because rolling with the punches gets you the education you are seeking without provoking a confrontation that could be upsetting and costly.

"I'm not yelling at you, I'm yelling with you."

©The New Yorker Collection 2001 David Sipress from cartoonbank.com. All Rights Reserved.

Conflict Rituals

When people have been in a relationship for some time, their communication often develops into **conflict rituals**—unacknowledged but very real patterns of interlocking behavior.[41] Consider a few common rituals:

- A young child interrupts her parents, demanding to be included in their conversation. At first the parents tell the child to wait, but she whines and cries until the parents find it easier to listen than to ignore the fussing.

■ A couple fights. One partner leaves. The other accepts the blame for the problem and begs forgiveness. The first partner returns, and a happy reunion takes place. Soon they fight again.

■ A boss flies into rage when the pressure builds at work. Recognizing this, the employees avoid him as much as possible. When the crisis is over, the boss compensates for his outbursts by being especially receptive to employee requests.

There's nothing inherently wrong with the interaction in many rituals, especially when everybody involved accepts them as ways of managing conflict.[42] Consider the preceding examples. In the first, the little girl's whining may be the only way she can get the parents' attention. In the second, both partners might use the fighting as a way to blow off steam, and both might find that the joy of a reunion is worth the grief of the separation. In the third, the ritual might work well for the boss (as a way of releasing pressure) and for employees (as a way of getting their requests met).

Rituals can cause problems, though, when they become the *only* way relational partners handle their conflicts. As you learned in chapter 1, competent communicators have a large repertoire of behaviors, and they are able to choose the most effective response for a given situation. Relying on one ritual pattern to handle all conflicts is no more effective than using a screwdriver to handle every home repair or putting the same seasoning on every dish you cook: What works in one situation isn't likely to work in many others. Conflict rituals may be familiar and comfortable, but they aren't the best way to resolve the various conflicts that are part of any relationship.

INVITATION TO INSIGHT

YOUR CONFLICT RITUALS

Describe two conflict rituals in one of your important relationships. One of your examples should consist of a positive ritual and the other of a negative ritual. For each example, explain

1. A subject that is likely to trigger the conflict (e.g., money, leisure time, affection)

2. The behavior of one partner that initiates the ritual

3. The series of responses by both partners that follows the initiating event

4. How the ritual ends
   Based on your description, explain an alternative to the unsatisfying ritual, and describe how you might be able to change the way you manage the conflict in a more satisfying way.

VARIABLES IN CONFLICT STYLES

By now you can see that every relational system is unique. The communication patterns in one family, business, or classroom are likely to be very different from those in any other. But along with the differences that arise in individual relationships, there are two powerful variables that affect the way people manage conflict: gender and culture. We will now look at each of these variables and see how they affect how conflict is managed.

Gender

Men and women often approach conflicts differently. Even in childhood, males are more likely to be aggressive, demanding, and competitive, whereas females are more likely to be cooperative. Studies of children from preschool to early adolescence have shown that boys try to get their way by ordering one another around: "Lie down." "Get off my steps." "Gimme your arm." By contrast, girls are more likely to make proposals for action, beginning with the word "Let's": "Let's go find some." "Let's ask her, 'Do you have any bottles?'" "Let's move *these* out *first*."[43] Whereas boys tell each other what role to take in pretend play ("Come on, be a doctor"), girls more commonly ask each other what role they want ("Will you be the patient for a few minutes?") or make a joint proposal ("We can both be doctors"). Furthermore, boys often make demands without offering an explanation ("Look, man. I want the wire cutters right now."). By contrast, girls often give reasons for their suggestions ("We gotta *clean* 'em first . . . 'cause they got germs.").

Differences like these often persist into adulthood. One survey of college students revealed that men and women viewed conflicts in contrasting ways.[44] Regardless of their cultural background, female students described men as being concerned with power and more interested in content than relational issues. Phrases used to describe male conflict styles included: "The most important thing to males in conflict is their egos." "Men don't worry about feelings." "Men are more direct." By contrast, women were described as being more concerned with maintaining the relationship during a conflict. Phrases used to describe female conflict styles included: "Women are better listeners." "Women try to solve problems without controlling the other person." "Females are more concerned with others' feelings." When the actual conflict behaviors of both sexes are observed, women turn out to be more assertive than men about expressing their ideas and feelings, and men are more likely to withdraw from discussing issues.[45]

These sorts of differences don't mean that men are incapable of forming good relationships. Instead, their notions of what makes a good relationship are different. For some men, friendship and aggression aren't mutually exclusive. In fact, many strong male relationships are built around competition—at work or in athletics, for example. Women can be competitive, too, but they also are more likely to use logical reasoning and bargaining than aggression.[46] When men communicate with women, they become less aggressive and more cooperative than they are in all-male groups.

Most theorists suggest that the primary reason for differences in conflict style is socialization.[47] Some social scientists have proposed that a "threshold of assertiveness" may exist for people, especially women, allowing them to behave in an assertive way up to a point, but no further. Because women have been typically perceived as more compliant and cooperative, they may have seen themselves as reaching this threshold sooner than men, at which time they back off. Being less assertive may not feel right to women who justifiably think that they shouldn't be held to a different standard than men. Nonetheless, this is one case where gender equity doesn't produce the best results: Both women and men appear less tolerant of assertive behavior when it comes from a woman than from a man.[48]

In contrast with the "men are from Mars, women are from Venus" view of conflict, a look at the entire body of research on gender and conflict suggests that the differences in how the two sexes handle conflict are rather small, and sometimes quite different from the stereotypical picture of aggressive men and passive women.[49] Contrary to common wisdom, men are more likely to withdraw from discussing personal issues. One reason why women may complain more than their male partners is because they have more reasons to do so. In many relationships, women do more of the work than men, so it stands to reason that they are more likely to object to the situation.[50]

In other cases, people may *think* that there are greater differences in male and female ways of handling conflicts than there actually are.[51] People who assume that men are aggressive and women accommodating may notice behavior that fits these stereotypes ("See how much he bosses her around. A typical man!"). On the other hand, behavior that doesn't fit these stereotypes (accommodating men, pushy women) goes unnoticed.

Where men and women do have characteristically different conflict styles, the reasons may have little to do with gender. The situation at hand has a greater influence on shaping the way a person handles conflict.[52] For example, both men and women are more likely to respond aggressively when attacked by the other person. (Recall the discussion of defensive spirals in chapter 9.) In fact, researchers exploring how married couples handle disagreements found that the importance of gender in determining conflict style is "dwarfed" by the behavior of the other person.[53]

What, then, can we conclude about the influence of gender on conflict? Research has demonstrated that there are, indeed, some small but measurable differences in the two sexes. But, although men and women may have characteristically different conflict styles, the individual style of each communicator—regardless of gender—and the nature of the relationship are more important than gender in shaping the way he or she handles conflict.

Culture

The way in which people manage conflict varies tremendously depending on their cultural background. The straight-talking, assertive approach that characterizes many North Americans is not the universal norm.[54]

Perhaps the most important cultural factor in shaping attitudes toward conflict is an orientation toward individualism or collectivism.[55] In individualistic cultures like the United States, the goals, rights, and needs of each person are considered important, and most people would agree that it is an individual's right to stand up for himself or herself. By contrast, collectivist cultures (more common in Latin America and Asia) consider the concerns of the group to be more important than those of any individual. In these cultures, the kind of assertive behavior that might seem perfectly appropriate to a North American would seem rude and insensitive.

Another factor that distinguishes the assertiveness that is so valued by North Americans and northern Europeans is the difference between high- and low-context cultural styles.[56] Recall from our discussion in chapter 6 that low-context cultures like the United States place a premium on being direct and literal. By contrast, high-context cultures like Japan value self-restraint and avoid confrontation. Communicators in these cultures derive meaning from a variety of unspoken rules, such as context, social conventions, and hints. Preserving and honoring the face of the other person are a prime goal, and communicators go to great lengths to avoid any communication that might risk embarrassing a conversational partner. For this reason, what seems like "beating around the bush" to an American would be polite to an Asian. In Japan, for example, even a simple request like "close the door" would be too straightforward.[57] A more indirect statement such as "It is somewhat cold today" would be more appropriate. To take a more important example, Japanese are reluctant to say "no" to a request. A more likely answer would be "let me think about it for a while," which anyone familiar with Japanese culture would recognize as a refusal. When indirect communication is a cultural norm, it is unreasonable to expect more straightforward approaches to succeed. When people from different cultures face a conflict, their habitual communication patterns may not mesh smoothly. The challenge faced by an American husband and his Taiwanese wife illustrates this sort of problem:

> The husband would typically try to confront his wife verbally and directly (as is typical in the United States), leading her to either become violently defensive or withdraw completely from the discussion. She, on the other hand, would attempt to indicate her displeasure by changes in mood and eye

LOOKING AT DIVERSITY

Bridging the Gap between Cultures

John S. Yoo *was born in South Korea. He came to the United States at age twenty-seven, first living in Kansas and then moving to Los Angeles. He has worked as a community organizer for the Los Angeles County Sheriff's Department, a staff writer for the Korean Journal, and a law and politics specialist for the Korean-American Coalition. Yoo has earned master's degrees from the University of Southern California and the Claremont Graduate School, and he is presently working on a Ph.D. in criminal justice and public law.*

The 4.29 Merchant Consumer Relations Center is named after the date of the riots that consumed Los Angeles in 1992. One of the many contributing factors to those events which destroyed thousands of Korean-owned businesses was the mistrust and misunderstanding between some Korean American merchants and the African American customers they served in the inner city. Both store owners and customers face a lot of pressure in this environment: they have different native languages and communication styles, and many times they have a hard time understanding each other very well. Also, the merchants work very long hours with little financial rewards, and many customers have suffered from financial hardships and social oppression. This kind of situation has the potential to create hostility, and even violence.

Our center aims to resolve disputes between merchants and consumers in impoverished urban areas before they get out of hand. We also provide counseling services for dealing with discontented consumers. We work on educating merchants on how to respond in heated situations, such as when a customer accuses a merchant of overcharging for a purchase or when a merchant suspects a customer of shoplifting.

Since preventing problems is better than reacting to them, we teach merchants how to build working relationships with consumers before friction develops. For example, we explain how getting to know customers and speaking courteously to them can create goodwill. We suggest that merchants who make contributions to the communities they serve earn appreciation and respect that can lead to better relations, and better profits, too.

We have found that most of the conflicts which arise between Korean Americans and African Americans center around communication, not ethnic differences. For this reason, we use mediation as a tool for dealing with merchant-customer disputes. In a typical situation we use two mediators, one Korean American and the other African American. In this way, both the people involved in the dispute feel like they have someone who they can trust and who understands them. In one recent case, a customer of a liquor store thought he overheard a Korean American merchant use a racial slur against an African American man who had shoplifted some beer. A member of our center and a representative from the African American community met with the customer and the store owner. After this conversation, the customer realized he had misunderstood the store owner's expression of anger and frustration, and the issue was resolved peacefully. I think the main ingredient in the success of cases like this is that everyone involved feels like they are treated with respect by people who take their concerns seriously.

contact (typical of Chinese culture) that were either not noticed (or uninterpretable) by her husband. Thus, neither "his way" nor "her way" was working and they could not see any realistic way to "compromise."[58]

It isn't necessary to look at Asia to encounter cultural differences in conflict. Americans visiting Greece, for example, often think they are witnessing an argument when they are overhearing a friendly conversation.[59]

A comparative study of American and Italian nursery school children showed that one of the Italian children's favorite pastimes was a kind of heated debating that Italians call *discussione* but that Americans would call arguing. Likewise, research has shown that the conversations of working-class Jewish speakers of eastern European origin used arguments as a means of being sociable.

Within the United States, the ethnic background of communicators also plays a role in their ideas about conflict. When members of a group of African-American, Mexican-American, and Anglo-American college students were asked about their views regarding conflict, some important differences emerged.[60] For example, Anglo Americans seem more willing to accept conflict as a natural part of relationships, whereas Mexican Americans describe the short- and long-term dangers of conflict. Anglos' willingness to experience conflicts may be part of their individualistic, low-context communication style of speaking directly and avoiding uncertainty. It's not surprising that people from more collective, high-context cultures that emphasize harmony among people with close relationships tend to handle conflicts in less direct ways. With differences like these, it's easy to imagine how two friends, lovers, or fellow workers from different cultural backgrounds might have trouble finding a conflict style that is comfortable for them both.

Despite these differences, it's important to realize that culture isn't the only factor that influences the way people approach conflict or how they behave when they disagree. Some research suggests that our approach to conflict may be part of our biological makeup.[61] Furthermore, scholarship suggests that a person's self-concept is more powerful than his or her culture in determining conflict style.[62] For example, an assertive person raised in an environment that downplays conflict is still likely to be more aggressive than an unassertive person who grew up in a culture where conflicts are common.

Beyond individual temperament, the environment in which we are raised can shape the way we approach conflict. Parental conflict style plays a role. Some research has revealed a significant relationship between the ways a mother handles conflict and the style of her adult children.[63] Interestingly, there was no significant relationship between a father's conflict style and that of his children.

Beyond the family, the "culture" of each relationship can shape how we approach conflict.[64] You might handle conflicts calmly in a job where rationality and civility are the norm, but shriek like a banshee at home if that's the way you and a relational partner handle conflicts.

METHODS OF CONFLICT RESOLUTION

No matter what the relational style, gender, or culture of the participants, every conflict is a struggle to have one's goals met. Sometimes that struggle succeeds, and sometimes it fails. In the remainder of this chapter we'll look at various methods of conflict resolution and see which ones are most promising.

Win-Lose

In **win-lose problem solving,** one party gets what he or she wants, whereas the other comes up short. People resort to this method of resolving conflicts when they perceive a situation as being an "either-or" one: Either I get what I want, or you get what you want. The most clear-cut examples of win-lose situations are certain games such as baseball or poker, in which the rules require a winner and a loser. Some interpersonal issues seem to fit into this win-lose framework: two coworkers seeking a promotion to the same job, or a couple who disagree on how to spend their limited money.

Power is the distinguishing characteristic in win-lose problem solving because it is necessary to defeat an opponent to get what one wants. The most obvious kind of power is physical. Some parents threaten their children with warnings such as "Stop misbehaving, or I'll send you to your room." Adults who use physical power to deal with each other usually aren't so blunt, but the legal system is the implied threat: "Follow the rules, or we'll lock you up."

"It's not enough that we succeed. Cats must also fail."

©The New Yorker Collection 1997 Leo Cullum from cartoonbank.com. All Rights Reserved.

Real or implied force isn't the only kind of power used in conflicts. People who rely on authority of many types engage in win-lose methods without ever threatening physical coercion. In most jobs, supervisors have the authority to assign working hours, job promotions, and desirable or undesirable tasks and, of course, to fire an unsatisfactory employee. Teachers can use the power of grades to coerce students to act in desired ways.

Intellectual or mental power can also be a tool for conquering an opponent. Everyone is familiar with stories of how a seemingly weak hero defeats a stronger enemy through cleverness, showing that brains are more important than brawn. In a less admirable way, passive-aggressive crazymakers can defeat their partners by inducing guilt, avoiding issues, withholding desired behaviors, pseudoaccommodating, and so on.

Even the usually admired democratic system of majority rule is a win-lose method of resolving conflicts. However fair it may be, with this system one group is satisfied and another is unsatisfied.

In some circumstances the win-lose method may be necessary, as when there are truly scarce resources and only one party can achieve satisfaction. For instance, if two suitors want to marry the same person, only one can succeed. And to return to an earlier example, it's often true that only one applicant can be hired for a job. But don't be too willing to assume that your conflicts are necessarily win-lose: As you'll soon read, many situations that seem to require a loser can be resolved to everyone's satisfaction. There is one situation when win-lose is the best method. Even when cooperation is possible, if the other person insists on trying to defeat you, the most logical response might be to defend yourself by fighting back.

A final and much less frequent justification for trying to defeat another person occurs when the other party is clearly behaving in a wrong manner and when defeating that person is the only way to stop the wrongful behavior. Few people would deny the importance of restraining a person who is deliberately harming others, even if the person's freedom is sacrificed in the process. The danger of forcing wrongdoers to behave themselves is the wide difference in opinion between people about who is wrong and who is right. Given this difference, it would seem only justifiable in the most extreme circumstances to coerce others into behaving as we think they should.

Lose-Lose

In **lose-lose problem solving,** neither side is satisfied with the outcome. Although the name of this method is so discouraging that it's hard to imagine how anyone could willingly use it, in truth lose-lose is a fairly common way to handle conflicts. In many instances the parties will both strive to be winners, but as a result of the conflict, both end up losers. On the international level many wars illustrate this sad point. A nation that gains military victory at the cost of thousands of lives, large amounts of resources, and a damaged national consciousness hasn't truly won much. On an interpersonal level the same principle holds. Most of us have seen battles of pride in which both parties strike out and both suffer.

Compromise

Unlike lose-lose outcomes, a **compromise** gives both parties at least some of what they wanted, though both sacrifice part of their goals. People usually settle for compromises when it seems that partial satisfaction is the best they can hope for. Although a compromise may be better than losing everything, this method hardly seems to deserve the positive image that it has with some people. In his valuable book on conflict resolution, Albert Filley makes an interesting observation about our attitudes toward this method.[65] Why is it, he asks, that if someone says, "I will compromise my values," we view the action unfavorably, yet we view favorably parties in a conflict who compromise to reach a solution? Although compromises may be the best obtainable result in some conflicts, it's important to realize that both people in a conflict can often work together to find much better solutions. In such cases *compromise* is a negative word.

THE FAR SIDE® BY GARY LARSON

© 1991 FarWorks, Inc. All Rights Reserved/Dist. by Creators Syndicate

"OK, crybaby! You want the last soda? Well, let me GET IT READY FOR YOU!"

The Far Side by Gary Larson ©1991 FarWorks, Inc. All Rights Reserved. Used with permission.

Most of us are surrounded by the results of bad compromises. Consider a common example: the conflict between one person's desire to smoke cigarettes and another's need for clean air. The win-lose outcomes of this issue are obvious: Either the smoker abstains, or the nonsmoker gets polluted lungs—neither very satisfying. But a compromise in which the smoker gets to enjoy only a rare cigarette or must retreat outdoors and in which the nonsmoker still must inhale some fumes or feel like an ogre is hardly better. Both sides have lost a considerable amount of both comfort and goodwill. Of course, the costs involved in other compromises are even greater. For example, if a divorced couple compromise on child care by haggling over custody and then grudgingly agree to split the time with their children, it's hard to say that anybody has won.

Some compromises do leave both parties satisfied. You and the seller might settle on a price for a used car that is between what the seller was asking and what you wanted to pay. Although neither of you got everything you wanted, the outcome would still leave both of you satisfied. Likewise, you and your companion might agree to see a film that is the second choice for both of you in order to spend an evening together. As long as everyone is satisfied with an outcome, compromise can be an effective way to resolve conflicts.

Let us begin anew, remembering on both sides that civility is not a sign of weakness.

John F. Kennedy

Win-Win

In **win-win problem solving** the goal is to find a solution that satisfies the needs of everyone involved. Not only does each party avoid trying to win at the other's expense, but also they believe that by working together it is possible to find a solution that goes beyond a mere compromise and allows all parties to reach their goals. Consider a few examples:

Gordon was a stamp collector; his wife, Elaine, loved to raise and show championship beagles. Their income didn't leave enough money for both to practice their hobbies, and splitting the cash they did have wouldn't have left enough for either. *Solution:* Put all the first year's money into the puppies, and then after they were grown, use the income from their litters and show prizes to pay for Gordon's stamps.

Marta, a store manager, hated the task of rescheduling employee work shifts to accommodate their social and family needs. She and her staff developed an arrangement in which employees arranged schedule swaps on their own and notified her in writing after they were made.

Wendy and Kathy were roommates who had different study habits. Wendy liked to do her work in the evenings, which left her days free for other things, but Kathy felt that nighttime was party time. *Solution:* Monday through Wednesday evenings Wendy studied at her boyfriend's place while Kathy did anything she wanted. Thursday and Sunday Kathy agreed to keep things quiet around the house.

The point here isn't that these solutions are the correct ones for everybody with similar problems: The win-win method doesn't work that way. Different people might have found other solutions that suited them better. The win-win method gives you a way of creatively finding just the right answer for your unique problem. By using it you can tailor-make a way of resolving your conflicts that everyone can live with comfortably.

You should understand that the win-win method doesn't call for compromises in which the participants give up something they really want or need. Sometimes a compromise is the only alternative, but in the method we're talking about you find a solution that satisfies everyone—one in which nobody has to lose.

Although a win-win method sounds ideal, it is not always possible, or even appropriate. Table 10-3 lists some factors to consider when deciding which method to use when facing a conflict. There will certainly be times when compromising is the most sensible method. You will even encounter times when pushing for your own solution is reasonable. Even more surprisingly, you will probably discover that there are times when it makes sense to willingly accept the loser's role.

When we think about cooperation at all, we tend to associate the concept with fuzzy-minded idealism or, at best, to see it as workable only in a very small number of situations. This may result from confusing cooperation with altruism. It is not at all true that competition is more successful because it relies on the tendency to "look out for number one" while cooperation assumes that we primarily want to help each other. Structural cooperation defies the usual egoism/altruism dichotomy. It sets things up so that by helping you I am helping myself at the same time. Even if my motive initially may have been selfish, our fates now are linked. We sink or swim together. Cooperation is a shrewd and highly successful strategy.

Alfie Kohn

TABLE 10-3 Choosing the Most Appropriate Method of Conflict

CONSIDER DEFERRING TO THE OTHER PERSON	CONSIDER COMPROMISING	CONSIDER COMPETING	CONSIDER COOPERATING
When you discover you are wrong	When there is not enough time to seek a win-win outcome	When the issue is important and the other person will take advantage of your noncompetitive approach	When the issue is too important for a compromise
When the issue is more important to the other person than it is to you	When the issue is not important enough to negotiate at length		When a long-term relationship between you and the other person is important
When others need to learn by making their own mistakes	When the other person is not willing to seek a win-win outcome		When the other person is willing to cooperate
When the long-term cost of winning may not be worth short-term gains			

WIN-WIN COMMUNICATION SKILLS

Win-win problem solving is clearly superior to win-lose and lose-lose problem solving. Why, then, is it so rarely used? There are three reasons. The first is lack of awareness. Some people are so used to competition that they mistakenly think that winning requires them to defeat their "opponent."

Even when they know better, another reason prevents many people from seeking win-win solutions. Conflicts are often emotional affairs, in which people react combatively without stopping to think of better alternatives. Because this kind of emotional reflex prevents constructive solutions, it's often necessary to stop yourself from speaking out aggressively in a conflict and starting an escalating spiral of defensiveness. The time-honored advice of "counting to ten" applies here. After you've thought about the matter, you'll be able to *act* constructively instead of *reacting* in a way that's likely to produce a lose-lose outcome.

A third reason why win-win solutions are rare is that they require the other person's cooperation. It's difficult to negotiate constructively with someone who insists on trying to defeat you. In this case, use your best persuasive skills to explain that by working together you can find a solution that satisfies both of you.

In spite of these challenges, it is definitely possible to become better at resolving conflicts. In the following pages we will outline a method to increase your chances of being able to handle your conflicts in a win-win manner. As you read the following steps, try to imagine yourself applying them to a problem that's bothering you now.

Step 1—Identify Your Problem and Unmet Needs

Before you speak out, it's important to realize that the problem that is causing conflict is yours. Whether you want to return an unsatisfactory piece of merchandise, complain to noisy neighbors because your sleep is being disturbed, or request a change in working conditions from your employer, the problem is yours. Why? Because in each case *you* are the person who "owns" the problem—the one who is dissatisfied. You are the one who has paid for the unsatisfactory merchandise; the merchant who sold it to you has the use of your good money. You are the one who is losing sleep as a result of your neighbors' noise; they are content to go on as before. You are the one who is unhappy with your working conditions, not your employer.*

---

* Of course, others involved in the conflict may have problems of their own. For instance, the merchant, the noisy neighbors, and your employer may all be bothered by your requests. But the fact remains that the reason you are speaking up about these matters is because you are dissatisfied. Thus, the problem is at least initially yours.

I will not play at tug
o' war.
I'd rather play at hug
o' war,
Where everyone hugs
Instead of tugs,
Where everyone giggles
And rolls on the rug,
Where everyone kisses,
And everyone grins,
And everyone cuddles,
And everyone wins.

© 1974 by Evil Eye Music, Inc. Used by permission of HarperCollins Publishers.

Realizing that the problem is yours will make a big difference when the time comes to approach the other party. Instead of feeling and acting in an evaluative way, you'll be more likely to state your problem in a descriptive way, which will not only be more accurate but also reduce the chance of a defensive reaction.

After you realize that the problem is yours, the next step is to identify the unmet needs that make you dissatisfied. For instance, in the barking dog example, your need may be to get some sleep or to study without interruptions. In the case of a friend who teases you in public, your need would probably be to avoid embarrassment.

Sometimes the task of identifying your needs isn't as simple as it first seems. Behind the apparent content of an issue is often a relational need. Consider these examples:

> A friend hasn't returned some money you lent long ago. Your apparent need in this situation might be to get the money back. But a little thought will probably show that this isn't the only, or even the main, thing you want. Even if you were rolling in money, you'd probably want the loan repaid because of your most important need: *to avoid feeling victimized by your friend's taking advantage of you.*

> Someone you care about who lives in a distant city has failed to respond to several letters. Your apparent need may be to get answers to the questions you've written about, but it's likely that there's another, more fundamental, need: *the reassurance that you're still important enough to deserve a response.*

As you'll soon see, the ability to identify your real needs plays a key role in solving interpersonal problems. For now, the point to remember is that before you voice your problem to your partner, you ought to be clear about which of your needs aren't being met.

Step 2—Make a Date

Destructive fights often start because the initiator confronts a partner who isn't ready. There are many times when a person isn't in the right frame of mind to face a conflict, perhaps owing to fatigue, being in too much of a hurry to take the necessary time, being upset over another problem, or not feeling well. At times like these it's unfair to "jump" a person without notice and expect to get full attention for your problem. If you do persist, you'll probably have an ugly fight on your hands.

After you have a clear idea of the problem, approach your partner with a request to try to solve it. For example, "Something's been bothering me. Can we talk about it?" If the answer is "yes," you're ready to go further. If it isn't the right time to confront your partner, find a time that's agreeable to both of you.

Our marriage used to suffer from arguments that were too short. Now we argue long enough to find out what the argument is about.

Hugh Prather

Step 3—Describe Your Problem and Needs

Your partner can't possibly meet your needs without knowing why you're upset and what you want. Therefore, it's up to you to describe your problem as specifically as possible. The best way to deliver a complete, accurate message is to use the assertive clear message format. Notice how well this approach works in the following examples:

Example 1

"I have a problem. It's about your leaving dirty clothes around the house after I've told you how much it bothers me (*behavior*). It's a problem because I have to run around like crazy and pick things up whenever guests come, which is no fun at all (*consequence*). I'm starting to think that either you're not paying attention to my requests or you're trying to drive me crazy (*thoughts*), and either way I'm getting more and more resentful (*feeling*). I'd like to find some way to have a neat place without my having to be a maid or a nag."

Example 2

"I have a problem. When you drop by without calling ahead, and I'm studying (*behavior*), I don't know whether to visit or ask you to leave (*thought*). Either way, I get uncomfortable (*feeling*), and it seems like whatever I do, I lose: Either I have to put you off or get behind in my work (*consequences*). I'd like to find a way to get my studying done and still socialize with you (*intention*)."

Example 3

"Something is bothering me. When you tell me you love me and yet spend almost all your free time with your other friends (*behavior*), I wonder whether you mean it (*thought*). I get insecure (*feeling*), and then I start acting moody (*consequence*). I need some way of finding out for sure how you feel about me (*intention*)."

Step 4—Consider Your Partner's Point of View

After stating your problem and describing what you need, it's important to make sure that your partner has understood what you've said. As you can remember from the discussion of listening in chapter 7, there's a good chance—especially in a stressful conflict—that your words will be misinterpreted.

It's usually unrealistic to insist that your partner paraphrase your statement, and fortunately there are more tactful and subtle ways to make sure that you've been understood. For instance, you might try saying, "I'm not sure I expressed myself very well just now—maybe you should tell what you heard me say so I can be sure I got it right." In any case, be absolutely sure that your partner understands your whole message before going any further. Legitimate agreements are tough enough without getting upset about a conflict that doesn't even exist.

After you have made your position clear, it's time to find out what your partner needs to feel satisfied about this issue. There are two reasons why it's important to discover your partner's needs. First, it's fair. Your partner has just as much right as you to feel satisfied, and if you expect help in meeting your needs, it's reasonable that you behave in the same way. But in addition to fairness, there's another, practical reason for concerning yourself with what your partner wants. Just as an unhappy partner will make it hard for you to become satisfied, a happy partner will be more likely to cooperate in letting you reach your goals. Thus, it's in your own self-interest to discover and meet your partner's needs.

You can learn about your partner's needs simply by asking about them: "Now I've told you what I want and why. Tell me what you need to feel OK about this." After your partner begins to talk, your job is to use the listening skills discussed earlier in this book to make sure that you understand.

Step 5—Negotiate a Solution

Now that you and your partner understand each other's needs, the goal becomes finding a way to meet them. This is done by developing as many potential solutions as possible and then evaluating them to decide which one best meets everyone's needs. Probably the best description of the win-win approach has been written by Thomas Gordon in his book *Parent Effectiveness Training*.[66] The following steps are a modification of this approach.

1. *Identify and define the conflict.* We've discussed identifying and defining the conflict in the preceding pages. These consist of discovering each person's problem and needs, setting the stage for meeting all of them.

2. *Generate a number of possible solutions.* In this step, the partners work together to think of as many means as possible to reach their stated ends. The key concept here is quantity: It's important to generate as many ideas as you can think of without worrying about which ones are good or bad. Write down every thought that comes up, no matter how unworkable: Sometimes a far-fetched idea will lead to a more workable one.

3. *Evaluate the alternative solutions.* This is the time to talk about which solutions will work and which ones won't. It's important for all parties to be honest about their willingness to accept an idea. If a solution is going to work, everyone involved has to support it.

4. *Decide on the best solution.* Now that you've looked at all the alternatives, pick the one that looks best to everyone. It's important to be sure that everybody understands the solution and is willing to try it out. Remember that your decision doesn't have to be final, but it should look potentially successful.

Step 6—Follow Up the Solution

You can't be sure that the solution will work until you try it. After you've tested it for a while, it's a good idea to set aside some time to talk over its progress. You may find that you need to make some changes or even rethink the whole problem. The idea is to keep on top of the problem, to keep using creativity to solve it.

As you think about applying this method, it is important to keep two points in mind. First, realize the importance of following every step. Each one is essential to the success of your encounter, and skipping one or more steps can lead to misunderstandings that might cause the conversation to degenerate into a negative spiral. After you have practiced the method a number of times and are familiar with it, this type of problem solving will become almost second nature. You will then be able to approach your conflicts without following this step-by-step approach. But for the time being try to be patient and trust the value of the pattern.

Second, realize that this method is not likely to flow smoothly from one step to another in real life. You can expect and prepare for a certain amount of resistance from the other person. As Figure 10-1 shows, when

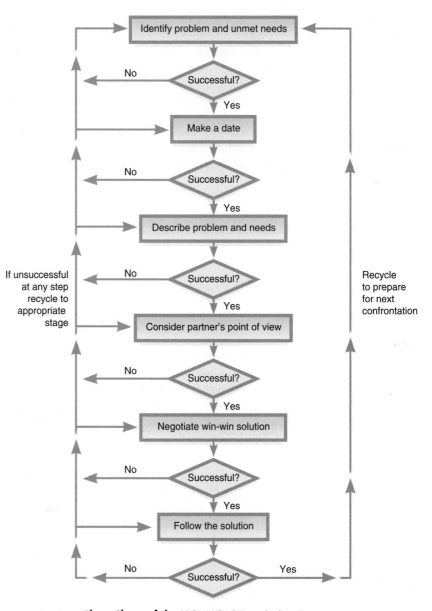

FIGURE 10-1   **Flow Chart of the Win-Win Negotiation Process**

Adapted from Rory Remer and Paul deMesquita, "Teaching and Learning Skills of Interpersonal Confrontation" in *Intimates in Conflict: A Communication Perspective* edited by Cahn ©1990 p. 227.

Win-Win Problem Solving

It is 7:15 A.M. on a typical school day. Chris enters the kitchen and finds the sink full of dirty dishes. It was her roommate Terry's turn to do them. She sighs in disgust and begins to clean up, slamming pots and pans.

Terry Can't you be a little more quiet? I don't have a class till 10:00, and I want to catch up on sleep.

Chris (*Expressing her aggression indirectly in a sarcastic tone of voice*) Sorry to bother you. I was cleaning up last night's dinner dishes.

Terry (*Misses the message*) Well, I wish you'd do it a little more quietly. I was up late studying last night, and I'm beat.

Chris (*Decides to communicate her irritation more directly, if aggressively*) Well, if you'd done the dishes last night, I wouldn't have had to wash them now.

Terry (*Finally realizes that Chris is mad at her, responds defensively*) I was going to do them when I got up. I've got two midterms this week, and I was studying until midnight last night. What's more important, grades or a spotless kitchen?

Chris (*Perpetuating the growing defensive spiral*) I've got classes, too, you know. But that doesn't mean we have to live like pigs!

Terry (*Angrily*) Forget it. If it's such a big deal, I'll never leave another dirty dish!

Chris and Terry avoid one another as they get ready for school. During the day Chris realizes that attacking Terry will make matters only worse. She decides on a more constructive approach that evening.

Chris That wasn't much fun this morning. Want to talk about it?

Terry I suppose so. But I'm going out to study with Kim and Alisa in a few minutes.

Chris (*Realizing that it's important to talk at a good time*) If you have to leave soon, let's not get into it now. How about talking when you get back?

Terry OK, if I'm not too tired.

Chris Or we could talk tomorrow before class.

Terry OK.

Later that evening Terry and Chris continue their conversation.

Chris (*Defines the issue as her problem by using the assertive clear message format*) I hated to start the day with a fight. But I also hate having to do the dishes when it's not my turn (*behavior*). It doesn't seem fair for me to do my job and yours (*interpretation*), and that's why I got so mad (*feeling*) and nagged at you (*consequence*).

Terry But I was studying! You know how much I have to do. It's not like I was partying.

Chris (*Avoids attacking Terry by sincerely agreeing with the facts and explaining further why she was upset*) I know. It wasn't just doing the dishes that got me upset. It seems like there have been a lot of times when I've done your jobs and mine, too.

Terry (*Defensively*) Like when?

Chris (*Gives specific descriptions of Terry's behavior*) Well, this was the third time this week that I've done the dishes when it's your turn, and I can think of a couple of times lately when I've had to clean up your stuff before people came over.

Terry I don't see why it's such a big deal. If you just leave the stuff there, I'll clean it up.

Chris (*Still trying to explain herself, she continues to use "I" language.*) I know you would. I guess it's harder for me to put up with a messy place than it is for you.

Terry Yeah. If you'd just relax, living together would be a lot easier!

Chris (*Resenting Terry's judgmental accusation that the problem is all hers*) Hey, wait a second! Don't blame the whole thing on me. It's just that we have different standards. It looks to you like I'm too hung up on keeping the place clean . . .

Terry Right.

Chris . . . and if we do it your way, then I'd be giving up. I'd have to either live with the place messier than I like it or clean everything up myself. Then I'd get mad at you, and things would be pretty tense around here. (*Describes the unpleasant consequences of not solving the problem in a mutually satisfactory way*)

Terry I suppose so.

Chris We need to figure out how to take care of the apartment in a way that we can both live with. (*Describes the broad outline of a win-win solution*)

Terry Yeah.

Chris So what could we do?

continued

Win-Win Problem Solving

Terry (*Sounding resigned*) Look, from now on I'll just do the dishes right away. It isn't worth arguing about.

Chris Sure it is. If you're sore, the apartment may be clean, but it won't be worth it.

Terry (*Skeptically*) OK; what do you suggest?

Chris Well, I'm not sure. You don't want the pressure of having to clean up right away, and I don't want to have to do my jobs and yours, too. Right?

Terry Yeah. (*Still sounding skeptical*) So what are we going to do—hire a housekeeper to clean up?

Chris (*Refusing to let Terry sidetrack the discussion*) That would be great if we could afford it. How about using paper plates? That would make cleaning up from meals easier.

Terry Yeah, but there would still be pots and pans.

Chris Well, it's not a perfect fix, but it might help a little. (*Goes on to suggest other ideas*) How about cooking meals that don't take a lot of work to clean up—maybe more salads and less fried stuff that sticks to pans. That would be a better diet, too.

Terry Yeah. I do hate to scrub crusty frying pans. But that doesn't do anything about your wanting the living room picked up all the time, and I bet I still wouldn't keep the kitchen as clean as you like it. Keeping the place super clean just isn't as big a deal to me as it is for you.

Chris That's true, and I don't want to have to nag you! (*Clarifies the end she's seeking*) You know, it's not really cleaning up that bothers me. It's doing more than my share of work. I wonder if there's a way I could be responsible for keeping the kitchen clean and picking up if you could do something else to keep the workload even.

Terry Are you serious? I'd love to get out of doing the dishes! You mean you'd do them . . . and keep the place picked up . . . if I did something else?

Chris As long as the work was equal and you really did your jobs without me having to remind you.

Terry What kind of work would you want me to do?

Chris How about cleaning up the bathroom?

Terry Forget it. That's worse than doing the dishes.

Chris OK. How about cooking?

Terry That might work, but then we'd have to eat together all the time. It's nice to do our own cooking when we want to. It's more flexible that way.

Chris OK. But what about shopping? I hate the time it takes, and you don't mind it that much, do you?

Terry You mean shop for groceries? You'd trade that for cleaning the kitchen?

Chris Sure. And picking up the living room. It takes an hour each time we shop, and we make two trips every week. Doing the dishes would be much quicker.

Terry All right!

The plan didn't work perfectly: At first Terry put off shopping until all the food was gone, and Chris took advantage by asking Terry to run other errands during her shopping trips. But their new arrangement proved much more successful than the old arrangement. The apartment was cleaner and the workload more even, which satisfied Chris. Terry was less the object of Chris's nagging, and she had no kitchen chores, which made her happier. Just as important, the relationship between Chris and Terry was more comfortable—thanks to win-win problem solving.

Using your **Looking Out/ Looking In** *CD-ROM, click on* Scenarios, *then click "Win-Win Problem Solving" to watch and analyze a dramatized version of this conversation.*

---

a step doesn't meet with success, simply move back and repeat the preceding ones as necessary.

Win-win solutions aren't always possible. There will be times when even the best-intentioned people simply won't be able to find a way of meeting all their needs. In times like these, the process of negotiation has to include some compromises. But even then the preceding steps haven't been wasted. The genuine desire to learn what the other person wants and to try to satisfy those wants will build a climate of goodwill that can help you find the best solution to the present problem and also improve your relationship in the future.

SKILL BUILDER

WIN-WIN SOLUTIONS AND YOU

1. Make a list of the situations in your life in which a conflict of needs is creating tension between you and someone else.

2. Analyze what you're doing at present to resolve such conflicts, and describe whether your behavior is meeting with any success.

3. Pick at least one of the situations you just listed, and, with the other people involved, try to develop a win-win solution by following the steps listed in the preceding pages.

4. After working through steps 1 to 5, disclose the results of your conference to the class. After you've had time to test your solution, report the progress you've made, and discuss the follow-up conference described in step 6.

CONSTRUCTIVE CONFLICT: QUESTIONS AND ANSWERS

After learning about win-win negotiating, people often express doubts about how well it can work. "It sounds like a good idea," they say, "but . . ." Three questions arise more than any others, and they deserve an answer.

Isn't the Win-Win Approach Too Good to Be True?

Research shows that seeking mutual benefit not only is desirable—but also it works. In fact, the win-win approach produces better results than a win-lose approach.

In a series of experiments, Robert Axelrod presented subjects with a bargaining situation called "prisoner's dilemma," in which they could choose either to cooperate or betray a confederate.[67] There are three types of outcome in prisoner's dilemma: One partner can win big by betraying a confederate, both can win by cooperating, or both can lose by betraying one another.

Although cynics might assume that the most effective strategy is to betray a partner (a win-lose approach), Axelrod demonstrated that cooperation is actually the best hard-nosed strategy. He staged a tournament in which participants played against a computer that was

© 2001 from cartoonbank.com. All Rights Reserved.

programmed to represent several negotiating strategies. The winning strategy was one called "Tit-for-Tat." It starts out by cooperating and continues to cooperate until the other player betrays it. After that, the program always does what the other player did on the previous move. It never punishes an opponent more than once for a betrayal, and it will always cooperate if the other player does.

A win-win Tit-for-Tat strategy succeeds for several reasons.[68] First, it isn't a patsy. It responds quickly to betrayal, discouraging others from taking unfair advantage. At the same time, it is quick to forgive. It doesn't hold a grudge: As soon as the other party cooperates, it does, too. Finally, it isn't too sneaky. By making its behavior obvious and predictable, Tit-for-Tat creates an atmosphere of trust.

There are certainly some conflicts that can't be resolved with win-win approaches. Only one suitor can marry the prince or princess, and only one person can be hired for the advertised job. Furthermore, it's impossible to reach a win-win solution when your partner refuses to cooperate. Most of the time, however, good intentions and creative thinking can lead to outcomes that satisfy everyone's needs.

Isn't the Win-Win Approach Too Elaborate?

The win-win approach is detailed and highly structured. In everyday life you may rarely use every step: Sometimes the problem at hand won't justify the effort, and at other times you and your partner might not need to be so deliberate to take care of the problem. Nonetheless, while learning to use the approach try to follow all the steps carefully. After you have become familiar and skillful at using them all, you will be able to use whichever ones prove necessary in a given situation. For important issues, you are likely to find that every step of the win-win approach is important. If this process seems time-consuming, just consider the time and energy that will likely be required if you *don't* resolve the issue at hand.

Isn't Win-Win Negotiating *Too* Rational?

Frustrated readers often complain that the win-win approach is so sensible that only a saint could use it successfully. "Sometimes I'm so angry that I don't care about being supportive or empathetic or anything else," they say. "I just want to blow my top!"

When you feel like this, it's almost impossible to be rational. At times like these probably the most therapeutic thing to do is get your feelings off your chest in what George Bach calls a "Vesuvius"—an uncontrolled, spontaneous explosion. A Vesuvius can be a terrific way of blowing off steam, and, after you do so, it's often much easier to figure out a rational solution to your problem.

So we encourage you to have a Vesuvius, with the following qualifications: Be sure that your partner understands what you're doing and realizes that whatever you say doesn't call for a response. Your partner should let you rant and rave for as long as you want without getting defensive or "tying in." Then when your eruption subsides, you can take steps to work through whatever still troubles you.

Is It Possible to Change Others?

Readers often agree that win-win problem solving would be terrific—if everyone had read *Looking Out/Looking In* and understood the method. "How can I get the other person to cooperate?" the question goes.

Though you won't always be able to gain your partner's cooperation, a good job of selling can do the trick most of the time. The key lies in showing that it's in your partner's self-interest to work together with you: "Look, if we can't settle this, we'll both feel miserable. But if we can find an answer, think how much better off we'll be." Notice that this sort of explanation projects both the favorable consequences of cooperating and the unfavorable consequences of competing.

You can also boost the odds of getting your partner's cooperation by modeling the communication skills described in this book. You've read that defense-arousing behavior is reciprocal, but so is supportive communication. If you can listen sincerely, avoid evaluative attacks, and empathize with your partner's concerns, for example, there's a good chance that you'll get the same kind of behavior in return. And even if your cooperative attitude doesn't succeed, you'll gain self-respect from knowing that at least you behaved honorably and constructively.

> No one said it would be easy,
> but no one said it would be this hard.
> No one said it would be easy,
> but no one thought we'd come this far.
>
> Sheryl Crow

SUMMARY

Conflict is a fact of life in every interpersonal relationship. The way in which conflicts are handled plays a major role in the quality of a relationship. When managed constructively, conflicts can lead to stronger and more satisfying interaction; but when they are handled poorly, relationships will suffer.

There are four approaches that a person can take when faced with a conflict. A nonassertive approach avoids the conflict altogether. A directly aggressive approach attacks the other party, whereas a passive-aggressive approach expresses hostility obliquely. An indirect approach hints about the nature of a problem, whereas an assertive approach confronts the issue directly but without attacking the other party. A complete assertive message describes the behavior in question, at least one interpretation, the speaker's feelings, the con-

sequences of the situation, and the speaker's intentions in making the statement.

The way a conflict is handled is not always the choice of a single person because the parties influence one another as they develop a relational conflict style. This style may be complementary, symmetrical, or parallel; it can involve a combination of intimate and aggressive elements; and it can involve constructive or destructive rituals. Besides being shaped by the relationship, a conflict style is also shaped by a person's gender and cultural background.

There are three outcomes to conflicts: win-lose, lose-lose, and win-win. A win-lose approach often disintegrates into a lose-lose outcome in which all the parties suffer. Win-win outcomes are often possible, if the parties possess the proper attitude and skills.

KEY TERMS

accommodation	conflict ritual	nonassertion
assertion	consequence statement	parallel conflict style
avoidance	crazymaking	passive aggression
behavioral description	direct aggression	relational conflict style
complementary conflict style	indirect communication	symmetrical conflict style
compromise	intention statement	win-lose problem solving
conflict	lose-lose problem solving	win-win problem solving

LOOKING OUT/LOOKING IN ONLINE

Use your *Looking Out/Looking In* CD-ROM for quick access to the electronic resources that accompany this chapter. Included on this CD-ROM are additional study aids and links to the *Looking Out/Looking In* Web site at the Wadsworth Communication Café. The CD-ROM is your gateway to a wealth of resources that will help you understand and further explore the material in this chapter. **Video clips** under *Communication Scenarios* on the CD illustrate the skills introduced in this chapter. Click on the Web site link to complete self-study **review quizzes** to help you master new concepts; access a **feature film database** to locate clips and entire movies that illustrate communication principles; find Internet material via the maintained **Web site links;** and complete **online activities** to help you master new concepts.

INFOTRAC COLLEGE EDITION EXERCISES

Use the InfoTrac College Edition password that was included free with a copy of this new text to answer the following questions. These questions can be completed online and, if requested, submitted to your instructor under InfoTrac College Edition Activities at the *Looking Out/Looking In* Web site.

1. The Nature of Conflict

Use PowerTrac to search for the term "workplace conflict." Find and read one of the articles within this area that provides useful information for you. Summarize the key points the article makes, and explain how you can apply them in your work. Do the points you read here support information in this chapter? How?

2. Direct Aggression

Locate and read the article "It's in Our Nature: Verbal Aggressiveness as Temperamental Expression" by Michael J. Beatty and James C. McCroskey. (Hint: Use PowerTrac and search for this article by either author or title.) What is the thesis of this article? How conclusive is the evidence offered by the authors to support it? What do you think personally about the authors' thesis? To what

degree does the article explain aggressive behavior? To what degree does it provide a legitimate excuse for aggression?

3. Variables in Conflict Styles

Locate and read the article "Conflict Behaviors Toward Same-Sex and Opposite-Sex Peers Among Male and Female Late Adolescents" by Esin Tezer and Ayhan Demi. (Hint: Use PowerTrac and search for this article by either author or title.) Answer the following questions: What conflict styles have social science researchers found to be used by college-age men and women? What role does gender play in the choice of conflict style?

READINGS

Canary, Daniel J., William R. Cupach, and Susan J. Messman. *Relationship Conflict*. Thousand Oaks, Calif.: Sage, 1995.

This brief book summarizes the research on conflict. Chapter topics include conflict in a variety of interpersonal relationships, including friendships, parent-child, and romantic.

Cupach, William R., and Daniel J. Canary. *Competence in Interpersonal Conflict*. New York: McGraw-Hill, 1997.

Canary and Cupach offer a useful overview of what social scientists have learned about the nature of interpersonal conflict and how to manage it.

Fisher, Roger, and Scott Brown. *Getting Together: Building a Relationship That Gets to Yes*. Boston: Houghton Mifflin, 1988.

This outstanding book offers specific guidelines for managing conflicts constructively. The authors focus on ways to improve the ability to solve such problems as sorting out relational issues from content-related disputes, balancing emotion and reason, and learning how to be trustworthy without being naive.

Fisher, Roger, and Scott Brown. *Getting to Yes: Negotiating Agreement without Giving In*. Boston: Houghton Mifflin, 1981.

This is perhaps the best of the expanding collection of books on the subject of negotiating. Fisher and Brown show that you needn't choose between being an aggressive, demanding negotiator and a pushover. Their discussion of principled negotiation shows how to seek win-win solutions whenever possible and what to do when you face a partner who seems interested only in winning at your expense.

Hocker, Joyce L., and William W. Wilmot. *Interpersonal Conflict*, 6th ed. New York: McGraw-Hill, 2001.

A thorough survey of the nature of interpersonal conflict and how it can be resolved. This is an ideal second step for readers who want to explore the subject in further detail.

FILMS

In addition to the films suggested here, go to the **Film in Communication Database** at the *Looking Out/Looking In* Web site to locate movie clips that illustrate different interpersonal communication conflict styles.

Dysfunctional Conflict

American Beauty (1999) Rated R

From outside, Lester and Carolyn Burnham (Kevin Spacey and Annette Bening) look like the perfect couple: attractive, with good jobs and an immaculate suburban home. But we soon learn that life isn't as good as it seems. The Burnhams' relationship with their daughter Jane (Thora Birch) is superficial. Carolyn is in denial about Lester's crisis, and she ignores his pleas to recapture their lost love. As the film relentlessly moves toward a stunning conclusion, we are presented with a portrait of American family members who alternate between avoidance and aggression without demonstrating any apparent skill at managing the serious conflicts that face them.

Culture and Conflict

The Joy Luck Club (1993) Rated R

The Joy Luck Club tells a series of stories involving four Chinese women and their daughters. The mothers all flee difficult situations in China to start new lives in the United States, where they raise their daughters with a mixture of Chinese and American styles. Many of the movie's conflicts are rooted in cultural value clashes.

The mothers were raised in the high-context, collectivist environment of China, where open conflict is discouraged and individual needs (particularly of women) are submerged for the larger good. To achieve their goals, the mothers use a variety of indirect and passive-aggressive methods. Their daughters, raised in the United States, adopt a more low-context, direct form of communication. They are also more assertive and aggressive in their conflict styles, particularly when dealing with their mothers.

The daughters have a harder time dealing with the men in their lives. For example, Rose (Rosalind Chao) begins her relationship with Ted (Andrew McCarthy) very assertively, telling him candidly what she thinks and how she feels about him (he is charmed by her directness). They marry, and she becomes an accommodator, constantly submerging her needs for his. Rather than liking Rose's accommodating, Ted comes to despise it. He exhorts her to be more assertive: "Once in a while, I would like to hear what you want. I'd like to hear your voice, even if we disagree." He then suggests that they separate.

Several of the stories have happy endings. In Rose's case, she fights for her rights with Ted—and ultimately they reconcile. In fact, each woman in the movie takes a stand on an important issue in her life, and most of the outcomes are positive. The women in *The Joy Luck Club* learn to both embrace and reject aspects of their cultural heritage as they attempt to manage their conflicts effectively.

LOOKING OUT/LOOKING IN COMMUNICATION VIDEO

Using your *Looking Out/Looking In* CD-ROM, click on *Communication Scenarios* and then click on the "Win-Win Problem Solving" icon to watch and analyze a dramatized version of the conversation featured in the Communication Transcript on pages 443–444.

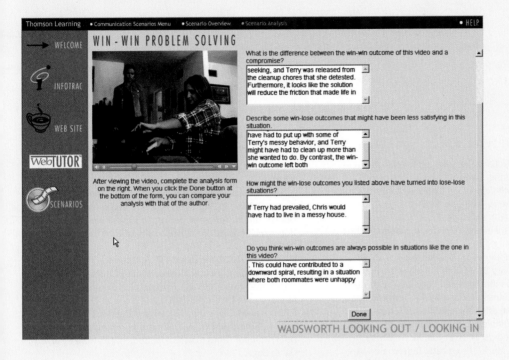

ENDNOTES

ENDNOTES FOR CHAPTER 1

1. J. B. Ross and M. M. McLaughlin, eds., *A Portable Medieval Reader* (New York: Viking, 1949).
2. S. Schachter, *The Psychology of Affiliation* (Stanford, Calif.: Stanford University Press, 1959), pp. 9–10.
3. VPI, *Wisconsin State Journal*, Sept. 7, 1978.
4. J. McCain, *Faith of My Fathers* (New York: Random House, 1999), p. 212
5. Three articles in *The Journal of the American Medical Association* 267 (January 22/29, 1992) discuss the link between psychosocial influences and coronary heart disease: R. B. Case, A. J. Moss, N. Case, M. McDermott, and S. Eberly, "Living Alone after Myocardial Infarction" (pp. 515–519); R. B. Williams, J. C. Barefoot, R. M. Califf, T. L. Haney, W. B. Saunders, D. B. Pryon, M. A. Hlatky, I. C. Siegler, and D. B. Mark, "Prognostic Importance of Social and Economic Resources among Medically Treated Patients with Angiographically Documented Coronary Artery Disease" (pp. 520–524); and R. Ruberman, "Psychosocial Influences on Mortality of Patients with Coronary Heart Disease" (pp. 559–560). See also J. T. Cacioppo, J. M. Ernst, M. H. Burleson, M. K. McClintock, W. B. Malarkey, L. C. Hawkley, R. B. Kowalewski, A. Paulsen, J. A. Hobson, K. Hugdahl, D. Spiegel, and G. G. Berntson, "Lonely Traits and Concomitant Physiological Processes: The MacArthur Social Neuroscience Studies," *International Journal of Psychophysiology* 35 (2000): 143–154.
6. S. Cohen, W. J. Doyle, D. P. Skoner, B. S. Rabin, and J. M. Gwaltney, "Social Ties and Susceptibility to the Common Cold," *Journal of the American Medical Association* 277 (1997): 1940–1944.
7. R. Narem, "Try a Little TLC," *Science* 80 (1980): 15.
8. J. Lynch, *The Broken Heart: The Medical Consequences of Loneliness* (New York: Basic Books, 1977), pp. 239–242. See also A. J. Kposowa, "Marital Status and Suicide in The National Longitudinal Mortality Study," *Journal of Epidemiology and Community Health* 54 (2000): 254–261.
9. Lynch, op cit.
10. W. D. Rees and S. G. Lutkins, "Mortality of Bereavement," *British Medical Journal* 4 (1967): 13.
11. R. Shattuck, *The Forbidden Experiment: The Story of the Wild Boy of Aveyron* (New York: Farrar, Straus & Giroux, 1980), p. 37.
12. A. M. Nicotera, "Where Have We Been, Where Are We, and Where Do We Go?" in A. M. Nicotera and associates, eds., *Interpersonal Communication in Friend and Mate Relationships* (Albany: State University of New York Press, 1993).
13. R. B. Rubin, E. M. Perse, and C. A. Barbato, "Conceptualization and Measurement of Interpersonal Communication Motives," *Human Communication Research* 14 (1988): 602–628.
14. S. Duck and G. Pittman, "Social and Personal Relationships" in M. L. Knapp and G. R. Phillips, eds., *Handbook of Interpersonal Communication*, 2nd ed. (Newbury Park, Calif.: Sage, 1994).
15. S. Ball-Rokeach, "Belonging in the 21st Century: The Case of Los Angeles," Annenberg School for Communication, 2000. http://www.metamorph.org/whitepaper12.html.
16. J. Rochmis, "Humans Do *Many* Things," *Wired Magazine* online. http://www.wired.com/news/culture/0,1284,34387,00 .html (June 12, 2000).
17. National Communication Association, *How Americans Communicate*, 1999. http://www.natcom.org/research/Roper/how_americans_communicate.htm.
18. W. Goldschmidt, *The Human Career: The Self in the Symbolic World* (Cambridge, Mass.: Basil Blackman, 1990).
19. J. L. Winsor, D. B. Curtis, and R. D. Stephens, "National Preferences in Business and Communication Education: An Update," *Journal of the Association for Communication Administration* 3, 170–179. See also M. S. Peterson, "Personnel Interviewers' Perceptions of the Importance and Adequacy of Applicants' Communication Skills," *Communication Education* 46 (1997): 287–291.
20. J. Flanigan, "For All of Us, the Future of Labor Lies in Learning," *Los Angeles Times*, Sept. 5, 1993, p. D5.
21. R. M. Kanter, "The New Managerial Work," *Harvard Business Review* 66 (November–December 1989): 85–92.
22. A. H. Maslow, *Toward a Psychology of Being* (New York: Van Nostrand Reinhold, 1968).

23. C. E. Shannon and W. Weaver, *The Mathematical Theory of Communication* (Urbana, Ill.: University of Illinois Press, 1949).

24. K. R. Colbert, "The Effects of Debate Participation on Argumentativeness and Verbal Aggression," *Communication Education* 42 (1993): 206–214.

25. The issue of intentionality has been a matter of debate by communication theorists. For a sample of the arguments on both sides, see M. T. Motley, "On Whether One Can(not) Communicate: An Examination via Traditional Communication Postulates," *Western Journal of Speech Communication* 54 (1990): 1–20; J. B. Bavelas, "Behaving and Communicating: A Reply to Motley," *Western Journal of Speech Communication* 54 (1990): 593–602; and J. Stewart, "A Postmodern Look at Traditional Communication Postulates," *Western Journal of Speech Communication* 55 (1991): 354–379.

26. E. M. Rogers and D. L. Kincaid, *Communication Networks: Toward a New Paradigm for Research* (New York: Free Press, 1981), pp. 43–48, 63–66.

27. See, for example, R. K. Shelly, "Sequences and Cycles in Social Interaction," *Small Group Research* 28 (1997): 333–356.

28. M. Dainton and L. Stafford, "The Dark Side of 'Normal' Family Interaction" in B. H. Spitzberg and W. R. Cupach, eds., *The Dark Side of Interpersonal Communication* (Hillsdale, N.J.: Erlbaum, 1993).

29. See T. Clevenger, Jr., "Can One Not Communicate? A Conflict of Models," *Communication Studies* 42 (1991): 340–353. For a detailed rationale of the position argued in this section, see G. H. Stamp and M. L. Knapp, "The Construct of Intent in Interpersonal Communication," *Quarterly Journal of Speech* 76 (1990): 282–299.

30. For a thorough discussion of communication difficulties, see N. Coupland, H. Giles, and J. M. Wiemann, eds., *"Miscommunication" and Problematic Talk* (Newbury Park, Calif.: Sage, 1991).

31. For a similar list of characteristics, see J. C. McCroskey and V. P. Richmond, *Fundamentals of Human Communication: An Interpersonal Perspective* (Prospect Heights, Ill.: Waveland, 1996).

32. J. C. McCroskey and L. Wheeless, *Introduction to Human Communication* (Boston: Allyn and Bacon, 1976), p. 5. See also D. H. Cloven and M. E. Roloff, "Sense-Making Activities and Interpersonal Conflict: Communicative Cures for the Mulling Blues," *Western Journal of Speech Communication* 55 (1991): 134–158. See also D. Stiebel, *When Talking Makes Things Worse! Resolving Problems When Communication Fails* (Kansas City, Mo.: Andrews and McMeel, 1997).

33. M. V. Redmond, "Interpersonal Communication: Definitions and Conceptual Approaches" in M. V. Redmond, ed., *Interpersonal Communication: Readings in Theory and Research* (Fort Worth: Harcourt Brace, 1995), pp. 4–11.

34. For a discussion of personal relationships between teachers and students, see A. Bainbridge Frymier and M. L. Houser, "The Teacher-Student Relationship as an Interpersonal Relationship," *Communication Education* 49 (2000): 207–219.

35. See, for example, G. R. Miller and M. Steinberg, *Between People: A New Analysis of Interpersonal Communication* (Chicago: SRA, 1975); and J. Stewart and C. Logan, *Together: Communicating Interpersonally*, 5th ed. (New York: McGraw-Hill, 1998).

36. For further discussion of the characteristics of impersonal and interpersonal communications, see Arthur P. Bochner, "The Functions of Human Communication in Interpersonal Bonding" in C. C. Arnold and J. W. Bowers, eds., *Handbook of Rhetorical and Communication Theory* (Boston: Allyn and Bacon, 1984), p. 550; S. Trenholm and A. Jensen, *Interpersonal Communication*, 2nd ed. (Belmont, Calif.: Wadsworth, 1992), pp. 27–33; J. Stewart and G. D'Angelo, *Together: Communicating Interpersonally*, 5th ed. (New York: McGraw-Hill, 1998), p. 5.

37. J. Wood, *Relational Communication*, 2nd ed. (Belmont, Calif.: Wadsworth, 1997).

38. K. J. Gergen, *The Saturated Self: Dilemmas of Identity in Contemporary Life* (New York: Basic Books, 1991), p. 158.

39. K. O'Toole, "Study Takes Early Look at Social Consequences of Net Use," *Stanford Online Report* Feb. 16, 2000. http://www.stanford.edu/dept/news/report/news/february16/internetsurvey-216.html.

40. "Surveying the Digital Future," UCLA Center for Communication Policy, October 2000. www.ccp.ucla.edu. Accessed Oct. 25, 2000.

41. "Pew Internet and American Life Project," Pew Charitable Trusts, May 2000. http://www.pewinternet.org/. Accessed Oct. 25, 2000.

42. See, for example, J. B. Walther, "Computer-Mediated Communication: Impersonal, Interpersonal, and Hyper-personal Interaction," *Communication Research* 23 (1996): 3–43; and J. B. Walther and J. K. Burgoon, "Relational Communication in Computer-Mediated Interaction," *Human Communication Research* 19 (1992): 50–88.

43. M. Marriott, "The Blossoming of Internet Chat," *New York Times* online, July 2, 1998. http://www.nytimes.com/library/tech/98/07/circuits/articles/02/chat.html.

44. D. Tannen, "Gender Gap in Cyberspace," *Newsweek* (May 16, 1994): 52–53.

45. D. Kirkpatrick, "Here Comes the Payoff from PCs," *Fortune* (March 23, 1992): 93–102.

46. See P. Watzlawick, J. H. Beavin, and D. D. Jackson, *Pragmatics of Human Communication* (New York: Norton, 1967); and W. J. Lederer and D. D. Jackson, *The Mirages of Marriage* (New York: Norton, 1968).

47. See, for example, R. A. Bell and J. A. Daly, "The Affinity-Seeking Function of Communication" in M. V. Redmond, ed., *Interpersonal Communication: Readings in Theory and Research* (Fort Worth: Harcourt Brace, 1995).

48. M. Dainton, "Everyday Interaction in Marital Relationships: Variations in Relative Importance and Event Duration," *Communication Reports* 11 (1998): 101–143.

49. T. S. Lim and J. W. Bowers, "Facework: Solidarity, Approbation, and Tact," *Human Communication Research* 17 (1991): 415–450.

50. M. T. Palmer, "Controlling Conversations: Turns, Topics, and Interpersonal Control," *Communication Monographs* 56 (1989): 1–18.

51. Watzlawick, Beavin, and Jackson, op. cit.

52. D. Tannen, *That's Not What I Meant! How Conversational Style Makes or Breaks Your Relations with Others* (New York: Morrow, 1986), p. 190.

53. For a thorough review of this topic, see B. H. Spitzberg and W. R. Cupach, *Handbook of Interpersonal Competence Research* (New York: Springer-Verlag, 1989).

54. See J. M. Wiemann, J. Takai, H. Ota, and M. Wiemann, "A Relational Model of Communication Competence" in B. Kovacic, ed., *Emerging Theories of Human Communication* (Albany: SUNY Press, 1997).

55. See Y. Y. Kim, "Intercultural Communication Competence: A Systems-Theoretic View" in S. Ting-Toomey and F. Korzenny, eds., *Cross-Cultural Interpersonal Communication* (Newbury Park, Calif.: Sage, 1991); and G. M. Chen and W. J. Sarosta, "Intercultural Communication Competence: A Synthesis" in B. R. Burleson and A. W. Kunkel, eds., *Communication Yearbook 19* (Thousand Oaks, Calif.: Sage, 1996).

56. J. K. Burgoon and N. E. Dunbar, "An Interactionist Perspective on Dominance-Submission: Interpersonal Dominance as a Dynamic, Situationally Contingent Social Skill," *Communication Monographs* 67 (2000): 96–121.

57. M. J. Collier, "Communication Competence Problematics in Ethnic Relationships," *Communication Monographs* 63 (1996): 314–336.

58. L. Chen, "Verbal Adaptive Strategies in U.S. American Dyadic Interactions with U.S. American or East-Asian Partners," *Communication Monographs* 64 (1997): 302–323.

59. B. H. Spitzberg, "An Examination of Trait Measures of Interpersonal Competence," *Communication Reports* 4 (1991): 22–29.

60. L. K. Guerrero, P. A. Andersen, P. F. Jorgensen, B. H. Spitzberg, and S. V. Eloy, "Coping with the Green-Eyed Monster: Conceptualizing and Measuring Communicative Responses to Romantic Jealousy," *Western Journal of Communication* 59 (1995): 270–304.

61. See B. J. O'Keefe, "The Logic of Message Design: Individual Differences in Reasoning about Communication," *Communication Monographs* 55 (1988): 80–103.

62. See, for example, A. D. Heisel, J. C. McCorosey, and V. P. Richmond, "Testing Theoretical Relationships and Non-Relationships of Genetically-Based Predictors: Getting Started with Communibiology," *Communication Research Reports* 16 (1999): 1–9; and J. C. McCroskey and K. J. Beatty, "The Communibiological Perspective: Implications for Communication in Instruction," *Communication Education* 49 (2000): 1–6.

63. J. Ayres and T. Hopf, *Coping with Speech Anxiety* (Norwood, N.J.: Ablex, 1993). See also M. Allen, J. Bourhis, T. Emmers-Sommer, and E. Sahlstein, "Reducing Dating Anxiety: A Meta-Analysis," *Communication Reports* 11 (1998): .

64. M. A. deTurck and G. R. Miller, "Training Observers to Detect Deception: Effects of Self-Monitoring and Rehearsal," *Human Communication Research* 16 (1990): 603–620.

65. R. B. Rubin, E. M. Perse, and C. A. Barbato, "Conceptualization and Measurement of Interpersonal Communication Motives," *Human Communication Research* 14 (1988): 602–628.

66. D. B. Wackman, S. Miller, and E. W. Nunnally, *Student Workbook: Increasing Awareness and Communication Skills* (Minneapolis: Interpersonal Communication Programs, 1976), p. 6.

67. D. E. Ifert and M. E. Roloff, "The Role of Sensitivity to the Expressions of Others and Ability to Modify Self-Presentation," *Communication Quarterly* 45 (1997): 55–67.

68. J. M. Wiemann and P. M. Backlund, "Current Theory and Research in Communication Competence," *Review of Educational Research* 50 (1980): 185–199. See also M. V. Redmond, "The Relationship between Perceived Communication Competence and Perceived Empathy," *Communication Monographs* 52 (December 1985): 377–382; and M. V. Redmond, "The Functions of Empathy (Decentering) in Human Relations," *Human Relations* 42 (1989): 593–605.

69. R. Martin, "Relational Cognition Complexity and Relational Communication in Personal Relationships," *Communication Monographs* 59 (1992): 150–163. See also B. R. Burleson and S. E. Caplan, "Cognitive Complexity" in J. C. McCroskey, J. A. Daly, M. M. Martin, and M. J. Beatty, eds., *Communication and Personality: Trait Perspectives* (Creskill, N.Y.: Hampton Press, 1998), pp. 233–286.

70. Burleson and Samter, op. cit., p. 22.

71. B. D. Sypher and T. Zorn, "Communication-Related Abilities and Upward Mobility: A Longitudinal Investigation," *Human Communication Research* 12 (1986): 420–431.

72. Research summarized in D. E. Hamachek, *Encounters with the Self*, 2nd ed. (Fort Worth: Holt, Rinehart and Winston, 1987), p. 8. See also J. A. Daly, A. L. Vangelisti, and S. M. Daughton, "The Nature and Correlates of Conversational Sensitivity" in M. V. Redmond, ed., *Interpersonal Communication: Readings in Theory and Research* (Fort Worth: Harcourt Brace, 1995).

73. D. A. Dunning and J. Kruger, *Journal of Personality and Social Psychology* (December 1999): .

74. Adapted from the work of R. P. Hart as reported by M. L. Knapp in *Interpersonal Communication and Human Relationships* (Boston: Allyn and Bacon, 1984), pp. 342–344. See also R. P. Hart and D. M. Burks, "Rhetorical Sensitivity and Social Interaction," *Speech Monographs* 39 (1972): 75–91; and R. P. Hart, R. E. Carlson, and W. F. Eadie, "Attitudes toward Communication and the Assessment of Rhetorical Sensitivity," *Communication Monographs* 47 (1980): 1–22.

ENDNOTES FOR CHAPTER 2

1. D. Carbaugh, *Situating Selves: The Communication of Social Identities in American Scenes* (Albany: SUNY Press, 1996).

2. D. Hamachek, *Encounters with the Self*, 3rd ed. (Fort Worth: Holt, Rinehart and Winston, 1992), pp. 5–8. See also J. D. Campbell and L. F. Lavallee, "Who Am I? The Role of Self-Concept Confusion in Understanding the Behavior of People with Low Self-Esteem" in R. F. Baumeister, ed.,

Self-Esteem: The Puzzle of Low Self-Regard (New York: Plenum Press, 1993), pp. 3–20.

3. J. F. Rosenblith, *In the Beginning: Development from Conception to Age Two* (Newbury Park, Calif.: Sage, 1992).

4. C. H. Cooley, *Human Nature and the Social Order* (New York: Scribner's, 1912).

5. A. L. Vangelisti and L. P. Crumley, "Reactions to Messages That Hurt: The Influence of Relational Contexts," *Communication Monographs* 65 (1998): 173–196.

6. K. Voss, D. Markiewicz, and A. B. Doyle, "Friendship, Marriage and Self-esteem," *Journal of Social and Personal Relationships* 16 (1999): 103–122.

7. S. J. Paxton, H. K. Schutz, E. H. Wertheim, and S. L. Muir, "Friendship Clique and Peer Influences on Body Image Concerns, Dietary Restraint, Extreme Weight-Loss Behaviors, and Binge Eating in Adolescent Girls," *Journal of Abnormal Psychology* 108 (1999): 255–266.

8. J. B. Miller, "Learning from Early Relationship Experience" in S. Duck, ed., *Learning about Relationships* (Newbury Park, Calif.: Sage, 1993).

9. T. Adler, "Personality, Like Plaster, Is Pretty Stable over Time," *APA Monitor* (October 1992): 18.

10. J and R. W. Robins, "A Longitudinal Study of Consistency and Change in Self-Esteem from Early Adolescence to Early Childhood," *Child Development* 64 (1993): 909–923.

11. J. D. Brown, N. J. Novick, K. A. Lord, and J. M. Richards, "When Gulliver Travels: Social Context, Psychological Closeness, and Self-Appraisals," *Journal of Personality and Social Psychology* 62 (1992): 717–734.

12. P. N. Myers and F. A. Biocca, "The Elastic Body Image: The Effect of Television Advertising and Programming on Body Image Distortions in Young Women," *Journal of Communication* 42 (1992): 108–134.

13. D. Grodin and T. R. Lindlof, *Constructing the Self in a Mediated World* (Newbury Park, Calif.: Sage, 1995).

14. J. D. Brown and T. A. Mankowski, "Self-Esteem, Mood, and Self-Evaluation: Changes in Mood and the Way You See You," *Journal of Personality and Social Psychology* 64 (1993): 421–430.

15. M. A. Gara, R. L. Woolfolk, B. D. Cohen, and R. B. Goldston, "Perception of Self and Other in Major Depression," *Journal of Abnormal Psychology* 102 (1993): 93–100.

16. B. Bower, "Truth Aches: People Who View Themselves Poorly May Seek the 'Truth' and Find Despair," *Science News* (August 15, 1992): 110–111; and W. B. Swann, R. M. Wenzlaff, D. S. Krull, and B. W. Pelham, "Allure of Negative Feedback: Self-Verification Strivings among Depressed Persons," *Journal of Abnormal Psychology* 101 (1992): 293–306.

17. L. C. Miller, L. L. Cooke, J. Tsang, and F. Morgan, "Should I Brag? Nature and Impact of Positive and Boastful Disclosures for Women and Men," *Human Communication Research* 18 (1992): 364–399.

18. W. W. Wilmot, *Relational Communication* (New York: McGraw-Hill, 1995), pp. 35–54.

19. J. Servaes, "Cultural Identity and Modes of Communication" in J. A. Anderson, ed., *Communication Yearbook 12* (Newbury Park, Calif.: Sage, 1989), p. 396.

20. A. Bharti, "The Self in Hindu Thought and Action" in *Culture and Self: Asian and Western Perspectives* (New York: Tavistock, 1985).

21. W. B. Gudykunst and S. Ting-Toomey, *Culture and Interpersonal Communication* (Newbury Park, Calif.: Sage, 1988).

22. L. A. Samovar and R. E. Porter, *Communication between Cultures* (Belmont, Calif.: Wadsworth, 1991), p. 91.

23. D. Klopf, "Cross-Cultural Apprehension Research: A Summary of Pacific Basin Studies" in J. Daly and J. McCroskey, eds., *Avoiding Communication: Shyness, Reticence, and Communication Apprehension* (Beverly Hills, Calif.: Sage, 1984).

24. S. Ting-Toomey, "A Face-Negotiation Theory" in Y. Kim and W. Gudykunst, eds., *Theory in Interpersonal Communication* (Newbury Park, Calif.: Sage, 1988).

25. L. C. Lederman, "Gender and the Self" in L. P. Arliss and D. J. Borisoff, eds., *Women and Men Communicating: Challenges and Changes* (Fort Worth: Harcourt Brace, 1993), pp. 41–42.

26. For more examples of gender-related labels, see A. Wittels, *I Wonder . . . A Satirical Study of Sexist Semantics* (Los Angeles: Price/Stern/Sloan, 1978).

27. M. Knox, J. Funk, R. Elliotoo, and E. G. Bush, "Gender Differences in Adolescents' Possible Selves," *Youth and Society* 31 (2000): 287–309.

28. C. J. Smith, J. A. Noll, and J. B. Bryant, "The Effect of Social Context on Gender Self-Concept," *Sex Roles* 40 (1999): 499–512.

29. J. Kolligan, Jr., "Perceived Fraudulence As a Dimension of Perceived Incompetence" in R. J. Sternberg and J. Kolligen, Jr., eds., *Competence Considered* (New Haven, Conn.: Yale University Press, 1990). See also A. L. Vangelisti, S. D. Corbin, A. E. Lucchetti, and R. J. Sprague, "Couples' Concurrent Cognitions: The Influence of Relational Satisfaction on the Thoughts Couples Have As They Converse," *Human Communication Research* 25 (1999): 370–398.

30. B. Zimmerman, A. Bandura, and M. Martinez-Pons, "Self-Motivation for Academic Attainment: The Role of Self-Efficacy Beliefs and Personal Goal Setting," *American Educational Research Journal* 29 (1992): 663–676.

31. G. Downey and S. I. Feldman, "Implications of Rejection Sensitivity for Intimate Relationships," *Journal of Personality and Social Psychology* 70 (1996): 1327–1343.

32. P. D. MacIntyre and K. A Thivierge, "The Effects of Speaker Personality on Anticipated Reactions to Public Speaking," *Communication Research Reports* 12 (1995): 125–133.

33. C. L. Kleinke, T. R. Peterson, and T. R. Rutledge, "Effects of Self-Generated Facial Expressions on Mood," *Journal of Personality and Social Psychology* 74 (1998): 272–279.

34. R. Rosenthal and L. Jacobson, *Pygmalion in the Classroom* (New York: Holt, Rinehart and Winston, 1968).

35. P. D. Blank, ed., *Interpersonal Expectations: Theory, Research, and Applications* (Cambridge, England: Cambridge University Press, 1993).

36. Ibid., pp. 5–6.

37. C. M. Shaw and R. Edwards, "Self-Concepts and Self-Presentations of Males and Females: Similarities and Differences," *Communication Reports* 10 (1997): 55–62.

38. C. M. Scotton, "The Negotiation of Identities in Conversation: A Theory of Markedness and Code Choice," *International Journal of Sociological Linguistics* 44 (1983): 119–125.

39. E. Goffman, *The Presentation of Self in Everyday Life* (Garden City, N.Y.: Doubleday, 1959), and *Relations in Public* (New York: Basic Books, 1971).

40. J. Stewart and C. Logan, *Together: Communicating Interpersonally*, 5th ed. (New York: McGraw-Hill, 1998), p. 120.

41. M. R. Leary and R. M. Kowalski, "Impression Management: A Literature Review and Two-Component Model," *Psychological Bulletin* 107 (1990): 34–47.

42. V. Brightman, A. Segal, P. Werther, and J. Steiner, "Ethological Study of Facial Expression in Response to Taste Stimuli," *Journal of Dental Research* 54 (1975): 141.

43. N. Chovil, "Social Determinants of Facial Displays," *Journal of Nonverbal Behavior* 15 (1991): 141–154.

44. See, for example, R. A. Giacalone and P. Rosenfeld, eds., *Applied Impression Management: How Image-Making Affects Managerial Decisions.* (Newbury Park, Calif.: Sage, 1991).

45. D. Morier and C. Seroy, "The Effect of Interpersonal Expectancies on Men's Self-Presentation of Gender Role Attitudes to Women," *Sex Roles* 31 (1994): 493–504.

46. M. Leary, J. B. Nezlek, D. Downs, et al., "Self-Presentation in Everyday Interactions: Effects of Target Familiarity and Gender Composition," *Journal of Personality and Social Psychology* 67 (1994): 664–673.

47. M. Snyder, *Public Appearances, Private Realities: The Psychology of Self-Monitoring* (New York: W.H. Freeman, 1987).

48. The following discussion is based on material in Hamachek, *Encounters with the Self*, 3rd ed., pp. 24–26.

49. L. M. Coleman and B. M. DePaulo, "Uncovering the Human Spirit: Moving beyond Disability and 'Missed' Communications" in N. Coupland, H. Giles, and J. M. Wiemann, eds., *"Miscommunication" and Problematic Talk* (Newbury Park, Calif.: Sage, 1991), pp. 61–84.

50. J. W. Vander Zanden, *Social Psychology*, 3rd ed. (New York: Random House, 1984), pp. 235–237.

51. D. Brouwer, "The Precarious Visibility Politics of Self-Stigmatization: The Case of HIV/AIDS Tattoos," *Text and Performance Quarterly* 18 (1998): 114–136.

52. J. Coupland, "Past the 'Perfect Kind of Age'? Styling Selves and Relationships in Over-50s Dating Advertisements," *Journal of Communication* 50 (2000): 9–30.

53. S. Lyall, "Personal Ads: Flatulent British Gnome, Toothless, Does Not Seek Romantic Sunsets," *New York Times* (February 14, 1999): 7.

54. P. B. O'Sullivan, "What You Don't Know Won't Hurt Me: Impression Management Functions of Communication Channels in Relationships," *Communication Monographs* 26 (2000): 403–432.

55. D. Chandler, "Personal Home Pages and the Construction of Identities on the Web." http://www.aber.ac.uk/~dgc/ webident .html. Accessed July 11, 2000.

ENDNOTES FOR CHAPTER 3

1. The graphic demonstrations of factors influencing perception in this and the following paragraph are borrowed from Dennis Coon's *Introduction to Psychology*, 9th ed. (Belmont, Calif.: Wadsworth, 2001).

2. G. W. Allport, *The Nature of Prejudice* (New York: Doubleday Anchor, 1958), p. 185.

3. M. Hewstone and R. Brown, "Contact Is Not Enough" in M. Hewstone and R. Brown, eds., *Contact and Conflict in Intergroup Encounters* (Oxford, England: Basil Blackwell, 1986), p. 29. See also H. Giles, N. Coupland, J. Coupland, A. Williams, and J. Nussbaum, "Intergenerational Talk and Communication with Older People," *International Journal of Aging and Human Development* 33 (1992): 251–297.

4. B. Allen, "Diversity and Organizational Communication," *Journal of Applied Communication Research* 23 (1995): 143–155. See also R. Buttny, "Reported Speech in Talking Race on Campus," *Human Communication Research* 23 (1997): 477–506.

5. M. L. Hecht, M. J. Collier, and S. A. Ribeau, *African American Communication: Perspectives, Principles, and Pragmatics* (Hillsdale, N.J.: Lawrence Erlbaum, 1993).

6. M. Allen, "Methodological Considerations When Examining a Gendered World" in D. Canary and K. Dindia, eds., *Handbook of Sex Differences and Similarities in Communication* (Mahwah, N.J.: Lawrence Erlbaum, 1998) pp. 427–444.

7. M. L. Inman and R. S. Baron, "Influence of Prototypes on Perceptions of Prejudice," *Journal of Personality and Social Psychology* 70 (1996): 727–739.

8. P. Watzlawick, J. Beavin, and D. D. Jackson, *Pragmatics of Human Communication* (New York: Norton, 1967), p. 65.

9. V. Manusov, "It Depends on Your Perspective: Effects of Stance and Beliefs about Intent on Person Perception," *Western Journal of Communication* 57 (1993): 27–41.

10. T. Adler, "Enter Romance, Exit Objectivity," *APA Monitor* (June 1992): 18.

11. J. K. Alberts, U. Kellar-Guenther, and S. R. Corman, "That's Not Funny: Understanding Recipients' Responses to Teasing," *Western Journal of Communication* 60 (1996): 337–357. See also R. Edwards, R. Bello, F. Brandau-Brown, and D. Hollems, "The Effects of Loneliness and Verbal Aggressiveness on Message Interpretation," *Southern Communication Journal,* 66 (2001): 139–150.

12. See T. N. Bradbury and F. D. Fincham, "Attributions in Marriage: Review and Critique," *Psychological Bulletin* 107 (1990): 3–33; and V. Manusov, "An Application of Attribution Principles to Nonverbal Behavior in Romantic Dyads," *Communication Monographs* 57 (1990): 104–118.

13. For a detailed description of how the senses affect perception, see N. Ackerman, *A Natural History of the Senses* (New York: Random House, 1990).

14. J. Piaget, *The Origins of Intelligence in Children* (New York: International Universities Press, 1952).

15. C. Cooper and C. McConville, "Interpreting Mood Scores: Clinical Implications of Individual Differences in Mood Variability," *British Journal of Medical Psychology* 63

(1990): 215–225. See also J. Mendlewicz and H. M. van Praag, eds., *Biological Rhythms and Behavior* (New York: Karger, 1983).

16. See, for example, J. C. Hoffmann, "Biorhythms in Human Reproduction: The Not-So-Steady States," *Signs* 7 (1982): 829–844.

17. J. W. Bagby, "A Cross-Cultural Study of Perceptual Predominance in Binocular Rivalry," *Journal of Abnormal and Social Psychology* 54 (1957): 331–334.

18. R. Armao, "Worst Blunders; Firms Laugh through Tears," *American Business* (January 1981): 11.

19. R. Harrison, "Nonverbal Behavior: An Approach to Human Communication," in R. Budd and B. Ruben, eds., *Approaches to Human Communication* (New York: Spartan Books, 1972).

20. E. T. Hall, *The Hidden Dimension* (New York: Doubleday Anchor, 1969), p. 160.

21. H. Giles, N. Coupland, and J. M. Wiemann, "Talk Is Cheap . . . But 'My Word Is My Bond': Beliefs about Talk," in K. Bolton and H. Kwok, eds., *Sociolinguistics Today: International Perspectives* (London: Routledge & Kegan Paul, 1992).

22. A. Fadiman, *The Spirit Catches You and You Fall Down* (New York: Farrar, Straus and Giroux, 1997), p. 33.

23. J. Horn, "Conversation Breakdowns: As Different as Black and White," *Psychology Today* 8 (May 1974): 30.

24. P. Andersen, M. Lustig, and J. Anderson, "Changes in Latitude, Changes in Attitude: The Relationship between Climate, Latitude, and Interpersonal Communication Predispositions," paper presented at the annual convention of the Speech Communication Association, Boston, 1987; and P. Andersen, M. Lustig, and J. Andersen, "Regional Patterns of Communication in the United States: Empirical Tests," paper presented at the annual convention of the Speech Communication Association, New Orleans, 1988.

25. See S. A. Rathus, *Psychology*, 5th ed. (Fort Worth: Harcourt Brace Jovanovich, 1993), pp. 640–643; and C. Wade and C. Tavris, *Psychology* (New York: Harper & Row, 1987), pp. 488–490.

26. S. L. Bem, "Androgyny and Gender Schema Theory: A Conceptual and Empirical Integration" in T. B. Sonderegger, ed., *Nebraska Symposium on Motivation: Psychology and Gender* (Lincoln: University of Nebraska Press, 1985).

27. P. G. Zimbardo, C. Haney, and W. C. Banks, "A Pirandellian Prison," *New York Times Magazine*, April 8, 1973.

28. See, for example, P. Baron, "Self-Esteem, Ingratiation, and Evaluation of Unknown Others," *Journal of Personality and Social Psychology* (1974): 104–109.

29. D. E. Hamachek, *Encounters with Others: Interpersonal Relationships and You* (New York: Holt, Rinehart and Winston, 1982), p. 3.

30. For a summary of the narrative paradigm, see E. Griffin, *A First Look at Communication Theory*, 3rd ed. (New York: McGraw-Hill, 1997), pp. 322–332. For a more detailed description, see W. R. Fisher, *Human Communication as Narrative: Toward a Philosophy of Reason, Value, and Action* (Columbia, S.C.: University of South Carolina Press, 1987).

31. See, for example, E. Stone, "Family Ground Rules" in K. Galvin and P. Cooper, eds., *Making Connections: Readings in Relational Communication* (Los Angeles: Roxbury, 1996).

32. P. M. M. Sias, "Constructing Perceptions of Differential Treatment: An Analysis of Coworkers Discourse," *Communication Monographs* 63 (1996): 171–187.

33. J. C. Pearson, "Positive Distortion: 'The Most Beautiful Woman in the World'" in K. M. Galvin and P. Cooper, eds., *Making Connections: Readings in Interpersonal Communication* (Beverly Hills, Calif.: Roxbury, 1996), pp. 175–181. See also S. L. Murray, J. G. Holmes, and D. W. Griffin, "The Benefits of Positive Illusions: Idealization and the Construction of Satisfaction in Close Relationships," *Journal of Personality and Social Psychology* 70 (1996): 79–98.

34. Pearson, op. cit., p. 177.

35. D. Hamachek, *Encounters with the Self*, 3rd ed. (Fort Worth: Harcourt Brace Jovanovich, 1992).

36. For a review of these perceptual biases, see Hamachek, *Encounters with the Self*. See also Bradbury and Fincham, op. cit. For an example of the self-serving bias in action, see R. Buttny, "Reported Speech in Talking Race on Campus," *Human Communication Research* 23 (1997): 477–506.

37. B. Sypher and H. E. Sypher, "Seeing Ourselves as Others See Us," *Communication Research* 11 (January 1984): 97–115.

38. Reported by D. Myers, "The Inflated Self," *Psychology Today* 14 (May 1980): 16.

39. See, for example, A. Sillars, W. Shellen, A. McIntosh, and M. Pomegranate, "Relational Characteristics of Language: Elaboration and Differentiation in Marital Conversations," *Western Journal of Communication* 61 (1997): 403–422.

40. J. B. Stiff, J. P. Dillard, L. Somera, H. Kim, and C. Sleight, "Empathy, Communication, and Prosocial Behavior," *Communication Monographs* 55 (1988): 198–213.

41. This research is described by D. Goleman in *Emotional Intelligence* (New York: Bantam, 1995), p. 98.

42. M. Davis, "The Heritability of Characteristics Associated with Dispositional Empathy," *Journal of Personality* 62 (1994).

43. B. Burleson, J. Delia, and J. Applegate, "The Socialization of Person-Centered Communication: Parental Contributions to the Social-Cognitive and Communication Skills of Their Children" in M. A. Fitzpatrick and A. Vangelisti, eds., *Perspectives in Family Communication* (Thousand Oaks, Calif.: Sage, 1995).

44. R. Lennon and N. Eisenberg, "Gender and Age Differences in Empathy and Sympathy" in N. Eisenberg and J. Strayer, eds., *Empathy and Its Development* (Cambridge, England: Cambridge University Press, 1987).

45. T. Adler, "Look at Duration, Depth in Research on Emotion," *APA Monitor* (October 1990): 10.

46. N. D. Feshbach, "Parental Empathy and Child Adjustment/Maladjustment" in Eisenberg and Strayer, op. cit.

47. See, for example, "Diversity in the Communication Curriculum: Impact on Student Empathy," *Communication Education* 46 (1977): 234–244.

48. P. Reps, "Pillow Education in Rural Japan" in *Square Sun, Square Moon* (New York: Tuttle, 1967).

ENDNOTES FOR CHAPTER 4

1. R. J. Sternberg, *Beyond I.Q.* (New York: Cambridge University Press, 1985).
2. D. Goleman, *Emotional Intelligence: Why It Can Matter More Than I.Q.* (New York: Bantam, 1995).
3. P. Ekman, R. W. Levenson, and W. V. Friesen, "Autonomic Nervous System Activity Distinguishes among Emotions," *Science* 221 (September 16, 1983): 1208–1210.
4. C. L. Kleinke, T. R. Peterson, and T. R. Rutledge, "Effects of Self-Generated Facial Expressions on Mood," *Journal of Personality and Social Psychology* 74 (1998): 272–279.
5. S. Valins, "Cognitive Effects of False Heart-Rate Feedback," *Journal of Personality and Social Psychology* 4 (1966): 400–408.
6. P. Zimbardo, *Shyness: What It Is, What to Do about It* (Reading, Mass.: Addison-Wesley, 1977), p. 53.
7. Ibid., p. 54.
8. D. Goleman, *Emotional Intelligence: Why It Can Matter More Than I.Q.* (New York: Bantam, 1995).
9. J. M. Gottman, L. F. Katz, and C. Hooven, *Meta-Emotion: How Families Communicate Emotionally* (Mawah, N.J.: Lawrence Erlbaum, 1997).
10. R. Plutchik, "A Language for the Emotions," *Psychology Today* 14 (February 1980): 68–78. For a more detailed explanation, see R. Plutchik, *Emotion: A Psychoevolutionary Synthesis* (New York: Harper & Row, 1980).
11. C. R. Bush, J. P. Bush, and J. Jennings, "Effects of Jealousy Threats on Relationship Perceptions and Emotions," *Journal of Social and Personal Relationships* 5 (1988): 285–303.
12. M. Mikulincer and J. Segal, "A Multidimensional Analysis of the Experience of Loneliness," *Journal of Social and Personal Relationships* 7 (1990): 209–230.
13. Plutchik, "A Language for the Emotions."
14. W. B. Gudykunst and Y. K. Young, *Communicating with Strangers*, 2nd ed. (New York: McGraw-Hill, 1995), pp. 173–174.
15. S. Ting-Toomey, "Intimacy Expressions in Three Cultures: France, Japan, and the United States," *International Journal of Intercultural Relations* 15 (1991): 29–46. See also C. Gallois, "The Language and Communication of Emotion: Universal, Interpersonal, or Intergroup?" *American Behavioral Scientist* 36 (1993): 309–338.
16. J. W. Pennebaker, B. Rime, and V. E. Blankenship, "Stereotypes of Emotional Expressiveness of Northerners and Southerners: A Cross-Cultural Test of Montesquieu's Hypotheses," *Journal of Personality and Social Psychology* 70 (1996): 372–380.
17. Ibid., p. 176. See also C. Gallois, "The Language and Communication of Emotion: Universal, Interpersonal, or Intergroup?" *American Behavioral Scientist* 36 (1993): 309–338.
18. H. C. Triandis, *Culture and Social Behavior* (New York: McGraw-Hill, 1994), p. 169. See also F. M. Moghaddam, D. M. Taylor, and S. C. Wright, *Social Psychology in Cross-Cultural Perspective* (New York: Freeman, 1993).
19. D. Matsumoto, "Ethnic Differences in Affect Intensity, Emotion Judgments, Display Rule Attitudes, and Self-Reported Emotional Expression in an American Sample," *Motivation and Emotion* 17 (1993): 107–123.
20. See, for example, A. W. Kunkel and B. R. Burleson, "Assessing Explanations for Sex Differences in Emotional Support: A Test of the Different Cultures and Skill Specialization Accounts," *Human Communication Research* 25 (1999): 307–340.
21. D. J. Goldsmith and P. A. Fulfs, "You Just Don't Have the Evidence": An Analysis of Claims and Evidence in Deborah Tannen's *You Just Don't Understand* in M. E. Roloff, ed., *Communication Yearbook 22* (Thousand Oaks, Calif.: Sage, 1999), pp. 1–49.
22. D. F. Witmer and S. L. Katzman, "On-Line Smiles: Does Gender Make a Difference in the Use of Graphic Accents?" *Journal of Computer-Mediated Communication* 2 (1999) (Online).
23. J. Hall, "Gender Effects in Decoding Nonverbal Cues," *Psychological Bulletin* 85 (1978): 845–857.
24. J. Swenson and F. L. Casmir, "The Impact of Culture-Sameness, Gender, Foreign Travel, and Academic Background on the Ability to Interpret Facial Expression of Emotion in Others," *Communication Quarterly* 46 (1998): 214–230.
25. K. Floyd, "Communication Affection in Dyadic Relationships: An Assessment of Behavior and Expectancies," *Communication Quarterly* 45 (1997): 68–80.
26. S. E. Snodgrass, "Women's Intuition: The Effect of Subordinate Role on Interpersonal Sensitivity," *Journal of Personality and Social Psychology* 49 (1985): 146–155.
27. S. B. Shimanoff, "Commonly Named Emotions in Everyday Conversations," *Perceptual and Motor Skills* 58 (1984): 514. See also J. M. Gottmann, "Emotional Responsiveness in Marital Conversations," *Journal of Communication* 32 (1982): 108–120.
28. S. B. Shimanoff, "Degree of Emotional Expressiveness as a Function of Face-Needs, Gender, and Interpersonal Relationship," *Communication Reports* 1 (1988): 43–53.
29. C. A. Stearns and P. Stearns, *Anger: The Struggle for Emotional Control in America's History* (Chicago: University of Chicago Press, 1986).
30. S. B. Shimanoff, "Rules Governing the Verbal Expression of Emotions between Married Couples," *Western Journal of Speech Communication* 49 (1985): 149–165.
31. S. Duck, "Social Emotions: Showing Our Feelings about Other People" in *Human Relationships* (Newbury Park, Calif.: Sage, 1992). See also S. B. Shimanoff, "Expressing Emotions in Words: Verbal Patterns of Interaction," *Journal of Communication* 35 (1985): 16–31.
32. E. S. Sullins, "Emotional Contagion Revisited: Effects of Social Comparison and Expressive Style on Mood Convergence," *Personality & Social Psychology Bulletin* 17 (1991): 166–174.
33. Goleman, op. cit., p. 115.

34. L. B. Rosenfeld, "Self-Disclosure and Avoidance: Why Am I Afraid to Tell You Who I Am?" *Communication Monographs* 46 (1979): 63–74.

35. T. DeAngelis, "Illness Linked with Repressive Style of Coping," *APA Monitor* (1992): 14–15. See also T. J. Mayne, "Negative Affect and Health: The Importance of Being Earnest," *Cognition and Emotion* 13 (1999): 601–635.

36. A. W. Seigman and T. W. Smith, *Anger, Hostility, and the Heart* (Hillsdale, N.J.: Lawrence Erlbaum, 1994).

37. E. Kennedy-Moore, E. and J. C. Watson, *Expressing Emotion: Myths, Realities, and Therapeutic Strategies* (New York: Guilford, 1999).

38. S. Nelton, "Emotions in the Workplace," *Nation's Business* (February 1996): 25–30.

39. M. Booth-Butterfield and S. Booth-Butterfield, "Emotionality and Affective Orientation" in J. C. McCroskey, J. A. Daly, M. M. Martin, and M. J. Beatty, eds., *Communication and Personality: Trait Perspectives* (Creskill, N.Y.: Hampton, 1998).

40. B. J. Bushman, R. F. Baumeister, and A. D. Stack, "Catharsis, Aggression, and Persuasive Influence: Self-Fulfilling or Self-Defeating Prophecies?" *Journal of Personality and Social Psychology* 76 (1999): 367–376.

41. S. A. McCornack and T. R. Levine, "When Lovers Become Leery: The Relationship between Suspicion and Accuracy in Detecting Deception," *Communication Monographs* 57 (1990): 219–230.

42. J. Bourhis and M. Allen, "Meta-Analysis of the Relationship between Communication Apprehension and Cognitive Performance," *Communication Education* 41 (1992): 68–76.

43. M. L. Patterson and V. Ritts, "Social and Communicative Anxiety: A Review and Meta-Analysis" in B. R. Burleson, ed., *Communication Yearbook 20* (Thousand Oaks, Calif.: Sage, 1997).

44. D. R. Vocate, "Self-Talk and Inner Speech" in D. R. Vocate, ed., *Intrapersonal Communication: Different Voices, Different Minds* (Hillsdale, N.J.: Erlbaum, 1994).

45. J. Ayers, T. Keereetaweep, P. Chen, and P. A. Edwards, "Communication Apprehension and Employment Interviews," *Communication Education* 47 (1998): 1–17.

46. M. Booth-Butterfield and M. R. Trotta, "Attributional Patterns for Expressions of Love," *Communication Reports* 7 (1994): 119–129.

47. A. L. Vangelisti, S. D. Corgin, A. E. Lucchetti, and R. J. Sprague, "Couples' Concurrent Cognitions: The Influence of Relational Satisfaction on the Thoughts Couples Have As They Converse," *Human Communication Research* 25 (1999): 370–398.

48. J. A. Bargh, "Automatic Information Processing: Implications for Communication and Affect" in H. E. Sypher and E. T. Higgins, eds., *Communication, Social Cognition, and Affect* (Hillsdale, N.J.: Erlbaum, 1988).

49. A. Beck, *Cognitive Therapy and the Emotional Disorders* (New York: International Universities Press, 1976).

50. S. Metts and W. R. Cupach, "The Influence of Relationship Beliefs and Problem-Solving Relationships on Satisfaction in Romantic Relationships," *Human Communication Research* 17 (1990): 170–185.

51. A. Meichenbaum, *Cognitive Behavior Modification* (New York: Plenum, 1977). See also A. Ellis and R. Greiger, *Handbook for Rational-Emotive Therapy* (New York: Springer, 1977) .

52. A. Chatham-Carpenter and V. DeFrancisco, "Pulling Yourself Up Again: Women's Choices and Strategies for Recovering and Maintaining Self-Esteem," *Western Journal of Communication* 61 (1997): 164–187.

ENDNOTES FOR CHAPTER 5

1. Sacks, *Seeing Voices: A Journey into the World of the Deaf* (Berkeley: University of California Press, 1989), p. 17.

2. M. Henneberger, "Misunderstanding of Word Embarrasses Washington's New Mayor," *New York Times* online, January 29, 1999. http://www.nyt.com.

3. T. L. Scott, "Teens before Their Time," *Time* (November 27, 2000): 22.

4. T. Wallsten, "Measuring the Vague Meanings of Probability Terms," *Journal of Experimental Psychology* 115 (1986): 348–365.

5. Reprinted in *Newsweek*, March 7, 1994, 54, and *Time*, October 11, 1993, 24.

6. J. K. Alberts, "An Analysis of Couples' Conversational Complaints," *Communication Monographs* 55 (1988): 184–197.

7. M. L. Hecht, M. J. Collier, and S. A. Ribeau, *African American Communication: Ethnic Identity and Cultural Interpretation* (Newbury Park, Calif.: Sage, 1993), pp. 84–89.

8. N. Coupland, J. M. Wiemann, and H. Giles, "Talk as 'Problem' and Communication as 'Miscommunication': An Integrative Analysis" in N. Coupland, J. M. Wiemann, and H. Giles, eds., *"Miscommunication" and Problematic Talk* (Newbury Park, Calif.: Sage, 1991).

9. W. B. Pearce and V. Cronen, *Communication, Action, and Meaning* (New York: Praeger, 1980). See also V. Cronen, V. Chen, and W. B. Pearce, "Coordinated Management of Meaning: A Critical Theory" in Y. Y. Kim and W. B. Gudykunst, eds., *Theories in Intercultural Communication* (Newbury Park, Calif.: Sage, 1988).

10. E. K. E. Graham, M. Papa, and G. P. Brooks, "Functions of Humor in Conversation: Conceptualization and Measurement," *Western Journal of Communication* 56 (1992): 161–183.

11. M. G. Marcus, "The Power of a Name," *Psychology Today* 9 (October 1976): 75–77, 106.

12. A. Mehrabian, "Interrelationships among Name Desirability, Name Uniqueness, Emotion Characteristics Connoted by Names, and Temperament," *Journal of Applied Social Psychology* 22 (1992): 1797–1808.

13. C. A. VanLear, "Testing a Cyclical Model of Communicative Openness in Relationship Development," *Communication Monographs* 58 (1991): 337–361.

14. M. Hecht and S. Ribeau, "Sociocultural Roots of Ethnic Identity," *Journal of Black Studies* 21 (1991): 501–513.

15. K. Foss and B. Edson, "What's in a Name? Accounts of Married Women's Name Choices," *Western Journal of Speech Communication* 53 (1989): 356–373.

16. K. L. Dion, "What's in a Title? The Ms. Stereotype and Images of Women's Titles of Address," *Psychology of Women Quarterly* 11 (1987): 21–36.

17. See, for example, R. K. Aune and Toshiyuki Kikuchi, "Effects of Language Intensity Similarity of Perceptions of Credibility, Relational Attributions, and Persuasion," *Journal of Language and Social Psychology* 12 (1993): 224–238.

18. H. Giles, J. Coupland, and N. Coupland, eds., *Contexts of Accommodation: Developments in Applied Sociolinguistics* (Cambridge, England: Cambridge University Press, 1991).

19. M. Weiner and A. Mehrabian, *A Language within Language: Immediacy, a Channel in Verbal Communication* (New York: Appleton-Century-Crofts, 1968).

20. J. J. Bradac, J. M. Wiemann, and K. Schaefer, "The Language of Control in Interpersonal Communication" in J. A. Daly and J. M. Wiemann, eds., *Strategic Interpersonal Communication* (Hillsdale, N.J.: Erlbaum, 1994), pp. 102–104. See also S. H. Ng and J. J. Bradac, *Power in Language: Verbal Communication and Social Influence* (Newbury Park, Calif.: Sage, 1993), p. 27.

21. L. A. Hosman, "The Evaluative Consequences of Hedges, Hesitations, and Intensifiers: Powerful and Powerless Speech Styles," *Human Communication Research* 15 (1989): 383–406.

22. L. A. Samovar and R. E. Porter, *Communication between Cultures*, 4th ed. (Belmont, Calif.: Wadsworth, 2001), pp. 58–59.

23. J. Bradac and A. Mulac, "Attributional Consequences of Powerful and Powerless Speech Styles in a Crisis-Intervention Context," *Journal of Language and Social Psychology* 3 (1984): 1–19.

24. J. J. Bradac, "The Language of Lovers, Flovers [sic], and Friends: Communicating in Social and Personal Relationships," *Journal of Language and Social Psychology* 2 (1983): 141–162.

25. D. Geddes, "Sex Roles in Management: The Impact of Varying Power of Speech Style on Union Members' Perception of Satisfaction and Effectiveness," *Journal of Psychology* 126 (1992): 589–607.

26. S. L. Kirkland, J. Greenberg, and T. Pyszczynski, "Further Evidence of the Deleterious Effects of Overheard Derogatory Ethnic Labels: Derogation beyond the Target," *Personality and Social Psychology Bulletin* 12 (1987): 216–227.

27. E. S. Kubany, D. C. Richard, G. B. Bauer, and M. Y. Muraoka, "Impact of Assertive and Accusatory Communication of Distress and Anger: A Verbal Component Analysis," *Aggressive Behavior* 18 (1992): 337–347.

28. T. Gordon, *P.E.T.: Parent Effectiveness Training* (New York: Wyden, 1970), p. 145.

29. R. Raskin and R. Shaw, "Narcissism and the Use of Personal Pronouns," *Journal of Personality* 56 (1988): 393–404; and A. L. Vangelisti, M. L. Knapp, and J. A. Daly, "Conversational Narcissism," *Communication Monographs* 57 (1990): 251–274.

30. A. S. Dreyer, C. A. Dreyer, and J. E. Davis, "Individuality and Mutuality in the Language of Families of Field-Dependent and Field-Independent Children," *Journal of Genetic Psychology* 148 (1987): 105–117.

31. J. M. Honeycutt, "Typological Differences in Predicting Marital Happiness from Oral History Behaviors and Imagined Interactions," *Communication Monographs* 66 (1999): 276–291.

32. R. F. Proctor and J. R. Wilcox, "An Exploratory Analysis of Responses to Owned Messages in Interpersonal Communication," *ETC: A Review of General Semantics* 50 (1993): 201–220; and Vangelisti et al., *Conversational Narcissism*, op. cit.

33. See, for example, D. Tannen, *You Just Don't Understand: Women and Men in Conversation* (New York: William Morrow, 1990).

34. D. J. Goldsmith and P. A. Fulfs, "'You Just Don't Have the Evidence': An Analysis of Claims and Evidence in Deborah Tannen's *You Just Don't Understand*" in M. E. Roloff, ed., *Communication Yearbook 22* (Thousand Oaks, Calif.: Sage, 1999).

35. See, for example, A. Haas and M. A. Sherman, "Conversational Topic As a Function of Role and Gender," *Psychological Reports* 51 (1982): 453–454; and B. Fehr, *Friendship Processes* (Thousand Oaks, Calif.: Sage, 1996).

36. R. A. Clark, "A Comparison of Topics and Objectives in a Cross Section of Young Men's and Women's Everyday Conversations" in D. J. Canary and K. Dindia, eds., *Sex Differences and Similarities in Communication: Critical Essays and Empirical Investigations of Sex and Gender in Interaction* (Mawah, N.J.: Erlbaum, 1998).

37. J. T. Wood, *Gendered Lives: Communication, Gender, and Culture* (Belmont, Calif.: Wadsworth, 1994), p. 141.

38. M. A. Sherman and A. Haas, "Man to Man, Woman to Woman," *Psychology Today* 17 (June 1984): 72–73.

39. J. D. Ragsdale, "Gender, Satisfaction Level, and the Use of Relational Maintenance Strategies in Marriage," *Communication Monographs* 63 (1996): 354–371.

40. Clark, op. cit.

41. Haas and Sherman, "Conversational Topic as a Function of Role and Gender."

42. Research summarized by D. Tannen, *You Just Don't Understand: Women and Men in Conversation* (New York: William Morrow, 1990).

43. J. Sachs, "Young Children's Language Use in Pretend Play" in S. U. Philips, S. Steele, and C. Tanz, eds., *Language, Gender, and Sex in Comparative Perspective* (Cambridge, England: Cambridge University Press, 1987).

44. For a summary of research on differences between male and female conversational behaviors, see H. Giles and R. L. Street, Jr., "Communication Characteristics and Behavior" in M. L. Knapp and G. R. Miller, eds., *Handbook of Interpersonal Communication* (Beverly Hills, Calif.: Sage, 1985), pp. 205–261; and A. Kohn, "Girl Talk, Guy Talk," *Psychology Today* 22 (February 1988): 65–66.

45. V. deKlerk, "Expletives: Men Only?" *Communication Monographs* 58 (1991): 156–169.

46. A. Mulac, "The Gender-Linked Language Effect: Do Language Differences Really Make a Difference?" in D. J. Canary and K. Dindia, op cit.

47. L. L. Carli, "Gender, Language, and Influence," *Journal of Personality and Social Psychology* 59 (1990): 941–951.

48. D. J. Canary and K. S. Hause, "Is There Any Reason to Research Sex Differences in Communication?" *Communication Quarterly* 41 (1993): 129–144.

49. C. J. Zahn, "The Bases for Differing Evaluations of Male and Female Speech: Evidence from Ratings of Transcribed Conversation," *Communication Monographs* 56 (1989): 59–74. See also L. M. Grob, R. A. Meyers, and R. Schuh, "Powerful/Powerless Language Use in Group Interactions: Sex Differences or Similarities?" *Communication Quarterly* 45 (1997): 282–303.

50. J. T. Wood and K. Dindia, "What's the Difference? A Dialogue about Differences and Similarities between Women and Men" in Canary and Dindia, op cit.

51. C. J. Zahn, "The Bases for Differing Evaluations of Male and Female Speech: Evidence from Ratings of Transcribed Conversation," *Communication Monographs* 56 (1989): 59–74.

52. J. T. Wood, *Gendered Lives: Communication, Gender, and Culture* (Belmont, Calif.: Wadsworth, 1994).

53. D. Tannen, *Talking from 9 to 5: Women and Men in the Workplace: Language, Sex and Power* (New York: William Morrow, 1994).

54. D. G. Ellis and L. McCallister, "Relational Control Sequences in Sex-Typed and Androgynous Groups," *Western Journal of Speech Communication* 44 (1980): 35–49.

55. For a thorough discussion of the challenges involved in translation from one language to another, see L. A. Samovar and R. E. Porter, *Communication between Cultures* (Dubuque, Iowa: W.C. Brown, 1991), pp. 165–169.

56. The examples in this paragraph are taken from D. Ricks, *Big Business Blunders: Mistakes in International Marketing* (Homewood, Ill.: Dow Jones-Irwin, 1983), p. 41.

57. N. Sugimoto, "'Excuse me' and 'I'm sorry': Apologetic Behaviors of Americans and Japanese," paper presented at the Conference on Communication in Japan and the United States, California State University, Fullerton, California, March 1991.

58. A summary of how verbal style varies across cultures can be found in chapter 5 of W. B. Gudykunst and S. Ting-Toomey, *Culture and Interpersonal Communication* (Newbury Park, Calif.: Sage, 1988).

59. E. Hall, *Beyond Culture* (New York: Doubleday, 1959).

60. L. Leets and H. Giles, "Words As Weapons—When Do They Wound? *Human Communication Research* 24 (1997): 260–301; and L. Leets, "When Words Wound: Another Look at Racist Speech," paper presented at the annual conference of the International Communication Association, San Francisco, May 1999.

61. A. Almaney and A. Alwan, *Communicating with the Arabs* (Prospect Heights, Ill.: Waveland, 1982).

62. K. Basso, "To Give Up on Words: Silence in Western Apache Culture," *Southern Journal of Anthropology* 26 (1970): 213–230.

63. J. Yum, "The Practice of Uye-ri in Interpersonal Relationships in Korea" in D. Kincaid, ed., *Communication Theory from Eastern and Western Perspectives* (New York: Academic Press, 1987).

64. L. Martin and G. Pullum, *The Great Eskimo Vocabulary Hoax* (Chicago: University of Chicago Press, 1991).

65. H. Giles and A. Franklyn-Stokes, "Communicator Characteristics" in M. K. Asante and W. B. Gudykunst, eds., *Handbook of International and Intercultural Communication* (Newbury Park, Calif.: Sage, 1989).

66. L. Sinclair, "A Word in Your Ear" in *Ways of Mankind* (Boston: Beacon Press, 1954).

67. B. Whorf, "The Relation of Habitual Thought and Behavior to Language" in J. B. Carrol, ed., *Language, Thought, and Reality* (Cambridge, Mass.: MIT Press, 1956).

68. H. Hoijer, quoted in T. Seinfatt, "Linguistic Relativity: Toward a Broader View" in S. Ting-Toomey and F. Korzenny, eds., *Language, Communication, and Culture: Current Directions* (Newbury Park, Calif.: Sage, 1989).

69. H. Rheingold, *They Have a Word for It* (Los Angeles: Jeremy P. Tarcher, 1988).

70. D. A. Prentice, "Do Language Reforms Change Our Ways of Thinking?" *Journal of Language and Social Psychology* 13 (1994): 3–19.

71. "Most Blacks Prefer 'Black' to 'African American,'" *Society* 28 (May/June 1991): 2–3. See also D. Niven and J. Zilber, "Preference for African American or Black," *Howard Journal of Communications* 11 (2000): 267–277.

ENDNOTES FOR CHAPTER 6

1. Research summarized by J. K. Burgoon, "Nonverbal Signals" in M. L. Knapp and G. R. Miller, eds., *Handbook of Interpersonal Communication* (Newbury Park, Calif.: Sage, 1994), p. 235.

2. B. M. DePaulo, "Spotting Lies: Can Humans Learn to Do Better?" *Current Directions in Psychological Science* 3 (1994): 83–86.

3. Not all communication theorists agree with the claim that all nonverbal behavior has communicative value. For a contrasting opinion, see Burgoon, "Nonverbal Signals," pp. 229–232.

4. F. Manusov, "Perceiving Nonverbal Messages: Effects of Immediacy and Encoded Intent on Receiver Judgments," *Western Journal of Speech Communication* 55 (Summer 1991): 235–253.

5. R. Birdwhistell, *Kinesics and Context* (Philadelphia: University of Pennsylvania Press, 1970), chapter 9.

6. P. Ekman, W. V. Friesen, and J. Baer, "The International Language of Gestures," *Psychology Today* 18 (May 1984): 64–69.

7. E. Hall, *The Hidden Dimension* (Garden City, N.Y.: Anchor Books, 1969).

8. A. M. Warnecke, R. D. Masters, and G. Kempter, "The Roots of Nationalism: Nonverbal Behavior and Xenophobia," *Ethnology and Sociobiology* 13 (1992): 267–282.

9. Hall, *The Hidden Dimension.*

10. D. L. Rubin, "'Nobody Play by the Rule He Know': Ethnic Interference in Classroom Questioning Events" in Y. Y. Kim, ed., *Interethnic Communication: Recent Research* (Newbury Park, Calif.: Sage, 1986).

11. S. Weitz, ed., *Nonverbal Communication: Readings with Commentary* (New York: Oxford University Press, 1974).

12. J. Eibl-Eibesfeldt, "Universals and Cultural Differences in Facial Expressions of Emotions" in J. Cole, ed., *Nebraska*

Symposium on Motivation (Lincoln, Neb.: University of Nebraska Press, 1972).

13. M. Booth-Butterfield and F. Jordan, "'Act Like Us': Communication Adaptation among Racially Homogeneous and Heterogeneous Groups," paper presented at the Speech Communication Association meeting, New Orleans, 1988.

14. D. Morris, *Manwatching: A Field Guide to Human Behavior* (New York: Abrams, 1977).

15. For a comprehensive summary of male-female differences and similarities in nonverbal communication, see P. A. Andersen, *Nonverbal Communication: Forms and Functions* (Mountain View, Calif.: Mayfield, 1999), p. 107. For a detailed summary of similarities and differences, see D. J. Canary and T. M. Emmers-Sommer, *Sex and Gender Differences in Personal Relationships* (New York: Guilford, 1997).

16. Andersen, op cit., p. 107.

17. J. T. Wood and K. Dindia, "What's the Difference? A Dialogue about Differences and Similarities between Women and Men" in D. J. Canary and K. Dindia, *Sex Differences and Similarities in Communication* (Mahwah, N.J.: Erlbaum, 1998).

18. J. K. Burgoon and B. A. LePoire, "Nonverbal Cues and Interpersonal Judgments: Participant and Observer Perceptions of Intimacy, Dominance, Composure, and Formality," *Communication Monographs* 66 (1999): 105–124.

19. "Smile When You Write That," *Los Angeles Times*, March 18, 1999: C2.

20. M. T. Motley, "Facial Affect and Verbal Context in Conversation: Facial Expression as Interjection," *Human Communication Research* 20 (1993): 3–40.

21. M. Moore, "Nonverbal Courtship Patterns in Women: Context and Consequences," *Ethology and Sociobiology* 6 (1985): 237–247.

22. See, for example, K. Drummond and R. Hopper, "Acknowledgment Tokens in Series," *Communication Reports* 6 (1993): 47–53; and H. M. Rosenfeld, "Conversational Control Functions of Nonverbal Behavior" in A. W. Siegman and S. Feldstein, eds., *Nonverbal Behavior and Communication*, 2nd ed. (Hillsdale, N.J.: Erlbaum, 1987).

23. J. Hale and J. B. Stiff, "Nonverbal Primacy in Veracity Judgments," *Communication Reports* 3 (1990): 75–83; and J. B. Stiff, J. L. Hale, R. Garlick, and R. G. Rogan, "Effect of Cue Incongruence and Social Normative Influences on Individual Judgments of Honesty and Deceit," *Southern Speech Communication Journal* 55 (1990): 206–229.

24. J. K. Burgoon, T. Birk, and M. Pfau, "Nonverbal Behaviors, Persuasion, and Credibility," *Human Communication Research* 17 (1990): 140–169.

25. D. D. Henningsen, M. G. Cruz, and M. C. Morr, "Pattern Violations and Perceptions of Deception," *Communication Reports* 13 (2000): 1–9.

26. See, for example, B. M. DePaulo, "Detecting Deception Modality Effects" in L. Wheeler, ed., *Review of Personality and Social Psychology*, vol. 1 (Beverly Hills, Calif.: 1980); and J. Greene, D. O'Hair, M. Cody, and C. Yen, "Planning and Control of Behavior during Deception," *Human Communication Research* 11 (1985): 335–364.

27. P. Kalbfleisch, "Deceit, Distrust, and Social Milieu: Applications of Deception Research in a Troubled World," *Journal of Applied Communication Research* (1992): 308–334.

28. D. B. Buller, J. Comstock, R. K. Aune, and K. D. Stryzewski, "The Effect of Probing on Deceivers and Truthtellers," *Journal of Nonverbal Behavior* 13 (1989): 155–170. See also D. B. Buller, K. D. Stryzewski, and J. Comstock, "Interpersonal Deception: I. Deceivers' Reactions to Receivers' Suspicions and Probing," *Communication Monographs* 58 (1991): 1–24.

29. D. A. Lieberman, T. G. Rigo, and R. F. Campain, "Age-Related Differences in Nonverbal Decoding Ability," *Communication Quarterly* 36 (1988): 290–297.

30. S. A. McCornack and M. R. Parks, "What Women Know That Men Don't: Sex Differences in Determining the Truth behind Deceptive Messages," *Journal of Social and Personal Relationships* 7 (1990): 107–118.

31. M. A. deTurck, "Training Observers to Detect Spontaneous Deception: Effects of Gender," *Communication Reports* 4 (1991): 81–89.

32. A. E. Lindsey and V. Vigil, "The Interpretation and Evaluation of Winking in Stranger Dyads," *Communication Research Reports* 16 (1999): 256–265.

33. G. Y. Lim, G. Y. and M. E. Roloff, "Attributing Sexual Consent," *Journal of Applied Communication Research* 27 (1999): 1–23.

34. D. Druckmann, R. Rozelle, and J. Baxter, *Nonverbal Communication: Survey, Theory, and Research* (Beverly Hills, Calif.: Sage, 1982), p. 52.

35. M. Motley and C. Camden, "Facial Expression of Emotion: A Comparison of Posed versus Spontaneous Expressions in an Interpersonal Communication Setting," *Western Journal of Speech Communication* 52 (1988): 1–22.

36. M. L. Knapp and J. Hall, *Nonverbal Communication in Human Interaction*, 3rd ed. (Fort. Worth: Harcourt Brace Jovanovich, 1992), pp. 466–477.

37. J. A. Hall, "Gender, Gender Roles, and Nonverbal Communication Skills" in R. Rosenthal, ed., *Skill in Nonverbal Communication: Individual Differences* (Cambridge, Mass.: Oelgeschlager, Gunn, and Hain, 1979), pp. 32–67.

38. Summarized in Burgoon, "Nonverbal Signals," op. cit.

39. M. Argyle, F. Alkema, and R. Gilmour, "The Communication of Friendly and Hostile Attitudes" Verbal and Nonverbal Signals," *European Journal of Social Psychology* 1 (1971): 385–402.

40. M. T. Palmer and K. B. Simmons, "Communicating Intentions through Nonverbal Behaviors: Conscious and Nonconscious Encoding of Liking," *Human Communication Research* 22 (1995): 128–160.

41. A. Mehrabian, *Silent Messages*, 2nd ed. (Belmont, Calif.: Wadsworth, 1981), pp. 47–48, 61–62.

42. M. B. Myers, D. Templer, and R. Brown, "Coping Ability of Women Who Become Victims of Rape," *Journal of Consulting and Clinical Psychology* 52 (1984): 73–78.

See also C. Rubenstein, "Body Language That Speaks to Muggers," *Psychology Today* 20 (August 1980): 20; and J. Meer, "Profile of a Victim," *Psychology Today* 24 (May 1984): 76.

43. J. M. Iverson, "How to Get to the Cafeteria: Gesture and Speech in Blind and Sighted Children's Spatial Descriptions," *Developmental Psychology* 35 (1999): 1132–1142.

44. Andersen, op. cit., p. 37.

45. P. Ekman and W. V. Friesen, "The Repertoire of Nonverbal Behavior: Categories, Origins, Usage, and Coding," *Semiotica* 1 (1969): 49–98.

46. P. Ekman and W. V. Friesen, "Nonverbal Behavior and Psychopathology" in R. J. Friedman and M. N. Katz, eds., *The Psychology of Depression: Contemporary Theory and Research* (Washington, D.C.: J. Winston, 1974).

47. Ekman, *Telling Lies*, p. 107.

48. P. Ekman and W. V. Friesen, *Unmasking the Face: A Guide to Recognizing Emotions from Facial Clues* (Englewood Cliffs, N.J.: Prentice-Hall, 1975).

49. Ibid., p. 150.

50. S. F. Davis and J. C. Kieffer, "Restaurant Servers Influence Tipping Behavior," *Psychological Reports* 83 (1998): 223–226.

51. E. H. Hess and J. M. Polt, "Pupil Size As Related to Interest Value of Visual Stimuli," *Science* 132 (1960): 349–350.

52. E. T. Hall, *The Silent Language* (New York: Fawcett, 1959).

53. For a summary, see Knapp and Hall, op. cit., pp. 344–346.

54. A. Mehrabian and M. Wiener, "Decoding of Inconsistent Communications," *Journal of Personality and Social Psychology* 6 (1967): 109–114; see also A. Mehrabian and S. Ferris, "Interference of Attitudes from Nonverbal Communication in Two Channels," *Journal of Consulting Psychology* 31 (1967): 248–252.

55. A. R. Trees, "Nonverbal Communication and the Support Process: Interactional Sensitivity in Interactions between Mothers and Young Adult Children," *Communication Monographs* 67 (2000): 239–261.

56. D. Buller and K. Aune, "The Effects of Speech Rate Similarity on Compliance: Application of Communication Accommodation Theory," *Western Journal of Communication* 56 (1992): 37–53. See also D. Buller, B. A. LePoire, K. Aune, and S. V. Eloy, "Social Perceptions As Mediators of the Effect of Speech Rate Similarity on Compliance," *Human Communication Research* 19 (1992): 286–311; "The Effects of Vocalics and Nonverbal Sensitivity on Compliance: A Speech Accommodation Theory Explanation," *Human Communication Research* 14 (1988): 301–332.

57. Ekman, *Telling Lies*, p. 93.

58. P. A. Andersen, "Nonverbal Communication in the Small Group" in R. S. Cathcart and L. A. Samovar, eds., *Small Group Communication: A Reader*, 4th ed. (Dubuque, Iowa: W.C. Brown, 1984).

59. K. J. Tusing and J. P. Dillard, "The Sounds of Dominance: Vocal Precursors of Perceived Dominance during Interpersonal Influence," *Human Communication Research* 26 (2000): 148–171.

60. M. Zuckerman and R. E. Driver, "What Sounds Beautiful is Good: The Vocal Attractiveness Stereotype," *Journal of Nonverbal Behavior* 13 (1989): 67–82.

61. S. H. Ng and J. J. Bradac, *Power in Language: Verbal Communication and Social Influence* (Newbury Park, Calif.: Sage, 1993), p. 40.

62. H. Giles, K. Henwood, N. Coupland, J. Harriman, and J. Coupland, "Language Attitudes and Cognitive Mediation," *Human Communication Research* 18 (1992): 500–527.

63. R. Heslin and T. Alper, "Touch: A Bonding Gesture" in J. M. Wiemann and R. P. Harrison, eds., *Nonverbal Interaction* (Beverly Hills, Calif.: Sage, 1983), pp. 47–75.

64. Ibid.

65. J. Burgoon, J. Walther, and E. Baesler, "Interpretations, Evaluations, and Consequences of Interpersonal Touch," *Human Communication Research* 19 (1992): 237–263.

66. C. R. Kleinke, "Compliance to Requests Made by Gazing and Touching Experimenters in Field Settings," *Journal of Experimental Social Psychology* 13 (1977): 218–223.

67. F. N. Willis and H. K. Hamm, "The Use of Interpersonal Touch in Securing Compliance," *Journal of Nonverbal Behavior* 5 (1980): 49–55.

68. A. H. Crusco and C. G. Wetzel, "The Midas Touch: Effects of Interpersonal Touch on Restaurant Tipping," *Personality and Social Psychology Bulletin* 10 (1984): 512–517.

69. D. Kaufman and J. M. Mahoney, "The Effect of Waitresses' Touch on Alcohol Consumption in Dyads," *Journal of Social Psychology* 139 (1999): 261–267.

70. H. Bakwin, "Emotional Deprivation in Infants," *Journal of Pediatrics* 35 (1949): 512–521.

71. T. Adler, "Congressional Staffers Witness Miracle of Touch," *APA Monitor* (February 1993): 12–13.

72. M. S. Driscoll, D. L. Newman, and J. M. Seal, "The Effect of Touch on the Perception of Counselors," *Counselor Education and Supervision* 27 (1988): 344–354; and J. M. Wilson, "The Value of Touch in Psychotherapy," *American Journal of Orthopsychiatry* 52 (1982): 65–72.

73. For a summary, see Knapp and Hall, *Nonverbal Communication in Human Interaction*, pp. 93–132.

74. V. Ritts, M. L. Patterson, and M. E. Tubbs, "Expectations, Impressions, and Judgments of Physically Attractive Students: A Review," *Review of Educational Research* 62 (1992): 413–426.

75. W. Thourlby, *You Are What You Wear* (New York: New American Library, 1978), p. 1.

76. L. Bickman, "The Social Power of a Uniform," *Journal of Applied Social Psychology* 4 (1974): 47–61.

77. S. G. Lawrence and M. Watson, "Getting Others to Help: The Effectiveness of Professional Uniforms in Charitable Fund Raising," *Journal of Applied Communication Research* 19 (1991): 170–185.

78. H. Fortenberry, J. Maclean, P. Morris, and M. O'Connell, "Mode of Dress As a Perceptual Cue to Deference," *The Journal of Social Psychology* 104 (1978).

79. A. Vrij and L. Akehurst, "The Existence of a Black Clothing Stereotype: The Impact of a Victim's Black Clothing on Impression Formation," *Psychology, Crime and Law* 3 (1999): 227–237.

80. L. Bickman, "Social Roles and Uniforms: Clothes Make the Person," *Psychology Today* 7 (April 1974): 48–51.

81. M. Lefkowitz, R. R. Blake, and J. S. Mouton, "Status of Actors in Pedestrian Violation of Traffic Signals," *Journal of Abnormal and Social Psychology* 51 (1955): 704–706.

82. L. E. Temple and K. R. Loewen, "Perceptions of Power: First Impressions of a Woman Wearing a Jacket," *Perceptual and Motor Skills* 76 (1993): 339–348.

83. T. F. Hoult, "Experimental Measurement of Clothing as a Factor in Some Social Ratings of Selected American Men," *American Sociological Review* 19 (1954): 326–327.

84. Hall, *The Hidden Dimension.*

85. M. Hackman and K. Walker, "Instructional Communication in the Televised Classroom: The Effects of System Design and Teacher Immediacy," *Communication Education* 39 (1990): 196–206. See also J. C. McCroskey and V. P. Richmond, "Increasing Teacher Influence through Immediacy" in V. P. Richmond and J. C. McCroskey, eds., *Power in the Classroom: Communication, Control, and Concern* (Hillsdale, N.J.: Erlbaum, 1992).

86. C. Conlee, J. Olvera, and N. Vagim, "The Relationships among Physician Nonverbal Immediacy and Measures of Patient Satisfaction with Physician Care," *Communication Reports* 6 (1993): 25–33.

87. E. Sadalla, "Identity and Symbolism in Housing," *Environment and Behavior* 19 (1987): 569–587.

88. A. Maslow and N. Mintz, "Effects of Aesthetic Surroundings: Initial Effects of Those Aesthetic Surroundings upon Perceiving 'Energy' and 'Well-Being' in Faces," *Journal of Psychology* 41 (1956): 247–254.

89. J. J. Teven, and M. E. Comadena. "The Effects of Office Aesthetic Quality on Students' Perceptions of Teacher Credibility and Communicator Style," *Communication Research Reports* 13 (1996): 101–108.

90. R. Sommer, *Personal Space: The Behavioral Basis of Design* (Englewood Cliffs, N.J.: Prentice-Hall, 1969).

91. D. I. Ballard and D. R. Seibold, "Time Orientation and Temporal Variation across Work Groups: Implications for Group and Organizational Communication," *Western Journal of Communication* 64 (2000): 218–242.

92. R. Levine, "The Pace of Life across Cultures" in J. E. McGrath, ed., *The Social Psychology of Time* (Newbury Park, Calif.: Sage, 1988).

93. R. Levine and E. Wolff, "Social Time: The Heartbeat of Culture," *Psychology Today* 19 (March 1985): 28–35.

ENDNOTES FOR CHAPTER 7

1. L. Barker, R. Edwards, C. Gaines, K. Gladney, and R. Holley, "An Investigation of Proportional Time Spent in Various Communication Activities by College Students," *Journal of Applied Communication Research* 8 (1981): 101–109.

2. Research summarized in A. D. Wolvin and C. G. Coakley, "A Survey of the Status of Listening Training in Some Fortune 500 Corporations," *Communication Education* 40 (1991): 152–164.

3. K. J. Prager and D. Buhrmester, "Intimacy and Need Fulfillment in Couple Relationships, *Journal of Social and Personal Relationships* 15 (1998): 435–469.

4. A. L. Vangelisti, "Couples' Communication Problems: The Counselor's Perspective," *Journal of Applied Communication Research* 22 (1994): 106–126.

5. A. D. Wolvin, "Meeting the Communication Needs of the Adult Learners," *Communication Education* 33 (1984): 267–271.

6. B. D. Sypher, R. N. Bostrom, and J. H. Seibert, "Listening Communication Abilities and Success at Work," *Journal of Business Communication* 26 (1989): 293–303. See also E. R. Alexander, L. E. Penley, and I. E. Jernigan, "The Relationship of Basic Decoding Skills to Managerial Effectiveness," *Management Communication Quarterly* 6 (1992): 58–73.

7. J. L. Winsor, D. B. Curtis, and R. D. Stephens, "National Preferences in Business and Communication Education: An Update," *Journal of the Association for Communication Administration* 3 (1999): 170–179.

8. S. Johnson and C. Bechler, "Examining the Relationship between Listening Effectiveness and Leadership Emergence: Perceptions, Behaviors, and Recall," *Small Group Research* 29 (1998): 452–471.

9. V. Marchant, "Listen Up!" *Time* 153 (June 28, 1999): 74.

10. C. Flexer, "Commonly-Asked Questions about Children with Minimal Hearing Loss in the Classroom," *Hearing Loss* (February 1997): 8–12.

11. L. R. Smeltzer and K. W. Watson, "Listening: An Empirical Comparison of Discussion Length and Level of Incentive," *Central States Speech Journal* 35 (1984): 166–170.

12. M. Pasupathi, L. M. Stallworth, and K. Murdoch, "How What We Tell Becomes What We Know: Listener Effects on Speakers' Long-Term Memory for Events," *Discourse Processes* 26 (1998): 1–25.

13. M. H. Lewis and N. L. Reinsch, Jr., "Listening in Organizational Environments," *Journal of Business Communication* 23 (1988): 49–67.

14. J. B. Elshtian, "Feminist Discourse and Its Discontents: Language, Power, and Meaning" in N. O. Keohane, M. Z. Rosaldo, and B. C. Gelpi, eds., *Feminist Theory: A Critique of Ideology* (Chicago: University of Chicago Press, 1982).

15. D. Borisoff and L. Merrill, "Gender Issues and Listening" in D. Borisoff and M. Purdy, eds., *Listening in Everyday Life: A Personal and Professional Approach* (Lanham, Md.: University Press of America, 1991).

16. A. Mulac, J. M. Wiemann, S. Widenmann, and T. W. Gibson, "Male/Female Language Differences and Effects in Same-Sex Dyads: The Gender-Linked Language Effect," *Communication Quarterly* 55 (1988): 315–355.

17. A. T. Beck, *Love Is Never Enough* (New York: Harper & Row, 1988).

18. S. L. Bem, *The Lenses of Gender: Transforming the Debate on Sexual Inequality* (New Haven, Conn.: Yale University Press, 1993).

19. J. E. Williams and D. L. Best, *Measuring Sex Stereotypes: A Thirty Nation Study* (Beverly Hills, Calif.: Sage, 1982).

20. D. Borisoff and D. F. Hahn, "Listening and Gender: Values Revalued" in M. Purdy and D. Borisoff, eds., *Listening in Everyday Life: A Personal and Professional Approach*, 2nd ed. (Lanham, Md.: University Press of America, 1997).

21. M. D. Phillips, J. T. Lurito, M. Dzemidzic, M. J. Lowe, Y. Wang, and V. P. Mathews, "Gender Based Differences in

Temporal Lobe Activation Demonstrated Using a Novel Passive Listening Paradigm," paper presented at the 86th annual meeting of the Radiological Society of North America, Chicago, November 2000.

22. R. L. Hotz, "Women Use More of Brain When Listening," *Los Angeles Times* (November 29, 2000): A1.

23. A. L. Vangelisti, M. L. Knapp, and J. A. Daly, "Conversational Narcissism," *Communication Monographs* 57 (1990): 251–274.

24. K. B. McComb and F. M. Jablin, "Verbal Correlates of Interviewer Empathic Listening and Employment Interview Outcomes," *Communication Monographs* 51 (1984): 367.

25. A. Mulac, J. M. Wiemann, S. J. Widenmann, and T. W. Gibson, "Male/Female Language Differences and Effects in Same-Sex and Mixed-Sex Dyads: The Gender-Linked Language Effect," *Communication Monographs* 55 (1988): 315–335.

26. A. Wolvin and C. G. Coakley, *Listening*, 3rd ed. (Dubuque, Iowa: W.C. Brown, 1988), p. 208.

27. R. Nichols, "Listening Is a Ten-Part Skill," *Nation's Business* 75 (September 1987): 40.

28. L. J. Carrell and S. C. Willmington, "A Comparison of Self-Report and Performance Data in Assessing Speaking and Listening Competence," *Communication Reports* 9 (1996): 185–191.

29. J. Brownell, "Perceptions of Effective Listeners: A Management Study," *Journal of Business Communication* 27 (1990): 401–415.

30. N. Spinks and B. Wells, "Improving Listening Power: The Payoff," *Bulletin of the Association for Business Communication* 54 (1991): 75–77.

31. D. Carbaugh, "'Just Listen': 'Listening' and Landscape among the Blackfeet," *Western Journal of Communication* 63 (1999): 250–270.

32. R. Remer and P. DeMesquita, "Teaching and Learning the Skills of Interpersonal Confrontation" in D. Cahn, ed., *Intimates in Conflict: A Communication Perspective* (Norwood, N.J.: Erlbaum, 1991), p. 242.

33. B. Burleson and W. Samter, "Cognitive Complexity, Communication Skills, and Friendship," paper presented at the 7th International Congress on Personal Construct Psychology, Memphis, August 1987.

34. See, for example, J. Ekenrode, "Impact of Chronic and Acute Stressors on Daily Reports of Mood," *Journal of Personality and Social Psychology* 46 (1984): 907–918; A. D. Kanner, J. C. Coyne, C. Schaefer, and R. S. Lazarus, "Comparison of Two Modes of Stress Measurement: Daily Hassles and Uplifts versus Major Life Events," *Journal of Behavioral Medicine* 4 (1981): 1–39; A. DeLongis, J. C. Coyne, G. Dakof, S. Polkman, and R. S. Lazarus, "Relation of Daily Hassles, Uplifts, and Major Life Events to Health Status," *Health Psychology* 1 (1982): 119–136.

35. C. J. Notarius and L. R. Herrick, "Listener Response Strategies to a Distressed Other," *Journal of Social and Personal Relationships* 5 (1988): 97–108.

36. D. J. Goldsmith and K. Fitch, "The Normative Context of Advice as Social Support," *Human Communication Research* 23 (1997): 454–476. See also D. J. Goldsmith and E. L. MacGeorge, "The Impact of Politeness and Relationship on Perceived Quality of Advice about a Problem," *Human Communication Research* 26 (2000): 234–263.

37. D. J.Goldsmith, "Soliciting Advice: The Role of Sequential Placement in Mitigating Face Threat," *Communication Monographs* 67 (2000): 1–19.

38. D. J. Goldsmith and E. L. MacGeorge, "The Impact of Politeness and Relationship on Perceived Quality of Advice about a Problem," *Human Communication Research* 26 (2000): 234–263.

39. S. J. Messman, D. J. Canary, and K. S. Hause, "Motives to Remain Platonic, Equity, and the Use of Maintenance Strategies in Opposite-Sex Friendships," *Journal of Social and Personal Relationships* 17 (2000): 67–94.

40. A. W. Kunkel and B. R. Burleson, "Assessing Explorations for Sex Differences in Emotional Support," *Human Communication Research* 25 (1999): 307–340.

41. W. Samter, B. R. Burleson, and L. B. Murphy, "Comforting Conversations: The Effects of Strategy Type on Evaluations of Messages and Message Producers," *Southern Speech Communication Journal* 52 (1987): 263–284.

42. M. Davidowitz and R. D. Myrick, "Responding to the Bereaved: An Analysis of 'Helping' Statements," *Death Education* 8 (1984): 1–10.

43. Adapted from B. R. Burleson, "Comforting Messages: Features, Functions, and Outcomes" in J. A. Daly and J. M. Wiemann, eds., *Strategic Interpersonal Communication* (Hillsdale, N.J.: Erlbaum, 1994), p. 140.

44. Research summarized in J. Pearson, *Communication in the Family* (New York: Harper & Row, 1989), pp. 272–275.

45. See J. Bruneau, "Empathy and Listening: A Conceptual Review and Theoretical Directions," *Journal of the International Listening Association* 3 (1989): 1–20; and K. N. Cissna and R. Anderson, "The Contributions of Carl R. Rogers to a Philosophical Praxis of Dialogue," *Western Journal of Speech Communication* 54 (1990): 137–147.

46. C. R. Rogers, "Reflection of Feelings," *Personal-Centered Review* 1 (1986): 375–377.

47. L. A. Hosman, "The Evaluational Consequences of Topic Reciprocity and Self-Disclosure Reciprocity," *Communication Monographs* 54 (1987): 420–435.

48. R. A. Clark and J. G. Delia, "Individuals' Preferences for Friends' Approaches to Providing Support in Distressing Situations," *Communication Reports* 10 (1997): 115–121.

49. See, for example, R. Silver and C. Wortman, "Coping with Undesirable Life Events" in J. Garber and M. Seligman, eds., *Human Helplessness: Theory and Applications* (New York: Academic Press, 1981), pp. 279–340; and C. R. Young, D. E. Giles, and M. C. Plantz, "Natural Networks: Help-Giving and Help-Seeking in Two Rural Communities," *American Journal of Community Psychology* 10 (1982): 457–469.

50. Clark and Delia, op. cit.

51. See research cited in B. Burleson, "Comforting Messages: Their Significance and Effects" in J. A. Daly and J. M. Wiemann, eds., *Communicating Strategically: Strategies in Interpersonal Communication* (Hillside, N.J.: Erlbaum, 1990). See also J. L. Chesbro, "The Relationship between Listening Styles and Conversational Sensitivity," *Communication Research Reports* 16 (1999): 233–238.

ENDNOTES FOR CHAPTER 8

1. See, for example, D. Byrne, "An Overview (and Underview) of Research and Theory within the Attraction Paradigm," *Journal of Social and Personal Relationships* 14 (1999): 417–431.
2. F. E. Aboud and M. J. Mendelson, "Determinants of Friendship Selection and Quality: Developmental Perspectives" in W. M. Bukowski and A. F. Newcomb, eds., *The Company They Keep: Friendship in Childhood and Adolescence* (New York: Cambridge University Press, 1998).
3. B. R. Burleson and W. Samter, "Similarity in the Communication Skills of Young Adults: Foundations of Attraction, Friendship, and Relationship Satisfaction," *Communication Reports* 9 (1996): 127–139.
4. K. J. Prager and D. Buhrmester, "Intimacy and Need Fulfillment in Couple Relationships," *Journal of Social and Personal Relationships* 15 (1998): 435–469.
5. C. E. Crowther and G. Stone, *Intimacy: Strategies for Successful Relationships* (Santa Barbara, Calif.: Capra Press, 1986), p. 13.
6. D. Morris, *Intimate Behavior* (New York: Bantam, 1973), p. 7.
7. K. Floyd, "Meanings for Closeness and Intimacy in Friendship," *Journal of Social and Personal Relationships* 13 (1996): 85–107.
8. M. R. Parks and K. Floyd, "Making Friends in Cyberspace," *Journal of Communication* 46 (1996): 80–97.
9. L. A. Baxter, "A Dialogic Approach to Relationship Maintenance" in D. Canary and L. Stafford, eds., *Communication and Relational Maintenance* (San Diego: Academic Press, 1994).
10. J. T. Wood and C. C. Inman, "In a Different Mode: Masculine Styles of Communicating Closeness," *Applied Communication Research* 21 (1993): 279–295; K. Floyd, "Gender and Closeness among Friends and Siblings," *Journal of Psychology* 129 (1995): 193–202.
11. See, for example, K. Dindia, "Sex Differences in Self-Disclosure, Reciprocity of Self-Disclosure, and Self-Disclosure and Liking: Three Meta-Analyses Reviewed" in S. Petronio, ed., *Balancing Disclosure, Privacy and Secrecy* (Mahwah, N.J.: Lawrence Erlbaum, 2000).
12. See, for example, K. Floyd, "Gender and Closeness among Friends and Siblings," *Journal of Psychology* 129 (1995): 193–202.
13. S. Swain, "Covert Intimacy in Men's Friendships: Closeness in Men's Friendships" in B. J. Risman and P. Schwartz, eds., *Gender in Intimate Relationships: A Microstructural Approach* (Belmont, Calif.: Wadsworth, 1989).
14. M. T. Morman and K. Floyd, "Affection Communication between Fathers and Young Adult Sons: Individual and Relational-Level Correlates," *Communication Studies* 50 (1999): 294–309.
15. L. Stafford, M. Dainton, and S. Haas, "Measuring Routine and Strategic Relational Maintenance: Scale Revision, Sex versus Gender Roles, and the Prediction of Relational Characteristics," *Communication Monographs* 67 (2000): 306–323.
16. C. K. Reissman, *Divorce Talk: Women and Men Make Sense of Personal Relationships* (New Brunswick: Rutgers University Press, 1990).
17. J. Adamopoulos, "The Emergence of Interpersonal Behavior: Diachronic and Cross-Cultural Processes in the Evolution of Intimacy" in S. Ting-Toomey and F. Korzenny, eds., *Cross-Cultural Interpersonal Communication* (Newbury Park, Calif.: Sage, 1991). See also G. Fontaine, "Cultural Diversity in Intimate Intercultural Relationships" in D. D. Cahn, ed., *Intimates in Conflict: A Communication Perspective* (Hillsdale, N.J.: Erlbaum, 1990).
18. J. Adamopoulos and R. N. Bontempo, "Diachronic Universals in Interpersonal Structures," *Journal of Cross-Cultural Psychology* 17 (1986): 169–189.
19. M. Argyle and M. Henderson, "The Rules of Relationships" in S. Duck and D. Perlman, eds., *Understanding Personal Relationships* (Beverly Hills, Calif.: Sage, 1985).
20. W. B. Gudykunst and S. Ting-Toomey, *Culture and Interpersonal Communication* (Newbury Park, Calif.: Sage, 1988), pp. 197–198.
21. S. Faul, *The Xenophobe's Guide to the Americans* (London: Ravette, 1994), p. 3.
22. C. W. Franklin, "'Hey Home—Yo Bro': Friendship among Black Men" in P. M. Nardi, ed., *Men's Friendships* (Newbury Park, Calif.: Sage, 1992).
23. H. C. Triandis, *Culture and Social Behavior* (New York: McGraw-Hill, 1994), p. 230.
24. K. Lewin, *Principles of Topological Psychology* (New York: McGraw-Hill, 1936).
25. E. M. Eisenberg, "Jamming: Transcendence through Organizing," *Communication Research* 17 (1990): 139–164.
26. See, for example, R. Bellah, W. M. Madsen, A. Sullivan, and S. M. Tipton, *Habits of the Heart: Individualism and Commitment in American Life* (Berkeley: University of California Press, 1985); R. Sennett, *The Fall of Public Man: On the Social Psychology of Capitalism* (New York: Random House, 1974); and S. Trenholm and A. Jensen, "The Guarded Self: Toward a Social History of Interpersonal Styles," paper presented at the Speech Communication Association meeting, San Juan, Puerto Rico, 1990.
27. See, for example, M. E. Roloff, *Interpersonal Communication: The Social Exchange Approach* (Beverly Hills, Calif.: Sage, 1981).
28. M. L. Knapp and A. L. Vangelisti, *Interpersonal Communication and Human Relationships*, 4th ed. (Boston: Allyn & Bacon, 2000).
29. D. J. Canary and L. Stafford, eds., *Communication and Relational Maintenance* (San Diego: Academic Press, 1994).
30. For a discussion of relational development in nonintimate relationships, see A. Jensen and S. Trenholm, "Beyond Intimacy: An Alternative Trajectories Model of Relationship Development," paper presented at the Speech Communication Association annual meeting, New Orleans, 1988.
31. C. R. Berger, "Communicating under Uncertainty" in M. E. Roloff and G. R. Miller, eds., *Interpersonal Processes: New Directions in Communication Research* (Newbury Park, Calif.: Sage, 1987). See also C. R. Berger and R. J. Calabrese, "Some Explorations in Initial Interaction and Beyond: Toward a Developmental Theory of Interpersonal Communication," *Human Communication Research* 1 (1975): 99–112.

32. Knapp and Vangelisti, *Interpersonal Communication and Human Relationships*, p. 37.

33. W. B. Gudykunst and S. Ting-Toomey, *Culture and Interpersonal Communication* (Newbury Park, Calif.: Sage, 1988), p. 193.

34. S. Stewart, H. Stinnett, and L. B. Rosenfeld, "Sex Differences in Desired Characteristics of Short-Term and Long-Term Relationship Partners," *Journal of Social and Personal Relationships* 17 (2000): 843–853.

35. L. Pratt, R. L. Wiseman, M. J. Cody, and P. F. Wendt, "Interrogative Strategies and Information Exchange in Computer-Mediated Communication," *Communication Quarterly* 47 (1999): 46–66.

36. J. H. Tolhuizen, "Communication Strategies for Intensifying Dating Relationships: Identification, Use and Structure," *Journal of Social and Personal Relationships* 6 (1989): 413–434.

37. L. A. Baxter, "Symbols of Relationship Identity in Relationship Culture," *Journal of Social and Personal Relationships* 4 (1987): 261–280.

38. C. J. S. Buress and J. C. Pearson, "Interpersonal Rituals in Marriage and Adult Friendship," *Communication Monographs* 64 (1997): 25–46.

39. R. A. Bell and J. G. Healey, "Idiomatic Communication and Interpersonal Solidarity in Friends' Relational Cultures," *Human Communication Research* 18 (1992): 307–335.

40. M. Roloff, C. A. Janiszewski, M. A. McGrath, C. S. Burns, and L. A. Manrai, "Acquiring Resources from Intimates: When Obligation Substitutes for Persuasion," *Human Communication Research* 14 (1988): 364–396.

41. D. H. Solomon, "A Developmental Model of Intimacy and Date Request Explicitness," *Communication Monographs* 64 (1997): 99–118.

42. J. K. Burgoon, R. Parrott, B. A. LePoire, D. L. Kelley, J. B. Walther, and D. Perry, "Maintaining and Restoring Privacy through Different Types of Relationships," *Journal of Social and Personal Relationships* 6 (1989): 131–158.

43. S. Petronio, "The Boundaries of Privacy: Praxis of Everyday Life" in S. Petronio, ed., *Balancing the Secrets of Private Disclosure* (Mahwah, N.J.: Lawrence Erlbaum, 2000), pp. 37–49.

44. J. A. Courtright, F. E. Miller, L. E. Rogers, and D. Bagarozzi, "Interaction Dynamics of Relational Negotiation: Reconciliation versus Termination of Distressed Relationships," *Western Journal of Speech Communication* 54 (1990): 429–453.

45. D. M. Battaglia, F. D. Richard, D. L. Datteri, and C. G. Lord, "Breaking Up Is (Relatively) Easy to Do: A Script for the Dissolution of Close Relationships," *Journal of Social and Personal Relationships* 15 (1998): 829–845.

46. S. Metts, W. R. Cupach, and R. A. Bejllovec, "'I Love You Too Much to Ever Start Liking You': Redefining Romantic Relationships," *Journal of Social and Personal Relationships* 6 (1989): 259–274.

47. See, for example, L. A. Baxter and B. M. Montgomery, *Relating: Dialogues and Dialectics* (New York: Guilford, 1996); W. K. Rawlins, *Friendship Matters: Communication, Dialectics, and the Life Course* (New York: Aldine de Gruyter, 1992); B. H. Spitzberg, "The Dark Side of (In)Competence" in W. R. Cupach and B. H. Spitzberg, eds., *The Dark Side of Interpersonal Communication* (Hillsdale, N.J.: Lawrence Erlbaum, 1993).

48. Summarized by L. A. Baxter, "A Dialogic Approach to Relationship Maintenance" in D. J. Canary and L. Stafford, eds., *Communication and Relational Maintenance* (San Diego: Academic Press, 1994).

49. Morris, *Intimate Behavior*, pp. 21–29.

50. T. D. Golish, "Changes in Closeness between Adult Children and Their Parents: A Turning Point Analysis," *Communication Reports* 13 (2000): 78–97.

51. D. Barry, *Dave Barry Turns 40* (New York: Fawcett, 1990), p. 47.

52. C. A. VanLear, "Testing a Cyclical Model of Communicative Openness in Relationship Development," *Communication Monographs* 58 (1991): 337–361.

54. E. M. Griffin, *A First Look at Communication Theory*, 4th ed. (New York: McGraw-Hill, 2000).

55. B. M. Montgomery, "Relationship Maintenance versus Relationship Change: A Dialectical Dilemma," *Journal of Social and Personal Relationships* 10 (1993): 205–223.

56. D. O. Braithwaite, L. A. Baxter, and A. M. Harper, "The Role of Rituals in the Management of the Dialectical Tension of "Old" and "New" in Blended Families," *Communication Studies* 49 (1998): 101–120.

57. See A. Christensen and J. Jacobson, *Reconcilable Differences* (New York: Guilford, 2000).

58. R. L. Conville, *Relational Transitions: The Evolution of Personal Relationships* (New York: Praeger, 1991), p. 80.

59. I. Altman and D. A. Taylor, *Social Penetration: The Development of Interpersonal Relationships* (New York: Holt, Rinehart and Winston, 1973). See also D. A. Taylor and I. Altman, "Communication in Interpersonal Relationships: Social Penetration Processes" in M. E. Roloff and G. R. Miller, eds., *Interpersonal Processes: New Directions in Communication Research* (Newbury Park, Calif.: Sage, 1987).

60. J. Luft, *Of Human Interaction* (Palo Alto, Calif.: Natural Press, 1969).

61. J. C. Pearson, *Communication in the Family*, 2nd ed. (New York: HarperCollins, 1993), pp. 292–296.

62. K. Dindia, M. A. Fitzpatrick, and D. A. Kenny, "Self-Disclosure in Spouse and Stranger Interaction: A Social Relations Analysis," paper presented at the annual meeting of the International Communication Association, New Orleans, 1988; and S. W. Duck and D. E. Miell, "Charting the Development of Personal Relationships" in R. Gilmour and S. W. Duck, eds., *Studying Interpersonal Interaction* (New York: Guilford., 1991), pp. 133–144.

63. S. Duck, "Some Evident Truths about Conversations in Everyday Relationships: All Communications Are Not Created Equal," *Human Communication Research* 18 (1991): 228–267.

64. Adapted from V. J. Derlega and J. Grezlak, "Appropriateness of Self-Disclosure" in G. J. Chelune, ed., *Self-Disclosure* (San Francisco: Jossey-Bass, 1979).

65. See V. J. Derlega and A. L. Chaikin, *Sharing Intimacy: What We Reveal to Others and Why* (Englewood Cliffs, N.J.: Prentice-Hall, 1975).

66. H. L. Wintrob, "Self-Disclosure as a Marketable Commodity," *Journal of Social Behavior and Personality* 2 (1987): 77–88.

67. E. Aronson, *The Social Animal*, 7th ed. (New York: W.H. Freeman, 1999).

68. F. D. Fincham and T. N. Bradbury, "The Impact of Attributions in Marriage: An Individual Difference Analysis," *Journal of Social and Personal Relationships* 6 (1989): 69–85.

69. V. G. Downs, "Grandparents and Grandchildren: The Relationship between Self-Disclosure and Solidarity in an Intergenerational Relationship," *Communication Research Reports* 5 (1988): 173–179.

70. L. B. Rosenfeld and W. L. Kendrick, "Choosing to Be Open: Subjective Reasons for Self-Disclosing," *Western Journal of Speech Communication* 48 (Fall 1984): 326–343.

71. E. M. Eisenberg and M. G. Witten, "Reconsidering Openness in Organizational Communication," *Academy of Management Review* 12 (1987): 418–428.

72. L. B. Rosenfeld and J. R. Gilbert, "The Measurement of Cohesion and Its Relationship to Dimensions of Self-Disclosure in Classroom Settings," *Small Group Behavior* 20 (1989): 291–301.

73. T. E. Runge and R. L. Archer, "Reactions to the Disclosure of Public and Private Self-Information," *Social Psychology Quarterly* 44 (December 1981): 357–362.

74. C. L. Kleinke, "Effects of Personal Evaluations" in *Self-Disclosure* (San Francisco: Jossey-Bass, 1979).

75. L. B. Rosenfeld and G. I. Bowen, "Marital Disclosure and Marital Satisfaction: Direct-Effect versus Interaction-Effect Models," *Western Journal of Speech Communication* 55 (1991): 69–84.

76. A. Jaksa and M. Pritchard, *Communication Ethics: Methods of Analysis*, 2nd ed. (Belmont, Calif.: Wadsworth, 1993), pp. 65–66.

77. D. O'Hair and M. J. Cody, "Interpersonal Deception: The Dark Side of Interpersonal Communication?" in B. H. Spitzberg and W. R. Cupach, eds., *The Dark Side of Interpersonal Communication* (Hillsdale, N.J.: Erlbaum, 1993).

78. R. E. Turner, C. Edgely, and G. Olmstead, "Information Control in Conversation: Honesty Is Not Always the Best Policy," *Kansas Journal of Sociology* 11 (1975): 69–89.

79. J. Bavelas, "Situations That Lead to Disqualification," *Human Communication Research* 9 (1983): 130–145.

80. W. C. Rowatt, M. R. Cunningham, and P. B. Druen, "Lying to Get a Date: The Effect of Facial Physical Attractiveness on the Willingness to Deceive Prospective Dating Partners," *Journal of Social and Personal Relationships* 16 (1999): 209–223.

81. D. Hample, "Purposes and Effects of Lying," *Southern Speech Communication Journal* 46 (1980): 33–47.

82. S. A. McCornack and T. R. Levine, "When Lies Are Uncovered: Emotional and Relational Outcomes of Discovered Deception," *Communication Monographs* 57 (1990): 119–138.

83. S. Metts, W. R. Cupach, and T. T. Imahori, "Perceptions of Sexual Compliance-Resisting Messages in Three Types of Cross-Sex Relationships," *Western Journal of Communication* 56 (1992): 1–17.

84. J. B. Bavelas, A. Black, N. Chovil, and J. Mullett, *Equivocal Communication* (Newbury Park, Calif.: Sage, 1990), p. 171.

85. Ibid.

86. W. P. Robinson, A. Shepherd, and J. Heywood, "Truth, Equivocation/Concealment, and Lies in Job Applications and Doctor-Patient Communication," *Journal of Language and Social Psychology* 17 (1998): 149–164.

87. M. T. Motley, "Mindfulness in Solving Communicators' Dilemmas," *Communication Monographs* 59 (1992): 306–314.

88. S. B. Shimanoff, "Degree of Emotional Expressiveness as a Function of Face-Needs, Gender, and Interpersonal Relationship," *Communication Reports* 1 (1988): 43–53.

89. A. P. Hubbell, "I Love Your Family—They Are Just Like You": Lies We Tell to Lovers and Perceptions of Their Honesty and Appropriateness," paper presented at the annual meeting of the International Communication Association, San Francisco, May 1999. See also S. A. McCornack, "Information Manipulation Theory," *Communication Monographs* 59 (1992): 1–16.

90. P. Andersen, *Nonverbal Communication: Forms and Functions* (Menlo Park, Calif.: Mayfield, 1999), pp. 297–298.

ENDNOTES FOR CHAPTER 9

1. J. Veroff, E. Douvan, T. L. Orbuch, and L. K. Acitelli, "Happiness in Stable Marriages: The Early Years" in T. N. Bradbury, ed., *The Developmental Course of Marital Dysfunction* (New York: Cambridge University Press, 1998).

2. D. J. Canary and T. M. Emmers-Sommer, *Sex and Gender Differences in Interpersonal Relationships* (New York: Guilford, 1997).

3. J. J. Teven, M. M. Martin, and N. C. Neupauer, "Sibling Relationships: Verbally Aggressive Messages and Their Effect on Relational Satisfaction," *Communication Reports* 11 (1998): 179–186.

4. R. Guzley, "Organizational Climate and Communication Climate: Predictors of Commitment to the Organization," *Management Communication Quarterly* 5 (1992): 379–402.

5. D. Pincus, "Communication Satisfaction, Job Satisfaction, and Job Performance," *Human Communication Research* 12 (1986): 395–419.

6. K. Ellis, "Perceived Teacher Confirmation: The Development and Validation of an Instrument and Two Studies of the Relationship to Cognitive and Affective Learning," *Human Communication Research* 26 (2000): 264–291.

7. A. L. Vangelisti and S. L. Young, "When Words Hurt: The Effects of Perceived Intentionality on Interpersonal Relationships," *Journal of Social and Personal Relationships* 17 (2000): 393–424.

8. K. Cissna and E. Seiberg, "Patterns of Interactional Confirmation and Disconfirmation" in M. V. Redmond, ed., *Interpersonal Communication: Readings in Theory and Research* (Fort Worth: Harcourt Brace, 1995).

9. M. W. Allen, "Communication Concepts Related to Perceived Organizational Support," *Western Journal of Communication* 59 (1995): 326–346.
10. B. Bower, "Nice Guys Look Better in Women's Eyes," *Science News* (March 18, 1995): 165.
11. E. Seiberg, "Confirming and Disconfirming Communication in an Organizational Setting" in J. Owen, P. Page, and G. Zimmerman, eds., *Communication in Organizations* (St. Paul, Minn.: West, 1976), pp. 129–149.
12. See, for example, A. Holte and L. Wichstrom, "Disconfirmatory Feedback in Families of Schizophrenics," *Scandinavian Journal of Psychology* 31 (1990): 198–211.
13. A. S. Rancer, R. L. Kosberg, and R. A. Baukus, "Beliefs about Arguing as Predictors of Trait Argumentativeness: Implications for Training in Argument and Conflict Management," *Communication Education* 41 (1992): 375–387.
14. E. O. Onyekwere, R. B. Rubin, and D. A. Infante, "Interpersonal Perception and Communication Satisfaction as a Function of Argumentativeness and Ego-Involvement," *Communication Quarterly* 39 (1991): 35–47.
15. D. A. Infante, B. L. Riddle, C. L. Horvath, and S. A. Tumlin, "Verbal Aggressiveness: Messages and Reasons," *Communication Quarterly* 40 (1992): 116–126.
16. D. A. Infante and W. I. Gorden, "Argumentativeness and Affirming Communicator Style as Predictors of Satisfaction/Dissatisfaction with Subordinates," *Communication Quarterly* 37 (1989): 81–90.
17. A. L. Vangelisti, "Messages That Hurt" in W. R. Cupach and B. H. Spitzberg, eds., *The Dark Side of Interpersonal Communication* (Hillsdale, N.J.: Erlbaum, 1994).
18. W. W. Wilmot, *Dyadic Communication* (New York: Random House, 1987), pp. 149–158.
19. C. Burggraf and A. L. Sillars, "A Critical Examination of Sex Differences in Marital Communication," *Communication Monographs* 54 (1987): 276–294. See also D. A. Newton and J. K. Burgoon, "The Use and Consequences of Verbal Strategies during Interpersonal Disagreements," *Human Communication Research* 16 (1990): 477–518.
20. J. L. Hocker and W. W. Wilmot, *Interpersonal Conflict*, 4th ed. (Dubuque, Iowa: Brown & Benchmark, 1995), p. 34.
21. Ibid., p. 36.
22. G. H. Stamp, A. L. Vangelisti, and J. A. Daly, "The Creation of Defensiveness in Social Interaction," *Communication Quarterly* 40 (1992): 177–190.
23. D. R. Turk and J. L. Monahan, "'Here I Go Again': An Examination of Repetitive Behaviors during Interpersonal Conflicts," *Southern Communication Journal* 64 (1999): 232–244.
24. J. Powell, *Why Am I Afraid to Tell You Who I Am?* (Chicago: Argus Communications, 1969), p. 12.
25. L. Festinger, *A Theory of Cognitive Dissonance* (Stanford, Calif.: Stanford University Press, 1957).
26. See, for example, W. R. Cupach and S. J. Messman, "Face Predilections and Friendship Solidarity," *Communication Reports* 12 (1999): 117–124.
27. A. M. Nicotera, *Interpersonal Communication in Friend and Mate Relationships* (Albany: State University of New York, 1993).
28. J. Gibb, "Defensive Communication," *Journal of Communication* 11 (September 1961): 141–148. See also W. F. Eadie, "Defensive Communication Revisited: A Critical Examination of Gibb's Theory," *Southern Speech Communication Journal* 47 (1982): 163–177.
29. R. F. Proctor and J. R. Wilcox, "An Exploratory Analysis of Responses to Owned Messages in Interpersonal Communication," *ETC: A Review of General Semantics* 50 (1993): 201–220.
30. T. C. Sabourin and G. H. Stamp, "Communication and the Experience of Dialectical Tensions in Family Life: An Examination of Abusive and Nonabusive Families," *Communication Monographs* 62 (1995): 213–243.
31. Research summarized in J. Harwood, E. B. Ryan, H. Giles, and S. Tysoski, "Evaluations of Patronizing Speech and Three Response Styles in a Non-Service-Providing Context," *Journal of Applied Communication Research* 25 (1997): 170–195.
32. C. E. Beck and E. A. Beck, "The Manager's Open Door and the Communication Climate" in K. M. Galvin and P. Cooper, eds., *Making Connections: Readings in Relational Communication* (Los Angeles: Roxbury, 1996).
33. Adapted from M. Smith, *When I Say No, I Feel Guilty* (New York: Dial Press, 1975), pp. 93–110.
34. W. L. Benoit and S. Drew, "Appropriateness and Effectiveness of Image Repair Strategies," *Communication Reports* 10 (1997): 153–163. See also Stamp et al., *Creation of Defensiveness.*

ENDNOTES FOR CHAPTER 10

1. J. L. Hocker and W. W. Wilmot, *Interpersonal Conflict*, 6th ed. (New York: McGraw-Hill, 2001), pp. 21–30. See also P. M. Buzzanell and N. A. Burrell, "Family and Workplace Conflict: Examining Metaphorical Conflict Schemas and Expressions across Context and Sex," *Human Communication Research* 24 (1997): 109–146.
2. S. Metts and W. Cupach, "The Influence of Relationship Beliefs and Problem-Solving Responses on Satisfaction in Romantic Relationships," *Human Communication Research* 17 (1990): 170–185.
3. Hocker and Wilmot, *Interpersonal Conflict*, pp. 20–28.
4. For a summary of research detailing the prevalence of conflict in relationships, see W. R. Cupach and D. J. Canary, *Competence in Interpersonal Conflict* (New York: McGraw-Hill, 1997), pp. 5–6.
5. W. L. Benoit and P. J. Benoit, "Everyday Argument Practices of Naive Social Actors" in J. Wenzel, ed., *Argument and Critical Practices* (Annandale, Va.: Speech Communication Association, 1987).
6. W. Samter and W. R. Cupach, "Friendly Fire: Topical Variations in Conflict among Same- and Cross-Sex Friends," *Communication Studies* 49 (1998): 121–138.

7. S. Vuchinich, "Starting and Stopping Spontaneous Family Conflicts," *Journal of Marriage and the Family* 49 (1987): 591–601.

8. J. M. Gottman, "Emotional Responsiveness in Marital Conversations," *Journal of Communication* 32 (1982): 108–120. See also W. R. Cupach, "Communication Satisfaction and Interpersonal Solidarity as Outcomes of Conflict Message Strategy Use," paper presented at the International Communication Association conference, Boston, May 1982.

9. P. Koren, K. Carlton, and D. Shaw, "Marital Conflict: Relations among Behaviors, Outcomes, and Distress," *Journal of Consulting and Clinical Psychology* 48 (1980): 460–468.

10. Hocker and Wilmot, *Interpersonal Conflict*, p. 37.

11. J. M. Gottman, *Marital Interaction: Experimental Investigations* (New York: Academic Press, 1979). See also D. A. Infante, S. A. Myers, and R. A. Buerkel, "Argument and Verbal Aggression in Constructive and Destructive Family and Organizational Disagreements," *Western Journal of Communication* 58 (1994): 73–84.

12. S. E. Crohan, "Marital Happiness and Spousal Consensus on Beliefs about Marital Conflict: A Longitudinal Investigation," *Journal of Science and Personal Relationships* 9 (1992): 89–102.

13. D. J. Canary, H. Weger, Jr., and L. Stafford, "Couples' Argument Sequences and Their Associations with Relational Characteristics," *Western Journal of Speech Communication* 55 (1991): 159–179.

14. M. E. Roloff and D. H. Cloven, "The Chilling Effect in Interpersonal Relationships: The Reluctance to Speak One's Mind" in D. D. Cahn, ed., *Intimates in Conflict: A Communication Perspective* (Hillsdale, N.J.: Erlbaum, 1990).

15. G. R. Birchler, R. L. Weiss, and J. P. Vincent, "Multimethod Analysis of Social Reinforcement Exchange between Maritally Distressed and Nondistressed Spouse and Stranger Dyads," *Journal of Personality and Social Psychology* 31 (1975): 349–360.

16. For a detailed discussion of the drawbacks of nonassertion, see Roloff and Cloven, "The Chilling Effect in Interpersonal Relationships."

17. D. D. Cahn, *Conflict in Intimate Relationships* (New York: Guilford, 1992), p. 100.

18. D. A. Infante, "Aggressiveness" in J. C. McCroskey and J. A. Daly, eds., *Personality and Interpersonal Communication* (Newbury Park, Calif.: Sage, 1987).

19. D. A. Infante, A. S. Rancer, and F. F. Jordan, "Affirming and Nonaffirming Style, Dyad Sex, and the Perception of Argumentation and Verbal Aggression in an Interpersonal Dispute," *Human Communication Research* 22 (1996): 315–334.

20. D. A. Infante, T. A. Chandler, and J. E. Rudd, "Test of an Argumentative Skill Deficiency Model of Interspousal Violence," *Communication Monographs* 56 (1989): 163–177.

21. M. M. Martin, C. M. Anderson, P. A. Burant, and K. Weber, "Verbal Aggression in Sibling Relationships," *Communication Quarterly* 45 (1997): 304–317.

22. J. W. Kassing and D. A. Infante, "Aggressive Communication in the Coach-Athlete Relationship," *Communication Research Reports* 16 (1999): 110–120.

23. B. K. Houston, M. A. Babyak, M. A. Chesney, and G. Black, "Social Dominance and 22-Year All-Cause Mortality in Men," *Psychosomatic Medicine* 59 (1997): 5–12.

24. "Marital Tiffs Spark Immune Swoon," *Science News* (September 4, 1993): 153.

25. D. R. Turk and J. L. Monahan, "'Here I Go Again': An Examination of Repetitive Behaviors during Interpersonal Conflicts," *Southern Communication Journal* 64 (1999): 232–244.

26. T. C. Sabourin, D. A. Infante, and J. E. Rudd, "Verbal Aggression in Marriages: A Comparison of Violent, Distressed but Nonviolent, and Nondistressed Couples," *Human Communication Research* 20 (1993): 245–267.

27. Cahn, *Conflict in Intimate Relationships*, pp. 29–30.

28. B. H. Spitzberg, D. J. Canary, and W. R. Cupach, "A Competence-Based Approach to the Study of Interpersonal Conflict" in D. D. Cahn, ed., *Conflict in Personal Relationships* (Hillsdale, N.J.: Erlbaum, 1994), p. 191.

29. M. J. Beatty, K. M. Valencic, J. E. Rudd, and J. A. Dobos, "A 'Dark Side' of Communication Avoidance: Indirect Interpersonal Aggressiveness," *Communication Research Reports* 16 (1999): 103–109.

30. J. Jordan and M. E. Roloff, "Acquiring Assistance from Others: The Effect of Indirect Requests and Relational Intimacy on Verbal Compliance," *Human Communication Research* 16 (1990): 519–555.

31. C. Tavris, "Anger Defused," *Psychology Today* 16 (November 1982): 34.

32. Spitzberg, Canary, and Cupach, "A Competence-Based Approach," p. 190.

33. Adapted from S. Miller, E. W. Nunnally, and D. B. Wackman, *Alive and Aware: How to Improve Your Relationships through Better Communication* (Minneapolis, Minn.: International Communication Programs, 1975). See also R. Remer and P. deMesquita, "Teaching and Learning the Skills of Interpersonal Confrontation" in Cahn, *Intimates in Conflict*.

34. J. K. Alberts, "An Analysis of Couples' Conversational Complaints," *Communication Monographs* 55 (1988): 184–197.

35. J. K. Alberts and G. Driscoll, "Containment versus Escalation: The Trajectory of Couples' Conversational Complaints," *Western Journal of Communication* 56 (1992): 394–412.

36. Hocker and Wilmot, *Interpersonal Conflict*; M. L. Knapp, L. L. Putnam, and L. J. Davis, "Measuring Interpersonal Conflict in Organizations: Where Do We Go from Here?" *Management Communication Quarterly* 1 (1988): 414–429.

37. C. S. Burggraf and A. L. Sillars, "A Critical Examination of Sex Differences in Marital Communication," *Communication Monographs* 53 (1987): 276–294.

38. M. Gottman and L. J. Krokoff, "Marital Interaction and Satisfaction: A Longitudinal View," *Journal of Consulting and Clinical Psychology* 67 (1989): 47–52; G. R. Pike and A. L. Sillars, "Reciprocity of Marital Communication,"

Journal of Social and Personal Relationships 2 (1985): 303–324.

39. M. A. Fitzpatrick, "A Typological Approach to Communication in Relationships" in B. Rubin, ed., *Communication Yearbook 1* (New Brunswick, N.J.: Transaction Books, 1977).

40. M. A. Fitzpatrick, J. Fey, C. Segrin, and J. L. Schiff, "Internal Working Models of Relationships and Marital Communication," *Journal of Language and Social Psychology* 12 (1993): 103–131. See also M. A. Fitzpatrick, S. Fallis, and L. Vance, "Multifunctional Coding of Conflict Resolution Strategies in Marital Dyads," *Family Relations* 21 (1982): 61–70.

41. Hocker and Wilmot, *Interpersonal Conflict*, p. 142.

42. Cupach and Canary, p. 109.

43. Research summarized by D. Tannen in *You Just Don't Understand: Women and Men in Conversation* (New York: William Morrow, 1989), pp. 152–157, 162–165.

44. M. J. Collier, "Conflict Competence within African, Mexican, and Anglo-American Friendships" in S. Ting-Toomey and F. Korzenny, eds., *Cross-Cultural Interpersonal Communication* (Newbury Park, Calif.: Sage, 1991).

45. D. J. Canary, W. R. Cupach, and S. J. Messman, *Relationship Conflict* (Newbury Park, Calif.: Sage, 1995).

46. See M. J. Papa and E. J. Natalle, "Gender, Strategy Selection, and Discussion Satisfaction in Interpersonal Conflict," *Western Journal of Speech Communication* 52 (1989): 260–272.

47. See, for example, J. C. Pearson, *Gender and Communication*, 2nd ed. (Dubuque, Iowa: W.C. Brown, 1991), pp. 183–184.

48. Spitzberg, Canary, and Cupach, "A Competence-Based Approach," p. 190.

49. B. M. Gayle, R. W. Preiss, and M. A. Allen, "A Meta-Analytic Interpretation of Intimate and Non-Intimate Interpersonal Conflict" in M. A. Allen, R. W. Preiss, B. M. Gayle, and N. Burrell, eds., *Interpersonal Communication: Advances through Meta-Analysis* (New York: Lawrence Erlbaum, 2001).

50. D. J. Canary and K. Dindia, Sex Differences and Similarities in Communication: Critical Essays and Empirical Investigations of Sex and Gender in Interaction (Mahwah, N.J.: Lawrence Erlbaum, 1998).

51. M. Allen, "Methodological Considerations When Examining a Gendered World" in D. Canary & K. Dindia, eds., *Handbook of Sex Differences and Similarities in Communication* (Mahwah, N.J.: Lawrence Erlbaum, 1998).

52. Research summarized in W. R. Cupach and D. J. Canary, *Competence in Interpersonal Conflict* (New York: McGraw-Hill, 1997), pp. 63–65.

53. C. S. Burggraf and A. L. Sillars, "A Critical Examination of Sex Differences in Marital Communication," *Communication Monographs* 54 (1987): 276–294.

54. For a more detailed discussion of culture, conflict, and context, see W. B. Gudykunst and S. Ting-Toomey, *Culture and Interpersonal Communication* (Newbury Park, Calif.: Sage, 1988), pp. 153–160.

55. S. Ting-Toomey, "Managing Conflict in Intimate Intercultural Relationships" in D. D. Cahn, ed., *Conflict in Personal Relationships* (Hillsdale, N.J.: Erlbaum, 1994).

56. See, for example, S. Ting-Toomey, "Rhetorical Sensitivity Style in Three Cultures: France, Japan, and the United States," *Central States Speech Journal* 39 (1988): 28–36.

57. K. Okabe, "Indirect Speech Acts of the Japanese" in L. Kincaid, ed., *Communication Theory: Eastern and Western Perspectives* (San Diego: Academic Press, 1987), pp. 127–136.

58. G. Fontaine, "Cultural Diversity in Intimate Intercultural Relationships" in Cahn, *Intimates in Conflict*.

59. The following research is summarized in Tannen, *You Just Don't Understand*, p. 160.

60. Collier, "Conflict Competence."

61. See, for example, K. J. Beatty and J. C. McCroskey, "It's in Our Nature: Verbal Aggressiveness as Temperamental Expression," *Communication Quarterly* 45: 466–460.

62. J. G. Oetzel, "Explaining Individual Communication Processes in Homogeneous and Heterogeneous Groups through Individualism-Collectivism and Self-Construal," *Human Communication Research* 25 (1998): 202–224.

63. M. M. Martin, C. M. Anderson, P. A. Burant, and K. Weber, "Verbal Aggression in Sibling Relationships," *Communication Quarterly* 45 (1997): 304–317.

64. S. J. Messman and D. J. Canary, "Patterns of Conflict in Personal Relationships" in B. H. Spitzberg and W. R. Cupach, eds., *The Dark Side of Close Relationships* (Mahwah, N.J.: Lawrence Erlbaum, 1998).

65. A. C. Filley, *Interpersonal Conflict Resolution* (Glenview, Ill.: Scott, Foresman, 1975), p. 23.

66. T. Gordon, *Parent Effectiveness Training* (New York: Wyden, 1970), pp. 236–264.

67. R. Axelrod, *The Evolution of Cooperation* (New York: Basic Books, 1984).

68. M. Kinsley, "It Pays to Be Nice," *Science* 222 (1984): 162.

GLOSSARY

Abstraction ladder   A range of more to less abstract terms describing an event or object.

Accenting   Nonverbal behaviors that emphasize part of a verbal message.

Accommodation   A nonassertive response style in which the communicator submits to a situation rather than attempt to have his or her needs met.

Active listening   Restating a speaker's thoughts and feelings in the listener's own words.

Advising response   A helping response in which the receiver offers suggestions about how the speaker should deal with a problem.

Affection   The social need to care for others and to be cared for by them.

Affinity   The degree to which persons like or appreciate one another.

Ambiguous response   A disconfirming response with more than one meaning, leaving the other party unsure of the responder's position.

Ambushing   A style in which the receiver listens carefully in order to gather information to use in an attack on the speaker.

Analyzing statement   A helping style in which the listener offers an interpretation of a speaker's message.

Androgynous   Possessing both masculine and feminine traits.

Apathy   A defense mechanism in which a person avoids admitting emotional pain by pretending not to care about an event.

Assertion   A direct expression of the sender's needs, thoughts, or feelings, delivered in a way that does not attack the receiver's dignity.

Attending   The process of filtering out some messages and focusing on others.

Attribution   The process of attaching meaning to behavior.

Avoidance   A nonassertive response style in which the communicator is unwilling to confront a situation in which his or her needs are not being met.

Avoiding   A stage of relational development immediately prior to terminating in which the parties minimize contact with one another.

Back   The region in which behavior will not be perceived by an audience. *See* Front.

Behavior   Observable actions that can be interpreted as communicative messages.

Behavioral description   An account that refers only to observable phenomena.

Body orientation   Type of nonverbal communication characterized by the degree to which we face forward or away from someone.

Bonding   A stage of relational development in which the parties make symbolic public gestures to show that their relationship exists.

Breadth   First dimension of self-disclosure involving the range of subjects being discussed.

"But" statements   Statements in which the word "but" cancels out the expression that preceded it.

Certainty   Attitude behind messages that dogmatically imply that the speaker's position is correct and that the other person's ideas are not worth considering. Likely to generate a defensive response.

Channel   The medium through which a message passes from sender to receiver.

Chronemics   The study of how humans use and structure time.

Circumscribing   A stage of relational development in which partners begin to reduce the scope of their contact and commitment to one another.

Cliché   A ritualized, stock statement delivered in response to a social situation.

Cognitive complexity   The ability to construct a variety of frameworks for viewing an issue.

Cognitive conservatism   The tendency to seek and attend to information that conforms to an existing self-concept.

Cognitive dissonance An inconsistency between two conflicting pieces of information, attitudes, or behaviors. Communicators strive to reduce dissonance, often through defense mechanisms that maintain an idealized presenting image.

Communication A continuous, transactional process involving participants who occupy different but overlapping environments and create relationships through the exchange of messages, many of which are affected by external, physiological, and psychological noise.

Communication climate The emotional tone of a relationship between two or more individuals.

Communication competence The ability to accomplish one's personal goals in a manner that maintains a relationship on terms that are acceptable to all parties.

Compensation A defense mechanism in which a person stresses a strength in one area to camouflage a shortcoming in some other area.

Competitive symmetry A relational condition in which both parties strive to gain control.

Complaining A disconfirming response that implicitly or explicitly attributes responsibility for the speaker's displeasure to another party.

Complementary communication Communication in which one partner consistently occupies a powerful position, while the other responds in a subservient manner.

Complementary conflict style A relational conflict style in which partners use different but mutually reinforcing behaviors.

Complementary relationship One in which the distribution of power is unequal, with one party occupying a "one-up" and the other a "one-down" position.

Complementing Nonverbal behavior that reinforces a verbal message.

Compromise An approach to conflict resolution in which both parties attain at least part of what they wanted through self-sacrifice.

Computer-mediated communication (CMC) Communication between individuals that is conducted via computer channels such as e-mail, chat, and instant messaging.

Confirming communication A message that expresses caring or respect for another person.

Conflict An expressed struggle between at least two interdependent parties who perceive incompatible goals, scarce rewards, and interference from the other party in achieving their goals.

Conflict ritual An unacknowledged repeating pattern of interlocking behavior used by participants in a conflict.

Congruency The matching of verbal and nonverbal messages sent by a communicator.

Connotation The emotional associations of a term.

Consequence statement An explanation of the results that follow from either the behavior of the person to whom the message is addressed or from the speaker's interpretation of the addressee's behavior. Consequence statements can describe what happens to the speaker, the addressee, or others.

Content message A message that communicates information about the subject being discussed. *See also* Relational message.

Contradicting Nonverbal behavior that is inconsistent with a verbal message.

Control The social need to influence others.

Controlling communication Messages in which the sender tries to impose some sort of outcome on the receiver, usually resulting in a defensive reaction.

Convergence The process of adapting one's speech style to match that of others with whom the communicator wants to identify. *See also* Divergence.

Conversational control The power to determine who speaks in a conversation.

Counterfeit questions Questions that disguise the speaker's true motives, which do not include a genuine desire to understand the other person. *See* Sincere questions.

Crazymaking *See* Passive aggression.

Debilitative emotions Emotions that prevent a person from functioning effectively.

Deception cues Nonverbal behaviors that signal the untruthfulness of a verbal message.

Decision control The power to influence which person in a relationship decides what activities will take place.

Decoding The process in which a receiver attaches meaning to a message. Synonymous with *Interpreting.*

De-escalatory conflict spiral A communication spiral in which the parties slowly lessen their dependence on one another, withdraw, and become less invested in the relationship.

Defense mechanism A psychological device used to maintain a presenting self-image that an individual believes is threatened.

Defensive listening A response style in which the receiver perceives a speaker's comments as an attack.

Defensiveness The attempt to protect a presenting image a person believes is being attacked.

Denotation The objective, emotion-free meaning of a term. *See also* Connotation.

Depth A dimension of self-disclosure involving a shift from relatively nonrevealing messages to more personal ones.

Descriptive communication Messages that describe the speaker's position without evaluating others. Synonymous with "I" language.

Desired self   The person we would like to be. It may be identical to or different from the perceived and presenting selves.

Dialectical tensions   Inherent conflicts that arise when two opposing or incompatible forces exist simultaneously.

Differentiating   A stage of relational development in which the parties re-establish their individual identities after having bonded together.

Direct aggression   A criticism or demand that threatens the face of the person at whom it is directed.

Disconfirming communication   A message that expresses a lack of caring or respect for another person.

Disfluency   A nonlinguistic verbalization, for example, um, er, ah.

Displacement   A defense mechanism in which a person vents hostile or aggressive feelings on a target that cannot strike back, instead of on the true target.

Divergence   Speaking mannerisms that emphasize a communicator's differences from others. *See also* Convergence.

Double message   Contradiction between a verbal message and one or more nonverbal cues.

Dyad   Two individuals communicating. The interaction may or may not be interpersonal in nature.

Emblems   Deliberate nonverbal behaviors with precise meanings, known to virtually all members of a cultural group.

Emotional contagion   The process by which emotions are transferred from one person to another.

Emotive language   Language that conveys the sender's attitude rather than simply offer an objective description.

Empathy   The ability to project oneself into another person's point of view, so as to experience the other's thoughts and feelings.

Encoding   The process of putting thoughts into symbols, most commonly words.

Ends   The ultimate goal a person is seeking. Ends are often confused with means, resulting in unproductive conflicts. *See also* Means.

Environment   The field of experiences that leads a person to make sense of another's behavior. Environments consist of physical characteristics, personal experiences, relational history, and cultural background.

Equality   A type of supportive communication described by Gibb, suggesting that the sender regards the receiver as worthy of respect.

Equivocal language   Ambiguous language that has two or more equally plausible meanings.

Escalatory conflict spiral   A communication spiral in which one attack leads to another until the initial skirmish escalates into a full-fledged battle.

Euphemisms   Pleasant terms substituted for blunt ones in order to soften the impact of unpleasant information.

Evaluative communication   Messages in which the sender judges the receiver in some way, usually resulting in a defensive response.

Experimenting   An early stage in relational development, consisting of a search for common ground. If the experimentation is successful, the relationship will progress to intensifying. If not, it may go no further.

External noise   Factors outside the receiver that interfere with the accurate reception of a message.

Face   The socially approved identity that a communicator tries to present. *See also* Impression management.

Face-threatening act   Behavior by another that is perceived as attacking an individual's presenting image, or face.

Facework   Verbal and nonverbal behavior designed to create and maintain a communicator's face and the face of others.

Facilitative emotions   Emotions that contribute to effective functioning.

Factual statement   A statement based on direct observation of sense data.

Fallacy of approval   The irrational belief that it is vital to win the approval of virtually every person a communicator deals with.

Fallacy of catastrophic expectations   The irrational belief that the worst possible outcome will probably occur.

Fallacy of causation   The irrational belief that emotions are caused by others and not by the person who has them.

Fallacy of helplessness   The irrational belief that satisfaction in life is determined by forces beyond one's control.

Fallacy of overgeneralization   Irrational beliefs in which (1) conclusions (usually negative) are based on limited evidence or (2) communicators exaggerate their shortcomings.

Fallacy of perfection   The irrational belief that a worthwhile communicator should be able to handle every situation with complete confidence and skill.

Fallacy of shoulds   The irrational belief that people should behave in the most desirable way.

Feedback   The discernible response of a receiver to a sender's message.

Feeling statement   An expression of the sender's emotions that results from interpretation of sense data.

Front   Publicly visible behavior. *See also* Back, Face.

Gestures   Motions of the body, usually hands or arms, that have communicative value.

Gibb categories Six sets of contrasting styles of verbal and nonverbal behavior. Each set describes a communication style that is likely to arouse defensiveness and a contrasting style that is likely to prevent or reduce it. Developed by Jack Gibb.

Hearing The physiological dimension of listening.

High-context cultures Cultures that avoid direct use of language, relying on the context of a message to convey meaning.

"I" language A statement that describes the speaker's reaction to another person's behavior without making judgments about its worth. *See also* "You" language.

Ideal self The person each wishes to be. *See also* Perceived self and Presenting self.

Identity *See* Presenting Self.

Identity management The communication strategies people use to influence how others view them.

Illustrators Nonverbal behaviors that accompany and support verbal messages.

Impersonal communication Behavior that treats others as objects rather than individuals. *See* Interpersonal communication.

Impersonal response A disconfirming response that is superficial or trite.

Impervious response A disconfirming response that ignores another person's attempt to communicate.

Impression management *See* Identity management.

Inclusion The social need to feel a sense of belonging in some relationship with others.

Incongruous response A disconfirming response in which two messages, one of which is usually nonverbal, contradict one another.

Indirect communication An oblique way of expressing wants or needs in order to save face for the recipient.

Influence *See* Control.

Initiating The first stage in relational development, in which the parties express interest in one another.

Insensitive listening Failure to recognize the thoughts or feelings that are not directly expressed by a speaker; instead, accepting the speaker's words at face value.

Insulated listening A style in which the receiver ignores undesirable information.

Instrumental goals Goals aimed at getting others to behave in desired ways.

Integrating A stage of relational development in which the parties begin to take on a single identity.

Intensifying A stage of relational development preceding integrating, in which the parties move toward integration by increasing the amount of contact and the breadth and depth of self-disclosure.

Intention statement A description of where the speaker stands on an issue, what he or she wants, or how he or she plans to act in the future.

Interaction constructs Perceptual schema that categorize people according to their social behavior.

Interactive communication model A characterization of communication as a two-way event in which sender and receiver exchange messages in response to one another.

Interpersonal communication In a quantitative sense, communication (usually face-to-face) between two individuals. (*See also* Dyad.) In a qualitative sense, communication in which the parties consider one another as unique individuals rather than objects. It is characterized by minimal use of stereotyped labels; unique, idiosyncratic rules; and a high degree of information exchange.

Interpersonal relationship An association in which the parties meet each other's social needs to a greater or lesser degree.

Interpretation The process of attaching meaning to sense data; synonymous with *Decoding*.

Interrupting response A disconfirming response in which one communicator interrupts another.

Intimacy A state of personal sharing arising from physical, intellectual, and/or emotional contact.

Intimate distance One of Hall's four distance zones, ranging from skin contact to eighteen inches.

Irrelevant response A disconfirming response in which one communicator's comments bear no relationship to the previous speaker's ideas.

"It" statements Statements that replace the personal pronoun "I" with the less immediate word "it," often reducing the speaker's acceptance of responsibility for the statement.

Johari Window A model that describes the relationship between self-disclosure and self-awareness.

Judging response A reaction in which the receiver evaluates the sender's message either favorably or unfavorably.

Kinesics The study of body position and motion.

Leakage Nonverbal behaviors that reveal information a communicator does not disclose verbally.

Lie A deliberate attempt to hide or misrepresent the truth.

Linear communication model A characterization of communication as a one-way event in which a message flows from sender to receiver.

Linguistic determinism The theory that a culture's world view is unavoidably shaped and reflected by the language its members speak.

Linguistic relativism   A more moderate form of linguistic determinism which argues that language exerts a strong influence on the perceptions of the people who speak it.

Listening   Process that consists of hearing, attending, understanding, responding, and remembering an aural message.

Lose–lose problem solving   An approach to conflict resolution in which neither side achieves its goals. Sometimes lose–lose outcomes result from both parties seeking a win–lose victory over one another. In other cases, the parties settle for a lose–lose outcome (for example, compromise) because they cannot find any better alternative.

Low-context cultures   Cultures that use language primarily to express thoughts, feelings, and ideas as clearly and logically as possible.

Manipulators   Movements in which one part of the body grooms, massages, rubs, holds, fidgets, pinches, picks, or otherwise manipulates another part.

Means   Ways of achieving one's ends. There are usually several means to an end. Unproductive conflicts often occur when people argue over a limited number of means rather than focus on finding the best ones to achieve their ends.

Membership constructs   Perceptual schema that categorize people according to the groups to which they belong.

Message   Information sent from a sender to a receiver.

Metacommunication   Messages (usually relational) that refer to other messages: communication about communication.

Microexpressions   Brief facial expressions.

Mixed emotions   Emotions that are combinations of primary emotions. Some mixed emotions can be expressed in single words (that is, *awe, remorse*), whereas others require more than one term (that is, *embarrassed and angry, relieved and grateful*).

Narrative   A perception of the world shared by a collection of people. Narratives can be described in terms of a dramatic theme.

Negotiation   A process in which two or more parties discuss specific proposals in order to find a mutually acceptable agreement.

Neutrality   A defense-arousing behavior described by Gibb in which the sender expresses indifference toward a receiver.

Neutralized symmetry   A relational condition in which the balance of control shifts between the partners according to the issue at hand.

Noise   External, physiological, and psychological distractions that interfere with the accurate transmission and reception of a message.

Nonassertion   The inability to express one's thoughts or feelings when necessary. Nonassertion may be due to a lack of confidence or communication skill or both.

Nonverbal communication   Messages expressed by other than linguistic means.

One-way communication   Communication in which a receiver provides no feedback to a sender.

Operational definition   A definition that refers to observable referents rather than using other words with no apparent concrete meanings.

Organization   The stage in the perception process that involves arranging data in a meaningful way.

Paralanguage   Nonlinguistic means of vocal expression: rate, pitch, tone, and so on.

Parallel conflict style   A relational conflict style in which the approach of the partners varies from one situation to another.

Parallel relationship   One in which the balance of power shifts from one party to the other, according to the situation.

Paraphrasing   Restating a speaker's thoughts and/or feelings in the listener's own words.

Passive aggression   An indirect expression of aggression, delivered in a way that allows the sender to maintain a façade of kindness.

Passive listening   *See* One-way communication.

Perceived self   The person we believe ourselves to be in moments of candor. It may be identical with or different from the presenting and ideal self.

Perception checking   A three-part method for verifying the accuracy of interpretations, including a description of the sense data, two possible interpretations, and a request for confirmation of the interpretations.

Perceptual schema   Cognitive frameworks that allow individuals to organize perceptual data that they have selected from the environment.

Personal distance   One of Hall's four distance zones, ranging from eighteen inches to four feet.

Personality   A relatively consistent set of traits exhibited by a person across a variety of situations.

Phonological rules   Linguistic rules that govern how sounds are combined to form words.

Physical avoidance   A defense mechanism whereby the person steers clear of people who attack a presenting self to avoid dissonance.

Physical constructs   Perceptual schema that categorize people according to their appearance.

Physiological noise   Biological factors in the receiver that interfere with accurate reception of a message.

Pillow method   A method for understanding an issue from several perspectives rather than with an egocentric "I'm right and you're wrong" attitude.

Posture   The way in which individuals carry themselves—erect, slumping, and so on.

Powerless speech mechanisms   Ways of speaking that may reduce perceptions of a communicator's power.

Pragmatic rules   Linguistic rules that help communicators understand how messages may be used and interpreted in a given context.

Presenting self   The image a person presents to others. It may be identical with or different from the perceived and ideal self.

Primary emotions   Basic emotions. Some researchers have identified eight primary emotions: joy, acceptance, fear, surprise, sadness, disgust, anger, and anticipation.

Problem orientation   A supportive style of communication described by Gibb in which the communicators focus on working together to solve their problems instead of trying to impose their own solutions on one another.

Prompting   Using silences and brief statements of encouragement to draw out a speaker.

Proprioceptive stimuli   Sensations activated by movement of internal tissues (for example, upset stomach, pounding heart).

Provisionalism   A supportive style of communication described by Gibb in which the sender expresses a willingness to consider the other person's position.

Proxemics   The study of how people and animals use space.

Pseudolistening   An imitation of true listening in which the receiver's mind is elsewhere.

Psychological constructs   Perceptual schema that categorize people according to their apparent personalities.

Psychological noise   Forces within a communicator that interfere with the ability to express or understand a message accurately.

Public distance   One of Hall's four distance zones, extending outward from twelve feet.

Punctuation   The process of determining the causal order of events.

Qualitative interpersonal communication   *See* Interpersonal communication.

Quantitative interpersonal communication   *See* Interpersonal communication.

Questioning response   A style of helping in which the receiver seeks additional information from the sender. Some questioning responses are really disguised advice.

Rationalization   A defense mechanism in which logical but untrue explanations maintain an unrealistic desired or presenting self-image.

Receiver   One who notices and attends to a message.

Reference groups   Groups against which we compare ourselves, thereby influencing our self-concept and self-esteem.

Reflected appraisal   The theory that a person's self-concept matches the way the person believes others regard him or her.

Regression   A defense mechanism in which a person avoids assuming responsibility by pretending that he or she is unable to do something instead of admitting to being simply unwilling.

Regulating   One function of nonverbal communication, in which nonverbal cues control the flow of verbal communication among individuals.

Relational conflict style   A pattern of managing disagreements that repeats itself over time in a relationship.

Relational maintenance   Communication aimed at keeping relationships operating smoothly and satisfactorily.

Relational message   A message that expresses the social relationship between two or more individuals.

Relationship   *See* Interpersonal relationship.

Relative words   Words that gain their meaning by comparison.

Remembering   Ability to recall information.

Repeating   Nonverbal behaviors that duplicate the content of a verbal message.

Repression   A defense mechanism in which a person avoids facing an unpleasant situation or fact by denying its existence.

Respect   The social need to be held in esteem by others.

Responding   Giving observable feedback to the speaker.

Role constructs   Perceptual schema that categorize people according to their social position.

Sapir–Whorf hypothesis   Theory of linguistic determinism in which language is determined by a culture's perceived reality.

Sarcasm   A potential defensive reaction in which an individual redirects a perceived threat to his or her presenting self by attacking the critic with contemptuous, often ironical remarks.

Selection   The first stage in the perception process in which some data are chosen to attend to and others to ignore.

Selective listening   A listening style in which the receiver responds only to messages that interest him or her.

Self-actualization   One of Maslow's five needs; the desire to reach one's maximum potential.

Self-concept   The relatively stable set of perceptions each individual holds of himself or herself.

Self-disclosure   The process of deliberately revealing information about oneself that is significant and that would not normally be known by others.

Self-esteem   The part of the self-concept that involves an individual's evaluations of his or her self-worth.

Self-fulfilling prophecy   A prediction or expectation of an event that makes the outcome more likely to occur than would otherwise have been the case.

Self-monitoring   The process of attending to one's behavior and using these observations to shape the way one behaves.

Self-serving bias   The tendency to interpret and explain information in a way that casts the perceiver in the most favorable manner.

Self-talk   The nonvocal process of thinking. On some level, self-talk occurs as a person interprets another's behavior.

Semantic rules   Rules that govern the meaning of language, as opposed to its structure. *See also* Syntactic rules.

Sender   The creator of a message.

Sex role   The social orientation that governs behavior, rather than the biological gender.

Significant other   A person whose opinion is important enough to affect one's self-concept strongly.

Sincere questions   Questions that are aimed at soliciting information that enable the asker to understand the other person. *See* Counterfeit questions.

Social comparison   Evaluation of oneself in terms of or by comparison to others.

Social distance   One of Hall's distance zones, ranging from four to twelve feet.

Social exchange theory   A socioeconomic theory that suggests people seek relationships in which the rewards they receive from others are greater than or equal to the costs they encounter.

Social penetration   A model that describes relationships in terms of their breadth and depth.

Spiral   A reciprocal communication pattern in which each person's message reinforces the other's. *See also* De-escalatory conflict spiral, Escalatory conflict spiral.

Spontaneity   A supportive communication behavior described by Gibb in which the sender expresses a message without any attempt to manipulate the receiver.

Stage-hogging   A listening style in which the receiver is more concerned with making his or her own point than in understanding the speaker.

Stagnating   A stage of relational development characterized by declining enthusiasm and standardized forms of behavior.

Static evaluation   The tendency to view people or relationships as unchanging.

Stereotyping   Categorizing individuals according to a set of characteristics assumed to belong to all members of a group.

Strategy   A defense-arousing style of communication described by Gibb in which the sender tries to manipulate or deceive a receiver.

Submissive symmetry   A relational condition in which both parties strive to shift control to the other person.

Substituting   Nonverbal behavior that takes the place of a verbal message.

Superiority   A defense-arousing style of communication described by Gibb in which the sender states or implies that the receiver is not worthy of respect.

Supportive responses   Responses that demonstrate solidarity with a speaker's situation.

Symmetrical communication   Communication in which the power is distributed evenly between the parties.

Symmetrical conflict style   A relational conflict style in which both partners use the same tactics.

Symmetrical relationship   A relationship in which the partners seek an equal amount of control.

Sympathy   Compassion for another's situation. *See also* Empathy.

Syntactic rules   Rules that govern the ways symbols can be arranged, as opposed to the meanings of those symbols. *See also* Semantic rules.

Tangential response   A disconfirming response that uses the speaker's remark as a starting point for a shift to a new topic.

Terminating   The concluding stage of relational development, characterized by the acknowledgement of one or both parties that the relationship is over.

Territory   A stationary area claimed by an individual.

Transactional communication model   A characterization of communication as the simultaneous sending and receiving of messages in an ongoing, irreversible process.

Two-way communication   An exchange of information in which the receiver deliberately provides feedback to a sender.

Uncertainty reduction   The process of getting to know others by gaining more information about them.

Understanding   Occurs when sense is made of a message.

Verbal abuse   A disconfirming response intended to cause psychological pain to another.

Verbal aggression   A defense mechanism in which a person avoids facing unpleasant information by verbally attacking the confronting source.

"We" statement   Statement that implies that the issue is the concern and responsibility of both the speaker and receiver of a message. *See also* "I" language and "You" language.

Whorf–Sapir hypothesis   The theory that the structure of a language shapes the worldview of its users.

Win–lose problem solving   An approach to conflict resolution in which one party reaches its goal at the expense of the other.

Win–win problem solving   An approach to conflict resolution in which the parties work together to satisfy all their goals.

"You" language   A statement that expresses or implies a judgment of the other person. *See also* Evaluative communication, "I" language.

PHOTO CREDITS

xx   Carmen Lomas Garza "Cakewalk." Reprinted with permission of the publisher, Children's Book Press, San Francisco, CA. Art copyright © 1990 by Carmen Lomas Garza.

2   © Bettye Lane/Photo Researchers

5   "Lunch Counter" © Mary Monge

6   "The Color of Love" © 1996 Suzanne Tornquist

9   "Eddie Diptych" © Estate of Roy Lichtenstein

13   "People Whispering Under Window with Bird" Detail. Dave Cutler/SIS

17   "Living with Remote Man" © 1997 Erika Oller

21   Charlie Hill "Morning Mail" SuperStock

24   "Do You Want to Dance?" © Antionette Simmons Hodges

32   Mixed media 3D construction Maria Rendon © 1994

44   watercolor of head being constructed © Lonni Sue Johnson

49   Illustration by Blair Drawson

52   "The Juggler" © 1999 Tom Curry

54   "Stripes" Colored drawing by: Bernard A. Poulin

56   Norman Rockwell "Girl at Mirror" Printed by permission of the Norman Rockwell Family Trust. Copyright © 2002 the Norman Rockwell Family Trust. Photo courtesy of The Norman Rockwell Museum at Stockbridge.

62   Borislav Sajtinac "Mausegrusse" Edition Inkognito

72   Kasmir Malevich "Female Torso II" Russian State Museum, St. Petersburg, Russia/SuperStock

80   "Mona Lisa" © 1988, Paul Giovanopoulos. Photo credit: Aaron Miller.

83   Edward Hopper "Soir Bleu" 1914. Oil on canvas 36 X 72 inches. Collection of Whitney Museum of American Art. Josephine N. Hopper Bequest 70.1208. Photograph © 2001: Whitney Museum of American Art

92   Private Collection/Diana Ong/SuperStock

94   M.C. Escher's "Relativity" © 2001 Cordon Art B.V. - Baarn, Holland. All rights reserved.

109   Robert Campbell, Jr. "Aboriginal Change in Lifestyle" 1987. Courtesy of the artist and Roslyn Oxley9 Gallery

115   Betty Biggs "Resplendence" © 1998

122   "I Know How You Must Feel, Brad!" © Estate of Roy Lichtenstein

124   Xavier Jones/SuperStock

134   © Rosanne Percivalle

141   Clive Smith "Held" By permission of Clive Smith and Galerie de Bellefeuille, Montreal.

146   Martiros Saryan "Street in Cairo" Private Collection, Moscow, Russia/SuperStock

150   Private Collection/Pablo Rivera/SuperStock

153   Will Terry "Firehead"

163   Diana Ong/SuperStock

174   "Men of Letters" © Bob Milnazik

176   Pieter Bruegel d.Ä.: Tower of Babel. Museum of Fine Arts, Vienna

177   © Sandy Novak

180   Sir Frank Dicksee "La Belle Dame Sans Merci" Detail. City of Bristol Museum and Art Gallery/Bridgeman Art Library

187   "Evening Song" © Jeanine M. Frazier

192   "Walking in Beauty" © 1997 Dorothy Strait

200   Tsing-Fang Chen "Love Above Confrontation"/SuperStock

208   "No Worries" © Tom Ratliffe

215   Rufino Tamayo *Man and Woman (Hombre y mujer)*, 1981, oil on canvas, 124.8 X 180 cm. Tate Gallery, London/Art Resource. © Inheritors of the artist in support of the Fundación Olga y Rufino Tamjayo, A.C.

220   Georges de la Tour, "The Cheat" Musee du Louvre, Paris/Giraudon, Paris/SuperStock

229   "Geisha with Braces" © Jeff Sedlik

233   "Above the Sea" © Eric Zenner 1997

235   © Eric Jaquier/Stock, Boston

241   "Couple with Their Feet Up" © Jonathan Sobol

243   Roswita Szyszka "Linear Retrospect" www.RSzyszka.com

244   "Untitled" 1987 © The Estate of Keith Haring

246   © J. L. Anderson/H. Armstrong Roberts

248   Eugene Weston III

249   George Tooker "The Subway" 1950. Egg tempera on composition board. Sight: 18 1/8 X 36 1/8 inches. Collection of Whitney Museum of American Art. Purchase, with funds from the Juliana Force Purchase Award. 50.23. Photograph © 2001: Whitney Museum of American Art

254   "Follow the Leader" graphite drawing. Carol V. Gray © 1997

257   © 2002 Brad Holland

259   "Separation" Living artist: Tomyé

266   "Soup Cans" Illustration by Craig Frazier with permission from INVESCO Funds

270   Mary Hearne "Secrets"

273   Rhoda Yanow "Conversation"

274   Gustav Igler "In Detention" oil on canvas, 1881. Galerie G. Paffrath

276   Mike Mazzachi/Stock, Boston

278   "Cocktail Party II" Dale Kennington/SuperStock

291   "Conversation" Daniel Nevins/SuperStock

294   "The Saturday Club" Dale Kennington/SuperStock

295   "Summer Supper" © Tracey Brown

303   M. C. Escher's "Bond of Union" © 2001 Cordon Art B.V. - Baarn, Holland. All rights reserved.

304   Joy Zemel "Two Women with the Black Cat on the Table" oil on canvas, 26" X 32". Reproduced by permission of the artist.

312   53912/13 "Taos People at a Round Dance" 1935 by Tonita Lujan (Khup Khu), Taos Pueblo. Museum of Indian Arts and Culture/Laboratory of Anthropology, Museum of New Mexico. Photograph by Blair Clark.

318   Gustav Klimt "The Three Ages of Woman" detail. Gallery of Modern Art, Rome/ET Archive, London/SuperStock

319   Barbara Kruger "Untitled" (You contruct intricate rituals which allow you to touch the skin of other men). 37" by 50" photograph. 1980. Collection: Museum of Fine Arts, Boston, Massachusetts. Courtesy: Mary Boone Gallery, New York.

330   "Prince Rahotep and his wife Nofret" Egyptian Antiquities Museum, Cairo, Egypt/Ben Mangor/SuperStock

332   Janette Ostier Gallery, Paris, France/Giraudon, Paris/SuperStock

337   © Emanuel Dimitri Volakis

338   Alexej von Jawlensky "Head" Christie's Images/SuperStock

345 © Mick Wiggins

366 "Latino Lovers Under the Sheets" Karen Boyhen © 2000

369 Mary Hearne "Recess"

379 Edward Hopper "Sunday" 1926, oil on canvas, 29 X 34, The Phillips Collection, Washington, DC

381 Kasimir Malevich "Three Girls" Russian State Museum, St. Petersburg, Russia/SuperStock

387 Maxfield Parrish "Dream Days (The Magic Ring)" 1901. Photo courtesy of the Archives of the American Illustrators Gallery, New York City © 2000, by ASaP of Holderness, NH 03245/ www.americanillustrators.com

388 Henry Moore "Seated Figure" Christie's Images/SuperStock. The work illustrated on page 388 has been reproduced by permission of the Henry Moore Foundation.

400 Theodor Geisel "My Petunia Can Lick Your Geranium" From The Secret Art of Dr. Seuss. Copyright © 1995 by Dr. Seuss Enterprises, L.P. Reprinted by permission of Random House, Inc.

403 © Edel Rodriguez

405 Corbis/Bettmann

408 Stephen Schildbach "Direct Aggression"

412 Frank Siteman/Stock, Boston

415 Carolina Larrea "Arvores" Kactus Foto, Santiago, Chile/SuperStock

431 "The Dispute" Explorer/SuperStock

441 Theo Rudnak "Shaking Columns"

CREDITS

PREFACE **xvii** *Peanuts* by Schulz © 1970. Reprinted permission of United Feature Syndicate, Inc.

CHAPTER 1 **2** "The Silencing" From *Newsweek* 6-18-73 © 1973 *Newsweek*, In. All rights reserved. Reprinted by permission. **11** *Zits* by Scott and Borgman. Reprinted with special permission by King Feature Syndicate. **15** Drawing by Bruce Kaplan. © The New Yorker Collection 1996 Bruce Eric Kaplan from cartoonbank.com. All rights reserved. **19** Drawing by Aaron Bacall. © The New Yorker Collection 1997 Aaron Bacall from cartoonbank.com. All Rights Reserved. **21** "The Electronic Block Party" © 1999 by the New York Times Co. Reprinted by permission. **25** "You Drawing by Mike Ewers. Used with permission. **29** From *The Accidental Tourist* by Anne Tyler. © 1985 by Anne Tyler Modarressi. Used by permission of Alfred A. Knopf, a division of Random House, Inc. **36** *Calvin and Hobbes* © Watterson. Reprinted with permission of Universal Press Syndicate. All rights reserved.

CHAPTER 2 **48** Figure adapted from H. M. Johnson (1998) *How Do I Love Me?* 3rd ed. Salem, Wisconsin: Sheffield Publishing Co. Used by permission. **51** Poem, "Once Riding In Old Baltimore" by Countee Cullen from *On These I Stand: An Anthology of the Best Poems of Countee Cullen.* **53** *Ziggy* by Tom Wilson. © Ziggy and Friends, Inc. Reprinted with permission of Universal Press Syndicate. All rights reserved. **54–55** "Cipher in the Snow" by Jean Mizer from *Today's Education.* Used with permission. **57** Drawing by Barbara Smaller © The New Yorker Collection 2000 Barbara Smaller from cartoonbank.com. All Rights Reserved. **63** *Cathy* © Cathy Guisewite. Reprinted with permission of Universal Press Syndicate. All rights reserved. **65** Drawing by Ed Frascino. © The New Yorker Collection 1991 Ed Frascino from cartoonbank.com. All Rights Reserved. **68** © Gahan Wilson. Used with permission. **75** Drawing by Dana Fradon. © The New Yorker Collection 1983 Dana Fradon from cartoonbank. com. All Rights Reserved. **78** Drawing by

Wm. Hamilton. © 2001 from cartoonbank.com. All Rights Reserved. **80–81** Excerpt from *Person to Person* by Barry Stevens. © 1967 Real people Press. Used with permission. **86** Drawing by Peter Steiner. © The New Yorker Collection 1993 Peter Steiner from cartoonbank.com. All Rights Reserved.

CHAPTER 3 **94** M. C. Escher's "Relativity" © 2001 Cordon Art V. B. -Baarn -Holland. All rights reserved. **100** *Farcus*® by David Waisglass and Gordon Coulthart is reprinted with permission from LaughingStock Licensing Inc., Ottawa, CanadaCanada. All rights reserved. **102** *Sally Forth* by Greg Howard; © 1982. Reprinted with special permission of King Feature Syndicate. **107** Excerpt from pp. 103-4 from *That's Not What I Meant* by Deborah Tannen © 1986 by Deborah Tannen. Reprinted by permission of HarperCollins Publishers, Inc. William Morrow **112–113** Article: "Field Experiment: Preparation for the Changing Police Role" by Fred Ferguson. Used courtesy of the author. **114** Drawing by John Jonik published in *Psychology Today* 1984. Reprinted by permission of John Jonik. **117** Drawing by Lorenz. Reprinted with permission of the *Saturday Evening Post.* **125** Drawing by William Steig. © The New Yorker Collection 1997 William Steig from cartoonbank.com. All Rights Reserved.

CHAPTER 4 **139** Drawing by Robert Weber. © The New Yorker Collection 1981 Robert Weber from cartoonbank. com. All Rights Reserved. **141** Lyrics by Tom Waits "Emotional Weather Report" Fifth Floor Music © 1975. Used by permission. All rights reserved. **147** Drawing by Jack Ziegler. © The New Yorker Collection 1991 Jack Ziegler from cartoonbank.com. All Rights Reserved. **149** Drawing by Victoria Roberts. © The New Yorker Collection 1995 Victoria Roberts from cartoonbank.com. All Rights Reserved. **150** Poetry by Yevgeny Yevtushenko. From *Yevgeny Yevtushenko: The Collected Poems, 1952–1990* edited by Albert C. Todd, © 1991 by Henry Holt and Company, Inc. Reprinted by permission of Henry Holt and Company, Inc. **151** Drawing by Leo Cullum. © 2001 Leo Cullum from

cartoonbank.com. All Rights Reserved. **157** *Zits* by Scott and Borgman. Reprinted with special permission of King Feature Syndicate. **166** Drawing by Steve Delmonte. © 2001 Steve Delmonte. Used by permission.

CHAPTER 5 **178** *Calvin and Hobbes* © Watterson. Reprinted with permission of Universal Press Syndicate. All rights reserved. **179** Drawing by Schochet. From *The Wall Street Journal.* Permission, Cartoon Feature Syndicate. **180** From *Conversation and Communication* by J. A. M. Meerloo, © 1952 by International Universities Press Inc. Used with permission. **183** Drawing by Leo Cullum. © 2001 Leo Cullum from cartoonbank.com. All Rights Reserved. **187** Article by Carla Hall, *Los Angeles Times* staff writer © 1997, *Los Angeles Times.* Reprinted by permission. **191** Drawing by Handelsman. © The New Yorker Collection 1996 J. B. Handelsman from cartoonbank.com. All Rights Reserved. **192** Article: "Changing the 'S' Word" by Christina Koenig. By permission of Christina Koenig. **197** Drawing by Marian Henley. © 2001 Marian Henley from cartoonbank.com. All Rights Reserved. **199** Excerpt from *I And Thou: Here And Now* by Claudio Naranjo. Used courtesy of the author. **206** Drawing by Mick Stevens. © The New Yorker Collection 1992 Mick Stevens from cartoonbank.com. All Rights Reserved. **213** "The Drawing by Leo Cullum. © 2001 Leo Cullum from cartoonbank.com. All Rights Reserved.

CHAPTER 6 **222** From "A Scandal in Bohemia from *The Adventures of Sherlock Holmes* by Sir Arthur Conan Doyle. Used by permission. **224** Table: "Types of Communication" adapted from *Together: Communicating Interpersonally* by John Stewart and Gary D'Angelo. © 1980 by Addison-Wesley. Used courtesy McGraw-Hill Inc. **225** Drawing by Gahan Wilson. Reproduced by Special permission of *Playboy* magazine: © 1977 by Playboy. **226** *Dilbert* drawn by Scott Adams. *Dilbert* reprinted by permission of United Feature Syndicate, Inc. **228** Table from *Interracial Communication Theory Into Practice (with InfoTrac),*

1st edition, by M. P. Orbe and T. M. Harris © 2001. Reprinted with permission of Wadsworth, an imprint of Wadsworth Group, a division of Thomson Learning. Fax 800-730-2215. **229** Article by Valerie Reifman, *Los Angeles Times* staff © 1999, *Los Angeles Times*. Reprinted by permission. **234** Poem: "Nothing" from *Love Poems for the Very Married* by Lois Wyse. © 1976 by Lois Wise. Used by permission of HarperCollins. **235** Poem: "Flags: From *Even As We Speak* by Ric Masten. Reprinted by permission of the publisher, Sunflower Ink, Palo Colorado Road Carmel, CA 93925. **236** Drawing by Robert Mankoff. © 2001 Robert Mankoff from cartoonbank.com. All Rights Reserved. **240** Excerpt: "Black Men and Public Spaces" by Brent Staples from *Life Studies* edited by D. Cavitch. © 1992 Brent Staples. Used by permission of the author. **246** Article: "The Look of a Victim" from *Introduction to Nonverbal Communication* by L. Malandro & L. Baker © 1982. Reprinted courtesy of the Random House, Inc. **250** *Cathy* © Cathy Guisewite. Reprinted with permission of Universal Press Syndicate. All rights reserved. **252** Chart: " A Comparison of the Ideal Speakers' Voice Types in Mexico and the United States" adapted from "Communicative Power: Gender and Culture as Determinants of the Ideal Voice" in *Women and Communicative Power: Theory, Research and Practice* edited by Valentine and Hoar. © 1988 by the SCA. Reprinted with permission. **253** Reprinted from Thomas Hurka, *Principles: Short Essays on Ethics* (Toronto: Harcourt Brace, © 1994) pp. 201-3 **255** *Cathy* © Cathy Guisewite. Reprinted with permission of Universal Press Syndicate. All rights reserved. **256** Drawing by Schwadran from *The Wall Street Journal*, permission, Cartoon Features **259** From *W. H. Auden: Collected Poems* by W. H. Auden, edited by Edward Mendelson. © 1965 by W. H. Auden. Reprinted by permission of Random House, Inc. **261** Lyrics from "Stickshifts and Safety Belts" written by John McCrea - Stamen Music - Performed by CAKE on the CD *Fashion Nugget*.

CHAPTER 7   268 Poem: "Conversations" by Ric Masten from *Dragonflies, Codfish*

& *Frogs* by Ric Masten. Reprinted by permission of publisher, Sunflower Ink, Palo Colorado Road, Carmel, CA 93923. **271** Drawing by Robert Mankoff. © The New Yorker Collection 2000 Robert Mankoff from cartoonbank.com. All Rights Reserved. **275** *Calvin and Hobbes* © Watterson. Reprinted with permission of Universal press Syndicate. All rights reserved. **276** Selected song lyrics: From "Everybody's Talkin'" by Fred Neil. © 1967 Third Story Music. Used by permission. **278** From W. H. Auden: *Collected Poems* by W. H. Auden, edited by Edward Mendelson © 1965 by W. H. Auden. Reprinted by permission of Random House, Inc. **279** "At a Lecture Only 12% Listen" from *The San Francisco Sunday Examiner and Chronicle*. Reprinted by permission. **281** Poem: "Deafness Lite" by Sal Parlato, Jr. Reprinted with permission, *Silent News*. **283** Article excerpt: "Lend an Ear" by Roberta Israeloff. Pub: 7-13-99 in *Woman's Day*. Used by permission. **285** Drawing by Ted Goff. © 2001 Ted Goff from cartoonbank.com. All Rights Reserved. **289** From Don Fabun *Communication: The Transfer of Meaning* © 1968 by Kaiser Aluminum and Chemical Corp. Adapted by permission Allyn and Bacon. **291** Excerpt: "Finding Common Ground Through Listening" by Ellen Goodman. © 1987, The Boston Globe Newspaper Co./ Washington Post Writers Group. Reprinted with permission. **295** Article: "They Learn to Aid Customers by Becoming Good Listeners" by Beth Mohr. From the *San Diego Union* © 1976. Reprinted with permission. **299** *Zits* by Scott & Borgman. Reprinted with special permission of King Feature Syndicate. **300** Poem: "So Penseroso" from *Verses From 1929 On* © 1935 by Ogden Nash. Used by permission Little Brown and Company. **304** Selected lyrics: "Trouble Me" by Natalie Merchant and Dennis Drew. Reprinted by permission of Christian Burial Music. **305** Selected lyrics: From "Everybody Hurts" by William Berry, Michael Stipe, Peter Buck, & Mike Mills. © 1992 Night Garden Music (BMI) All rights administered by Warner-Tamerland Publishing Corp. All rights reserved. Used by permission Warner Bros. Publications U.S. Inc. Miami FL 33014.

CHAPTER 8   315 Drawing by John O'Brien. © The New Yorker Collection 1998 John O'Brien from cartoonbank. com. All Rights Reserved. **321** *Sally Forth* by Greg Howard. Reprinted with special permission of King Feature Syndicate. **324** Drawing by J. B. Handlesman. © The New Yorker Collection 1996 J. B. Handlesman from cartoonbank.com. All Rights Reserved. **325** Figure: "Stages of Relational Development" from *Interpersonal Communication and Human Relationships* (4th edition) by Mark L. Knapp and Anita L. Vangelsti. © 2000 by Allyn & Bacon. Adapted by permission. **326** The Far Side® by Gary Larson © 1991 FarWorks, Inc. All Rights Reserved. Used with permission. **328** *Zits* by Scott & Borgman. Reprinted with special permission of King Feature Syndicate. **330** Excerpt: From *The Accidental Tourist* by Anne Tyler, © 1985 by Anne Tyler Modarressi. Used by permission of Alfred A. Knopf, a division of Random House, Inc. **333** Drawing by Tom Cheney. © The New Yorker Collection 1997 Tom Cheney from cartoonbank. com. All Rights Reserved. **334** Figures: From "Testing a Cyclical Model of Communication Openness in Relationship Development: Two Longitudinal Studies" by C. A. VanLear. Published in *Communication Monographs* 59 (199) © Speech Communication Association. **335** *Zits* by Scott & Borgman. Reprinted with special permission of King Feature Syndicate. **338** Poem: "Looking Out, Looking In" from *Stark Naked* by Ric Masten. Reprinted by permission of publisher, Sunflower Ink, Palo Colorado Road, Carmel, CA 93923. **341–3** Figure: "The Johari Window Model" from *Group Processes: An Introduction to Group Dynamics* by Joseph Luft. Used courtesy of the author. **346** Drawing by Jack Ziegler. © The New Yorker Collection 1984 Jack Ziegler from cartoonbank.com. All Rights Reserved. **348** Drawing by Stan Hunt. © The New Yorker Collection 1982 Stan Hunt from cartoonbank.com. All Rights Reserved. **352** Drawing by Leo Cullum. © The New Yorker Collection 2000 Leo Cullum from cartoonbank.com. All Rights Reserved. **353** Table: "Types of White Lies and Their Frequency" from "White Lies and

Interpersonal Communication: A Taxonomy and Preliminary Investigation of Social Motivations" *Western Journal of Speech Communication* 48 (1984) **355** Article: "Is Misleading Your Spouse Fraud or Tact?" by Maria Cone. © *L. A. Times* 1993 Reprinted by permission. **356** Figure: "Dimensions of Truthfulness and Equivocation" adapter from *Equivocal Communication* by J. B. Bavelas, A. Black, N. Chovil and J. Mullett. © 1990 by Sage Publications, Inc. Used courtesy of publisher. **357** *Dilbert* by Scott Adams. Reprinted by permission of United Feature Syndicate, Inc.

CHAPTER 9 371 Poem: "Notice Me" from *The Voice of the Hive* by Ric Masten. Reprinted by permission of the publisher, Sunflower Ink, Palo Colorado Road, Carmel, CA 93923. **372** Drawing by Jack Ziegler. © The New Yorker Collection 1997 Jack Ziegler from cartoonbank.com. All Rights Reserved. **373** Table: "Positive and Negative Reciprocal Communication Patterns" adapted from *Competence in Interpersonal Conflict* by W. R. Cupach and D. J. Canary, © 1997. Reproduced by

permission The McGraw-Hill Companies. **375** Poem: From *Knots* by R. D. Laing © 1970 by R. D. Laing. Reprinted by permission of Pantheon Books, a division of Random House, Inc. and courtesy of Tavistock Publications Ltd. **379** Song lyric: "I Am a Rock" by Paul Simon. © 1965 by Paul Simon. Used by permission. **380** Table: "The Gibb Categories of Defensive and Supportive Behaviors" from "Defensive Communication" by Jack R. Gibb. © 1961 in the *Journal of Communication*, Vol. 11:3. Used courtesy of the author and publisher. **384** Column: "How to Argue Effectively" by Dave Barry, a humor columnist with the *Miami Herald*. © 1980 by Dave Barry. Reprinted with the author's permission. **385** Drawing by Al Ross. © The New Yorker Collection 1983 Al Ross from cartoonbank.com. All Rights Reserved. **394** *Peanuts* by Schulz reprinted by permission of United Features Syndicate, Inc.

CHAPTER 10 406 Table: "Individual Styles of Conflict" adapted with permission from *The Assertive Woman* by Stanlee Phelps and Nancy Austin. 3rd edition, © 1997 by Impact Publishers,

Inc., P. O. Box 1094, San Luis Obispo, CA 93406. Further reproduction prohibited. **407** *Peanuts* by Schulz reprinted by permission of United Features Syndicate, Inc. **424** *Cathy* © Cathy Guisewite. Reprinted with permission of Universal Press Syndicate. All rights reserved. **427** Drawing by David Sipress © The New Yorker Collection 2001 David Sipress from cartoonbank.com. All Rights Reserved. **434** Drawing by Leo Cullum © The New Yorker Collection 1997 Leo Cullum from cartoonbank.com. All Rights Reserved. **435** *The Far Side* by Gary Larson © 1991 FarWorks, Inc. All Rights Reserved. Used with permission. **438** Poem: "Hug O'War" by Shel Silverstein from *Where the Sidewalk Ends* © 1974 by Evil Eye Music, Inc. Used by permission of HarperCollins Publishers. **442** Figure: "Flow Chart of the Win-Win Negotiation Process" adapted from Rory Remer and Paul deMesquita, "Teaching and Learning Skills of Interpersonal Confrontation" in *Intimates in Conflict: A Communication Perspective* edited by Cahn © 1990 **445** Drawing by Bruce Kaplan © 2001 from cartoonbank.com. All Rights Reserved.

NAME INDEX

SUBJECT INDEX

couple communication (*continued*)
  conflict style-variables 429–31
  intimate and aggressive styles of conflict 426–8
crazymakers 411
crazymaking 409–10
crisis tickler (crazymaker) 411
criticism (nondefensive responses) 387–396
  agree with critic 393–6
  seek more information 387–393
cultural differences
  and perception checking 121
  "Empathy and the Golden Rule" (ethical challenge) 123
  in perception 105–10
cultural influence, intimacy and 321–2
cultural rules in perception checking 121
culture
  communication and multiple identities 74
  conflict style variables, and 431–3
  development of self-concept, and 48–53
  differences in perception checking, and 121
  emotional expression, and 144–6
  "Empathy and the Golden Rule" (ethical challenge) 123
  influence on communication 61
  influence on identity 60–62
  influence on interpretation in perception process 101–3
  influence on self-concept, and 60–62
  interpreting others emotions, and 146
  "Kholoud Elayyan: Identity and a Sense of Mission" (looking at diversity) 79
  "Lend An Ear" (reading) 283
  perception organization by membership, and 97
  perception process, and 96–97
  self-esteem and social comparison, and 53
  shapes male-female behavior (nonverbal) 230–1
  social expectations and self-concept, and 57–58
  "Speaking and Listening with a 'Talking Stick'" (invitation to insight) 284
  stereotyping in perception process, and 98–100
culture and impression management 84–85
culture and language 190–2, 210–4
  "Challenging the 'S' Word" (reading) 192
  high context cultures 211–4
  "Language and Heritage" (reading) 215
  linguistic determinism 214
  linguistic relativism 216–7
  "Low- and High-Context Communication Styles" (table) 211
  low-context cultures 211–4
  "Mikako Garara: 'Speaking' the Culture" (looking at diversity) 212
  powerful speech 195
  Sapir-Whorf hypothesis 216–7
  syntactic rules, and 186
culture and nonverbal communication 226–9
"Cyclical Phases . . . in Relationships" (figure) 334

D

debilitative emotions 156–7
deceiving (nonverbal) 234–7
decision control 26–27
decodes 8
de-escalatory conflict spiral 374
defense mechanisms 376–80
  three basic types 376–8
    attacking the critic 376–7
    avoiding dissonant information 378
    distorting critical information 377–8
"Defense Mechanism Inventory" (invitation to insight) 380
defense reduction-use "I" language 201
defensive behaviors (Gibb categories) 380–6
defensive listening 276–7
defensiveness 9
  causes and remedies 375–96
  definition 375
"Defensiveness Feedback" (invitation to insight) 385
definition of communication 12–13
deliberate vs. unconscious (nonverbal) 242
demonstrative pronoun (language) 193
description (supportive behavior) 381–2
descriptive communication 380–1
dialectical tensions 332–6
  connection vs. autonomy 332–3
  openness vs. privacy 333–4
  predictability vs. novelty 333
differentiating (relational stage) 329
dimensions of a message
  content 24
  relational 24–25
"Dimensions of Truthfulness and Equivocation" (figure) 356
Diner (film) gender and intimacy 262–3
direct aggression 408–9

"Dirty Fighting with Crazymakers" (ethical challenge) 411
disclaimers 194–5
disclosure 18
disconfirming messages 370–2
"Disconfirming Messages" (reading) 370–1
disfluencies (nonverbal) 250
displacement (defense mechanism) 378
disruptive language 195–8
"Distance Makes a Difference" (invitation to insight) 258
distance (nonverbal) 258–60
  intimate 259
  personal 259–60
  public 260
  social 260
distorted feedback 56–57
distorting critical information (defense mechanism)
  compensation 377–8
  rationalization 377
  regression 378
"Distribution of Control in Relationships" (table) 27
divergence 193–4
Doctor, The (film) building empathy 132
"Down-to-Earth Language" (skill builder) 185
dyad, definition of 16–17
dyadic communication 16

E

effective communicator 30–38
effects of lying 354–5
"'Ego Boosters' and 'Ego Busters'" (invitation to insight) 49
"Electronic Block Party, The" (reading) 20
elements of "I" language 200–1
elements of perception checking 120–1
e-mail 19–21
  emoticons and smileys 232
  emotional intimacy via 318
  expressing nonverbal messages 232
  its asynchronous nature 20
  physical appearance doesn't matter (cartoon) 255
  speeds up relational development 326
emblems (nonverbal) 245
emoticons and smileys (nonverbal e-mail) 147, 232
emotion and nonverbal communication 231–2
emotional coaching (parenting style) 140
emotional contagion 148–9
emotional dismissing (parenting style) 140